Baedeker
Turkey

GW00500505

WARNING

In view of the present highly tense situation in eastern and south-eastern Anatolia with the Kurdish part of the population, visitors are strongly advised to exercise the utmost care and restraint, and even to refrain from visiting these areas. In the first place the visitor runs the risk of being caught up in an attack by Kurdish militia, and secondly it must be realised that the Turkish security forces deal severely with any rebellious activity by the Kurds or their sympathisers. Therefore visitors should avoid taking sides with the Kurdish cause.

As these risks exist everywhere in Turkish Kurdistan, before embarking on a planned visit to this area visitors should enquire of the appropriate authorities – administrative headquarters, military posts, police-stations or information offices – as to the possibility of the proposed visit being subject to restrictions or even prohibition and to adhere strictly to any instructions. Useful information can also be obtained from the Ministry of Tourism in Ankara (see Practical Information: Information).

Baedeker's
TURKEY

Imprint

269 illustrations, 99 maps, drawings and plans. 1 large map at end of book

Original German text: Dr Volker Höhfeld, Vera Beck, Astrid Feltes, Prof. Dr Wolfgang Hassenpflug, Prof. Dr Manfried Korfmann, Dr Günter Ludwig.
Introductory section and "Turkey from A to Z" are partly based on Baedeker's Motoring guide to Turkey and on the Baedeker guide-books "Turkish Coasts" and "Istanbul".

Editorial work (German edition): Baedeker Redaktion (Astrid Feltes)
English edition: Crispin Warren

Cartography: Gert Oberländer, Munich; Mairs Geographischer Verlag, Ostfildern (large map)

General direction (German edition): Dr Peter Baumgarten
(English edition): Alec Court

Source of Illustrations: Archiv für Kunst und Geschichte (3), Baumgarten (1), Börner (1), Feltes (146), Hackenberg (31), Hartmann (3), Historia-Photo (5), Höfeld (56), Information Department of the Turkish Consulate General (Munich) (2), Jansen (1), Paysan (2), Schäfer (2), Stetter (4), Strobel (8), Süddeutscher Verlag (2), Ullstein Bilderdienst (2)

English translation: Wendy Bell, Brenda Ferris, Paul Fletcher

Following the tradition established by Karl Baedeker in 1844, sights of particular interest and hotels and restaurants of particular quality are distinguished by either one or two asterisks.
To make it easier to locate the various places listed in the "A to Z" section of the Guide, their co-ordinates on the large country map are shown at the head of each entry.
Only a selection of hotels, restaurants and shops can be given; no reflection is implied therefore on establishments not included.
In a time of rapid change it is difficult to ensure that all the information given is entirely accurate and up-to-date, and the possibility of error can never be entirely eliminated. Although the publishers can accept no responsibility for inaccuracies and omissions, they are always grateful for corrections and suggestions for improvement.

1st English edition in this format 1994

© Baedeker Stuttgart
Original German edition

© 1994 Jarrold and Sons Limited
English language edition worldwide

© 1994 The Automobile Association
United Kingdom and Ireland

Prentice Hall General Reference
US and Canadian edition

PRENTICE HALL and colophon are registered trademarks of Simon & Schuster, Inc.

Distributed in the United Kingdom by the Publishing Division of the Automobile Association, Fanum House, Basingstoke, Hampshire RG21 2EA

Licensed user:
Mairs Geographischer Verlag GmbH & Co., Ostfildern-Kemnat bei Stuttgart

The name *Baedeker* is a registered trade mark
A CIP catalogue record of this book is available from the British Library

Printed in Italy by G. Canale & C.Sp.A – Borgaro T.se –Turin

ISBN US and Canada 0–671–89686–5
    UK 0 7495 0863 9

Contents

The Principal Places of Tourist Interest at a Glance

(Continued on page 571)

Preface

This guide to Turkey is one of the new generation of Baedeker guides.

These guides, illustrated throughout in colour, are designed to meet the needs of the modern traveller. They are quick and easy to consult, with the principal places of interest described in alphabetical order, and the information is presented in a format that is both attractive and easy to follow.

The subject of this guide is Turkey, both the European and Asiatic parts of the country.

The guide is in three parts. The first part gives a general account of the country, its topography, political and geographical divisions, climate, flora and fauna, population, religion, state and administration, economy, history, famous people, culture and art history. A brief selection of quotations and a number of suggested itineraries provide a transition to the second part, in which the country's places of tourist interest – towns, scenery and archaeological sites – are described. The third part contains a variety of practical information. Both the sights and the practical information are listed in alphabetical order.

The new Baedeker guides are noted for their concentration on essentials and their convenience of use. They contain numerous specially drawn plans and colour illustrations; and at the end of the book is a large map making it easy to locate the various places described in the "A to Z" section of the guide with the help of the co-ordinates given at the head of each entry.

Facts and Figures

The vast rectangle of Turkey, protruding peninsula-like from the western rim of Asia but with its foothold on the mainland of Europe, serves as a major bridge between different cultures and economic regions. Thrace and the area around the Sea of Marmara in particular have played a vital and unique role as intermediary between Europe and Asia, with an impact on world history that has endured from earliest antiquity right up to the present. The seaway through the straits also links the Aegean and eastern Mediterranean with the waters of the Black Sea and since the times of colonisation by the Ancient Greeks has carried the flow of ideas and influence towards the north-east, not least through the spread of Christianity from Byzantium into Eastern Europe. Although most of its geography puts Turkey among the mountainous countries of the Near East, its bridgehead position has from time immemorial brought it into close contact with the West so that the culture of present-day Turkey draws heavily on Europe. This also finds political expression in its associate status with the European Community and membership of NATO, the North Atlantic Treaty Organisation.

General

The enormous expanse that is the Republic of Turkey stretches in a long rectangle from from west to east, from Thrace in the south-eastern corner of Europe, via the Sea of Marmara and the peninsula of Asia Minor into the distant reaches of Anatolia in the Near East. Measured from its farthest points in each direction it lies between longitude 25° 45' and 44° 48' E and between latitude 42° 06' and 35° 51' N.

Geographical position

More than two-thirds of Turkey's well-drawn frontiers are coastline. These stretch for fully 6000km/3730 miles along the Aegean, eastern Mediterranean and Black Sea, contrasting with only 2753km/1710 miles of land frontier (the Sea of Marmara is wholly Turkish on all sides), a ratio of about 2 to 1 as between coastal and landlocked.

Frontiers

Turkey's neighbours are Greece in the west, Bulgaria in the north-west, Georgia and Armenia in the north-east, Iran in the east, Iraq in the south-east and Syria in the south.

Neighbours

Extending for more than 1500km/930 miles from east to west and between 500 and 600km/310 and 370 miles from north to south, Turkey covers a total area of 774,815sq.km/299,078sq.miles. This is divided between its European territory of 23,764sq.km/9.172sq.miles (Avrupa Türkiyesi, Thrace) and its territory in Asia Minor (Anatolia, from the Greek for land of the sunrise), over 30 times greater at 751,051sq.km/290,000sq.miles. These two parts of Turkey are separated by the Dardanelles, the Sea of Marmara and the Bosphorus, although this is no great divide since both people and landscape share the same features on either side. Another 11,500sq.km/4427sq.miles of Turkey's surface area is taken up by its many lakes and barrages.

Territorial area and distribution

In the 16th and 17th c. the Ottoman Empire, at its peak, extended over a vast expanse of more than 5 million sq.km/1.9 million sq.miles; by the beginning of the 20th c. this had shrunk to just under 3 million sq.km/1.2 million sq.miles. Further territory was lost in the Tripolitanian and Balkan wars but

Territorial area past and present

◀ *Tuff pyramids near Zelve in Cappadocia*

General

Plateau in the Taurus

the most drastic reduction was to be at the end of the First World War when Turkey not only permanently lost the vast expanse of the Syro-Arabian tableland but also had to give up the whole of the north-east to Armenia, the south-east to the Mosul region and a strip 50–100km/30–60 miles wide west of this to Syria, then under French mandate, while Smyrna (İzmir), with a hinterland of some 100 by 150km/60 by 90 miles on the west coast of Asia Minor, and almost the whole of Thrace in European Turkey, as far as the Çatalca Line only 40km/25 miles from İstanbul, were assigned to Greece which thus extended along a broad front to the Black Sea. This sweeping reduction in national territory, imposed by the Treaty of Sèvres (1920), was bitterly resisted by the Turks and their leader Kemal Atatürk (Mustafa Kemal Paşa), who succeeded in recovering all these areas through the Treaty of Lausanne (1923), securing Turkey a unified natural Lebensraum. This was subsequently enlarged by the addition of the Hakkâri region in the extreme south-east (1926) and the important sanjak of Alexandretta, the Hatay region (1939).

Present-day Turkey thus commands a national territory that is large-scale yet compact and bounded by very well-defined frontiers. Compared with the unwieldy expanse of the Ottoman Empire, made difficult to rule because of its far-flung outposts, modern Turkey's relatively smaller size makes for a more unified nation, enabling an empire which held sway over many different peoples to be transformed into a true nation state with, since 1923, Ankara as its capital.

Within its vast area Turkey's mainly Muslim population numbers over 58.5 million (1992) and has a high degree of national unity. It is thus the most populous state not only in the Near East but also in south-eastern Europe. With its great geographical diversity – warm wet regions on the coast and a dry interior, fertile albeit narrow coastal plains, immense rolling uplands and rugged mountain ranges, plus ample sources of mineral wealth – Turkey can draw on a well-matched range of complementary natural resources and also entertain prospects of significant future development.

Topography

Historical Background

The Ottoman Empire which in 1453, with the conquest of Constantinople, was poised to exploit the fragmented remains of the Byzantine Empire and triumph over the Christian culture of the West with the Islamic culture of the East, found itself faced five hundred years later with its own empire in ruins.

Ottoman Empire

However, there were already signs in the 19th c., during the reigns of Sultans Mahmut II, Abdulmecit and Abdulaziz, that Turkey was changing from being the sick man of Europe, its corrupt and hidebound Sultanate making it easy prey for others' colonial ambitions, to becoming a stable state on more modern lines.

In the light of 20th c. pressures for change and the need to model itself on the western industrial nations Turkey has since sought to achieve greater political, economic and social cohesion. When in October 1923 the Republic of Turkey arose from the ashes of the Ottoman Empire it needed to shake off the legacy of its eventful past and find recognition as a progressive nation in the world of modern states.

Republican Turkey

Atatürk was fully aware of this and sought through his "Kemalist" social and economic reforms to lay the foundations for just such a modern industrial state. To date, however, the loss of major parts of empire in the past and drastic inroads into its Islamic traditions have combined with internal and external policy issues such as Cyprus, the Kurdish question, and an impoverished economy, to bring about a cultural identity crisis for modern republican Turkey.

Geographical features

Framed pincerlike by the rugged Pontine Mountains of the Black Sea in the north, with peaks topping 3500m/11,500ft, and the Taurus Mountains, soaring to over 4000m/13,200ft, in the south and south-east, the great basin of the high plateau (1000m/3280ft) at the heart of Anatolia has seen much ancient settlement and been home to many advanced civilisations.

Anatolia

Along with the farmland of eastern Thrace these vast, gently rolling upland steppes and shallow depressions form the breadbasket of the nation, rendering it almost self-sufficient in grain. The surrounding mountains hold the wealth of minerals and thermal springs that go hand in hand with spectacular volcanic activity and strong earthquakes along tectonic fault lines. Another striking feature is the sharp division and carving up of the landscape into nigh on impassable mountains and massifs and flat-bottomed depressions and basins. This means that nearly all the larger rivers have to negotiate these obstacles on their way from their upland sources down to the sea, often passing through narrow gorges from one basin to the next. Others end up in one of the many shallow lakes in the centre of the country from which no rivers flow apart from those which drain away through underground karst systems.

The deep depressions between the ridges and trenches of Western Anatolia's uplands and the host of smaller intramontane basins provide land suitable for intensive cultivation of the fresh fruit and vegetables which go to supply the needs of the expanding urban population in Turkey's growing number of large towns and cities.

Western Anatolia

In the east the rugged barriers of the Pontine and Taurus mountains merge around the great basin of Lake Van with the wild mountain country, mighty volcanoes and steppe-like basalt plateaus of Kurdistan and ancient Armenia. Till now this has been Turkey's economic backwater, with as yet

Eastern Anatolia

Topography

unexploited stocks of minerals and broad high prairies where wandering
herdsmen graze their stock.

Coastal areas

Turkish Asia Minor, extending over 1500km/930 miles east to west and
600km/370 miles north to south, is bounded to the north, south and east by
four seas – the Black Sea, the Mediterranean and Aegean and the Sea of
Marmara – and has a total of over 8000km/5000 miles of coastline. The
tourist potential of its beaches is consequently enormous. So far the fertile
farms on the floodplain and along the coast carry the areas largely dependent on irrigation with intensive cultivation for export, the domestic market,
and homegrown industry, and these will be joined by large sections of
south-eastern Anatolia's flatlands as the many dams of GAP, the South-
eastern Anatolia Project, come on stream.

Contrasts

All this means that Anatolia breaks down into countless different-sized
areas of landscape which, even though they might be right next to one
another, can be sharply contrasting in their natural resources, economic
potential and physical features, since the way the basic relief is structured
clearly determines climate and vegetation and restricts what can and cannot be grown.
Thus only the narrow coastal fringes in the south, west and on the Black
Sea tend to be subtropical. The coastal areas are also those that get the
most rainfall since they benefit most from the steep mountain ranges,
without which Turkey would be much dryer than it is, and which generally
rise up abruptly without any transitional slopes.
On the other hand, Central Anatolia and the south-east, far from the sea, are
extremely dry in summer. Whereas the annual rainfall in the Pontine and
Taurus mountains can be as much as 2000mm/79 inches, and parts of the
north are densely wooded with beech, oak and pines allowing the cultivation of hazelnuts and tea, the rainfall in Central Anatolia around Tuz Gölü
(Salt Lake) and in the hot south-east, where it is dry in summer, very cold in
winter and no trees grow, can often be barely 300mm/11 inches.

Inland Waters

Lakes

Alongside the smaller depressions ringed by mountains in the eastern
highlands, one of which holds Lake Van (1646m/5400ft; 3738sq.km/
1443sq.miles), and the high country lakes in the western Taurus (Burdur
845m/2773ft, 202sq.km/780sq.miles; Egredir 916m/3000ft, 486sq.km/
188sq.miles; Beyşehir 1121m/4124ft, 650sq.km/250sq.miles), the whole of
south-western Central Anatolia – an area of some 70,000sq.km/
27,000sq.miles – constitutes a self-contained region undrained by rivers on
account of the lack of rainfall. It also holds the great lake of Tuz Gölü ("salt
lake", 925m/3036ft, 1397sq.km/539sq.miles). The only other notable Turkish freshwater lake is Lake Sapanca (40m/131ft, 40sq.km/15sq.miles) which
is a continuation of the Gulf of İzmit.
Since the Seventies, as part of its GAP irrigation and hydro-electric
schemes, the South-eastern Anatolia Project has been responsible for
creating a massive network of reservoirs, chief among them the Atatürk
reservoir (over 800sq.km/309sq.miles), on the Euphrates (Fırat) and Tigris
(Dicle) and their tributaries.

Rivers

The only river whose course can be traced back through the whole of the
Taurus mountains to the self-contained tableland of Central Anatolia is
the Çakit Çay. This carves its passage down to the Adana Plain through the
mountains in a great gorge in the Cilician Pass region. A number of large
rivers flow through northern Anatolia's well-watered mountain fringe to
the Black Sea: Sakarya (824km/512 miles), Kızılırmak (ancient Halys,
1182km/734 miles), Yeşilırmak (468km/290 miles) with Kelkit Çay
(373km/232 miles) and Çoruk (376km/234 miles, 355/220 of them in Turkey).
The Aras (920km/572 miles in total, 441/274 in Turkey) flows off to the east,

12

the Dicle (Tigris, 452km/281 miles of its total 1900km/1181 miles in Turkey) and the Fırat (Euphrates, for 971km/603 miles of its total 2800km/1740 miles) run south, while the Ceyhan (509km/316 miles) and the Seyhan (560km/348 miles) enter the eastern Mediterranean. The rivers of the Aegean hinterland also draw on a large area; they include the meandering Menderes (the classical Maeander, 529km/329 miles), the Gediz (350km/217 miles) and the Ergene (281km/175 miles), largest tributary of the Meriz (Maritza).

The volume of water in the rivers can vary considerably according to the season, especially in the dry areas. Unexpectedly heavy summer downpours can lead to extensive local flooding even in the dry interior. The incredible volume of water in the Manavgat which emerges into the Mediterranean east of Antalya is due to the underground streams flowing from the karst systems which drain the Taurus uplands, and these feed other rivers on the Antalya Plain in the same way. In addition to rainfall distribution the nature of the widespread karst-type limestones also contributes to the dry conditions and lack of rivers, particularly in the western and central Taurus mountains and the south-eastern foothills, as well as in some parts in the north-west.

Geological Features

Turkey, in terms of its geology and general land formation, is part of the great belt of mountain chains girding the Ancient World. Its only expanse of the Syro-Arabian tableland is the broad strip in the south-east, but even here, at its edge, the effects of young Alpidic mountain formation are still visible, so that this also has the appearance of the foreland to the belt of mountain chains, the main feature being diverging outlying ridges which enclose plateaux or large basins and then come together to form a single range of hills before separating again. Their presence in this type of arrangement is best explained in general terms by the earlier existence of a number of ancient massifs as intermediary mountain formations or "geotumors", with the outlying hills around them, and in the more specific sense also by the curved course of the outlying ranges which in Turkey would be the Northern Anatolian threshold mountains on the one side and the Taurus mountain systems on the other, southern side of the massifs.

Turkey as a whole

The first of these massifs, in the south-west of Turkey, is the south-western Anatolia massif, formed of granite, gneiss, phyllites and mostly edged with marble (also the Lydia-Caria massif or Menderes massif, thought to be a geotumor). It is caused by the extension of the Western Taurus on a line north-east running along the south-eastern side of the massif far into the interior. On the massif's northern side the mountain ranges south of the Sea of Marmara, usually running west to east, lead into the Pontine chains bordering Northern Anatolia, linking up with one another on the eastern side of this ancient massif in the more scattered hills of Western Anatolia, towards the northern and southern ranges of the interior and in the watershed of the rivers draining into the Aegean.

South-western Anatolia massif

To the east the plateau of the interior is taken up with the Central Anatolian massif, enclosing the central steppe tableland (Lycaonian Massif) and the beginnings of the ancient fold country, rich in granite, of the Kızılırmak (Halys massif, Kırşehir massif). Here too ancient, probably Palaeozoic rocks – gneiss, crystalline schists, phyllites, quarzite and marble, transformed by penetrating intrusions of granite and syenite – form the bedrock; however this is only orographically apparent in individual mountain outcrops and is usually enclosed in younger strata (see below). The Central Anatolia massif is responsible for both causing the mountains bordering Northern Anatolian to curve outwards to their northernmost extent and for the great arc southwards of the Central Taurus in the south. In the east the two ranges of

Central Anatolia massif

Erosion of the Tuff in Cappadocia

mountains on the rim come so close together that the Northern Anatolian foothills and the Eastern Taurus merge to become a single much dissected set of hills. Finally the spurs of the Median massif in the extreme east again force the border ranges apart, the northernmost to the north-east, the southernmost to the south-east. Here the landscape is made up of upland basins with Tertiary infill, wide volcanic pavements, and towering volcanic mountains, including Mount Ararat, Turkey's highest peak at 5165m/16,950ft. The eastern end of the Taurus contains the ancient Bitlis massif.

With their inclusion in the tectonic array of mountains arching around the Mediterranean the "Taurides" of the Taurus mountains constitute the continuation of the "Dinarides", the Dinaric Alps which curve down from Croatia, Bosnia Herzegovina and Montenegro, arching through the Greek islands of Cos and Rhodes to the Western Taurus, and then crossing the Central Taurus, one arm also traversing Cyprus, with a continuation in the Eastern Taurus.

On the other side Northern Anatolia's Pontine Mountains north of the Paphlagonian Seam – a long rift valley consisting of a succession of basins and longitudinal valleys – are traversed by the "Pontides", the continuation of the "Balkanides". The ancient ridges of folded rock, the "Anatolides", in the area between these chains still represent part of the Northern Anatolian foothills in a northern zone reaching right up to the Paphlagonian Seam, whereas further south they form single massive outcrops rearing up out of the flatlands of the Central Anatolia plateau.

Central
Anatolia
plateau

Most of the Central Anatolia plateau, in the rain shadow of the surrounding mountains, is a landscape from which no rivers flow. Its vast expanses are built up of Teritary sedimentation deposited either horizontally or in flat layers. At around 800–1200m/2626–3938ft there are also outcrops of strata left by ancient Tertiary seas with occasional lignite deposits as well as gypsum and rock salt left by Oligocene and late Tertiary lakes and rivers.

These are accompanied by broad flattened strata of volcanic tufa. Young volcanic hills rise up out of these broad flatlands. These include on the eastern rim of the undrained area the Erciyas Dağı (3916m/12,852ft), west of Niğde the Melendiz Dağı (2935m/9633ft) and the Hasan Dağı (2271m/7453ft) at Karaman. Their jagged shapes distinguish them from the outcrops of the ancient bedrock already mentioned such as the Elma Dağı (1855m/6088ft), south-east of Ankara, with its flatter Palaeozoic rock formation. On the other hand broad shallow depressions or "ovas" are the result of more recent sinking processes. Several of these depression zones hold salt lakes including the largest of them, Tuz Gölü. The nature of the bedrock can also lend itself to startling erosion by heavy downpours at the end of long dry summers, when the rush of water often scours out very characteristic furrows in the slopes and, as at Göreme in Ürgüp, forms conical pinnacles of tufa.

Right from the south-eastern shore of the Sea of Marmara, where the first of the chain of hills and mountains begins, the Pontine Mountains bordering Northern Anatolia are a range of mountains in their own right, starting at the mouth of the Sakarya where they first curve north as low hills running as far the the mouth of the Kızıl Irmak. North of the Paphlagonian Seam, here tracking through a series of basins, they are composed of ancient folded Palaeozoic cores but also contain Ereğli's important coal deposits, a number of granite massifs and the sandstones, marls, shales and clays of Flysch deposits. River erosion has eaten into the landscape to create an often jagged mountain relief but one that is frequently topped by flat uplands, plateaux that have been left behind. The peaks here are only moderately high, and the Ilgaz Mountains are the only ones reaching up to 2565m/8418ft. After the relatively low-lying Flysch highlands around Samsum the Pontine Mountains in their eastern range as they curve round, swinging southwards, soon tower upwards to form the higher ranges of the Zigana region. Here in the main they are granite but also contain Flysch and late volcanic rocks. The highest peaks are in the Kaçkar range (3548m/11,645ft). Their rugged forms can be traced back to considerable glacial action in the Ice Ages. The Kelkit Çay and Çoruh rivers run through stretches of broad valleys along the Paphlagonian Seam.

This rift valley which runs for a total of 1100km/684 miles through Northern Anatolia is an important earthquake line – a fault zone half a mile across – where displacement in the vertical reaches up to 1m/3ft and in the horizontal as much as 4.3m/14ft has been recorded following major earthquakes. The total horizontal displacement for the period between 1939 and 1967 actually amounted to 18m/59ft! Other earthquake lines include the tectonic faults in western Turkey and, more especially, the south-eastern Taurus foreland.

The western section of the Taurus Mountains in the south of the central plateau show the adaptation to the south-western Anatolia massif already mentioned. West of the Gulf of Antalya they stretch inland verging south-west to north-east as far as the Afyon-Karahisar region. In the Ak Dağı this mountain massif, mostly of Mesozoic limestones, reaches its highest point in the Bey Dağlan (3085m/10,125ft). In the centre, where this massif converges with the bow of the Central Taurus, there is a region of high isolated lakes (Burdur, Eğridir, Beyşehir). The limestone chains of the Central Taurus, here at their start, first run south-east from their meeting point with the Western Taurus, getting higher all the time so that the individual massifs generally top 2500m/8205ft. Hence the outlying Sultan Dağı, mainly composed of older rocks, reaches 2581m/8471ft and, in the Şeytan Dağı, Üç Tepe peaks at 3036m/9964ft. East of the broad Antalya plain from Alanya to Silifke the southern edge of the mountains is formed by the Palaeozoic coastal chains and their many valleys. After the height loss of the Central Taurus between Karaman and Silifke with flat layered Miocene strata the north-eastern section begins its further spread with the Bolkar Dağı. The main mountain range is of palaeozoic and chalk strata. Three to four chains

Northern Anatolia
border mountains

Taurus Mountains

Mountain scenery south of Beyşehir

run parallel with one another, merging together towards the north-east and gaining in height as they go, with Mededsiz in the Bolkar Dağ towering up to 3585m/11,766ft. The Taurus name is recalled in the Toros Dağ group. Eastwards of them the Çakit Çay flows through the only valley in the whole mountain system which cuts across from the central plateau to the coast. The most imposing of the other mountain groups is Ala Dağı (Cilician Ala Dağ), with peaks of 3700–3900m/12,143–12,800ft, and already running south to north.

Misis Dağı, east of the Adana Plain, and Amanos Dağı, across the Gulf of İskenderun, herald the beginning of the chains of the Eastern Taurus. These run inland, towards the north-east to start with, and can be separated into the inner and outer Eastern Taurus, or Anti Taurus as they are often also called. Many of the mountains in this eastern section top 3000m/9850ft, while the Sat Dağı and Cilo Dağ, which already form part of the ranges bordering Iran, can exceed 4000m/13,130ft.

Glaciers still cover the summits of mountains such as Ala Dağ and Cilo Dağ, a reminder that the higher mountain ranges throughout the Taurus and in the eastern Pontine have often been shaped by Ice Age glaciation, lending them a generally Alpine appearance. The process of solifluxion, as soil saturated with meltwater moves over the frozen subsoil, has also left some amazing sights and phenomena up on these lofty mountain tops.

Geographical Regions

Seven main regions

Turkey can be broken down into seven main regions, each of which has more or less the same natural features and a common pattern of other factors:

- Thrace and Marmara Region
- Ege Region
- Mediterranean Coast and Taurus
- Inner Anatolia
- Black Sea Coast and North Anatolia Border Region
- East Anatolian Uplands
- South Anatolia

Regions of Turkey

Thrace and the Marmara Region

Thrace and the Marmara region – the Thracian steppe tableland and the area south of the Sea of Marmara with its alternating pattern of hills and low-lying basins – are two territories of very different character which through proximity and close connections of many kinds can be seen as forming a larger unity.

Thrace

The Thracian tableland is continued beyond the Bosporus (once a river valley running from the Golden Horn to the Black Sea) by the Bithynian or Kocaeli Peninsula, a region of very similar topography. The Dardenelles were once also a valley traversed by a river, and here too the rolling uplands of the southern Marmara region continue on the Gallipoli (Gelibolu) Peninsula on the north side of the straits.

Bosporus
Bithynian
Peninsula
Dardanelles

Gallipoli

The northern part of the Sea of Marmara (280 × 76km/174 × 47 miles; 11,352sq.km/4383sq.miles) is a rift valley extending from west to east and going down to considerable depths, much of it below 1000m/3300ft, with maximum depths reaching 1350m/4430ft. This forms the most westerly element in a sequence of troughs and basins some 1000km/600 miles long (Paphlagonian Seam) which plays an important part in the conformation of Northern Anatolia. Out of the relative shallows – less than 50m/165ft below sea level – along its northern coast emerge the Princes' Islands, built up of hard quartzites which have resisted erosion. In the shallow waters of the southern part of the sea are the Island of Marmara and a number of smaller islands. The Sea of Marmara, a typical inter-continental sea, lies wholly within Turkey.

Sea of Marmara

Princes' Islands

Island
of Marmara

Thrace is mostly a region of steppe tableland at between 100 and 200m/330 and 660ft traversed by broad valleys: an erosion plain thrust upwards in geologically recent times overlaying Late Tertiary marine sediments, mainly Miocene limestones, marls and clays, with sands and gravels

THRACE
Steppe
tableland

Geographical Regions

brought down from the Istranca Hills by rivers. The Istranca range to the north-east of the Thracian tableland and rising in the forest zone to a height of 1031m/3383ft, consists basically of Palaeozoic rocks and represents a continuation of the dome formation of the Balkan mountains. To the south-west of the tableland, between Tekirdağ and the Gulf of Saros, is the Genos range, an upland region of flysch and limestone with recent folding which rises to some 945m/3100ft; this is continued by lower hills along the Gallipoli Peninsula, which has a broad strip of Late Tertiary sediments along the Dardanelles. Raised beaches at different heights – ranging between 6 and 7m/20 and 23ft and 110m/360ft above sea-level – bear witness to changes in the level of the sea. A last post-glacial rise in sea-level associated with world oceanic changes converted the estuaries of rivers

Coastal lagoons

flowing into the Sea of Marmara into coastal lagoons extending far inland, as at Büyük Çekmece and Küçük Çekmece to the west of İstanbul. To the west of the Bosporus and on the Kocaeli Peninsula on the Asia Minor side, the Thraco-Bithynian erosion plain, thrust upward at a late geological period, cuts Early Palaeozoic (Silurian, Devonian) folded rocks. In the eastern part of the Kocaeli Peninsula the tableland is thrust up higher, much dissected and extensively forested.

With a continental temperature pattern and annual precipitation between 40 and 60cm/16 and 24in., falling mainly in winter, the Thracian tableland is a great expanse of arable and pasture land, stripped of its forests by 600 years of human activity (with only the Ergeni area perhaps originally unforested), where the traditional agriculture has been improved by the growing of sugar-beet and sunflowers.

Except for the Istranca Hills, the Black Sea coast and the interior of the Kocaeli Peninsula, which are thinly settled, Thrace is well populated, with numbers of small and medium-sized towns distributed fairly regularly over its area. Two places merit special mention – the city of İstanbul, with its

İstanbul

great past and its present potential, its influence reaching out over the

Edirne

Bosporus into Anatolia, and Edirne (ancient Adrianopolis), the oldest of the Ottomans' strongholds, a city resplendent with works of art and architecture.

West of the
Sea of Marmara

The region south of the the Sea of Marmara shows a mixed pattern of hills and depressions, mostly running from west to east and a result of geologically recent upward and downward movements. The Gulf of İzmit, a recent

BITHYNIA

depression, is continued eastward by Lake Sapanca and, beyond this, the Adapazarı basin on the Lower Sakarya. A first ridge of hills to the south is followed by a second depression, consisting of the Gulf of Gemlik and its continuation, Lake İsnıl. A second ridge, extending farther west along the Sea of Marmara as a range of coastal hills of moderate height, is succeeded by a third depression consisting of the Bursa Basin and Lakes Apolyont and Manyas. In the mountains to the south of this depression the highest peak

Ulu Dağ

is Ulu Dağ (2543m/8344ft), the Mysian or Bithynian Olympus, with corries around its summit formed by two small glaciers during the Ice Age. Farther west, in the Troad, the pattern of relief is more irregular.

The Marmara region enjoys a Mediterranean climate. While the hills are covered with forests of pine and oak, the fertile basins between them have flourishing olive and fig groves, fruit orchards, vineyards, fields of corn and tobacco, as well as great expanses of grazing for sheep and cattle, consequently giving these basins a greater than average density of population.

Bursa

The region's main town is Bursa, with its mosques and sultans' tombs, in a lovely setting on the slopes of Ulu Dağ.

TROAD
Troy

The greatest of the many great sites of the past in the historic landscape of the Troad is ancient Troy, with its many levels of human settlement from prehistoric to Classical times.

Aegean Region

Aegean Coast

The Aegean region extends from the coast to the ranges of hills that make up the mountain barrier of western Anatolia, the watershed between the coastal region and the arid interior. Here, too, the land is broken up by depressions running from west to east, with between them mountain ranges, mostly of ancient rocks and often steeply scarped and rising to considerable heights (1000–2000m/3300–6600ft; Boz Dağ 2157m/7077ft). To the west the hills are continued by long peninsulas with much-indented coasts and by the Greek islands. The fertile rift valleys are watered by large rivers – the Gediz, the Küçük Menderes and the Büyük Menderes, the Meander of classical times – and covered with great fig plantations, olives, vineyards (used to make raisins as well as wine) and fields of tobacco, cotton and grain.

Thanks to its mild Mediterranean climate, this area has enjoyed human settlement and civilisation since the earliest times. It holds many magnificent remains of the past – Pergamum, Ephesus, Priene, Miletus, Didyma, Hieropolis, Aphrodisias and many more – and encompasses the ancient kingdoms of Mysia, Ionia, Lydia and Caria. Nowadays its various districts are centered on medium-sized towns which are the focus for the local industries Its major centre of population is the great port and industrial city of İzmir, Turkey's third largest city, with some 2,500,000 people living in and around it.

MYSIA, IONIA, LYDIA, CARIA

İzmir

Pamukkale, the "cotton castle" next to ancient Hieropolis, opposite Denizli in the valley of the Büyük Menderes, is the site of a magnificent natural pheonomenon where warm mineral springs bubble over the stalactites fringing its cascade of limestone travertines.

Pamukkale

Mediterranean Coast and Taurus Mountains

The south coast of Anatolia, much indented in its western section on which verge the ranges of the Western Taurus, here running almost due north-south, has only two large, widely arched bays between here and the Gulf of İskenderun – the Gulfs of Antalya and Mersin.

South coast of Anatolia

Eventide on the Gulf of Antalya

Geographical Regions

Western Taurus

The limestone mountains of the Western Taurus rear up steeply, directly from the coast, to heights of 2000m/6500ft or more, with some peaks towering to over 3000m/9800ft. Farther north they rise out of the broad coastal plain of Antalya and continue into the upland region of the interior with its many lakes. Here the Western Taurus gives place to the great arc of

Central Taurus

the Central Taurus, also built up of limestone, which runs south-east, east, north-east and finally north-north-east, and after a zone of lesser peaks reaches its highest points between Karaman and Silifke, attaining 3583m/11,756ft in Bolkar Dağ (Medetsiz) and over 3800m/12,500ft in the Cilican Ala Dağ.

PAMPHYLIA

East of Alanya, between the limestone mountains of the Central Taurus and the coast, is a lower range of wooded hills, formed of Palaeozoic crystalline schists and much dissected by valleys, which falls steeply down to the sea, leaving room only round the river estuaries for small areas of cultivable land – ricefields, banana plantations, groundnuts, vegetables grown in hothouses. There is a striking contrast between the seaward slopes of these hills, with their plentiful rainfall, and the arid inland side. On the southern slopes a lower vegetation zone reaching up to 700m/2300ft and in

The Principal Mountains, Rivers and Lakes in Turkey

places up to 1000m/3300ft, with plants sensitive to cold, olives and Aleppo pines (pinus brutia) interspersed with deciduous trees (oaks, planes, nut trees), followed by a zone of pines, cedars and junipers extending up to the treeline at 2200–2400m/7200–7900ft. The highest parts (Ala Dağ) run into the permanent snow region, with glaciers and patches of hard-frozen snow. On the northern side the pattern is very different: the steppe extends to the foot of the mountains, and only above 1200–1400m/3900–4600ft) where it is wet enough for trees, is there a zone of natural forest, although most of this has been destroyed.

The western part of the large coastal depression around the Gulf of Antalya consists of extensive travertine plateaux, in two stages – 200–250m/660–820ft and 40–120m/130–390ft. The big river plains spreading out to the east of this benefit from the climate and are intensively farmed, producing citrus fruit (particularly in the western part, near the coast), cotton, cereals and groundnuts. These plains are also used for winter grazing by the nomads who move up into the hills in summer. Large modern industrial sites (textiles, rubber, chromium) have sprung up on the travertine plateaux in the western half of the depression.

Coastal plain around the Gulf of Antalya

The Antalya Plain, long settled by man, was the heartland of the ancient region of Pamphylia and holds impressive remains of the cities of Perge, Aspendos and Side. The upland region to the west was part of Caria, while the region to the north belonged to Isauria. The town of Antalya, formerly Adalia, was founded in the 2nd c. B.C. by Attalos II of Pergamum, who named it Attaleia, and along with nearby Termessos and Phaselis, it still has much to show of its classical past.

CARIA
ISAURIA

CILICIA

The great Adana Plain, a recent infill plain, lies on the Gulf of Mersin and together with the low and gently sloping plateaux of Late Tertiary lime-stones and the hilly country of the hinterland forms the fertile and densely populated region of Çukurova. The rivers Seyhan (with a large dam) and Ceyhan flow down from the Central and Eastern Taurus with their abundant rainfall. The Çakıt Çay cuts through the Taurus in a narrow gorge which is also used by the Baghdad Railway on a boldly engineered stretch of line.

Cilician Gates

This passage through the mountains is within the Cilician Pass region, but the original pass – the Cilician Gates of antiquity – is a narrow gorge in a little valley which runs up from the Adana Plain to the Takir Pass (1200m/3900ft) and continues from there to meet the Çakıt Çay at Pozantı where road and rail converge, making it the real junction for the Cilican Pass region. Railroad and highway then continue together, running west and then north-west on the line of an old caravan route and drove road, going north over a low pass into a large basin on the west side of Ala Dağ and from there continuing farther into the interior.

Çukurova

In the Çukurova region plantations of citrus fruits and olives, vineyards, market gardens and the production for export of water-melons, auber-gines, tomatoes, etc., which ripen very early here, testify to the favourable climate. Cereals (wheat, barley, oats) are grown in winter when the nomads also move down here to their winter grazing grounds. Çukurova's main claim to fame, however, is as Turkey's major source of cotton. Most of the large plantation-holders are on the plain, but there are also small peasant holdings on the lower plateaux and upland regions, up to a height of about 500m/1640ft. The cotton harvest brings in large numbers of seasonal work-ers, and as an industry cotton is responsible for many local factories. The villages on the plain have square houses built of mud brick with the unusual feature of wooden shelters on their flat roofs to sleep under on the hot summer nights.

Mersin, Tarsus,
Adana

The main towns are Mersin with its large modern port, ancient Tarsus, and Adana on the River Seyhan. In antiquity the region was part of Cilicia, bounded on the west by Pisidia.

Central Anatolia

Plateau
GALATIA
CAPPADOCIA

The Central Anatolia plateau, north of the middle section in the great curve of the Taurus, is immediately a very different landscape. A vast dry virtually riverless area, it extends over the whole south-west of central Turkey and stretches eastwards as far as Erciyas Dağı. To the north the plateau gradu-ally merges with the foothills of Northern Anatolia, drained by the river systems of the Sakarya and the Kızılırmak running down into the Black Sea. The scenic features of Central Anatolia's landscape of broad rolling plains, at an altitude of between 800 and 1200m/2626 and 3938ft, also include rugged volcanic mountain ranges of tufa and lava, smoother ancient mountain massifs that soar, island-like, out of the plain, and the broad depressions of "ovas", bordered by gentle slopes.

Throughout the region the climate is typically continental, with hot sum-mers and cold winters. In the rain shadow of the surrounding mountains precipitation is nowhere greater than 400m/15¾in., and no trees occur naturally throughout the whole of the centre below the dryness limit at 1000–1400m/3282–4595ft.

The depressions hold salt lakes and marshes such as Tuz Gölü and Akşehir Gölü in the west and Sultan Sazlığı south of Erciyas Dağı. Farmers grow arable crops on the steppeland, and tend their herds of sheep and goats, including the famous Angoras. Their square houses have flat roofs and are built of mudbrick or stone if there are volcanic rocks nearby.

Most of the population live around the edge of the region. Here too are the major remains of the ancient civilisations: Boğazkale, the Hatusa of the Hittites north-east of Ankara, Alaçahüyük in the east and Gordium in the west in what was Phrygia. Roman cities include Ancyra (Ankara), Caesarea (Kayseri), Tyana (near Niğde) and Doylaeum (Eskişehir), while testimony to the Byzantine and Seljuk Empires can also be found in Ankara, Konya, Niğde and Kayseri as well. The better conditions around the rim of the plateau also account for the ring of large towns found there today – Eskişehir, Konya, Niğde, Kayseri and, chief among them, Ankara, much expanded and now Turkey's capital and second largest city.

Areas of ancient settlement round the rim

Eşkisehir, Konya, Niğde, Kayseri, Ankara

Amid the hills and valleys of Cappadocia, about 90km/56 miles south-west of Kayseri, the famous moonscapes of tufa pinnacles and hollowed-out caves of Göreme are among the highlights of Central Anatolia.

Göreme

Black Sea Coast and Mountains of Northern Anatolia

From the mouth of the Sakarya in the west to the frontier with Georgia in the east Turkey's Black Sea coast is flanked by an 1100km/685 miles long barrier of hills and mountains, ranging between 150 and 200km/95 and 125 miles across and consisting of a series of chains, mostly running parallel to the coast, with large longitudinal valleys and basins sunk into the floor of the Paphlagonian Seam. From the coastal region, which has plenty of rain throughout the year, especially in autumn and winter, the amount of rainfall gets less as it approaches the interior. On the coast the annual rainfall at the western end is 1000mm/40in., and in the mountains it reaches 1500mm/60in. but around Samsun, where the coast runs south-east, it sinks below 800mm/30in., while at the east end, in the Pontic region, it is over 2000mm/80in. The better climate on the coast is reflected in the vegetation, with trees susceptible to frost, such as the olive, occurring at the lower levels. Mixed deciduous forest, with a dense undergrowth of mostly rhododendrons, extends up to 1000m/3300ft, to be succeeded by hardy firs and pines. Further inland fir and scrub-oak replace the moisture-loving trees of the coast until eventually the only forest cover is on the northern mountain slopes where there is higher rainfall.

Pontine Mountains

At the western end of the coast, round Zonguldak, are large deposits of coal. Here, too, with the opening out of the Sakarya Valley into a basin at Adapazarı, begins a succession of large basins enclosed by hills – Düzce (100m/330ft), Bolu (700m/2300ft), Reşadiye (900m/2950ft) and Gerede (1300m/4265ft). The type of farming here differs markedly according to altitude and ranges from the intense cultivation of maize, tobacco and other crops in the lower of the basins to the growing of wheat and barley and the pasture land found in Gerede, which is the highest. The Kastamonu Basin (700m/2300ft) lies slightly farther north. While the coastal hills are still under 2000m/6560ft, the Ilgaz Massif south of Kastamonu rises to 2565m/8416ft, and Karoğlu Tepe south-east of Bolu to 2378m/7802ft.

Western section Zonguldak

Basin landscapes

Samsun, the main town on the Black Sea coast and an important exporter, lies in the fertile tobacco-growing low plain around the mouths of the Kızılırmak and the Yesilırmak.

Samsun

The taller mountain chains of the Zigana district, to the east, rise up to over 3000m/9850ft, soaring to 3937m/12,917ft in the Kaçkar range, where they become high Alpine peaks, their rugged forms carved out by glacial action – begun during the Ice Ages but still continuing today. One of the most important cash crops grown in the densely populated coastal region is tea, a major export as well as a source of domestic supply. Hazelnuts are another crop grown here, as they are all along the coast.

Eastern section Zigana distric

Trabzon

The main town on the eastern Black Sea coast is ancient Trebizond, now the port of Trabzon.

Eastern Anatolia

Plateau and
volcanic peaks

Ararat

Lake Van

Erzerum
Aras Trench

The central plateau which lies between the Taurus in the south and the Pontine Mountains in the north broadens out as the Eastern Taurus gradually swing south-east and the mountains along the Black Sea coast follow the coastline north-east. The northern part of this plateau south of the Kaçkar chain is covered by great pavements of lava and tufa, the result of young volcanic action, and is dotted with isolated volcanic peaks, most of them over 3000m/9850ft, of which the southernmost is Tendürük (3542m/11,625), north-east of Lake Van. Mount Ararat (Büyük Ağrı Dağ) soars to a majestic 5165m/16,952ft at a point where two fault lines meet. The system of Pontine chains that border Northern Anatolia continues over the top of the volcanic floor in the area north of the Aras district, while in the south the Taurus system carries on south of Lake Van (1648m/5408ft) to form the Hakkâri Mountains, at their highest in the glaciated peak of Cilo Dağı (4119m/13,519ft).

Eastern Anatolia has Turkey's most continental climate, with very hot summers, very cold winters, and rainfall so low that no trees grow on the plains or in the valleys. The southern Taurus foreland gets its water supply from the upper reaches of the Fırat (Euphrates) with the Murat and the Dicle (Tigris). The Aras (the Araxes of Classical times) rises in the high country in the basin of Erzerum (1950m/6400ft) and runs east in a tectonic depression – the Aras Trench – 160km/100 miles wide then turns south-east along the line of its tributary, the Arpa flowing in from the left, to form the boundary with Armenia and Iran before entering the Caspian Sea as it leaves Iranian territory. Most of the people who live here are farmers or herders. From 1878 to 1923 Kars, the north-east part of the region, was ruled by the Russians.

South-eastern Anatolia

Amanos
Mountains

Taurus foreland

MESOPOTAMIA
Tigris and
Euphrates

Diyarbakır

Nemrut Dağı
Harran
Karkamış

The Amanos mountains on the east side of the Gulf of Iskenderun stretch inland north-north-east to join the eastern ranges of the Taurus. The final spurs of the great Syrian rift valley, east of the Amanos, here extend into Turkey as far as the basin of Maras (Kahramanmaraş). Further east again the south-eastern Taurus foreland, 500km/310 miles long and 100–150km/62–93 miles across, already shows the flat layering of strata typical of the Syrian tableland. These are also accompanied by very young fold axes, outlying foothills from the folds of the Taurus. Recent volcanic action was responsible for Karaça Dağı (1919m/6298ft) which also marks the start of the lava pavements which stretch eastwards as far as Diyarbakır and south-westwards to the limestone tables of the Tektek Dağı. From here and far to the west karst formations feature among the limestone tables and rocky outcrops. The Fırat (Euphrates) and Dicle (Tigris) carve out their courses on either side of the high plains (500–700m/1640–2300ft) of Mesopotamia.

In this dry region of very hot summers trees only occur above 800m/2626ft. The local farmers grow mainly wheat or graze sheep, but this part of Turkey owes its major economic importance to the presence of oil. Diyarbakır, the regional capital, is connected to the main line through Malatya from Sivas and Eastern Anatolia, and the Baghdad railway runs eastwards along its southern border. Other important towns include Gaziantep, Şanlıurfa and, well to the west, Antakya, the Antioch of antiquity.

Chief among the region's historic sites are the ruins and colossi around the tomb of Antiochus I, King of Commagene atop Nemrut Dağı near Eski Kahta (in antiquity Arsemeia on the Nymphaios), along with Harran, mentioned in the Old Testament, and the Hittite capital of Karkamış, both close by the frontier with Syria.

GAP – South-eastern Anatolia Project

GAP (Güneydoğu Anadolu Projesi), Turkey's South-eastern Anatolia Project, is by far the country's biggest and most ambitious capital project. Designed to harness the waters of the Tigris and the Euphrates for the supply of both irrigation and electricity, it extends for over 74,000sq.km/28,564sq.miles from the Syrian border around the middle reaches of the two rivers up into the Taurus and Hakkâri mountains to the north, west and east, taking in large parts of the provinces of Urfa (Şanlıurfa), Mardin, Diyarbakır, Şırnak, Batman and Siirt.

This mammoth project encompasses dams, reservoirs and power plants on the Tigris, Euphrates and several other rivers, irrigation works, agricultural programmes and infrastructural improvements in transport and industry, as well as health and education programmes.

The most important elements of GAP are the irrigation projects and the hydro-electric plant. The largest of the reservoir dams is the Atatürk Barajı, designed primarily to alleviate the water shortage of the region and to improve farming by using modern methods to increase the cultivable area to a total of 1,856,627ha/4,587,725acres. The projects on the lower Turkish Euphrates alone will be responsible for 706,208ha/1,745,040acres of new irrigated land. GAP will entail a further 13 irrigation projects, three of them on the Euphrates and seven on the Tigris, as well as 21 dams and 17 hydro-electric plants capable of generating an additional 26 billion kilowatts – equivalent to Turkey's entire electricity supply for 1981.

Atatürk Dam (power plant, Urfa tunnel)	Individual projects
Karakaya Dam (power plant)	
Sınır-Fırat Dam (power plant)	
Suruç-Bazıkı irrigation project (three reservoirs)	
Adıyaman-Kahta project (four dams, five power plants)	
Adıyaman-Göksu-Araban irrigation project (several dams)	
Gaziantep project (three dams)	
Tigris-Kralkızı project (three dams, three power plants)	
Batman project (dam, power plant)	
Silvan project (two dams, power plant)	
Garzan project (dams, power plant)	
Ilısu Dam (power plant)	
Cizre Dam (power plant)	

The plan is to make the whole of the 47% of the region's potential farmland currently fallow suitable for cultivation. This will more than double Turkey's cotton output (including for export), treble its pistachio crop and increase its rice production for home consumption by more than 85%. The new irrigated cultivable areas will be greater than all those already existing in the country put together. **Plan**

The GAP project was first embarked on in the early Seventies and is expected to be completed within twenty years. **Completion period**

The capital cost, in 1991 values, is estimated to be the equivalent of one year's national budget for Turkey; this breaks down to about 60% for irrigation works and 40% for power plants. **Cost**

The core of the South-eastern Anatolia Project is Atatürk Barajı, the great Atatürk Dam east of Adıyaman across the waters of the central Euphrates (Fırat Nehri); this is designed to provide irrigation for 52% of the total new acreage. In doing so the dam is associated with a number of other individual projects: **Atatürk Barajı (Atatürk Dam)**

Urfa Tunnel[1] and power plant
Harran-Urca-Ova irrigation works
Mardin-Ceylanpınar irrigation works
Siverek-Hilvan irrigation works
Bozova irrigation works

[1]The twin pipelines of the Urfa tunnel will carry the water for the Harran

25

South-east Anatolia Project GAP – Karakaya Reservoir

Ovası from the Atatürk reservoir to the low-lying plain between Şanlıurfa (Urfa) and Harran.

Technical data Atatürk Dam	Height of the dam	169m/555ft
	Width of dam parapet	15m/49ft
	Breadth of dam across	1614m/5297ft
	Reservoir surface area	817sq.km/315sq.miles
	Volume of water in reservoir	48470cu.m/171,196cu.ft
	Maximum capacity	84,500cu.m/2,984,540cu.ft
	Irrigated surface area	92,338ha/2,107,222acres
	Catchment area	92,338sq.km/35,642sq.miles
	Power plant generated capacity (8×300MW)	2400MW
	Annual power supply	8.9 bio kWh
Urfa Tunnel	Length of tunnel	26.4km/16.4 miles
	Volume of throughput	328cu.m/11,584cu.ft/sec

Main barrages along the **Euphrates** and its tributaries

From north to south: Keban Barajı · Karakaya Barajı · Atatürk Barajı · Birecik Barajı · Karkamış Barajı · Büyük Çayı Barajı · Kâhta Barajı · Sırımtaş Barajı · Koçalı Barajı · Sürgü Barajı · Çataltepe Barajı · Besni Barajı · Çamgazi Barajı · Kayacık Barajı · Kemlin Barajı · Seve Barajı · Hacıdır Barajı · Siverek Barajı · Kale Barajı

Main barrages along the **Tigris** and its tributaries

From north to south: Hazae Gölü (lake source) · Krlkızı Barajı · Dicle Barajı · Dipni Barajı · Devegeçidi Barajı · İlisu Barajı · Cizre Barajı · Silvan Barajı · Kayser Barajı · Batman Barajı · Ayşehatun Barajı · Kor Barajı · Garzan Barajı · Ceffan Barajı · Dilaver Barajı · Göksu Barajı

Other reservoirs

Kartlkaya · Harmancık · Tozlucva · Aylan · Taşbasan · Derik · Mardin

Small basins

Diner · Camurlu · Kesmekaya · Alancık · Uğurlu · Uzunpınar · Özenpınar · Uzunca · Mavigöl · Demirkapı · Taşli · Buğur · Ballıcar · Cöye · Gölebakan ·

Büyükkazanlı · Tanrıverdı · Tazonu · Gürseli · Demirci · Koşunlu · Gölcük ·
Demirli

Climate

General

What distinguishes Turkey's climate is the marked contrast between the
coastal regions and the interior.

The western and southern coasts have the hot dry summers and warm wet
winters of the Mediterranean climate, while the Black Sea coast, with its
Pontic climate, has wet summers as well as winters.

The interior has a continental climate, shielded by its mountains from the
sea, although the climate on the plateau of Western Anatolia is distinctly
different from that of the high country of Eastern Turkey which is colder and
gets more rain and snow.

The south-east of the country, around the upper reaches of the Tigris and
Euphrates, has hot summers and a climate all of its own.

The climate tables show what the climate is like in the different regions of
Turkey in terms of temperature and rainfall from January (J) to December
(D).

The orange curve stands for the temperatures in celsius, with the upper
edge of the band representing average maximum daytime temperatures,
and the lower edge average minimum night-time temperatures. The
breadth of the band is an indication of the daily variation in temperature,
while the steepness of the curve shows just how much temperatures vary
over the year. In many years these figures can vary but the more rarely this
occurs the greater the variation will be.

The blue columns show the monthly rainfall in millimetres.

These tables can also be used to estimate what the climate will be like for
the parts of the country between these particular measuring points. Here a
few other pointers can be helpful as well:

● On the coast or inland:
   Daily and annual temperature variations are less on the coast than they
   are inland because of the sea's influence. Winds off the sea bring
   cooling breezes onland in the daytime and are replaced by warm winds
   off the land at night.
● Leeward or windward side of mountains:
   When they meet mountains winds chill as they rise higher, forming
   rainclouds as they cool down and thus bringing rain to the windward
   side. On the other side, to the lee of the mountains, the air heats up as it
   descends and the clouds disperse.
● Altitude:
   Temperatures fall with a rise in altitude. Depending on the season and
   the humidity the drop in temperature can be by as much a whole degree.
   Precipitation increases with altitude, and this can be seen from the
   vegetation, even in the heat of summer, as evidenced by the tree growth
   around the tops of the mountains rising up out of the central plains.

The typical weather pattern for Turkey is determined by the movement of
air on a grand scale in an overwhelmingly southerly direction.

The winds in the summer – from June/July to September – are northerlies,
sucked in by the heated-up landmasses of the Sahara and Arabia. On
Turkey's north coast these winds blow onland, causing clouds and rainfall
on the mountain slopes. Low pressure areas, which have freshened over
the Black Sea, also bring rain, even in summer, to the Pontine Mountains.
Central Anatolia, on the other hand, is in the rainshadow, on the leeside of

**Climatic
contrasts**
Coastal regions

Interior

South-east

Climate tables
Temperatures
and rainfall

Climatic factors

**Seasonal weather
patterns**
Summer

Climate

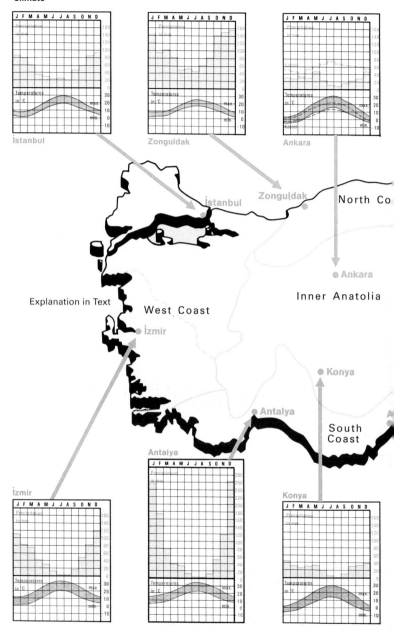

İstanbul

Zonguldak

Ankara

İstanbul

Zonguldak

North Co

Ankara

Inner Anatolia

Explanation in Text

West Coast

İzmir

Konya

Antalya

South Coast

Antalya

İzmir

Konya

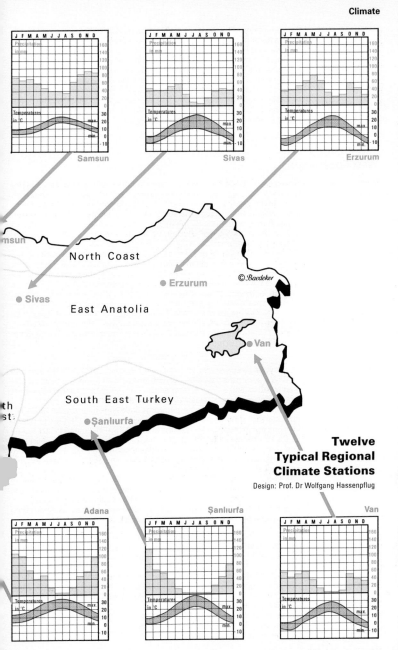

North Coast

East Anatolia

South East Turkey

© Baedeker

**Twelve
Typical Regional
Climate Stations**

Design: Prof. Dr Wolfgang Hassenpflug

Samsun

Sivas

Erzurum

Adana

Şanlıurfa

Van

Climate

the mountains. The western and southern coasts have none of these factors for bringing winds inland, apart from the gentle local winds off land and sea, and consequently get virtually no rain in summer.

In winter Turkey's weather is dominated by the strong and extensive high pressure area over northern Asia. The interior is bitterly cold, with no wind and no rain. The winter rain typical of the Mediterranean falls when this dominant weather pattern is interrupted by low pressure areas which form or freshen over the seas around Turkey. This is when snow falls up in the mountains. The Cyprus Low is well known for moving east and bringing plenty of winter rain and snow to south-eastern Turkey.

West Coast (Aegean)

Mediterranean climate

Turkey's west coast has a Mediterranean climate with wet winters and dry summers, although the temperatures are generally lower than on the south coast. In the valleys running west to east the Mediterranean climate penetrates well inland because the surrounding ridges are colder and wetter. Hence Bursa, which is only 100m/328ft above sea level, has a rainfall of 730mm/2¾in. as against Uludağ, up in the mountains (1920m/6310ft), which gets 1544mm/61in.

The west coast climate gets increasingly wetter towards the north. In the Marmara region the Mediterranean and Pontic climatic factors cut across one another. The Black Sea coasts on either side of the Bosporus and the shores of the Sea of Marmara are exposed to cold fronts in winter from the Balkans. In the west to east mountain areas the northern "hazelnut" slopes, which get north winds in summer, also tend to get some rain at that time of year, whereas the lee of the hills, facing south, the "olive" side, tend to be dry. Here the maximum altitude for growing olives – the sign of a Mediterranean climate – is 100–200m/328–656ft as compared with 400m/1313ft in the central Aegean area.

İzmir
(sea level)

January air temperatures in İzmir range between 4°C/39°F at night and 13°C/55°F during the day, although extreme cold air fronts can be accompanied by frosts and a drop in temperature to −5°C/23°F. In July and August temperatures range between 20°C/68°F and 33°C/91°F.

By February the mean sea temperatures have sunk to as low as 13°/55°FC, then start to climb again in April (15°C/59°F) and May (18°C/64°F) before levelling out in the summer months at over 20°C/68°F (June 21°C/69°F, July 23°C/73°F, August 23°C/73°F, September 22°C/71°F, October 20°C/68°F).

The annual number of hours of sunshine amounts to 2929, 113 and 131 of them in December and January respectively, and 380 hours each for July and August.

The annual rainfall of 652mm/25in. covers 60 days – 10 days each in December and January, four days each in May and October, two days each in June and September and less than one day in July and in August.

In summer the annual north-westerly "etesians" over the Aegean bring cooling and often gusty breezes in their wake.

İstanbul
(40m/131ft)

Summer daytime temperatures in İstanbul stay below the 30°C/86°F mark, and the daily temperature variation throughout the year is less than in İzmir.

Water temperatures are much lower than further south, at 8°C/46°F from January to March, 11°C/52°F in April, 15°C/59°F in May, 20°C/68°F in June, 22°C/71°F in July, 23°C/73°F in August, 21°C/69°F in September and 19°C/66°F in October.

Hours of sunshine total 2480 for the year, with 70 of them in December, 80 in January, 364 in July and 350 in August.

Annual rainfall is 667mm/26in.

South Coast (Mediterranean coast)

Antalya (40m/131ft) **and Adana** (24m/79ft)

Turkey's south coast has a typical Mediterranean climate of wet winters Mediterranean
and hot summers. It owes this to its south-facing position and the fact that it climate
is sheltered from the cold north winds by the Taurus Mountains – which
mark the weather divide – while at the same time benefitting from the
climatic advantages of being on a sea where the water temperature never
drops below 16°C/60°F, even in winter. Its pleasant climate is also reflected
in the vegetation. Here olive trees, typical for this kind of weather pattern,
grow up to an altitude of 700m/2300ft. Citrus groves, notoriously sensitive
to the cold, grow in the narrow confines of the coastal plains, as they do
along the southern reaches of the west coast as far as Kuşadası. Cold air
fronts in winter and a drop in temperature to −10°C/21°F only happen once
in every 40 to a hundred years. However every now and then short sharp
frosts can strike when cold air gets over the sheltering mountains and,
despite warming up as it descends, reaches the coastal lowlands in the
form of the "Poyraz", the Turkish equivalent of the Bora on the Dalmatian
coast.

Nearness to the sea means that even in winter night-time temperatures Temperatures
never drop below 5°C/41°F, while daytime temperatures peak at 15°C/59°F.
The variation in July and August is between 22°C/71°F at night and
34°C/93°F in the day. Close to the coast pleasant cooling breezes blow in
from the sea by day, with the process reversed by night.
In the spring water temperatures climb more slowly than air temperatures
(April 17°C/62°F, May 20°C/68°F, June 23°C/73°F). In July they reach
25°C/77°F, August 27°C/80°F, September 26°C/78°F, November still
20°C/68°F, then in December 18°C/64°F.
Antalya gets almost as many hours of sunshine a year as Şanlıurfa in
south-eastern Turkey – 142 hours in December, 153 in January and 387 in
July. Potential evaporation, at 1000mm/39in., is accordingly on the same
scale.

Most of the rain comes in the winter months, when the "Cyprus Low" Rainfall
sweeps plenty of rain in along the coast and as far inland as the farthest
reaches of the Eastern Taurus and up into the "fertile crescent" of Upper
Mesopotamia and Iran; the mountain slopes to windward are particularly
well watered. East of Antalya the Taurus range running north-west/south-
east actually gets over 2000mm/78in. of rain a year, thus giving Turkey's
highest annual rainfall, on a par with the eastern stretches of the Black Sea
coast. The number of rainy days changes very little from year to year
(Antalya 1057mm/41in. a year on 57 days, Adana 619mm/24in. on 51 days).
From time to time Turkey's coastline experiences short-lived but very
heavy downpours – about every ten years not only the south coast but also
the north coast and less frequently the west coast can expect over
100mm/4in. a day (maximum for Antalya 290mm/11in., Rize 244mm/9in.
and İzmir 231mm/9in.) during their rainy season.

North Coast (Black Sea coast)

Zonguldak (42m/138ft) **and Samsun** (40m/131ft)

Turkey's Black Sea coast has a climate all its own, unlike those of the west Pontic climate
and south coasts. This is the Pontic climate which is much wetter overall,
especially in summer, and has much more even temperatures throughout
the year, hence the narrowness of the orange band on the climate tables.

Air temperatures only range between 2–3°C/35–37°F at night and Temperatures
9–10°C/48–50°F during the day in winter, and between 17–18°C/62–64°F and
25–26°C/77–78°F in summer.

31

Climate

Sea temperatures, measured at Trabzon, are at their lowest (8°C/46°F) in February and March, compared with 9°C/48°F in April, 14°C/57°F in May, 20°C/68°F in June, 24°C/75°F in July and August, 22°C/71°F in September and 19°C/66°F in October.

Rainfall

The coast gets rain all year round, but rainfall is at its lowest in July/August, followed by the maximum figure in the autumn. Northerlies blowing off the sea bring cloud up to a height of 2000m/6564ft, turning to heavy rain as they encounter low pressure squalls from the north-west. Consequently the north-west facing coast around Zonguldak and Trabzon, further east, gets more rain than the areas around Samsun which face more directly into the wind. Rainfall is greater at the eastern end of the coast than the western end because the air masses have warmed up and been charged with more moisture as they have travelled the greater distance over the Black Sea (Zonguldak 1179mm/46in. a year on 110 days, Samsun 739mm/29in. on 92 days, Rize, east of Trabzon, 2415mm/95in.). Turkey's heaviest rainfall is recorded at Kemalpaşa on the Georgian frontier which gets 2652mm/104in. a year.

Central Anatolia

Ankara (900m/2954ft) **and Konya** (1025m/3364ft)

Continental climate

The great plateau of Anatolia, lying as it does at an altitude of from 900m/2954ft to over 1000m/3282ft and shielded by the Pontine Mountains in the north and the Taurus in the south, has a continental climate of moderately cold and wet winters and hot dry summers.

Temperatures

Cloudless skies and long hours of sunshine mean wide swings in daily and yearly temperature, hence the relatively steep curve and wide breadth of the orange band in the climate tables. From December to March nighttime temperatures fall to below freezing, while the top daytime figures remain well above.
East of Konya, however, the narrow stretch on the northern slopes of the Taurus has comparatively warm winters thanks to warm dry "foehn" winds like those on the north side of the Alps.
In the cold winter air the inversions that often occur in the valleys and basins can turn pollutants from towns and industries into smog when warm air up above traps the colder air nearer the ground.

Rainfall

The rainfall comes almost entirely in the winter months, amounting to somewhere between 300mm/11in. and 500mm/19in. (Ankara 344mm/13in. on 68 days, Konya 333mm/13in. on 50 days), although at Tuz Gölü and several other places it can be even less than that.
Winter sees only a thin covering of snow, which soon vanishes with the rapid alternation of frost and thaw (Ankara 24 days with snow, Konya 22 days).
The maximum rainfall is in the spring, when local warm depressions, at a time when the land has already warmed up and the seas are still cold, can combine with cold fronts to bring violent squally showers which now and again turn into heavy downpours (maximum figure for Ankara: 69mm/2¾in. a day). Drought and failure of the grain harvests can result if the rainfall gets concentrated in this way, draining away to no good effect, or if there is no rain after March or it is well below average.

Eastern Anatolia

Sivas (1185m/3889ft), **Erzerum** (1951m/6403ft) **and Van** (1732m/5684ft)

Climate variation

Climatic conditions can vary considerably within a small area depending on altitude and position in relation to the mountains. Basin and valley locations are dryer and hotter while places in the mountains are wetter and cooler. The climate tables are for basin locations.

Temperatures are very much dictated by altitude. At Erzerum, for example, even the top daytime temperatures from December to February are below freezing. This whole region can reckon on getting over 130 days of frost a year.
Temperatures in summer range between a minimum of 10–13°C/50–55°F at night and a maximum 26–28°C/78–82°F during the day.

Temperatures

On average the low-lying locations only get an annual precipitation of 300–400mm/12–16in. (Sivas 422mm/17in. on 53 days, Erzerum 540mm/21in. on 89 days, Van 395mm/16in. on 70 days) but those at higher altitudes get over twice as much – 1000–2000mm/39–79in. in the Eastern Taurus and 600–1000mm/24–39in. in the Taurus of the interior, thus providing the headwaters feeding the Tigris and Euphrates.
Spring is the season of the heaviest rainfall. Sivas gets nine days of rain in May, Erzerum eleven and Van 16 in April.
Winter precipitation comes down as snow which can often lie in thick drifts at above 1500m/4923ft, blocking the high passes and leading to avalanches. West of an imaginary line from Trabzon to Lake Van the snow stays around for 30 to 60 days a year, while to the east it remains for at least two months and more.

Precipitation

South-eastern Turkey

Şanlıurfa (540m/1772ft)

This part of the country, south of the Eastern Taurus, is the hottest in all Turkey. Here the sun shines for 3214 hours of the year, with 408 hours in July alone, while December and January still get 126 and 124 hours respectively.

Hot summer-type climate

Moving inland from the southern flanks of the Taurus, temperatures increase steadily as the terrain flattens out towards Arabia, peaking at their highest for the whole country on the Syrian border. At Şanlıurfa in July and August they exceed 38°C/100°F during the day and fall to 23°C/73°F at night, while the top temperatures recorded between June and September are over 40°C/104°F. In winter even the lowest nighttime temperatures remain above freezing, and January is the only month when the top daytime temperatures just fall below the 10°C/50°F mark.

Temperatures

The reverse of temperature, rainfall gets progressively less from the edge of the Taurus to the frontier with Syria. Şanlıurfa still has 461mm/18in. a year but the figure on the Syrian border to the south-west is less than 300mm/12in. The need for irrigation is correspondingly greater. Potential evaporation here annually is 1100mm/43in., two to three times greater than the amount of rainfall.
On average snow cover is present for only 2.7 days a year, and just over half that is in January.

Precipitation

Flora and Fauna

Flora

The difference in landscape between Turkey's dry interior and lush coasts is most marked in the vegetation. It is only around the perimeter that trees can grow naturally everywhere up to the timberline, here dependent on

Vegetation

temperature. In the interior, as in the south-eastern foreland, timber only appears above a certain altitude but here this also has a lower limit set by the dryness factor. No trees occur naturally throughout the vast plains of south-western Central Anatolia, nor are they to be found in the basins and valleys of the higher upland and mountain country of Eastern Turkey.

Dryness limit

The dryness limit in the south-eastern Taurus foreland between the Tigris and Euphrates is at 800m/2626ft; in the interior of Anatolia it gets higher from west to east, climbing rapidly from 800–1000m/2626–3282ft to 1200–1400m/3938–4595ft in the main part of Central Anatolia, getting progressively higher still towards the east until it appears at 1800m/5908ft around Lake Van and even as high as 2100m/6892ft in the mountains of the extreme east.

Timberline

The timberline marking the upper limit follows the same course as the dryness limit, progressing from 2000–2200m/6562–7218ft in the western mountains up to 2600–2800m/8530–9186ft in the ranges on the extreme east. Unlike the coastal fringe trees can only grow in the Anatolian heartland in the belt of altitude between the two limits. Undergrowth, drawing as it does on a groundwater supply, only appears along the rivers. Naturally occurring timber is therefore only possible over about two-thirds of the whole country's surface area; about a quarter is natural steppe while the rest is high mountains or open water. Erosion and the destruction of woodland, and conversion to farming and grazing have combined to bring about a drastic reduction in all forms of tree cover, and that includes maquis and other kinds of scrub.

Vegetation zones

Like anywhere else, Turkey's natural vegetation is ruled by the height it grows at, how much rain it gets and which season the rain falls in.
The climatic differences between the Black Sea and the Mediterranean coasts are naturally also reflected in different forms of vegetation.

Aleppo pine

Reed beds and forest

Hibiscus   *Oranges ripening*

The pattern of vegetation on the Black Sea coast is much like that of Central Europe. Fir, spruce, beech, oak, plane, elm, lime, ash and maple still flourish in those heavily wooded areas that have survived the depradations of intensive cultivation along the coast. Rhododendrons grow in profusion, as well as other evergreen shrubs like laurel and arbutus.

North coast

Under the pressure of its expanding population the Black Sea region is steadily losing its once luxuriant wild woods to the advance of cultivated fields and plantations, where the main crops grown are maize and hazelnuts. Figs, which are particularly hardy trees, thrive all along Turkey's northern coastline, while mandarin oranges are found in the more sheltered parts and tea is grown round Rize. Olives can also grow in some parts of the region but rarely above 100–200m/330–660ft.

The vegetation on Turkey's south and west coasts is typical of the Mediterranean, especially the ubiquitous thick evergreen scrub of the maquis. This contains the whole range of characteristic Mediterranean species – holmoak, with its small shiny prickly leaves, arbutus, carob, briar, or tree heath, and myrtle – dotted with patches of light woodland or cultivation. Although centuries of slash-and-burn for farming have considerably reduced the original tree cover Turkey's coastline still has more wooded countryside than the other countries on the Mediterranean. The main forest tree is "pinus brutia", a variety of the Aleppo pine. The stone pine, also widespread, has large round cones containing edible seeds rather like hazelnuts. The most important of the cultivated trees is the olive which grows well on the west coast up to about 400m/1300ft, on the south coast up to 700m/2300ft and in sheltered spots even up to 1000m/3300ft. Other crops grown on the fertile coastal plains, with or without irrigation, include citrus fruit, wine grapes, figs, vegetables and, to an increasing extent, cotton and bananas.

South and west coasts

The basin landscapes in Turkey's interior are overwhelmingly treeless steppe, originally grassland but steadily depleted by overgrazing to

Anatolia

35

become semi-desert, with shrubby wormwood, spiny cushions, thistles, spurges, etc.

Natural steppe vegetation – grasses, wormwood, crocus and other bulbs – only occurs in the Ergene basin in the very centre, on the Anatolian plateau around Eskişehir, Konya, and Nevşehir, in a few depressions in the east and around the foothills of the Eastern Taurus. Spring transforms the steppe into a verdant, blossoming landscape which then turns bleak and sere with the coming of summer.

Trees such as black pine, fir, cedar and oak still grow on some of the mountainsides in the interior. The Pontine Mountains fringing the north coast have predominantly mixed woodland – firs, beech and oak – with here and there a stand of juniper. Clusters of spiny cushions are common in the rugged high mountain region.

Fauna

Wild animals

Turkey has a wealth of different species but their numbers have been drastically reduced by mankind. It is a country which holds the creatures of three different continents, with Africa represented by species such as porcupine and mongoose south of the Taurus, Asia by animals who have found their way here from the semi-deserts such as the camel – nowadays more likely to be encountered as a beast of burden – gerbil, wolf, fox and jackal, while the mountains still harbour bear, deer and wild boar and, in the Taurus, the occasional leopard and other wild cats.

Along the coasts recent decades have also taken a heavy toll on the wildlife. The burning of forests and the total lack of any controls on hunting – open season on any creature all year round – mean that deer, wild sheep and goats have become a rare sight indeed. The dense woods of the Black Sea coast are the only place where anyone is more likely to come across deer and some of the smaller mammals.

Tortoise

Donkeys

Those humble beasts of burden, the donkey and the mule, patiently bear their loads throughout the country.

Tortoises

Tortoises are remarkably common all along Turkey's south and west coasts, while loggerhead turtles breed in the Dalyan Delta.

Birds

The autumn migration of birds of prey and storks over the Bosporus is one of the great spectacles of the bird world. Black kites are also a familiar sight around İstanbul, and white storks breed in all the wetlands.

Marine life

Although fishermen not infrequently resort to dynamite and dragnets some parts of the coast still boast a surprising variety of marine creatures in great numbers. Hence the eastern Mediterranean still has its dolphins as well as mackerel, bass, moray eel, nearly all the sea bream, crustaceans and, a real speciality, the dark red parrot-fish, the only representative of its tropical family to have established itself in the Mediterranean.

Population

Evolution

Despite a process of evolution that goes back over thousands of years, including no less than four millennia of recorded history and which involved massive movements of peoples, their co-existence and assimilation

An evening occupation

A woman wearing Turkish trousers

– Hittites, Phrygians, Persians, Macedonians, Greeks, the Celtic Galatians, Romans, Arabs, Seljuk and Ottoman Turks – the people of Turkey are relatively homogeneous in terms of physical characteristics, mostly Near Eastern in their looks, of medium height and a sturdy build, square featured and with dark hair and eyes.

After the Ottoman Empire had been cut back to the country's present boundaries, the forces of nationalism strengthened their position through pogroms against the Armenians, the emigration and deportation of Greeks living in Asia Minor, then only allowed to stay on in certain zones (İstanbul and the Aegean islands of İmroz and Bozcaada), and restricting where the Kurds could settle while, on the other hand, securing the return of over a million muhacir Muslims from Bulgaria, Yugoslavia, Greece and Romania.

Due chiefly to a higher number of births than deaths, Turkey's population more than tripled in just over fifty years this century, shooting up from a good 13.6 million in 1927 to 44.7 million in 1980, and already topping 58.5 million in 1992, showing an annual average growth rate of 2.4% between 1980 and 1990. Over 10% of Turkey's population live in the European part, Avrupa Türkiyesi.

Growth and numbers

Population density for the country as a whole works out at 75.5 to the square kilometre/195 to the square mile, a figure in which the low population density of the interior and especially the mountainous east and the dry south-west is offset against those areas around Turkey's perimeter, already densely populated and where the growth rate is still on the increase, such as the eastern Black Sea coast, the stretch from Ereğli to Zonguldak, the low-lying lands of Marmara and the Aegean, and the plains behind Antalya, Adana and İskenderun, plus the Hatay at Antakya.

Density

Over 90% of the population are Turks, at least 7% Kurds (officially "mountain Turks") and an estimated 1.6% Arabs; other ethnic minorities living in

Nationalities

37

Religion

Turkey include Circassians (Cherkess), Georgians, Laz, Armenians, Abkhazians, Chechens, Yezidians, Greeks, Bulgarians, Albanians and Jews.

Some statistics
Turkey has an active population of over 20 million, with 47% making their living from the land, barely 20% in industry and just 1% in tourism. Well over a million Turks live and work abroad.
The proportion of the population living in towns has risen from 18.8% in 1927 to 60% in 1992.
Average life expectancy is 67, the literacy rate is 19%, infant mortality 6% and the official unemployment figure 8%.

Language
The official language is Turkish; the minorities use their own languages among themselves.

Education
Under Atatürk's secular reforms school attendance is officially compulsory from the age of six to 14 but in practice this only applies to the primary school years. Schooling is free and co-educational. Although vocational training is not wholly in place there are adequate secondary schools.
The whole country has close on 30 universities and colleges. Particular emphasis is placed on teacher training, and adult education also plays an important role.

Religion

Over 97% of Turks are Muslims, predominantely Sunnite with about 27% Alevi (Shiite); there are also small minorities of Jews and Orthodox, Catholic, and Protestant Christians.

Islam

Islam is the youngest of the world religions. It is the faith preached by Mohammed Ibn Abdallah, later to be known as the Prophet Mohammed, who was born in Mecca about A.D. 570, a member of the Quraysh tribe. Through long journeys with trading caravans and his own deep interest in religion he acquired a knowledge of the faiths practised in his own and other lands, so that his teachings contain concepts drawn from Judaism, Christianity, the Persian religion, and various Arab tribes. Above all, they incorporated and further developed monotheism as a doctrine.

Monotheism
The prime creed of Islam is that of total monotheism – there is but one God, and that God is Allah. Man is but the subject of that one god, Allah, the all-knowing and all-powerful, the creator of all things. Man's fate (Kismet, Mektub) lies entirely in Allah's hands, it is predetermined and man can do nothing to change it. It is this belief which also accounts for the fatalism found in Muslim countries and which rules the lives of individuals as well as the State (although not officially in Turkey since its secularisation by Kemal Atatürk). This much is quite clear from the very word Islam itself, meaning as it does "surrender to God".

Prophets
Islam's second fundamental tenet is that God's laws are conveyed through the prophets to whom God's word had been revealed. These include figures from the Old and the New Testament – Abraham, Isaac and Moses, Jesus and John the Baptist. Mohammed himself is among their number, but considered the last and the greatest of them all. He first began preaching his new faith in Mecca around 607. This brought him into conflict with his fellow Meccans, who worshipped many different pagan gods, and in 622 he was forced to flee to Yathrib, thereafter named Medinet en Nebi (city of the Prophet), Medina for short. The Muslim era, and calendar, is dated from the "hijra", as the year of Mohammed's flight from Mecca is called, since the founding of the religious community in Medina marked the first

acceptance of Muhammad's doctrine and acknowledgement that he was the messenger of God.

The sacred book of Islam is the Koran, to which has been added the Sunna. The Koran contains the word of God as vouchsafed by the Angel Gabriel to his prophet Muhammad. The Koran is divided into 114 chapters called suras. These are arranged not chronologically but according to length so that suras praising God can be in among descriptions of Hell and Paradise or rules and commandments governing daily behaviour.

Koran

Although Mohammad is said to have dictated the angel's revelations to his scribe, no complete collection existed on his death, and initially they were handed on by word of mouth. The final form of the Koran, still in use today, was eventually compiled by the third Caliph (Uthman; 644–656). This Arabic text is the only valid and sacred one, since this was the language in which God's word was revealed.

Sunna is Arabic for "rule" in the sense of "ways of behaviour", "the path one should follow". The Sunna is thus a body of traditional Islamic law based on the words and acts of the Prophet Mohammed, describing the rules he and his wife observed in their daily lives and their treatment of others, and serving as rules for Muslims to live their own lives by. Originally this too was handed down by word of mouth. It was first written down in the 9th c.

Sunna

Muslims who observe the Koran and the Sunna call themselves Sunnites, and nowadays this is the sect to which most Turkish Muslims belong.

Sunnites

Shiites, who observe the Koran but not the Sunna, belong to the second great sect of Islam. The split began with Ali, Mohammed's cousin and son-in-law, who became fourth Caliph (i.e. successor of Mohammed) in 656. The rift was finally sealed with Ali's murder in 661 and the flight of his followers. Ali maintained that only blood relatives of the Prophet could be his successors. Consequently he and his adherents, the Shiites (in Arabic "Shiat Ali", the party of Ali), did not recognise the three Caliphs who preceeded him – Abu Bakr (632–634), Omar (d.644) and Othman (d.656). Moreover Ali saw himself as the Prophet's first rightful successor. The Shiites likewise refused to recognise any Caliphs who succeeded him unless they were of his blood. They held the same view of the Sunna since besides the rules of Mohammed it also contained those of his successors. The Shiites, however, do venerate the first leaders descended from Ali, the Imams, and await their salvation from the Mahdi, the last Imam, who is to establish a kingdom of apocalyptic righteousness in this world. Most present-day Shiites regard him to be the twelfth true successor of Mohammed (twelfth Shia), although a lesser number, the Ismailites, consider he will be the seventh Shia. The Imams are venerated as saints, the Shiite religious beliefs entailing a substantially greater degree of mysticism than those of the Sunni Muslims.

Shiites

The codes of the Koran and the Sunna, taken together, form the Shariah, or Islamic holy law, although in Turkey this has been replaced with civil and criminal codes on the European model.

Shariah

Islam also enjoins its believers to spread the faith and in the past this was enforced by the "Jihad", the waging of "holy war" against the infidel. Nowadays this is only taken to be a duty to defend oneself against the hostile unbeliever. Some particularly enlightened Muslim theologians now interpret this phrase in the Koran as "to strive on the path to Allah", i.e. the duty to strive to conquer one's own shortcomings.

Holy War

Besides the five "Pillars of the Faith" (see Baedeker Special, The Five Pillars of Islam), there are many other important ordinances that the good Muslim must observe in his private life such as prohibitions against alcohol and the eating of pork, usury and all forms of gambling. Animals must be slaughtered according to fixed rules, and there must be no consumption of blood or blood products.

Religious ordinances

The Five Pillars of Islam

The **five pillars of Islam** are the duties of the faith imposed on its followers by the Koran. They are *Shahidah*, the profession of faith, *Salat*, prayer, *Sakat*, alms-giving, *Saum*, fasting, and *Hadj*, pilgrimage to Mecca.

Shahidah is the profession of faith that "there is no God but Allah and Mohammed is his prophet". This must be repeated, in Arabic, many times during the day and is intoned to the faithful five times daily, from the minaret of the mosque, with the Muezzin, nowadays more likely to be a tape recording or via a loudspeaker than the unaided human voice. It is "cradle-song, dirge, password, war cry and hallelujah" all in one. Anyone who pronounces the Shahidah before Muslim witnesses thereby embraces Islam.

Salat, the duty of prayer, must also be performed by believers five times a day. They are summoned by the call to prayer (Adhan) of the Muezzin at dawn, midday, three in the afternoon, sunset and then two hours later.
The practice of religion being founded, according to the Koran, on cleanliness, before prayer face, mouth, hands and feet must be clean (hence the fountain for ritual bathing in the mosque courtyard; if no water is available the purification can be symbolic and, say, sand can be used), clothing must be clean (hence footwear is always removed), and the ground upon which the believer prays must also be clean (hence the use of some form of prayer carpet). The believer must also give a mute declaration of his intention to pray.

The believer must pray facing in the direction of Mecca and also take up strictly prescribed prayer positions.

Postures for Islamic Prayers

© *Baedeker*

1 Standing upright, the hands raised to shoulder level and facing the front (with the thumbs behind the lobes of the ears), he says '"Alláhu ákbar" (Allah is great).
2 Still standing, with the arms hanging down or with the right hand placed over the left in the middle of the body, he recites the first sura of the Koran (*Fatikhaj*) and then the other sura or verses.
3 Bowing, with hands on knees, he praises Allah.
4 There follow further expressions of praise while in a prostrate attitude, with the forehead touching the ground.
5 After every other prayer and also after the last one he recites the creed, with the forefinger of the right hand placed on his knee.
6 At the conclusion of the prayers, while still kneeling, he greets the protecting angel, or the others at prayer, by looking over his right and his left shoulder.

Muslims need only visit a mosque for the midday prayers on Fridays. In the mosque the direction to pray to (kıbla) is marked by a special niche (mihrab); otherwise the faithful judge the direction of Mecca by the position of the sun.

N.B. Muslim prayers contain no forms of intercession or request.

Sakat, the duty to give alms, is the most important command of Islam along with profession of the faith and the duty of prayer. Mohammed himself had already ordained this in Medina and introduced it as a form of tax. This was originally conceived as the only tax for Muslims and the whole community (umma), as laid down in Sura 9.60 of the Koran:

"Alms are for the poor and the needy;
And those employed to administer them (i.e. officials and the Caliphs, their successors, relations and their empowered representatives);
For those whose hearts have been reconciled to Truth (won for the cause of Islam);
For those in bondage (for purchasing the freedom of Muslim slaves)
And in debt;
In the cause of God (Holy War);
And for the wayfarer (travellers, pilgrims):
Thus is it ordained by God!
God is full of knowledge and wisdom!"

The alms tax was 10% of the harvest, livestock and their offspring, and 2.5% of savings, holdings of gold, silver and money, of the merchant's goods and yields. This tax is still levied today in many of the oil-rich states of the Persian Gulf and the Middle East. Nowadays Turkish believers, like those of many other Muslim countries, give their alms direct to the poor.

Saum, the month of fasting during Ramadan – a basic concept borrowed by Mohammed from Judaism – is specifically ordained in the second Sura of the Koran. Ramadan has to be the ninth month of the Islamic calender because this was the month when the Angel Gabriel appeared to Mohammed.

However, fasting is only mandatory during the day, i.e. from sunrise to sunset, but it also extends beyond eating and drinking to other worldly pleasures such as smoking and sex.

Those exempt from this duty are children – uncircumcised boys (i.e. under 7) and pre-pubescent girls – the old and the sick, travellers, nurses and pregnant women.

Hadj, the duty of pilgrimage to Mecca, is connected with the ancient Arabic pre-Islamic ritual of veneration of a great black meteorite (Hadja) contained within the holy shrine (Kaba) in the central courtyard of the great mosque at Mecca in Saudi Arabia. Muslims hold the Kaba to be a shrine erected by Abraham and Ishmael.

The prescribed month for the pilgrimage is Dulhija, the twelfth month in the Muslim calendar. Every Muslim, unless prevented by sickness or poverty, is expected to make the pilgrimage to Mecca once in his life; thereafter he is entitled to the honorary title of "El Hadj".

Relations between men and women

Lastly, the Koran and the Sunna also rule on the relations between men and women. The Koran specifically states that a woman is inferior to a man (Suras 4 and 33). He must however protect her and support her and may not ill-treat her. Suras 4.4 and 4.25 to 4.27 allow a man to have four wives and any number of concubines but all his wives must be treated in every way equally.

Simply on material grounds (bride price, the cost of weddings) marriage with more than one wife was out of the question for most Muslims. In modern republican Turkey monogamy is the law, but apart from that the position of women remains firmly anchored in many respects in the traditional social framework. Hence Turkey's policies on training and education are still very much on the traditional Islamic lines and not entirely welcoming where women are concerned.

The Koran also prescribes the wearing of the veil for women (Sura 33, 59), although even in Turkey there is heated and ongoing debate on precisely this point and differing schools of thought on the matter.

State and Society

Constitution and Government

According to its constitution the Republic of Turkey – officially "Türkiye Cumhuriyeti" – is a "national, democratic, secular and socialist republic". The legislature is the Greater National Assembly, consisting of the Parliament, with 450 members elected every four years by proportional representation, and the Senate, with 150 directly elected members, 15 appointed by the head of state and a number of senators for life.

The head of state is the President who is elected by the Greater National Assembly and may only serve for one 7-year term of office.

The Cabinet (Prime Minister and ministers) requires a vote of confidence from the whole assembly.

Political parties

Turkey's main political parties, in descending order of magnitude according to the number of members of Parliament elected in 1991, are the Party of the Right Way (DYP), the Motherland Party (ANAP), the Social Democratic People's Party (SHP), the People's Workers' Party (HEP), the Party of the Democratic Left (DSP), the Nationalist Labour Party (MÇP) and the Islamic fundamentalist Salvatione Party (RP).

Under the new constitution of 1923 the Turkish legal system was restructured and secularised, with criminal and civil law based largely on the codes of Italian and Swiss law respectively.

Membership of international organisations

Turkey is a member, inter alia, of the United Nations (UN) and various UN affiliates, the World Health Organisation (WHO), General Agreement on Tariffs and Trade (GATT), International Monetary Fund (IMF), Organisation for Economic Co-operation and Development (OECD), the North Atlantic Treaty Organization (NATO), since 1952, and, since 1990, the European Conference on Security and Co-operation.

Turkey is one of the states seeking entry to the European Community, with whom, since 1963, it has a Treaty of Association.

In 1991 Turkey was responsible for setting up an Economic Community of the countries bordering the Black Sea. This has its headquarters in İstanbul.

Diplomatic relations

Turkey maintains diplomatic relations with most of the world's countries.

Kurds

The Kurdish peoples have no state of their own. They are Muslims, with a Persian language, and live in mountainous Kurdistan, the frontier zone of south-eastern Turkey, which holds almost half their population, around their stronghold of Diyarbakır, Iran, and Iraq, with very small numbers in Syria.

The Turkish State does not recognise the Kurds as a national minority, considering them "mountain Turks" with no special rights. The Turkish

Language Law of 1983 forbids the speaking of their language in public, and rigorous repression of their independence aspirations has led to the radicalisation of their struggle for autonomy. PKK, the militant Kurdish Workers' Party, is banned in Turkey, and its members and sympathisers are ruthlessly hunted down by the national security forces.

Turkey's prime administrative unit is the province, formerly "vilâyet" in Turkish, now the "il". Up until a few years ago there were 67 of these provinces, numbered in alphabetical order, i.e. from Adana (01) to Zonguldak (67), but recently another six were created, bringing their number up to 73. Vehicle registrations use the same system of numbering.

These 73 provinces are subdivided into a total of 580 smaller districts ("ilçe", previously "kaza") and then 880 smaller units ("bucak", previously "nahiye").

Special development projects are planned for the provincial capitals which between them are responsible for administering over 35,000 towns and villages.

Economy

Situation and Trends

In economic terms Turkey ranks as a fast developer, one of those developing countries forging ahead to become an industrial nation.

Although the bulk of the population still live in the countryside and work on the land, there has been a marked shift towards industry and the services sector over the past 30 years, bringing with it a general change in people's way of life. Nowadays what most rural Turks hanker after is the urban lifestyle.

Flight from the land

However, the country has some worrying socio-economic factors to contend with: the decline from west to east, contrasts between periphery and interior, disturbing rates of unemployment, high inflation (1980–91, between 70 and 120%!), large budget deficits (5.7% of the gross domestic product in 1992) and a balance of trade which in 1991 was in the red to the tune of 7.8 billion dollars – all problems that beset its path to fully developed status. The high growth rates between 1980 and 1987, averaging up to 7%, tended to mask the country's underlying economic crisis. The Gulf War also dealt this growth rate a considerable blow, forcing it down to below 1%. Despite rising tax receipts the already considerable national debt has continued to accumulate, shooting up from 16.5 billion dollars in 1984 to 57 billion in 1991. In 1988 the gross national product was already 80% below that of Portugal, and on average earned income was half what it had been in real terms in 1978.

Economic facts and figures

The gross domestic product in 1991 was made up of 50.1% from services, 26.6% from industry, 16.8% agriculture and 6.5% building and construction.

Spurred on by the pressures of economic necessity and its expanding population the Turkish government, not to mention the man in street, are pinning their hopes on their application for full membership of the European Community. A package of special new measures including income tax reform, introduction of VAT at 12.5% (1985), improved banking laws and liberalisation of the money market (1980) has been designed to put the economy on a sounder footing and to bring Turkish financial systems into line with those of the industrialised western nations.

Attempts at consolidation

Economy

International
Vehicle
Nationality Plate

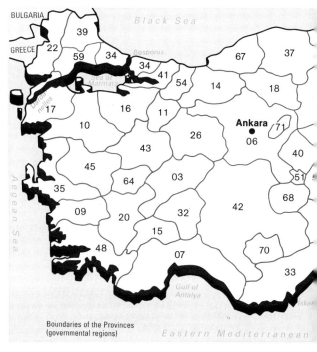

Boundaries of the Provinces
(governmental regions)

Administrative Districts

01 Adana	13 Bitlis	25 Erzurum
02 Adıyaman	14 Bolu	26 Eskişehir
03 Afyon	15 Burdur	27 Gaziantep
04 Ağrı	16 Bursa	28 Giresun
05 Amasya	17 Çanakkale	29 Gümüşhane
06 Ankara	18 Çankırı	30 Hakkâri
07 Antalya	19 Çorum	31 Hatay (Antakya)
08 Artvin	20 Denizli	32 Isparta
09 Aydın	21 Diyarbakır	33 İçel (Mersin)
10 Balıkesir	22 Edirne	34 İstanbul
11 Bilecik	23 Elazığ	35 İzmir
12 Bingöl	24 Erzincan	36 Kars

Gainful employment

Of the 20.1 million Turks over the age of 12 in gainful employment in 1992 about 40% worked on the land (farming, forestry, hunting and fishing, about 72% in 1965), 15% in industry (7% in 1965) and only 0.8% in mining and quarrying, 16.3% in trade and commerce, 4.5% in building and construction and 18.3% in the rest of the services sector.

Unemployment

Due to lengthening life expectancy and a falling death rate, overpopulation and greater mechanisation, unemployment in the countryside is above the national average. Besides creating a society where services are mostly at a lower level as well as being more thinly spread, this has also resulted in a noticeable flight from the rural areas to parts of the country where the economic prospects are better.

Republic of Turkey
Türkiye Cumhuriyeti

37 Kastamonu	49 Muş	62 Tunceli
38 Kayseri	50 Nevşehir	63 Sanlıurfa
39 Kırklareli	51 Niğde	(Urfa)
40 Kırşehir	52 Ordu	64 Uşak
41 Kocaeli (İzmit)	53 Rize	65 Van
42 Konya	54 Sakarya (Adapazarı)	66 Yozgat
43 Kütahya	55 Samsun	67 Zonguldak
44 Malatya	56 Siirt	68 Aksaray
45 Manisa	57 Sinop	69 Bayburt
46 Kahramanmaraş	58 Sivas	70 Karaman
(Maraş)	59 Tekirdağ	71 Kırıkkale
47 Mardin	60 Tokat	72 Batman
48 Muğla	61 Trabzon	73 Şırnak

It was hoped that the numbers of Turks going to work abroad would take the pressure off a domestic labour market which between 1975 and 1988 had seen a tenfold increase in unemployment. In 1988 almost 2.5 million Turks were living abroad, 60% of them – a workforce of half a million – in Western Germany alone. Their return to Turkey speeded up with the change in European attitudes to immigrant workers compared with the mid-Seventies, and opportunities of alternative employment in the oil states of the Arab countries were drastically reduced by the Gulf War.

Turks working abroad

Since the Sixties the number of towns and cities has doubled due to the soaring population and, to a large extent, the flight from the land. Big cities like İstanbul, Ankara and İzmir, with populations running into millions,

Urban concentration

have had to absorb a flood of humanity moving in from the countryside, mostly to settle in the booming shantytowns, the "gecekondu", so called because houses there spring up overnight.

Over half Turkey's population now lives in towns with annual growth rates up to 7% (about 2% in the interior). This means that despite the size of the country in many places its population, now grown to 58.5 million, is living in very cramped conditions – in the Fatih quarter of İstanbul, for example, there are just on 50,000 people to the square kilometre/130,000 to the square mile, compared with a national figure of 75.5/195. About a third of the total population and more than 60% of the towns are crowded into the areas of industrial concentration and the more prosperous west and south, as well as in and around the nation's capital Ankara.

Agriculture

Importance

Because Turkey is so mountainous, much of it at altitudes too cold for any form of cultivation, there is less land which is either very fertile or lends itself to intensive farming. Nevertheless, despite being prone to drought, Turkey is a country which is capable of sustaining its own population. In fact, not only is it self-sufficient, it also produces enough for export, through the use of subsidy, of products such as cotton and hazelnuts. Although so far only about 30% of farming land is irrigated the annual growth rate for farm products is around 3%. If, however, the grain harvest falls short because of insufficient rainfall, for example, there is a growing trend towards imports for domestic consumption.

Between 1980 and 1987 agriculture's share of the gross domestic product fell from 23 to 17%, and this has been matched over the past 15 years by a

Women harvesting grain by Lake Van

fall of around 15% in the numbers employed in farming. Nevertheless this sector of the economy still officially accounts for close on half the workforce.

In 1985 32.5% of the country was down to agriculture, 24.8% to forestry, 16.3% to grazing and pastureland, with a further 26.4% not suitable for cultivation.

Cultivable agricultural area (CAA)

Of the cultivable area 62.4% went on arable farming, 24.3% on crop rotation (including fallow periods), 11.1% on orchards and other forms of plantation and only 2.4% on vegetables.

The laws on land inheritance have resulted in a relatively high proportion (30%) of holdings under 2ha/5 acres. These smallholdings account for only 4% of the CAA and are often merely subsistence farming. On the other hand, 35% of farmland is farmed by only 6% of all landowners – large farmers with more than 20ha/49 acres – although this imbalance is gradually being redressed.

The high ground of the Anatolian plateau in the heart of Turkey is mostly used for arable (wheat, rye, maize, pulses) and livestock farming. This largely takes the form of grazing for sheep and goats, despite the growing encroachment into prairieland for cultivation. Extensive livestock farming is also on the increase in the north and north-east. Vineyards are quite common on slopes up to 2000m/6564ft.

Regional concentration

Cotton

Technological advances, especially the introduction of pumping engines, have helped to add to the traditional areas where irrigation was responsible for such cash crops as rice, fruit, and vegetables. These can now be grown in what was far from suitable terrain, thanks mainly to the hothouse culture of early vegetables, and the use of plastic sheeting along the coasts, along with irrigation for sugar beet outside the central depressions, and the large-scale growing of cotton.

The bread basket of the nation, where the most cereals are grown, is to be found in the flatlands of Thrace, which, like the west, also has a good sunflower crop, and in central Anatolia. The climate on the coastal plains favours the growing of olives, figs, grapes (for wine and for raisins), citrus fruit, bananas, peanuts and hazelnuts, maize and tobacco, not to mention tea, a local crop since 1892.

The fields of poppies used to make opium have been officially banned since 1972.

Traditional farming methods such as ploughing by hand and threshing with sledges have steadily given way to tractors, mechanical harvesters and, above all, the combustion engine. The fivefold increase in agricultural land between 1987 and 1927, when it only totalled 4.4 million ha/10.8 million acres, along with the virtual doubling of afforestation between 1960 and 1987, bringing the total wooded area up to 201,990sq.km/77,968sq.miles at the expense of pastureland and steppe grazing, have resulted in acute overgrazing combined with soil erosion as the numbers of livestock have risen accordingly – since 1927 the national stock of sheep and goats has gone up from 19.7 to 53.5 million (1984), and cattle and buffalo from 7.5 to 12.9 million.

Mechanisation and overgrazing

The two-field rotation system of alternating farm crops with fallow periods is still widely practised. This is due largely to inability to pay for expensive artificial fertiliser and the use of dried cowdung ("tezek") for fuel because of

Rotation and cash crops

47

Economy

the lack of firewood. Although average wheat yields are still relatively low at 2000kg/39cwt per ha, the planned expansion of sugarbeet output from 3.4 million t. (1969) to 11.5 million t. (1988) has changed the face of vast expanses of countryside as crop rotation has come into play. One reason for the often uneconomical style of farming is the predominance of small landholdings: about three quarters of all farmers have plots with a culti-vable area of less than 7.5ha/18.5 acres. However these peasant farmers are also increasingly turning over to cash crops, most of which go for export and can yield them a higher return. They can also count on the added inducement of State aid in the form of subsidy.

GAP · South-eastern Anatolia Project

Another force to be reckoned with is the prospect of the additional 1.6 million ha/3.9 million acres of agricultural land likely to come from the irrigation projects associated with GAP, the South-eastern Anatolia Project (Güneydoğu Anadolu Projesi), and the dams this will create in the upper reaches of the Tigris and Euphrates.

Timber

Measures such as planned forestry, restrictions on woodland grazing, bans on taking trees for firewood, and education of the local people have suc-ceeded not only in transforming poor scrub into usable timber but also in doubling the country's wooded area between 1950 and 1988 to over 20 million ha/49.4 million acres, despite the fact that as much as 1.5% of Turkey's forests may be destroyed every year – 1400 forest fires were responsible for the loss of 18,200ha/45,000 acres in 1988 alone. More than half the woodland is only good for firewood. Sweet chestnuts and, up to quite high altitudes, hazelnuts accompany the main tree species such as firs and beeches in the north, various pines and junipers in the dry interior, Aleppo pines, planes and other deciduous trees junipers and cedars in the central and western Taurus, oaks in the east, south-east and dry inner edges of the mountains, holm-oaks in the west. The farmers plant plenty of robinia and eucalyptus but their most common tree is poplar, grown for firewood close to the villages.

Mining

Mineral resources

Turkey, with its ancient mountains and Tertiary infills, is rich in minerals, but lack of knowhow and the inability to develop them have meant that they have yet to be exploited to the full. Ores such as lead and copper, already known and made use of by our prehistoric ancestors, occur in mostly small pockets over a wide range. The Turkish Government made the devel-opment of mining a national priority, particularly after the Second World War, assigning a crucial role in this to the Institute for Site Exploration (MTA · Maden Tetkik ve Arama Enstitüsü, founded in 1934) and the Eti Bank, the largest of Turkey's State Economic Enterprises which takes in energy as well.

Besides deposits aplenty of sulphur, lead, tungsten, nickel, antimony, cobalt, zinc, mercury, magnesite, borazite, bauxite, asbestos, emery and meerschaum, there are significant reserves of iron ore (1.3 billion t.), copper (205 million t.), manganese (3.5 million t.), tungsten (10.5 million t.) and chromium (26.1 million t.). Divriği, near Sivas, has large fields of high-grade iron ore, chromium is present throughout the country, and the main sources of copper are at Ergani (Diyarbakır) and Murgul, on the Black Sea.

The coal at Zongaduldak on the Black Sea was discovered in the 19th c. Development of this into a major coalmining area made possible the opening up of the large iron ore field at Divriğli in eastern Anatolia. In 1967 the high-yielding brown coal deposits at Tuncdilek, near Kütahya, were supplemented by the discovery of further brown coal reserves (about 1 billion t.) at Elbistan, west of Malatya.

48

Energy

Turkey's main energy resources lie in its brown coal (7.5 billion t.) and hard coal (1.4 billion t), its oilfields, such as those around Batman and Kahta (30 million t.), with an annual output of about 3 million t. – 12% of the country's oil needs – and its potential for hydroelectric power.
The exploitation of the rich natural gas fields in parts of the country, around Adıyaman for example, is still in its early stages.
Its thermal waters are also reckoned to provide Turkey with the world's largest geothermic energy source, and one which is likely to stand it in good stead in the future.

Energy sources

Turkey currently has four large refineries: Ramandağı, in the Batman oil-field, Aliağa (İzmir), İpraz (İzmit) and İçel, in the port of Mersin.

Petroleum refineries

Despite the growing importance of hydro-electric power – already supplying almost 20% of Turkey's energy output in 1980 – much of the national electricity supply still relies on coal, and around 10% of the coal produced still goes to coal-fired power stations.

Power

The first coal-fired power station went up in 1948 on the western edge of the Zonguldak coalfield. This was subsequently extended in the mid-Fifties and joined by others sited at Tunçbilek (Kütahya), Soma (İzmir), Manisa, İzmit, Silantar (İstanbul), Ankara and near Elbistan.

Turkey's biggest hydro-electric power station is currently being built on the Euphrates as part of the South-eastern Anatolia Project and will eventually produce 2400MW using eight turbines.

Hydro-electric power

Up until 1950 Turkey's hydro-electric power was supplied only by a great many small plants dotted across the country, most of them built after 1926. Nowadays this power source is increasingly taking the form of large plants used both for irrigation and flood protection. The first of these was the Seyhan barrage, built at Adana in 1956, to be followed in stages mainly by dams across valleys in the Taurus and the Pontine Mountains. These already total 200, with another 85 in the pipeline, plus 50 smaller generator stations on rivercourses with the appropriate gradients. The GAP project will provide 17 major hydro-electric plants generating no less than 26,127 billion KW a year in total.

Nuclear power plants such as Taşucu in southern Anatolia are either at the planning stage or already under construction by various different international consortia.

Nuclear energy

Industrial Sector

From early beginnings with foodstuffs and textiles, starting in the Twenties and then speeding up after 1950, Turkey has gradually been constructing itself a major industrial base. In 1933 the State first assumed the role of funder of industrial development by setting up the State Economic Enterprises and founding the Sümer Bank, in its day the country's second largest economic enterprise after the Etibank, established in 1934 to cater for mining and electricity supply. Even today the Sümer Bank still mainly controls the nationalised chemical, textile and iron and steel industries, not to mention building and construction.
Turkish industry is primarily based on processing the country's own agricultural and mineral raw materials. Thus the cement industry, initiated by Atatürk, is already an exporter. Iron ore from Divriği goes for smelting at Karabük, Zonguldak and Ereğli, close to the Zonguldak coalfields. Turkey's heavy industry is concentrated in and around this area and further afield at Kırıkkale east of Ankara, Yarmıca (İzmit), Samsun, Elazığ and near Iskenderun. The other ores are not all smelted in Turkey. Some copper, for example, is exported as ore. Mineral raw materials also provide a basis for the chemicals industry.

Industry

Collecting salt at the Tuz Gölü

The size of the textile industry is closely allied to Turkey's much expanded cotton production. Textiles constitute the country's second largest industrial employer after the food and drink industry, with which it shares the distinction of broadly catering for all Turkey's needs from within its own sector. As more sugarbeet is grown and many more new sugar plants are built Turkey could become entirely self-sufficient here too.

In 1983 a series of sweeping reforms were brought in to make Turkish industry more competitive on world markets. Subsidies were dismantled, import restrictions lifted, nationalised undertakings privatised and the free movement of capital introduced. However, industrial development continues to be dogged by problems with capital investment and by the underlying skills shortages on the labour market, particularly in mining and heavy industry where workers tend to be employed on a seasonal basis or alternate between stints of paid employment and working on their own land in their home village. The hoped-for success of the Anatolian hinterland has yet to materialise and the situation of industrial concentration in the northwest, west, around Ankara and in the Çukurova has barely altered, with these areas still accounting for almost three-quarter of the country's industrial wealth creation. Turkey's capital investment in its energy supply programme also has to be seen against this background. By the turn of the century the massive network of dams and reservoirs of the South-eastern Anatolia Project (GAP) on the Tigris and Euphrates is due to be supplying 24 billion KW. Another added resource will come from the planned exploitation of the country's hitherto undeveloped brown coal and oil reserves.

Manufacturing

The flagging manufacturing sector was first given a boost under Adnan Menderes in the Fifties then, after 1980, substantially strengthened under Turgut Özal who encouraged the growth of private enterprise, especially where manufactured goods were concerned.

Manual crafts

Despite having to compete with mass-produced foreign imports since the 19th c. Turkey's manual crafts continue to flourish, especially in the making of copperware, pottery and carpets. Nowadays, however, Turkish carpets are increasingly being produced in co-operatives run on industrial lines, and plant dyes are relatively rarely used.

Trade

For some years Turkey has sought to compete on world markets by heavily subsidising its exporters. About a third of its manufactured goods go for export, along with close on a quarter of agricultural products and food-stuffs. Clothing and textiles come third with about 20%.
There is a substantial deficit on the balance of trade. In 1992 the value of imports, at 22.4 billion US dollars, exceeded that of exports by just on $8 billion. This reflected a long-standing deficitary trend in the volume of external trade, most of it with the EC countries, and which has grown from $2.9 billion in 1980 to $14.5 billion in 1992.

Exports

The chief imports are capital goods (tools and machinery) and fuel (oil, etc.), followed by manufactured goods and chemical products.

Imports

Transport

In order to achieve its economic development goals Turkey puts a good third of all public investment into improving its transport infrastructure, spending on capital projects such as roadbuilding in the east of the country and the modernisation and expansion of the rail network. One important factor in this is the growth of foreign tourism.

Capital investment

Passenger transport plays hardly any role in the very loose-knit rail net-work, although the modernisation of the track between Ankara and İstanbul may well be an indication of change in things to come. Where rail transport is important is in the movement of bulk freight in, for example, the mining industry.
To cater for European interests concerned with getting their raw materials to the Aegean ports a number of lines were built in the western Anatolian valleys in the second half of the 19th c., then towards the end of the century a start was made on the important trunk line from Haydarpaşa (İstanbul) via Eskişehir, Kütahya, and Afyon, to Konya in Central Anatolia. Its extension through the Cilician Gates in the eastern section of the Central Taurus via the Çukurova to Aleppo in Syria and Baghdad in Iraq earned itself the title of the Baghdad line. This laid the foundation for the eventual building of railroads across the Asia Minor peninsula as far as the borders with Iran, Armenia, and Georgia, and up to the Black Sea coast.
The only part of Turkey with a denser railroad pattern is western Anatolia where a line linking the fertile valleys runs north/south from Bandırma on the Sea of Marmara to the Büyük Menderes (Meander), with a number of branch lines running east to connect with the Baghdad railroad. Eskişehir, the major junction on the Baghdad line, is also the start of what is still the only rail link connecting western Turkey with its eastern frontiers. After passing through Ankara this branches north at Çetinkaya, east of Sivas, and runs via Erzincan and Erzerum to Georgia. Further south at Malatya the main line branches east via Lake Van to Iran, and a branchline off this route goes as far as Siirt, via Diyarbakır. The dry heart of central Anatolia is encircled by the Baghdad line in the west and south and the main east/west trunkline in the north, connected by a loopline which joins the main line at Ulukısla, just before the Cilician Pass region. Two important lines run north from the central railroad to the Black Sea coast, one from Ankara to the Zonguldak coalfields and the other from Sivas to Samsun. The whole track network, state-run since 1947, totals 8430km/5238 miles.

Rail transport

Transport in Anatolia relies chiefly on its steadily expanding network of metalled roads from which it is also increasingly possible to gain access to

Roads

many of the more out of the way villages. The bulk of the traffic – chiefly passenger vehicles but also a good deal of freight – is carried on a series of trunk roads, most of them quite good, and these routes are constantly being extended.

Since 1950 the road network, originally centred almost exclusively on Ankara, has been substantially expanded, and has grown from 18,335km/11,393 miles in 1923 to 58,600km/36,414 miles in 1991, of which 46,170km/28,690 miles are tarmac and 9560km/5940 miles are at least metalled. This has been accompanied in many cases by schemes for road-widening, straightening and general technical improvements. In addition there are at least 1200km/746 miles of dirt "dry weather" roads and a further 1450km/901 miles of farmtrack, although these are not suitable for ordinary vehicles.

Vehicles and accidents

Since 1950 the number of vehicles on the road has shot up from 26,457 to 2.25 million – about 55% cars, 20% trucks, 7% buses. The accident total has risen accordingly, from about 40,000 in 1981 to well over 100,000 today. However, considering the number of vehicles for its size and population, road accidents in Turkey are still well below the European average.

Shipping

Turkey has a fleet of over 3800 vessels. This also represents a clear increase, and is an important factor in the economy given the growth in the export trade and the country's position as a link between the Black Sea and the Mediterranean. Gross tonnage has gone up from 216,458 tonnes in 1923 to 3.4 million in 1988, since when it has remained more or less the same.

Air transport

Turkish Airlines (THY, Türk Hava Yolları), the State airline, carry most of the domestic air traffic. The main airports at İstanbul (Yeşilköy), Ankara (Esenboğa), Adana and İzmir (Adnan Menderes) are particularly important for international flights between Europe and the Middle East. Besides the airports in most of the provincial centres a couple of new airports have been added more recently at Dalaman (Muğla) and Antalya to serve the tourist resorts on the south coast.

Tourism

Foreign tourism

Over the past decade the number of foreign tourists has soared to over 4 million a year. Although this suffered a setback in 1991 following the Gulf War, by 1992 it was back up to 3 million visitors from Europe alone. Despite the fact that foreign tourism has quadrupled since 1976 the number of beds available has only tripled.

Domestic tourism

It is also worth pointing out that the bulk of holidaymakers in Turkey are the Turks themselves. This applies both to those taking the traditional break from the summer heat up in the mountains ("yayla") and the growing numbers who head for the beaches of the Aegean and the Mediterranean ("plaj").

Environmental impact

This massive growth in tourism also has its more disturbing aspects. These include the unsightly overdevelopment of long stretches of coastline and the damage to the environment caused by a glaring lack of waste disposal facilities combined with the failure of local investors to face up to the problem.

Winter sports

A new trend in Turkish tourism is the development of winter sports resorts in popular mountain centres such as Uludağ (Bursa), Palondöken Dağları (Erzerum), Sarıkamış (Van), Saklıkent (Antalya) and Kartalkaya (Bolu).

History

Asia Minor already has human settlement in the Stone Age. The first evidence of settled communities dates from the Neolithic period (4th/3rd millennium B.C.); headmen live in small, well-fortified centres and the local culture, which still lacks writing, is Sumerian-influenced.

Prehistory

Waves of Hittites – an Indo-European people – invade Anatolia and eventually gain control of the indigenous peoples.

2000 B.C. onwards

Labarnas (whose name becomes the title of later Hittite kings) founds the Hatti kingdom, the Old Hittite Kingdom. His successors are responsible for much expansion of the original territory around the capital, Hattusa (Hattusas; about 200km/125miles east of today's Ankara).

c. 1650–
c. 1460 B.C.

After a period of weakness a new dynasty in Hattusa brings a resurgence: establishment of the New Hittite Kingdom, and its greatest ruler Suppiluliuma I (1380–46) reorganises the state and greatly extends the kingdom's frontiers.
Hittite power gradually declines towards the turn of the 13th c. The end comes with the onslaught of warring bands of Thracians who are also responsible for the downfall of the city of Troy described in Homer's Iliad (Troy VI).

c. 1460–
c. 1200 B.C.

During the great Aegean Migration the west coast of Anatolia (Asia Minor) is settled by Greeks (Ionians, Aeolians, Dorians). The development of the Greek cities here runs broadly parallel with what is happening on the mainland, and after 700 B.C. they thus play a major part in Greek colonisation. Miletus, the leading political and cultural city state on the west coast, is responsible in its own right for over 90 Greek colonies on the shores of the Black Sea.

c. 1200–
c. 1000 B.C.

The Phrygians, also Indo-Europeans, succeed in bringing together Central Anatolia's smaller powers to form one large kingdom (capital Gordium). The reign of King Midas, famed for his legendary wealth, ends with defeat at the hands of the Cimmerians.

c. 800–c. 680 B.C.

The Cimmerians are driven out only to be replaced by the Lydians who take over from the Phrygians as the dominant force in Anatolia, and also seize the Greek cities on the west coast, with the notable exception of Miletus. The Lydians were probably the first people to turn the pieces of metal used as currency into coins by stamping their imprint on them (7th c.)

c. 680–546 B.C.

A pre-emptive strike on the Persians by the Lydian King Croesus fails and the Persians absorb the Greek cities on the west coast into their empire.

546 B.C.

Revolt by the cities of Ionia on the west coast, headed by Miletus, sparks off the Persian Wars. These last until 478. The Persians eventually put down the uprising and destroy Miletus.

500–494 B.C.

Persian rule gradually becomes less tightly structured as the satraps and the provinces they govern gain greater independence. Alexander the Great consequently succeeds in liberating the people of Anatolia from the Persians in a relatively short sharp campaign.

334–323 B.C.

After Alexander's death in 323 the Greek dynasties headed by his generals who becomes his successors, the Diadochoi, set up their own rival kingdoms in Anatolia.

323–281 B.C.

History

281–263 B.C.   After no single one of the Diadochoi manages to gain overall control the
                    Seleucids succeed in establishing their rule over almost the whole of
                    Anatolia. The coastal cities in the south and south-west initially fall to
                    the Seleucids, only to have them replaced by Egyptian influence.
                    Several places such as Pontos and Bithnyia on the north coast take advan-
                    tage of the power vacuum to set themselves up as independent city states.

263–133 B.C.   The kingdom of Pergamum becomes the dominant power in western
                    Anatolia. Its kings ally themselves with the Romans in the fighting with the
                    Seleucids, and the last king bequeaths his kingdom to Rome.

129 B.C.   The Romans declare western Anatolia a Roman province which they call
                    "Asia".

63 B.C.   The Roman general Pompeius starts imposing Roman administration on
                    Anatolia, creating a series of "client states" on the borders of the Roman
                    provinces strung out along most of the coastline.
                    Roman rule brings with it a period of cultural and economic prosperity for
                    western Anatolia.

from A.D. 47   Paul's missionary journeys signal the arrival of Christianity in Asia Minor.

c. A.D. 250   The political centre of gravity shifts increasingly to the north-west in the
                    decades to follow: the Emperor Diocletian (284–305) creates a new capital
                    in Anatolia at Nicomedeia (now İzmit) following the administrative split of
                    the Roman Empire into eastern and western halves.

330   Constantine the Great (324–37) chooses the provincial town of Byzantium
                    as capital of the Roman Empire, renaming it Constantinople (now İstanbul).

394–95   After the division of the Empire by Theodosius the Great, Anatolia becomes
                    the heartland of the eastern realm of the Roman (Byzantine) Empire, a state
                    founded on Roman law and government, Greek language and culture, and
                    the Christian faith.

1025   The late Byzantine state reaches the apogee of its glory under Basil II
                    (976–1025), but decline sets in after his death as conflicts between the civil
                    bureaucracy and the military help to undermine Byzantium's fiscal and
                    fighting power.

1071   The Seljuk Turks under Alp Arslan inflict a decisive defeat on the Byzantine
                    mercenaries at the Battle of Manzikert and proceed to conquer large parts
                    of Central Anatolia, even advancing as far as the Mediterranean.

1203–04   The Fourth Crusade proves a disaster for Byzantium when the Crusaders
                    capture Constantinople and Baldwin I establishes his Latin Kingdom there,
                    taking in north-western Anatolia. It is 1261 before this reverts to Byzantium.

1453   The Ottoman Turks, who have been a growing threat to Byzantium with
                    their expansion since the late 13th c., finally take Constantinople (29 May),
                    thus putting an end to the Byzantine Empire. The city is renamed İstanbul
                    (Islamboul, the City of Islam) and becomes the capital of the Ottoman
                    Empire.

1520–66   The Ottoman Empire reaches its peak during the reign of Suleyman the
                    Magnificent. Besides ruling over the whole of Asia Minor it also takes in the
                    lands between the Tigris and the Euphrates, Syria, Egypt and North Africa
                    as far as Morocco (1580), stretches to its cornerstones of Hungary and the
                    vassal state of Transylvania in the north, and contains large areas on the
                    northern shores of the Black Sea within its sphere of influence which also
                    extends as far as the Caspian Sea in the east.

1683   The decline in Ottoman power sets in with the failure of the Second Siege of
                    Vienna (the first unsuccessful siege had been in 1529), and large parts of

the empire are to be surrendered in the years to come. This external decline is mirrored by disintegration from within as the sultans increasingly withdraw from active involvement in the business of government and cease to take part in military campaigns. Meanwhile the provincial governors are gaining in power.

The Ottoman Empire becomes increasingly dependent on the European Great Powers for protection against Russia (Russo-Turkish Wars). The political rapprochement is also reflected in domestic reforms and there is growing European cultural influence.

from 1800

The Treaty of the Dardanelles with Britain, France, Austria and Prussia bans the passage of any non-Turkish warships through the straits.

1841

Crimean War. Britain, France and Italy come to the rescue of the Ottoman Empire when it is attacked by the Russians.

1853–56

The Treaty of Paris, which ends the Crimean War (1853–56), guarantees the independence of the Ottoman Empire, but Turkey's financial dependence on the Western Powers increases.

1856

Adoption of the first Ottoman constitution. Although suspended a year later it provides for parity of religions and nations within the empire.

1876

Turkey is forced to cede sovereignty over Cyprus to Britain.

1878

The "Young Turks", an opposition movement against the autocratic rule of the Sultan and undue influence by foreigners, forces restoration of the 1876 Constitution.

1908

Turkey, by now the "Sick Man of Europe", enters the First World War as one of the Central Powers; the Ottoman troops have one early success when they defeat the ANZAC troops at Gallipoli during their defence of the Dardanelles, but the final year of the war brings defeat and ultimately surrender.
The Mudros Armistice (October 30th 1918) effectively signifies the end of the Ottoman Empire.

1914–18

Mustafa Kemal Pasa (b. 1881 in Salonica, d. 1938 in İstanbul) sets about organising national resistance in a War of Independence against the Allies who now control much of his country.

1919

Kemal convenes the Grand National Assembly in Ankara and is made head of a new government to replace that of the Sultan.

1920

The Greeks speedily occupy large parts of western Anatolia but are then driven out by the Turks. The evacuation of Smyrna (İzmir) in September 1922 ends 3000 years of Greek settlement on the west coast of Anatolia.

1920–22

On November 1st Mustafa Kemal announces the abolition of the Sultanate.

1922

With the Lausanne Peace Treaty (July 24th) the Allies recognise Turkey's sovereignty, but force it to give up the non-Turkish parts of the former Ottoman Empire. The Republic of Turkey is proclaimed on October 29th and Mustafa Kemal becomes its first President (the surname Atatürk – father of the Turks – is bestowed on him in 1934). In the years that follow he brings in his far-reaching "Kemalist" reforms: elimination of Islamic law, abolition of polygamy, political rights for women, introduction of the Latin alphabet, modern labour and social legislation, etc.
Ankara becomes the capital of the Turkish Republic.

1923

On Atatürk's death Ismet Inönü succeeds him as President, bringing further democratic reforms.

1938

1939–45	Turkey remains neutral during the Second World War until the closing weeks when it declares war on Germany.
1947	An aid agreement with the United States ties Turkey in more closely with the Western system of alliances.
1950	Celal Bayar, leader of the Democrat Party, becomes President when his party wins the general election and he appoints Adnan Menderes as Prime Minister.
1952	Turkey joins NATO.
1960	Anti-democratic measures by Menderes such as Press censorship lead to student riots and evenutally a military coup headed by General Cemal Gürsel, who takes over the government. Menderes is arrested and executed with two of his ministers. Britain grants Cyprus independence on August 16th. The fact that the Turkish Cypriot minority only have autonomous rights in matters of culture and religion results in a constant near-civil war struggle between Turkish and Greek Cypriots.
1961	Adoption of a new more liberal constitution guaranteeing the rights of the individual and providing for far-reaching education and social reform.
1965	Süleyman Demirel becomes Prime Minister with the election victory of the Justice Party.
1966	Cevdet Sunay succeeds the gravely ill Cemal Gürsel as President on March 28th. Growing radicalism on the political scene.
1973	Admiral Fahri Korutürk is elected President on April 6th. New Land Reform Law (July). Repeal of the martial law dating from 1971. The first bridge over the Bosporus is opened to traffic on October 30th.
1974	In the October elections the Republican People's Party emerges as the largest single party and its leader Bülent Ecevit becomes Prime Minister, forming a coalition government with aid of the Islamic fundamentalist National Salvation Party. Ecevit orders Turkish troops into Cyprus after a coup sponsored by the Greek junta in Athens threatens to topple President Makarios. The coup collapses but the Turkish troops continue to occupy the northern part of the island. Ceasefire negotiations agree on the Attila line as the frontier between north and south. Ecevit is forced to resign in September in the aftermath of the Cyprus situation.
1975	The six-month Government crisis ends with the formation of a right-wing coalition led by Demirel as Prime Minister (March 31st). Severe earthquake rocks eastern Anatolia.
1976	Negotiations between Greece and Turkey over the Aegean continental shelf in Bern, the Swiss capital. Another bad earthquake in eastern Anatolia (Van).
1977	Bloodshed and unrest in a number of Turkey's big cities. Fresh government crisis: Ecevit and Demirel both unable to form an ongoing government.
1978	Ecevit becomes Prime Minister again (January 5th), with Evren the new chief of general staff. Cyprus conference in Montreux. Growing terrorism from extremists both on the right and the left (riots in December in Kahramanmaraş · Maraş). The Government imposes martial law on many of the provinces.

Martial law extended due to continued unrest.   1979
In October Demirel succeeds Ecevit as Prime Minister.
Pope John Paul II pays an official visit to Turkey (November 28th), the first
Pope to do so, going to Ankara, İstanbul and Ephesus (Selçuk), and holding
talks with the Orthodox Patriarch of Constantinople on a rapprochement
between their two Churches, which have been apart since 1054.

More acts of terrorism and further extension of martial law (2300 deaths   1980
since November 1979).
The army seizes power in a bloodless coup (September 12th). Parliament is
dissolved and the country is run by the National Security Council, headed
by the coup leader, General Kenan Evren. The new government which is
formed, with Bülent Ülüsü as Prime Minister, proclaims martial law in the
country's 67 provinces, bans activity by political parties and trade unions,
curbs Press freedom and arrests many politicians.
Amnesty International accuses the military junta of torturing activists im-
prisoned following earlier radical acts of terrorism.
Kenan Evren takes over from Ihsan S. Çağlayangil who has been acting
president.

President Kenan Evren inaugurates "Atatürk Year".   1981
Dissolution of all political parties on October 16th.

A national referendum on November 7th overwhelmingly endorses a new   1982
draft Constitution. At the same time General Evren is voted in as President
for a seven-year term. Although the Constitution guarantees basic human
rights it still leaves the generals with a large say in policy.

After May 16th new electoral laws permit the establishment of political   1983
parties subject to certain conditions.
The general election on November 6th is won by ANAP, the Motherland
Party, and technocrat Turgut Özal becomes Prime Minister.
On November 15th the Parliament of the Turkish-held part of Cyprus votes
for independence as the " Turkish Republic of Northern Cyprus" with Rauf
Raşit Denktaş as "President". This is regarded as legally invalid by the UN
Security Council and remains recognised only by Turkey.

In January hundreds of political prisoners go on hunger strike, and some   1984
die, in protest at the inhuman conditions in Turkish prisons. Martial law is
suspended in a number of provinces.

In the dispute with Greece over exploitation of the Aegean shelf tempo-   1987
rarily Turkey abandons planned oil exploration in the international waters
around the Greek Islands.
On April 14th Turkey officially applies to become the 13th Member State of
the European Community.
A controversial change in electoral law allows the ANAP a fresh win in the
Parliamentary elections and Özal stays on as Prime Minister.

At the end of January an international economic forum in Davos, Swit-   1988
zerland, concludes with a declaration by Prime Minister Özal for Turkey and
the then Prime Minister Papandreou for Greece that their two countries will
seek to achieve lasting peaceful relations in future.
The second bridge over the Bosporus is opened on July 3rd.
About 100,000 Kurds cross into Turkey, fleeing from Iraq.

Local election victory for SHP, the Social Democratic People's Party, led by   1989
Erdal Inönü.
Expulsion of over 200,000 Turks from Bulgaria (July).
In October Turgut Özal is elected President and Yıldırım Akbulut Prime
Minister.
The EC Commission turns down talks on Turkey's membership of the
Community (December).

1990	Completion in August of the Atatürk Dam on the Euphrates (Fırat). a key part of GAP, the South-eastern Anatolia Project. The Turkish Parliament allows the Government to send troops to the Gulf. At the special Paris Summit on European security and co-operation in November Turkey signs the "Paris Charter for a new Europe", whereby the signatories pledge themselves to uphold democracy and the rule of law, to observe human rights and to promote friendly relations with one another.
1991	Turkey strengthens its relations with the states of the former Soviet Union and Iran. More than 200,000 Kurds enter Turkey by the end of April, fleeing persecution in Iraq during and after the Gulf War. The conservative DYP, the Party of the Right Way, emerges the victor from the parliamentary elections on October 20th with 27% of the votes cast; the ANAP which has held power for eight years only manages 24%. Süleyman Demirel of the DYP heads the coalition government.
1992	An agreement on economic co-operation between the countries bordering the Black Sea initiated by President Özal is initialled in İstanbul on February 2nd, and signed by eleven States on July 25th. Following continual raids by Kurdish guerrillas on Turkish garrisons and police stations, the air force steps up raids on Kurdish villages near the Turkish-Iraqi border. In late April and early May Prime Minister Demirel visits Azerbaijan and the central Asian republics of the Commonwealth of Independent States, with the exception of Tajikistan. An agreement is reached with Syria on joint exploitation of the waters of the Euphrates following the official opening of the Atatürk Dam on July 24th.
1993	After the sudden death of President Turgut Özal in Ankara on April 17th Süleyman Demirel is elected his successor for a 7-year term. With her election to the chair of the Party of the Right Way economist Tansu Çiller (b. 1946) becomes Turkey's first woman government chief.

Rulers

Byzantine Emperors

306–337	Constantine I	641	Constantine II
337–361	Constantine II	641	Heracleonas
361–363	Julian the Apostate	641–668	Constantine III
363–364	Jovian	668–685	Constantine IV
364–378	Valens	685–695	Justinian II (first reign)
378–395	Theodosius the Great	695–698	Leontinus
395–408	Arcadius	698–705	Tiberius II Aspimar
408–450	Theodosius II	705–711	Justinian II
450–457	Marcian		(second reign)
457–474	Leo I	711–713	Philippicus Bardanes
474	Leo II	713–715	Anastasius II
474–491	Zeno	715–717	Theodosius III
491–518	Anastasius I	717–741	Leo III
518–527	Justin I	741–775	Constantine V
527–565	Justinian I	775–780	Leo IV
565–578	Justin II	780–797	Constantine VI
578–582	Tiberius I Constantine	797–802	Irene
582–602	Maurice	802–811	Nicephorus I
602–610	Phocas	811–813	Michael I
610–641	Heraclius	813–820	Leo V

820–829	Michael II	1081–1118	Alexius I Comnenus
829–842	Theophilus	1118–43	John II Comnenus
842–867	Michael III	1143–80	Manuel I Comnenus
867–886	Basil I	1180–83	Alexius II Comnenus
886–912	Leo VI	1183–85	Andronicus I Comnenus
912–913	Alexander	1185–95	Isaac II Angelus (first reign)
913–959	Constantine VII Porphyrogenitus	1195–1203	Alexius III Angelus
	(Romanus I Lecapenus	1203–04	Isaac II Angelus (second reign;
	co-emperor 919–944)		Alexius IV Angelus co-emperor)
959–963	Romanus II	1204	Alexius V Ducas
963–969	Nicephorus II Phocas	1204–22	Theodore I Lascaris (in Nicaea)
969–976	John I Tzimisces	1222–54	John III Ducas Vatatzes
976–1025	Basil II		(in Nicaea)
1025–28	Constantine VIII	1254–58	Theodore II Lascaris
1028–34	Romanus III Argyrus		(in Nicaea)
1034–41	Michael IV	1258–61	John IV Lascaris (in Nicaea)
1041–42	Michael V	1261–82	Michael VIII Palaeologus
1042	Theodora and Zoë	1282–1328	Andronicus II Palaeologus
1042–55	Constantine IX	1328–41	Andronikos III Palaeologus
1055–56	Theodora (second reign)	1341–91	John V Palaeologus
1056–57	Michael VI	1347–54	John VI Cantacuzene
1057–59	Isaac I Comnenos		(Anti-emperor)
1059–67	Constantine X Ducas	1376–79	Andronicus IV Palaeologus
1067	Eudocia Ducaena	1390	John VII Palaeologus
1067–71	Romanus IV Diogenes	1391–1425	Manuel II Palaeologus
1071–78	Michael VII Ducas	1425–48	John VIII Palaeologus
1078–81	Nicephorus III Botaniates	1448–53	Constantine XI Dragases

Latin Emperors

1204–05	Baldwin I of Flanders	1221–28	Robert de Courtenay
1205–16	Henry of Flanders	1228–61	Baldwin II
1217	Pierre de Courtenay		(1231–37 Jean de Brienne)
1217–19	Yolande		

Ottoman Sultans

1290–1326	Osman I	1640–48	Ibrahim (the Terrible)
1326–59	Orhan	1648–87	Mehmed IV
1359–89	Murad I	1687–91	Süleyman II
1389–1402	Beyazıd I	1691–95	Ahmed II
1413–21	Mehmed I	1695–1703	Mustafa II
1421–51	Murad II	1703–30	Ahmed III
1451–81	Mehmed II	1730–54	Mahmud I
	(Fâtih the Conqueror)	1754–57	Osman III
1481–1512	Beyazıd II	1757–74	Mustafa III
1512–20	Selim I	1774–89	Abdül Hamid I
1520–66	Süleyman I	1789–1807	Selim III
	(Kanuni, the Magnificent)	1807–08	Mustafa IV
1566–74	Selim II	1808–39	Mahmud II
1574–95	Murad III	1839–61	Abdül Mecid I
1595–1603	Mehmed III	1861–76	Abdül Aziz
1603–17	Ahmed I	1876	Murad V
1617–18	Mustafa I (first reign)	1876–1909	Abdül Hamid II
1618–22	Osman II	1909–18	Mehmed V
1622–23	Mustafa I (second reign)	1918–22	Mehmed VI
1623–40	Murad IV	1922–23	Abdül Mecid II (Caliph only)

Historic Kingdoms and Provinces (Map pp.64–65)

Armenia

See A to Z

Bithynia

Characteristics

The ancient province of Bithynia in north-western Anatolia centered on the fertile plain bordered by the Sea of Marmara and the Bosporus in the west and the Black Sea in the north and, inland, stretched as far as the mountain passes east of Bolu and, to the south, down to the Uludağ mountains south of the Gulf of İzmit and the Köroğlu Dağlari hills. Geologically speaking parts of its north-western edge still belong to Thrace, while to the east and south chalk and palaeozoic slate and limestone come together to form hills and mountains, peaking in the Uludağ, the classical Bithnyian Olympus (2500m/8205ft). Verdant forests of beech, pine, fir, oak and rhododendron grow on Bithnyia's well-watered Black Sea slopes and farming benefits from the sunshine higher up. More intensive farming in some parts is carried out by such settlers such as the Muhacir who were driven out of the Balkans, Caucasus, Crimea, etc. when the Ottoman Empire was stripped of these provinces in the late 19th c. One of Turkey's most densely settled areas, the Bithnyian plain nowwadays carries the main routes from İstanbul to Ankara and also forms part of the industrial sector of the north-west, much of it concentrated around İzmit, Adapazarı and Bursa.

History

At the crossroads of Europe and Asia Minor, the territory of ancient Bithynia was constantly being fought over. Settled originally by the Thracians, around 550 B.C. it was taken by the Lydians then later by the Persians. Since the wooded mountains of the north remained outside the dominion of Alexander the Great and his successors, Bithynia under the Seleucids was able to develop more or less independently and by the 2nd c. B.C. had become a kingdom in its own right, flourishing around its ancient capitals of Nikomedeia (İzmit) and Nicaea (İznik). In 74 B.C. it was made a Roman province. The Greek colony founded on the Bosporus around 675 B.C., where the İstanbul suburb of Kadıköy stands today, became the Romans' capital and in the Byzantine era, when it was the seat of the archbishopric, provided the venue for the fourth ecumenical council in 451. In the 11th c. Bithynia was ruled by the Seljuks. Since the 14th c. it has been Ottoman, and, in Bursa, it also supplied the Ottomans' first capital.

Cappadocia

See A to Z

Caria

Characteristics and History

The ancient coastal province of Caria, in the south-western corner of Asia Minor, lay more or less between the Maeander (Büyük Menderes) and the Dalaman/Koca Çayı rivers. Nowadays rather off the beaten track, Caria was very important in ancient times because of the many harbours along its deeply indented coast, its relatively dense population, and the routes along the valley of the Maeander, with Miletus at its mouth. No clear picture has emerged of the Carians who originally lived there and their inscriptions have yet to be deciphered. Their national shrine was the temple of Zeus Labrayndos (with the double axe) at Mylasa (Milas).

Ancient authors speak of the Carians as early pre-Greek Aegean seafarers, pushed south from their island homes and the coasts of the Troad by the

Early Christian wall-painting in a Cappadocian cave church near Göreme

Greeks and only living as loosely federated tribes with their own culture in a few cities (Mylasa/Milas, Alinda/Çina, Alabanda). In the late 7th c. B.C. Caria's cities were ruled by the Lydians, in the 6th c. by the Persians, and it was 387 B.C. before they gained their freedom and were able to join other regions of Asia Minor in the Delian League. The ensuing Persian satrap dynasty and the Diadoch battles, which brought a limited degree of Hellenisation in speech and writing to Caria, even after the advent of Alexander, were finally put an end to by Rome in 129 B.C. From 27 B.C. onwards Caria was to enjoy over two centuries of prosperity under Roman rule while managing to retain its own culture, writing and pre-Indo-European language.

Cilicia

The ancient kingdom of Cilicia in Asia Minor was the area known to the Assyrians as Khilakku in the west and Kue in the east. The western half, Cilicia Tracheia ("rough Cilicia"), is the rugged and still largely inaccessible and undeveloped section of the Taurus stretching inland from Anamur, while to the east is the fertile Cilician plain of Çukurova, with its fields of grain and cotton and its banana and citrus groves. This division of what is now a flourishing agricultural region, with a well developed industrial base, still persists today, when Cilicia roughly falls into two Turkish provinces, İçel, with its capital at Mersin, and Adana, the area around the industrial city of the same name at the heart of the Cilician plain.

Characteristics

Cilicia was never a kingdom in its own right for very long. It was too much of a buffer state, too often a prey to the power struggles of neighbouring kingdoms. There is no doubting the fact, however, that this was among the regions that served as the cradle of ancient civilisations from the earliest times. On the Çukurova plain alone, between Mersin and Toprakkale, there are 150 historic sites, some dating as far back as the neolithic, chalcolithic

61

Ancient theatre at Aphrodisias

and bronze ages, along with major ruins from the Hittites right up to Classical Greece and Rome. For thousands of years people have lived on these fertile alluvial plains in the Taurus foreland, the legacy of the "rivers of Paradise", as the Arabian geographers called the Seyhan and the Ceyhan.

History

Some of Cilicia was probably for a time part of the independent kingdoms of Arzawa and then Kizzuwadna (from about 1650 B.C.), buffer states between the Hittites and the Mitanni. From 1196 B.C. it belonged for *c.* 400 years to the late Hittite Kueli kingdom. After the established order in Anatolia was destroyed in the late 7th c. B.C. by invading Scythian and Cimmerian "barbarians" from southern Russia, a kingdom of Cilicia south of the Taurus was one of the new political power structures which soon emerged as regions sought to establish their own identity. The Cilician kings who ruled in Tarsus as vassals of the Persians managed to retain a certain degree of independence and succeeded in expanding their territory as far as Cappadocia and Pamphylia.

Around 103 B.C. Cilicia came under the sway of the Romans. However, it was not until 66 B.C., when Pompey rooted out and destroyed the ferocious pirates from their lairs in the west, that Tarsus was made the capital of the Roman province of Cilicia. This ushered in a long period of prosperity, ended only in the 7th c. A.D. by the Arabs sweeping up from the south. The Armenian kingdom of Cilicia (until 1375, Little Armenia) started to develop in the late 11th c., with support from the Crusaders after 1199, and Armenians were in fact to continue living in the Taurus mountains north-east of Adana and in Kahramanmaraş (Maraş) around Hacin until their deportation earlier this century.

Between 1352 and 1378 the Ramazanoğlu nomads succeeded in winning for themselves a princedom from the Turcoman tribes who had been gradually moving in since 1185 from the north-east, and this was to survive for about 250 years despite its absorption into the Ottoman Empire in 1517.

With time, and against a background of growing political uncertainty (uprisings at Celäli and Saruca/Sebkan), the demands of these wandering herdsmen led to the flat parts of Cilicia near the coast being turned over to winter pastures, where fewer and fewer people settled, and it was only when the nomadic way of life had to be abandoned in the late 19th c. that farming returned to the coastal plain again.

Commagene

Described by Strabo as a small but fertile country between the south-eastern Taurus and the Euphrates, Commagene was nearly always a buffer between much mightier realms and only managed to retain its relatively brief independence, squeezed as it was between Parthia and Rome, by an adroit marriage policy, careful manoeuvring, and astute alliances, thus exploiting the weaknesses of the great power blocks.

Characteristics and History

Until the coming of the Romans the abundance of its natural resources of timber and good grazing land made Commagene the richest kingdom in the arid south-east. Its capital Samosata (Samsat), named after Samos I (3rd c. B.C.), commanded a strategic crossing over the Euphrates, and it was this that enabled Ptolemeus, the local ruler, to take advantage in 163 B.C. of the power struggle between Alexander's successors to make himself king of a small dominion which gradually developed into an independent state. Its temporary subjection by the Armenians was ended by the Roman Lucullus in 69 B.C., and during the reign of Commagene's best remembered ruler, Antiochus I – responsible for the unique site of Nemrut Dağ – Pompeii secured the country's independent statehood which was to last until Vespasian absorbed it into the Roman province of Syria in 72 A.D.

Galatia

Ancient Galatia, at the centre of Asia Minor with its capital Ancyra (Ankara), was part of Phrygia and Cappadocia in early antiquity. The first Galatians crossed the straits from Europe into Anatolia in 278 B.C. These Gallic tribes of eastern Celts had been forced back to the Danube by Alexander the Great and Lysimachus and descended on Macedonia in 279 only to be soundly beaten at the Dardanelles. King Nicomedes of Bithynia brought them in as mercenaries the following year to provide support in his power struggle with the Seleucid Antiochos I, and the arrival of these Celtic hordes made serious inroads into the flourishing civilisations of Asia Minor. The local rulers, summoning up their own forces, succeeded in containing the "barbarians" in the area between Pergamon, Bithynia, Pontus and Cappadocia, and Antiochos I defeated them in the famous Ankara "Battle of Elephants". Employed as mercenaries by the Hellenistic kings they renewed their pillaging raids on Anatolia's cities until Attalos I, King of Pergamum (241–197 B.C.), defeated them in two battles between 235 and 225 B.C. (monument in Pergamon) and forced them to settle. For over a thousand years the Galatians lived around the Phrygian city of Ancyra, hence the name of the region. M. Vulso was finally responsible for the collective defeat of their tribes in 189 B.C., and it was around A.D. 55 that the Apostle Paul wrote his famous Epistle to the Galatians concerning the independence of his Gospel and the freedom from Jewish law of any Galatians he converted to Christianity.

Characteristics and History

Ionia

The offshore islands and the fertile plain along Turkey's south-western Aegean coast formed the ancient region of Ionia. The people who colonised the area in the 1st c. B.C. were probably the first Greeks to move into Asia Minor. Immensely rich in culture, especially in archaic times, Ionia

Characteristics and History

originally embraced all the cities of Ephesus, Erythrae, Clazomenae, Colophon, Lebedos, Miletus, Myus, Priene and Teos, then added Chios, Phocaea and Samos to form the Ionian League. Its religious centre was the shrine of Poseidon in the Panionion on Mount Mykale. The cities soon enjoyed great prosperity thanks to their position on the trade routes from the east. This contact with the old civilisations of the Orient led to a great flowering of cultural life in Ionia, which became the home of poets (Homer probably lived in Smyrna around 800 B.C.), philosophers (Thales, Heracleitus of Ephesus, Pythagoras of Samos), historians (Herodotus) and physicians (Hippocrates). Its artists were equally gifted, producing paintings and sculpture of a breathtaking lightness and grace. It is to the supple spirit of the Ionians that the Greek architecture owes its originality, elegance and charm. On the darker side partisan infighting undermined their great democracies and opened the way to rule by tyrants. Ionia was to play its last real role on the stage of world history with the Ionian uprising of 500–494 B.C., which saw the destruction of Miletus by the Persians. Following Alexander's conquest of Asia the Ionian cities enjoyed their second flowering when they produced such marvels as the Temple of Diana (Artemis) at Ephesus, one of the seven wonders of the ancient world.

Isauria

Characteristics and History

The Taurus mountain country north of Pamphylia and Cicilia, around today's small towns of Mut, Ermenek, Hadım, Bozkır, Seydişehir and Beyşehir, was known to the ancients as Isauria. A landscape of mountains and hollows around Lake Beyşehir (Kireli Gölü) and Lake Suğla (Karaviran

Historical Regions of Turkey

GEORGIA
Artvin
nsun
Ordu • Rize
Giresun Trabzon *Lasistia* Kars • ARMENIA
ısya • Gümüşhane
• Tokat *Pontos* • Erzurum • Ağrı
• Erzincan
Sivas *Armenia*
Tunceli IRAN
ppadocia Bingöl • Muş Lake Van
• Elazığ Bitlis • Van
Malatya • Diyarbakır
Adıyaman Siirt Hakkâri
anmaraş *Kommagene* • Mardin
Şanlıurfa *Mesopotamia*
en Gaziantep
kya IRAQ
SYRIA

Gölü), Isauria, together with adjoining Pisidia in the east, forms part of the upland lake district which gradually gives way to the high plateau of Lycaonia to the north and east, and its relative remoteness was only ended with the building of the Anatolian railroad and the line to Eğridir along the Maeander valley.

Comparatively little is known of the original Isaurians apart from the fact that they were a rough people, a law unto themselves, who were feared far and wide as notorious pirates. Around the middle of the 1st c. B.C. Marcus Aurelius Polemo, one of the high priests of the temple city of Olba on the Taşili plateau, had succeeded in uniting their savage tribes of the Taurus into one independent kingdom. The Byzantine emperor Leo I used these warlike tribesmen to break the power of the Ostrogoths. Upon his death in 474 his successor was a former leader of the Isaurians, Tarasikodissa, who had changed his name to Zenon. The Isaurians had finally become somewhat more civilised during the early Byzantine era, but under Zenon they turned out to be as much of a threat as the Ostrogoths had been before them, and their level of culture, in the eyes of the Byzantines, was still well below that of the Goths. Although it was Zenon who was responsible for building the great Byzantine basilica over the catacombs of St Thekla at Silifke, his successor, Athanasios, after prolonged hostilities, found himself forced to despatch the unruly Isaurians to Thrace and settle them there.

Lazistan

Lazistan, the land of the Lazes on the narrow scenic Black Sea coast east of Trabzon and the easternmost of the Pontine provinces, was until the early

Characteristics
and History

65

Historic Kingdoms and Provinces

Middle Ages the ancient kingdom of Colchis, the green rainsoaked land ruled by King Aietes when Jason and the Argonauts came here in search of the Golden Fleece, and the home of Medea, the legendary princess of the Medeans. The main coastal town is Rize, and further inland there is the lovely little mountain town of Artvin (see entry) on the Çoruh Nehri. The Lazes, many of them blonde and blue-eyed, are still a substantial ethnic minority with a language of their own. They were Orthodox Christians from the early 6th c. who formed their own kingdom until the 10th c., conquest by Mehmed II in 1461 led to their division into as many valley princedoms as there were valleys and their conversion to Islam, so that now they are as fanatically Sunni Muslim as they once were Christian. The Turks called their country "Çengelistan", land of the barbed hook, on account of their contrariness and inaccessibility. Until and into the 19th c. Lazistan was an Ottoman province in its own right and fully independent of İstanbul, and even then its people were moving abroad in search of work, travelling to neighbouring Georgia.

Lydia

Characteristics

With good reason many scholars include the Ionian fringe of the Aegean around İzmir (Smyrna) when they speak of ancient Lydia. It has a similar landscape, is also historically closely interwoven and its influence lent a finer gloss to the innately less refined architecture and sculpture of the Lydians. Here lie Anatolia's largest and most densely populated lowland plains, matched only by Cilicia's Çukurova, and which within Lydia as the seat of early civilisation achieved political and economic significance earlier than the hinterland. This coastal region is the most highly indented section of the Turkish coast, thus having the most harbours, and is divided up into many highly individualistic self-contained units which in ancient times set themselves apart from the actual Lydian hinterland as the special province of the twelve Ionian city states. Central western Lydia held the ancient capital of Sardes, its wealth based on the gold found in the river Pactolos (Sart Çayı), foreign trade, and the skill of its artists and craftsmen (paintings, bronze and gold jewellery). By contrast the core of Ionia, with the ancient centre of Ephesus, stretched between the Gediz (Hermos) river in the north and Küçük Menderes (Caestros) in the south. The less densely populated hill country in the east, with its upland pastures and fields of grain, heralds the steppe-like nature of neighbouring Phrygia – broken up by the Katakekaumene, the "burnt land" of the ancients, the badlands of basalt clinker and lavafields around Kula.

History

Although Lydia first appeared as a historical entity in the early 7th c. B.C. when, following the destruction of the Phrygian kingdom by the Cimmerians, its Mermnades dynasty ruled over a large and strong realm with its capital at Sardes, Lydia's historical origins in the 14th/13th c. B.C. are shrouded in legend. It is said to have been ruled by the famous Atyad dynasty, identified with the Arzawa referred to in Hittite inscriptions. Following the invasion of the Thracians around 1200 B.C. their successors were the mythical ruling family of the Heraklides, descendants of Hercules. Lydia later became a Persian satrapy and then shared the fate of the rest of Asia Minor.

The Lydians' language, known only from 65 inscriptions dating from the 6th/4th c. B.C., shows clear Hittite influence, and they were as famous for their crafts as they were for their legendary King Croesus, defeated in 546 B.C. by the Persians. In terms of culture they lay somewhere between Greece and the Near East.

Lycaonia

Characteristics and History

Few travellers will be aware of the name of Lycaonia, the ancient province that existed high on the great plateau of Central Anatolia, rimmed by the

Central Taurus in the south and centred on classical Iconeum (Konya).
Ringed round by mountains its plains are by far the dryest on the plateau
and in summer its vast vistas of treeless steppe recall nothing so much as
the deserts of Arabia, but in spring this dry-farming country becomes one
great green sea, due largely to artificial irrigation, since this is one of the
great breadbaskets of Turkey. A mountain town, a garden-like oasis,
guards each of the main passes leading out of Lycaonia – Konya on the
route to Pisidia and Phrygia, Niğde and Aksaray on the roads to Cappadocia, Ereğli keeping watch before the Cilician Gates and Karaman on the
Barbarossa line to Kalykadnos.
Although Lycaonia may well have been the cradle of Anatolian pre-history
(Çatalhüyük) it never played an important role in classical times. Its major
independent kingdoms only developed for any duration under the Seljuks
and their successors.

Lycia

The broad peninsula in the extreme south of what was the Turcoman Tekke
principality in south-western Anatolia, and which now takes in parts of the
provinces of Antalya, Muğla, Burdur and Denizli, with a coastline only
recently opened up to tourism, was known to the ancients as Lycia. Brimful
of culture and history, it has one of Turkey's most contrasting and varied
landscapes. Western Lycia, with its three limestone massifs underlying a
hilly, plateau-like countryside, still remains largely devoid of traffic, while
on its sea-facing flanks clumps of many different kinds of trees, colourful
fruit groves and fields of grain alternate with the marshy humid swamps
that persist in the face of modern drainage.
Inland Lycia's high pastures, at 900–1200m/2954–3938ft, are distinctly
dryer by contrast, and the roads here have to snake in and out, up and
down, around the bare hill country, largely treeless but by no means
monotonous. Eastern Lycia is taken up with the mountain wall of the Bey
Dağları, towering up to 2375m/7795ft over the Gulf of Antalya. The town of
Termessos high on its wooded slopes for a long time held the ancient
Solymians after they had been driven out by the Lycians.
The real cultural centre of the region is undoubtedly southern Lycia, a place
full of contrasts and almost comparable with Lazistan. No other place has
such a rapid transition within such a narrow fringe as takes place here,
changing as it does from bare mountain heights at 3000m/9846ft, above
hills covered with pasture and pine, oak and juniper, to chalk cliffs clad with
a maquis of myrtle and laurel above coastal plains and valleys, glowing
with heat in the summer.

Characteristics

The Lycians who emerged as the frontrunners among the sharply divided
population groupings who lived here in the 6th/5th c. B.C. had come over
from Crete and according to classical tradition called themselves "Tra-
mils". The Pisidians and Solymians, long resident on the peninsula, were
driven out into the mountains upcountry. From 540 B.C. Lycia was ruled by
the Persians and then by the Seleucids. In the 5th c. the Lycian cities gained
a degree of independence by banding together in the Attic League and
made a name for themselves through piracy as fine seafarers, but the
Second Pirate Wars put a stop to that.
Since its mountains divided Lycia into many different small units it was
always difficult to get its people to unite into a single state. Since the most
distant past the history of Lycia has therefore been dogged by feudalism,
vested interests, and fragmentation, although it did develop its own writing
and language. As late as the 10th c. A.D. the Lycian language, which had
much in common with the Indo-European Hittite dialect of Luwian, was still
being used in some isolated valleys. The region also evolved a typically
Lycian style of art, heavily influenced by Ionian and Anatolian forms, which
is seen at its best in the reliefs and architecture of the monumental Lycian
rock tombs dating from the 6th c. B.C. onwards.

History

Mesopotamia

Characteristics

Mesopotamia, Greek for "the land between the rivers", strictly speaking means the country between the central and upper reaches of the Tigris and the Euphrates, but in more general terms reaches as far as the foothills of the mountain boundaries. The Euphrates enters Mesopotamia when it leaves the Gerger gorge, the end of its wild passage through the Taurus, while for the Tigris its entry into Mesopotamia is reckoned to be the start of its course through the ravines crisscrossing the tablelands south of Ergani. As the north-western continuation of the Persian Gulf, Mesopotamia is a large geological depression between the deserts of Arabia in the south-west, the oxbow of the Taurus in the north, and the Zagros ranges in the north-east. Upper Mesopotamia – south of the Eastern Taurus and east of the Amanos mountains – is the only section of this great region that belongs to Turkey. By far the greater part – all of the south and most of the middle – lies in Iraq.

In the north Mesopotamia is high plains country, dissected by river valleys, a country of karst formations and horst mountains (Mardin foothills/Tur Abdin), limestone plateaux (Urfa Yalası, Gaziantep Yaylası, upper Tigris basin), black lava pavements (Karacadağ), and rolling valley plains (Urfa-Harran Ovası), bitterly cold in winter, with some snowfall, and unbearably hot and dry in summer.

History

Around 2000 B.C. Upper Mesopotamia was inhabited by the Hurrians, incomers from the Caucassus, then between 1450 and 1350 B.C. it was the centre of the Mitanni realm. In 1200 B.C. it fell to the Semitic Assyrians and the ending of their empire was followed by a brief period of interim rule from New Babylon. The Persians were here in 539 B.C. then after the death of Alexander the Great the Seleucids. The Parthians profited from their downfall to conquer the area, and their rule was interrupted by a brief spell of Roman occupation between 114 and 117 A.D. The Persian Sassanids in the 3rd c. were succeeded by the Byzantines in the 6th c., only for them to be

A sunshade-tent in Mesopotamia

replaced a century later by the Arab Caliphs. With their decline in the 10th/11th c. local Arab and Turkish rulers took it in turns until the whole region fell to the now much stronger Ottomans. In the late 19th/early 20th c. the dismantling of the Ottoman Empire brought with it considerable resistance from the local Turks against British and French colonial ambitions.

Mysia

The hilly countryside of ancient Mysia leaves little room for farming. Manufacturing industry is rare and restricted to a few places such as Bursa, Balıkesir and Bandırma. Intensive use is made of the coastal plains (Biga, Bergama, Edremit, Skamander) and some of the large intramontane basins (Bursa, Apolyont, Manyas, Balıkesir), which are more densely populated as a result.

Mysia effectively falls into a western and an eastern half, either side of the Simav Çayı (Makestos) which down through the ages has provided a route between İzmir and the Marmara region, while the extension of the Gulf of Edremit is another dividing line, this time running west to east. But whereas both northern sections benefit from the rainfall generated by the Sea of Marmara the south-east of the region is much drier. The coastal foothills are thickly planted with olive trees and oak groves (*quercus aegilops*), while the well-watered hills of the hinterland are partly covered with lovely forests of summer oak, shady beech and rhododendron. In the southern part of Mysia, once the province of Pergamum, there is space for farming, settlement and lines of communication. Here pines and sweet chestnuts join the treecover on the hills.

The mountainous south-east and north-west still have few roads and a sparse population, especially since the people of the mountain villages are now leaving them to work in the big cities or the tourist resorts on the coast. Towering massifs like those of the Kaz Dağı (Mount Ida; 1769m/5806ft) in

Characteristics

Taurus Mountains near Termessos . . .   *. . . and Olympus*

the west, Alaçam Dağı (2089m/6856ft) in the south, Eğrigöz Dağı, with its twin peaks (2072m/6800ft), towards the plains of Phrygia in the east, and Uludağ, the Mysian Olympus (2543m/8346ft) in the north provide the setting for a rugged landscape of wooded mountains and hills.

History
Mysia was at the heart of the great kingdom of Pergamum. This also embraced the Troad peninsula and was at its height in the 3rd c. B.C. when it was ruled by its powerful kings, the Attalids. Other important cities of the time include Kyzikos (near Bandırma), Lampsakos (Lapseki on the Dardanelles) and Adramyttion (Edremit).

Relatively little is known of the Mysian language and culture although it would appear from a brief inscription from the 4th/3rd c. B.C. that Mysian was a dialect somewhere between Lydian and Phrygian.

Pamphylia

Characteristics
The rich plain of Pamphylia, curving around the top of the Gulf of Antalya between Antalya (Adalia, Attaleia) in the west and Alanya (classical Coracesium, the "crow's nest", famous for its pirates) in the east, against the impressive backdrop of the Bey Dağları (over 2000m/6564ft) in the west and the Central Taurus in the north, nestles almost like a piece of North Africa between its mountains and the Mediterranean. The white chalkfaces of the low foothills of the mountain country of Pisidia in the north are covered with pines and maquis, their lower slopes dotted with the ruins of ancient castles and classical cities and the many villages crowding the well-watered valley floors. The Pamphylian plain itself is rich alluvial farmland, given over to the intensive cultivation of vegetables, cotton, citrus fruits, and bananas. Towards Lycia in the west, however, the subsoil is of limestone tufa, and here the cultivated travertine terraces start right at the foot of the mountains, falling steeply to the sea and the ancient harbour of Antalya.

History
In classical times Pamphylia's most important cities were Adalia, Alanya, Perge, Aspendos and Side. The main period of settlement is thought to have been when Greek refugees mingled with the local peoples having fled here following the fall of Troy around 1184 B.C. – the name Pamphylia is ancient Greek for "land of all tribes" and an indication of just how colourful a mixture this must have been. Ruled in turn by the Lydians, Persians, Alexander the Great, Antigonos I, one of his successors, the Seleucids and Egypt's Ptolimites, it enjoyed a brief period of independence until the west of the region was ceded to the King of Pergamum in 188 B.C. The Romans made it the heart of the military province of Cilicia, then merged it with Lycia in the 1st c. A.D. to form a single province which reached the height of its prosperity in the 2nd c. A.D. Earlier this part of the coast had also been notorious for its pirates who were to plague the Romans until their reign of terror was ended by Pompey. He also took the local cult of Mithraism back with him to Rome, and for a long time Mithras was the official protector of the Roman empire and the great rival of the Christian religion. This local attachment to Mithraism made it particularly difficult for the early Christians to gain general acceptance of their new religion. As a consequence the Crusaders set up numerous small Christian enclaves, each with its castle, along the coast of Pamphylia and Cilicia. The Italians seized on this fact, as "heirs to the Roman Empire" and representatives of the Church of Rome, to lay claim to these coasts in the Turkish War of Liberation earlier this century.

Paphlagonia

Characteristics
The westernmost of the ancient countries of the Pontus, with mountains 2000m/6564ft high, Paphlagonia lies between the Filyos (Yenice İrmağı) in

the west, with the coalfields of Ereğli–Zonguldak, and the Halys (Kızılırmak) in the east. The high wide plains are framed by the Küre Dağları (2019m/6626ft) in the north, the İlgas Dağları (2546m/8356ft) in the south and the Köroğlu Dağları (2013m/6607ft) in the east. There is little room for proper harbours along the steep coast and the hinterland only becomes less forbidding at the start of the ancient Pontus beyond the Kısılırmak in the east. The dry interior begins behind the narrow woodland zone of the coastal hills. Three farmland belts with hamlets and small weaving towns run parallel with the evergreen coastline, and here on the undulating chalk uplands irrigation is used to grow grain, maize, cotton, rice, fruit and tobacco. On the dryer, southern side of the mountains the valleys of the Araç Çayı and the Gökırmak are Paphlagonia's economic backbone, while the high plains of İflani/Devrekanı lie at the core of the plateau. This high country is also the location of Kastamonu, ancient capital of the province, and Safranbolu, the gateway to western Paphlagonia and once Anatolia's centre for saffron-growing. The valley dwellers of the Ulu Çay (Gerede Çayı), Devrez Irmak and part of the lower Kızılırmak in the south live in a similar succession of small market towns. There the rainfall can be as little as 400mm/15in. a year in parts, and the dry steppe gradually gains the upper hand with the transition to Central Anatolia. Down through the ages the people of this sparsely settled region have been considered wild and strange, and were already called "Paphlasians", i.e. speakers of a barbaric tongue, by the ancient Greeks who colonised the area.

Paphlagonia came under Lydian rule in the 6th c. B.C., then become Persian and, following Alexander's campaigns, Macedonian. It was only during the Hellenistic period, when the local dynasty of Ariarathes was in power, that it became a kingdom in its own right, later to be taken by the Romans under Augustus as part of the province of Galatia.

History

Phrygia

Ancient Phrygia in the west of the Anatolian plateau, the country around the sources of the Sakarya Nehri within the triangle of the modern cities of Afyon, Eskişehir and Ankara, was named after the western Indo-Europeans who came here from Europe around 1200 B.C. and left their mark as skilled craftsmen with a culture of their own. It was a country clearly with many towns and cities, lying on the routes to the east from Lydia and Caria. Today it has only three major cities: Afyon, the opium city, Eskişehir, a hub of industry and the main railroad junction, and Kütahya, a centre for ceramics and the mining of brown coal. Here in many places the westerlies and southerlies can still carry rain deep into the mountains, bringing denser settlement and a greater degree of cultivation in their train. This farming potential enabled Phryia even in early classical times to develop a powerful kingdom of its own with many towns and cities. Its fringes, where east met west, were a battleground for Persians and Lydians, Romans and Galatians, Arabs and Romaioi, Crusaders and Seljuks, Ottomans and Mongols, Byzantines and Turks. Ruins and age-old monuments abound up on the rolling plateau around the upper reaches of the Sakarya, with here and there towering rocky outcrops and a few scraggy trees, although nowadays signs of settlement are few and far between.

Characteristics

The Phrygian language, which died out in the 6th c. A.D., was closely related to Greek, as can be seen from 80 ancient Phrygian inscriptions (7th–4th c. B.C.), written in a script rather like Greek, and over 110 neo-Phrygian writings in Greek from Roman times.

Language

As Thracian invaders the Phrygians played a decisive role in the destruction of the Hittite Kingdom and the fall of Troy. Their independent Phrygian kingdom of the 8th and 7th c. B.C. maintained close contacts with the Aryans in the east and the Greeks in the west. Its early history is only briefly

History

chronicled (Herodotus), recounting the suicide of its last king, Midas, in Gordium when it fell to the Cimmerians (676 B.C.). With the establishment of the Galatians in eastern Phrygia the fertility cult of Cybele, the mother goddess, spread widely amongst town dwellers, while countryfolk tended to worship Men the moon god, ruler of Paradise and the Underworld. In 188 B.C. Phrygia came under Pergamum, followed by Rome, who made it a province in 133 B.C.

Montanism
Novatianism

The early spread of Christianity here was largely due to St Paul but the 2nd c. A.D. also saw the development of two extreme sects: Montanism, derived from the locally born Prophet Montanus who preached that the end of the world was nigh, and Novationism, named after the Roman theologian and later Bishop Novatian, whose followers called themselves "the pure", in Greek "katharoi" – hence the Cathar heresy of the Middle Ages – and refused to allow any lapsed Christians back into the Church.

Pisidia

Characteristics

The Taurus mountain country of ancient Pisidia, now parts of the modern provinces of Burdur, Isparta, Denizli and Antalya, lies between the Pamphylian coastal plain and the Phrygian plateau and the massifs of Lycia and "rough" Cilicia, starting in the south as the landscape becomes more forbidding and ending in the high mountain chains of the interior (Sultan Dağları, Karakus Dağları, Söğut Dağı, Dedegöl Dağları). Stretching from Lake Beyşehir in Isauria to Kastel Daği in bordering Phrygia it is a high plains country, dotted with lakes and shallow depressions, patchy farmland and pasture. The central and eastern parts of the plateau in the middle make up a region of chalk ridges overlooking poljes and karst gullies where whole lakes drain away underground. The south sees little traffic and its sparse population live in a few islands of cultivation. Despite the fact that it remained untouched by foreign cultures until the coming of the Romans, Pisidia is rich in antiquities, many of them the ruins of fortified strongholds. Rushing rivers bite deep into rugged mountains full of narrow canyons, caves, and underground streams, and where beech, cedar, pine, spruce and oak alternate with "yayla", i.e. summer pastures.

History

The mountain fastnesses of the Pisidians, a long-established and proverbially warlike people, remained for centuries untouched by outside influences. Its inaccessibility and the fierce resistance of its people meant that Pisidia was able to avoid outright conquest by the Persians and Alexander the Great, and Greek and Roman culture only succeeded in gaining a foothold when it became an ally of the Romans. The interpretation of Pisidian as a language is still in dispute since only brief extracts have been found to date, but it seems to bear some similarity to that of the Indo-Europeans.

Pontus

Characteristics

The heartland of the ancient kingdom of Pontus on the rugged eastern coast of the Black Sea – antiquity's Pontus Euxinus – lies between the mouth of the Halys (Kızılırmak) and the Çoruh Nehri. This coastal strip between its only ports of note – Pontos, Trabzon and Samsun – has also been known from time to time as "East Pontus" as opposed to western Pontine Paphlagonia. Narrow and mountainous, it was for centuries exposed to the influence of Greek colonists and the seafaring peoples of the Black Sea.

Despite its deep mountain valleys, the west, the "land of life" of the Canık, with its less steep, trachytic lava pavements, tends to appear a more hospitable countryside of fields, pastures, and parkland. Here the alluvial plains of the Iris (delta of the Yeşilırmak and the setting for the legendary Amazons) provide the only fertile coastal lands of any size in the north

Pontus, and this is where up until 1806 the town of Bafra was the capital of an independent Canık with its tiny mountain strongholds, feudal castles and ruins. The eastern part of the Pontus is more a region of spectacular natural beauty, rich in forests and minerals, where three mountain ranges, towering up to 3000m/9846ft, stand between the dry hinterland and the sea.

Maize and hazelnuts grow on the rain-soaked slopes of the northern and eastern Pontus, thickly wooded right down to the sea in places with dense forests and undergrowth of beech, pine, rhododendron and azalea. This is the land of classical Chalybe, of the ironsmiths, with everywhere in the woods remains of ancient foundries and mines (Gümüşhane = Silver House). Also typical of the Pontus are the scattered hamlets and farmsteads clinging to the steep valley sides and mountain slopes. More extensive farmland, and hence greater density of population, only begins in the southern basins – Bayburt's Hart Ovası, Suşehri Ovası, Merzifon's Suluova, Erbaa's Taş Ovası, Niksar Ovası, Tokat's Kaz Ovası, Turhal and Zile, Amasya Ovası.

The Greeks had founded city colonies such as Sinope (Sinop), Amisos (Samsun), Kerasos (Giresun) and Trapezius (Trabzon) on the Black Sea coast in the 6th c. B.C. After Alexander the Great's defeat of the Persians a larger kingdom, with its capital at Amaseia (Amasya), was created in 281 B.C. by Mithridates II, the first to call himself King of Pontus. Later Mithridates VI Eupator the Great (120–63 B.C.) chose Amisos (Samsun) as his capital, extended his realm to the neighbouring districts and threatened the Roman Empire in Greece. Julius Caesar put an end to the expansionist ambitions of the Pontine rulers and their allies (Tigranes, Pharnakes) at the battle of Zela (Zilve: "veni, vidi, vici"). The western Black Sea coast (Bithynia and Pahplagonia) became the Roman province of Bithynia et Pontus, while the section east of the Halys (Kızılırmak) went to the Galatian ruler Deiotarus and the local ruler Polemo, eventually also becoming Roman (Province of Galatia) in 32 and 63 B.C. respectively.

After the fall of Constantinople to the Crusaders in 1204 two fleeing princes of the imperial Comnenos dynasty, David and Alexius I, founded their own flourishing Pontic empire here, with its capital at Trebizond (Trabzon), and this was to survive for over 250 years until its absorption into the Ottoman empire in 1462.

History

Thrace

For the very earliest Greeks Thrace was the whole of the Balkan Peninsula, including Macedonia, in the east of Illyria, then later just its eastern half south of the Danube. The Roman province of Thrace only covered the region between the Balkan mountains and the Sea of Marmara (Propontis), and since the Ottoman conquest it has simply been the area south of the Rhodope Mountains, belonging to Greece in the west and Turkey in the east.

Modern Thrace, the part of Turkey in Europe, is made up of the provinces of Edirne, Kırklareli, Tekirdağ˘ and İstanbul. It is a dry country where the high hills in the north and west keep the rainfall at bay. The highest parts are the İstranca mountains (Yıldız Dağı) bordering the Black Sea in the north-east and the Kuru Dağı/Işıklar Dağı in the south-west, but here too there is relatively little tree cover. The "Thracian triangle" between Edirne, İstanbul and Gelibolu (Gallipoli) has much in common with the Anatolian plateau, a kind of broken table landscape, here drained by the Maritza, Ergene Nehri and their tributaries, flat dry-farming country, with much grain grown on the approaches to İstanbul. It has always been of strategic rather than economic importance, lying as it does at the crossroads of the land routes between Europe and Asia and the sea routes between the Black Sea and the Mediterranean through the Bosporus and the Dardanelles.

Characteristics

King Tereus founded the first great kingdom of Thrace around 450 B.C. Under his successors it reached to the Danube, the Sea of Marmara, the

History

Aegean and the Black Sea but was never an independent country again after 342 B.C. Despite becoming part of the Roman and then Byzantine empire its strategic position meant it was often the prey of other nations – Huns, Goths, Slavs, Bulgarians – until finally falling to the Ottomans in 1358. Although Bulgaria captured large parts of Thrace in the first of the Balkan Wars, in the second it lost the western section around Kavalla to Greece, followed by the whole of the coastal strip during the First World War.

Troad

See A to Z, Troia

Famous People

The following famous people were all connected with Turkey in some way or other, whether as the place of their birth or death, or because they lived or worked there.

Alexander the Great, one of the world's greatest military commanders, was born in Pella in northern Greece, the son of King Philip II of Macedon and Olympiás, daughter of King Neoptolemos. Between 342 and 340 B.C. his tutor was the philosopher Aristotle. Alexander had already distinguished himself in battle at Chaironaia in 338 B.C. when he secured the throne as Alexander III by eliminating his rivals after the death of his father in 336 B.C. at the hands of Pausanias, possibly a hired assassin. Appointed Commander of the Corinthian League he moved first against the Thracians and the Illyrians and put down a rising by the Thebans (335 B.C.). As supreme commander of the Greeks in 334 B.C. Alexander, with his army of 35,000 men, embarked on a campaign of "Hellenistic revenge" against the Persians, crossing the Hellespont (Dardanelles), winning the battle on the Granikos in the spring, occupying Gordium (the story of him cutting the legendary Gordian knot is without historical foundation), then marching over the Taurus mountains to Cilicia and defeating Darius III, the Persian king, in November of 333 at Issus, north of present-day Iskenderun. This left the way open to Egypt where he founded the city of Alexandria and had his divine origins and claim to power confirmed by the oracle of Zeus Ammon at the Siwa oasis.

Alexander the Great (356–323 B.C.)

From Egypt Alexander and his army marched to Babylonia, where he again defeated Darius, this time decisively, at Gaugamela on the Mossul plain, now in Iraq. He carried on into Persia (Iran) and finally began his Indian campaign (327–325 B.C.), getting as far as the Hindu Kush and the Punjab before his exhausted men forced him to turn back at the Indus delta. Sailing back for part of the return journey through the Persian Gulf, Alexander and his remaining men made the gruelling crossing of the desert and eventually reached Babylon where he died of a fever while preparing for an Arabian campaign.

Alexander's declared policy, in part already embarked upon, of conciliation and of consolidating the great new empire he had created from so many disparate pieces, was doomed to failure. His empire fragmented almost immediately as rival claims were lodged by his successors.

The Turkish statesman Mustafa Kemal Pasa was born in 1880 or 1881 in Salonika in Macedonia, attended the Military Academy in Constantinople, took part in the Young Turk Rising of 1908–09 alongside Enver Pasa, fought against the Italians in 1912 in Cyrenaica and was a divisional commander in Gallipoli in the First World War. When western Turkey was occupied by the Greeks in 1918 he withdrew to Anatolia, where he organised resistance to Allied and Greek forces in May 1919 and broke off relations with the Sultan's government. In 1920 he set up a provisional government in Ankara, and in 1921–22 he secured victory over the Greeks; he was granted the honorific title of Gazi in 1921. In November 1922 he succeeded in abolishing the Sultanate. The following year he proclaimed the Republic of Turkey, and was elected its first President on October 29th 1923.

Kemal Atatürk (1880 or 1881–1938)

Kemal Pasa's aim was to create a secular Turkish nation state, and the national renewal was to be achieved by a fundamental Europeanisation of Turkish society. He made Ankara the new capital of Turkey and carried through comprehensive political and cultural reforms – legal system, social position of women, education policy, introduction of the Latin alphabet, reform of the calendar, etc.

Famous People

Alexander the Great   *Kemal Atatürk*   *Beyazid I*

In 1934 he assumed the patronymic Atatürk ("Father of the Turks"). He remained President of the Republic until his death in İstanbul on November 10th 1938. His remains were reinterred in the Atatürk Mausoleum in 1953. Atatürk's philosophy and ideas, or Kemalism as they came to be called, still hold good, subject to certain limitations, in the Turkey of today.

Beyazid I (c. 1354–1403)	The Ottoman Sultan Beyazid I, Yıldırım the Thunderbolt, who ruled from 1389, was the eldest son and heir of Sultan Murad I. The conqueror of Bulgaria and Serbia, he made Wallachia a vassal state and penetrated down into Greece, although he failed to capture Constantinople. In the autumn of 1396 he defeated the crusader army led by Sigismund, King of Hungary, at Nicopolis on the Danube, but was defeated in his turn by Tamerlane and his Mongols at Ankara in the summer of 1402. He died Tamerlane's prisoner at Akşehir on March 8th 1403.
Beyazid II (c. 1448–1512)	The Ottoman Sultan Beyazid II Veli, the Holy One, was born in Demotika (now Didimotichon, in the Greek district of Evros), and succeeded his father Mehmed II Fâtih (see entry) in 1481. He waged frontier wars in the Balkans (1482 conquest of Hercegovina) but was unsuccessful against the Egyptian Mameluks in Cilicia, brought Moldova (now part of Romania) under his sway and moved on Venice, capturing their Greek outposts. It was during his Sultanate that the Ottomans first attacked Transylvania and Austria. In 1512 his son Selim I (see entry) rose against him and forced him to abdicate with the help of the janissaries. Beyazid II died on May 26th 1512 close to his birthplace.
Celaleddin Rumi	See entry
Constantine the Great (c. 288–337 A.D.)	Born in what is now Nis in Serbia around A.D. 288, the Roman Emperor Constantine (I) the Great moved the capital of the Empire in 330 from Rome to Byzantium, which was then renamed Constantinopolis/Nova Roma (İstanbul after 1453). With the Edict of Milan, already promulgated in 313 and giving Christianity official recognition, he inaugurated the first steps toward it becoming the only state religion. In Constantinople during his reign the foundation stone was laid for Hagia Sophia (Ayasofya), the forum was completed and the Serpentine Column was brought to the Hippodrome from Delphi. Constantine is a saint in the Greek and Russian Orthodox and Armenian Churches.
Mehmet Akıf Ersoy (1873–1936)	Born in İstanbul, the writer Mehmet Akıf Ersoy received an excellent education on traditionally Islamic lines, attended the Veterinary Academy in 1894, worked in the border provinces of what was then the Ottoman Empire and spent some time in Germany in the First World War. Although initially a

supporter of Pan-Islamism he joined the Freedom Movement and became a member of the newly created Republic's first Parliament. He spent the last ten years of his life in Cairo, Egypt, as a lecturer in literature.

In his early years Ersoy wrote lyrical poetry of a religious nature. Throughout the seven volumes of poetry between 1911 and 1933 which form his collected works he used the classical Turkish metre but fashioned his material with naturalistic means. "İstiklâl Marşi", his freedom song, was made the Turkish national anthem in 1921 (see Quotations).

Mehmet Akıf Erskoy died in his home city of İstanbul on December 27th 1936.

Eyüp Ensari, a trusted companion of the Prophet Mohammed and standard-bearer for the first Holy Army of Islam, was commander of the Arab forces during their first siege of Constantinople in 674–678 when he is said to have lost his life and been buried on the site of the present mosque in the İstanbul suburb of Eyüp on the western bank of the Golden Horn. This is İstanbul's most sacred mosque and is especially revered as one of the holy sites of Islam.

Eyüp Ensarı
(7th c. A.D.)

Herodotus, according to Cicero the "father of history", was born in Dorian Halicarnassus (now Bodrum), but had to leave after taking part in an uprising against the tyrant Lygdamis. He travelled widely in Egypt, Africa, Asia Minor and eastern Europe, then lived for a time in Athens, greatly respected and honoured, before moving in 444 B.C. to settle in the newly founded Athenian colony of Thourioi (Thurii) in southern Italy. His history of the wars between Greece and Persia, divided in later years into nine books named after the Muses, incorporated observations made on his travels as well as a record of the political events. Later study has confirmed in many respects the accuracy of his work, which is a valuable source of information on the Greek settlements in Asia Minor as well as on the lands and peoples of Africa and the Near East.

Herodotus
(c. 490–
425/420 B.C.)

Born January 20th 1902 in Saloniki (Greek Thessaloniki) the son of a doctor from an aristocratic family, Nazım Hikmet (Nâzı, Hikmet Ran) first attended the Naval College in İstanbul before spending between 1921 and 1928 in the Soviet Union, where he studied in Moscow at the Communist University for "Eastern Workers". A member from 1924 of the illegal Turkish Communist Party, after his return to Turkey he was arrested many times for subversive activities and eventually sentenced to 28 years imprisonment in 1937. Freed under an amnesty in 1950 he lived in Sofia, Warsaw and Moscow, where he died on June 3rd 1963.

Nazım Hikmet
(1902–63)

İHis works of poetry mean that Hikmet is credited with being the founder of the new Turkish verse. He started out with patriotic poems then became acquainted with the Expressionist and Dada movements in the experimental literary circles of Moscow in the Twenties. He was the first Turkish poet to abandon the classical metre, turning increasingly to free verse liberally sprinkled with slang and more down-to-earth expressions. The influence of Mayakovsky, the Russian poet, clearly had a hand in Hikmet becoming the leading poetry exponent of the Turkish moderns around 1930, although during his years in exile it was his agitprop side that inevitably came to the fore. His great body of work has been translated into many languages but its publication was banned in Turkey between 1950 and 1964, and is still viewed with unease even today.

The city of Smyrna (İzmir) in Asia Minor claims, probably with some justification, to be the birthplace of Homer, legendary author of the "Iliad" and the "Odyssey" and the West's earliest epic poet. Tradition has it that he was a blind "rhapsode", a wandering reciter of poetry who travelled around the Ionian cities. The Ionian "sons of Homer" existed as a guild from about 700 B.C., based more particularly on the island of Chios. However, it has always been a matter of debate whether Homer actually was a historical figure, especially since it was doubted whether one single person

Homer
(c. 8th c. B.C.)

Homer

İsmet İnönü

Mehmed II

was capable of being solely responsible for two such great works. A late 18th c. German scholar advanced the theory that the Iliad and the Odyssey were collections of individual lays, thus making Homer a kind of collective term for more ancient epic verse.

Nowadays it is generally held that Homer was a real person who lived and wrote on the west coast of Asia Minor and was associated in many ways with the island of Chios. His great works probably also incorporated many older and shorter legendary epics, with the Iliad thought to have been written before the Odyssey although both works were much amended and expanded at a later date. Homer is also credited with the "Homeric Hymns and Epigrams" and the comic epics of the Fool Margites and the War of Frogs and Mice ("Batrachomyomachia").

İsmet İnönü
(1884–1973)

Born Mustafa İsmet Pasa on September 25th 1884 in the Aegean port of Smyrna, then Greek, now İzmir in Turkey, the Turkish soldier and statesman took part in the Young Turks' revolution in 1908 and joined Mustafa Kemal (Atatürk)'s freedom movement in 1920, becoming Chief of the General Staff of the Kemalist forces in the wars with Greece (1920–22/23) when in 1921 he won several battles around İnönü in the province of Bilecik, subsequently taking the name of the village for his surname.

As Turkish Foreign Minister (1922–24) he signed the Lausanne Peace Treaty in 1923, then as Prime Minister (1923/24 and 1925–37) he had a large share in the reforms carried out by Kemal Atatürk within Turkey. After Atatürk's death in 1938 İnönü became President of the Republic and Chairman of the CHP, the Republican People's Party. Singlemindedly he carried on the policy of reform (greater press freedom, introduction of the multi-party system, etc.) and managed largely to keep Turkey out of the Second World War, only coming in on the side of the Allies in 1945. After defeat by the Democratic Party in the 1950 elections he became leader of the Opposition. Following the military putsch in 1960 he returned as Prime Minister from 1961 to 1965. As an opponent of Bülent Ecevit's increasingly social democratic party line he eventually stood down from chairing the CHP and left the party. Ismet İnönü had been serving as a Senator in the Grand National Assembly since 1972 when he died on December 25th 1973 in Ankara.

Mausolus
(4th c. B.C.)

Mausolus, the satrap who became king of an independent Caria after the greater loosening of ties with the Persian Empire in 362 B.C., had his capital at Halicarnassus, now Bodrum. His "Mausoleion", the magnificent tomb begun during his lifetime and completed after his death (353 B.C.) by his widow, and sister, Artemisia, was one of the Seven Wonders of the World (see p. 86) and gave its name to any "mausoleum" of a like kind thereafter.

Mehmed II
(1432–81)

Sultan Mehmed II Fâtih (Mehmed the Conqueror), born in Adrianople (Edirne) in 1430, and, after 1451, the seventh Sultan of the Ottoman Empire,

Mevlana   *Nasrettin Hoca*   *St Nicholas*

captured Constantinople after a two-month siege in 1453, renaming it İstanbul, also thereafter known in the West as Stamboul. He took possession of the famous church of Hagia Sophia for Islam, but allowed the Genoese in Galatia continuing freedom to trade, subject to their surrender of all weapons and the payment of official tolls and taxes, and permitted recognition of the Greek Orthodox Church, also transferring to the anti-Roman church Patriarch Gennadios civil jurisdiction over the Greek Christians. İstanbul was resettled with the recall of Greeks who had fled before the Ottoman advance, thus bringing into being the Phanariotentum, named after Phanar, the Greek quarter.

Mehmed II made İstanbul the capital of the Ottoman Empire and the spiritual centre of Islam. He died in the city on May 3rd 1481 and his türbe, or tomb, reconstructed in the 18th c., lies within the great Mehmed Fâtih mosque.

The mystic poet and philosopher Celaleddin Rumi was probably born in September 1199 or 1200, and not 1207 as was previously supposed, in Balkh, Afghanistan. As the son of Bahreddin Valed, one of Islam's learned men and teachers, he first studied in the Muslim faith in his home town then followed his family via Nishapur in Persia, Bagdad, Mecca, Medina, Jerusalem, Damascus and Aleppo, then Malatya, Erzincan, Sivas, Kayseri, and Niğde, to Karaman. He assumed his father's role and in 1233 was invited by the Seljuk Sultan Alaeddin Keykubad to the court at Konya.

Mevlana (Celaleddin Rumi; *c.* 1200–73)

His encounter in Konya with Şemseddin, a dervish or "holy man" from Tabris in Persia, changed his life, setting him on the mystic philosophical path of Sufism (from the Arabic "sufi", originally a wool-clad Muslim ascetic), to which he also brought concepts of tolerance for other religions, preaching a doctrine of absolute perfection and all-embracing love in passionate self-abandonment, which found its fulfilment in the enraptured trance dance of the dervishes. Thus, under his honorary title "Mevlâna", the Master, he became the founder of the Sufi brotherhood of the Mevlevî, the whirling dervishes, so-called because of the spinning dance performed in flowing robes every Friday, often with musical accompaniment, as a devotional ritual to achieve a spiritual state of ecstasy. Guided by his basic tenet "be not without love that ye may live, and die in love that ye may not die", he was preacher, philosopher and mystic poet all in one.

Celaleddin Rumi died on December 17th 1273 in Konya where his tomb can be found today in the tekke, the dervish convent of the Order of Whirling Dervishes founded by his son Veled in 1284. This is still one of Turkey's most revered places of pilgrimage, despite the fact that Atatürk (see entry), in his secularisation of the country, banned all religious sects in 1925 and with them the Mevlevî, declaring the convent a museum in 1927.

Famous People

Midas
(c. 738–700 B.C.)

Midas, son of Gordius and the last and most famous of the Phrygian kings, ruled over the whole of Asia Minor as far as Cilicia. The "Midas touch" legend has it that in return for sending back the drunken Silenus to Dionysus the god granted Midas his wish that everything he touched would turn to gold. Another legend is that because Midas voted against Apollo in a music contest between him and Pan, Apollo, in revenge, caused Midas to grow ass's ears, which Midas sought in vain to hide under a Phrygian cap. An ally of the Urartian kingdom, Midas forged a pact in 717 B.C. with the king of Carcemish on the Euphrates against his Assyrian adversary, Sargon II, who then went on to take the old Hittite capital. The onslaught of the Cimmerians (c. 700–670 B.C.) and the Scythians brought the break-up of the Phrygian empire and Midas attempted suicide by drinking bull's blood. The Phrygian kingdom continued in existence until about 650 B.C. when it was absorbed by the Lydians, although Phrygian culture continued to live on for many years to come.

Mehmet Namık Kemal
(1840–88)

Born December 21st 1840 in Rodostó (now Tekirdağ¨), the scion of an aristocratic line of officials, Mehmet Namık Kemals is regarded as one of Turkey's great poets of the people. After a private education he worked as a civil servant in İstanbul where he was also employed on "Tasvir-i Efkâr", the journal published by İbrahim Şinasi (see entry), which he also took over in 1865.

Already in his youth one of the fiercest opponents of the despotic Sultans, the critical nature of Namık Kemal's journalism forced him to flee to Paris in 1867 and then London where along with Ziya Pasha he published "Hürriyet" (Freedom), the exiles' anti-government journal. After an 1870 amnesty brought him back to Turkey, the performance in early April 1873 of his freedom play "Vatan yahud Silistre" (Homeland or Silistra) in İstanbul's Gedikpaşa theatre led to unrest, the banning of the play and his banishment to Cyprus where he spent the years until 1876 in Famagusta prison. After his release following the deposing of Sultan Abdul Aziz he left Cyprus, helped to found the Young Turks in Paris in 1876 and then, after a brief period on the constitution commission, was banished in 1877 to the Aegean island of Mytilene. Becoming governor there in 1879 he was transferred to Rhodes in 1884 and Chios in 1887 where he died from tuberculosis on December 2nd 1888.

With their pretensions to romanticism and often downright sentimentality, Namık Kemal's poetry and prose, including "İntibah", the first "modern" Turkish novel, served as a clarion call to the stirrings of Ottoman patriotism and helped to unleash the Young Turk movement, thus paving the way for Atatürk's revolutionary reforms.

Nasrettin Hoca
(c. 1208–c. 1284)

Turkey's most famous folk hero, Nasrettin Hoca (or Nasrettin Efendi) was a semi-legendary joker, and supposedly lived, and died, in Akşehir as a Hodja, a kind of Muslim cleric.

Seen as the personification of the Turkish national character, a whole host of stories were handed down, making their first written appearance in 1571, featuring his jokey homespun philosophy, many of which have become common sayings. Tamerlane, the Mongolian conqueror, is said to have looked upon him as his wise fool and jester (see Quotations).

İsa Necatî
(15th/16th c.)

Born the son of slave at a date unknown, but probably in Edirne, the Turkish poet İsa Necatî was, so tradition has it, in the service of a wealthy woman who secured him a good education. It is known that he was a scribe and poet in Kastamonu and was clerk to the divan (council of state) of Sultans Mehmed II and Beyazid II (see entries). He died in İstanbul on March 17th 1509.

İsa Necatî is considered one of the 15th c.'s most important "divan poets". Unlike many of his contemporaries he did not model himself on the Persian masters but instead penned realistically worded poems which also addressed social problems.

Behçet Necatigil
(1916–79)

The writer Behçet Necatigil from İstanbul, where he was later to become a lecturer in Turkish language and literature, is accounted to be among the

Turgut Özal   *Sinan*   *Suleiman I*

leading innovators of modern Turkish poetry – there has been a Necatigil
poetry prize since 1980. Besides also working as a lexicographer and
translator, he was the first Turk to write literary plays for radio.
Necatigil died in İstanbul on December 13th 1979.

Tradition has it that St Nicholas, whose feast day is December 6th, was born
at Patara in Lycia and in the early 4th c. was Bishop of Myra (now Kale, also
in Lycia), where his loving kindness brought him to the aid of many in
distress. The legend, however, probably developed round a historical figure, Abbot Nicholas of Sion, near Myra, whose death is recorded as having
been on December 10th 564. The saint's tomb in Antalya was plundered in
the early Middle Ages, and in 1087 his relics were taken to Bari in southern
Italy. Veneration of St Nicholas as patron saint of children, as well as
seamen, merchants, and pawnbrokers, began with the Greek and Russian
Churches of the 6th c., reaching Italy in the 9th c., whence it spread to the
rest of Europe where as Santa Claus he came to play such an important part
in Christmas.

St Nicholas
(3rd/4th c.)

Osman I, to whom the Ottoman dynasty owes its name, succeeded his
father Ertugrul, a famous chieftain of horsemen and warlord of a small
Bithynian fief in western Anatolia. By seizing Byzantine's strongholds he
extended his father's domain and after 1290 was able to call himself an
independent Emir, thus laying the foundations of the Ottoman empire.
Also known as "Osman Ghazi" (foremost among warriors), Osman I died in
1326 in present-day Söğüt.

Osman I
(1258–1326)

Osman Hamdi Bey was born in İstanbul where he was to make a name for
himself as a promoter of the arts. He founded an art college there in 1880
and committed himself in 1881 to establishing a museum of art history. He
played a large part in the excavations of the Sidon necropolis in the
Lebanon, where the sarcophagus of Alexander the Great (see entry), now
in İstanbul's Archaeological Museum, was found in 1887.

Osman Hamdi
(1842–1910)

Born in Malatya in eastern Anatolia on October 13th 1927, Turgut Özal
studied electrical engineering at İstanbul Technical University until 1950
before turning to economics. In Ankara from 1967 to 1971, he was State
Planning's Under Secretary of State, and chaired the national commission
for economic co-ordination, the Finance Committee and other bodies, then
from 1971 to 1973 served on the special projects advisory council of the
World Bank in Washington DC. On returning to Turkey he held a number of
top jobs in the private sector before becoming head of the State Planning
Office in 1979. After the coup the following year Özal moved up as acting
Prime Minister under Bülent Ülüsü but stepped down in the summer of

Turgut Özal
(1927–93)

1982; in 1983 he was elected Chairman of the Motherland Party, the ANAP (Anavatan Partisi), becoming Prime Minister following their election victory in November that year. He strove to improve Turkey's relations with Western Europe, continuing to pursue his country's long-term goal of membership of the European Community. In 1988, mainly with a view to lessening the tensions surrounding Cyprus and the Aegean continental shelf, he met with Andreas Papandreou, then Greek Prime Minister, in Davos, Switzerland (January), and Brussels (April) before travelling to Greece in June, thus becoming the first Turkish Prime Minister in 36 years to visit Athens. In July he was also the first Prime Minister of the avowedly secular Republic of Turkey to make the Muslim pilgrimage to Mecca.

On October 31st 1989 the Grand National Assembly elected him President and in March 1991 he was his country's first head of state to visit Russia. Although his party's failure to win the Parliamentary elections in October of that year undermined his position the Economic Co-operation Treaty he had initiated for the Black Sea countries was signed by eleven states in İstanbul on June 25th 1992.

Turgut Özal's jetsetting diplomacy eventually took its toll and he died suddenly on April 17th 1993 in Ankara.

Heinrich
Schliemann
(1822–90)

The archaeologist Heinrich Schliemann was born in Mecklenburg, Germany, on January 16th 1822. Family circumstances compelled him to leave school and join the business world. His gift for languages – he eventually mastered 15 – was a great asset in his subsequent career, and he soon rose to the top in an Amsterdam business house. He went on to found his own business in St Petersburg in 1847 and succeeded in amassing a considerable fortune enabling him from 1858 onwards to devote himself entirely to archaeology. Having travelled widely and studied archaeology and languages in Paris, he settled in Athens in 1868. Convinced that Homer's works were based on historical fact he anticipated modern archaeologists by studying literary sources, examining the topography of the site and where necessary carrying out test digs before starting on the actual excavation. Where he fell short of modern standards was in his failure fully to record the evidence destroyed by his excavations.

Schliemann's great find was Troy (1870–82 and 1890), but his other excavations included Mycenae (1876), Orchomenos (1880–86) and Tiryns (1884–85). He presented his main finds to museums in Germany and Greece; the famous Priam's Treasure from Troy went to Berlin, probably vanishing to Moscow after the Second World War, and gold jewellery from Mycenae to Athens and the National Archaeological Museum.

Heinrich Schliemann died in Naples on December 26th 1890 on a return trip from Germany to Athens, where he is buried.

Selim I
(1467 or 1470
–1520)

Ottoman Sultan from 1512, Selim I Yavuz, the Grim, came from Pontic Amasya and was responsible for the triumph of Sunni orthodoxy by his ruthless suppression of the Shiah Turcomans in Anatolia, bringing him into conflict with the Shiites of Persia whom he forced to cede part of Ajerbijan before going on to conquer Mesopotamia, Syria, Palestine and Egypt. Here he took the capital Cairo in May 1517 and executed the last of the Mamluks the following month. The holiest sites of Islam thus came under his sway, and he assumed the title of Caliph.

Selim I, who was also a writer of Persian verse, died in 1520, probably from the plague, near Çorlu en route from İstanbul to Edirne.

Sinan
(c. 1497–
1587 or 1588)

Sinan, the greatest architect of the Ottoman Empire, is presumed to have been born in an Anatolian village near Kayseri. The son of Christian Greek or Armenian parents, he was eventually sent to İstanbul where he received a Muslim education and was trained as a Janissary. From 1521 he served as an engineer under Suleiman the Magnificent (see entry) in various military campaigns before his appointment in 1538 as chief architect for the whole of the Empire, a function he performed under three Sultans, Suleiman I, Selim II and Murad III.

His buildings ranged from the grandest and greatest of mosques to a whole host of other important public buildings – between 1528 and 1588 he was responsible for no less than 477. Still standing today there are over 150 large (Camii) and small mosques (Mesçit), over 70 medreses, 38 palaces, over 30 caravanserai, 25 mausolea, plus innumerable schools, public baths (hamam), almshouses, hospitals and dervish cloisters, as well as bridges and aqueducts, including one 265m/870ft long from Mağlova to İstanbul. More than half Sinan's buildings are in and around what was then the glittering capital of the empire, İstanbul. This "Ottoman Michelangelo" only began working on mosques when he was barely 50, basing himself largely on the multi-domed style of the Hagia Sophia, but as a well-travelled man he was also familiar with the work of the Seljuks, the tombs of Anatolia, early Christian cave churches in Cappadocia and traditional Armenian architecture.

His most outstanding works include the Princes' Mosque, Şehzade Camii, and the Mosque of Suleiman the Magnificent, Süleymaniye Camii, both in İstanbul, but he himself considered his masterpiece to be the Mosque of Selim II, Selimiye Camii, in Edirne. Much venerated, Hoca Mimar Sinan died in 1587 or 1588 in İstanbul.

Born in İstanbul the son of an officer, İbrahim Şinasi was a civil servant who received government funding to study finance in Paris from 1849 to 1855. The two journals he helped to found – "Tercüman-i Ahval" (1860) and "Tasvir-i Efkâr" (1862) – served as a platform for his progressive views that Turkey should model itself more on European lines. Banished as a result he spent the years from 1865 to 1869 back in Paris again.

İbrahim Şinasi (1826–71)

Beginning around 1860 İbrahim Şinasi's writings opened up Turkish literature's modern phase. He translated French classics into his mother tongue and "Şair Evlenmesi", 1860, was the first original Turkish comedy. Although his poetry is still in the traditional verse form it is already imbued with new thought processes. His prose signals the first move away from what had been the highly florid Turkish style of writing to a plainer use of language. İbrahim Şinasi died on September 13th 1871 in İstanbul.

The only son of Selim I (see entry), Suleiman I was probably born on November 6th 1494 at Trebizond (Trabzon) on the Black Sea. He became Sultan in 1520 and is known as "Kanuni", the Lawgiver, in his homeland, but for Europeans this most expansionist and accomplished of the Ottoman rulers has always been "Suleiman the Magnificent". During the course of his substantial extension of the Ottoman Empire he captured Belgrade in 1521 and Rhodes in 1522, forcing the Knights of St John to leave for Malta, defeated and killed King Lewis of Hungary at Mohács in 1526, taking Buda in 1529 and unsuccessfully besieging Vienna in September and October of that year, and Transylvania came into his possession in 1562. His domain extended far to the eastward and into Egypt and Persia, while his fleet was master of the Red Sea (including Yemen and Aden) and virtually the whole of the Mediterranean, waging war on the coasts of North Africa, Italy and Dalmatia under the command of its fearsome admiral Kair ad-Dín (Barbarossa).

Suleiman the Magnificent (1494–1566)

Within the empire Suleiman was responsible for transforming the army and the judicial system. Under his rule its capital, İstanbul, was to flourish as never before and become a great centre for the creative arts (Suleiman himself was a poet and an accomplished goldsmith) and for a grand building programme spearheaded by Sinan, his Chief Architect (see entry). Suleiman died on September 6th 1566 during the war with Austria outside Sziget, then in Hungary, now Sighetul Marmaţiei in Romania, which two days later fell to the Ottomans. He is buried in the largest of Sinan's mausolea situated within the complex of the Sülemaniye Camii mosque in İstanbul.

Famous People

Thales
(c. 650–
c. 560 B.C.)

The Greek philosopher, astronomer, mathematician and natural scientist Thales of Miletus was probably of Phoenician origin. One of the Seven Sages of antiquity, he was the first of the Ionian physical scientists who decided the material basis of the world was water. He believed there was life even in inorganic matter, and attributed all motion to a soul which directed all things. As an astronomer he is said to have predicted the solar eclipse of 585 B.C. The theorem that bears his name – all triangles inscribed in a semicircle contain a rightangle – was already known to the Babylonians.

Xenophon
(c. 430–425–
c. 355 B.C.)

The Greek historian Xenophon, a youthful adherent of Socrates, took part in 401 B.C. in the campaign of the Persian Cyrus the younger against his brother, King Artaxerxes II Mnemon. After Cyrus had fallen at Kunaxa Xenophon led the rearguard of the Greek soldiers through Armenia in winter to the Black Sea at Trebizond (now Trabzon), and joined up with the Spartan king Agesilaus, campaigning with him against the Persians in the west of Asia Minor and also fighting on the Spartan side in the battle of Koroneia (394 B.C.). This led to his being banned from Athens and he then lived and wrote on his estates at Scillus, south of Olympia, which the Spartans had given him, until he had to leave for Corinth following the collapse of Spartan rule. It is unclear whether he was ever allowed to return to Athens before his death, which probably occurred in Corinth.

All of Xenophon's writings have survived. Chief among them are "Anabasis", eight volumes on the Persian expedition under Cyrus and the long march with the 10,000 Greek mercenaries, and "Hellenica", a history of Greece from 411/410 B.C. which follows on from Thucydides' "History of the Peloponnesian War", but he also wrote biographies of Cyrus and Agesilaus, treatises on horsemanship and state finance and, more importantly, his works featuring Socrates, "Symposium" and "Memoirs".

Yunus Emre
(13th/14th c.)

The birthplace of the folk poet Yunus Emre is thought to have been the Anatolian village of Sarıköy. Little is known of his life in any detail but as a wandering Sufi who had travelled through Syria and Azerbaijan he eventually came to Konya where he is said to have become acquainted with Mevlava Celaleddin Rumi (see entry). He is also supposed to have been a pupil of the founder of the Bektashi order of dervishes.

His mystical and sometimes passionate verse centres entirely on people and the greatest of their capacities which is to love. In contrast with many of the "divan poets", whose highly artificial language was larded with alien Persian and Arabic, Yunus Emre wrote in the simple tongue of the Anatolian people, thus earning himself a universal appeal which has endured to this day.

Yunus Emre is supposed to have died at a ripe old age in 1321, and Karaman claims to be his burial place.

UNESCO declared 1991 "Yunus Emre Year".

Mehmet Emin
Yurdakul
(1869–1944)

The poet Mehmet Emin Yurdakul, born in İstanbul and the self-taught son of a fisherman, embarked on a career as a civil servant before becoming Governor of various Turkish provinces.

In his poetry he used a simple and direct form of Turkish, albeit in the traditional verse form, to portray the plight of the ordinary people, endearing himself with his countrymen right up to the present. As the "bard of Turkdom", with his patriotic and often emotive poems, in a style that marked an important new poetry phase, he gave a vital boost to nationalism, although this diminished in vigour with the early days of the Republic.

Art and Culture

As countless discoveries can testify, the coast of Anatolia was settled from the very earliest times. A great diversity of peoples and cultures, from the Stone Age to the present day, have left their mark on the vast peninsula of Asia Minor. There is hardly anywhere else in the world with such striking transitions from one culture to another; in many places remains of Greek, Roman, Byzantine, Seljuk and Ottoman civilisations exist side by side, often with one building superimposed upon the foundations of those that have gone before.

With a history of human settlement going back more than 7000 years, Asia Minor still retains many magnificent reminders of its past civilisations. Parts of the country abound with "hüyüks", mounds as high as 20m/65ft, veritable treasure troves containing the remains of prehistoric and early historical communal settlements.

A wealth of cultural heritage

Major Historical Periods and Cultures

The oldest Stone Age settlement to have been unearthed in Anatolia to date is near Antalya, and its tools, weapons and unpainted ceramics give some idea of the culture of this early period.

Prehistoric

The many regional centres that grew up in Asia Minor during the Bronze Age included the first two levels of Troy – Troy I (after 3000 B.C.) and Troy II (after 2500 B.C.). It was in this second level that Schliemann found the gold and jewellery which he thought belonged to Priam and the Trojans of Homer's Iliad.

Anatolia's historical period begins with the Hittites who started arriving in Asia Minor towards the end of the 3rd millennium B.C., and who were the first people in this part of the world to employ a form of writing, using the cuneiform script which they introduced from Mesopotamia in the 18th and 17th c. B.C. They also used hieroglyphics rather like those of the Cretans.

Hittite

Hittite art developed from interaction between the culture of the native Anatolian Hattites and that of the incoming Indo-European Hittites. Its main features were already present as early as as the 18th c. B.C., but it was at its peak between c. 1450 and 1200 B.C., when the Hittites were building great temples and palaces and amazing fortifications. The outstanding feature of their architecture was its asymmetrical nature. Support was provided by square pillars rather than rounded columns; also characteristic were the large window openings with low parapets.

The grand reliefs carved on palace portals and rockfaces show how the Hittite sculptors followed set formulae and rules in their work and this is reflected in the stylised representation of human and animal forms, as well as hairstyles and clothing.

The Urartu civilisation (900–600 B.C.) of the successors to the Hurrians was very much influenced by the Assyrians and centred on the Urartian upland steppe kingdom in present-day Armenia and around Lake Van in the easternmost part of Anatolia.

Urartu

The remarkable culture created by the Phrygians in central Asia Minor (750–500 B.C.) owed much to Greek influence but also derived substantially from that of the late Hittites and Urartu. The Phrygians themselves were originally Thracians who were probably partly responsible for the destruction of the Hittite kingdom, although in archaeological terms they can only be traced back to the mid-8th c. B.C.). Their relatively short-lived kingdom was founded by Midas in the second half of the 8th c. and came to

Phrygian

a sudden end with the invasion of the Cimmerians *c.* 675 B.C. Their culture lived on, however, and in the 6th c. produced magnificent monuments which are amongst the most impressive to be found in present-day Anatolia. These are chiefly in the western part of the central plateau, the most important discoveries being those from Gordium, the Phrygian capital, and other Phrygian cities such as Alışar, Boğazkale, Alaca, Pazarlı and Ankara.

Lydian,
Lycian,
Carian

The Dark Ages which followed the downfall of the Hittites around 1190 B.C. lasted longer in some parts of Asia Minor than in others. With the 8th c. B.C. the culture that came to dominate south-western Anatolia was that of Lydia, Lycia and Caria. Few traces remain apart from their unique rock tombs, burial vaults, etc.

By the middle of the 7th c. B.C. the cultural history of Anatolia was one of growing Hellenisation. However, these local civilisations were able to continue in their own style until the arrival of Alexander the Great and the subsequent supremacy of Greek culture in most of Anatolia.

Hellenistic

The early Greek settlements on the west coast of Asia Minor (1050–750 B.C.) were originally quite primitive, and their art was modelled on that of their homeland, but as this eastern, Hellenistic, arm of Greek civilisation grew in political importance, so its cultural significance grew along with it. In this the Ionians played a leading role, and their Hellenistic culture, an amalgam of local and Greek influences, with influences from trade with the east and other distant shores, reached its peak between 650 and 494 B.C. when it differed markedly from that of mainland Greece. Typical features of Hellenistic sculpture, for example, are the radiant expression on the faces of the figures and the elaborate folding of the drapery. What was much more significant, however, was the Ionic contribution to Greek architecture. The slender proportions of Asia Minor's Ionic order toned down the stocky and heavier features lent to Greek architecture by the Doric order. Nowadays it is difficult to get a real impression of what Ionia's magnificent works of architecture must have been like since all that is left are fragments of the kind that can be seen in museums such as those in İstanbul, İzmir, Selçuk (Ephesus), etc.

Although eastern Greek art produced little work in its own distinctive style after the destruction of Miletus (494 B.C.), the cities of western Asia Minor were still among the leading artistic and cultural centres of the Hellenistic period, i.e. the last three centuries B.C. While Ionic continued to exist alongside Doric, individual buildings during this period, unlike previous centuries, were no longer treated in isolation but seen as one element in an architectural scheme as a whole, and this is still apparent today in, for example, the layout of Priene. Another feature of Hellenistic architecture is the way that ornament and decoration became more important than pure functionalism, producing more grandiose architecture as a result. Here the classic example is Pergamum, at one time covered with all kinds of elaborate decoration.

The Seven Wonders of the Ancient World

Mausoleum
of Halicarnassus
Temple of Diana
at Ephesus

Two of the Seven Wonders of the classical world of the 3rd c. B.C., were in Asia Minor – the Mausoleum of King Mausolos of Caria at Halicarnassus (Bodrum), and the great Temple of Diana/Artemis at Ephesus (Selçuk).

Statue of Zeus
at Olympia
Colossus of
Rhodes

Another two were in Ancient Greece – Phidias' statue of Zeus at Olympia on the Pelopponese, and the Colossus of Rhodes, an enormous figure astride the entrance to the harbour of the Aegean island of Rhodes.

Pyramids
of Giza
Pharos
lighthouse outside
Alexandria
Hanging Gardens
of Babylon

The other three were the Pyramids of Giza (near Cairo) and the Pharos (lighthouse) of Alexandria, both in Egypt, and the Hanging Gardens of Babylon, in present-day Iraq.

Apart from the pyramids next to nothing has survived of these famous monuments.

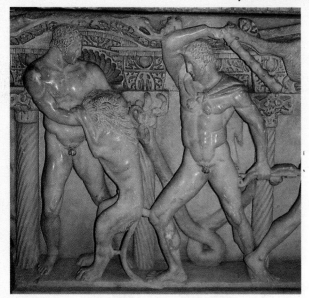

Detail of relief on the Roman Hercules sarcophagus of Konya

The Hellenistic tradition in art and architecture carried on almost without
interruption into Roman times, leaving the Roman era in Asia Minor with
no distinctive style of its own, but it was this period of Roman rule which
was to bequeath some of the finest and best preserved theatres and other
buildings of antiquity such as those at Aphrodisias, Aspendos, Miletus and
Ephesus.

Roman art

Byzantine art developed during the 5th c. out of the Roman culture of late
antiquity, its Hellenistic foundations having been further enriched by Christianity. It achieved its great flowering in the reign of Justinian (526–
565). This was followed by a period of stagnation and, under the Iconoclast
Emperors (716–843), of decline. Then, in the late 9th c., there was a fresh
flowering of Byzantine art under the Macedonian dynasty. Although art
was still primarily in the service of the Church, the Iconoclast controversy
produced one positive effect in the emergence of a school of secular art
alongside religious art. This new heyday of Byzantine culture continued
into the 12th century, and thereafter there was a further period of brilliance
under the emperors who ruled between 1261 and 1453. The end came with
the Ottomans' capture of Constantinople.

Byzantine

The various phases of Byzantine art are primarily reflected in architecture,
above all, needless to say, ecclesiastical architecture.
Prior to Justinian the commonest church form was the basilica – a rectangular building with a flat roof borne on columns or pillars, usually divided
into a nave and two or more aisles – which had evolved from the Roman
meeting-hall. The church proper was entered by way of a square forecourt
surrounded by colonnades (the atrium) and a vestibule or narthex, and was
divided into two parts, the first part, for the lay congregation, being separated by a high screen from the part reserved for the clergy. This latter
section ended in the apse, which held the altar, the bishop's throne and

87

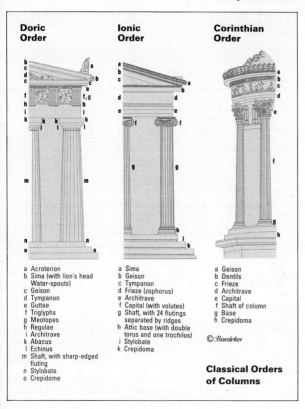

Doric Order

Ionic Order

Corinthian Order

a Acroterion
b Sima (with lion's head Water-spouts)
c Geison
d Tympanon
e Guttae
f Triglyphs
g Meotopes
h Regulae
i Architrave
k Abacus
l Echinus
m Shaft, with sharp-edged fluting
n Stylobate
o Crepidome

a Sima
b Geison
c Tympanon
d Frieze (zophorus)
e Architrave
f Capital (with volutes)
g Shaft, with 24 flutings separated by ridges
h Attic base (with double torus and one trochilus)
i Stylobate
k Crepidoma

a Geison
b Dentils
c Frieze
d Architrave
e Capital
f Shaft of column
g Base
h Crepidoma

© *Baedeker*

Classical Orders of Columns

benches for the officiating priests. The central aisle had a gently arched barrel roof, the side aisles pent roofs. There are often variations on this standard form: the building might not have an atrium, for example, or it could have a greater number of side aisles.

Once architectural solutions had been found for building sizeable domes Justinian's reign ushered in the domed basilica. This was an amalgam of the rectangular and the circular. The dome is seen as a break in the nave, and the wish to heighten its effect leads to the incorporation of barrel-roofed transepts, lateral side-domes, load-bearing arches and the like. Although this considerably modified the original basilica its basic structure is still recognisable in the narthex, apse and lateral aisles. The ultimate masterpiece of this new basic form was to be Hagia Sophia, famed the world over and built 532–537.

The third type of Byzantine church, the domed cross-in-square church, evolved after the 6th c. but did not reach full maturity until the Macedonian dynasty, whereupon it came to take precedence over all the earlier forms. The basic plan of this type of church is a Greek cross inscribed in a square, capped by a main central dome at the crossing point, with subsidiary domes at the ends of the cross and often also at the corners of the square. In

◄ *Acropolis of Pergamon (Bergama)*

later centuries, as the central dome became less prominent, attempts were made to make it stand out more by raising it on a tall drum but this had an adverse effect on the unity of the overall design.

Byzantine art also excelled in the applied arts and painting, where it produced icons, miniatures, frescoes and mosaics. It was this area of the arts which was to suffer at the hands of the Iconoclasts, who opposed what they saw as the excessive veneration accorded to images, and it was only after the resolution of the controversy in favour of holy images in the latter part of the 9th c. that Christian representational art recovered its momentum. Henceforth such holy images were not to be mere decoration but were intended to direct the thoughts of the faithful to the truths of salvation. Mosaic, with durable materials and striking light and colour effects, is particularly well suited for this purpose. Although previously it had been left to the artists to select their subjects and where they should be placed, after the Iconoclast controversy there were certain rules they had to abide by. Thus the highest point of the mosaic in the dome, seen as symbolising the vault of heaven, must always be Christ enthroned, surrounded by the Archangels, and attended by the Evangelists and the Apostles or Prophets.

The art of portraiture using the encaustic technique probably came to Byzantium from Egypt and led to the depiction of individual saints. Later portraits were painted in tempera on wood, and eventually oils were used as well. The earliest surviving icons of this kind date from the 11th c., but many more have come down from the 14th–16th c.
Illuminated manuscripts give some idea of the artistry of the Byzantine miniaturists, although those still extant are only copies of earlier examples. These illustrations are less closely prescribed in their form than mosaics, and therefore constantly striving for new ornamental forms and shapes.
Among the applied arts ivory-carving assumed particular significance alongside textiles and the work of gold- and silversmiths.

Seljuk

The Seljuk period heralded Byzantine Asia Minor's entry into the Islamic world. The Seljuks' occupation of Anatolia began in 1071 with the celebrated Battle of Manzikert in eastern Asia Minor, after which their victorious army swept across Anatolia as far as the Mediterranean coast. Seljuk art was thus able to cover the whole region but it tended to focus on central Anatolia, and especially its capital, Konya.
The heyday of Seljuk art was the first half of the 13th c., during which brief 50-year period the Seljuks were responsible for a great many buildings –

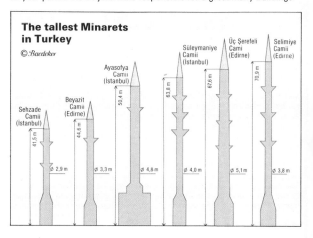

The tallest Minarets in Turkey
© Baedeker

Sehzade Camii (Istanbul) 41,5 m · ⌀ 2,9 m
Beyazit Camii (Edirne) 44,6 m · ⌀ 3,3 m
Ayasofya Camii (Istanbul) 50,4 m · ⌀ 4,8 m
Süleymaniye Camii (Istanbul) 63,8 m · ⌀ 4,0 m
Üç Şerefeli Cami (Edirne) 67,6 m · ⌀ 5,1 m
Selimiye Camii (Edirne) 70,9 m · ⌀ 3,8 m

Şehzade Mehmet Camii
İstanbul

İstanbul's
Princes' Mosque,
Şehzade Camii,
by the great
Sinan (see
Famous People)

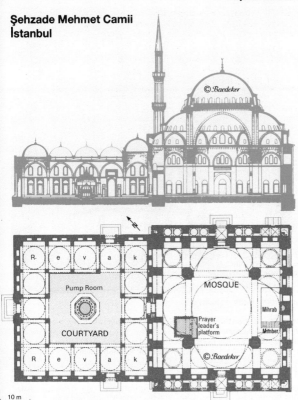

mosques and medreses (Koranic colleges), their minarets covered with glazed tiles, fortress-like caravanserais (inns), palaces and türbes (tombs). The Seljuks built a surprising variety of different kinds of mosque. Besides types of mosque already found in Islam, such as the courtyard mosque, Asia Minor produced a new design of its own, the basilican mosque. Instead of the usual broad prayer-hall this was a longitudinal structure with three or more aisles and had such typical features as the system of domes and the elaborate doorway found only in Asia Minor. This kind of doorway, which also appears in medreses, caravanserais and türbes, is a distinctive feature of Seljuk architecture, and with its arabesques, calligraphy and geometric designs shows off the whole range of the wealth of Seljuk ornament. Surprisingly this also includes figurative motifs, something found nowhere else in Islamic sacral art.

The most significant of the secular buildings is the "saray" or serail, a palace consisting not of one large building but a series of light, open pavilions or "kiosks". Another characteristic Islamic secular building is the caravanserai or "han". Placed at regular intervals along the main trade routes, these staging posts, defended like fortresses by massive towers, replaced the earlier primitive inns. Like the mosques, they have imposing and elaborately decorated doorways which show, even more strikingly

91

Serefeddin Camii in Konya

than in the sacred buildings, the Seljuk love of figurative images – lions are a particular favourite.

The Seljuks were also masters in the art of building fortifications – Alanya is a particularly striking example of a Seljuk fortified town.

The fine Seljuk carpets deserve a special mention. Asia Minor must have been the leading centre for knotted carpets from early times. The oldest of these, entirely of wool and using the "Turkish knot", stand out because of their borders, richly contrasting with the densely patterned central panels. Variations on one basic colour – different shades of green, blue or red – are especially popular.

Ottoman

With its capture of Constantinople in 1453 the Ottoman Empire was set on its course to become a world power, ushering in a great flowering of culture and the arts. The history of Ottoman art falls into a number of distinct phases with the early period in the 14th and 15th c. marked by a variety of trends, followed by the classical period in the 16th and 17th c. with a greater degree of uniformity, then, finally, the phase of strong European influence. The diversity of the early Ottoman period is particularly reflected in mosque architecture, which entered an entirely new phase. The basilica layout favoured by the Seljuks is replaced by the wide prayer-hall again, this time combined with a courtyard and a vestibule, now used in Asia Minor for the first time. The dome becomes more important, with a whole series of domes covering the colonnades in the courtyards of mosques and medreses. The façade is given a new look as bands of windows and facings of coloured marble are added to the elaborate Seljuk portal.

The classical period of Ottoman art, the 16th and 17th c., is characterised by a noticeably more uniform imperial style, extending to the farthest reaches of the vast Ottoman Empire but at its peak in İstanbul, the focus of its culture and power.

The most striking features of the Ottoman mosques are their imposing

Window decoration Topkapı Sarayı

Candalabrum Dolmabahçe Camii

central domes and exaggeratedly slender minarets. The trend towards the monumental is evident everywhere, with the enormous new complexes undoubtedly inspired by Hagia Sophia. The finest of these Ottoman mosques were the work of Sinan (see Famous People), the Ottomans' prolific chief architect who was responsible for no fewer than 477 buildings, in which he employed a whole variety of different layouts for his domed complexes.

Secular as well as sacred buildings were now marked by domes. These dominate the spacious hamams which, like the Roman baths, were divided into three parts – a room for changing and resting, a warm room and a hot room, but no cold room. Domes featured in the Ottoman palaces too, which were based on the more sprawling Seljuk model, but the precincts of these sarays now took in a much larger area. Tiles came to play a major part in the decoration of buildings, and were being used to cover large expanses of both the exterior and the interior. Their new ornamental style reflected European influence and was markedly more realistic, drawing on the superabundance of the country's native flowers. This new style is found in other forms of applied art as well. One lively example of this is the fine tableware. In fact from the first half of the 16th c. the production of pottery and glassware developed on an extraordinary scale in the famous İznik workshops, earning itself a reputation as far afield as Europe.

Knowledge of the earliest Ottoman skills as carpet makers stems from 15th c. European paintings depicting rugs such as those collected by King Henry VIII of England and painted by Holbein. These had purely geometric designs. Another important type is the prayer rug, its design featuring the mihrab, the prayer niche in a mosque which indicated the direction of Mecca towards which the faithful directed their prayers. Among other textile products, the Ottomans were renowned for their precious fabrics such as velvet and silk brocades. These, too, made use of the inevitable flower patterns.

Housing and Town Planning

Tulip period	The style of the final phase of Ottoman art, the early 18th c. "Tulip period", had a distinctly western stamp to it, with the emergence of strands of European Baroque, at their most visible in the swelling lines of roofs and other architectural details.
Turkish Rococo	Rococo itself arrived in the Ottoman Empire from France in the mid–18th c. and was enthusiastically taken up both by the Court and Turkey's artists, who developed its forms into a style that was very much their own.
Modern	With the 19th and 20th c. western architecture became steadily more influential, so that eventually the only characteristically eastern touches are in the decoration of the buildings.

Housing and Town Planning

Although many Turks still live in relatively small communities the towns and cities are expanding on a large scale.

Housing

The conventional form of Turkish dwelling in the west and the north continues to be wooden and half-timbered houses, with lots of big windows and various forms of pitched roof, and, in the interior and the south east, mud-brick or stone houses with small windows. Here houses in the countryside are all flat-roofed, with pitched roofs confined to the towns. Stone buildings tend to be found more in the volcanic parts of the dry country in the east.

As elsewhere in the East, the old town centres and villages have simply evolved without any formal planning. In the older quarters the houses huddle together along winding alleys, with hardly any windows on the front but looking out over walled gardens and courtyards at the back, forming residential quarters separate from the hurly burly of the bazaars and workshops where the business of the place is carried on. The newer parts of town tend to be more spacious and built on more regular lines. Gardens are everywhere in villages, towns and suburbs, while another characteristic feature, dominating town and country alike, is the mosque, with its minaret.

Building development

A great deal of building has gone on more recently, both rural and urban. The development being carried out all over Turkey includes improvements to the infrastructure such as new roads and better drainage, as well as new buildings for housing and industry, while hotels and holiday resorts are also springing up in many places catering for the burgeoning tourist trade.

Typical Islamic Buildings

Mosque

The most important of Islamic sacred buildings is the mosque – in Turkish the "mesçit", from the Arabic "masjid" for "place of prostration" (in prayer). The principal mosque in a town or city, where the faithful assemble for Friday prayers, is the "cami", from the Arabic "jemaa" for "place of congregational worship".

Courtyard

The outer aisles extend beyond the length of the prayer hall to form covered galleries on either side of the courtyard.

Entry to this courtyard is through an often elaborately decorated doorway set in a large outside wall. The grand, often marble, fountain in the centre of the courtyard is for the ritual ablutions which must be undergone before prayer.

Minaret

On a corner of the outer wall or side galleries stands the minaret – Turkish mosques often have two or more of them – from which the muezzin recites the call to prayer.

The prayer hall, the main part of the mosque, is square or rectangular and faces toward the kıbla, the direction of Mecca, which is indicated by the mihrab, or prayer niche. Next to the mihrab, usually at an angle to the kıbla wall, stands the pulpit, the mimber.

Prayer hall
kıbla
mihrab

mimber

Medrese

Another important sacred building is the medrese, from the Arabic "darasa", meaning to study, a Koranic college which can also cover the study of science and medicine as well as the Koran and Islamic law. This includes accommodation for students and a mosque-like prayer hall.

The medrese buildings are generally grouped around a central, rectangular courtyard and fountain, with the prayer hall at one end. The lecture rooms, library, and administrative offices are on the ground floor of the buildings around the courtyard, with the students' rooms, often no more than small cells, on the floor above.

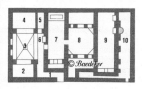

Turkish Bath — Hamam
Typical plan of a bath-house

1 Entrance
2 Supervisor's lodge
3 Inner courtyard
4 Rest room
5 Toilet
6 Well
7 Cold room
8 Warm room
9 Hot room
10 Heating area
   with stove
   and tank

Haman

As in the rest of the Islamic world, there are public and private bath-houses throughout Turkey. These "hamams" as they are called, both in Arabic and Turkish, are actually intended for purposes of Muslim ritual purification. Used by men and women at different times, the baths are modelled on those of the Romans, and divided into a cold room, a hot room, a steam bath and a rest room, together with a fountain, often of marble, and toilets. The way into the hamam is always circuitous to prevent passers-by seeing in from outside. In the usually tiled interior an attendant is on hand to see that the proprieties are observed.

Turkey in Quotations

Fynes Moryson
(1566–c. 1617))

Neither is the Art of Cookery greater in Turkey than with us in Wales, for Toasting of Cheese in Wales, and seething of Rice in Turkey, will enable a man freely to profess the Art of cookery.
An Itinerary, 1617

Lord Byron
(1788–1824)

Know ye the land where the cypress and myrtle
Are emblems of deeds that are done in their clime,
Where the rage of the vulture, the love of the turtle
Now melt into sorrow, now madden to crime? . . .
Where the virgins are soft as the roses they twine,
And all save the spirit of man is divine?
The Bride of Abydos, 1813

Thomas Hood
(1799–1845)

O Turkey! how mild are thy manners,
Whose greatest and highest of men
Are all proud to be rhymers and scanners,
And wield the poetical pen!
Poetry, Prose and Worse, 1836

Baedeker
(1914)

Special equipment for the journey is not necessary. For Constaninople a good, fairly light suit is recommended in normal circumstances, supplemented on windy boat or carriage trips and in the cooler period after sunset by a greatcoat. A soft felt hat is the most convenient form of headgear. The fez denotes a subject of the Sultan, and is, therefore, not appropriate for foreigners. During the rainy season rubber shoes are indispensable in Turkish towns which lack drainage. A black coat should be worn only for visits to high Turkish officials.

Laundry is competently washed, the charge being frequently based on the number of articles of whatever kind – approximately four francs the dozen. For travel in Asia Minor a suit must be of durable material, and sturdy footwear is necessary. Each traveller will come provided with binoculars, water-bottle, compass, flannel shirts and a heavy felt cloak. For long rides and overnight stops in peasants' houses, etc. a travelling-rug, cutlery, aluminium plates and cups, gaiters, a neck scarf, a tin of insect powder and a stout, easily lockable travelling-bag of soft leather which can be tied to the saddle are required. The local fare can be supplemented by tea, chocolate and biscuits brought from home. The offer of a cigarette (sigâra) is a good way of expressing thanks for small courtesies, a cup of coffee, etc. To carry weapons with you merely creates difficulties.
Constantinople and Asia Minor, 1914

Baedeker
(1914)

Mount Ararat
The best season for the ascent is August and September. Rugs, cooking utensils, tea, red wine, rice and two bags of coal must be carried. Information may be had from the frontier officer or from the village-chief at Araluikh. Each porter receives 5rb. for the whole excursion. – As the traveller may possibly be molested by the nomadic Kurds, he is advised to take a revolver and procure an escort of Cossacks from the frontier officer.
Russia with Teheran, Port Arthur and Peking, 1914

Dardanelles (Ancient Hellespont)

Lady Mary
Wortley Montagu
(1689–1762)

Since I have seen this streight, I find nothing improbable in the adventure of Leander or very wonderfull in the Bridge of Boats of Xerxes. 'Tis so narrow, 'tis not surprising a young Lover should attempt to swim it or an Ambitious King try to pass his Army over it. But then 'tis so subject to storms, 'tis no wonder the Lover perish'd and the Bridge was broken.

This morning I swam from Sestos to Abydos, the immediate distance is not above a mile, but the current renders it hazardous, so much so, that I doubt whether Leander's conjugal powers must not have been exhausted in his passage to Paradise.
Letter to Henry Drury, May 3rd 1810

Lord Byron
(1788–1824)

(Sestos) A naked point on the European side, so ugly compared with all around it as to attract particular attention, projects into the strait and here are the ruins of Sestos; here Xerxes built his bridge of boats to carry over his millions to the conquest of Greece; and here, when he returned with the wreck of his army, defeated and disgraced, found his bridge destroyed by a tempest, and in his rage, ordered the chains to be thrown into the sea, and the waves to be lashed with rods. From this point too, Leander swam the Hellespont for love of Hero, and Lord Byron and Mr Ekenhead for fun. Nearly opposite, close to the Turkish fort, are the ruins of Abydos. Here Xerxes, and Leander, and Lord Byron and Mr Ekenhead landed.

J. L. Stephens
(1805–52)

İstanbul

The streetes of this Citie are narrow, and shadowed with pentises of wood and upon both sides the way is raised some foot high, but of little breadth, and paved for men and women to passe, the middest of the street being left low and unpaved, and no broader, then for the passage of Asses or beasts loaded. In many places of the streetes lye carcasses, yea sometimes the bodies of dead men, even till they be putrified, and I thinke this uncleanlinesse of the Turks (who otherwise place Religion in washing their bodies, and keeping their apparrell, especially their Tulbent pure and cleane) is the chiefe cause that this Citie, though most pleasantly seated, yet above all the Cities of the world is continually more or lesse infected with the plague.
An Itinerary, 1617

Fynes Moryson

The walls of the Seraglio are like the walls of Newstead Gardens only higher, and much in the same order, but the ride by the walls of the city on the land side is beautiful, imagine, four miles of immense triple battlements, covered with Ivy, surmounted with 218 towers, and on the other side of the road Turkish burying grounds (the loveliest spots on earth) full of enormous cypresses. I have seen the ruins of Athens, of Epheses and Delphi, I have traversed great part of Turkey and many other parts of Europe and some of Asia, but I never beheld a work of Nature or Art, which yielded an impression like the prospect on each side, from the Seven Towers to the End of the Golden Horn.
Letter of Mrs Catherine Gordern, 1810

Lord Byron

Constantinople makes a noble picture. But its attractiveness begins and ends with its picturesqueness. From the time one starts ashore till he gets back again, he execrates it . . . it was, – well, it was an eternal circus. People were thicker than bees in those narrow streets, and the men were dressed in all the outrageous, outlandish, idolatrous, extravagant, thunder-and-lightning costumes that ever a tailor with the delirium tremens and seven devils could conveive of. There was no freak in dress too crazy to be indulged in; no absurdity too absurd to be tolerated; no frenzy in ragged diabolism too fantastic to be attempted. No two men were dressed alike. It was a wild masquerade of all imaginable costumes.
The Innocents Abroad, 1869

Mark Twain
(1835–1910)

Suggested Routes

The following suggestions offer some ideas for touring Turkey by road, Preface
using the map at the back of the book to check on the details, while leaving
the visitor the freedom to make his or her own plans and select a preferred
itinerary. The routes have been designed to take in all the major sights but a
detour will be necessary to get to some of the places listed in the guide. The
additional information required can be found under the separate headings
in the A to Z section, here printed in **bold**.

All the towns, villages, regions, rivers, etc. mentioned in the routes, and the
individual sights, whether under the main headings or as part of the
surroundings, are listed in the index at the end of the guide, making them
quick and easy to find.

General

Today's traveller in Turkey is much less likely to encounter the problems Driving out of town
with petrol/gas supply, road conditions, and uncertainties about estimated
time of arrival which used to be the order of the day for anyone trying to get
round Anatolia. New roads are constantly being built and the old ones
improved. Nowadays you can drive to even the remotest of villages,
though the roads you travel on can be an adventure in themselves!
Leadfree petrol/gas can still be quite difficult to find, but this is less likely to
be the case in future. Gas supply only becomes a problem if you spend a lot
of time away from the main roads, but if this should happen make sure you
carry some fuel in reserve or use diesel (derv), since this is available
everywhere in the countryside because all the farmers run their tractors on
it.
The local people can generally advise about the state of the roads. Away
from the intercity highways traffic is luckily still much lighter than on the
crowded roads of Europe so that giving a villager a free ride can bring with
it not only the inevitable invitation to tea but also often forge bonds of
lasting friendship. The country people are usually relatively poor, hence
unable to afford a dolmus (shared taxi), and there is not enough demand
for a proper local bus service.
In choosing the stages of your journey try to make your finishing point
somewhere with hotels – ports and seaside resorts along the coast, main
towns and tourist centres inland – since the network of places with a good
standard of accommodation is still comparatively thinly spread or concentrated in some regions and not others.

Thrace (European part of Turkey)

Apart from Edirne or the main highways from Greece and Bulgaria to
İstanbul and Gallipoli, Thrace is probably one of the least well known parts
of Turkey. At first sight it has few attractions to offer and its largely
treeless and rolling landscape, covered with fields of grain, makes no
particular impact on the visitor. Consequently a voyage of discovery off the beaten
track and into the altogether delightful hinterland of this region becomes all
the more appealing. It is usually also worth paying a bit more attention to
the places along the main highway.
Exploration of this tip of south-eastern Europe does not necessarily have to
start from the Balkans either – İstanbul can make a good jumping off point

◀ *Rocks in the Peristrema Valley*

too. If you are making your way, say, to the Dardanelles or Turkey's Aegean coast the route through Thrace and then across by ferry can prove quite an acceptable alternative to driving through the southern Marmara region.

1. From İstanbul to the Dardanelles on minor roads

From **İstanbul** north to Kilyos a route rich in history and with very little traffic winds its way through changing scenery on at times narrow country roads along the shore of the **Bosporus**, then through the Belgrade Forest and along the southern foothills of the still wooded Istranca Mountains via the little towns of Saray and Vize to Kırklareli and then on to **Edirne** or further south to the **Daradanelles**. This route characteristically alternates between corn prairie and wooded valleys harbouring tiny villages. Only at Uzunköprü, after this stretch, do you come to the broad expanses of the Ergene Valley with its rice paddies and further south, at Kesan, the wooded mountains of the Koru Dağı (National Park).

On the Gallipoli Peninsula not only is every mile steeped in history – it is no distance to a swim in the Aegean on one side, or the **Sea of Marmara** and the Dardanelles on the other, plus superb views out over the straits. There are two car ferries which make the crossing to Asia Minor: a very busy one from Eceabat to **Çanakkale**, and another from Gelibolu to Lapseki.

2. From İstanbul to Bulgaria via Edirne

The favourite route out of Turkey for migrant workers, the E80 is unquestionably the busiest road for passing through Thrace. Built like a motorway for much of the stretch from İstanbul to Edirne, it is already the preferred fast route between İstanbul and Europe, and with the completion of the planned improvements is likely to be even more so in future. Its heavy traffic makes it a road to avoid in the peak season, but even though this is destined to be an expressway, and already used as such, you will find it worth stopping off at Çorlu, Lüleburgaz, Babaeski, and, above all, **Edirne**.

3. From İstanbul to Greece via Tekirdağ

Anyone wanting to return to Europe on a quieter road should opt for the longer but certainly more interesting and, in the western section, substantially more traffic free route via the Greek part of Thrace. The first leg of this tour between İstanbul and Silivri is the same as the E80 to Edirne, so right from **İstanbul** you should take the more attractive road which follows the shoreline of the Sea of Marmara through the city's green suburbs as far as Küçükçakmece and then also avoid the new motorway as much as possible. This is the only way to get an impression of the summer vacation homes of the residents of İstanbul along the edges of the **Sea of Marmara**. These stretch in a more or less unbroken line of coastal resorts and holiday apartments from the capital to the provincial centre of Tekirdağ, after which the hills and artificial lakes around Malkara provide a welcome change. The stretch via Kesan and İpsala to the Greek frontier is less interesting, ending as it does in the broad valley and rice paddies of the Maritza (Meriç Nehri). The leg to Gelibolu offers an alternative to Route 1 from İstanbul to the Dardanelles, with a particularly pleasant variation after Tekirdağ along the seaside coast of Barbaros–Kumbağ via the newly built coastal stretch down to Şarköy and on to Gelibolu.

From the Bosporus into South-eastern and Eastern Anatolia

Turkey's main highways offer plenty of opportunities for exploring its vast hinterland in Asia Minor. There are various good places to start from, using their hotels as a base, but initially we have chosen only two for touring into Eastern Turkey, namely, İstanbul, and İzmir on the Aegean coast (see routes 17 and 18).

Unless you want to trust to luck and the uncertain standards of accommodation in a rural backwater you would do best to rely on finding somewhere to stay overnight between stages in one of the provincial centres or hotel complexes, in particular tourist highspots such as Bolu, Abant, Ankara, Cappadocia, Konya, etc. The suggested variations during the tour cover a good deal of the most scenic routes and take in many of the sights, some of them by small detours or excursions.

4. From İstanbul into the Çukurova via Bolu, Ankara and Aksaray

Anyone who prefers a straight through-run on good quality roads should opt for this route. If, however, you want to avoid getting caught up in heavy traffic you should steer clear of it at all possible and opt for one of the many recommended alternatives. This route through the ancient kingdoms of Bithynia, Paphlagonia and Galatia via Bolu to Ankara, then down through Central Anatolia and via Aksaray to Cilicia and on to Adana, is one of the main links for through traffic between Turkey's major economic centres – the north-east Marmara region, Ankara, the nation's capital, and Adana in the Çukurova. However, as the shortest line of communication between the north-west and the south-east, this route also offers in a relatively brief span a sight of the basic contrasts and characteristics of the countryside of Asia Minor, ranging from the temperate nature of the north-west and the dryness of the central plateau to the burning heat of the south, especially in summer. It includes several quite daunting mountain passes such as the crossing from **Bolu** through the Pontus, and the Cilician Gates through the Taurus, although these are by no means the most attractive ways of getting across the mountains as you journey from the north-west to the south-east of the country, as you will soon find out if you try one of the various alternatives.

Starting from **İstanbul** the route first passes through the impressive but unappealing industrial development along the road to Adapazarı (Sakarya) before entering the wooded mountain scenery of the Pontus, alternating between valleys and passes en route for Bolu, from where in May/June it is worth making the detour to Abant Gölü (hotel) or the Yedi-Göller National Park to see the rhododendrons in bloom – almost anywhere in the Pontus it is also worth making a sidetrip up into the alpine meadows, even if this means having to take unmetalled roads. After Bolu the route turns south through Kızılcahamam (National Park; hotel), bringing you already into the Mürted Ovası and the run-up to **Ankara**. The highlight of the journey from Ankara to the Taurus across the treeless steppes of Central Anatolia, dotted with wells and mudbrick villages, nearly always with something interesting to see, and roamed by flocks of sheep and (Angora) goats, is a visit to Tuz Gölü, the great Salt Lake, at, say, the salt pans of Şereflikoçhisar.

Aksaray, the next stop, is particularly interesting for its fine mosques and ruined churches. Then as the route enters the Taurus the main attraction is the old road through the Cilician Gates between Pozantı and Gülek – here the little place of Çiftehan provides a typical example of Turkish thermal baths. Beyond the mountains the Çukurova, the Cilician plain, with its hot and humid climate and the towns of **Adana**, **Tarsus**, and **Mersin**, is a centre for cotton, citrus fruit, and the textile industry. Its climate makes this an area to avoid in the summer months, when you would be well advised to follow the example of the locals and head for the cooler mountain air of the summer pastures, the yayla, up in the Taurus, although there is no guaranteeing the quality of the accommodation.

5. From İstanbul to Cappadocia and Adana via the Köroğlu Dağları

As far as
Cappadocia

This recommended tour is a variation running more or less parallel with
Route 4, seeking out scenic beauty and quiet places off the beaten track in
more remote areas, taking in little towns and picturesque villages as well as
an impressive range of still largely untouched cultural landscapes and
more elusive works of art. Cutting across the Bithynian Peninsula you
touch on the charming Black Sea towns of Sile, Agva and Kandıra before
turning south to Adapazarı and the Sakarya river, then following its gorge
down to Geyve. Passing by mountain villages deep in the forest you cross
the south-western ranges of the Pontus via Taraklı, Göynük and Uluhan on
minor roads, some of them no more than dirt roads in places, through pine,
beech and oak woods, before getting to the juniper groves at Nallıhan on
the dry southern slopes of the Pontus and running into the rice paddies on
the Nallıhan Çayı. From Nallıhan a very scenic stretch, starting with the
Çayırhan badlands, via Beyzapan – from where it is worth making a loop at
the right time of year to take in the ricefields on the Güdül Çayı – and Ayaş,
follows the southern chain of the mountains east, on a very scenic stretch
(badlands landscape at Çayırhan), to **Ankara**.
Although the road from Ankara to **Cappadocia** is undoubtedly shorter and
faster via Kırıkkale the prettier route is the southern one to **Kırşehir** via Bala,
Karakeçili and Kaman which, by turning off to Hacıbektas and Gülşehir,
soon brings you into the heart of the amazing tuffa moonscape country
around Göreme between Nevşehir, Avanos and Ürgüp.

Itineraries in
Cappadocia

Luckily the scenic sights and historic places of Capaddocia are relatively
close to one another, and the roads are quite good, making it easy to
explore the whole area using the towns with tourist hotels (Ürgüp, Avanos,
Gülşehir, Nevşehir, Ortahisar) as a base. However, if you want to avoid the
usual crowds it will pay you to spend several days here. We can recommend the following round trips:
1. Ürgüp – Ortahisar – Üçhisar – Göreme – Zelve – Avanos – Ürgüp
2. Ürgüp – Ortahisar – Göreme (steep gradient) – Avanos – Gülşehir –
   Nevşehir – Ürgüp
3. Ürgüp – Mustafapaşa – Soğanlı – Derinkuyu – Kaymaklı – Çardak (or
   Kavak) – Üçhisar – Ürgüp
4. Ürgüp – Aksalur (steep climb) – Incesu – Kayseri – Kayak Evi – Develi –
   Dörtyol – Ürgüp
5. Aksaray is the best starting point for the cave churches in the Peristrema
   valley but there is also a good circular route from Nevşehir via Derinkuyu, Gölçük, Çiftlik, Güzelyurt, Ihlara, Ağzıkarahan, Acıgöl and back to
   Nevşehir, or vice versa.

Southern part
of the route

This part of the itinerary leads more or less straight down south without
following the usual route. South of the potato fields of Nevşehir/Derinkuyu
it picks up the road through Çamardı which runs down the less frequented
but well opened-up Ecemis rift valley along the foot of the towering mountain wall of the 3734m/12,255ft high Ala Dağları to Pozantı and Tekir (Yaylası) and from there takes the new highway through the pass down as far as
the easily spotted turn-off beyond Gülek to Çamlıyayla, carrying on
through the lovely alpine meadows of the Taurus to Çamlıyayla (Namrun-
kale) before turning back and down again to **Tarsus**. From there it runs
through an extended industrial stretch of cotton fields and citrus groves
across the Çukurova to **Adana**, which lends itself to plenty of excursions
along the coast to places – with good fish restaurants – such as Tuzla,
Karata and Yumurtalık.

6. From İstanbul to Adana via Bursa, Kütahya and Konya

Another option for traversing Western Anatolia from the north-west to the
south-east is the faster route, in parts, to the Çukurova via Bursa, Afyon and

Konya, with the only rather bumpy ride being the section between Bursa and Tavşanlı, although the lovely scenery here more than makes up for this. The route starts from **İstanbul** with a short ferry ride (not many sailings a day), cutting out the tedious drive round the Bay of Kocaeli, over the **Sea of Marmara** to Mudanya. From there it carries on via **Bursa** through the lovely wooded mountains and valleys of north-western Anatolia and into the little-known forests and hills of Orhaneli on the upper reaches of the Kocasu Deresi to the pottery town of **Kütahya**, followed by the opium city of Afyon and the ancient centre of the whirling dervishes at **Konya** on the south-western edge of the Lycaonian tablelands of Central Anatolia. Places worth a visit en route include Bolvadın, just off the main road, Çay and **Akşehir**.

As the route continues across the flat steppes and cornfields of the north-eastern Konya Ovası just past Karapınar you come across the remarkable volcanoes and volcanic lakes (Gölü crater) of the Karacadağ region which you should definitely take a look at. A few miles further on you are already in the marshy environs of **Ereğli** (Konya Ereğlisi) where you join Route 4 over the Cilician Passes and through the Cilician Gates, bringing you to the mostly heavy traffic of the motorway from Pozantı through Tekir (Yaylası) to Tarsus and then the reasonably good trunk road across the Çukurova to **Adana**.

The cool summer resorts of the high pass country, the Tekir Yaylası, around Tekir off the Pozantı/Tarsus motorway, are a good base in summer and early autumn for making a high mountain tour either on foot (trekking) or in part by a heavy-duty vehicle, taking you through one of the south-facing valleys of the Taurus to scale the heights of the Bolkar Dağı (Mededsiz Tepe, 3585m/11,766ft). From here, on a clear day, there is a fantastic view over the high country of southern Central Anatolia. You can find a suitable vehicle almost anywhere in Tekir Yaylası. The way up the valley is first forest track then the bed of a stream and pathway up to the steep ascent below the region of the peak at around the timberline (about 2500m/8205ft). Make sure you take a local guide with you.

Mountain tour

7. From İstanbul to Sivas via Bursa, Eskişehir, Ankara and Kayseri

Another fast cross-country route, avoiding the usual trunkroads, takes you from İstanbul to Sivas in the north-west of Eastern Anatolia. This also starts with a short ferry ride, this time from Darıca over the Gulf of **İzmit** to Topçular near Yalova, then, apart from the section between Yalova and **Bursa**, continues on the less busy trunkroad via İnegol to **Eskişehir**, taking in the beautiful scenery of the high pass country between Bursa and Bozuyuk on the way, and across the broad, treeless expanses of the plateau of northern Central Anatolia, passing Sivrihisar's volcanic peaks, then Polatlı, and on to **Ankara**.

Along the way it is worth making the detour before Polatlı to **Gordion** on the upper reaches of the Sakarya. The next part of the route follows the well-beaten path to Kayseri via Kırıkkale, Keskin and Kırşehir.

Scenically the road becomes more interesting beyond Kayseri when you pick up the old caravan trail to Sivas running parallel with the rift valley of the Kızılırmak. Not only will you come across several well preserved Seljuk caravanserai – on the other side of relatively densely populated **Cappadocia** you pass through a typical part of the "empty quarter" of eastern Central Anatolia which from Kayadibi becomes south-western sectors of the gypsum karst country of Sivas. In order to enjoy this to the full it is better to take the traditional, more north-easterly, route from Hanlı past the Yassıbel Geçidi which meets up with the southbound road from Tokat to **Sivas** just west of Sivas at a Seljuk bridge over the Kızılırmak, rather than the new road due east which joins up with the Sivas/Gürün highway.

8. From İstanbul to Artvin along the Black Sea coast

Main route

Nowadays, with the gradual opening up of the **Black Sea Coast** to traffic, you can drive right along it with relative ease from İstanbul in the west to Artvin in the east.

This main route takes you from **İstanbul** to **Artvin** via İzmit and Adapazarı, then along the coast through Ereğli, **Zonguldak**, Amasra, Cide, Inebolu, Sinop, Samsun, Ünye, Ordu, Giresun, Tirebolu, **Trabzon**, Rize and Hopa. Along the way you can take in Turkey's lovely northern beaches, less popular with tourists because of the climate (Karasu, Akçakoca, Amasra, Cide, İnebolu, Abana, Sinop, the deltas of the Kızılırmak and Yeşilırmak and the bays of the eastern Black Sea coast). Here on the verdant, rain-soaked northern side of the Pontus you can explore the spectacular scenery of lush green jungle-like forests (beech, oak, pine, rhododendron, fern, tree heather, arbutus, laurel), lined with ancient fishing and trading ports and farming villages growing tea, tobacco and hazelnuts, all set against an everchanging backdrop of magnificent mountains. And almost every bend in the road on this route and its variations through the ancient kingdoms of Bithynia, Paphlagonia, Pontus, Colchis, Trebizond, Lazistan and south-western Georgia, with their eventful history and wealth of fascinating sites, has something of interest to offer.

Variations

On two sections of the Black Sea coast itinerary there are a couple of parallel, alternative routes which are worth considering: these entail, firstly, turning inland from Ereğli, away from the mining city of Zonguldak, to Bartın, and secondly, from Bartın via Devrekâni to Abana off the tourist track and through the high country of Eflani and the Küre Dağları.

Detour

If you need a change from the coastal route you can always make a detour up into one of the mountain valleys or transfer to Route 9 which runs parallel with the coast but further inland.

9. From İstanbul to Erzurum on minor roads inland through the Pontus

This attractive alternative route to the coastal itinerary also heads eastwards from İstanbul but mostly on roads which are less busy and more remote, taking you inland through the Pontus with its gorges, passes, high plateaux and basins, and an infinite variety of cultures and landscapes, to where its ranges join up with the Taurus at Erzurum.

The first part of the route is, like Route 8, the busy **İstanbul** to **İzmit** motorway, this time carrying on past Lake Sapanca and the Muhacir villages in the Adapazarı basin, via Akyazı, to **Bolu** in the green setting of the Köroğlu Dağları. Beyond Bolu take the road north-east, through the woods and plateaux of the northern Ilgaz Dağları, to Mengen, then east to Eskipasar and north again to Karabuk and Safranbolu, east through Iğdir and Araç to **Kastamonu** and then south to Tosya. From here you run along the fertile, rice-growing valleys of the Devrez Çayı and the Kılılırmak to Osmancık and Merzifon, emerging close to the treeless and much dryer southern slopes of the Pontus, thus dramatically illustrating the contrasting climates of northern Anatolia. This is no ordinary route but it is on good roads, as is its continuation beyond the forests and passes of Ladik, through the valley towns of Taşova, Erbaa, and Niksar, and the scenic gorge of the Kelkit Çayı as far as Koyulhisar and Şebinkarahisar. This is where the really adventurous driving begins, but it only lasts until just before Bayburt, on the upper Çoruh Nehri and the end of this leg.

The final stage, crossing the ranges of the southern Pontus, includes spectacular views at the top of the steep climb up Kop Geçidi before the road drops sharply down into the Aşkale basin and heads east again to **Erzurum**, in the heart of the Armenian highlands and at the source of the northern Euphrates.

Through the West and South-west of Asia Minor

Most tourists who want to get to know the western parts of Turkey take the same route as the long-distance buses, running either diagonally or down the coast between the main provincial centres – İstanbul, Bursa, Balıkesir, Çanakkale, Manisa, İzmir, Aydın and Muğla. This is undoubtedly the best course but only if you are in a real hurry, since many of the scenic and historical treasures are further off the beaten track on roads which will also get you to your destination, although maybe not as quickly. Once you have sampled the heavy traffic of the coast you will be only too glad to try a different road, and in Western Anatolia this usually presents no problem.

10. From İstanbul to Antalya along the Aegean coast

To get from **İstanbul** to the Dardanelles and the Aegean coast you can either start off with Routes 1 and 3 through Thrace, or cross to Asia Minor and into the southern Marmara region which also has plenty of attractions to offer.

To speed up the early stages it pays to take a ferry from the **Bosporus** to Mudanya (Route 6) or from Darıca to Yalova (Route 7) then drive down to **Bursa**, where Bithynia meets Mysia and the traditional western Anatolia coastal tour begins at the foot of Uludağ, the Mysian Olympus, continuing on good, if busy, roads down to Antalya. Between Bursa and Gönen the route runs across the lowland plain containing **Lake Apolyont** and Lake Manyas. Here you can choose between the lakes' northern and southern shores, although the smaller, more winding roads to the south are scenically much more interesting, with the stretch round Lake Apolyont taking you through the foothills of the Kızılelmadağı to Mustafakemalpaşa. The southern route around Lake Manyas will enable you to see something of newer Muhacir communities and to visit the little-known historical site of Eski Manyas.

The next stretch, taking in rice plains, the lower reaches of the Gönen Çayı and the Biga hills, leads down to the southern shore of the Dardanelles and on to **Çanakkale** and **Troy**, crossing the scenic mountain landscape of the Troad.

If you have already been to Troy and enjoy seeing unspoilt Turkish countryside you can cut out part of the coastal route and head south from Biga, through the Troad hills, to Çan, Bayramiç and Ezine, then take the narrow and occasionally less than perfect minor road via Geyikli, Alexandria Troas, Assos (Behramkale) and Ayvacık to rejoin the main route at Küçükkuyu on the **Edremit Körfezi**.

The Gulf of Edremit marks the start of the Aegean seaside resorts which have become so popular with foreign visitors, most of them at the end of access roads (Ören, Ayvalık, Dikili, Çandarlı, Foça, the Çeşme peninsula and Urla, Ilıca and Çeşme, Gümüldür, Kuşadası, Didim).

Strung out along this part of the Turkish coast there are a host of classical Ionian, Lydian and Carian cities and sites, including such famous ones as **Pergamum** (Bergama), **Sardes** (further inland), **Ephesus**, **Milete**, **Priene**, Didyma and Herklea ad Latmos.

The whole length of the coastline of south-western Anatolia, around **Milas**, Muğla, **Fethiye** and **Kaş**, though less sandy, with its many bays and rocky headlands is certainly more scenic than the northern and western Aegean coast. Tourist development here is still quite recent, especially in the section south-east of Muğla, the ancient centre of Menteşe, which up to now has made it a good recommendation for the discerning visitor. The opposite is true of already overcrowded resorts like **Bodrum**, **Marmaris** and now even Fethiye, while places such as Kalkan, Kaş and Finike, once well off the tourist circuit, are also gaining in popularity.

The mountainous and occasionally wooded Mediterranean lands of ancient Caria and Lycia, with their green covering of maquis, are packed with historic sites, especially Lycia, including such evocative names as Cnidus, Halicarnassus, Caunus, Termessos, Xanthus, Patara, Myra, Kekova, Limyra, Olympos and Phaselis. Here too many of these can only be reached by access roads (Bodrum, Marmaris, Kekova, Olympus) but generally speaking they are easy to drive on.

Longer stretches of beach occur again at the foot of the mighty Bey Dağları on the Gulf of Antalya between western Pamphylia's tourist hotspots of Kemer and Antalya.

One highly recommended alternative to this last section of the itinerary is to take the route from Kumluca up to Altınyaka which runs along the mountain roads of the Bey Dağları National Park before dropping down to **Antalya** again.

11. From İstanbul to Antalya through the mountain interior of Western Anatolia

This route, on good roads throughout, runs along the Gulf of **İzmit** to Adapazarı (Sakarya) then follows the Sakarya river down to Geyve, through Pamukova and on to **İznik** (Niceaea) on the lake of the same name.

The next stretch, leaving out the Biga peninsula, cuts diagonally across the hills of northwestern Anatolia via Yenişehir, **Bursa**, **Balıkesir** and Akhisar down to Manisa and **İzmir**, passing through the hinterland of Bithynia, Mysia and Lydia, mainly on a route shared in most parts by long-distance and tourist buses but which on the whole carries much less traffic than the coastal itinerary for Route 10. Here your road will take you, with the obvious exceptions of İznik, Bursa, Manisa, İzmir and Ephesus, to historic sites such as Yenişehir, Balıkesir and Akhisar whose charms are more hidden, and where you can take pleasure in constantly changing scenery, not least because of the contrasts between wooded mountains, river gorges, and the lakes and valleys of the high country.

The continuation of the route from İzmir again counts as one of the traditional tourist circuits. It follows the long, broad and fertile valley of the **Menderes**, the classical Maeander, climbing slowly but steadily upwards to the obligatory tourist highspot of **Pamukkale** near Denizli, then progresses into the salt lakes and limestone scenery of Western Pisidia via Dazkırı and on to the source of the Maeander at Dinar, almost on the edge of Lycaonia. From Dinar the route swings south down an old caravan trail to **Burdur** and Bucak, through the poljes of south-western Pisidia and north-western Pamphylia, before dropping down from the cooler uplands to the hot and humid plain of **Antalya**.

12. From İstanbul to Lycia on minor roads

This route through the western parts of Bithynia, Phrygia and Pisidia, avoids the main roads by, after the initial stretch from **İstanbul**, **İzmit** and Karamürsel, taking minor roads down to Lycia through agreeably varied countryside. Although the state of the road leaves something to be desired in some sections, this is more than made up for by the still generally unspoilt rural landscape of Western Anatolia, largely unknown to the visitor, but still with such historic attractions as. **İznik** (Nicaea) and **Pamukkale** (Hierapolis). These unique features of the western Anatolian hinterland go hand in hand with changing scenery ranging from the green forests of the north, the dry summer scrub of the hills, the grain prairies of the steppes of Central Anatolia, and the high mountains and maquis of the Mediterranean. You can experience wonderful views over Lake İznik on the journey over the Samanlı Dağı from Karamürsel, and enjoy crossing the eastern foothills of the wooded Uludağ from İnegöl to Domaniç, the hill country of Emet and the mountainous limestone slopes of Yaylacı Dağı via Cameli to **Fethiye**.

Other good stopping points en route include **İzmit**, Yenişehir, İnegöl and Tavşanlı.

13. From the Dardanelles to Lycia on minor roads

Another variation, which would particularly suit travellers coming from Greece who are already familiar with the shoreline of the west coast, is the inland route to Lycia, parallel with the coast, from **Çanakkale** on the Dardanelles. Take Route 10 through the Troad from Çanakkale as far as **Edremit** then turn inland to Ivrindi across the forested northern slopes of the Sabla Dağı.

From İvrindi there are two alternative routes south over the foothills of the Madras Dağı to the little towns of Soma and Kırkağac then down into the northern arm of the Gediz rift system and the fertile Akhisar Ovası.

Variations

Both legs, either via **Balıkesir** and Savaştepe or via Bergama (**Pergamum**) and Kınık, use lovely, remote – and hence time-consuming and very ordinary quality – roads through the frontier terrain between Mysia and Lydia. After that it is a quick run via Gölmarmara down to the Gediz valley and the royal tombs of Lydia's ancient capital, **Sardis**, off the İzmir/Ankara road near the town of Salihli. From there, on some quite adventurous roads, you travel through the beautiful pass country of the Boz Dağları and Lake Golçük then down again into the valley of the Kücükmenderes, the Little Maeander, at Birgi and Ödemiş, up again across the wooded mountain barrier of the Aydın Dağları and down again to **Nazilli** in the more built-up area of the **Menderes** valley, this time the Great Maeander.

East of Nazilli a minor road to Karacasu, Tavas, and Serinhisar along the picturesque Vandalas valley and over the wooded Kazıbeli passes skirts the classical ruined city of **Aphrodisias**. It also shows to advantage the many shallow upland depressions in the karst landscapes of western Pisidia and eastern Caria on the upper reaches of the Dalaman Çayı.

Two options present themselves for the route down to the main road from Antalya to Fethiye. You can either take the new road, the E87 via Çavdır to Söğüt, or choose the older, narrower and highly scenic route via Gölhisar and the Dirmil pass country as far as the valley of the Koca Çayı, which you then follow south-westwards, mostly down through the magnificent mountain country of the Ak Dağları spurs as far as Kemer where you can already smell the sea air of the Mediterranean. From there it is but a short distance across the passes to **Fethiye** and the coast.

14. From Çanakkale to Antalya on minor roads

There is a diagonal route, which hardly anyone uses, linking the Dardanelles with Antalya. Although most of the roads are narrow and full of bends they are usually well surfaced, mostly with tarmac. Like Route 12, this is full of variety but takes you down to the Turkish Riviera through Pamphylia rather than Lycia.

You start by crossing the lonely Troad hill country of **Çanakkale** via Çan, Balya and İvrindi to **Balıkesir**. The next rather indirect stretch on the old road into the Akhisar basin through the mountains of the Uludağ and the Simav Dağları crosses two wooded passes and touches Bigadiç and Sındırgı. Well away from the main traffic routes and travelling via Gördes you move through an area of the western Anatolian mountain country untouched by tourism, past the Demirköprü barrage into the vineyards of the Alaşehir depression which runs into the actual Gediz rift valley east of Salihli and is highly reminiscent of the hills of Tuscany. You cross the ranges of the Boz Dağları and the Aydın Dağları at the point where they merge on a scenic mountain road and beyond Buldan, in the Menderes valley, reach the thermal springs around **Pamukkale**, Sarayköy and Denizli.

Just as impressive as Route 12 heading south-west, this section also crosses the limestone mountain country of Pisidia with its extensive polje systems of Yeşilova, Tefenni and Korkuteli, but this time in an easterly direction until, north of the Bey Dağları, the road spirals down through the trees and maquis of the highlands, bare of farming other than fruit orchards, around the former summer pastures of the Pamphylian coastal cities to Döşemaltı, passing Termessos, high up in the mountains, and bringing you to **Antalya**, pearl of the Turkish Riviera, with its fascinating old town and lovely harbour.

15. From Antalya to Cappadocia through Lycaonia

The picturesque port of **Antalya** on the Turkish Riviera makes a particularly good starting point for tours of south-western Anatolia. Here, in Routes 15 and 16, we shall briefly introduce you to just two of them.

Undoubtedly one of the best routes through the southern part of South and Central Anatolia combines the sunny Mediterranean of the Turkish Riviera with the Isaurian lakes, the solitude of the Lycaonian steppes and the strange moonscapes of **Cappadocia**. Starting with Pamphylia's traditional coastal trail taking in Perge, Sillyon, Aspendos and **Side**, you then experience inland, between Manavgat, Akseki, Lake Beyşehir, the Suğla Basin and Bozkır, one of the most attractive mountain regions of the Central Taurus, with its maquis, groves of cedar and pine, juniper and oak, lonely valleys, deep poljes and wonderful views, leaving you with a magnificent impression of southern Turkey's high country which will stay with you long after you emerge at Kazım Karabekir onto the Konya Ovası's vast grain prairielands, dotted with massive volcanic outcrops.

You can also on this route visit such top historical sites as those at **Beyşehir**, the high plains town of **Karaman**, **Ereğli** (Konya Ereğlisi), Ulukışla, Bor, **Niğde**, İncesu and, of course, at the foot of the towering extinct volcano of Erciyes Dağı, the Seljuk city of **Kayseri**.

16. From Antalya to Cilicia through Pamphylia

Another of the traditional routes is the drive along the length of Turkey's south coast from Antalya in Pamphylia through southern Pisidia and "Rough" Cilicia to the Cilician Plain and **Adana**.

Even without the detour up the Köprülü into the Taurus and the Köprülü Canyon then over a gravelled road to Selge (highly recommended) this route is lined with famous and not so famous ruined sites of antiquity, such as Perge, Aspendos, **Side**, Anamurion, Seleukia, Kanlıdıvane, Kız Kalesi and Pompeiopolis to name but a few. You will come across handsome Armenian and Crusader castles, some great reminders of the heyday of the Ottoman Empire (caravanserais, Antalya, Alanya), and natural beautyspots (waterfalls at Antalya, Manavgat and Tarsus, potholes at Cennet Cehennem), while, on each side of the road, you will see the exotic crops grown in this part of the world – bananas, citrus fruit, pomegranates, cotton, peppers and groundnuts. But above all you will find long bathing beaches, inviting bays for swimming, and good hospitality, even though you may have to pay over the odds and the tourist places will be too full in the peak season and there are simply too many of them.

Besides **Antalya** and **Alanya** the main tourist centres on the Turkish Riviera are the thriving seaside resorts around Manavgat, Sorgun and **Side**, along with the coastal towns of Rough Cilicia between Taşucu (**Silifke**), Kızkalesi and Erdemli.

This is certainly the ideal stretch for anyone who loves the summer heat, enjoys the excitement of Mediterranean beach life, but is also looking for spectacular scenery. Despite the fact that holiday apartment blocks are mushrooming on a terrifying scale around Mersin, and the road from here to Adana is heavily industrialised, simply driving along the coast road between Alanya and Silifke, as it winds past Anamur, is enough to give you an idea of the scenic pleasures of the southern heights of the Taurus.

From the Aegean Coast to Eastern Anatolia

Several of the itineraries from Western Anatolia into the east and south-east have already been outlined in Routes 4 to 9 starting from İstanbul. The next two, which begin at İzmir, will take you right across the centre of Anatolia well into Armenia and Kurdistan. They have been deliberately designed to give you a north and a south option so that, despite similarities in the landscape, you can also choose between the cooler and wetter attractions of the north and the dryer features of the south. Parts of these routes cover the familiar cross-country highways used by visitors and commercial traffic alike, which, though faster roads, also carry a good deal of traffic. Other sections, however, take you away from the main roads as well so that you can enjoy the scenery of the more remote areas.

Foreword

17. The Northern Route: from İzmir to northeastern Anatolia

This cross-country route from **İzmir** (E88/E80) through the more northerly parts of Central Anatolia's high country often follows the well-trodden path taken for centuries by travellers from the Aegean to **Armenia**. As a result it passes through such important provincial towns and cities as Uşak, **Afyon**, **Ankara**, **Yozgat**, **Sivas**, **Erzincan** and **Erzerum**, which, because of the accommodation they can offer, make good places for an overnight stop. Along the way you pass from the everchanging landscapes of western Anatolia's partly still wooded mountains, basins and rivers (Gediz rift valley, volcanic region and source of the Gediz at Kula, upper valley of the Banaz Çayı) into the contrasting wide open spaces of the Lykaonian and Galatian steppes and depressions of the upper Sakarya Nehri between Afyon and Ankara, only briefly interrupted by the volcanic ridges around Sivrihisar. The western part of the road to **Ankara** is lined with various historic sites, chief among them **Sardes**, Pessinus and **Gordion**.
The next leg of the drive is almost equally impressive, crossing the colourful mountain country of Kırıkkale on the Kızılırmak and travelling over the lonely undulating uplands of the former nomadic grazing pastures of the Bozok Yaylası, passing Yerköy, Yozgat, Sorgun and Akdağmadenı, to the grain prairies of the Yıldızırmak at Yılkızeli and **Sivas** on the upper Kızılırmak, thus finally bringing you into Eastern Anatolia. The route – particularly attractive at this point – continues along the upper Kızılırmak, through the gypsum karst country, dotted with dolines and lakes, of Sivas, Hafık and Zara, and over the mighty mountain threshold of the Köse Dağları, the source of the headwaters of the northern Euphrates (Karasu), to **Erzincan**. The wonderful scenery goes some way to compensate for the lack of historic sites on this part of the route, but these start to appear again further down the road as, following the Euphrates (Karasu), it runs through Altıntepe and Tercan into Askale and then on to **Erzurum**.

If you then take the main road eastwards via Pasinler to Çobandede on the Araxes (Aras Nehri) you can choose at Horasan between two different routes: the northern road continues along the Araxes and then over the Güllü Dağları on the basalt plateaux of **Kars** and **Ani**, while the southern road (E80) crosses the south edge of the mighty Köse Dağı by the beautiful Saç pass, heading eastwards to Eleskirt and Ağrı where it picks up the Murat Nehri (Euphrates) and brings you via Taslıçay into the Doğubayazıt basin at the foot of Mount **Ararat**.

Variations

18. The Southern Route: from İzmir to Van

The southern route, from **İzmir** to Lake Van, besides taking in various cultural and historical sights, also passes through scenery which in parts is much more impressive than on the northern route. It also follows much busier trunk roads from west to east. This particularly applies to the most westerly section from **İzmir** down to **Ephesus** (Selçuk) then on to Söke.

Beyond Söke, where you cross over to the southern side of the Menderes valley, the route follows roads which are not only well away from the traffic but also run through pleasant countryside. This is particularly true of the road from **Aydın** through Çine to Muğla and above all the next stretch of the route via Kale, although this bit of road is still in a poor state.

The next leg, to **Konya** via Yeşilova, **Burdur**, Yalvaç, Şarkıkaraağaç and **Beyşehir**, takes you through the Isaurian/Pisidian lake district (Salda Gölü, Yaraşlı Gölü, Burdur Gölü, Eğridir-Hoyran Gölü and Beyşehir Gölü) and one of the loveliest parts of Turkey, lightly forested with juniper and oak, following parts of an ancient caravan trail but only touching on a few historical sights such as the towns of Yalvaç (Antioch), Beyşehir and Konya, or the region around Burdur.

An alternative and similarly recommended route from Burdur to **Beyşehir** is to take the road via Isparta and **Eğridir** round the southern edge of Lake Eğridir, thus giving you an opportunity to visit the Kovada Gölü National Park.

From Konya, via **Aksaray**, Acıgöl, Nevşehir, Ürgüp (**Göreme**) and İncesu, you cross the wide open spaces of the heart of Anatolia to **Kayseri**, passing through the wonders of **Cappadocia** on the Seljuk highway, with its caravanserais at, for example, Konya, Obruk, Sultanhanı and Ağzıkarahan.

Further east the traffic tends to thin out. The roads are usually in good condition, making for a faster run from Kayseri to Malatya across the Uzun Yayla, the upland pastures where the Çukurova nomads used to graze their flocks in summer, with a particularly impressive stretch between the Zıya-rettepese and Karahan passes.

Beyond **Malatya** (Melitene/Eskimalatya) you enter the mountains of Eastern Anatolia's Antitaurus and the country around the headwaters of the southern arm of the Euphrates, the Murat, which you pick up for the first time at **Elzazığ**, following its course past Bingöl and on to **Muş**, bringing you into the Lake Van region and the heartland of the ancient Urartu civilisation.

The route between Tatvan and Gevaş, along the southern shore of Lake Van, is one of magnificent scenery, with many former Christian churches and monasteries hidden away on the little islands out in the lake and on the slopes of Kavuşşahap Dağları, close to the shore, while from a distance you can already glimpse the great citadel which marks **Van** and the end of your journey.

From the Black Sea to the Mediterranean

Foreword

However impressive a drive from one end of Turkey to the other may be, travelling west to east, the best way to run the whole gamut of contrasting climate, vegetation, land use, culture and lifestyle, existing as they do behind mountain barriers, in rift valleys, on high plateaux, and within deep depressions, is to make the trip which takes you across the country from north to south. This will precisely show you its special climatic features and just how closely related they are to altitude and distance from the sea in the way the situation can change so rapidly over such short distances. You will still often be using the age-old routes across the mountains enclosing Central Anatolia, although the roads you will have been much improved compared with 50 years ago as the communications network has been expanded. The alternative routes you can take from north to south are nowadays correspondingly more varied than they were. Several of the more diagonal routes from the north-west to the south-east and north to south through the west of Turkey have already been featured under those starting from İstanbul (4 to 6 and 10 to 13) and Çanakkale (14 and 15). Those that follow will briefly outline a number of others more or less in succession according to the characteristics of the different regions. The only thing they have in common is that they all begin somewhere on the Black Sea so that they are comparable one with another, although each one has its own specific highlights.

19. From Bithynia to Lycia on minor roads

Starting from the relatively new Black Sea beach resort of Karasu (or from İstanbul) you can embark on an interesting journey across Western Anatolia from north to south which will give you a representative cross-section of the types of landscape in western Turkey as well as taking in several of the sightseeing highlights, while touching on the ancient kingdoms of Bithynia, Phrygia, Pisidia, Pamphylia and Lycia.
The first leg of the trip follows one of the main lines of communication between north and south along the Sakarya River through Adapazarı (Sakarya), Geyve (Pamukova), Osmaneli (Lefke), Bilecik and, some way from the main road, Söğüt, as far as İnönü (not far from **Eskişehir**) then, having crossed the threshold of Dutluca, switches over to the upper reaches of the Porsuk Çayı en route for **Kütahya**, famous for its pottery, before taking to a minor road through the hilly country of Arslanapa to the great classical temple ruins of Aezani in the Çavdarhisar basin on the upper Kocasu Deresi.
Next you climb the heights of the Karlık Dağı to get to Gediz, the picturesque old town which suffered the earthquake, then follow a quite tortuous mountain road which is not without its problems and is unmetalled in places through the region of thermal springs around Muratdağı via Karacahisar and Çamsu to Banaz on the upper Banaz Çayı and not far from the ruins of Flaviopolis. Another way to get from Gediz to Banaz is to take the route via Uşak. The very scenic minor road from Banaz to Flaviopolis meets up at Sandıklı, a thermal spa town, with the main road from Afyon to Dinar. Follow this south then take the south-east fork at Çobansaray, past Karakuyu Gölü and through Keçiborlu down into the Burdur Gölü basin and on to Isparta.
Beautiful mountain scenery awaits you on the next leg south around the Akdağ to the ruins of Sagalassos near Ağlasun and on to Bucak where the more adventurous would be well advised to make the detour to Kremna and Milyas.
The next stretch is no less attractive, passing through the Kestel polje system and over the karst plateaux and wooded foothills of Korkuteli and Elmalı.
The final highlight of the journey is the descent via Gömbe from this plateau to the Mediterranean through either the Karaovabeli pass to Kasaba and then **Kaş** or the Belpınar pass and down to Kalkan, although in summer you may well feel reluctant to exchange the cool alpine meadows you have just left for the sweltering humidity of the coastal resorts.

20. From Paphlagonia to the South-west on minor roads

This interesting tour down to the south-west is predominantly on minor but mostly quite passable roads and starts from the Black Sea resort of Akçakoca. Fairly early on you get the adventurous drive out of the Düzce Ovası past the Yığılca barrage through the uninhabited Karadere valley to **Bolu**, with the opportunity to make a detour to the Yedi Göller National Park.
The subsequent leg across the Köroğlu Dağları, with its high alpine meadows and pine, fig, and juniper forests, either via Seben or via Kıbrıscik and Beypazarı to Nallıhan, is among Western Anatolia's most scenic ways of

crossing the Pontus. The roads via Kıbrıscık can present a problem but are passable provide you are not in a bus. To be sure of somewhere to stay you should then make straight for **Eskişehir**. Another possibility is to cross the Sakarya barrage on the road to Mihalıççık and carry on to Alpu, with its meerschaum mines, not far from Eskişehir.

Although this has been largely a scenic tour so far the next stage via Seyitgazi and Kırka provides more chances for sightseeing with a sidetrip to **Midas Şehir** and a visit to the Phrygian rock monuments north of Afyon. Scenery comes once more to the fore as the route continues from Afyon through Şuhut and along the juniper-lined western shore of Lake **Eğridir** to İsparta and then the classical ruins of Sagalossos near Ağlasun.

From Eğridir you can also take a longer and more adventurous but highly recommended mountain route south on less good roads through the Kovada Gölü National Park as far as Sığırlık and then wind your way via Aşağıgökdere and Çamlıdere to Sagalossos.

The rest of the tour largely coincides with Route 19 but from Elmalı drops down to Finike on the Mediterranean through the cedars of the Avlan pass and past Arıkanda.

21. Through Paphlagonia and Galatia into Rough Cilicia

Another good route for crossing Asia Minor from the Black Sea to the Mediterranean begins in İnebolu. A steep climb from this lovely Black Sea town through the forests of the Küre Dağları takes you up onto the farming plateau of Devrekâne and to **Kastamonu**, the appealing old centre of Paphlagonia and a good base for excursions into the surrounding countryside.

The next leg brings a pleasing succession of different landscapes as you pass over the flat uplands of the northern Ilgaz Dağları to the Ilgaz Dağı pass in the wooded heights of the Ilgaz Dağı National Park, cross the Devrez Çayı valley at Ilgaz and then climb up again onto the slopes of the eastern Köroğlu Dağları. The impact made by the rest of this section is more one of wide open spaces, crossing the steppes of northern Central Anatolia via Çankırı and Kalecik to **Ankara** then passing through the Kurd mountain country from Haymana to Polatlı and skirting the vast, shallow basin of the upper Sakarya via Yenimehmetli and Yunak into the lake-filled depression of **Akşehir**. From here, again away from the main roads, you pass the Lycaonian steppes, crossing the wooded heights of the Sultan Dağları, to enter the lake district of Pisidia and the Kızıl Dağ National Park, running along the west shore of Lake Beyşehir beside the great wall of the Dedegöl Dağları. The excavations of the old Seljuk summer palace of Kubadabad Sarayı lie near the southern end of the lake, after which you come to the town of **Beyşehir**.

The following stretch southwards via Seydişehir in the Suğla Gölü basin through the Taurus will really put your vehicle to the test after Bozkır (gravel roads from Taşkent) but on the other hand you will be traversing one of the lonely regions of the Central Taurus, where at Hadim you will be quite close to the source of the Kalikadnos (Göksu Nehri), at Taşkent you will pass through one of Turkey's most picturesque little towns, and between there and Ermenek you will go through several breathtaking passes in the deep gorge of the Ermenek Çayı.

From Ermenek there are several options how to proceed. Firstly, you can follow the Ermenek valley, with its many views, on a good road to where it joins the Göksu river just before Mut. From Mut you can either take the main road through the Göksu canyon down to **Silifke** or carry on eastwards on a narrow little road which winds upwards again along the east flank of the Mut basin on the karst heights of the Taşeli plateau to the polje of Kırobaşı and then over the high ground, once trodden by the Crusader forces of Barbarossa on their way south, on a leisurely descent via Demircili to Silifke. En route, or when you are in Silifke, you should definitely make a detour to Uzuncaburç to see the ruins of the ancient city of Olba/ Diocaesarea.

The second option from Ermenek is to take a rather chancy gravel road (watch out for missing bridges!) which runs south-east, climbing the Moca pass up onto the alpine pastures of the Taşeli plateau where a narrow asphalt road leads to Gülnar.
From here there are three different routes, all of them by small and none too wide asphalt roads, which can bring you eventually to **Silifke**.
The most straightforward one takes you eastwards further across the plateau and more or less directly into Silifke.
A second road spirals southwards down through maquis and pines to the Mediterranean and Aydıncik which is on the coast road to Silifke.
The third route snakes north-east through lovely karst scenery and tall pines up to the northern end of the Göksu canyon and the main road running down to Silifke.

22. From Sinop through Central Anatolia into Rough Cilicia

There are two routes to the south which start in Sinop and initially run more or less parallel. The first stage of this, the more westerly route, taking several different passes through the Pontus, runs via Erfelek, Yenikonak, Boyabat and Osmancık to **Çorum**. It crosses several of the long Pontine valleys, including the winding course of the Kızılırmak with its rice paddies and old waterwheels.
The next stretch, from Çorum via Sungurlu and Delice to Keskin, the Hirfanlı barrage, the great Salt Lake and then to Konya, also takes in Alacahüyük and **Boğazkale** as places worth seeing – even though this may mean making a detour, they are not to be missed! The same applies to a visit to the saltpans of Yavşan Tuzlası south of Kulu (via Cihanbeyli) and the small hike from Ilica Yaylası to the travertine pillars not far from salty Bulak Gölü east of the highway to **Konya**, home of the whirling dervishes.
There are three different variations on the next stretch of the route from Konya through south-western Anatolia to **Karaman**, the ancient capital of Karamania.
The least interesting is the direct route south but anyone with a particular interest in archaeology should make the detour via Yarma to **Çatalhüyük** and Cumra, while the route through the summer pastures on the Konya plain via Hotamış, also off the road to Karapinar, to Binbirkilise on the Karadağ will especially appeal to scenery lovers. In any event the following stretch south to Mut and on to the Mediterranean is well worth experiencing at any time of year, passing as it does through the juniper and pinewoods of the Sertavul pass, with wonderful views into the dry Mut basin, then on through the scenic Göksu canyon to **Silifke**.
Once in Silifke you can explore the fascinating coastline of Rough Cilicia between Kız Kalesi and Taşucu with its castles, bays and classical ruins.

23. From Sinop to the Gulf of İskenderun on minor roads through Cappadocia and the Antitaurus

The second route from Sinop leads directly south over the lovely Dranoz pass to Boyabat then travels upstream along the Kızılırmak (rice-growing) via Durağan and along the new Altınkaya barrage to Vezirköprü, the spa town of Havza and then Merzifon to **Çorum**. The following winding stretch of poor road to **Yozgat** passes fairly close to the sites of the excavations at Alaca Hüyük and **Boğazkale**.
From Yozgat you can choose between the longer run on good roads via Sorgun and Sarıkaya to Boğazlıyan, or the shorter route, but on poorer

roads, over the high country of the nomads' former summer pastures of Bozok Yaylası, direct to Boğazlıyan. From here take the route via Himmetdede to get to Avanos and Ürgüp in the heart of **Cappadocia**.

The rest of the route via Saimbeyli, Feke, and Kozan down to the Cilician Plain is one seldom travelled by visitors and you should allow plenty of time for it. The roads are narrow and full of bends, occasionally very steep and only metalled in parts, with no overnight accommodation worth mentioning en route. Nevertheless it is unusually striking and dotted with a host of scenic and historical sights, passing through the Develi Ovası at the foot of the Erciyes Dağı and crossing various passes of the Tahtalı Dağları in the Antitaurus to both headwaters of the Seyhan Nehri – the Zamantı Nehri and Göksü (not to be confused with the river of the same name at Silifke) – into what was once the kingdom of Little Armenia. If you are looking for somewhere to stay overnight towards the end there is quite an acceptable hotel in Kadırlı – from where a poor dirtroad leads direct to Karatepe – which could prove a good alternative to the sweltering heat of **Adana**.

From Kadırlı you can take the route south via Hemit Kale which passes by Hierapolis Kastabala and leads down through Toprakkale, the Syrian Gates, Issos, and Payas to **İskenderun**.

24. From Samsun to Antakya via the Uzun Yayla

A thoroughly classic north/south route through Anatolia from the Black Sea to the Syrian border, with many historical highlights on the way, this itinerary starts from Samsun and proceeds via the staging posts of **Amasya**, **Tokat**, **Sivas** and **Kahramanmaraş** down to **Antakya** (Hatay) on the Orantes. Along the way, much of which covers the old caravan trails (Amasya – Tokat – Sivas), besides the many ancient Seljuk and Ottoman buildings in these historic towns you will also come across some magnificent caravanserais, including the one in Pazar. It is also worth making a sidetrip from Tokat to Sulusaray.

The road south via Gürün over the nomads' former great summer pastureland, the Uzun Yayla, to Pınarbaşı and Sarız leads to the bare northern ranges of the Antitaurus. From here you travel down through lovely wooded karst mountain country, via Göksun – from where it is worth paying a visit to Afşin in the Elbistan basin on a road to **Malatya** – into the valley of the upper Ceyhan Nehri and thence to **Kahramanmaraş** on the northern rim of the Maras trench.

Beyond Kahramanmaraş you follow the Maras trench, parts of it covered in vulcanite, down through Narlı and Hassa, both of which make good starting points for a trip to Yesemek, along a road lined with cotton fields, as far as the south-west end of the route at **Antakya**, where the Orantes forces its way between Musa Dağı and Ziyaret Dağı to enter the sea at Samandağ.

25. From Giresun or Ordu to Antakya on minor roads through Pontus and Commagene

You can enjoy scenic and historical highlights similar to those of Route 24 on a parallel itinerary starting from Giresun which also leads down to Antakya but is initially almost entirely on quite difficult minor roads through the mountains. That is especially true of the old pass road further east to Şebinkarahisar and into the Kelkit valley through the magnificent alpine meadows on the Şehitler pass, although you can avoid this by taking the parallel road to the west which has since been asphalted.

As an alternative you can start further west from Ordu where an asphalt route, likewise recommended for its scenery, runs through Ulubey, Gölköy and Mesudiye to Koyulhisar and Suşehri into the Kelkit valley.

The next stretch, from the Kelkit valley via Zara to **Divriği**, is almost exclusively on metalled roads, and is one of the loneliest but also the most impressive crossings of the eastern Pontus, passing through three passes in the gypsum karst mountains before Zara and then continuing across the Tecer Dağları, the Kulmaç Dağları and the eastern Uzun Yayla.

The scenery is no less attractive on the next leg down into the Malatya depression, running either alongside or close to the Euphrates (Fırat Nehri) via Kemaliye or over the more westerly bare mountains leading up to the Karababa pass direct to Arapkır and in the Euphrates valley parallel with the Karakay barrage through Yazıhan to **Malatya**. The new reservoir has closed off the old road through Eski Malatya (Arslantepe), so you now have to get there direct from Malatya.

Unfortunately there is only a very bad road through the Malatya Dağları to Adıyaman, but if you have a suitable vehicle for travelling cross-country you could try this lovely minor road from Yeşilyurt through Çelikan. A safer course is to take the longer way round on the Kahramanmaraş main road, along the Gölbaşı depression, as far as Gölbaşı and then go east to **Adıya-man**. Its various new hotels make this the best base for excursions around Commagene to places such as Nemrud Dağı and the Atatürk Reservoir on the Euphrates.

The stretch of route from Adıyaman to Gaziantep follows a road seldom taken by tourists across badlands and plateau landscapes to Besni, on the southern edge of the Göksü valley, and Araban on the Karasu, both rivers tributaries of the Euphrates, then to Yavuzeli and finally **Gaziantep**, Tur-key's modern city of the south-east where most of the country's pistachios are grown.

The rest of the route runs south through olive groves to Kilis and along Turkey's frontier with Syria, through Hassa, Kırıkhan and Reyhanlı (Tell Acana) in the Amik plain, mostly on narrow but reasonable roads to **Anta-kya** (Hatay). This makes a good base either as final destination or as the starting point for touring to Harbiya, on the Musa Dağı, or even to **İskende-run** or Seleukeia Pieria (near Samandağ) on the Mediterranean.

Through the South-east and East of Anatolia

As with journeys across the centre of Asia Minor from the Black Sea to the Mediterranean, you can enjoy similar scenic and cultural highlights by travelling from ancient Colchis in the north to Turkish Kurdistan and the frontiers with Syria and Iraq.

Foreword

Another good starting point for tours of eastern Turkey is Van in the Lake Van region and at one time centre of the Urartu civilisation. The communi-cations in this far east of the country have been much improved, making driving distinctly easier than it was a decade ago, thanks to the work being carried out for the GAP project and the programme to encourage tourism here and forge better links with the industrial and financial centres in western Anatolia. Nevertheless there are still many stretches of road that are not necessarily suitable for ordinary vehicles. This particularly applies to the mountains around Hakkâri or the triangle of Taurus regions around Sason between Bingöl, Bitlis and Siirt. What has proved a real boon for anyone travelling in eastern Anatolia is the extension of the highway across the Tendürek Dağı north-east of Lake Van from Muradiye to Doğu-bayazıt and the direct route from Tuzluca on the Armenian frontier through Digor to Kars. Brief itineraries for some of these routes are given below.

Adana makes a good starting point for anyone vacationing in the south of Turkey who wants to explore eastern Anatolia from there.

26. From Adana to Diyarbakır and Lake Van

Starting from **Adana** take the main highway which runs east across the cottonfields of the Çukurova, past Misis, Ceyhan and Toprakkale, over the Amanos mountains and into the Maraş trench. From here the highway, with its notoriously heavy flow of lorries, continues parallel with the Syrian border as far as Iraq. Leave it in the lowest point of the rift valley at the main junction with the road to Kahramanmaraş and head for Gölbaşı via Türko-ğlu and Pazarcık, up the fertile Aksu Çayı valley and across the oak scrub of the pass country to the Gölbaşı depression with its many lakes. From here good roads will take you into the heart of Commagene and **Adıyaman** and Kâhta where you can spend a couple of days in this beautiful and historic part of the country. The next leg of the route will take you first across the Euphrates (Fırat) to Siverek and then along the bleak northern spurs of the Karaca Dağı, where nomads still graze their flocks, to **Diyarbakır** on the Tigris (Dicle).

From Siverek you can also take a new road, which leads among other places to the Atatürk dam on the Euphrates, and travel south to **Şanlıurfa** to join up with Route 27 if you want to see something of, say, Harran, **Mardin** and the Tur Abdin.

The route from Diyarbakır is across broad gently rolling steppes over the foreland of the south-eastern Taurus, passing through Silvan, with its fascinating history, taking in the ancient bridge over the Batman Çayı and the local shrine of Ziyaret. The road, which is a good one, winds upwards along the scenic Bitlis Çayı, out of the heat of northern Mesopotamia into the cool of the Armenian highlands, until it reaches the old Kurdish town of **Bitlis** and the pass country of Tatvan, south-east of Lake Van.

The tour passes round the southern shore of the lake, ringed by the magnificent mountain scenery of the peaks of Kurdistan and at Gevaş you can already glimpse from afar the citadel crowning the old city of **Van** to the north. Once there if you have enough time you should take the boat trip out on the lake to the famous old Armenian church on Ahtamar Island.

27. From Adana to Mardin via Şanlıurfa (Urfa)

Like Route 26 this itinerary starts from **Adana** and takes the road east to Bahçe and the Maraş trench.

If you want a more interesting run take the minor narrow road before Bahçe and about 12½ miles past Osmaniye. This winds its way across the wooded Nurdağı pass to Fevzipaşa. Otherwise the rest of the road east to Mardin, running parallel with the Syrian border, is a good main road although rather monotonous and crowded with lorries. Although this traffic has been severely reduced following the Gulf War it is likely to build up again once sanctions on trade with Iraq are lifted.

The only attractive scenery is between the Maraş valley and Gaziantep on the heights of the Kartal Dağı and around the Euphrates near Birecik. The rest of the route is relatively lacking in variety as it crosses the tablelands of Şanlıurfa, Viranşehir and Kızıltepe.

In cultural and historical terms, however, this is a route that has much to offer and the places worth seeing along the way include Sakçağözü (Kara-höyük), **Gaziantep**, **Birecik**, **Şanlıurfa** (Urfa), Viransehir (Konstantina) and **Mardin**, as well as Tellbasar Kalesi, Rumkale, Karkamış and Tell Musa (Zeugma), which are some way from the road – and of course Harran, which is easy to get to from Şanlıurfa.

28. From the Black Sea to Harran and the Syrian frontier

This route from **Trabzon** to the Syrian frontier, through the western regions of old **Armenia** down to Mesopotamia, is one that strays from the beaten track in parts. The traditional way over the Pontus through the Zigana pass along the Maçka Çayı and the Harşit Çayı via Torul to Gümüşhane easily lends itself to a detour from Maçka to the Sumela monastery in the Altındere Vadisi National Park with its pines, beeches and rhododendrons. If you can manage it, rather than taking the new fast road over the Kalkanlı Dağları to Torul, opt for the old winding pass road alongside it, through the bustling picturesque Pontus villages with their hazel coppices and little plots of maize. More than any other this stretch clearly shows the rapid transition in climate and cultivation from northern to southern Pontus. **Gümüşhane** so far has no accommodation worth mentioning (Torul is much more attractive on the grounds of its setting alone). The first suitable place to stay, after taking only partly asphalted roads through the narrow gorge of the upper Harşit and the Kösedaği pass to Kelkit and the Otlukbeli pass at Yeniyol, is in the basin of **Erzincan**. Part of the next leg is not asphalted either. From Erzincan, where you should try to visit Altıntepe, it runs through the Alevi region of Dersim (Hozat) via Pülümür and **Tunceli**, continuing on to **Elazığ**. If you can arrange it, pay a visit to the Munzur Vadisi National Park in the valley of Ovacık and Tunceli's towering Munzur mountain range, but just for a hike since there is hardly any accommodation. Pertek should not be left out either, nor of course the Keban reservoir (ferry from Pertek to Elazığ) and ancient Harput above Elazığ.

South of Elazığ you enter the high wide valley which provides the lovely setting for Lake Hazar, the source of the Tigris (Dicle), which then bursts into life as it rushes down to Maden. The road to Siverek crosses the bleak and barren expanse of the broken limestone mountain country of Çermik. Beyond Siverek the low, basalt spurs of the volcanic Karaca Dağ and the Urfa plateau leading up to **Şanlıurfa** (Urfa) and the Harran depression are still among Turkey's least farmed regions, pending the completion of South-eastern Anatolia's GAP irrigation projects, yet both Şanlıurfa (Urfa, classical Edessa) and Harran, not far from the Syrian frontier, are among Turkey's traditional tourist destinations.

29. From Colchis to Mardin on minor roads

Another itinerary down to the Syrian border from the Black Sea, starting this time at Rize and mostly on minor roads, runs almost parallel with Route 26. It begins with an only partially hard-surfaced mountain road through wooded mountains and high peaks – parts of the road around the pass over the Ovitdağı (2600m/8533ft) are very poor indeed – through İkizdere in the Çoruh valley to İspir, from where dirtroads lead you through more passes, along remote small valleys and by little-known villages into the high-lying basin of **Erzurum** on the upper Karasu, not far from the source of the northern arm of the Euphrates.

An alternative route further west begins at Of and also traverses the high places of the northernmost of the Black Sea mountain ranges, this time via Çaykara and the Soğanlı pass – where you can make a sidetrip to the forests of Uzungöl – before reaching the Çoruh Nehri at Bayburt. The rest of the way to Erzurum via the Kop Dağı and Askale is described in Route 9.

Although most of the next leg, from Erzurum to Bingöl, is now on asphalt roads it covers a part of the country so far virtually unfrequented by tourists. This stretch, via Çat and Karlıova and crossing the Peri Suyu, runs through the colourful shrub terrain of the Şeytan Dağları.

The next stretch is also off the usual tourist circuit, heading south from Bingöl through Genç over the alpine pastures of the Akçara Dağı to the Berklin Çayı, the eastern source of the Tigris (Dicle Nehri), in the earthquake zone around Lice and Ceper.

Here you can choose between going straight ahead to Diyarbakır or taking the road leading westwards via Hanı and Dicle to Ergani and then turning south from there. This option means you can make a detour to visit the historically interesting little town of Eğil, in its picturesque setting above the Tigris gorge, before taking the fast main road to complete this leg of the journey at **Diyarbakır**, the capital of Turkish Kurdistan, ringed by massive black basalt walls and overlooking the green strip fringing the Tigris.

A scenic route from Diyarbakır carries on south-eastwards following the Tigris and then one of its tributaries across the limestone foothills to **Mardin**, the most Arab of Turkey's towns, high on a bluff with a wonderful view over the fields and flatlands of Syria. More modern accommodation is available somewhat further east, just beyond Nusaybin, right on the Syrian frontier and the busy highway into Iraq. This is also a good place from which to tour the Jacobite Christian areas of the Tur Abdin.

30. Tour of Eastern Anatolia

Although Doğubayazıt, Iğdır, Artvin, Erzurum and Ahlat all have the kind of accommodation which makes them good starting points for a tour of Eastern Anatolia, the best route for making the most of the variety and contrast in the sights worth seeing is the one beginning at **Van** and travelling in a clockwise direction.

You can start by touring along the shores of Lake Van, either by taking the northern route via Ercis and Adilcevaz so that you can familiarise yourself with the less well-known scenery of Turkey's largest lake and the mighty volcanoes of Süphan Dağı and Nemrut Dağı, or travelling round the southern shore, taking a boat trip out to Ahtamar, and then stopping overnight at Ahlat, where it is worth risking an excursion to the triple crater of Nemrut Dağı, but only if you go in a cross-country vehicle or a local minibus.

Just past Mus on the road from Tatvan on the western end of the lake you can take a seldom travelled road north along the Murat Nehri past Kale Kayalıdere and Varto then over the bar of the eastern Bingöl Dağları to Hınıs and later the upper course of the Araxes (Aras Nehri) which you follow downstream as far as the famous bridge at Çobandede when you turn west, via Pasinler (Hasan Kale), to get to **Erzurum**.

The monasteries and churches of south-western Georgia are reached from Erzurum by taking the road north to Artvin through Tortum, picking up the beautiful deepset River Tortum valley, with its lovely lake and magnificent waterfalls.

Artvin, overlooking the Çoruh valley, is a good stopover. From here you can get to Ardahan along bumpy, dusty roads through either Ardanuç or Şavşat leading up through the alpine meadows and woodland scenery of the Yalnızçam Dağları onto the bleak fastnesses of the Ardahan Yaylası and down into the Ardahan basin on the upper Kura, one of the largest rivers of the southern Caucasus.

There are two routes from Ardahan down to **Kars** and, further east and on the border, **Ani**. The eastern one passes the basalt-dark waters of Çıldır Gölü via Çıldır and Arpaçay, while the shorter one further west is a direct route over the Ardahan Yaylası via Susuz. South beyond Kars, on Turkey's frontier with Armenia, you pass through the region of Digor, full of Armenian monasteries and their ruins, then meet up again with the Araxes, this time following its valley eastwards as it widens out from Tozluca as far as Iğdır where Turkey's highest mountain, majestic Mount **Ararat** (Ağrı Dağ; 5137m/16,860ft), towers over the broad Iğdır basin.

The next leg over the Çilli pass to **Doğubayazıt** and then further south over the volcanic Tendürek pass to Muradiye crosses a region where even today you can still regularly encounter nomads. Besides containing İshak Paşa Sarayı, one of the great attractions of north-eastern Turkey, this region is packed with scenic charms, especially those met with when crossing the Tendürek Dağı and travelling by the waterfalls at Muradiye which must be among the highlights of this final stretch back to our starting point at **Van**.

31. Touring the mountain country of Turkish Kurdistan

When touring the mountain country of Hakkâri and Bitlis in the extreme south-east of Turkish Kurdistan your best chance of finding accommodation, apart from Van, is near Nusaybin. You can also find somewhere to stay in Hakkâri, Mardin and Siirt but it is unlikely to be very comfortable.

Completing a tour of this part of the world is also likely to be fraught with obstacles. Road conditions can be quite poor, especially between Hakkâri and Uludere, so you must have a sturdy vehicle suitable for driving cross-country. This is also one of the problem areas of Turkish Kurdistan and you are fairly certain to run into military checkpoints and roadblocks. Avoid using hire cars with a Turkish numberplate if at all possible.

Despite all this it is a region so remarkable for its variety and harsh beauty that it will only be missed out with reluctance. And it has some major historical sights awaiting the visitor in such places as Çavuştepe, Hoşap, Surb Batholomeos (Albayrak) and, further afield, Yanal. You will find other highlights of this tour beyond Cizre on the further stretch through the farmlands of the northern Syrian plain and the Tur Abdin at Nusaybin (Anastasiopolis), in the monasteries and sacred buildings around Midyat and **Mardin**, at Hasankeyf on the Tigris and at Aydınlar near Siirt.

The way back round again is no less attractive, through the narrow valley of the Bitlis Çayı via Baykan and Bitlis to the great peaks bordering Lake Van and along the southern shore to **Van**.

Important points
to bear in mind

32. Through Eastern Anatolia on minor roads

This route takes you mostly on minor roads from the lovely little town of **Artvin**, down through Eastern Anatolia to Lake Van. First follow the narrow canyon of the Çoruh Dağı upstream as far as Yusufeli to visit the Georgian churches at Peterekkale, Dörtkilise and around Barhal. To get to your next overnight stop at either Sarıkamış or Kars you can either take the road east, passing by Olur, to Bana (church) near Akşar, with a sidetrip to the church at İshan, or follow the Tortum valley upstream (waterfall, lake; sidetrips to Öşk Vank and Hahuli/Haho) towards Tortum as far as Aksukapı then take a narrow dirt road to Oltu. A third way is to take the good asphalt road from Tortum via Narman to Oltu and Bana. All three routes cross the majestic Kargapazar Dağları, the first mostly following the valley of the Oltu Çayı, but the best for scenery is undoubtedly the road through Tortum. Back up on the road to Göle you traverse the basalt highlands of the Kars Yaylası en route to **Kars**. From here you would be well advised to pay a visit to **Ani** right on the Armenian border before heading south.

There is a choice of two routes to Kağızman. You can either take the direct road over the Paslı pass and through Kötek or you can opt for the prettier way via Sarıkamış through the wooded Güllü Dağları to Karakurt and the beautiful canyon of the Araxes (Aras). Past Kağızman a winding dirt road, taxing the capabilities of both driver and vehicle, heads south through the high peaks of the Arasgüney Dağları and then follows the Cuma Çayı to Ağrı. The next stage to Tutak is on a good asphalt road snaking along the narrow valley of the upper Murat Nehri (source tributary of the Euphrates), followed by a rather uneventful stretch to Patnos, before meeting up with the Murat again at Malazgirt where the Seljuks decisively defeated the armies of Byzantium. From here you drive over the undulating high plains of Bulanık and Erentepe before plunging down from Karakale into the basin of **Muş** where you pick up Route 18 to **Van**.

Suggested Routes

From Ankara to the Black Sea through Northern Anatolia

These suggested routes are essentially ways of crossing the Pontus which take you through some of the beautiful scenery of Northern Anatolia, a region only recently opened up to tourism.

33. From Ankara to Ünye via Tokat

The first leg, between Ankara and Sungurlu, is the same as in Route 24 but in the opposite direction, and you should plan to include visits to Boğazkale and Alaca Hüyük.

From here head east-north-east and well away from the usual tourist circuit to Alaca and Aydıncık, over grain steppes and lightly wooded southern spurs of the Pontus, then on to Çekerek on the upper Çekerek İrmağı. Follow the river downhill as far as the village of Reşadiye before turning east onto a rather indifferent dirt road so that you can visit the village of Yalınazı and the nearby excavations at Maşat Hüyük, both of which are worth seeing.

The next stretch, on a narrow asphalt road, also has historical attractions at Zile, Pazar and, of course, **Tokat**.

The scenery is constantly changing on the rest of the route to the coast, passing by Comana Pontica, through Niksar and over the north Pontic high plains of Akkuş before dropping down through the hazel coppices on the northern flank of the mountains to Ünye and Black Sea.

34. From Ankara to Amasra through the eastern Köroğlu Dağları

The first stretch from **Ankara** takes narrow little-known asphalt roads northwards beyond the airport to Çubuk, from where you can get to both the Çubuk's artificial lakes as well as to Karagöl, some 19 miles away and a favourite spot for an outing by the people of Ankara into the woods of the eastern Köroğlu Dağları.

Next comes a lonely ride via Şabanözü and Orta over the mountain ridges to Çerkes where you follow the Devrez Çayı valley westwards. Turning north towards Eskipazar you cross a number of low passes and travel through deepset valleys before reaching Karabuk with beyond it Safranbolu, now classified a historical monument, before travelling down the wooded valley of the Gökirmak/Kocairmak to Bartin at the western end of the Küre Dağları, and a few miles beyond it the picturesque port of Amasra on the Black Sea.

Anamur Kalesi, a medieval pirates' stronghold ▶

Sights from A to Z

Adana

South coast (Eastern Mediterranean)
Province: Adana
Altitude: 25m/80ft
Population: 932,000, 1.9 million (with suburbs)

Situation and characteristics

The provincial capital of Adana, Turkey's fourth largest city (after İstanbul, Ankara and İzmir) and one of its most prosperous economic centres, lies in the south-east of the country in the Cilician Plain (known today as the Çukurova or "Hole Plain", and in antiquity as Aleion Pedion) below the southern slopes of the Taurus. It is built on both banks of the Seyhan (the ancient Saros), which is spanned by a number of bridges, some of them ancient, and a railway bridge. The town draws its subsistence from the fertile plain which extends in the form of a delta towards the Mediterranean. Its situation near the "Cilician Gate", from time immemorial the principal pass through the Taurus, and also on the Baghdad railway, were the chief stimuli to its economic development, as a result of which Adana has in recent years enjoyed an upswing in its economy (university since 1971) and a considerable increase in population. The principal sources of employment are food-canning and preserving factories, spinning and weaving mills, engineering plants, cement works and rail workshops. The corn and cotton trades are also important (Cotton Exchange). As well as being very hot the climate is humid and unhealthy (malaria).

History

Human settlement in Adana reaches far back into pre-Christian times. The Hittite town of Ataniya may have been situated on Velican Tepe, a hill about 12km/7½ miles outside the town. Under the Seleucids the town was known as Antiocheia on the Saros. In Roman times Adana, then called by its present name, was overshadowed by the regional capital Tarsus. Its real development began under Ottoman rule and, even more markedly, under the Turkish Republic.

Sights

Sights
Stone Bridge

Practically nothing remains of ancient Adana. All that it has to show is the 310m/340yd long Stone Bridge (Taş Köprü) over the Seyhan. Frequently destroyed and restored in the course of its history, the bridge preserves fourteen of its original 21 arches, including one (at the western end) which is believed to date from the time of the Emperor Hadrian (117–138).

Archaeological Museum

The Archaeological Museum contains a fine collection of prehistoric pottery from Cilicia, some Hittite items and interesting Turkish ethnographic material.

Ulu Cami

Enclosed within a high wall in the centre of the town stands Adana's most interesting medieval building, the 16th c. Ulu Cami (Great Mosque) with its medrese (theological college), türbe (tomb) and dersane (Koranic school). The main entrance is on the east side. Also on this side is a minaret (1507–08) with polygonal shaft, blind arcading and roofed gallery reminiscent of Syrian models. Along the north side runs a triple arcade of pointed arches, off which the various rooms of the medrese open. The türbe, with Syrian-style decoration, is faced with Ottoman tiles from İznik. On the west side are the dersane and a gatehouse with a conical dome.

Mosques

Two other mosques worth visiting are the Akça Mescit (1409; a mescit is a small mosque) and the 15th c. Ramazanoğlu Camii, both Syrian in style.

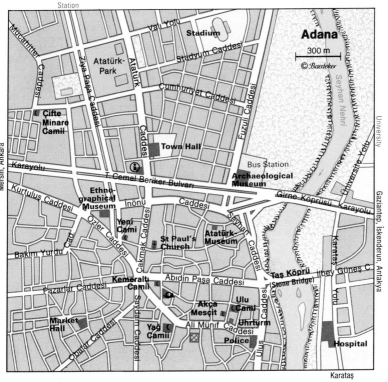

Surroundings

Eastwards from Adana the road to İskenderun crosses the Cilician Plain (Çukurova), to arrive after about 25km/15 miles at Misis (Yakapınar), the site of ancient Mopsuestia. The town extends on both banks of the Ceyhan, here spanned by a nine-arched Roman bridge. The main feature of interest in Misis is the Mosaic Museum, erected over the mosaic pavement of a small church, the latter having presumably been destroyed during the Arab incursions of the 8th c. The mosaics, built up from pieces of variously coloured stone and glass, date from the time of Bishop Theodore (4th c.).

Misis
(Mopsuestia)

About 11km/7 miles east of Misis, on the steep southern bank of the Ceyhan, a figure of the Hittite king Muwatalli (1315–1282 B.C.) can be seen carved into a smooth rock face rising above the river. On the top of a steep-sided crag on the north bank stands Yılanlıkale ("Snake's Castle"), an Armenian stronghold and Crusader castle of the 12th c. According to legend it was the residence of Sheikh Meran, half man, half snake, who was killed in the baths at Tarsus while seeking to carry off the king's daughter.

*Yılanlıkale
("Snake's Castle")

The main road continues to the chief town of the district Ceyhan (a short distance off the road to the right), some 35km/22 miles south of which, on the Gulf of İskenderun, lies the little port of Yumurtalık (previously called Ayas). In Marco Polo's time it was known as Layaze and was once the chief

Yumurtalık

123

Adana

port of Lesser Armenia. In addition to being a seaside resort popular with the local people, it is now the terminus of two oil pipelines from Iraq.

*Anavarza
(Anazarbus)

Beside the Sumbaş Çayi, near the village of Anavarza in Upper Çukurova, to the east of the Ceyhan–Kozan road, lie the easily recognised walled ruins of Anazarbus, at one time the minor capital of Lesser Armenia. Perched dizzily on an isolated crag some 200m/650ft directly above the town (and reached by steps from near the theatre) are extensive remains of the fortress (upper and lower fort). In addition to the ancient main street other town ruins include a Roman stadium, a theatre, an aqueduct, several churches and a fine gate to the south. The local open-air museum (situated away from the site itself, in the centre of the village) has some famous mosaics from the 3rd c.

Founded in the 1st c. B.C. Anazarbus was a Romano-Byzantine town. In the 12th c., after numerous disputes with Byzantium and with the aid of the Crusaders, it passed to Lesser Armenia, the principal capital of which was Sis (Sisium/Kozan). Although from 1199 onwards the Armenian princes styled themselves kings, they were always forced, in the final resort, to acknowledge Byzantine supremacy. While close links between the royal house and the Mongols preserved Anazarbus from destruction, in 1297 a Mongol prince had 40 Armenian noblemen, together with Hetum their king, murdered at a banquet in the town.

Hierapolis
Kastabala

5km/3 miles beyond the village of Yenice on the road from Osmaniya to Karatepe stand the ruins of Hieropolis (Kastabala). Between 52 B.C. and 17 B.C. this Cilician town became the centre of an independent principality under Tarcondimotus I. Rome (under Augustus) then restored its influence by making Tarcondimotus II, the new king, Governor of Cilicia in Anazarbus.

Kozan

Kozan (70km/43 miles north-west of Adana; pop. 50,000) occupies the site of ancient Sisium and in the 19th c. was still known as Sis. The fort, on a

Anavarza, the scene of a turbulent history

Adıyaman

hill-top south-west of the town, dates from the Byzantine period. The Armenian victory over Manuel I Comnenus (1143–80) led in 1199 to the establishment of the kingdom of Lesser Armenia, of which Sis became the capital. By 1375 however, shortly after the coronation of the last king, Leon V, it fell to the Mamelukes. Despite the schism in the Church (1441), Sis remained the centre of the Armenian Church until shortly after the First World War, the Catholicos of Sis being determined to preserve the status of his seat. Eventually, in 1921, increasing Islamic repression forced the head of the Armenian Church to flee the town, the patriarchate being transferred to Beirut. In the 19th c. Sis also became the capital of the Kozanoğulları, leaders of a large nomadic tribe forcibly resettled there from Cevdet Paşa.

About 27km/17 miles east of Ceyhan the road to İskenderun branches off to the right over the Toprakkale Pass. Describing Darius' march along this route through the foothills of Mount Amanos and the Misis Hills, the 2nd c. historian Arrian refers to the 2km/1¼ mile long defile between sheer rock walls 40–50m/130–165ft high as the Amanian Gates (Amaniae Pylae). Just off the Osmaniye road to the north, on a steep-sided basaltic cone some 76m/250ft high, are the conspicuous remains of a medieval settlement, possibly built on the site of ancient Augusta.

Toprakkale Pass, Toprakkale

Further along the Osmaniye road, a side turning branches off on the left to Karatepe (Black Hill), some 28km/17 miles north on the right bank of the Ceyhan Nehri. Excavated from 1949 onwards, the site has been extensively restored.
Karatepe was the walled stronghold of an 8th c. Hittite ruler called Azitawadda. The two main gates, on the north and south sides, are flanked by massive sphinxes while reliefs on the sills depict various gods, battle and hunting scenes, a ship with oarsmen, etc. There are two parallel inscriptions, one in Hittite hieroglyphic script, the other in Phoenician; these proved a valuable starting point for deciphering the hieroglyphic script. Little survives of the buildings within the town.

**Karatepe

From Sakarcalı (on the Ceyhan, 30km/19 miles south of Kadirli) a track follows the river to Hamide and, 70m/330ft above the village, the medieval Armenian castle of Amuda. In 1212 the Lesser Armenian King Leon I handed over the fortress with its massive keep and large courtyard to the Knights of the German Order. They built the tower, continuing in occupation (at Akkon's behest) until about 1291 (no later). Down at river level below the south side of the fortress can be seen the poorly preserved remains of a Hittite rock relief. Carved in the 13th c. B.C. it shows a warrior armed with a bow and lance.

Hemite Kalesi

Adıyaman

O 6

South-east Anatolia
Province: Adıyaman
Altitude: 725m/2380ft
Population: 102,000

See warning page 7

Adıyaman, capital of the province of that name, is situated within the plateau region of south-east Turkey, to the south of the east Taurus mountains. It lies on the western edge of a flat depression, the south-east limit of which is formed by the Euphrates. Although the town, the centre of an agricultural area (wine, cotton, apricots, pistachios), has little worth seeing, it makes an excellent base from which to explore the historic Kommagene sites.
Prior to the creation of the Turkish Republic Adıyaman was known as Hisn Mansur (Mansur's Castle), having begun life in 758 as a fortress (thugur) against the Byzantines. It was built under Caliph Marwan by the Omayyad leader Mansur Ben Ga'wana in succession to the earlier Roman town of Perre.

Situation and characteristics

Sights

Still surviving in the Old Town are the Ebu-Zer Gaffar Türbesi Mausoleum, dating from the Islamic period, and ruins of the Hisn Mansur fortress from the early Omayyad period, which latter underwent restoration at the hands of the Abbasid Caliph Haroun al-Rachid (786–809). Below the fortress stands the 14th c. Great Mosque (Ulu Cami) with three gates and encircling wall.

Surroundings

*Atatürk Barajı

About 30km/19 miles south of Adıyaman lies the 1614m/1 mile long, 169m/555ft high Atatürk Dam (formerly the Karabba Dam). With a volume of 48,470 million cu.m/63,400 million cu.yds and extending over an area of 817sq.km/315sq.miles, the reservoir produces 8900 million kWh of electricity annually. Completed in 1990 as part of the GAP Project (South-east Anatolian Project), the Atatürk Barajı is a key element in a whole series of dams on the Tigris and Euphrates. Altogether they irrigate some 1,856,627ha/4,587,725 acres of arable land as well as generating much-needed hydro-electric power.

Arsameia on the Euphrates

About 65km/40 miles north-east of Adıyaman, reached via a track off to the right some 18km/11 miles along the Gerger road, the Gerger Kalesi (lower and upper forts) stands guard high above the flooded Euphrates valley (Atatürk Dam). There are some Kommagene inscriptions (third gate) and a 2.7m × 4m/9ft × 13ft relief depicting the ruler Samos II. (Being carved in the rock at the western end of the castle crag, the latter is not easily accessible.) Inscriptions record that the founder was King Arsames of Kommagene in the 3rd c. B.C. and that the site was dedicated to the goddess Argandene.

Antiochos I and Hercules in Arsameia at the Nymphaios

126

Approximately 25km/15 miles north-east of Adıyaman, above the east bank of the Kâhta Çayı (Nymphaios) opposite Yeni Kale castle near Eski Kâhta, is a cult and burial site known today as Eski Kale (Mithridates I Kallinikos) and the summer residence of the Kommagene rulers founded in the 3rd c. B.C. by Arsames. In addition to the remains of steps and buildings on the summit plateau (mosaics from the 2nd c. B.C.), a number of reliefs and rock chambers are passed on the approach.

*Arsameia on the Nymphaios

Lower relief (II): the god Mithras-Helios (a further part depicting Antiochus II is missing); middle relief (I): (fragments) Mithridates and his son Antiochus I, antechamber (cult site of the god Mithras?) with, to the rear, a rock tunnel with fourteen steps leading to the burial chamber of Mithridates (?); upper relief (III): Dexiosis relief of king (Mithridates or Antiochus I) with the demigod Hercules (extending his right hand), inscription by Antiochus I, steeply-stepped, blocked, rock tunnel (158m/518ft deep), purpose unknown.

This well-preserved Roman bridge crossing the Cendere (the ancient Chabinas) at a point where the river emerges from an impressive gorge into the wide valley of the Kâhta Çayı, was built between A.D. 198 and 200 by the "legio XVI Flavia firma", stationed in Samosata (Samsat). According to an inscription four Kommagene towns financed the building of the single-arched bridge with its span of 34.2m/112ft. One of the original four dedicatory columns (to Septimus Severus, his wife Iulia Domna and their sons Caracalla and Geta), the one to Geta, was taken down in A.D. 212, part of an attempt to obliterate any reminder of Caracalla's having had his brother and co-ruler removed.

Cendere Köprüsü (Chabinas Bridge)

The Dikilitas tumulus, 6m/20ft high and 35m/115ft in diameter, located 60km/37 miles south-west of Adıyaman, is almost certainly the burial place of Mithridates II of Kommagene and his wife. Of the three original pairs of columns (from which the old name Sesönk = "three columns" was derived) only the southernmost survive complete with linking architrave. The outer chamber, with three tombs, is accessible. If driving there the best route, which even then is not without its problems, is via Şambayat, Beşyol and Zormagora (4km/2½ miles on foot).

Dikilitas

The village of Kocahisar, 70km/43 miles north-east of Adıyaman, is a convenient spot from which to visit the Mameluke fortress of Yeni Kale, built on a narrow mountain spur high above a Seljuk bridge spanning the Kâhta Çayı gorge. The complex was constructed on top of earlier foundations by Kara Sonkar (Governor of Aleppo, 1286), being altered and extended at the end of the 13th c. and in the mid 14th c. Water was brought up from the Kâhta Çayı via a stepped passage-way and stored in a cistern. For the "express" delivery of messages carrier pigeons were used, notably during Sultan Kala'un's decisive battle against the Mongols at Homs (1281).

*Eski Kâhta Yeni Kale

A short distance east of Dikilitas are the remains of a triple-arched bridge (centre arch, 31m/102ft, collapsed) over the Göksu, the ancient Singas, a tributary of the Euphrates. Up until the Middle Ages this was an important river crossing on the former military road from Samosata to Zeugma (60km/37 miles south-west of Adıyaman).

Göksu Köprüsü

Kâhta (formerly Kolik), 35km/22 miles east of Adıyaman, is the principal town of the district and the starting point for the drive through ancient Kommagene. Being short of hotel accommodation it has found itself increasingly eclipsed by the provincial capital.

Kâhta

This Kommagene tumulus 47km/29 miles north-east of Adıyaman was erected by Mithridates II (36–20 B.C.) for his mother Isias, his sister Laodike (d. 36 B.C., wife of the Parthian King Orodes IV), and his niece Aka. From the original three pairs of columns only four now survive, the southernmost being crowned by an eagle (Karakus = "black bird"), the north-easterly one by a bull. On the north-west side are a toppled lion and a column the inscription on which records details of the tomb.

*Karakuş Tapesi

Adıyaman

Cult figures on the Nemrut Daği (in foreground Antiochos I)

Nemrut Daği

Topping the karst limestone mountain of Nemrut Dağı (2150m/7056ft) in the south-eastern Taurus 90km/56 miles north-east of Adıyaman is the Hierothesion of the Kommagene King Antiochus I (69–38 B.C.), dedicated to his own glory and that of the gods. Antiochus' tomb is concealed somewhere inside the 50m/164ft high man-made burial mound, with its spectacular terraces on three sides (east, north and west). The 80m/260ft long north terrace, lined with (collapsed) columns, served as a place of assembly and arena for processions and other rituals.

On either side of the east terrace stand reliefs of the King's ancestors, paternal (Persian) to the north, maternal (Seleucid) to the south, framing the colossal figures of the gods (heads standing on the ground) facing the main altar. These include, in addition to eagles and lions, the Greco-Persian mixed deities Zeus-Oromasdes, Hercules-Verethragna-Artagnes-Ares, Apollo-Mithras-Helios-Hermes and Kommagene-Tyche, as well as Antiochus I himself.

A similar arrangement is repeated on the west terrace, which is some 10m/33ft lower than the east. Here the heads of the colossal statues are better preserved and there are also more of them. The "Lion Horoscope" with its astral motifs symbolises the deification of Antiochus I through the metamorphosis of king into star.

Samsat

The ruins of Samosata (3rd c. B.C.), the old Kommagene capital on the Euphrates, now mostly lie submerged beneath the waters of the Atatürk Barajı south-west of Kâhta. Only when the level in the reservoir is low does the 45m/148ft high castle hill, which in 1990 was still being excavated, break the surface of the water. The site is reached from Adıyaman by driving east to Arılı and then south along the new road to Yeni Samsat (about 65km/40 miles). From about 640 Samsat, like Adıyaman, was one of the frontier forts (thugur) constantly changing hands between Byzantium and the Arab and Turkoman invaders, sometimes under Christian occupa-

tion, sometimes Muslim.

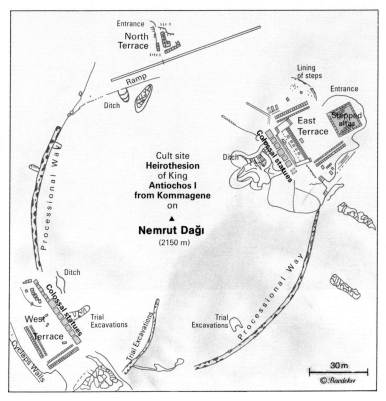

Cult site
Heirothesion
of King
Antiochos I
from Kommagene
on
▲
Nemrut Dağı
(2150 m)

North Terrace

Entrance

Ramp

Ditch

Lining of steps

Entrance

East Terrace

Stepped altar

Colossal statues

Ditch

Processional Way

Processional Way

West Terrace

Colossal statues

Ditch

Trial Excavations

Trial Excavations

Trial Excavations

Cyclops Walls

30 m

© Baedeker

tion (e.g. 700, 860, 1098) and at other times Muslim (10th c. Emirate of Aleppo; 12th c. Seljuks).

Afyon

F 5

West Anatolian highland
Province: Afyon Karahisar
Altitude: 1021m/3350ft
Population: 99,000

Afyon, the provincial capital, lies on the western edge of a large basin in the northern foothills of the Sandıklı Dağ. It is dominated by its citadel, built on top of a steep-sided, 226m/740ft high outcrop of black trachyte. Opium poppies grow in the countryside around the town, making the area one of the world's largest producers – hence also the town's name (meaning "black opium castle"). Cultivation and processing for the pharmaceutical industry are both strictly controlled; penalties for possessing drugs are severe and prove an effective deterrent.

Formerly a halt on the caravan route between the Aegean and Konya, Afyon remains an important road and rail junction to which cereals and

Situation and Characteristics

Afyon: the town and the castle hill

wool are brought for onward shipment. Merchandise produced in the town and surrounding countryside includes carpets and intarsia-work. The springs in the vicinity of Afyon are justly famous, the well-known "Kızılay" mineral water coming from this area for example.

History

Some historians identify Afyon's citadel hill with Hapanuva (mid 2nd c. B.C.), a fortress from which the Hittites held sway over the native Arzawa. Already settled in the Phrygian period when it was called Akroinos, the town was later absorbed into the Pergamene Empire, afterwards becoming a Roman possession and later, in 395, Byzantine. It achieved fame as a result of the battle (in 740) in which Leo III successfully repulsed an Arab incursion. The Seljuks under Alaeddin Keykubad I (1219–36) enlarged both the town and the fort, at that time known as Karahisar-Sahip after the Seljuk vizier Sahip Ata. In the 17th c. when the Ottoman Empire began to collapse, the town was the centre of a pasha revolt.

Sights

Old Town

The old part of the town with its narrow alleyways, interesting old houses and market, which is well worth visiting, clusters around the foot of the citadel hill.

Altıgöz Köprüsü

On the northern edge of the town, near the railway station, the Akar Çayı is spanned by a Seljuk bridge bearing an inscription from the year 1209.

Archaeological Museum

In addition to Islamic craftwork, archaeological finds from the Hittite, Phrygian, Hellenistic and Byzantine periods are on display in eight rooms of the Tas Medrese (İmaret Külliyesi/Gedik Ahmet Paşa Külliyesi; open: Tue.–Sun. 9am–noon, 1.30–5pm).

*Karahisar

Although probably standing on older (Cyclopean) foundations of the Hittite period, the fortress ruins, which now crown the isolated trachyte outcrop

An old-fashioned grain mill near Afyon

high above the centre of the town, date back to Alaeddin Keykubad I (1219–36). Vestiges of a tower (Kiz Kulesi) and remnants of substantial walls, cisterns, a palace and a small mosque (1235) survive. The hilltop also commands a fine view over the town.

The mosque, with a coloured marble portal, is typical of a 15th c. Ottoman stone building. Constructed in 1472 (renovated 1477), with a medrese and baths, it is also known as the Gedik Ahmet Paşa Külliyesi after its founder Mehmet, one of the conquering viziers. The medrese, asymmetric in plan, with an open schoolroom for summer use and an enclosed one for winter, now houses the ethnographic museum.

İmaret Külliyesi

The Wars of Liberation Museum, devoted to the historic Turkish victory at Dumlupınar (1922), occupies the former town hall.

İstiklâl Harbi Müzesi

This mosque (1710; in Kuyulu Cadde) is a shrine of major significance to the Dervish Order, being second only in importance to the Mevlana türbe and monastery at Konya. Many monks of the Order are buried here. Various items belonging to the Order can be seen on display in a small museum.

Mevlevihane Camii

Situated in the upper part of the Old Town, Afyon's Great Mosque (1272) with its plain exterior is one of the early Seljuk "forest mosques", so-called on account of their numerous columns. In this particular case, as many as 40 wooden pillars topped by stalactitic capitals support the decorated timber beams, thatch matting and thick layer of clay making up the flat roof of the nine-aisle prayer hall. The ceiling above the centre aisle is slightly raised and the white marble mihrab has a gilded calligraphic border. The main portal of the mosque is decorated with Seljuk wicker design.

*Ulu Cami

Standing in the main street (Cumhuriyet Meydanı) in the town centre near the park, the Zafer Anıtı Victory Memorial commemorates the Battle of

Zafer Abidesi

131

Dumlupınar (58km/36 miles north-west) where, on September 27th 1922, Kemal Paşa (Atatürk) vanquished the opposing Greek forces.

Surroundings

Acı Göl	This 153sq.km/59sq.mile salt lake (altitude: 836m/2742ft) south of Dazkırı dries out almost completely in summer, a white salt crust forming over it. Known in antiquity as Anaua Limnae, the historian Herodotus records that Xerxes and Alexander the Great both marched their armies along its shores.
Amorion	Remains of buildings and wall towers 80km/50 miles north-east of Afyon, near Emirdağ, are all that now mark the site of Amorion. It was once the key stronghold in the military district of Anatolikon, which the Byzantines established to defend their eastern border against the Arabs. After lengthy sieges and despite brave resistance, this important frontier fortress fell first in 716 to the Omayyad Caliph Süleiman and then again in 838 to Caliph Al-Mutasim. This last onslaught left the town completely destroyed and most of its inhabitants massacred. Captured officers spent seven years imprisoned in Samarra before being put to death for their faith. Since then they have been venerated by the Greek Orthodox Church as the 42 martyrs of Amorion.
Anıtkaya	Anıtkaya (formerly Eğret), a village 30km/19 miles north-west of Afyon, lays claim not just to one but two Seljuk caravanserais. The Eğret Hanı is a triple-aisled hall-like building dating from the 13th c., with a columned portal and interior arcades. The Yenice Köy Hanı, only 5km/3 miles north-west, is thought to be of Early Seljuk origin.
*Arslankaya (Kaya Kabartması)	Situated 40km/25 miles north of Afyon to the east of İhsaniye/Döger, this Phrygian site (not easy to find; guide recommended) was dedicated to the cult of Cybele. There is an altar with a niche and a shrine cut into a huge tuff monolith embellished with a relief. The figure of Cybele is flanked by two large lions (hence the name, meaning "lion-skin") with two sphinxes on the rock gable above.
*Arslantaş	The "Lion Stone", among a cluster of rocks known as "Asarlik" about 3km/2 miles west of Ayazını, is another Phrygian rock shrine. It too features a pair of lions in relief.
*Ayazını	Set in a delightful landscape 30km/20 miles north of Afyon, the village of Ayazını has numerous rock dwellings, also an Early Christian church with cruciform domed rock basilica and tombs dating from antiquity and the Byzantine period; it is very reminiscent of the troglodyte villages of Cappadocia. The well-preserved church with its high central dome has barrel vaulting, an apsis visible from the outside, rows of columns, and a baptistry chapel. Ayazını used to be called Metropolis and was for a time a bishopric.
Başkonutan Tarihi	Two large country areas, scene in 1922 of decisive engagements during the Turkish War of Liberation against the Greeks, are now National Parks (signposted). One lies immediately south of Afyon, the other north of Dumlupınar (53km/33 miles to the west).
Bolvadin	As well as two Ottoman caravanserais, Selcuklu Han and Kurşunlu Han, Bolvadin, 60km/40 mile east of Afyon, has a bridge built by Sinan (Kırkgöz Köprüsü), the Alaca Fountain, the Esireddin Ebheri Türbe, the Rüstempaşa Camii which are well worth a visit, and the Rüstempaşa Hanı (Ottoman caravanserai). Formerly a caravan halt, Bolvadin (Byzantine "Polybotum") was fortified against the Seljuks in the 12th c. though nothing from that period now survives.
Çay	The town of Çay occupies a verdant location on the south-east edge of the Afyon Ovası not far from Eber Gölü (967m/3173ft). Known in ancient times

as Julia Ipsus, it was here in 301 B.C. that the Macedonian Antigonus was killed in a power struggle between the diodochi. Outside the town there is an old bridge with 40 arches. Also worth seeing is the Seljuk Tas Camii (1278) with its fountain, richly ornamented portal and ruins of a domed medrese (13th c. tiles). Of the very neglected caravanserai from the same period only the hall and portal have survived.

Dinar, 120km/75 miles south of Afyon, lies at the foot of Samsun Dağ (to the north) and Ak Dağ (to the south), at the convergence of several roads. The principal town of its area, it is successor to the ancient Keleanai and the Hellenistic Apameia Kibotos, founded by Antiochus II Soter of Syria. Apameia Castle used to stand above Dinar on the site of the ancient settlement of Kelenai (remains of a theatre). Following the Battle of Magnesia (Manisa) in 190 B.C. Antiochus the Great took refuge in the Seleucid palace here. In Roman times Apameia was the most important trading centre east of Ephesus and was a bishopric until taken by the Seljuks in 1070. Kibotos (= "tub"), the second and unofficial part of its name, is believed to derive from Noah's Ark which, according to a somewhat fanciful Jewish tradition – there was a large Jewish community here – came to rest on this spot. Owing to the frequency of earthquakes (north-west edge of the Isparta arc) the town itself is devoid of historic monuments. There is much of interest to be seen in the surrounding countryside however (guide recommended).

Dinar

Not far from Dinar rise several sources of the Büyük Menderes (Great Maeander River), tributaries of which include the Orgas (flowing north), Obrimas (flowing south) and Marsyas. Between the Samsun-Ak Dağ and the Kır-Kızkuyu Dağ, two mountain ranges east of the town, stretches an extensive polje (depression), the Dombay Ovası, harbouring the very swampy Çapalı Gölü (ancient: Aulokrene reed lake). The basin traps water from a number of surface streams and large karst springs (Kavak Pınarı, Pınarbaşı), which then disappears into a karst swallow hole (ponor) at the foot of Akdağ on the western edge of the swamp before emerging again on the far (west) side of the uplands in the guise of sources of the Maeander. The river has three principal sources at the western foot of the Samsun-Ak Dağları: the southern source near Bülüç Alanı, the main source on the eastern outskirts of Dinar, and the northern source "Kapı Pınarı" 20km/12 miles north-west near Gökgöl which are all karst springs emitting substantial volumes of water, most of it drawn from the mountainous hinterland to the east via the karst drainage systems.

Sources of the Maeander

Also known as Kybele Kapıkaya or Büyük Kapıkaya, this Phrygian monument on open ground north-east of Liyen (40km/25 miles north of Afyon) is again of interest – a rock niche with a surround in geometric design (Maeander relief) and a carved figure of Cybele.

*Kapıkaya

One of the largest freshwater swamps in Turkey, covering an area of some 4100ha/10,000 acres, is found about 20km/12 miles south-west of Çay to the east of the Dinar/Karadilli road. Lying in a depression at an altitude of 1008m/3300ft, the surface of the swamp is almost completely covered with a carpet of reeds. Water-lilies grow where there is open water and myriads of frogs provide the staple diet for numerous herons and storks. Birds of prey are much in evidence, as are other water fowl including ducks (white-eyed pochard and white-headed duck), mute swans and ruddy shelduck (the latter breed in the Sultan Dağları).

Karamık swamps
Karamık
Bataklığı

Known in earlier days as İshaklı, Sultandağ (about 65km/40 miles east of Afyon) is situated in the northern foothills of the Sultan Dağ, on the old caravan route from Afyon to Konya. Not far away lies the Akşehir Gölü, part swamp, part freshwater lake teeming with fish. In the south of the town, in the courtyard of a two-storeyed mosque on the main street (eight-part cross vault, stalactitic dome), are the remains of a caravanserai, the İshaklı Han (or Sahibata Hanı; five-bay hall, elegantly articulated court portal) built

Sultandağ

in 1249/50 by the renowned master builder Ship Ata (Fahrettin Ali Ben Husain). The inner courtyard contains two double bowers with twin-bayed barrel vaulted arcades.

Usak

Extending south-west from the upper valley of the Gediz Çayi is a gently undulating upland region known as the Uşak highlands (altitude around 1200m/3900ft). The name derives from the town of Uşak (population: 105,000), the provincial capital and busy commercial centre of what is predominantly an agricultural region. Uşak itself is attractively situated astride a small river, at the foot of Elma Daği (Apple Mountain, 1805m/5924ft, north-east of the town). Well-known in the 16th and 17th centuries for its hand-woven carpets, traditional carpet manufacture is still important although more and more production is becoming factory rather than craftsman based.

In the section of the highlands west of Uşak between Gediz and the Gediz fault north of Alaşehir, especially around the small town of Kula (70km/43 miles west), the flat upland surface is overlaid with relatively young volcanic basalt and tuff eruptions. In some places the volcanic features – craters, cinder cones, lava streams, etc. – remain almost as if new. This is the Katakekaumene (Burnt Country) of the ancients. The uplands south and east of Uşak, through which the valley of the Banaz Çayi carves a swathe 30m/98ft deep, terminate abruptly in cliffs which meet almost at a right angle above the upper Maeander river.

Uşak itself, said to be of Seljuk origin, almost certainly stands on the site of the ancient, though not very important, Pelta. The present town, dominated by a dilapidated Byzantine citadel (Eucarpia), has few relics of the past, having been largely rebuilt in the 18th c. after a fire.

Ağri

See Ararat

Ahlat   S 5

East Anatolia (Lake Van)   See warning page 7
Province: Bitlis
Altitude: 1740m/5710ft
Population: 11,000

Situation and
Characteristics

Ahlat, centre of its district, lies about 70km/43 miles north-east of Bitlis on the western shore of Lake Van. It is a green sprawling place, parts of which still retain a village-like character. Reminders of the town's long history, some of them spectacular, are found everywhere. The area was very probably settled by about 900 B.C. by the Urartians. The Parthians then established a capital here, known as Hilyat in Roman sources and later as Chlat or Kelath to the Armenians. The Arabs called the town the Muslim enclave of the Kassite emirs of Malazgirt within otherwise Christian Armenia when they conquered it in the 7th c.

Under Sökman Arman, emir of the Azerbaijan ruler Kudbeddin Ismail, Ahlat became from about 1100 until 1207 capital of the principality of Armanshahlar, its power soon extending as far as Muş and Khoy. The title "Shah i-Arman" was then adopted by the Kurdish Ayyubids who arrived on the scene in 1209. Evliya Çelebi records that an earthquake in the 13th c. resulted in some 12,000 of the 300,000 inhabitants of the city emigrating to Egypt. Under Süleiman the Magnificent renewed building took place to the north of the site of the old village of Erkizan.

Sights

*Ahlat Kalesi

The one-time fortress situated directly on Lake Van has two sets of fortifications, inner and outer – the former (iç kale) smaller and fort-like, the latter, still partly inhabited, larger and more like a walled town. According to an inscription on the east gate of the ramparts, which were made even stronger by their round and square towers, construction began in 1554 under Süleiman and was completed under Selim II in 1568. Below the inner fort, which has its own ring wall, in the still inhabited part of the Old Town, are the remains of a bath house and two mosques. The more southerly of the two, the İskender Paşa Çamii, a domed mosque built between 1564 and 1570, is named after its founder, the then governor of the town. The Kadi Mahmut Çamii, also domed, standing a little to the north, was built in 1597.

The new museum building at the cemetery houses a small ethnographic collection and some Urartian finds from the 1st millennium B.C.

Ahlat Müzesi

Beyond the cemetery at the western exit of the old village stands the Bayındır Bey Türbesi, a mausoleum in front of a little mosque, its top resembling a monopteros with columns decorated with stalactitic capitals beneath a conical roof. According to the inscription the mausoleum was erected in 1491/92 for the Akkoyunlu governor, the Emir Bayındır of Roha and his son.

**Tombs

To the west outside the cemetery are the twelve-sided Erzen Hatun Türbe (1397; elegantly ornamented stonework) and the remains of the rectangular Şeyh Necmeddin Türbesi dating from the pre-Mongol period (1222). Further west again is the poorly preserved Hasan Padişa Türbesi (1275). The two-storey, 19m/62ft high Ulu Kümbet mausoleum south-west of the cemetery has a stalactitic frieze and inscribed band.

The angled roof of the Emir Ali Kümbeti, a tomb with a rather heavy-looking base beside a path to the west of the İki Türbe, rests on a low, ruff-like collar of masonry above pointed arches.

On the eastern edge of the most ancient of Ahlat's rural settlements, north of the track leading into the Old Town, two more tombs stand close together by the roadside. One, 14m/46ft high, originally built in 1279 for

Cemetery, with richly decorated Mihrab tombstones

Hasan Takın, was used for a second time in 1729 by Hasan Timor. The other, 12m/39ft high, was constructed in 1281 for the Emir Buğatay Ağa, whose wife Şirin Hatun was also interred there.

A vast cemetery with a multitude of impressive tombs with mihrabs, most dating from the 17th and 18th centuries, extends north-west of the Old Town. Each tomb bears rich ornamentation showing Armenian influence. Some of the red tuff sarcophagi on the west side of the cemetery, with prism lids and no gravestones, are said to date from the 12th c.; others, of grey tuff with pointed lids, in the north-east section of the grounds, also go back to the 11th/12th c. A number of the tombs with upright gravestones date from the 12th to 16th centuries.

Surroundings

Adilcevaz

The district town of Adilcevaz with its Byzantine-Seljuk fortress close to the lake (few remains), occupies the site of an Old Armenian settlement called Ardzgui 90km/60 miles north-east of Bitlis on the western shore of Lake Van. The presence of cuneiform inscriptions and the discovery of stones with Urartian carvings used in the construction of the castle (now on display in museums in Van and Ankara as well as in one of Adilcevaz's schools) strongly suggests that there was also a Urartian stronghold on this spot. The finding of a necropolis of the period only 300m/330yd from the lakeside lends additional support.

*Kefkalesi

In the hills above Adilcevaz, about 10km/6 miles further north, are the ruins of a Urartian town. Its lofty situation means that the final lap of the journey must be made on foot (with a guide, about half an hour). Scattered on a sizeable plateau at an altitude of 2200m/7220ft, the ruins date from the time of Rusa II (7th c. B.C.); they include remains of town defences made from massive blocks of stone, a fortress with a bastion, storerooms containing huge storage jars, and a vast 30-roomed palace. The most typically Urartian features are the corner projections on the rough-hewn stone blocks, partially decorated with reliefs. Many scholars identify this site with Qallania where, in 714 B.C. during the Eighth Campaign, Sargon II halted with his Assyrian troops. Further to the north-east, among the foothills of Süphan Dağ, there are traces of another Urartian building with Cyclopean walls (guide essential).

Below the ruins of the citadel stand the remnants of an 8th/9th c. Armenian monastery church known as "The Wonder of Ardzgui".

*Nemrut Dağı

At the western end of the lake, between Ahlat and Tatvan, towers the 2935m/9632ft volcanic cone of Nemrut Dağı. The huge summit caldera (diameter 7.5–8.5km/4½–5¼ miles; mean altitude 2300m/7550ft) is partially occupied by a freshwater lake (Nemrut Gölü up to 150m/490ft deep in places. There is still some volcanic activity at the eastern end of the caldera; as well as several minor lakes, some of which are temporary in nature, fresh tuff and cinder cones and young lava flows with miniature craters are very much in evidence. To the north, situated east of the main lake, is a smaller lake (İli Göl), 500m/550yd in diameter and 7–8m/23–26ft deep, where there are hot springs with temperatures up to 80°C/176°F. South-east of it and a little higher up are some sulphur vents (fumaroles, solfataras). The sides of the caldera rise wall-like in places to heights of more than 2800m/9190ft. In earlier days Nemrut Dağı was apparently well wooded though today it is virtually denuded of trees. Minibus trips are run from Ahlat and Tatvan and it is possible to go right down into the crater.

*Süphan Dağı

The ascent of the 4058m/13,318ft summit of this even more massive volcano, the fourth highest mountain in Turkey, takes two days and is best attempted between July and September. The approach from Adilcevaz (guide) is from the east via Aydınlar Köyü and Sekerpınarı Yaylası (half-way camp, 6–7 hours to the top). The huge main cone consists principally of andesite and obsidian. A lava plug, one kilometre in diameter rising steeply from the floor of the 1.5km/1 mile wide caldera, forms the actual summit cone. Above 3000m/9800ft cirques, small glaciers and snow fields are encountered, especially in the caldera.

Akhisar

See İzmir

Aksaray   K 5

Central Anatolia (Tuz-Gölü basin)
Province: Aksaray
Altitude: 980m/3216ft
Population: 92,000

This medium-sized town in its horticultural oasis has recently become a provincial capital. Situated on the banks of the Melendiz Suyu, below the step-fault marking the eastern edge of the Tuz-Gölü basin, Aksaray is dominated by the great volcanic pyramid and twin peaks of Hasan Dağ (Büyük Hasan Dağ 3268m/10,725ft, Küçük Hasan Dağ 3069m/10,072ft) and the bulky volcanic massif of Melendiz Dağ (2963m/9725ft). With the famous Cappadocian tuff cone region only a short distance away, Aksaray has attracted little attention, a situation which is now changing due to the increasing importance of its automotive industry.

Situation and Importance

In antiquity the town was called Garsaura. Many historians equate it with the even more ancient oriental town of Kursaura whose ruler is believed to have been a party to an alliance in the 3rd millennium B.C. against the Accadian King Naramsis. Following rebuilding the town was renamed Archelais by the Cappadocian King Archelaos. It came to enjoy considerable status as a frontier fortress against Lycaonia and a crossroads between Ephesus and the middle reaches of the Euphrates on the one hand and Ankara and Tyana (near Niğde) on the other.

History

During the Rum Sultanate (from the 11th c.) the Seljuk Sultan Kiliç Arslan II (1156–88) built a castle here, where Henry the Lion was fêted while returning home from a pilgrimage. Among the gifts lavished upon him were 30 magnificent horses with silver bridles (specially picked from among the 1800 in the Sultan's stables), six dromedaries, two leopards and six tents. In the 13th c. the town fell to the Mongols before passing in the 14th c. to the Karamanlidhes. The Ottomans resettled part of the population in İstanbul, hence that city's Aksaray district.

Sights

The İbrahim Kadıroğlu Medresesi Koranic school built by the Seljuks in the 12th/13th c. was restored in the mid 15th c. by the Karamanlidhes. A ruined Seljuk fortress dominates the town. The Kızıl Minare minaret (also called Eğri Minare), decorated with fine tiles, likewise dates from the Seljuk period. Unfortunately its mosque, the Kiliç Arslan II Mosque, has not survived. The stone-vaulted Ulu Cami in the town centre, built by the Karamanlidhes between 1433 and 1435, does however boast an exceptionally fine carved Seljuk staircase pulpit from the Kiliç Arslan II Mosque. The Zinciriye Medresesi Koranic school (with a beautiful portal), built by the local Karamanlis dynasty between 1336 and 1345, houses a small museum.

Surroundings

According to an inscription this impressive caravanserai with seven-sided corner towers, about 15km/9 miles east of Aksaray on the old caravan route

*Aızıkarahan

Aksaray

The Zinciriye Koran school houses an archaeological museum

from Konya to Kayseri, was built between 1231 and 1238 during the reign of Alaeddin Keykubad I. Also known as the Hoca Mesut Kervansarai it is one of three exceptionally well preserved Seljuk halts between Sivas and Konya. The arcaded courtyard has a small mosque (mesçid) in the middle. At right-angles to the huge entrance gate stands a vast hall with half a dozen transept-like bays either side of a central area. Daylight floods in through a dome over the penultimate "crossing". Both the main entrance and the hall portal are richly ornamented.

Akhisar

A Byzantine fort on top of a steep cliff stands guard over the village of Akhisar about 12km/7½ miles south-east of Aksaray. Of the various rock-cut churches in the neighbourhood, the 10th–11th c. Çanli Kilise (Bell Tower Church, several phases of construction), 7km/4 miles or so east of the village, gives the best idea of how the wall-paintings must once have looked. It is a Byzantine church with a two-storeyed narthex and three apses arranged around a central chamber.

°Belisırma

The valley-gorge of the Melendiz Suyu river between Ihlara and Selimiye takes its name from ancient Peristrema (Belisırma as it now is). With the exception of the Açikel Ağa Kilisesi (Church of Our Lord with the Open Hand), the numerous churches in and around the village are decorated with post-iconoclastic paintings (10th c. onwards). They include the Ala Kilise (White Church, superb façade), the Bahattin Samanlığı Kilisesi (Bahattin's Church with a Granary, scenes in dark colours of the Life of Christ), the Direkli Kilise (Columned Church, pictures of saints and martyrs), the Karagedikli Kilise (trachyte and brick Church of the Black Collar, remains of frescos) and the later Kırkdamaltı Kilise (Church under 40 Roofs/St George's Church, endowed between 1283 and 1295 by the Emir Basileios and his wife). The latter church is proof that even towards the end of the 13th c. there was still a Christian community here, though by then the area was part of the Seljuk Sultanate of Konya. In the 19th c. more churches were hollowed out of the cliffs by the Greeks.

138

In the steep rock walls of Peristrema Valley cave churches have been hewn

Up until 1921/22 there remained a considerable Greek minority in Gelveri, a village also known as Sivrihisar Geçidi (Sivrihisar Pass). As a result several well preserved churches have survived. One of them, below a cliff honeycombed with rock sanctuaries, was dedicated to Saint Gregory of Nazianz, reputedly born here in 328. It was converted to a mosque in 1896. Enthroned on a rock pyramid south-west of the village is a handsome monastery, the Yüksek Kilise (High Church).

Gelveri

South of the village of Helvadere (Valley of Turkish Honey), at the northern foot of Hasan Dağ about 45km/28 miles south-east of Aksaray, the ruins of a monastery lie hidden in a volcanic crater, access to which is via a narrow cleft in the rock. Known as "Viranşehir" (Destroyed City), there are other remains also, including those of a Byzantine fortress and two fine churches – the Kara Kilise (Black Church), a single-aisled basilica, and the cruciform Kemerli Kilise (Arcaded Church) constructed out of uniform blocks of trachyte.

Helvadere

A large number of typical Cappadocian-style rock-cut churches are found grouped around the village of Ihlara at the southern end of the Peristrema gorge. Most were decorated before the iconoclastic period (8th and 9th centuries) and, when later paintings are also taken into account, yield an excellent insight into the development of regional Cappadocian church art. The Ağaç Altı Kilise (Church under the Tree), the Eğri Tas Kilise (Church with the Crooked Stone, scenes of Jesus's youth), the Kokar Kilise (Fragrant Church, scenes from the life of Christ), the Pürenli Seki Kilise (Church with a Terrace) and the Yilanlı Kilise (Snake Church, with scenes of Hell) are all examples of this style. The Sümbülü Kilise (Hyacinth Church) provides a contrast with some outstanding Empire-style paintings in the south aisle and a superb façade the articulation of which shows Persian influence.

*Ihlara

The village of Mamasun nestles picturesquely in a narrow defile some 20km/12½ miles east of Aksaray. The tuff cliffs harbour several monasteries

Mamasun

hewn in the rock. Köy Ensesi Kilisesi (Village End Church), in the shape of a Greek cross, has carved choir screens and altar as well as fragments of late 10th c. frescos depicting the Twelve Apostles and the Archangels Michael and Gabriel. The village takes its name from a Caesarean (Kayseri) shepherd called Mames whose bones are preserved in the village mosque. He allegedly suffered a martyr's death after converting to Islam.

Aksaray

Selimiye

Byzantine Cave Churches in the Peristrema Valley

SELECTION
1 Koyunağlu Kilise
2 Güvercinlik Davullu K.
3 Ala K.
4 Eski Baca K.
5 Direkli K.
6 Bahattin Samanlığı
7 St. Georg
8 Bezir Ana K.
9 Karagedik K.

Yaprak Hisar

Belisırma

500 m
© Baedeker

10 Yılanlı Kilise
11 Sümbülü K.
12 Ağac Altı K.
13 Karanlık Kale K.
14 Pürenli Seki K.
15 Eğri Taş K.
16 Kokar K.
17 Kemer K.
18 St. Michael

Halvadere

Ihlara

Güzelyurt

**Peristrema Valley

Below Hasan Dağ, between the villages of Selimiye and Ihlara about 40km/25 miles south-east of Aksaray, the exceptionally lovely gorge of the Melendiz Suyu, bordered by willows, poplars and cypresses, cuts deep into the Cappadocian tuff. The steep cliffs on either side are a warren of Byzantine rock-cut monasteries and churches, 50 or so in all, access being on foot via hill paths from Ihlara or Belisırma (visitors are advised to hire a local guide.)

Two styles of decoration can be distinguished. The Byzantine Empire style predominates in the churches around Belisırma; in those nearer Ihlara the distinctive local Cappadocian-style frescos display Persian and Syrian influence.

**Sultanhanı

It was in about 1229 that Sultan Alaeddin Keykubad I had this huge caravanserai built on the main route between the capital Konya and the trade and administrative centre of Kayseri to the east. The 121m/132yd long fortified complex, strengthened by its 24 marble towers, covers an area of 4866sq.m/52,377sq.ft. In 1254 the caravanserai was badly damaged by fire, being restored between 1276 and 1278 by Keyhusrev III, then a puppet of the Mongol governor (Perwâne). More repairs were needed in the early 14th c. during the reign of the Seljuk Sultan Ma'sûd of Rum.

The complex is entered through an impressive marble gateway, 13m/43ft high and 11m/36ft wide, richly decorated with ornate designs (tendrils, whicker, rosettes, stalactites and arabesques). An inscription above the gate warns those who enter that "Allah is almighty". The thick walls filled with layers of mortar and rubble are typical of Early Seljuk ashlar building. The summer court, in the centre of which stands a pavilion mosque with twin staircases, measures 51m/167ft × 24m/79ft, not including the surrounding living quarters and arcades. The nine-bay winter hall with its magnificent, highly ornate portal and open octagonal drum with tent-roof over the central bay, measures 55m/180ft × 37m/121ft.

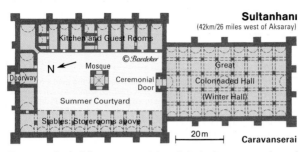

Sultanhanı
(42km/26 miles west of Aksaray)

© *Baedeker*

Kitchen and Guest Rooms

N

Mosque

Doorway

Ceremonial Door

Great Colonnaded Hall

(Winter Hall)

Summer Courtyard

Stables: Storerooms above

20 m

Caravanserai

The reason for building so many of these halts in the steppe regions of Anatolia was that, once away from areas of settlement, the wealthy merchants and their caravans on the long distance trade routes ran the gauntlet of predatory nomads. The caravanserais were therefore mostly bastion-like in design and equipped with a stout entrance gate which could be firmly secured. They were very much more than just temporary shelters for the night, with stabling, guest rooms, mosques, cooking facilities and baths; they were also self-contained settlements with a population of watchmen/guards, craftsmen (smiths, saddlers), grooms, labourers, butchers, bakers, cooks and kitchen staff, doctors and others. At the same time they were depots for merchandise and had their own marts with little shops. Travellers were allowed to stay for three days without charge. The cost of maintaining these hostelries was in part borne by the sultan in the interests of encouraging trade and in part, under the Seljuks, by levying an annual tax on every merchant and craftsman in the empire.

Aksaray: Entrance doorway . . .   *. . . and mosque of the caravanserai*

Akşehir   G 5

West Anatolian highland
Province: Konya
Altitude: 998m/3275ft
Population: 52,000

Situation and Importance

Situated at the mouth of a high-lying valley beneath the peaks of Sultan Dağı, this busy town, the principal one of its district, stands a short distance south of Akşehir Gölü on the northern edge of the Isaurian-Pisidian lake district, where the West Taurus mountains give way inland to the Inner Anatolian steppes. The town enjoys a reputation for its carpets and leather goods and was quite important in earlier days as a halt on the long distance route from Konya to İstanbul.

History

Akşehir, founded in the 3rd c. B.C. as Philomelion by the Macedonian prince Philomelos, was an important Phrygian town which later passed to Pisidia under Diocletian. It was here in 51 B.C. that Cicero meted out justice to the mutinous Roman cohorts and where, in 1403, Bayazit I, though later buried in Bursa, died a prisoner of the Mongols following his defeat by Tamerlane at the Battle of Ankara in 1402. For a long time the Mongols kept their notable prisoner – scourge of the East and the man who destroyed the Byzantine army at Nikopolis, holding numerous Byzantine noblemen captive in Bursa – confined in a cage-like litter in which they transported him about with their army. In 1190, while on the Third Crusade, the Emperor Friedrich I (Barbarossa) journeyed across country from Dinar to Akşehir, passing north of Lake Eğridir. Enduring great hardship he made his way to Ladik, Konya, Karaman and then Silifke where he drowned in the Göksu Nehri.
Nasrettin Hoca (see Famous People) the Turkish Eulenspiegel, born in about 1208, spent his working life in Akşehir, dying there in 1284/85.

Akşehir and Eber Gölü

The inland drainage system around Akşehir feeds twin lakes, Eber Gölü and Akşehir Gölü, the two being separated by a low sill and connected by a canal-like channel. When water levels rise, the slightly more elevated Eber Gölü overflows into the lower-lying Akşehir Gölü. With their extensive reed beds almost completely covering Eber Gölü and their abundance of nutrients, both provide ideal habitats for large numbers of reptiles, amphibians and birds.

Sights

*Nasrettin Hoca Türbesi

On the southern edge of the Old Town stands the türbe of the legendary Turkish humorist Nasrettin Hoca, a teacher at the Koranic school, who lived in Akşehir for more than 50 years until his death. A plaque above his grave in the lovingly tended columned pavilion (restored in 1905) declares "Here lies not a man but a philosophy!" Believed to have been born in 1208 in Horto near Sivrihisar, son of the Imam Abdullah, Hoca is the acknowledged doyen of Turkish folk humour. A scholar with a huge turban and whiter-than-white beard, he has achieved immortality through more than 500 anecdotes. With his sharp wit and subtle moral sense he stimulated his fellows to laugh and to ponder on every conceivable subject, even death. It seems wholly in keeping that, while the gate to the türbe is secured with a strong lock, the iron railings at the sides are missing and the tomb therefore quite open.

Seyğit Mahmut Hayrani Türbesi

Also in the southern part of the town is the tomb of the mystic Seyğit Mahmut. The octagonal mausoleum, built in 1224, was altered in 1409/10. Near-by is a small prayer mosque constructed from ancient stone.

Taş Medrese

The Koranic school, erected in 1216 by Sahib Ata using materials of more ancient origin, has an interesting gateway, two Byzantine colonnades in the inner courtyard and a Seljuk minaret of brick and fragments of tiles. Conversion of the building to a museum began in about 1986.

Surroundings

The site of the ancient town of Antiochia (Antiocheia) lies some 35km/ 22 miles south-west of Akşehir near Yalvaç, on the border between Pisidia and Phrygia. It is located above the valley of the Yalvaçbeli Deresi while behind it, to the north-east, rises the 2531m/8306ft high Sultan Dağları. "Pisidiae" (or "ad Pisidium") was added to its name in ancient times to distinguish it from other Antiochs in Asia Minor.

Antiochia in Pisidia (Yalvaç)

According to the Greek geographer Strabo Antiochia was founded by colonists from Magnesia (on the lower Maeander, not far from Germencik, near Aydın). In fact it is more likely to have been founded by one of the diadochi, either Seleukos I Nikator (312–280 b.c.) or his son Antiochus I Soter (280–261 b.c.), colonists brought from Magnesia to settle the town. Following the victory of the Roman general Scipio over the Seleucid Antiochus the Great (222–187 b.c.) at the Battle of Magnesia on Sypilos (Manisa) in 190/89 b.c., Antiochia temporarily gained independence, later being absorbed into the Roman Empire in 25 b.c. The cult of the Pisidian god Men Askaenos is known to have flourished in Antiochia early in its history, centred on a large priestly sanctuary where great numbers of unfortunates were kept as temple slaves (hierodules). Presided over by a eunuch priest the cult was notorious for its horrific cruelties and dissipation. Both St Paul and St Barnabas preached in Antiochia while on the first of their missionary journeys through Asia Minor. They succeeded in making converts among the town's large Jewish population, from whom they were eventually forced to flee. Antiochia grew to be the principal town in northern Pisidia, the seat of a metropolitan, producing by the 6th c. no less than thirteen distinguished bishops. The reasons for its eventual decline still remain obscure. Some historians suggest it was destroyed by the Arabs in the 8th c. Alternatively a combination of factors such as earthquakes, war and economic difficulties may have brought about its downfall. Highly prosperous in its heyday, the city's remains are still imposing.

During excavations here in 1912 the British archaeologist W. M. Ramsay discovered the "Monumentum Antiochenum", another copy of the Latin inscription known as the Testament of Augustus preserved in the "Monumentum Ancyranum" (see Ankara).

Little of note survives from the acropolis apart from the remains of the propylaeum, the monumental entranceway dating from the time of Augustus and leading to Augustus Square. It was in the propylaeum that the Testament of Augustus was found in 1912 (see above). On the east side of the square, strikingly positioned against a backdrop of vertical cliffs, are twin-storeyed colonnades with Ionic and Doric columns. In the centre stands the Temple of Augustus.

Acropolis Propylaeum

This splendid temple, of which significant remains can still be seen, is believed to stand on ground once occupied by a Men cult site.

Temple of Augustus

To the west and north-west of the square in front of the propylaeum (Tiberius Square) are two ruined Byzantine churches, one of which, a basilica, is believed to be the oldest Christian church in Asia Minor. On the east side are the remains of a theatre, marble seats from which were removed in about 1836 to provide building materials for houses in Yalvaç.

Tiberius Square

The largest and most interesting surviving structure is the aqueduct. Supported on several mighty arches it carried water from the Sultan Dağları across a deep valley to the high ground behind the town for storage in a great cistern in the upper town.

Aqueduct

The upper town, which affords some fine views, was once encircled by strong walls. Their course is still easily followed though the walls themselves are mostly in disrepair.

Town walls

Alanya

G/H 7

South coast (Eastern Mediterranean)
Province: Antalya
Altitude: 0–120m/0–395ft
Population: 30,000

Situation and
** Characteristics

Alanya (previously Alaja) lies on the east side of the Gulf of Antalya below a rocky promontory of marble crowned by a Seljuk castle. Away from the coast the land rises almost without interruption to the summit of Ak Daǧı (2647m/8685ft), a bare karstic peak forming part of the Taurus range. With its delightful setting and subtropical climate – dry summers and very mild winters – Alanya is popular for both winter holidays and as a seaside resort. A fine beach offers some of the best bathing in Turkey. In addition to this there is the attraction of the town's Seljuk architecture.

History

Known in antiquity as Korakesion (Coracesium), Alanya was a Cilician frontier fortress on the border with Pamphylia. In the 2nd c. B.C. Diodoros Tryphona, a pirate chief, erected a fortress on the hill; this stood until destroyed by Pompey in the final stages of his campaign against the Mediterranean pirates. Passing into Roman hands the town was later given by Antony to Cleopatra. It became a place of real consequence only after coming under Seljuk rule in 1221. Alaeddin Keykubad constructed a great stronghold on the promontory (completed in 1231) and transformed the town into an important naval base.

Sights

Old Town

Alanya's somewhat rambling Old Town dating from Seljuk and Ottoman times lies sandwiched between the lower and middle (south) walls of the

Panorama of Alanya from the castle hill

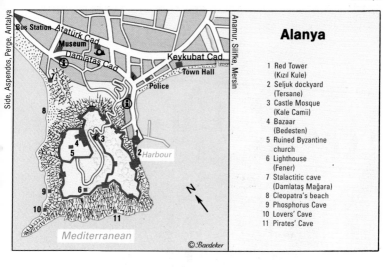

Alanya

1 Red Tower
  (Kızıl Kule)
2 Seljuk dockyard
  (Tersane)
3 Castle Mosque
  (Kale Camii)
4 Bazaar
  (Bedesten)
5 Ruined Byzantine
  church
6 Lighthouse
  (Fener)
7 Stalactitic cave
  (Damlataş Mağara)
8 Cleopatra's beach
9 Phosphorus Cave
10 Lovers' Cave
11 Pirates' Cave

© Baedeker

fortress on the eastern slopes of the promontory. The fortress itself stands
on even more ancient foundations. The more modern town extends along
the shore north-east of the promontory, ending among fruit orchards.

A road winding its way through the Old Town climbs the citadel hill
(250m/820ft) to the courtyard of the upper fortress, at the north end of
which stands the castle mosque (Kale Camii). In the same courtyard are a
ruined cruciform Byzantine church and, at the southern end, a lighthouse
erected in 1720. Adjoining the west wall is the citadel proper, in a good state
of repair. It affords superb panoramic views over the Mediterranean coastal plain, taking in the scattered houses of Alanya, the fruit orchards and the
Ak Dağı Massif.

Citadel hill
*View

Another road runs south along the shore of the promontory to the Kızıl Kule
(Red Tower; restored in 1948), a 46m/150ft high octagonal structure with
sides 12.5m/40ft in length. The massive corner bastion was built for Alaeddin Keykubad in 1225 by the Aleppo architect Ebu Ali, who was also
responsible for the castle at Sinop. The purpose of the tower was to protect
the Seljuk dockyard immediately to the south.

Red Tower

The Seljuk dockyard, quarried out of the rock in about 1227 and recently
restored, has five vaulted galleries 42.5m/140ft long and 7.7m/25ft wide
with linking arched entrances. Here Alaeddin Keykubad built the warships
which enabled him to extend his power across the eastern Mediterranean.
Timber for the ships came from the Taurus mountains, abundantly wooded
at that time. The dockyards remained in use until about 1950.

Seljuk dockyard

In 1948 workmen quarrying at the foot of the promontory on its north-west
side, at the end of the west beach, discovered the Damlataş Cave containing huge stalagmites nearly 15m/50ft high (damlataş = "limestone
formation"). Inside the cave the temperature remains a constant 22°C/72°F
summer and winter. The radioactivity and high carbon dioxide content of
the atmosphere (five times higher than in the open air) make the cave
popular with local people suffering from asthma or bronchitis.

Stalactitic
cave

A short distance north of the cave entrance there is a small archaeological
and ethnographic museum, opened in 1967.

Museum

145

Alanya

Ruins of a Byzantine church in the castle courtyard

Surroundings

Syedra

On the shores of a small bay about 35km/22 miles from Alanya lie the ruins of ancient Syedra. Remnants of the lower town (baths, necropolis, parts of walls) can be seen close to the road and on the adjoining hillside while, higher up and a little to the north-east, the site of the acropolis overlooks the Sedir Çayi from the top of steep rocky cliffs. More ruins are found at Belen/Demirtaş (Yenidamlar).

Gazipaşa
(Selinus)

Some 50km/30 miles south-east of Alanya on the coast road along the "Turkish Riviera" is the little town of Gazipaşa. The town itself stands about 3km/2 miles inland from the sea, on an alluvial plain formed by a number of streams flowing into the Mediterranean at this point. Here the headland known to the ancients as Cape Selindi falls steeply to the sea in almost vertical cliffs, its summit crowned by a ruined castle. In antiquity this was the site of the Phoenician town of Selinús (sela = "cliff"). In A.D. 117 the Emperor Trajan died here while returning from his Parthian campaign. For a period thereafter the town was known as Traianopolis.

Antiocheia
ad Cragum

The ruins of this ancient town are situated about 65km/40 miles east of Alanya, off the coast road near the village of Güney. The Roman town, known in antiquity as Cragus, stood high above the cliff which drops sharply to the sea. Quite substantial remains survive from the acropolis and there are more ruins on the slope down to the harbour. These include the agora (colonnade) and other remnants of the lower town. They are overlooked by a medieval castle.

*Anamur

Continuing east the coast road makes its way towards Cape Anamur, the most southerly point of Asia Minor, known in antiquity as Anamurion (remains of fortifications, theatres, baths, necropolises). Anamur (pop. 29,000) lies on the east side of the cape, at the foot of the Taurus mountains about 4km/2½ miles upstream from the mouth of the Sultan Suyu. 7km/4½ miles further on, beyond the turn-off to Ermenek, Anamur Castle (Anamur Kalesi, Mamure Kalesi), makes an imposing sight on a headland jutting into the sea. The fortress was one of the most notorious and feared of corsair strongholds in the early Middle Ages and was subsequently enlarged and strengthened by the Crusaders. It is encircled by formidable walls, with 36 round or square towers mostly excellently preserved, and parapet walks reached by staircases inside the walls. The main entrance to the castle, which has three courts or wards, is through a tower on the west side. (Arabic inscription.)

Amasya   L 3

Central South Pontus (Black Sea)
Province: Amasya
Altitude: 450m/1477ft
Population: 56,000

The provincial capital of Amasya nestles picturesquely in the narrow transverse valley of the Yeşilırmak (the ancient Iris) at the southern edge of the Pontus Mountains. Amasya's impressive setting is best appreciated from the vantage point of the fortress, the remains of which survive enthroned above the town. There are two distinct parts to Old Amasya. North of the river lies the earlier once walled Old Town, still with a large number of old dwelling houses. South of the river is an area which, though less ancient, nevertheless has many historic buildings both religious and secular. Despite the damage wrought by severe earthquakes in 1734, 1825 and 1935, and by a fire in 1915, Amasya remains one of the most rewarding towns in Turkey to visit. The surrounding countryside is also famed for its wealth of fruit trees and its mulberry plantations (silk manufacture).
Situation and *Importance

From its source on the north-western slopes of the 2812m/9229ft Köse Dağı, the Yeşilırmak (Green) river winds its way for a total of 520km/323 miles to the Black Sea. It begins by flowing westwards through a series of depressions running parallel to the main North Anatolian fault (the 31sq.km/12sq.mile Almuş Baraji and the Tokat and Turhal basins). Turning north it next cuts through the Buzluk Dağ by means of a narrow transverse valley into the Amasya Ovası basin, from which it escapes north-eastwards, via a second, equally deep and narrow valley, into the Taşova depression. Here it is joined by the west-flowing Kelkit Çayı before traversing the main northern ridge, passing through a third mountain gorge where in 1981 the 135m/443ft high Hasan Uğurlu dam was constructed creating a 23sq.km/9sq.mile reservoir linked to the 10sq.km/4sq.mile Ayvacık, Belhor and Suat Uğurlu Dam. The river finally escapes the mountains south of Çarşamba. Between Samsun in the west and Terme in the east it forms a large alluvial delta with numerous lagoons from whence it spills out into the Black Sea.
Yeşilırmak (River)

The origins of Amasya's citadel probably go back to pre-Hellenistic times. In the 3rd c. B.C. the town became the capital of the Pontic kingdom, after the last of the Greek tyrants of Kos was executed by Antigonus in 302 B.C. His opportunist nephew Mithridates, fleeing with a large following into the Pontus Mountains, captured the fortress at Amasya and proclaimed himself king. The Pontic dynasty he founded lasted until after 70 B.C., ending with the death of Mithridates VI Eupator, killed in the Third Mithridatic War against the Romans, led by Lucullus. Pharnaces, a son of Mithridates, attempted to regain his father's kingdom, but was defeated by Julius Caesar at the Battle of Zela in 47 B.C. Following this the town was absorbed into the Roman Empire.
History
Amasya was the birthplace of the celebrated geographer Strabo (64–20 B.C.) who, journeying the length and breadth of the ancient known world, recorded his findings in his seventeen volume "Oikomene". From 1243

Amasya: façades of houses by the River Yeşilırmak

onwards the region was under Mongol rule, a high-point being reached when Eretua was governor. During this period (1335–52) Amasya prospered. The town eventually fell to the Ottomans in 1392 and was occupied by Bayazit I. His son Mehmet I (reigned 1413–21) successfully defended the Amasya citadel against the Mongol prince Timur Lenk (Tamerlane, the Lame; 1402–04).

In the Middle Ages Amasya's prosperity was such as to warrant comparison with Baghdad. But with political, economic and cultural power concentrated increasingly in the west of the Empire, Amasya gradually declined into a provincial town. A substantial part of its architectural heritage has however been preserved.

Sights

Old Town

The oldest part of Amasya, at one time walled, extends below the citadel on the north side of the Yeşilırmak. Until quite recently many of the houses backing onto the river still retained their massive waterwheels (norias) which scooped up water and deposited it into irrigation channels. Sadly almost all have now vanished. Even so, the partly restored rows of houses along the riverside make a picture-postcard scene.

* Amasya Kalesi

Immediately north and high above the town stands Amasya's citadel with upper and lower levels from where there is an excellent view. The remains of defensive walls dating from Roman times can be seen running down the steep rocky slopes on either side. A third stretch of wall along the Yeşilırmak to the north completed the Old Town's defences. The citadel ruins can be reached on foot from the east end of the Kızlar Sarayı, the ascent of the steep rock steps taking a little over half an hour. Taxis provide a rather less strenuous alternative with a climb of no more than 20m/66ft to the citadel tower from the parking place.

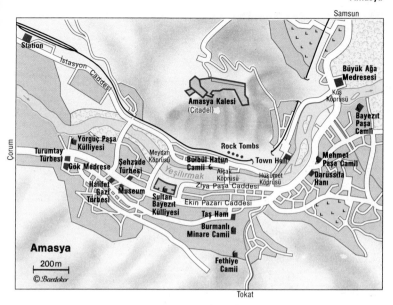

Tokat

At the time of the Pontic kings a temple dedicated to the Persian god Ahura Mazda (corresponding to Zeus Stratios) stood on the double summit. Later there was an acropolis here, with substantial defence-works including towers and ring walls. Vestiges of these can still be seen in the Turkish citadel. Three stairways tunnelled in the rock lead down towards the river, possibly providing access to cisterns intended to safeguard the water supply. Some historians on the other hand believe the tunnels were blind passages leading to Mithraic cult sites. No exits have ever been discovered.

On the left bank of the Yeşilırmak, about 2km/1¼ miles north of the town, there is a rock tomb, later used in the Byzantine period as a chapel, with remains of wall-paintings. As well as inscriptions in Greek its rock façade has corner pillars and string courses to the windows.

Ayınlı Mağara

The interesting octagonal Koranic school, also known as Kapı Ağası Medresesi, was founded in 1488 by Hüseyin Ağas, Chief White Eunuch to Bayazit II. An unusually high iwan (central dome with half-domes either side) dominates the rear of the courtyard. The restored building has recently been returned to its original use. Visitors are allowed a brief glimpse into the classrooms.

Büyük Ağa Medresesi

This small mosque, erected by the Seljuk bey Necmettin Ferun in 1242 for the Sultan Keyhusrev II, is situated in the southern part of the town, a short distance above the Tas Hanı. It owes its name to the spiral decoration on the minaret.

Burmanlı Minare Camii

Also known as Timar or Bimar Hanı this Old Turkish building on the south-east bank of the Yeşilırmak was erected in 1308–09. It was originally a hospital (dar üs-sifa = "lunatic asylum") and medical school founded by the Mongol Ilkhan Ölceytü and his wife Yıldız Hatun. By assassinating the last Seljuk sultan, Ölceytü finally brought to an end the long rule of the Sultans of Rum. The hanı has a magnificent portal.

Darüssifa Hanı

A flock of sheep trots behind the leading wether

*Rock tombs

Cut into the cliffs below the citadel are tombs of the Pontic kings (333 to 44 B.C.), some of the tombs being as much as 12m/39ft high. They are reached by crossing the Alçak Köprü and continuing through the Old Town (İçeri Şehir Mahallesi) by a road where the old royal palace (Kızlar Sarayı) once stood, its walled garden extending down to the river. The five sepulchral chambers, in groups of two and three respectively, date from the 3rd and 2nd centuries B.C. Two of the tombs can be entered. Linked by narrow steps they are hewn from the solid rock, with vaulted ceilings, smooth walls and stone plinths on which the sarcophagi were laid. Dowel holes in the façades and walls point to the tombs having been richly ornamented (marble panels/flagstones). The westernmost tomb also served as a place of burial in Byzantine times. The fifth tomb (Pharnaces I, 185–159 B.C.) was left unfinished. From the western group of tombs a stepped passageway gives access to one of the three tunnels originating in the citadel and leading to cisterns or, in the opinion of some scholars, a Mithraic shrine.

Kızlar Sarayı

The scant remains of the royal palace and gardens cannot begin to convey their former splendour.

Fethiye Camii

This small mosque, on the upper slope of the hill to the south of the town, was originally a Byzantine church (early 7th c). It was converted to a mosque in 1117. Badly damaged by fire in 1915, only the apse and some sections of wall survive. The minaret was built in 1812.

*Gök Medrese

The partly restored Gök Medrese was built by the Seljuk provincial governor Turumtay (see Turumtay Türbesi below) in 1266/67. The very striking three-aisled former Koranic school with its fifteen small domes is particularly noteworthy for its fine stalactitic portal and carved wooden doors. The interior of the medrese is simply furnished. Three İlkhlan mummies are buried here.

To the right of the entrance to the Koranic school can be seen the Turumtay Türbesi (erected in 1279), mausoleum of the (embalmed) founder of the Gök Medrese.

This mausoleum in the Üçler quarter south of the main road is believed to date from about 1145. It was built for a vizier of the Damishmendid emir, Melik Gazi. His remains are interred in a superbly ornamented marble coffin (rams' heads and Medusa heads between flower tendrils) presumed to have come from a Late Roman necropolis. Adjoining the türbesi are the ruins of yet another old medrese.

Halifet Gazi
Türbesi

Below the citadel, in the Hatuniye district, on the Yeşilırmak embankment not far from the Bülbül Hatun Camii, stands a superb old Ottoman town house of 1872. Beautifully restored and now open as a museum, it was the home of a court pharmacist Hasan Talât Efendi who, as Aziz Mahmud Efendi, became established in Amasya in the 1860s. He built the house after being banished from the sultan's palace.

*Hazeranlar
Konağı

The comfortably appointed, solidly built, two-storeyed house has a large forecourt and a cellar running from one end of the building to the other (now used for lectures/displays). The rooms on the ground floor, grouped around a spacious hall, were chiefly intended for domestic use and comprised kitchens, servants' quarters, dining-rooms and lavatory. The private accommodation, also leading off a generously-sized hall, was on the first floor. It included a winter and coffee room, bedrooms with showers and baths, a dressing room, a large reception-cum-living area and a ladies' drawing-room.

Built in 1486 by a councillor of Bayazit II's son Ahmet, the Mehmet Paşa Camii stands close to the Timar Hanı on the south-east bank of the Yeşilırmak.

Mehmet Paşa
Camii

Following restoration of the Gök Medrese, Amasya's museum was moved to a new building on the main road facing the Sultan Bayazit Külliyesi. In addition to ancient artefacts it also has an ethnographic collection.

Museum

This türbesi, hidden away in an alley to the west of the Sultan Bayazit Külliyesi, was probably the tomb of one of Bayazit I's sons. Dating from 1513 it is also known as the Şehzade Osman Türbesi.

Şehzade
Türbesi

The sons of three Ottoman sultans – Mehmet I, Bayazit I and Bayazit II – lie buried in the Şehzadeler Türbesi (1410), situated on the main road opposite the Şehzade Türbesi.

Şehzadeler
Türbesi

Rising conspicuously on the west side of the town centre, between the Yeşilırmak and the main road, the Sultan Beyazit Külliyesi was founded in 1486 by Ahmed, son of Bayazit II. The mosque has two domes, one in front of the other. Complementing them are a pair of minarets each with its own distinctive ornamentation. The prayer hall, entered through a five-bay portico, has windows with surrounds of blue glazed tiles.

*Sultan Beyazit
Külliyesi

In front of the mosque, flanked by fine trees, stands an ablutions fountain (or şadırvan). The grounds of the mosque also contain a library; among the 20,000 volumes are some valuable Koranic scripts. To the west, in front of a türbe, is the Bayazit Medresesi.

Erected in 1279, the mausoleum to the right of the entrance of the Gök Medrese is the tomb of the Koranic school's founder (embalmed).

Turumtay
Türbesi

This much venerated mosque, built between 1430 and 1438 by Yörgüç Paşa, teacher to Sultan Mehmet I, is tucked away to the north of the main road on the most westerly outskirts of the town. As well as a room containing three türbes (to the right of the vestibule), the complex of buildings also includes a hospital and a Koranic school.

Yörgüç Paşa
Külliyesi

Surroundings

Ezinepazarı	On the left of the Tokat road about 25km/15½ miles south-east of Amasya stands a simple 13th c. Seljuk han, now used as a byre. Built about 1240 by Mahperi Hatun, mother of the Seljuk Sultan Keyhusrev II, it was once the last caravanserai before Amasya.
Gümüşhacıköy	The Köprülü Mehmet Paşa Camii and the Mehmet Köprüsü (1666), about 62km/38 miles north-west of Amasya, were the work of a single founder. The mosque, like the bridge, dates from the 17th c.
Göynücek	Some 44km/27 miles south-west of Amasya the remains of a citadel stand guard over the district town of Göynücek and the gorge-like valley of the Çekerek İrmağı (the ancient Skylax). Two rock stairways are tunnelled in the cliffs.
Kocagöl	This little mountain lake, also known as Borabay Gölü, is set in the picturesque eastern foothills of Ak Dağ near the town of Taşova about 70km/43 miles north-east of Amasya. It is a favourite spot with local people because of its lovely wooded surroundings.
Merzifon	Before being rechristened Neapolis by Pompey, Merzifon, a district centre about 50km/31 miles north-west of Amasya, was known in antiquity as Phazemon. Some of its Byzantine churches were converted to mosques by the Ottomans. The best known Ottoman building is the Kara Mustafa Paşa Camii (founded in 1666/67) which has a square domed hall. The Murat Camii, built by Murat II, dates from 1427. The nearby Çelebi Mehmet Medresesi, named after Mehmet II, was constructed during the rule of the Emir Unmar. Its square inner court, all four sides of which have exceptionally high iwans, lacks the usual arcades. The old system for heating the cells around the courtyard has survived. Rising above the medrese is the town's clocktower, erected in 1866. Shaped like a minaret the tower is built of brick with a wooden structure above the gallery.

Anamur

See Alanya, Surroundings

Ani   T 3

North-eastern Anatolia
Province: Kars
Altitude: 1750m/5743ft
Village: Ocaklı (population: 1100)

Situation and ** Importance	The ruins of the Old Armenian capital of Ani lie almost on the Turko-Armenian border, near the village of Ocaklı some 45km/28 miles east of Kars. Here, in an area of gently undulating treeless steppe, a rock plateau roughly in the shape of an acute-angled triangle lies bounded by deep river gorges on all three sides – the valleys of the Bostanlar Çayı (Alaca Su = "bright water") to the west, the Migmig Çayı (Valley of the Flowers) to the north-east, and the Arpa Çayı (Barley Stream) to the south-east. Only on its north side is the plateau linked to the surrounding tableland; secured against attack from this direction by walls, it is hard to imagine a more strategic site for a medieval town.
N.B.	Although a special pass was formerly needed for visiting the ruined town, since 1991 regulations have been relaxed somewhat. If necessary permis-

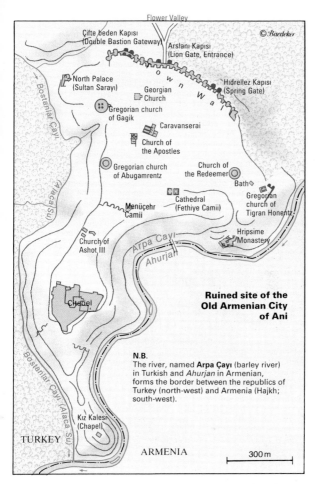

Flower Valley

Çifte beden Kapısı
(Double Bastion Gateway)

© *Baedeker*

Arslanı Kapısı
(Lion Gate, Entrance)

North Palace
(Sultan Sarayı)

Georgian
Church

Hıdrellez Kapısı
(Spring Gate)

Gregorian church
of Gagik

Caravanserai

Church of
the Apostles

Gregorian church
of Abugamrentz

Church of
the Redeemer

Bath

Cathedral
(Fethiye Camii)

Gregorian
church of
Tigran Honentz

Menüçehr
Camii

Church of
Ashot III

Arpa Çayı

Ahurjan

Hripsime
Monastery

Bostanlar Çayı

Alaca Su

**Ruined site of the
Old Armenian City
of Ani**

Citadel

N.B.
The river, named **Arpa Çayı** (barley river)
in Turkish and *Ahurjan* in Armenian,
forms the border between the republics of
Turkey (north-west) and Armenia (Hajkh;
south-west).

Bostanlar Çayı (Alaca Su)

Kız Kalesi
(Chapel)

TURKEY

ARMENIA

300 m

sion can be obtained from the police authorities in Kars (Emniyet Müdür-lüğü) using forms available from the tourist information office (Danışma Bürosu). Because the site is right on the Armenian frontier (the Arpa Çayı forms the actual boundary) the use of cameras may be forbidden depending on the political situation at the time. Photographic equipment must then be left at the police post in the village of Soylu. Otherwise the taking of photographs is permitted on the site, though not without restriction. Photographs, sometimes rather poor in quality, are also available from the museum in Kars.

Because of the military presence (observation post) there is no public access to part of the site, in particular to some of the churches along the Arpa Çayı, to the citadel or to the southernmost section of the town. Most of the rest of the ruins can be reached by following a made-up signposted path round the site.

Ani

History   The southern tip of the basalt plateau was probably settled as early as the Chalcolithic period and early Bronze Age; it is likely that the Urartians had a fortress there too. In the 8th c. the Bagratids (from south-west Georgia) extended and strengthened their rule, entering into treaties with the Arabs. In 722 the settlement which had grown up around the fort passed into the possession of their Armenian line (see Artvin, and Armenia). Under Ashot Msaker (809–827) it blossomed into a town which Ashot III (953–977) later chose for his seat. Then in 961/62, with the blessing of Ananias, Catholicos of Armenia, Ani became the Bagratid capital in place of Kars, Ashot taking the title of king. As first great patron of the infant metropolis, Ashot erected a number of public and ecclesiastical buildings, simultaneously encouraging commerce and trade. Ani developed into a flourishing cultural and economic centre. At the height of its splendour the town is thought to have boasted a population numbering 100,000, and as many as 1000 churches. Such was the pressure on space that some inhabitants were forced to live in cave dwellings in the Alaca Suyu gorge. Smbat II (977–989) fortified the town with walls and in 993, by adding substantially to its already considerable endowment of ecclesiastical buildings, his successor Gagik I (989–1020) induced the Armenian catholicos to make Ani his seat (replacing Arkina). The Armenian Empire, however, was even then on the verge of decline, Ani – and Armenia generally – soon to be cast in the role of bastion against a succession of Seljuk, Turkoman and Mongol invaders. In 1048, just three years after the first Byzantine governor had been installed, Turkoman nomads appeared at the gates. Having fallen to Alp Arslan in 1064, Ani found itself with a Seljuk governor Seddat Ogulları. Although he and his successor, the Emir Seddadi Abul Aşvâroğlu Menüçehr, attempted to stem the tide with a substantial programme of new building, there was large-scale migration from Armenia to Cilicia. In the 12th c. the kings of Georgia enjoyed periodic success against the Seljuks (defeat of the Emir of Erzurum in 1162). As a result, at the end of the century, under the feudal princes of the Armenian-Georgian Zakhariad family, Ani experienced a second flowering which not even the sack of the town in 1236 by the Mongols under Genghis Khan's son Oktai Khan could halt. The town grew to be a provincial capital and, despite a devastating earthquake in 1319 which caused many people to leave, was not finally abandoned until the 16th c. It was rediscovered by European scholars in the first half of the 19th c.

Excavations   H. F. B. Lynch's plan (1894) of the ruins was based on the findings of the earliest excavations, conducted by Hermann Abich in 1844. Further research was then carried out by the Russians in the period between the Russo-Turkish War (of 1877/78) and the onset of the First World War. More recent investigations by the Turkish Historical Society and Kemal Balkan, in 1944 and 1965, brought Bronze Age and Seljuk finds to light.

Sights

Arslanı Kapısı   The main gate into the town bears a relief of a lion and hence is known as the Lion Gate.

*Church of the Holy Apostles (Mestaba Kervansaray)   This badly ruined church, square in plan, with four conchas and two entrances, was originally built in 1031. It had smaller domed chambers with their own apses between the main apses and the outer walls. The church, altered and extended after 1064, was converted by the Seljuks into a caravanserai and tax office (mestaba kervansaray). Parts of the centrally-planned building, and also the later hall, survive. Typical Seljuk stalactitic ornamentation and decorative borders are still clearly visible in places, particularly in the south-east portal (note the Armenian inscriptions) and the dome. The black and red stone church is decorated with star motifs and embellished with spiral columns. South of the church (which is also called St John's Church, or Arak Elots Kilisesi) there is a further tomb-like structure.

Ani: scanty remains of the Apostles' Church

The grey minaret, known also as the Cami Minaresi, belonged to a mosque of which virtually nothing apart from the minaret remains.

Boz Minare Camii

Situated outside the town walls to the north-west this church is thought to date from the 11th/12th c. It is a hexagonal building on a central plan with a dome and triangular niches. The twelve-sided interior is painted with frescos. The upper storey, supported on timberwork, rests on walls reinforced by columns.

Çoban Kilisesi

Not the easiest of the ruined buildings to locate, this mosque dates from 1195. Coloured mosaics adorn the main hall. The prayer court and outer courtyard have both disappeared completely.

Ebül Muammeran Camii

Decorated with mosaics and graced by a tower, the 13th c. Seljuk Ejderha Kulesi next to the Lion Gate was actually a hospital, the first of its kind in Anatolia.

Ejderha Kulesi

The Keseli Kilise or Church of Our Saviour was begun in 1036. Its founders, the Pahlavuni family, decreed that prayers should be offered there until Christ's second coming. A segment on the east side of the centrally-planned, circular building with eight apses, has collapsed. The 13th c. paintings adorning the interior can still be made out despite having been whitewashed over. The elegantly ornamented exterior has blind arcading, originally comprising nineteen arches.

*Church of Our Saviour

This church, dedicated to St Gregory Lusavoriç and also known as the Polatoğlu Kilisesi, was founded in 944 by Gregory Abugamrentz for his siblings Hamze and Seta. Centrally planned it has a tall, twelve-sided drum, quatre-foil ground plan, several apses and six horseshoe-shaped conchas. The east apse, and lateral chambers either side, protrude slightly from an otherwise regular façade. Above the south-west entrance is an Armenian

Church of St Gregory Abugamrentz

Ani

Outer walls of Church of the Redeemer

Gregorian church with Byzantine frescoes

inscription. Piles of rubble to the north of the church mark the remains of the Stepanos and Kristapor chapels and the Abugamrentz family tomb (erected in 1040).

Church of
St Gregory of
Gagik

Modelled on the famous Zwartnotz cathedral in Armenia, this large and now badly ruined church was built between 1001 and 1010 by King Gagik I. Circular in plan, with two entrances and a small apsidal chapel, it collapsed just three years after completion and was never restored.

**Church of
St Gregory of
Tigran Honentz

One of the most interesting of Ani's churches, St Gregory of Tigran Honentz (also called the Şirli Kilise), stands close to the edge of the Arpa Çayı gorge. Founded in 1215 it is another domed, centrally-arranged building, but with a cruciform ground plan, a tall delicately ornamented drum, and twin-aisled narthex to the west. The interior of the narthex, and of the church proper up into the dome, are finely decorated with murals of Byzantine influence, some with Armenian and Georgian inscriptions. Subjects depicted include the annunciation, the nativity and the death of Mary, the conversion of King Tiridates to Christianity by Gregory the Illuminator, and various saints and evangelists. There are also imitations of Sassanid decorative motifs. The exterior is adorned with animal reliefs (on the well preserved south façade) and a corded design on the blind arcading. Sassanid embellishment to the right of the doorway reflects the building's subsequent use as a mosque.

Hıdrellez Kapısı
(Satrançlı
Kapısı)

Formerly the entrance to a palace, the Spring or Chessboard Gate (the latter name owed to the geometric pattern of the stonework) is situated 250m/275yd east of the Lion Gate. Embellished with serpents and a bull's head it is thought to date from the time of the Vatchoutanz family (8th c.) whose heraldic beasts these were. The ruined Mama Hatun and Chanuche towers to the left of the gate are remnants of the earliest sections of the double ramparts, built about 980.

Originally endowed by Tigran Honentz this poorly preserved monastery, centrally planned with a tent spire and six apses, dates from the 13th c. According to legend the nun Hripsime, accompanied by her abbess and another maiden called Shogagat, fled to Armenia to escape the attentions of Diocletian, only to find herself subjected to the equally unwelcome advances of King Tiridates. When he too was rejected, Tiridates had all three women put to death. 7th c. chapels are said to stand over their graves.

Hripsime Monastery Monastery of the Virgin

Even without its dome and supporting drum, both of which have collapsed, this solid, triple-aisled church with a nave of suitably cathedral-like proportions, still manages to dominate the ruined city. Founded by King Smbat and Queen Gadarine, it was built between 989 and 1001, replacing the Church of Ashot III as Ani's principal church. The architect was the famous Trdat, commissioned by the Byzantine Emperor Basil II to save the dome of Hagia Sophia from collapse following the earthquake of 989. Having been plundered by the Seljuks, the cathedral was converted into a mosque in 1064. The raised sanctuary has survived. Graceful blind arcading articulates the exterior.

* Fethiye Camii Cathedral

This small 13th c. hexagonal chapel, with a conical dome, stands on the southernmost point of the plateau. Byzantine palm motifs decorate the twin pillars and blind arcading of the centre section.

Kız Kalesi Fortress of the Virgin

Built in 1074 by Ani's first Seljuk governor, the Menüçehr Camii with its octagonal minaret is thought to be the oldest Seljuk mosque in Anatolia. Situated on the edge of the gorge, south of the city wall, the multi-storeyed building, which has a crypt with tombs, was severely damaged sometime around 1890. Although the windows and interior (columned hall) are Persian in style, the use made of different coloured stone to relieve the façade is typical of Christian Armenian churches.

* Menüçehr Camii

Thought to have been five-storeyed originally, this 11th or 12th c. Seljuk sultan's palace of stone and timber construction has lost its upper floors. The façade above the entrance gate with its pointed arch is a lovely chequered pattern of black and red.

North palace Sultan Sarayı

In 1965 excavations near the Ebül Muammaran Camii close to the town gate uncovered a bath house, probably constructed between 1080 and 1090 during Menüçehr's governorship. With typical Turkish ground plan, heating system and decor, the baths have four wash rooms built onto the corners of a square sweat room. In 1966 another Seljuk bath house was discovered, on a higher site to the north of St Gregory's of Tigran Honentz. Copper coins bearing the names of the Seljuk sultan Meleksah and the Emir Saddadi Abul Aşvâroğlu Menüçehr, governor of Ani, were also unearthed.

Selçuk Hamamları

Construction of the 2.5km/1½ miles of defensive wall along the so-called "Valley of the Flowers" north of the town was begun by Ashot III in 972. Over 8m/26ft high, and reinforced by ditches up to 10m/33ft deep at some points, the walls were further strengthened and extended between 977 and 990 by Smbat II. They were restored in the 11th c. under the Seljuk governor Menüçehr. Seven of the original gates survive, these being, from northwest to south-east, the Eğribucak Kapısı, Çifte Beden Kapısı, Arslan Kapısı, Hıdrellez (or Satrançlı) Kapısı, Acemağılı Kapı, Migmig Suyu Kapısı, Baı Sekisi Kapısı and Divin Kapısı.

Walls

The citadel, to the south of the town, is one of the oldest complexes of buildings in Ani. Enclosed within its protective walls are the ruins of the old two-storeyed Bagratid palace and two churches, the Kamsarakan Kilisesi (the palace church) and the Sarayı Kilisesi (the fortress church). The palace church, single-aisled, with plain reliefs and an apse, was endowed by Prince Kamsarakan in 622. The palace, with reception rooms, baths, under-

Citadel

floor heating and a theatre stage, was erected over the remains of an even
earlier edifice which also dated back to the Kamsarakan period.

Surroundings

Beş Kilise

In Armenian times a rocky projection in a deep gorge near the village of Beş
Kilise (about 30km/19 miles south-east of Kars and 4km/2½ miles from the
Digor road) was the site of the monastery of Chtskonk. Only a church
survives from the former complex of buildings. Dedicated to St Sergius it is
also known as the Karakale (Black Fort).

Chochavank

Downstream of the Arpa Çayı Barajı, east of the Arpa Çayı, about 4km/2½
miles from the Horomos Manastiri, stands a church built by monks sometime around 985/989. It has a lion carved in relief above the gable door.

Digor

Digor, on the site of Tekor, an Old Armenian settlement, had until relatively
recently a 5th c. Armenian church. Converted to a domed basilica in 986 the
church was long considered one of the finest examples of Armenian religious architecture. It collapsed however in 1912 and was never rebuilt, the
rubble being used as a quarry. Now little more than the outline remains.
East of the town, near the village of Harabıdigor, there is an interesting
church dedicated to St Sergius. Two other villages, Agrak (south-east) and
Nahçivan (south) also have churches worth visiting. The Turkish writer
Dede Korkut, famous for his folk tales, is said to have lived in Digor.

Horomos
Manastiri

Overlooking the valley of the Arpa Çayı about 10km/6 miles north-east of
Ani are the remains of a 10th c. Georgian monastery. Having being
enlarged and extended by the Armenian king Hovhannes Smbat III (1020–
42), it became the pantheon of the latter-day kings of Ani, among them
Ashot IV. The monastery complex, still an important centre of Christianity
as late as the 18th c., includes three churches worth seeing: St John's
Church, endowed by Smbat III, the body of which is smaller than the great,
hall-like narthex; the domed 10th c. St Menas' Church, with a narthex, apse
and two lateral chambers; and the star-shaped Church of the Shepherd
which has lost its conical roof.

Kilittaşı

Kilittaşı, a small village by the Arpa Çayı, lies off the main Tuzluca road just
90km/60 miles south-east of Kars (via Digor). The modern village occupies
the site of the Old Armenian Bagaran, residence in the 9th c. of the Bagratid
ruler Ashot the Great (856–90). Still standing from that period are remains
of the former Monastery of St John, square in plan with four apses, built
between 624 and 631 and renovated in the 13th c. Further upstream, not far
from the village of Mirikarabağ, are the ruins of Mren Cathedral, a centrally
planned, three-aisled building with a dome, two chapels and an apse, the
drum of the dome being supported on four massive pillars. There are bas
reliefs and remnants of frescos dating from between 638 and 640. Because
of its proximity to the Turko-Armenian border visitors to Mren require a
special permit.

Tuzluca

Huge rock-salt caves, some natural, others the result of salt mining, dominate the scenery around the little town of Tuzluca, 100km/62 miles or so
south-east of Kars. About 10km/6 miles north of the town, where the road
climbs towards Digor, a magnificent view is obtained over the Arpa Çayı/
Aras Nehri basin and across into Armenia as far as Erevan. The Turko-
Armenian frontier follows the line of the rivers either side of their confluence; great caution should be exercised if taking photographs in the vicinity of the border.

Ankara H 3/4

Northern Central Anatolia on the southern edge of the Pontus Mountains
Province: Ankara
Altitude: 835–1000m/2740–3282ft
Population: 2.6 million

Situated where Central Anatolia merges with the southern Pontus Mountains, Ankara, capital of the Turkish Republic, is the country's second largest city, an administrative centre with a population both young and modern in outlook. Its position as the seat of government, and the cultural, economic and political status which goes with it, are the result of the vision and determination of Mustafa Kemal Atatürk, who in 1923, mainly for strategic regions, chose to make what was then a provincial town of 30,000 inhabitants the country's capital. Ankara today is home not only to the Turkish parliament and its government departments and ministries but also to foreign embassies and a highly respected university.

Situation and
**Importance

The city, in a delightful setting encircled by mountains, has a temperate semi-arid continental-type climate with warm dry summers and cold wet

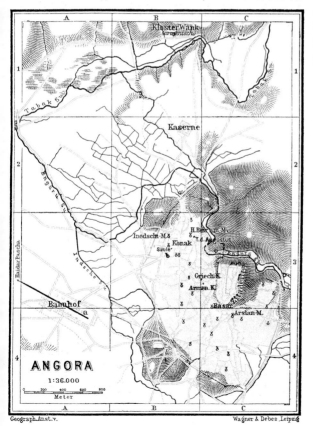

Historical plan of
Angora (Ankara)
from Baedeker's
guidebook
"Constantinople
and Asia Minor"
(2nd edition;
Leipzig 1914)

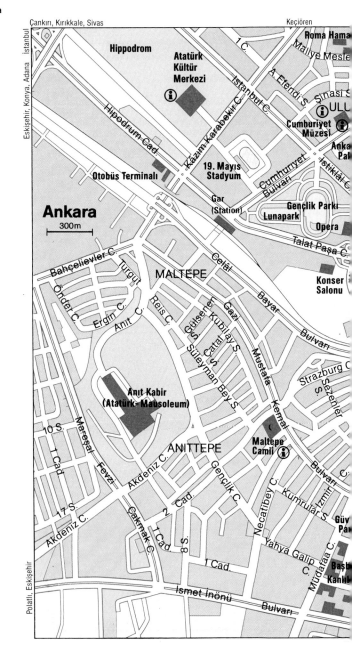

Çankırı, Kırıkkale, Sivas

Keçiören

Roma Hama

Maliye Mesle

Hippodrom

Atatürk
Kültür
Merkezi

İstanbul C.

A. Efendi S.

Sinasi S

ULL

Cumhuriyet
Müzesi

Anka
Pal

Kâzım Karabekir C.

Hipodrum Cad.

Otobüs Terminalı

19. Mayıs
Stadyum

Gar
(Station)

Cumhuriyet
Bulvarı

İstiklal C.

Gençlik Parkı
Lunapark

Opera

Ankara

300m

Talat Paşa C.

Bahçelievler C.

Turgut

MALTEPE

Celal

Bayar

Konser
Salonu

Önder C.

Ergin C.

Anıt C.

Reis C.

Gülsener

Kubilay S.

Gazi

Çatal S.

Öğd.

Süleyman Bey S.

Mustafa

Bulvarı

Strazburg C

Sezenler
S.

Kemal

Anıt Kabir
(Atatürk- Mausoleum)

10 S.

Mareşal

Fevzi

Akdeniz C.

ANITTEPE

Gençlik C.

Maltepe
Camii

Bulvarı

C.

17 S.

Necatibey C.

Kumrular S.

İzmir

Güv
Pa

T Cad.

Akdeniz C.

Çakmak C.

2 Cad.

T Cad.

8 S.

1 Cad.

Yahya Galip C.

Müdafaa C.

Başb

Kanlıb

İsmet İnönü
Bulvarı

Eskişehir, Konya, Adana İstanbul

Polatlı, Eskişehir

winters. In earlier days the Ankara basin (Mürted Ovası) was subject to frequent sandstorms while the poorly-drained marshlands of the Ankara Çayı flood plain held the threat of malaria. Added to which there was an acute shortage of clean drinking water. When Ankara became the new capital a series of urban building projects was undertaken, part of a comprehensive development scheme drawn up by the German town planner H. Jansen. Several reservoirs were also constructed – the Çubuk dams (15km/9 miles and 50km/31 miles north of Ankara), the Kurtboğazı dam (50km/31 miles north-west) and the Bayındır dam (20km/12½ miles east) – despite which water supplies have barely kept pace with the ever-growing demand.

*Townscape

As with İstanbul, İzmir and other Turkish cities, the lure of employment in its industries and rapidly developing service sector draws huge numbers of people to Ankara from the countryside. About 60% of Ankarans live in suburbs known as "gecekondu" (= built overnight), in simple housing much like that seen in Turkish villages. The modern face of the city shows itself in the broad avenues of the post-1923 planned New Town and in other more recent city-centre developments. Here are found the wide boulevards, the pedestrian precincts, the streets of western-style shops and boutiques, the luxury hotels and top-class restaurants which are the hallmark of a confident, forward-looking metropolis. The rapidly expanding capital is still plagued with serious problems with its water supplies in summer, and by atmospheric pollution during temperature inversions in winter. With its extremely heavy traffic and reliance on lignite as a fuel, Ankara recently had the dubious honour of being declared the city with the world's poorest air quality. A planned shift to natural gas should alleviate the situation.

In the meantime the population of greater Ankara continues to grow and probably now already exceeds three million. The urban sprawl extends from Yenikent, near Sincan in the Mürted Ovası, eastwards for more than 50km/31 miles to the Bayındır dam, and from Bağlum in the north, southwards for 35km/22 miles to Gölbaşı, a popular destination for day-trippers, on the Mugan Gölü.

It is often said that Ankara is not worth visiting. This is far from true. On the contrary, the old quarter around the citadel offers the discerning traveller an insight into a three thousand year-old cultural history which is still in some respects alive today.

Transport

When Ankara became the capital of Turkey transport links were almost non-existent – it was the terminus of the Anatolian railway, a branch of the Baghdad line. Expansion of the rail network, giving access to the Soviet Union, Syria and Iran, followed the opening up of the country by long-distance roads. Now flights between the capital and all the main provincial towns have been augmented by recently instituted air services to international airports around the world. Thus Ankara today is the hub of nearly all Turkey's major transport and communications links and, as the geographical, political, economic and intellectual centre of the Republic, has largely emerged from the shadow of "the secret capital" – İstanbul.

History

Neolithic finds from the area around Ankara testify to early settlement by Hittite farmers in about 2500 B.C. The first town of any importance known to have existed here was in the Phrygian period (about 1200 B.C.). The name Ankyra, first recorded as belonging to an Achaemenid staging post on the imperial route from Susa to Sardes, may also date from this time. Phrygia's decline saw Ankara become part of the Lydian Empire before the Lydians, led by, among others, Croesus (560–46 B.C.), were themselves defeated in the wars against the Persians (559–29 B.C.). Subsequently the town passed, as did Anatolia as a whole, to the Achaemids.

After 227 B.C. the Tectosages, a Galatian tribe who had migrated across the Dardanelles, made Ankara their capital, calling it Galatia. Victory over the Galatians in 189 B.C. then brought the city, the region and the whole

kingdom of Galatia, under Roman rule. After periods in the possession of
the Pergamum Empire and the Pontic King Mithridites the Great (until
74 B.C.) Roman rule resumed, and under Augustus (Greek: Sebastos) the
town, now with some 200,000 inhabitants and known as Sebaste Tec-
tosagum, became the capital of the Roman province of Galatia. A later
emperor, Caracalla (211–17) rebuilt the walls of the citadel and constructed
a large public baths.

With the arrival of Christianity Ankara became the seat of a metropolitan. It
was the venue of several Councils of the Church, including those of 314 and
358, and when the empire split into East and West in 395 it was absorbed by
Byzantium. Then followed centuries in which Islamic occupation alternated
with Christian reconquest until the final triumph of the Ottomans in 1403.
Situated as it was on the great Anatolian caravan route, the city, now
known as "Engüriye" (Angora to Europeans), enjoyed almost undisturbed
peace and prosperity under Ottoman rule.

Following the demise of the Ottoman Empire, the Grand National
Assembly, convened under the terms of the National Pact, met for the first
time in Ankara on April 23rd 1923. On October 13th that same year Ankara
was proclaimed capital and a few days later the new Turkish Republic was
born. A competition was held for the design of a modern metropolis with a
population expected to reach 300,000 by 1990. Building began in 1928, the
prize-winning scheme having been submitted by the German town planner
H. Jansen and architects C. Holzmeister, P. Bonantz and B. Taut.

Sights

This small 13th c. mosque south of the Arslanhane Camii was renovated in
1413, resulting in the building seen today. Endowed by the Ahi brotherhood it is a typical "forest mosque", with a flat timber ceiling supported on
twelve wooden columns. Note also the carving on the staircase pulpit and
window shutters (1413/14).

Ahi Elvan Camii

On the İstanbul Caddesi, the main road west out of Ankara, the Çubuk Çayı
is spanned by an old seven-arch bridge. An inscription on its west side
attributes its construction to the Seljuk governor Kızılbey in 1222.

Ak Köprü

Although restored in intervening centuries, the Alaeddin Camii, in the inner
citadel immediately behind the Parmak Kapı, was built in 1178 at the time of
the Seljuk Sultan İzz Eddin Kiliç Aslan II. The carving on the staircase pulpit
is particularly fine.

Alaeddin Camii

The Atatürk Mausoleum (open: daily 10am–noon, 2–6pm, all day Mon.),
symbol of the new Ankara, is located on the Anit Tepesi, beyond the railway
station, about 2.5km/1½ miles south-west of Ulus Meydanı. Designed by
the Turkish architect Emil Onat and erected between 1944 and 1953, the
mausoleum is a notable example of modern Turkish architecture. The
complex comprises a Path of Honour flanked by reclining Hittite lions, a
Court of Honour, the Atatürk Mausoleum itself and a museum.

*Anıt Kabir

A flight of 33 steps made from Cappadocian tufa leads up between the
Tower of Liberation and Tower of Independence to the 260m/285yd-long
Path of Honour. On either side of the 30m/33yd-wide avenue stand sculpted
groups of three female and three male figures representing the transition
from Ottoman traditionalism to the modernity of Atatürk's Turkish Republic. At the far end the entrance to the Court is guarded by two more towers
symbolising the simple Turkish soldier and the defence of national rights.
The Court, with colonnaded buildings on three sides, also has towers at
each corner signifying Peace, Victory, Revolution and the Republic.

The colonnaded hall on the east side of the Court houses the Atatürk
Museum, an interesting collection of mementos and memorabilia including many personal effects. The edifice on the south side is the mausoleum
of Turkey's second president, İsmet İnönü.

Anit Kabır, the landmark of Ankara

Atatürk's historic limousine

On the north side, reached by a second massive flight of 33 steps, stands the Atatürk Mausoleum, 55m/180ft wide, 72m/236ft long and 21m/69ft high. Bas reliefs on the front of the platform terrace either side of the steps depict scenes from the War of Liberation (Battle on the Sakarya, Battle of Dumlupınar). Above them burn eternal flames. Inscriptions flank the mausoleum entrance: to the right an excerpt from Atatürk's great speech delivered on the tenth anniversary of the founding of the Republic, to the left his exhortation to Turkish youth. At the rear inside the hall, in a niche with gilded top and elaborate front railing, stands the 40 tonne white marble sarcophagus of the Republic's founder. His remains were brought here from their temporary resting place in the Ethnographic Museum on November 10th 1953, the fifteenth anniversary of his death.

** Arkeoloji Müzesi (Hittite Museum)

The Mahmut Paşa Bedesteni (1464–71) with its crown of ten domes was once a covered bazaar where cloth made from angora wool was traded. Situated below the citadel, on its south-west side, the old building was converted in 1951 into the now world-famous Museum of Anatolian Civilisations, also known as the Hittite Museum (open: 9am–5.30pm, in winter 9am–5pm, closed Mon.).

The collection, divided into ten departments, comprises an enormous number of exceptionally impressive archaeological finds from the paleolithic period to classical times. These include neolithic artefacts from Çatalhüyük, in particular bulls' heads, reliefs, wall paintings and a picture of Kara Dağı erupting. Pride of place, however, belongs to the Hittite collection, the most comprehensive of its kind in the world. There are orthostatic reliefs, large sculptures (middle room), clay tablets and numerous smaller items, from sites such as Boğazkale (Hattuşaş), Alacahüyük, Alisar, Karatepe, Karkamış, Kültepe (Kaneş), Malatya (Arslantepe) and Ankara. Other exhibits in the museum come from the Assyrian trading colonies (Kültepe) and Phrygian cities such as Arslantaş and Gordion. Because of the sheer size of the collection visitors are advised to buy a detailed guidebook, available in the museum.

Kurşunlu Han

Adjoining the Mahmut Paşa Bedesteni on its north-east side is the Kurşunlu Han, also part of the museum but used for research and other such activities rather than for displaying the collection itself. The building incorporates a laboratory, library, lecture hall, and workshops. Documentary and other evidence suggests that the caravanserai dates from before 1450 and was erected by another of Mehmet the Conqueror's Grand Viziers, Mehmet Paşa. The income from the 58-roomed two-storeyed han with its cellars, stabling and shops funded a free kitchen for the poor of Üskükar.

Statues on the Road of Honour   *Cult figure in the archaeological museum*

Built in 1289 at the time of the Emir Şeref Eddin, the Arslanhanı Camii, on the south side of the citadel hill, is Ankara's oldest mosque. Prior to the construction in the 1970s of the Kocatepe Camii it was also the largest. Originally called the Ahi Şeref Eddin Camii after its founder, the mosque became known as the Arslanhanı Camii on account of a Roman stone-carving of a lion which once stood in the courtyard. The mosque is part of a complex (külliye) of several buildings all endowed by Şeref Eddin. These include a medrese and an early 14th c. octagonal Seljuk broach-roof türbe on Roman foundations, situated across the alleyway immediately on the left next to the mosque entrance. The main portal of the mosque has stalactitic decoration and incorporates pieces of Byzantine and Roman masonry. Although in plan the mosque is a typical five-aisle Seljuk basilica, the ceiling over centre aisle being slightly raised, the multi-columned prayer hall reveals it as one of the few "forest mosques" in Anatolia, the ceiling of elaborate stepped timbering being supported on two dozen wooden columns with Romano-Byzantine capitals. Note also the prayer niche of blue faience tiles with pierced stucco stalactitic vaulting, and the staircase pulpit (1209) in richly carved walnut.

*Arslanhanı Camii

This wide tree-lined thoroughfare, Ankara's main traffic artery and princi-pal shopping street, runs for 5km/3 miles from north to south linking the Old City (Ulus Meydanı) and New Town. At day's end the section between Lozan Meydanı (Lausanne Square) and İsmet İnönü Meydanı is crowded with people taking the evening air. South of Ulus Meydanı both sides of the boulevard are lined with public buildings including the opera house, the Turkish broadcasting corporation, the university, as well as banks and insurance company offices. The New Town proper begins south of the railway viaduct at Lozan Meydanı. Here there is a huge replica of a "sun-disc", one of the famous Hittite ritual "standards" discovered at Alaca-hüyük, examples of which are on display in the Hittite Museum. From the

Atatürk Bulvarı

Museum Entrance

Mahmut Paşa Bedesteni

Ticket Office · Café · Altsteinzeit · New Stone Age · Copper Age · Classical Age · Late Hittite · Urartian · Early Bronze Age · Age · Phrygian · Caravanserai © Baedeker · Assyrian Trading Colony · Hittite Old Kingdom Great Kingdom

Ankara Archaeological Museum Arkeoloji Müzesi

Museum of Anatolian Culture Anadolu Medeniyetleri Müzesi

Hittite Museum

square an extensive pedestrian precinct with restaurants and shops, mainly on the left of the road, stretches parallel with the Atatürk Bulvarı to well beyond Kızılay Meydanı.

Immediately south-west of the square lies the government quarter, with fine buildings housing various government departments and ministries. Most were designed between 1928 and 1935 by the German architect Clemens Holzmeister. Above them towers the Turkish Parliament building (viewing possible) on the İsmet İnönü Bulvarı. Further up the hill are the districts of Kavaklıdere, where many foreign countries have their embassies, and Çankaya, a residential area in which are located the Presidential Palace (Cumhurbaskanlığı Köşkü, built by Holzmeister in 1932) and the Atatürk Evi.

Atatürk Çiftliği

A visit to the Atatürk Orman Çiftliği, a model farm which at one time lay within the afforested area outside the city, is one of Ankara's most popular outings. It has good restaurants and a swimming pool shaped like the Black Sea.

Atatürk Evi

This house, Atatürk's residence in the early days of the Republic, stands in the park behind the Presidential Palace. It is now a museum with a collection of memorabilia of the founder of modern Turkey (open: Sat., Sun. 2–5pm).

*Caracalla Baths

About 300m/330yd north of Ulus Meydanı in Çankırı Caddesi (south side) are the remains of the Roman baths (open: daily 8.30am–5.30pm) constructed by the emperor Caracalla between 212 and 217. The baths, probably dedicated to Aesculapius, god of health, were burnt down in the 10th c. They originally comprised several changing rooms and at least ten rooms containing baths with water at different temperatures. These would have ranged from a frigidarium (cold), to a piscina (swimming pool), tepidarium (lukewarm) and caldarium (hot). In front of the comparatively well-preserved lower floor of the baths with its covered passageways and

Aslanhanı Camii

Prayer niche in the "Forest Mosque"

heating system, can be seen the palaestra, where bathers did their exercises. Also on display are fragments of columns and capitals as well as some interesting Byzantine gravestones.

The 12.5 million cu.m/16.3 million cu.yd capacity Çubuk Barajı I, situated about 10km/6 miles north of the city centre not far off the Çubuk road, was the first of several reservoirs designed to secure the capital's water supply. Constructed between 1929 and 1939 it also serves local people as a recreation area (several restaurants near the dam at the south-west end). Because it was found to be gradually silting up, a number of other reservoirs have since been built in the vicinity of Ankara. These include the Çubuk Barajı II (24.6 million cu.m/32 million cu.yd; about 50km/31 miles north of the city) and the Bayındır Barajı (20km/12½ miles east) where there are tea houses and a swimming pool.

Çubuk Barajı I

In the 1930s a solitary black pine (pinus negra) growing on a north-facing slope half way up Ankara's "Apple Mountain" (Elma Dağ: 1862m/6111ft; a few kilometres south-east of the city) came suddenly to scientific prominence. With the help of other evidence it enabled the geographer Herbert Louis to demonstrate that large parts of Central Anatolia were formerly forested.

Elma Dağ

From 1938 to 1953 the body of Mustafa Kemal Atatürk lay in state beneath the dome in the central hall of the Ethnographic Museum (next to the Halk Evi; open: 9am–12.30pm, 1.30–5.30pm, in winter 9am–noon, 12.30–5pm., closed Mon.). Gracing the forecourt is a monumental equestrian statue of Atatürk (1927) by the Italian sculptor Canonica, with scenes of the War of Independence depicted in relief. Today the museum's ten departments house a comprehensive collection of Turkish crafts dating back to Seljuk times; they include costumes, household utensils, weaponry, musical instruments, carpets, rugs and woodcarvings. Particularly noteworthy are

Etnografya Müzesi

167

Ankara

Ethnographical Museum

Clock-tower on the citadel wall

the throne of the Seljuk Sultan Keyhusrev III (1264–83) and the sarco-phagus of Ani Şeref Eddin.

Gençlik Parkı

The "Youth Park" (entrance free), a large green expanse south of Ulus Meydani in the heart of Ankara, was another of Atatürk's inspirations. Laid out as part of the development of the New Town it replaced what had previously been a swamp. Together with the adjoining "Luna Parkı" (entrance fee), the Gençlik Parkı with its tea gardens and restaurants, fountains and artificial lakes (pedalos) is a source of great pleasure to Ankarans – as also is its "Wedding House" to the capital's bridal couples.

Hacı Bayram Camii and Hacı Bayram Türbesi

Hacı Bayram, founder of the Bayramı order of dervishes in Ankara, is revered as one of the country's holiest men. Active here around the turn of the 14th/15th c., he was pronounced a "veli" following his death in 1430. His tomb (open: Wed.–Sun. 8–11am, Mon.–Sun. 3–5pm) and the adjacent mosque (1427) which he endowed (adjoining the Temple of Augustus) are among the most visited places of pilgrimage in Turkey and the scene of much devotional activity. The türbe door and window frames are elaborately carved in the Early Ottoman manner. The beautifully ornate wooden doors are now in the safekeeping of the Ethnographic Museum.

Museum of Modern Art

Built in 1925 the Halk Evi (or People's House), a short distance to the north on a small rise beyond the university, was converted into the Museum of Modern Art in 1976 (open: 9am–12.30pm, 1.30–5.30pm, in winter 9am–noon, 12.30–5pm). Several richly furnished rooms are hung with works by Ottoman artists of the 19th and 20th centuries.

*Hisar (Citadel)

The Old City and its fortress, the Ankara Kalesi, beseiged and stormed on many occasions, are built on a 120m/394ft high andesite ridge facing the oldest of Ankara's gecekondu quarters, Altındağ. The foundations are believed to date back to the Galatians. The double walls of the citadel, made

168

Old Town quarter around the citadel hill

from large blocks of stone and pieces of antique masonry, were probably constructed by Michael II (820–29) in the aftermath of two successful assaults by the Arabs under Haroun al-Rachid. Many of the houses squeezed into the area between the walls are now historic monuments protected by UNESCO.

From the old horse market (At Meydanı) where grain and spices are traded, the lower gate, the Hisar Kapısı, with a clock tower, leads into the tortuous alleyways of the outer fortress (diş kale); from there via another gate, the Parmak Kapısı with double bays offset for added security, the inner fort (iç kale) is reached. This probably dates from the time of Heraclius (640/41). The Sark Kale, a tower linking the inner and outer defences, was strengthened in the 9th c., the resulting walls being up to 8m/26ft thick. It is possible to climb the south-east citadel wall (east tower) at this point, to be rewarded with what is surely the most impressive of all views over the city. On its north side the inner ring wall, once boasting 42 towers, abuts the Ak Kale (or White Fortress) access to which requires a permit from the Department of Antiquities.

Still in the Old Town, the rectangular Hükümet Meydanı, 200m/220yd or so north-east of Ulus Meydanı, is adorned with the 15m/49ft high Julian's Column (also known as the Belkis Minaresi), probably erected in A.D. 362 to commemorate the visit of the Emperor Julian Apostatas. The shaft of the column is horizontally grooved and the Byzantine capital embellished with a leaf pattern.

Hükümet Meydanı

This square, situated at the intersection of Atatürk Bulvarı, Gökalp Caddesi (east) and Gazi Mustafa Kemal Bulvarı (west), lies at the very heart of the New Town. Lined with modern shops and offices its real name is Hürriyet Meydanı (Independence Square). The unofficial name by which it is universally known was taken from a building belonging to the Red Crescent (the Islamic equivalent of the Red Cross) which once stood on the north-

Kızılay Meydanı

west corner. In the southern corner stands a memorial (1932–36), designed by Holzmeister and executed by A. Hanak, symbolising the three national virtues: patriotism, creativity and the desire for peace.

Kocatepe Camii

Located in the Kocatepe district east of Kızılay Meydanı the new Ottoman-style Kocatepe Camii is the largest mosque in Turkey. Built in the 1970s it is the most obvious manifestation of the Islamic revival to be seen in Ankara today.

*Ögüst Mabedi

About 400m/435yd north-east of Ulus Meydanı, next to the Hacı Bayram Camii, are the remains of what is unquestionably the most important ancient building in Ankara, the "Temple of Augustus and of Rome" (open: daily 8.30am–6pm except Mon. and Tue. afternoons). Converted in the 4th c. into a Christian church having a rectangular choir with light and dark stone patterning, it was first built in the 2nd c. B.C. as an Ionic dipteros with pronaos, cella and rear hall (presumably of Pergamum influence). Originally dedicated to the Phrygian gods Men (moon) and Cybele (earth mother, fertility), it was restored under Augustus and became a joint shrine to the first Roman emperor and to the goddess of the city of Rome. A combination of earthquakes and despoliation (the stone was used in building the adjacent Hacı Bayram Mosque) have left the temple in a severely ruined state.

The walls of the temple vestibule are inscribed with the historic "testament" of the Emperor Augustus (RES GAESTAE DIVI AUGUSTI or MONUMENTUM ANCYRANUM). Dating from the time of the emperor Tiberius (A.D. 14–37) the inscription, in Greek (exterior right) and Latin (inside), is a copy of the deposition which Augustus intended for the front of his mausoleum on the Field of Mars in Rome but which was never in fact found there. Apart from fragments unearthed in Antiochia (near Yalvaç in Pisidia) and Apollonia (near Uluborlu in Phrygia) the inscription in Ankara is the only extant copy. It was rediscovered in 1555 by Busbek, emissary of the Habsburg Emperor Ferdinand I, while on his way to the court of Süleiman the Magnificent. The text was definitively analysed by Th. Mommsen from plaster casts made by Carl Humann in 1882. The magnitude of Augustus's political achievement is clearly revealed in the list of his deeds and exploits. There is also mention of the census carried out at the time of Christ's birth.

Opera house

Ankara's opera house, in the Atatürk Bulvarı immediately adjacent to Gençlik Parkı, was the first to be built in Turkey. Designed by the German architect P. Bonatz it was created from a former exhibition hall.

Tabiat Tarihi Müzesi

The mining institute (M.T.A. Genel Müdürlüğü; Maden Tektik ve Arama Enstitüsü), 5km/3 miles outside Ankara on the Eskişehir road, has a small but interesting museum with numerous fossils.

Ulus Meydanı

Situated at the heart of the "Ulus" district immediately to the west below the citadel, this square, with its bronze equestrian statue of Mustafa Kemal Atatürk (1926) by the Austrian sculptor Krippel, is the focal point of Old Ankara. Among the streets radiating off it are the Hisarparkı Caddesi (east), on either side of which lies the city's traditional business quarter, and the Cumhuriyet Bulvarı (south-west). To the right on the Bulvarı is a venerable old building where, until 1925, the Turkish parliament used to meet and where, on April 23rd 1923, the Grand National Assembly convened for the first time. Resplendent opposite stands the city's oldest hotel, the Ankara Palas, where Atatürk and his closest advisers gathered for discussions during the Republic's early years.

Yeni Cami

The red porphyry "New Mosque", opposite the central prison in the easterly district of Dörtyol, was founded in 1565 by Cenabi Ahmet Paşa, governor of Ankara under Süleiman I. It was probably the work of the great Ottoman master builder Sinan or one of his pupils. The pulpit and prayer niche are of white marble. Next to the mosque there is a türbe.

Surroundings

Ayaş, about 70km/43 miles west of Ankara, principal town of its district, has some typical Pontic half-timbered houses, an old and interesting wooden mosque, and well-known thermal springs. There are more mineral springs at Ayaş İçmecesi, a small place some 20km/12½ miles further west.

Ayaş

In otherwise treeless steppe country near the village of Beynam, about 35km/22 miles south-east of Ankara on the road to Bala and Kırşehir, are vestiges of a large forest, further evidence that vast areas of Central Anatolia were at one time densely wooded.

* Beynam Ormanı

The district town of Beypazarı, on the site of the ancient Lagania Anastasio-polis, enjoys a lovely setting (scenic rock formations) on the southern edge of the Pontus Mountains about 100km/62 miles west of Ankara. It boasts not only an interesting Old Town with Pontic-style houses but also a number of 15th c. mosques (including the Ala Eddin Camii) and an Ottoman caravanserai, the Sulu Han.

* Beypazarı

The verdant countryside around Şehler Yaylası, a resort in the hills just to the south of Çamlıdere about 100km/62 miles north-west of Ankara, is a popular place of escape in summer. Şehler Yaylası is also the venue for a famous wrestling competition held annually in a large wooden arena set among the trees.

Çamlıdere

One of western Anatolia's most intriguing landscapes is encountered a few kilometres west of the small lignite mining town of Çayırhan, where the Nallıhan road crosses the northern arm of the Sakarya Dam (Sarıyer Barajı; 84sq.km/32sq.miles, 1.9 billion cu.m/2.5 billion cu.yd). On both sides of the road different coloured layers of clay and marl lie exposed, producing a striking effect. (N.B. In wet weather the softened clays become treacherous.)

Çayırhan

A very famous gold and electrum Hittite statuette (Bronze Age, c. 2000 B.C., now in the Hittite Museum) was discovered in a grave near the village of Hasanoğlan (or Hasanoğlu) some 37km/23 miles east of Ankara. Nearby is a weathered rock relief, possibly Roman, and in the village itself Roman milestones from the 1st c. A.D.

Hasanoğlan

North of the district town of Haymana, in Haymana-Kurd territory about 60km/37 miles south-west of Ankara, the remains of a Hittite shrine (death cult) are to be found at Gavur Kalesi (Fortress of the Infidels) near Derköy. The site, on a 60m/200ft rock plateau further fortified with cyclopean walls, was occupied also in Phrygian and Roman times. Among the features dating from the Hittite period is a huge tomb, the underground burial chamber of which retains its false vaulting. It is known from textual sources that the ashes of the dead were interred in tombs like these following cremation. The site is approached along a paved processional route above which there is a rock relief, carved at the height of the New Kingdom, depicting the weather god Teshub and his son Sharma in the presence of an enthroned goddess.
Haymana itself has a thermal bath (the ancient Myrica Therma) beneficial for rheumatic and gynaecological complaints.

Haymana

About 85km/53 miles north-east of Ankara the ruins of a fortress of Roman origin can be seen on a volcanic cone overlooking the district town of Kalecik; they are thought to be ancient Acitoriciacum. The Byzantines enlarged the stronghold in the 11th c. to secure the nearby ford over the Kızılırmak against the Danishmendids. Segments of the bastion and foundations still survive, fashioned from huge blocks of volcanic rock. Spanning the Kızılırmak is an Ottoman bridge.

Kalecik

1400m/4600ft up in the eastern Köroğlu Dağları, roughly 64km/40 miles north of the capital, there are a number of popular summer resorts with

Karagöl

171

springs, pools and a small mountain lake (Karagöl) with crystal-clear water. The main resort is Kızıkuyu (Karagöl).

Karaoğlan

Although this 20m/65ft high hüyük (old settlement mound; east of the Konya road, 30km/19 miles south of Ankara) has little to show today in the way of ruins, it has yielded relics of every era from the Copper Age to Seljuk times. The foundations of a Phrygian citadel were exposed during excavations between 1937 and 1945 (finds in the Hittite Museum).

Kızılcahamam

Occupying the site of ancient Manegordos, Kızılcahamam is the centre of a rice growing area in the Kırmır Çayı valley 75km/47 miles north of Ankara. It is well known as a spa for treating rheumatic and gynaecological complaints (baths in the upper part of the town) and as a source of (bottled) mineral water. Kızılcahamam also has several carbonated radioactive thermal springs (50°C/122°F) containing arsenic, bromine and iron. The forested valley south-west of the town is now a conservation area and nature reserve (Soğuksu Milli Parkı).

*Soğuksu Milli Parkı

The 1050ha/2600 acre national park west of Kızılcahamam was established in 1959 to safeguard the natural forest of the upper Kırmır Çayı catchment area and create a groundwater reservoir. Whole villages had to be re-sited in the process. With its open-air theatre, cafés and picnic places the park is popular for excursions. Ranging in altitude from 950m to 1716m/3120ft to 5630ft, the tree cover is predominantly coniferous forest but with some stands of oak (quercus pubescens). Wolves, foxes, wild boar, brown bears and more than 160 species of birds, including such birds of prey as Egyptian vultures, booted eagles and buzzards, live here in the wild.

Antakya (Hatay) M 7

South coast (Eastern Mediterranean)
Province: Hatay
Altitude: 0–92m/0–300ft
Population: 124,000

Situation and
**Importance

Antakya, known in antiquity as Antioch (Antiocheia) and more recently as Hatay, is the chief town of the frontier province of that name in south-eastern Turkey. It lies surrounded by extensive olive groves some 30km/20 miles from the Mediterranean in the alluvial plain of the Asi (the ancient Orontes) at the foot of Mount Habib Neccar (ancient Mons Silpius).
Few vestiges remain of Antioch's former importance as one of the commercial and cultural centres of the Hellenistic World. It now gains a relatively modest subsistence from its administrative functions, its garrison and the traffic passing through the town on the way to the countries of the Levant. It is not on the railway and no longer has a harbour.

History

In 307 B.C. Antigonos, one of Alexander the Great's generals, founded the town of Antigoneia on a site rather higher up the Orontes than present-day Antakya. Then in 301 B.C. Seleukos Nikator (305–280), founder of the Macedonian dynasty in Syria, established a new settlment on the site of the present town, naming it Antiocheia in honour of his father. The new town flourished, thanks to its situation at the intersection of the road down the Mediterranean coast and the caravan route from its port of Seleukeia into Mesopotamia. In the 2nd c. B.C. it was said to have a population of some 500,000 and to be exceeded in size only by Rome itself; it had aqueducts, a system of street-lighting and a colonnaded street 6.5km/4 miles long, and was much criticised by contemporaries for its luxurious way of life. It was celebrated throughout the East for its games in honour of Apollo. Even after its conquest by Rome in 64 B.C. it continued to enjoy a large measure of autonomy.
Antioch played an important part in the history of early Christianity. The Apostle Paul made several missionary journeys here (Acts 11:26, 14:26,

15:30, 35, 18:22) and the term "Christians" (Christianoi) was first used in Antioch (Acts 11:26). In the reign of Diocletian the Christians were ruthlessly persecuted and their churches destroyed, but his successor Constantine made Christianity the state religion and caused the churches to be rebuilt. Antioch became the seat of a Patriarch.

The decline of Antioch began with its conquest and destruction by the Mamelukes in 1266. The harbour at Seleukeia silted up and Antioch gradually sank to being a provincial town of no importance.

Sights

The repeated destructions it has suffered in the course of an eventful history have left Antakya with little to show of the splendid buildings of the ancient city, which occupied an area more than ten times the size of the present town. One notable feature that has survived however is the four-arched bridge built by Diocletian (284–305) over the Asi, which in spite of repeated restorations has substantially preserved its original form. On one of the piers is a carving of a Roman eagle.

Between the hospital and the Habib Neccar Camii are the ruins of an aqueduct, known as the Memikli Bridge, built in the reign of Trajan (2nd c.) In Kurtulus Caddesi stands the Habib Neccar Camii, a mosque converted from a Byzantine church which still contains the tombs of saints. The minaret is 17th c.

Historic buildings

Near the bridge over the Asi can be found an interesting Archaeological Museum. It is notable particularly for its collection of 50 very fine mosaics from Roman houses in the surrounding area – the largest such collection in the world – with lively representations of mythological scenes. The museum also contains a variety of finds from the Amuq Plain (particularly from Tell Açana) and a number of Roman sarcophagi.

** Archaeological Museum

On a rocky plateau on the south side of the town are the ruins of the Citadel, originally built in the 11th c. and later enlarged. Only scanty remains of the fortifications survive since, during the occupation of the town by the troops of Mehmet Ali, the Egyptian viceroy who, between 1830 and 1840, led a revolt against the Sultan, great stretches of the walls were pulled down and the stone used for building barracks. From the top there are splendid views.

Citadel

The town walls, built of fine limestone from Mons Silpius, have totally disappeared from the plain. Originally extending from the Orontes up on to the high ground and beyond, they are said to have had 360 towers, as high as 25m/80ft on the hills, and to have been broad enough for a four-horse chariot to be driven along the top.

Town walls

Surroundings

The Grotto of St Peter is reached by taking the road which runs east to Aleppo from the Orontes bridge. In some 3km/2 miles a narrow road (signposted) goes off on the right and leads through suburban gardens to a hill with a car park. Nearby, on a terrace commanding extensive views, is the Grotto of St Peter, a cave in which the Apostle is said to have preached and which in the 13th c. was converted into a church with a Gothic façade. At the far end stands an altar, behind which, to the right, is a trickle of water regarded by both Christians and Muslims as having curative virtues. From the cave a narrow rocky path leads in some 200m/220yd to a likeness carved from the rock, the origin and significance of which remains unknown. The relief was described in the 11th c. by the Byzantine historian Malalas.

* Grotto of St Peter

Near the village of Demirköprü, 15km/9½ miles east of Antakya, the Orontes is spanned by a medieval limestone bridge, which Baldwin IV

Demirköprüköy

Archaeological Museum · Antakya

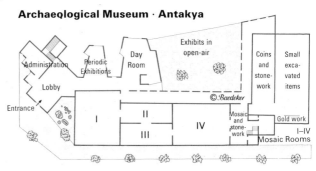

renovated in 1161. An earthquake in 1837 left the two towers of the bridge in ruins. Immediately south of the bridge lies the Tell Açana archaeological site and on the south side of the Reyhanlı road a few kilometres further east the Tell Taynat settlement mound. The latter, extending for some 500m×620m/547yd×678yd, was excavated between 1935 and 1938 by McEwan and Braidwood. First settled around 3000 B.C. it remained inhabited for about a thousand years during which time the summit plateau came to be occupied by a citadel with a large south-facing palace and a temple with a vestibule. Magnificent column bases found here can be seen in the Archaeological Museum in Ankara. At Tell Cüydeyde, another site in the vicinity, archaeologists have uncovered levels forming a continuous series from 4500 B.C. through to A.D. 600 (ceramic finds).

Roman mosaic in the Archaeological Museum

174

Peter's grotto

Gariz Tunnel in Samandağ

The town of Reyhanlı (population: 37,000) sprang up in the 19th c. follow-ing the enforced settlement of the Reyhanlı nomads. Nearby, in addition to numerous rock tombs, are the ruins of the Roman town of Emma (Yenişe-hir; 2km/1¼ miles), scene of many a crucial conflict down the centuries. Here Aurelian defeated Queen Zenobia of Palmyra in 272 and, in 1134, Baldwin III vanquished the Arabs. The fortress, burnt down in 1139, was rebuilt only to be destroyed for a second time by an earthquake in 1171. Some few remains can still be seen.

Reyhanlı

From the old bridge over the Orontes the Yayladağı road runs 8km/5 miles south to the residential suburb of Harbiye. 1km/¾ mile further on is a car park, below which, on the right, is the Grove of Daphne. In this shady grove of laurels, oaks and cypresses a beautiful waterfall cascades down over the rocks in an intricately patterned sheet of water. To this grove, according to the Greek legend, the coy nymph Daphne was pursued by Apollo, and here at her pleading Zeus changed her into a laurel tree; in compensation for his loss Apollo was to have a temple in his honour. The grove was regarded as sacred by local people and important games were held there. The town was a favoured place of residence for upper-class Greeks and Romans, and "Daphnici mores" became a synonym for relaxed moral standards.

Grove of Daphne

About 8km/5 miles beyond Karaçay a poor road turns off towards the Musa Dağı, leading after 11km/7 miles to a 13th c. Crusader church. After the Armenian pogroms which followed the First World War the Armenian minority took refuge in the Musa Dağı. The story of their suffering is told by Franz Werfel in his historical novel "The Forty Days of Musa Dağı". On the 1281m/4202ft high summit is a basilica dedicated to Saint Simeon Stylite the Younger who, inspired by the example of an older namesake (Qaalat Siman/St Simeon in Syria) reputedly spent his life perched on top of a tall column erected on the spot now occupied by the church.

Yoğun Oluk

Antalya

* Samandağ/
Seleukeia
Piereia

From the fork at the western end of Samandağ (Seleukeia; 26km/16 miles), a metalled road leads north-west over an alluvial plain and past a beautiful beach to the village of Mağaracık (7km/4½ miles). Here can be seen the remains of the once-considerable town of Seleukeia Piereia, the port of Antioch, founded by Seleukos Nikator about 300 B.C. In its heydey Seleukeia had a population of 30,000. To the right are a ruined aqueduct, with tombs cut in the rock face above, and the old harbour, now silted up. A notable feature is the canal, driven through solid rock at the time of the Roman emperors Vespasian and Titus in an unsuccessful attempt to save the harbour.

Bakras Kalesi

Some 8km/5 miles west of the İskenderun road about 28km/17 miles north of Antakya stands the ruined Crusader castle "Gaston" at Bakras. It fell to Saladin in 1188, to the Lesser Armenian King Levon II in 1191 and to the Mamelukes under Baibar in 1268. The site is thought by many historians to be that of Pagrae, to which Strabo refers.

Terbezek

Reached via a poor track running west off the Maraş road a few kilometres north of Kırıkhan are the ruins of the Templar Crusader castle of Trapesak (Terbezek or Darbsek Kale-si; about a kilometre north of the village). The castle played a key role in defending the Crusader kingdom of Antiochia (Antakya) against Saladin who, after a hard fought struggle, managed to take it for a short time in 1188. In 1268 it fell to the Mamelukes. Their leader Baibar garrisoned troops there, renaming it Darsak.

Gündüslü

Near the village of Gündüslü about a kilometre west of the Maraş highway north of Kırıkhan there are three cave tombs with long inscriptions in Greek and some badly damaged reliefs.

Sultankalesi

About 20km/12½ miles due north of Kırıkhan stands a third castle, Sultankalesi, with an impressive south gate (bastions), square north tower, chapel and cistern. Situated high up (1250m/4102ft) in the Amanus Mountains near the village of Cıvlan (Sıvlan), it was probably built during the Byzantine period to guard the pass, one of the routes through the Amanus from the Maraş trench to İskenderun.

Antalya   F 7

South coast (Eastern Mediterranean)
Province: Antalya
Altitude: 0–40m/0-130ft
Population: 250,000

**Situation and
Importance

The provincial capital of Antalya is delightfully situated at the innermost point of the Gulf of Antalya (Antalya Körfezi) on Turkey's southern coast. Against a backdrop of mountains – to the west the bare limestone massif of the Lycian Taurus (Bey Dağları) plunging steeply down from 3086m/10,125ft; to the east the Lower Cilician Taurus – the town clusters around the picturesque Old Harbour lying at the foot of a 23m/75ft high cliff. Between the town and the high ridge of hills to the west, the broad pebbly Konyaaltı beach – a major attraction for holidaymakers – extends in a wide sweep. Thanks to its sheltered situation Antalya has a subtropical climate, with very mild wet winters and almost rainless summers. The town's new harbour is the only one of any size between İzmir and Mersin.

History

In the 12th c. B.C. Achaeans from the Peloponnese moved into Pamphylia (the region in which Antalya lies) and overlaid the indigenous population. A second wave of Greek immigrants followed in the 7th c. when the Ionians occupied the existing settlements and established new ones. During the struggles between Rome and Antiochos the Great the area became of the kingdom of Pergamum, the ruler of which, Attalos II Philadelphos (159–38),

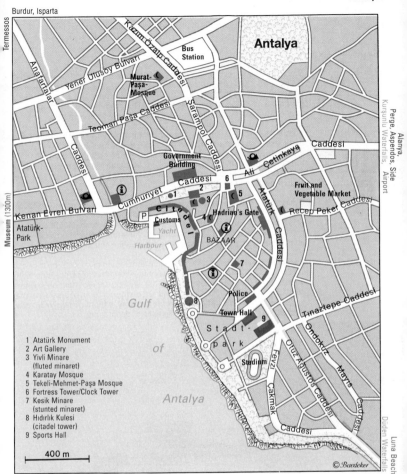

Burdur, Isparta

Termessos

Bus Station

Antalya

Kazım Özalp Caddesi

Yener Ulusoy Bulvarı

Murat-Paşa-Mosque

Anafartalar

Teoman Paşa Caddesi

Sarampol Caddesi

Alanya
Perge
Aspendos, Side
Kurşunlu Waterfalls, Airport

Caddesi

Government Building

Caddesi

Ali Çetinkaya

Caddesi

Cumhuriyet Caddesi

Kenan Evren Bulvarı

Museum (1300 m)

1
2
6
3
5
Fruit and Vegetable Market

Atatürk Caddesi

Recep Peker Caddesi

P
Customs

4 Hadrian's Gate

Atatürk-Park

Yacht Harbour

BAZAAR

Citadel

7

Gulf

8

Police

Town Hall

9

Stadt-park

Tınaztepe Caddesi

of

Stadium

Ömdokuz Mayıs Caddesi

Fevzi Çakmak

Otuz Ağustos Caddesi

İsli Caddesi

Antalya

Caddesi

Luna Beach
Düden Waterfalls

1 Atatürk Monument
2 Art Gallery
3 Yivli Minare
  (fluted minaret)
4 Karatay Mosque
5 Tekeli-Mehmet-Paşa Mosque
6 Fortress Tower/Clock Tower
7 Kesik Minare
  (stunted minaret)
8 Hıdırlık Kulesi
  (citadel tower)
9 Sports Hall

400 m

© Baedeker

founded the city of Attaleia, now Antalya, and made it capital of Pamphylia. In 133 Attaleia, together with the rest of the kingdom of Pergamum, passed into Roman hands, and thereafter formed part of the province of Asia. The Apostle Paul landed at Attaleia with his companions Barnabas and Mark on his first missionary journey to Asia Minor in A.D. 45–49. In the time of Hadrian the town was surrounded by a strong defensive wall. The Byzantines developed it still further, encircling it with a double ring of walls to repel Arab attacks in the 8th and 9th centuries.

During the Seljuk period (from 1207) a number of handsome mosques were built and the town's defences were strengthened. In Ottoman times the town – then also known as Adalia or Satalia – was divided into three, with separate areas for Christians, Muslims and those of other faiths. The

177

iron gates between them were closed every Friday from noon to 1pm because of a prophecy foretelling a Christian assault at that time.

Sights

*Old Harbour

Since the recent restoration of the picturesque quarter below the citadel (kaleiçi), the Old Harbour, nestling in its recess in the cliffs, and the area surrounding it, with hotels, restaurants, boutiques and bazaars, have become a busy focus of tourist activity. The citadel, on the clifftop overlooking the small-craft harbour, has also recently been restored.

*Yivli Minare

A little way north-east of the Old Harbour is Antalya's most striking landmark, the Yivli Minare (Fluted Minaret), a vigorous example of Seljuk architecture with a square base surmounted by an octagonal drum bearing the fluted shaft with its corbelled gallery round the top. The minaret, faced with brown tiles, belongs to a mosque converted from a former Byzantine church by Alaeddin Keykubad (1219–36).

Old Town

Other features of interest in the narrow bazaar-filled streets of the Old Town are a fortified gate with a clock-tower in the busy main square, the nearby Tekeli Mehmet Paşa Mosque, the Seljuk Karatay Mosque (1250) and, farther south, the Kesik Minare (Truncated Minaret) beside the ruins of an abandoned mosque which was once a Byzantine church.

*Hadrian's Gate

Considerable stretches of the Hellenistic and Roman town walls on the east side of the Old Town have been preserved, sometimes incorporating later building. The most notable part is the well-preserved Hadrian's Gate, erected in honour of the Emperor Hadrian on the occasion of his visit to the town in A.D. 130. This imposing marble gateway, with two massive towers flanking its three arches, has rich sculptural decoration.

Antalya: the Citadel on a steep rocky promontory dominating the harbour

View of the Old Town, with the Yivli Minaret in the foreground

Along the east side of Hadrian's Gate and the old town walls runs a broad avenue, Atatürk Caddesi, with dual carriageways separated by a double row of stately date palms. It sweeps southwards in a wide arc to the Town Hall and Municipal Park. The latter, extending to the cliff edge overlooking the Gulf, offers some splendid views. At the north-west corner of the park can be seen the 13m/43ft high Hıdırlık Kulesi, the stump of a tower which may once have been a Roman lighthouse.

Municipal Park

Definitely worth visiting is the Museum of Archaeology and Ethnography, situated some 2km/1¼ miles from the city centre on the western outskirts of the town. Founded in 1919, it was originally housed in the mosque adjacent to the Fluted Minaret, before being moved to its new premises in 1972. The collection is displayed in exemplary fashion, having been rearranged in 1985. The large archaeological section offers an excellent survey of the great periods in Pamphylia's history, from the neolithic on through the Bronze Age (urn burials) to Hellenistic and Roman times. Particularly notable are the gallery containing statues of divinities (mostly from Perge), the collection of items recovered by underwater archaeology, the Gallery of Roman Emperors, the magnificent series of sarcophagi, the mosaics from

*Archaeological Museum

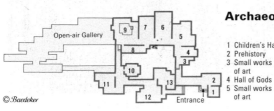

Archaeological Museum

1 Children's Hall
2 Prehistory
3 Small works of art
4 Hall of Gods
5 Small works of art
6 Imperial Hall
7 Sarcophagi
8 Icons
9 Mosaics
10 Coins
11–13 Ethnological department

© *Baedeker*

179

Seleukeia, and the fine coin collection with the Hoard of Probus, the Aspendos Hoard (silver), a Byzantine gold hoard found at Finike in 1959, and the Side Hoard (silver). There are also a number of icons.

The rich ethnographic section of the museum displays a great variety of material of the Turkish period – weapons, clothing, stockings, jewellery, domestic equipment, books, tiles, glass, porcelain, locks, musical instruments and carpets, together with a loom. (Open: 8am–noon, 1.30–5pm; closed Mon.)

Surroundings

* Termessos

Termessos, another important ancient site (Pisidian not Pamphylian) is situated in the mountains 30km/19 miles north-west of Antalya on the gentle slopes of Güllük Dağı (Solymos; 1650m/5415ft). This area is now a National Park. Little is known about the town's origins except that it was a Pisidian hill-fort reputedly besieged without success by Alexander the Great. The ruins seen today date from the 2nd and 3rd centuries A.D.; most notable are the theatre, the agora, a gymnasium, several pillared halls and a number of graves. A mountain road leads up to the site but the final two kilometres must be covered on foot. From the top there is a magnificent view of the Gulf of Antalya.

Saklıkent

In the last few years a small winter-sports centre has been built at an altitude of 2000–2400m/6500–7875ft near the village of Saklıkent (1850m/6071ft) in the northern Bey Dağları, about 70km/43 miles west of Antalya (via Çakırlar). Although chair-lift facilities are still modest the resort offers more than 2500 beds.

The remains of Termessos . . .   *. . . are overgrown with luxuriant vegetation*

The limestone country around Antalya is rich in karst springs, swallow-holes and waterfalls. Two large karst springs, Kırkgöz (close to a huge caravanserai dating from 1236) and Pınarbaşı, are located not far to the north-west of Antalya (follow the Burdur road for 11km/7 miles to where it forks, then take the old Korkuteli road instead of the fast new highway, continuing for a few kilometres beyond Döşemaltı). Water pours in abundance from these springs before disappearing behind the "regülatör" in the Bıyıklı Düdeni cave system. Some of the sink holes are massive, large enough to engorge a river or lake (up to 30,000l/6600galls per sec.). The lime deposits from these and other karst springs on the edge of the Taurus north and west of Antalya have built up, over a period of 1.5 to 2 million years, into vast travertine terraces similar to those at Pamukkale. Sometimes as much as 275m/900ft high and extending into the sea in places, they are found across a wide area approximately 35 x 20km/22 x 12½ miles, or 650sq.km/250sq.miles. The spring water from Bıyıklı flows underground for 14km/8½ miles, briefly surfacing again at Varsak Obruk (huge sink-hole) before resuming its subterranean course for a further 2km/1¼ miles, re-emerging finally with tremendous power at Düdenbaşı. Here it joins forces again with the water channelled off at the Bıyıklı regülatör and, together with the waters of the Düden Çayı, tumbles in a series of lovely cascades down a narrow gorge in the travertine. The upper falls (Düdenbaşı Şelalesi), just to the north-east of Antalya, are reached via a small road (Kızılırmak Caddesi) off the northern by-pass. The lower Düden Çayı falls (Düden Şelalesi), in the south-east part of the town itself, near a small park immediately beside the Lara Plajı coast road, plunge 20m/65ft over the edge of the travertine into the sea.

Karst springs
Düdenbaşı
Mağarası

The Karain cave, 27km/17 miles north-west of Antalya, near Döşemaltı, in the karst country around Şam Dağ, was inhabited by prehistoric man. It has yielded finds from both Lower and Middle palaeolithic, including bones and teeth belonging to Neanderthal man. Some of the finds are on show in a small but remarkably comprehensive museum on the site.

*Karain Mağarası

This cave lies hidden in the karst mountains 45km/28 miles north of Antalya, two hours away on foot from the village of Ahırtaş (turn north-east off the Burdur road a few kilometres beyond Döşemaltı, thence via Karatas or via Kovanlık, Camiliköy and Kilik). The cave, 600m/656yd long, 75m/82yd across and 35m/115ft high, with some colossal stalagmites, was investigated by K. Kökten, whose finds showed it to have been inhabited in prehistoric times. At the entrance is a huge cistern, also traces of a very early settlement.

Kocain Mağarası

With one lovely beach giving way to another, the 220km/137 miles of coastline on the Gulf of Antalya, from Kemer eastwards to beyond Gazipaşa, is known as the "Turkish Riviera".

Turkish Riviera

The west coast of the Gulf of Antalya, running almost due north–south, is fringed for some 50km/30 miles by a virtually uninterrupted line of delightful beaches, with the wooded hills of the Taurus rising immediately behind (Olimpos Bey Dağları National Park). About 50km/30 miles south of Antalya lies the up-and-coming holiday centre of Kemer, with hotels, holiday clubs, a modern yacht marina and good facilities for water sports. About 10km/6 miles further on there are more holiday facilities at Göynük and Beldibi (Stone Age site nearby).

*West coast of the Gulf of Antalya

Only 3km/1¾ miles south of Kemer are the ruins of the old Lydian port of Phaselis where, in 334–333 B.C., Alexander the Great set up his winter quarters. There are remains of a theatre, an aqueduct, temples, and a Hadrian's Arch erected in A.D. 114. There is also a museum.

Phaselis

Immediately west of the Gulf of Antalya, the 700sq.km/270sq.mile Olimpos Beydağları Milli Parkı (National Park) stretches from the coast into the

*Chimaera and Olympos

Ruins of Olympus in a picturesque setting

nearby mountains. Ancient Olympos, near the village of Çıralı in the southern section of the Park, about 50km/30 miles south of the new resort of Kemer, is the site of one of Nature's curiosities, the eternal flame of Chimaera (the fire-breathing monster of Greek mythology), a phenomenon mentioned in A.D. 300 by Bishop Methodius and by Beaufort on his travels in 1811. To reach the spot a strenuous climb of some 150m/500ft must first be made, followed by a further 150m/500ft of ascent above the ruins of Olympos. Natural gas escaping from eighteen or so holes and crevices in the rock has burned here since ancient times. Although barely discernible in daylight the flames are said to be visible far out to sea at night. The gases are still to be properly analysed but are known to include methane.

Olympos was once one of the most celebrated cities of the Lycian League before falling into the hands of pirates. They continued to plague it even after the successful campaign waged against them by the Romans in 78 B.C. In the end the city simply slipped into irreversible decline. During the imperial period Olympos was widely known as a cult site dedicated to the fire god Hephaistos (with a temple to Hephaistos at Chimaera, see above). There are also references in Plutarch to ritual feasts in honour of Mithras, Persian god of light.

The remains include those of a Roman theatre, a Byzantine basilica, a Roman temple, a bridge, defensive walls and chamber tombs. All are badly ruined and very overgrown; but standing in picturesque surroundings in a valley near the sea they are definitely worth a visit.

North coast of the Gulf of Antalya

From the eastern outskirts of Antalya a series of splendid beaches extend along the north shore of the Gulf (see above, "Turkish Riviera"). Lara Plajı is perhaps the best of them, with a number of new hotels.

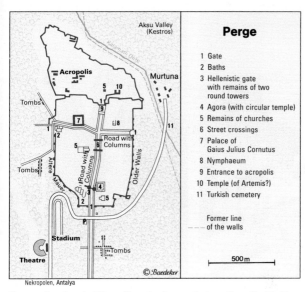

Nekropolen, Antalya

The remains of ancient Perge (Pergai or Pergae, first mentioned in the 4th c. B.C.) a Pamphylian city of particular importance in Roman imperial times, lies on a steep-sided hill on the north-western edge of the alluvial plain of the Aksu Çayı (the ancient Kestros) near the village of Murtuna, 18km/ 11 miles north-east of Antalya. The site is 4km/2½ miles from the river, which was navigable in ancient times, and 12km/7½ miles from the Mediterranean. Like most of the Greek colonies on the west and south coasts of Asia Minor, Perge found itself deprived of one of the main pillars of its existence as its harbour gradually silted up, leading in Byzantine times to its final decline. Perge had one of the oldest Christian communities in Asia Minor. Paul and Barnabas came here after their flight from Antioch in Pisidia and "spoke the word in Perga" (Acts 14:25).

**Perge

The lower town at Perge, once encircled by walls fortified with towers, is bounded to the north by a 50m/165ft hill on which the acropolis was built. Here stood the city's oldest buildings. At the south-east corner of the plateau are some remains which it is thought may be those of the famous Temple of Artemis to which Strabo refers. This however is far from certain. The site, parts of which are marshy, is entered through a gate in the walls, immediately beyond which are the remains of two round towers belonging to a gateway of the Hellenistic period. To the right of these towers lies the relatively small agora, with a circular temple. Across the centre of the site runs a colonnaded street 20m/65ft wide (many columns re-erected), which is continued at the foot of the acropolis by two branches leading east and west. Little is known of the buildings on either side of the colonnaded street. Remains of baths and of Byzantine churches have been identified at various points. On the north-west of the site are the excavated remains of the palace of Gaius Julius Cornutus. To the south-west, outside the walls of the lower town, is the well-preserved Roman stadium (234m/256yd long by 34m/37yd across, seating for 12,000) built in the 2nd c. A.D. The south end of the stadium was used for the gladitorial combats which were then popular. Under the seating on the east side are 30 rooms, originally used as shops. 200m/220yd farther south-west, built into the hillside, is the theatre, which dates from the 3rd c. A.D. Constructed of travertine and faced with marble, it

The ruins

Remains of two round towers . . .   *. . . on the Perge ancient site*

has 40 rows of seating, with a gangway between the upper and lower tiers, and could accommodate an audience of 13,000. Also outside the lower town are a number of sizeable necropolises.

**Aspendos   See Side

*Side   See entry

Aphrodisias   D 6

Western Anatolia (Menteşe highland)
Province: Aydın
Altitude: 548m/1800ft
Village: Geyre (3km/2 miles north-west; population: 1000)

Situation   The ruins of ancient Aphrodisias lie 82km/51 miles south-west of Denizli, where the heavily wooded southern foothills of Ak Dağ border on the broad valley of the Kekre Çayı. The site itself is located high in a side valley of the upper Dandalas Çayı (Vandalas Çayı), a tributary of the Büyük Menderes Nehri (Great Maeander River).

History   Chalcolithic finds show the area to have been settled in the 4th millennium B.C.; early Bronze Age pottery also suggests there was an Assyrian trading colony here during the Hittite period. There is a tradition that the settlement took its earliest recorded name, Ninoe, from the Assyrian King Ninos (Tukulti-Ninurta I, 1245–1208 B.C.); a more likely derivation however is from Nin (Ishtar) the Old Oriental goddess of love and war, with whom Venus, the Roman goddess of love, later became identified. Nin, daughter of the moon god Sin, was sister of the sun god Shamash and wife of Anu god of heaven. Her attributes were bestowed by the Greeks upon Aphrodite, goddess not simply of beauty and love but also of the Morning and Evening Star. The town only took the name Aphrodisias in Hellenistic times, having been known previously as Lelegonpolis, Megalopolis and probably also Plarasa. Through its sanctuary it became the centre of the wide-spread cult of Aphrodite, in addition to which it had famous schools of sculpture, medicine and philosophy. The pinnacle of its fortunes was reached under the Julian emperors when Aphrodisias enjoyed the patronage of Sulla, Caesar, Antony, and Augustus; it was Antony who granted sanctuary status to the temple. This is reflected in the fact that the surviving remains are almost all Roman, an exception being the town walls which are of later date (4th c.).

Seated Aphrodite

In the Early Christian-Byzantine era the town was first a bishopric and then the seat of the Metropolitan Bishop of Caria; it was also rechristened Stavropolis. From 540 (in the reign of Justinian), as capital of the province of that name, it became known simply as Caria (of which the name of the present village, Geyre, is a corruption). Despite having its fortifications strengthened in the latter part of the 7th c., in the 8th and 9th centuries the town succumbed to the Arabs. Its decline was accelerated by Ottoman rule until, in 1402, Tamarlane found no more than a village in the shadow of the ruined city. Excavation has proceeded in several stages, at first under the Turks in 1904/05, 1913 and 1937, then since 1961 by US archaeologists led by Kenan Erim.

Sights

The sprawling ruins of Aphrodisias lie at the foot of the 2308m/7575ft Baba Dağ (formerly Salbakos) to the south of the small modern village of Geyre (Geira, Gere; the old village was situated actually among the ruins). Finds from recent excavations are housed in a little museum built with American assistance. Modern research has transformed Aphrodisias from a place which few visited into one of the most important historic sites in Turkey. A partially excavated processional way equipped with a drainage system leads to the ruins.

**Ruins

The Roman agora, 120m/131yd wide and 205m/224yd long, with Doric portico along the north side and Ionic portico along the south, was renovated under Tiberius (14–37). Some of the columns still have their architraves in place. Twelve columns also survive from the colonnaded Portico of Tiberius.

To the south, on the far side of a large square, stand the ruins of the domed Byzantine Martyrs' Church (6th c.).

Apollo

The so-called "acropolis" is actually a hüyük or settlement mound. Excavation has shown it to have been inhabited in prehistoric times (from the 4th millennium B.C.).

Acropolis

The Temple of Aphrodite, an Ionic pseudo-dipteros of 8×13 columns, was built in about 100 B.C. over an earlier shrine (3rd c. B.C.) from which mosaics have survived. The temple, with pronaos and cella only, boasted a huge statue of Aphrodite, more than 3m/10ft tall, of which parts have been recovered. Of the fourteen columns still standing, two have their architrave in place. Like other temples dedicated to Aphrodite, this one can be presumed to have fulfilled a therapeutic sexual role, prostitution being a feature of the Aphrodite cult practised by priestesses and female temple slaves (hierodules). Following instructions from the Delphic Oracle, the patrons of the temple donated cult objects of various kinds: Sulla for instance gave a gold crown and double axe, Caesar a statue of Eros.

Temple of Aphrodite

In the 5th c. the Byzantines converted the pagan temple into a three-aisle basilica. Two centuries later the town was renamed Stavropolis (City of the Cross), further severing the links with its pagan past.

Sculptors' Workshop	Between the Temple to Aphrodite and the odeion are the remains of a sculptor's workshop – the school of sculpture at Aphrodisias contributed greatly to the cultural splendour of the city. Marble for use locally and almost certainly for export was quarried from the slopes of Baba Dağ to the east of the town.
Bishop's Palace	Excavation adjacent to the sculptors' workshop has uncovered a 5th c. bishop's palace with a peristyle court with columns of blue marble, kitchen quarters with a fine dining-room, and an audience chamber with three conchas and marble intarsia floor.
Hadrian's Baths	On the west side of the agora are baths built at the time of Hadrian (117–38), with interesting basins, heating system, changing rooms and a latrine. Some fine sculptures were uncovered here during excavation.
*Museum	In addition to small archaeological finds the museum on the site mainly houses sculptures from the celebrated Aphrodisias school – heads of muses, statues of emperors, clothed figures, etc. Particularly noteworthy are the Zoilos frieze, the portrait statue of the writer Pausanias, a reproduction of Polyclitus's famous discus thrower and a copy of the statue of Aphrodite from the temple.
Odeion	The best preserved structure on the site is the Roman odeion to the south of the Temple of Aphrodite. The little concert hall almost certainly doubled as a buleuterion (council chamber) and was decorated with reliefs and statues. Today the orchestra with its mosaic floor is usually flooded, leaving frogs to croak their own chorus from among the water plants.
*Propylon	The now reconstructed 2nd c. tetrapylon (pylon or gateway), originally with four rows of four columns, led to the Temple of Aphrodite. The columns on the east side have spiral fluting.

The reconstructed Propylon once led to the sanctuary

Not far from the museum are the remains of a shrine dedicated to the worship of the Roman emperors. The complex, built in A.D. 50, consisted of a podium temple reached via steps from the east end of an elongated court. Along the north and south sides of the court ran three-storeyed porticos, the columns in each tier being of a different Classical Greek order – Doric (lower tier), Ionic (middle tier) and Corinthian (upper tier). Between the columns of the middle and upper tiers on the south side were reliefs depicting scenes from mythology and history.

Sebasteion

The stadium at Aphrodisias ranks as perhaps the best preserved of all those surviving from antiquity. Built around an arena 270m/295yd long and 54m/59yd wide with semi-circular ends, its 22 rows of seats could accommodate more than 30,000 spectators.

**Stadium

The best preserved sections of the 3.5km/2 miles of defensive walls are found along the north-east of the site. Erected at the time of Constantine the Great (306–37) they incorporate masonry from the ancient buildings. Above the northernmost of the three gateways is an inscription which originally read "May fortune favour the glorious metropolis of Aphrodisians". In the 7th c. "Aphrodisians" was changed to "Stavropolitans".

The walls

Large enough to seat an audience of 10,000 the Late Hellenistic theatre with double proscenium, situated on the eastern slope of the "acropolis" mound, was restored and enlarged under Marcus Aurelius (161–80). The lower part of the stage and auditorium are well preserved. In a side entrance are carved transcriptions of imperial decrees and letters addressed to the city and its chief luminary and magistrate Zoilos. They include the so-called "Diocletian Price Edict" which, in an attempt to curb runaway inflation, introduced a regime of fixed prices. The large court in front of the theatre was paved with marble slabs in the 4th c. South-east of it lie the ruins of a columned, three-aisled basilica and a gymnasium; closer at hand are the remains of the theatre baths.

*Theatre

The well preserved ancient stadium of Aphrodisias

Lake Apolyont · Uluabat Gölü   D3

Southern Marmara region
Province: Bursa
Altitude: 5m/16ft
Size: 134sq.km/52sq.miles
Length: 23km/14 miles
Width: 12km/7½ miles
Depth: maximum 4m/13ft, average 2m/6½ft

Situation and Importance

Lake Apolyont (or Uluabat Gölü as it is officially known, Uluabat being a village on the north-west shore) is located in one of the large depressions which run parallel to the Pontic Mountains westward as far as the Sea of Marmara. These basins, reaching deep inland, are occupied by shallow lakes separated only by low-lying sills. With the Kara Dağ (833m/2734ft) forming a barrier against the Sea of Marmara to the north, and bounded by the Orhaneli upland in the south, the well-watered plains of the Marmara region are excellent for fruit and vegetable growing – olives and figs and mulberries for silk-worm breeding. Apolyont Gölü, shallower than Kuş/Manyas Gölü to the west, is rich in nutrients, the lake bottom being constantly churned up by wind and waves. Colonies of reeds, tamarisk swamps and carpets of waterlilies add to the picturesqueness of the scenery around the lake. A lock on the Koca Çay (the ancient Ryndakos) at Uluabat allows the water level to be regulated, a process which at one time was essential to the survival of the swamp crabs inhabiting the lake which were a valuable source of income for local fishermen. Today however disease has all but wiped out the crab population.

Though not a designated nature reserve Apolyont Gölü boasts a wide range of interesting flora and fauna. In addition to swamp crabs the latter include squacco and purple herons, little egrets and pelicans.

Sights

Apolyont, the fishing village from which the lake took its name, is now   *Apolyont
known as Gölyazı. Shaded by ancient plane trees it is attractively situated
about 5km/3 miles off the main road on the north-east shore, on a peninsula
linked to the mainland by a causeway. In antiquity the lake was called Lacus
Appolonia after Appolonia, a town famous for its temple cult and ruins
(including remains of a theatre, stadium and temple of Apollo from the 5th
c. B.C.) which today lie partly buried beneath the village.
There was very probably a Greek town here, resettled in Hellenistic times.
By the 14th c. it was described as virtually uninhabited and falling into
disrepair, with four ramparts and surrounded by water. In the 19th c. it was
said to be a prosperous small town with a mainly Greek population and a
castle.

Two important tombs dating from the mid 3rd millennium B.C. (roughly   Dorak
corresponding to Troy I/II; see Troy), one of a royal couple, the other of a
prince, were discovered at Dorak on the south side of the lake. The grave
goods, now in a private collection in İzmir, included superbly ornamented
swords and daggers, marble and amber sceptres with gold and silver
shafts, the remains of a throne, and a blade engraved with a ship's prow –
the earliest evidence yet found of a seagoing vessel apart from those of
ancient Egypt.

Earlier known as Mihaliç, Karacabey, the district's principal town, occupies   Karacabey
a site near that of ancient Miletopolis in the fertile plain of the Simav Çayı
(ancient Makestos). It was from Miletopolis, founded by colonists from
Miletus, that Manyas Gölü took its name.

From Karacabey a narrow asphalt road covers the 33km/20 miles to the   Kocaçay Deltası
sandy Yeniköy Plajı on the Sea of Marmara, from where the fascinating
Koca Çayı delta (into which the Apolyont Gölü drains) can be reached. It is
the largest river delta in the Marmara region, and the only one in which the
lagoons and surrounding forest are for the most part left to develop naturally. The primordial woodland of poplar, oak, ash and hawthorn is almost
jungle-like, with liana-festooned trees rising in tiers above smaller bushes.
Wild boar root about in the undergrowth, and snake-like lizards called
sheltopusiks, some more than a metre in length, inhabit the clearings. The
lagoons are the breeding ground of many kinds of waterfowl, and otters
and jackal are also found. In 1972, at Bayramdere, south-east of Yeniköy,
the Turkish forestry commission started a pheasant farm to bolster the
region's dwindling pheasant population. Indigenous stock have been
cross-bred with varieties introduced from Europe to produce a bird which
can survive in the open all the year round.

The village of Uluabat was the birthplace of Uluabatlı Hasan (Hasan of   Uluabat
Uluabat) who, in 1453, raised the Ottoman flag for the first time on the walls
of İstanbul. The name Uluabat means "big town", almost certainly a reflection of its closeness to ancient Miletopolis.

A few kilometres east of Uluabat, between the lake and the main Bursa   İssiz Han
road, stands an Ottoman caravanserai, İssiz Han. It is now used as an onion
store.

Ararat · Ağrı Dağı   U 4

Eastern Anatolia (Ararat highland)   **See warning page 7**
Province: Ağrı and Kars
Altitude: 5137m/16,860ft

The majestic double volcanic cone of Ararat (Late Tertiary) stands isolated   Situation and
on the outer rim of the great sweep of the Taurus Mountains in eastern   *Topography

Permanent snow crowns Ararat, the highest mountain in Turkey

Anatolia, at the south-eastern edge of the Ararat highland. It is a lava sheet plateau out of which rise a number of more recent, equally isolated volcanic massifs.

At 5137m/16,860ft the main peak, Great Ararat (Büyük Ağrı Dağı), is the highest mountain in Turkey; it is separated from the 3896m/12,786ft summit of Little Ararat (Küçük Ağrı Dağı) by a 2600m/8533ft high col. Because of its great height relative to the surrounding countryside – it rises almost 5200m/17,000ft above the İğdır basin to the north and 3500m/11,500ft above the Ararat highland – the visual impact of the mountain is immense. There is some dispute about its name: the Turkish Ağrı Dağı (Mountain of Pain, a reference to its steepness and roughness), only accurately describes parts of the upper slopes; another school of thought accordingly claims it was known in earlier times as "Eğri Dağı" (Lop-sided Mountain). The Armenians called it "Mother of Earth" and the Kurds "Mountain of Evil".

Physical geography

Great and Little Ararat are stratified volcanos with alternating layers of ash/tuff and trachyte/lava; both have concave truncated cones with central craters. On their flanks are a number of secondary vents as well as hot sulphurous springs and fumaroles. The most recent eruption was on June 6th 1840. The outpouring of lava and subsequent landslide destroyed a nearby monastery on the mountain's east flank and buried the village of Ahıra together with 2000 of its inhabitants. The monastery is said to have had in its possession a piece of wood from Noah's Ark. A huge nevé field and ice cap cover the main summit. The permanent snow line today is at about 4000m/13,100ft, leaving an area of almost 13sq.km/5sq.miles under perpetual snow and ice.

Importance

Since the 19th c. Ararat has been cast in a strategic role as a mountain barrier. In 1828 it was ceded to Russia by the Persians and for almost a century the Turko-Russian frontier ran over the top. Little Ararat marked the point at which Persia, the former Soviet Union (now the Armenian Republic) and Turkey all met. In 1920, as a result of the peace of Gümrü, Ararat passed in its entirety to Turkey. The present Turkish-Armenian frontier follows the line of the Aras Nehri and Arpa Çayı (see Ani) while the old frontier forms the provincial boundary between Ağrı and Kars.

The first person to climb Ararat was Pitton de Tournefort in 1707. The ascent takes three to four days, with at least one further day required for the descent (both ascent and descent take 8 hours from the second overnight camp). The climb can be attempted either from Doğubayazıt (south-west) or from Aralık near İğdır (north-west); guides can be hired in Doğubayazıt or İğdır. Anyone embarking on the climb will need a special permit from the Interior Ministry in Ankara. Further information is available from the Turkish Mountaineering Club, Dağcılık Federasyonu, B.T.G.M., Ulus İshanı A-Blok, Ulus, Ankara, tel. 41/108586–356.

Ararat is chiefly famous as the place where, according to the Old Testament (I. Moses 8:4), Noah's Ark finally came to rest, a claim based on a highly questionable interpretation of the biblical text. To the Hebrews Ararat was the land north of the Assur Empire, so the biblical reference was probably to the Armenian area as a whole i.e. to the Assyrian Ardardi/Uruartru (13th c. B.C.) or Accadian Urartu (from about 900 B.C.). Because the name had survived only as the name of the mountain, the interpreters of the bible were almost certainly misled. The legend of Noah and the Great Flood can itself be traced back to Sumerian sources dating from the 3rd millennium B.C.. In these a King Ziusudra of Shuruppak survives the Great Flood in an ark which, according to the Gilgamesh Epic (late 2nd millennium B.C.), came to rest on a mountain called Nisir (in Iranian Kurdistan). Armenians believe its resting place was Süphan Dağı, the extinct volcano near Lake Van, while for Muslims it was Cudi Dağı, in Mardin Province, near Cizre. Here, in 1953, fragments of timber thought to be 6500 years old were discovered in alluvial sand.

Although scholarly research has shown the Old Testament stories and the Gilgamesh Epic to be set much further south, over the last 140 years there have been several reported "sightings" of the Ark on Ararat. In 1833 a Turkish expedition reiterated, though without any new evidence, an old shepherds' tale of a wooden ship's prow protruding from the south glacier in summer. In 1892 the then Archdeacon of Jerusalem and Babylon put forward the thesis that the wrecked vessel does indeed lie hidden beneath the ice. In the First World War a Soviet air force officer called Roskovitzki claimed to have seen remains of a large shipwreck on the southern flank (photographs reportedly taken by a Soviet expedition are said to have been lost in the October Revolution). During the Second World War a Soviet and four American pilots reported similar sightings. In 1951 an American historian named Smith spent twelve days combing the mountain but found nothing. The Frenchman Navarra claims to have found remains of very old beams in a glaciated area. Since 1985 those searching for the Ark have concentrated their efforts on the col between Great and Little Ararat.

Ararat highland

Ağrı (pop. 58,000) lies in the middle of the Eleşkirt plain at the confluence of the Küpkıran Çayı and Murat Nehri (the southern headstream of the Euphrates). Known prior to the Turko-Russian War (1878) as Sorbulak, it was subsequently christened Karakilise (Black Church) by the occupying Russians on account of its Armenian church of dark-coloured basalt. Its name was changed to Ağrı in 1927 when it became capital of that province.

Diyadin, chief town of its district, is situated at the northern foot of the Ala Dağları, just 30km/19 miles or so north of where the Murat Nehri rises. It lies

Ascent

Noah's Ark

Ağrı

Diyadin

Old Doğubayzit, in the Ararat highlands

right on the line of the main north Anatolian fault (earthquakes, volcanic activity) and there are hot springs only 8km/5 miles from the town. The site was formerly that of an old town called Zarehaven which, though sacked by the Persians as early as the mid 4th c., was still in existence as a village until the 19th c.

Eleşkirt

Eleşkirt (pop. 12,000) sprawls across the almost circular bed of a former lake at an altitude of 1820m/5973ft (cereal growing and livestock rearing). It used to be called Alashgert (-kert or -gert being Armenian for town or citadel) and until the end of the 19th c. was just a village. The ruler at that time, a Kurdish derebey (autonomous local prince), held sway independently of the Ottoman Porte from his fortress at nearby Topprakale. An important inscription was discovered at Eleşkirt relating to King Menua of Urartu (c. 815–790 b.c.) whose capital was at Tushpa (now Van).

During his retreat from Persia Xenophon rested for a week on the Eleskirt plain with the exhausted remnants of the Ten Thousand, gathering strength for the next demanding stage of their forced march, the crossing of the Tahir Pass (the view from the pass is quite magnificent). Dominating the plain to the north is the 3432m/11,264ft volcanic peak of Büyükköse Dağı, its summit often still snow-covered in June.

Gürbulak

Near the frontier post on the Turko-Iranian border 35km/22 miles east of Doğubayazıt, there is a meteorite crater (signposted!).

Taşlıçay

At an altitude of 2241m/7355ft, Balik Gölü, north-east of Taşlıçay, is Turkey's highest lake. Reaching it involves a drive of some 28km/17 miles on a very minor road. The lake is set against a delightful backcloth of high mountains and its waters teem with fish. A small island has a ruin on it, probably an Armenian monastery.

Doğubayazıt

Dominated by the towering peak of Ararat, present-day Doğubayazıt, chief town of the Doğubayazıt basin, has only been in existence since after the

First World War. The chronology of settlement, precise location, even the name of its earliest predecessor, are shrouded in mystery, there being no written records prior to the region's absorption into the Ottoman Empire. Some 7km/4½ miles to the south-east, close to the remains of a Urartian settlement, are the ruins of a town dating from about 1064 (now called Eski Doğubayazıt), often, though wrongly, said to have been founded by Bayazit I sometime around 1390. It was abandoned in 1928 and its inhabitants forcibly resettled in the valley, ostensibly because there was too little scope for developing the existing town. The last remaining houses were demolished in 1945.

The old town of Bayazit was once an important staging post on the Silk Route, appearing in Armenian sources as "Darong". In the Ottoman era it was the provincial centre, a status it surrendered to Ağrı in 1927 (the name Doğubayazıt also dates from this time). The new town contains little of interest, but it does have some hotels and provides a base from which to attempt the ascent of Ararat. It makes its living from tourism and the through traffic to Iran.

From İğdır a track makes its way to the small Ararat village of Başköy (2100m/6892ft) at the mouth of the Ahira valley, a gorge-like defile full of volcanic lava slag. The entrance to the valley is pitted with caves, once the abode of Christian hermits. Five crosses are carved in the rock below the caves.

Başköy

Çakırtaş, a village about 7km/4½miles north of İğdır, has some interesting houses. Near the village is a conical türbe, the rear of which was damaged by a grenade during the War of Independence.

Çakırtaş

In 1913 a Late Urartian cemetery (7th c. B.C.) was discovered by Russian archaeologists at Malaklu, a village near İğdır. Finds from later Turkish excavations (1966) can be seen in the museum in Kars. İğdır, the local centre, lies in a large basin enjoying a micro-climate of hot summers and mild winters, in stark contrast to conditions in the mountains all around. Cotton, rice and fruit normally associated with warmer climes are commonly cultivated. Most of the inhabitants are Shiite Azerbaidjanis who migrated here from Russia and Iran between 1878 and 1920.

İğdır/Malaklu

South-east of Doğubayazıt, above a barren hillside dotted with the abandoned houses of the old town, are the ruins of the magnificent İshak Paşa Sarayı, half hill fortress and half oriental palace. Long ago a Urartian stronghold stood near this site, 300m/985ft above the plain. İshak Paşa Sarayi however was the replacement for a less ancient citadel, sometimes said to have been built by Bayazit I (1389–1403) to guard the Silk Route or perhaps to keep a watchful eye on Tamerlane. After Bayazit's defeat at Ankara in 1402, the Mongol leader is supposed to have kept him prisoner here until his death. Neither claim bears much examination since the region was not yet part of the Ottoman Empire at the time.

**İshak Paşa Sarayı

In fact the claim appears to be a case of mistaken identity. As the hold of the Mongol Ilkhan empire weakened in eastern Anatolia, the area fell under the sway of two brothers of the Mongol Jalairid dynasty, Ahmet and Bayazit. It was the Jalairid Bayazit who, in 1374, refurbished the existing (possibly Genoese) fortress at Darujnk (Darong) as a defence against Bayram Hoca (after which it became known as Bayazit Kalesi).

Although the keys of the fortress were surrendered to Selim I as early as 1514, the town itself became an Ottoman possession only in the mid 17th c. This followed a series of long drawn out and bloody confrontations with the Shiite Safavids from Persia, and a total of five different peace treaties.

At the end of the 18th c. İshak Paşa II, Kurdish emir and governor of Doğubayazıt from about 1769 until 1797, transformed the fortress into the extraordinary complex of buildings seen today, a project begun by his

İshak Paşa Sarayı, mountain fortress and oriental pleasure palace

father Hasan, a member of the Çıldıroğlu dynasty, and completed by his son Mehmut. Now in part restored, the palace with its outer and inner courtyards, flamboyant doorways, audience chambers, offices, kitchens, harem and men's quarters, is a curiously satisfying blend of Seljuk, Ottoman, Armenian, Georgian and Persian styles. It most definitely warrants a visit. Note in particular the very ornate türbe in front of the little domed cuboidal mosque.

On the far side of the small chasm east of the palace, beyond Eski Doğubayazıt's domed mosque (built by Selim the Grim in 1514), are the ruins of Bayazit's old fort, with circular towers. Local people still refer to it as Ceneviz Kalesi (the Genoese fort) as well as Bayazit Kalesi. To the left of the

Doğubayazıt

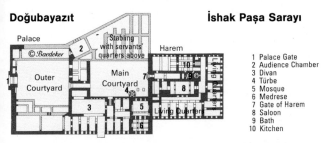

İshak Paşa Sarayı

1 Palace Gate
2 Audience Chamber
3 Divan
4 Türbe
5 Mosque
6 Medrese
7 Gate of Harem
8 Saloon
9 Bath
10 Kitchen

fort can be seen a partly completed relief, carved in the rock face either side of a Urartian rock chamber (9th c. B.C.).

Among several interesting natural features near the Ararat village of Yenidoğan are mountain tarns with fumaroles, coloured tufa cones and a small lake, Kop Gölü (at 4000m/13,128ft). A short distance below the lake stands a little fort, Koran Kalesi, with ruins of an Armenian church near by.

Yenidoğan

Armenia

P–U 3–5

Ararat highland (Turkish section: Eastern Anatolia) See warning page 7
Provinces: Ağrı, Bingöl, Erzurum, Muş and parts of Bayburt, Bitlis, Elazığ, Erzincan, Kars, Tunceli and Van.

From a geographical point of view Armenia corresponds roughly to the area covered by the Ararat highland (see Ararat, Surroundings), the mountainous region separating peninsular Asia Minor from Iran and the Armenian Republic (formerly part of the Soviet Union). Its boundaries are the Pontic Mountains, the eastern Taurus, the western Iranian chain and the mountain ranges south of Lake Van and the upper reaches of the Euphrates. Historically speaking, Armenian territory also included parts of north-east Anatolia (with the exception of Kolchis), the Armenian Republic and the Nakhchevan Autonomous Republic.

Situation and Topography

This is an area where spacious uplands dotted with numerous lakes alternate with extensive volcanic plateaux (Kars) deeply scored by gorge-like valleys. Above these rise isolated, extremely high volcanos such as Ararat and Aragats, as well as volcanic massifs and mountain ranges reaching well over 3000m/10,000ft in height. Lakes devoid of outlets, such as Lakes Van and Sevan, occupy large inward-draining depressions in between. A combination of high altitude and a dry and rigorous continental climate restricts agriculture to the lower-lying basins and valleys; considerable areas are covered by pastureland (irrigated for hay), while sizeable forests of oak, beech, ash, fir and spruce fringe the mountains. Throughout history the highland corridor and mountain passes of eastern Anatolia have formed the principal overland route from central Asia to the Mediterranean. As a result the region has always been plagued by instability and warring between neighbouring powers.

While Armenia's history goes back thousands of years, the exact origins of the Armenian people remain wrapped in uncertainty. It appears that by the 4th c. B.C. the region was inhabited by Indo-European speakers in close cultural contact with the Semitic tribes to the south.
Between 2000 and 1500 B.C. another Indo-European people, the Kurds, moved into the area from the north. Herodotus assumed the Armenians came to Asia Minor with the Phrygians in the 2nd millennium, claiming that

Early history

they learned the art of metalwork and building in stone from their Urartian neighbours. Xenophon describes them as a prosperous farming people, constantly at the mercy of the marauding Kurdish hill-tribes living in the mountains near by.

Armenia first appears as a name at the time of the Persian king Darius (521–485 B.C.). Politically the Armenian kings were almost always dependent on their more powerful neighbours, and the boundaries of their domains changed as often as their capitals.

Armenia first achieved independence following the victory of the Romans over the Seleucid Antiochos III. Tigranes (95–54 B.C.) established a flourishing kingdom in southern Armenia with its capital at Tigranocerte (see Diyarbakır, Silvan), before defeat in 69 B.C. left him a vassal of Rome. Later, under Vespasian, Armenia became a Roman province. Christianity took rapid hold in Armenia from the 2nd c. A.D. Gregory the Illuminator founded an independent Armenian Church and soon afterwards Christianity was adopted as the official religion. In the 5th c. Mesrop translated the Bible into Armenian. Christianisation also led however, in 387, to the partition of Armenia between Byzantium and Persia. Later the Armenian dynasties split up into ruling houses with considerable rivalry between them, as a result of which there was sometimes more than one Armenian Empire in existence at a time.

Since the First World War Armenia has been divided between the Soviet Union/Republic of Armenia, Iran and Turkey. Following an Armenian uprising in Van in 1915 and continuing support for Russia among Armenian guerillas in eastern Anatolia, virtually the entire Armenian population of Turkey was expelled, with the exception of a small minority living in İstanbul. Russia established its own Armenian Republic, which has now become independent.

Recent history

The influence of Gregory the Illuminator, Armenia's patron saint, led to Christianity being adopted as the official religion around 300. About a century later the monk Mesrop devised an Armenian script to facilitate translation of the Bible, drawing partly on a now lost alphabet of Iranian origin, but principally on Greek, and interposing fourteen new letters. Mesrop's achievement led to the emergence of a flourishing Armenian literature of epics, lyrics, novels, scientific treatises, chants and songs. In the 14th c. there arose a tradition of courtly minnesong, a form of secular folk literature.

Art and culture

The Armenians became highly skilled in the arts of gold and silverwork, book and manuscript illumination, miniature painting and musical composition.

The Armenians also evolved a characteristic style of ecclesiastical architecture, the principal features of which were a distinctive ground plan and construction of the walls (of lava and tufa). Unusual pyramidal and domed roofs, fanciful capitals and elaborate ornamentation reflecting Byzantine, Persian and Syrian-Arabic influences combined to produce a style which some art historians believe inspired the builders of Early Gothic.

Artvin

R 2

Black Sea region (East Pontus)
Province: Artvin
Altitude: 500m/1641ft. Population: 20,000

The small provincial capital of Artvin is situated in the far north-east corner of Turkey, separated from the coast by the first of the Pontic mountain

Situation and Importance

◄ *Hoşap (Van) mountain fortress, once a military observation post*

ranges. It makes an excellent base for forays into the surrounding country-side in search of some of the province's many ruined Early Christian and 9th–11th c. churches. These often lie off the beaten track, accessible only on foot or along dirt roads.

Located in the very heart of Turkish Georgia, this charming old town is also known as Çoruh (from the Çoruh Nehri) or Lazin (from Lazistan i.e. land of the Laz). Ascending in a series of south-west facing terraces, it clings to a steep hillside above the mouth of the Çoruh gorge.

Despite the steepness of its mountain slopes the area around Artvin – the "rain-covered Kolchis" of the Argonaut legend – is blessed with conditions ideal for the cultivation of a wide variety of fruit, vines, olives, hazelnuts and tea.

The history of Georgia

Relatively little is known about Artvin's past. Although the Muslim Laz (Chani) who inhabit the Black Sea coastal region form a distinctive ethnic group, they nevertheless share a common history with the other Caucasian peoples of Georgia. Once fought over by Romans and Sassanids (Persians), the area was conquered by the Arabs in the 7th c.; it remained under Arab rule for nearly three hundred years.

Turkish Georgia was the homeland of the Bagratid dynasty, who came from İspir. In the 10th c. the Armenian branch siezed control of parts of Armenia and the Transcaucasus; in the 12th and 13th centuries the Georgian Bagratids left an indelible mark on the whole of Christian Georgia.

The Arab invasions signalled the start of a lengthy period of decline, following which the Persians, Turks and Russians each sought to dominate the region. In 1071 the Artvin area, which from the 9th c. onwards, under the Bagratids, had became the political and cultural heartland of Georgia, fell to the Seljuk Alp Arslan. After the Seljuks had been driven out it became, under David the Restorer (David III, 1098–1125), the flourishing Bagratid kingdom of Georgia. This period of prosperity was cut short by the

Mountain pasture in the Giresun Dağlari near Artvin

Mongols who laid waste the land in 1386. In the 15th c. Tao Georgia became part of the Ottoman Empire. Following the Turko-Russian War of 1877/78 Artvin was in Russian hands until 1918.

Artvin's 16th c. Georgian fortress, perched on a cliff high above the river, is out of bounds to the public (military zone). The Salih Bey Camii, in the Çayazı area of the town, was built by Sivan in 1793(?). Salih Bey was Governor of the town.

Sights

Surroundings

On a clifftop overlooking the Köprüler Deresi gorge, not far from the little town of Ardanuç (about 30km/19 miles east of Artvin), are walls and stumps of towers belonging to a once mighty 12th c. fortress. Within the fort lie the ruins of an Armenian-Georgian church, a reminder that this was once the capital of the principality of Tao Georgia. Ashot Bagrationi the Great (780–826), founder of the ruling dynasty, skilfully preserved his relative independence by maintaining good relations simultaneously with Byzantium, the Emirs of Tiflis and the Caliphate. He styled himself Kuropalat (Guardian of palaces) and built numerous churches in his small realm.

Ardanuç

West of the mining town of Borçka there is an Ottoman bridge spanning a tributary of the Çoruh Nehri. Above the town, which in earlier times was also known as Yeniyol (New Way), stands a completely ruined fortress. In autumn the narrow gorge of the Çoruh Nehri between Artvin and the Turkish-Armenian border is visited by vast numbers of migrating birds.

Borçka

In Dört Kilise, a village overlooking the Çoruh about 5km/3 miles south of Yusefeli (the district town), are a ruined fortress and chapel. About 8km/5 miles further on, in a side valley, stands the Ohta Eklesia, a three-aisle Georgian basilica, rectangular in plan, dating from the 10th c. The ornate exterior and part of the stone-tiled roof have survived. Fragments of paintings can be seen inside the choir and a medallion portrait of the church's patron adorns the vaulting of the east window. The ruin north of the basilica was a chapel. These two are all that remain of the four churches which once stood here (Dört Kilise meaning "four churches").

*Dört Kilise

31km/20 miles east of Artvin in the valley of the Okçular Deresi is a ruined monastery, one of the most important of all those in the İmerhevi valley (see below). The chief point of interest today is a well preserved domed church, cruciform in plan, originally endowed by Smbat (923–985). Part of the church is now used as stabling, another part as a mosque. Note the south window, with figures of the Archangels Michael and Gabriel, also the relief of the founder on the drum.

Hamamlıköy

About 12km/8 miles south-east of Artvin, the Okçular Çayı flowing into the Çoruh Nehri from the north-east marks the entrance to a valley known locally as the İmerhevi Deresi. Because of its numerous churches and monasteries it used to be called the Sinai or Mt Athos of Georgia. A road runs the length of the valley, first to Şavşat and then past the 2640m/8664ft high Çam Gecidi to Ardahan. Along the route, particularly around Şavşat and Ardanuç, are several architecturally extremely interesting ruined churches (though some can only be reached on foot).

*İmerhevi valley

70km/43 miles south of Artvin, shortly before Kınalıçam, a turning off the main Erzurum road heads east along the Oltu Çayı valley towards Oltu. Not far along it, on the left, a dirt track leads north to İşhan, well worth visiting on account of its former cathedral, now a church. Several different phases of construction are easily recognisable. The horseshoe-shaped east apse, carved with rosettes and floral ornamentation, belonged to the original 7th c. building which had four conchas and multi-tiered blind arcading on

*İşhan

the exterior. The first alterations were carried out in 828, followed by more in 1032 (the dome being added and the west end extended). Now that the roofs over the aisles are missing, the drum with its twisted columns seems almost to hover above the crossing. Note in particular the painting in the dome of angels holding a cross, and the medallions painted with saints and patrons of the church adorning the window vaultings of the north transept, embellished with plant and wicker pattern motifs. Inside the roofless church there is now a small chapel.

*Kaçkar Dağları

Parallel to the eastern Black Sea coast runs a wall of mountains rising to heights in excess of 2000m/6500ft. This northernmost of the Pontic ranges forms the backbone of Turkish Georgia. Merging in the north into the Little Caucasus (now the Republic of Georgia), it attains its greatest altitude (3932m/12,905ft) in the Kaçkar Dağ massif, a triangle of mountains lying between Rize, Artvin and Bayburt. Bounded to the south-east by the deep Çoruh trench, from the coast the massif rises sharply to 2000m/6500ft, at which height the surface has been extensively eroded, creating a kind of tableland. The main summit (Kaçkar Dağ) lies only 35km/22 miles as the crow flies from the coast and the Çoruh valley.

Flora and flora

Caucasian spruce, Nordmann fir, forest pine, deciduous oak and Asian beech all flourish throughout the region, as do rhododendrons – the white-bloomed Caucasian rhododendron occuring extensively, the purply-violet and yellow-flowered Pontic variety forming an undergrowth beneath the beeches and pines. Both the woodland and high altitude zone are rich in wildlife, and brown bears, Caucasian chamois, bearded vultures, Caspian partridge and Caucasian black grouse are still found.

Hill walking

The Kaçkar range is magnificent mountain walking country, Parhal, a sprawling village in the Barhal Çayı valley, being a particularly good starting point. One six hour walk, filled with interest, goes from Parhal, via Kumru, Naznara and Amaneskit, first to a waterfall and then to Karagöl, a cirque lake 2600m/8533ft up. Another walk (of about ten hours) follows a track which can be used by vehicles as far as Olgunlar (Yaylalar), then continues upstream onto the Dilber Düzü (Dilber plateau; 2950m/9682ft); beyond, at 3250m/10,666ft, lies Deniz Gölü (full day's walk) and beyond that the summit of Kaçkar Dağ (3932m/12,905ft; two days needed).

*Parhal

From the Çoruh Nehri at Yusufeli a side valley runs north, penetrating deep into the mountains. About 15km/9 miles beyond Sarıgöl lies another village, Altıparmak (also called Barhal or Parchali), its square graced by a well-preserved 10th c. monastery church, still in use as a mosque. Founded by David Kuropalat and built in stone of different hues, the church resembles the basilica at Dört Kilise, even in much of its detail. Some traces of wall paintings survive. The windows are embellished with figurative motifs and reliefs. A path climbs up from the village to two more chapels. The lower of the two has only walls remaining, but the little basilica higher up boasts two small apses.

In a side valley off the Barhal Çayı, near to the village Yüksekoba, are the remains of another monastery, the Gudaschewi Manastırı.

Şavşat

Şavşat, also known as Yeniköy or Zavsat, a district centre about 63km/39 miles east of Artvin on the scenic road to Ardahan, is dominated on its east side by a massive ruined Georgian fortress. This is a relic of the days when it was the seat of the princes of Chavchetien, one of the small Georgian principalities which came into being when the country was partitioned in the 9th and 13th/14th centuries.

Yeni Rabat

About 15km/9 miles south-east of Ardanuç, the ruins of the Georgian Schatberdi Manastırı (or Yeni Rabat ie. new monastery) lie almost out of sight in a wooded hollow in the Yalnızçam Dağları, above the Köprüler Deresi. The church, endowed by Gregory Chandstili, has beautifully ornate window frames. Yeni Rabat was famous for its school of manuscript illuminators and some exquisitely illuminated Gospels produced here in the 9th and 10th centuries can be seen in the museum in Tiflis (in the Georgian Republic).

Aspendos

See Side

Assos

See Edremit Körfezi

Aydın   C 6

Western Anatolia
Province: Aydın
Altitude: 64m/210ft
Population: 107,000

The provincial capital of Aydın, largely modern but with an older nucleus, is situated on the northern edge of the Büyük Menderes plain, on the alluvial fan of the Tabakhane Deresi (the ancient Eudon). The town lies just off the Denizli highway, on the İzmir–Denizli–Afyon branch of the Anatolian railway. Located west of the Tabakhane are what were the old Turkish and Jewish quarters, to the east the Armenian and Greek. Driving in from the south however, past all the recent building, first impressions are of a newish town.

The Büyük Menderes plain, with Aydın at its centre, is a region of intensive cultivation where, in addition to the main crop cotton, Turkey's best grapes (wine, raisins) and best figs are also grown. Emery, occuring locally in the crystalline rock to the west of Aydın, makes this the country's principal source of the mineral. Straddling a tectonic fault-line (Menderes trench), the town is subject to frequent earthquakes. As recently as 1895 a quake near Aydın threw up a ridge a metre high.

Situation and Importance

Though built on a site immediately below that of ancient Tralles, the town is actually of Turkish origin. It was the seat of the emirs of Aydın, the first of whom, Mehmet Aydınoğlu, established the beylik (principality) of Aydın in 1307 and founded the Aydın Oğulları dynasty. The town was named Aydın Güzelhisar by Mehmet's father. When in 1424 the area came under Ottoman control, Aydın continued as an important regional centre. From the 18th c. until 1822, with the Ottoman Empire already in decline, its rulers were the Karaosmanoğlu derebeys.

The name Güzel Hisar, meaning "handsome fortress", refers in fact to the ruined Tralles. As far as the old beylik capital is concerned, several earthquakes and a devasting fire at the time of the Greek retreat in 1922, have left virtually no historic buildings standing. Only the mosques are of any real interest today.

History

Sights

The Ağaçarası (or Üveys Paşa) Camii in the Köprülü district is a splendidly baroque mosque dating from 1565. Also worth seeing is the domed 14th c. Alihan Kümbeti mausoleum in the Üveys Paşa quarter. Note the brick mosaic above the entrance, as well as the four tombs.

Ağaçarası Camii

Aydın

Cihanoğlu Camii

The Cihanoğlu (or Cihanzade) Camii, another exuberantly decorated building, square in plan, was erected in 1756. The sadirvan has a marble basin and twelve columns. The elaborate ornamentation of the mosque makes it one of the acknowledged masterpieces of the Turkish baroque style.

Museum

Aydın's museum is also worth visiting, situated just west of the town centre. While the majority of the exhibits come from Tralles it has, in addition, a section devoted to the ethnography of the area (open: 8.30am–noon; 1.30–5pm).

Osmanoğlu Külliyesi

The Osmanoğlu Hanı (Zinçirli Han), endowed by Nasuh Paşa, dates from between 1699 and 1707. As well as the caravanserai, a mosque, 20-roomed medrese and baths were all built at the same time. The Seljuk-style baths are now known as the Paşa Hamamı.

Süleiman Bey Camii

The Süleiman Bey Camii (1683), situated near the railway station, is one of the loveliest of all Aydın's mosques, another fine example of Turkish baroque. It has a şadırvan with a pyramidal domed roof.

*Tralles

The ruins of ancient Tralles stand encircled by olive groves 100m/328ft above Aydın on the steep mountain terrace known as Güzel Hisar (superb views). The site is in a restricted military zone and special permission is needed to visit it.

Originally founded by Argive colonists, at the time of its first mention (by Xenophon) Tralles was a fortified Persian military training area in the satrapy of the young Kyros. The town's surrender to Alexander the Great in 334 B.C. marked the start of a long period of prosperity and cultural vitality. It continued to flourish under Lysimachos, then under the Seleucids, when the town was known as Seleukia, and also under the kings of Pergamum, the Attalids, who maintained a palace here. Tralles figs were every bit as renowned then as they are today. The town was also famous for its school

A Turkish snack-bar

of philosophy. Having fallen to the Romans in 133 B.C., in 26 B.C. Tralles was devastated by an earthquake, being rebuilt largely through the beneficence of Augustus. The appreciative citizens renamed the city Caesarea, a name it retained until the late 1st c. In the 14th c. Güzelhisar (as it was then known) gave way to Aydın, newly established seat of the Aydın Oğulları built on the plain immediately below. Tralles's ancient buildings were pillaged for their stone.

The earliest excavations, undertaken in about 1888, bore little fruit, but in 1902/03 archaeologists from the Ottoman Museum in İstanbul uncovered the remains of baths and a stoá. The major find was a marble statue of a youth wearing a mantle (the Ephebe of Thalles, now in the Archaeological Museum in İstanbul).

Stripped of nearly all its stone (some of it still found in buildings in the old part of Aydın) the remains of the huge stadium are not particularly impressive. Beyond the stadium, to the north, lie the ruins of the theatre – substantial walls of masonry with a mortar and rubble core – built up against the side of the acropolis. Note especially the unusual tunnel under the orchestra. At one time the 280m/920ft high acropolis was supplied with water by means of a high-pressure conduit. Near the stadium are two ruined Early Byzantine churches with interesting ground plans. *(Visiting the ruins)*

A little to the right of the agora are three ruined arches which the Turks used to call "Üç Göz" (Three Eyes). These are now virtually the only remains of a large Late Roman gymnasium which had brick walls faced with marble.
The city walls, enclosing an oval area 1800m/1970yd long and 1000m/1094yd wide, have been reduced to just a few fragmentary remnants. On its east side Tralles was protected by the Tabakhne Çayı.

Balıkesir   C 4

Western Anatolian highland
Province: Balıkesir
Altitude: 120m/394ft
Population: 172,000

The name Balıkesir (or Balıkesri) is probably a Turkish corruption of the earlier "Paleo Kastro" (Old Fortress). Situated on the İzmir to Bursa road and surrounded by fertile countryside, the town has expanded considerably in the last three decades. In addition to its flourishing trade in local agricultural produce (tobacco, cotton, figs, etc.) Balıkesir has a substantial amount of industry, including textiles, engineering and vehicle manufacture. The countryside around the town is famous for its spas and mineral springs. *(Situation and Importance)*

The earliest known settlement on this ancient Mysian site was called Assuwa. Falling first to the Hittites, it later came under Lydian, Phrygian, Persian and then Roman control. No relics remain from this period. In 1303 it became the capital of the Karası beylik, before being taken by the Ottomans in 1363. It kept the name Karası right up until 1926. As the venue of a congress held to rally nationalist opposition to the Greek invasion of 1919, Balıkesir played an important part in the Turkish War of Independence. *(History)*

Sights

The Karası Bey (Kara İsa Bey) Türbesi in the Mustafa Fakir area bears the name of Balıkesir's founder, who lies buried there together with his five sons. The mausoleum was constructed eight years after his death in 1330. A Kufic inscription adorns the sarcophagus. *(Kara İsa Bey Türbesi)*

There are two Ottoman caravanserais in the town, the Hasan Paşa Hanı and İlyas Paşa Hani, both now converted to modern shops. *(Caravanserais)*

Balıkesir

Saat Kulesi

The Rococo- and Empire-style clock tower, on a hill in the town centre, was erected after an earthquake in 1987. It replaced an earlier one (1877) modelled on the Galata tower in İstanbul.

Yıldırım
Külliyesi

The Yıldırım Külliyesi comprises a medrese, a bath house and a mosque. The latter, several times restored, was endowed by Yıldırım Bayazit at the end of the 14th c.

Zaganos Paşa
Külliyesi

This mosque near the Kara İsa Bey Türbesi was founded in 1461 by a teacher of the Sultan Fatih Mehmet. In addition to the mosque, the complex consists of a bath house, fountain, mason's yard, a Koranic school with a library in the mosque, and the benefactor's türbe (1466). The pulpit of the mosque is inscribed with the date 865 H, i.e. 1446 (H being the year following the first Hadsh). Atatürk delivered his Friday Address here on February 7th 1923.

Surroundings

Balya

In earlier days this mining town, situated about 50km/30 miles north-west of Balıkesir, was known as Pazarköy or Balya Maden. The fort in the Kadiköy district possibly dates from Roman or perhaps Byzantine times. In the Hisar (Fortress) district there is a thermal bath fed by hot springs (50°C/122°F).

5km/3 miles or so from Balya at Hozluca there is another thermal bath with hot sulphur and carbon springs (80°C/176°F), beneficial to those with rheumatism and skin complaints. The hot springs at İlica, a little place 26km/16 miles north-east of Balya, are the best known of all in the Balya Dağ, ranging in temperature from 24°C/75°F to 63°C/145°F.

Bigadiç

On the east side of Bigadiç's town centre is a settlement mound, site of the former Byzantine town of Achyraos (remains of defences). More of the regions numerous medicinal baths are found at Hisar Köyü, a village about 15km/9 miles from Bigadiç. Here the hot springs (19.5°C/°67F–84°C/183°F) contain traces of carbon, sulphur, iron and magnesium sulphate, offering relief from rheumatism and skin complaints.

Pamukçu

Pamukçu, a spa about 18km/11 miles south of Balıkesir, has sulphur and chlorine springs providing treatment for diabetes as well as rheumatism and chronic intestinal conditions.

Panayır
(traditional
fairs)

Balıkesir province and immediately adjoining areas are now virtually the only part of Turkey where traditional panayır (fairs) still take place – of great interest from a socio-historical point of view. Dates on which fairs are held in the Balıkesir area include:
April 24th–26th Kepsut, 27th–29th Balya;
June 21st–23rd Balya-İlica;
August 7th–14th Dursunbey; 16th–20th Kepsut;
September 10th–13th Bigadiç, 17th–20th Savaştepe, 20th–22nd Balya, 25th–27th İvrindi.

Sındırgı
Hisaralan

The village of Emendere (İlıcalı), known for its radio-active hot springs, lies about 8km/5 miles south-east of the district town of Sındırgı. Another spa, with springs between 84°C/183°F and 96°C/204°F, is found 35km/22 miles further east, near the village of Hisaralan Kalesi. This village and the nearby fort (Hisaralan Kalesi) are on a site identified as that of Daskylcion, an ancient Persian settlement.

Bandırma   C 3

Southern Sea of Marmara
Province: Balıkesir
Altitude: 10m/32ft. Population: 77,000

This large port lies on a bay of the same name on the southern Sea of | Situation and
Marmara, facing the south-east side of the Kapıdağ peninsula. It has an | Importance
airport and is the terminus of the İzmir to Balıkesir railway. A busy commercial and industrial centre, it has a regular ferry service to İstanbul (the first
modern harbour was built in 1924). In 1943 a 2500ha/6180 acre farm was set
up on the southern outskirts of town to rear merino sheep. It has a stock of
about 5000 animals. Because of Bandırma's industries, its bay is not particularly attractive to holidaymakers. But there are still a number of sandy
beaches e.g. at Karşıyakaköyü, and also near the Kyzikos ruins (see below).

Little is known of the early history of the town or its origins. It was Mysian to | History
begin with, and later – probably in the guise of a small fishing village – part
of the kingdom of Kyzikos. In 1076, at the time of Sultan Süleiman Kutul-
muş, it came under the hegemony of the Seljuks of Rum. After their empire
collapsed, it was part of the Karası beylik (see Balıkesir). Under Ottoman
rule (until 1922) the population was predominantly Greek and Armenian. A
substantial section of the town was destroyed in a fire in 1874 and today
there is nothing much of interest to see.

Surroundings

South-east of Kuş/Manyas Gölü, near the village of Ergili (formerly Eski | Daskyleion
Köy, i.e. "old village"), are the remains of ancient Daskylos, founded in the
7th c. B.C. by the father of the Lydian King Gyges. Later the Persian satraps
of the small state of Phrygia made it into their capital. Pharnabazos built a
palace and had a splendid garden laid (foundation walls can still be seen).
Tomb reliefs and several imprints from Persian stone seals were also
uncovered during excavation; they are now in the archaeological
museums of İstanbul and Ankara.

About 26km/16 miles north-west of Gönen the Çanakkale road touches the | Denizkent
Sea of Marmara coast at Denizkent. Here miles of sandy beaches and
numerous holiday villages cater for mainly Turkish holidaymakers.
A short distance before Denizkent, on the left, is the Tahır Ovası model farm,
founded jointly by the Turkish agricultural ministry and the Germano-
Turkish Association. As well as breeding horses, sheep and plants it provides agricultural training.

Erdek, on the south-west corner of the Kapıdağ peninsula about 20km/14 | *Erdek
miles north-west of Bandırma, not only enjoys a pleasantly equable climate
but is blessed with an exceptionally attractive location as well. Since about
1950 it has proved more and more popular with the crowds of holidaymakers who come from the cities to the Sea of Marmara, and numerous
apartment blocks have been built to accommodate them. Until 1921 the
town was called Pithos and the population was mainly Greek. When the
Greeks left large parts of Pithos were burned down. Erdek arose from the
rubble, a new and to a large extent planned seaside town.
In antiquity Milesian settlers founded a colony called Artake on the site now
occupied by Erdek. Destroyed by the Persians, it subsequently took on the
modest role of a harbour for Kyzikos. Fishing for palamut, a short-finned
variety of tuna, must have been of considerable importance at the time
because the fish is featured on the kingdom's coinage.

Gönen

Intensive rice cultivation is the most striking feature of the wide Gönen plain, the cereal being grown in huge paddy fields along the length of the Gönen Çayı almost as far as its estuary near Denizkent. Gönen itself, a well-known thermal spa as well as the district town, is situated on the old Çannakale road, about 50km/30 miles south-west of Bandırma, right on the border of the Troas. Relics of the past include some remains from an ancient sacred spring dedicated to Artemis (Artemis Thermae; 5th c. mosaics in the Mosaic Museum in the spa area of the town). The hot springs (up to 82°C/179°F) assist the treatment of urinary, skin and nervous disorders. About 13km/8 miles south of Gönen, in the village of Eksidere in the Delical Dağ, there is another spa (Dağ İlıcası) with hot springs (43°C/109°F) said to help cure rheumatism, gynaecological and gastric complaints.

Other places of interest around Gönen include: the Yarasa Mağları bat caves, a short distance to the north-west at Dereköy; the İskender Köprüsü, a very ancient – possibly 4th c. B.C. – bridge at Güvercinli, about 11km/7 miles north; and the remains of a granite block fort at Babayaka, 7km/4 miles from the town.

Kapıdağ Yarımadası

The Kapıdağ peninsular north-west of Bandırma is linked to the mainland by a narrow isthmus. Mainly composed of granite (rock arch at ancient Dindymos), it is partly wooded, with mountains up to 782m/2566ft in height. When still an island in antiquity it was known as Arctonnesos, inhabited, according to legend, by Zeus's wetnurses transformed into bears.

Kyzikos

At the northern end of the isthmus between the Kapıdağ peninsula and the mainland, beside the Bandırma road about 10km/6 miles south-west of Erdek, lie the remains of the ancient trading colony of Kyzikos (or Belkis), known by the poetic name of Dindymos. It was probably settled from Miletus in the 2nd millennium B.C. and was certainly inhabited by Miletian settlers by 756 B.C. It is mentioned in the story of Jason and the Argonauts which tells how in error they killed the hospitable king who had earlier made them welcome. In 334 Alexander the Great built two bridges joining the southern tip of the island to the mainland. After Kyzikos declined, sand continuously washing up against the piles of the bridges caused the channel slowly to silt up and the isthmus was formed. Following Lucullus's decisive victory over Mithridates, Kyzikos became a "free" city and capital of Mysia. Badly damaged on several occasions by earthquakes (particularly in 543 and 1063) and by Arab assault (673), and further ravaged in fighting between Byzantines, Seljuks and Crusaders, it was finally abandoned in 1224. Little now remains to be seen, only a section of the walls, the site of the amphitheatre and some ruins of Hadrian's Temple to Zeus from which in the 16th c. columns were removed to embellish İstanbul's mosques. Finds from Kyzikos are displayed in the museum in Erdek.

Soğuksu

Situated about 10km/6 miles south-east of Manyas, below a flat-topped hill called Keltepe, Soğuksu takes its name from the cold freshwater springs which gush out above the village. On Keltepe itself are ruins of a much older and larger town, thought to have been ancient Poemanios (Poemanenos). This, some experts believe, was the principal settlement of the Poemanens, a people who for a time were under the sway of their more powerful neighbour Kyzikos (see above). The site was still inhabited in 1832, but by 1902 it was already abandoned and falling into ruin. Relics from this period can be seen among the remains, including two almost completely destroyed mosques, two ruined türbes and a crumbling fort (possibly Byzantine) on the spur occupied by the acropolis. From the latter there are splendid views of Kus Gölü and of the small village of Soğuksu below. The village was founded from nothing in the 19th c. by returning Circassian migrants.

***Kuş Cenneti**

This 52ha/128 acre nature reserve known as "Bird Paradise" was set up by the German hydrologist and zoologist Curt Crosswig in 1938. Frequented by some 250 different species of bird, the sanctuary has a small ornithological museum and an observation tower erected in 1952 by the Hydrology Department of the University of İstanbul. Occupying a largely unspoilt area of the lakeside near Siğircik in the north-east corner of Manyas Gölü (now renamed Kus Gölü, "Bird Lake"), it was designated a National Park in 1959 and awarded the Europa Diploma in 1976. Specially built hides enable resident species and migrant visitors to be observed without causing them the least disturbance. Herons (common herons, night-herons, purple-herons, squacco herons and little egrets) and spoonbills crowd together in the trees. The two species of pelicans, Dalmatian and pink, and the cormorants, on the other hand, keep themselves to themselves.

The story of Manyas, centre of its district and situated about 10km/6 miles south of Kuş Gölü, is typical of many a small Turkish town. The present community took root at the earliest towards the end of the 19th c. (probably around 1877), when 25 Tartar families, political returnees from Dobrudscha in Romania, took over what was a fair ground and established Tatarköy (Tartar Village). Although new, the village stood on the site of ancient Miletopolis and so could justifiably claim a much longer if somewhat confused history. In fact the name Miletopolis was still in use in a contracted form ("Maltepe") for the spot where the present town stands. Today very little is known about Miletopolis, few finds having ever come to light. Rather more is known of Manyas's immediate predecessor, Eski Manyas (see Soğuksu). There are two spas in the vicinity of Manyas, İlica (Hamamlı) near Çingir, and Kum İlıcası.

Manyas

The Manyas (Kuş) Panayırı, mentioned as early as the 17th c. by Evliya Celebi in his travelogue, is held twice a year (June 3rd–6th and September 15th–17th).

Lake Manyas (166sq.km/64sq.miles; maximum depth: 8m/26ft) nestles among hills about 20km/12½ miles south of Bandırma. The east side of the freshwater lake is now the Kuş Cenneti bird sanctuary (see above), while in the south there are some tamarisk swamps with waterlilies and reed beds. The lake is fed mainly by the Kadiköyü Deresi and teems with plankton, fish and birdlife. Known to the ancients as Lake Miletopolis it drains across the Kara Dere into the Koca Çayı.

Kuş (Manyas) Gölü

Of the 23 islands in the Sea of Marmara (see entry) the very mountainous Marmara Adası (Marmara Island) is much the best known. It is also the largest (118sq.km/45sq.miles) and gave the Sea of Marmara its name, being famous for its marble quarries (marmara = marble). Over the centuries it has supplied stone for everything from Roman sarcophagi to Ottoman mosques. An abundance of fish in the waters surrounding it provided an additional important source of prosperity. Today Marmara Adası is a popular holiday resort. A second island, Avşa, three nautical miles south, has also developed into a tourist resort. Very much smaller (21sq.km/8sq.miles) it contains just two villages and produces excellent wine. There are boats from Erdek and Bandırma.

Marmara Adalan

The district town of Susurluk, on the Balıkesir road about 55km/33 miles south of Bandırma, has few sights of interest apart from the Deveci Hanı, a 16th c. Ottoman caravanserai, and an Ottoman medrese with a little mosque. The countryside around the town however is dotted with well-known spas including Gökçedere İlıcası (30km/20 miles south-west, the water being a warm 25°C/77°F) and Kepekler Kaplıcası (Göbel, 10km/6 miles north, on the road to Bandırma; hot springs 45°C/113°F; treatment for rheumatism and sciatica). The waters at Ömerköy İlıcası (about 30km/ 19 miles south-west, on the railway line to Balıkesir) are beneficial for general aches and nervous disorders, while at Yıldız Kaplıcası (about 15km/10 miles south, on the Simav Çayı) there are therapeutic hot springs (74°C/165°F) for treating rheumatism, sciatica and similar complaints.

Susurluk

Bergama

See Pergamum

Beyşehir

G 6

Western Taurus (Isaurian-Pisidian lake district)
Province: Konya
Altitude: 1112m/3649ft
Population: 20,000

Situation and
Characteristics

The district town of Beyşehir, attractively situated at the south-east corner of Beyşehir Gölü at the point where the canalised Beyşehir Çayı enters the lake, is a busy market town, the economic centre of a sizeable agricultural basin. Lying at the junction of two ancient routes (Konya to İzmir and Konya to Antalya), it combines remnants of an old town (north-west on the lakeside) with a new town to the east. Stretching away north-east of the new town is the intensively cultivated Beyşehir Ovası, mainly given over to horticulture.

Beyşehir (Princely Town) was established in the 13th c. by a high official of the Seljuk imperial administration, the Emir Eşref, who made it his feudal seat. It probably occupies the site of ancient Parlais.

Sights

Eşrofoğlu Camii This seven-bay mosque is one of the loveliest wooden mosques in Anatolia. Endowed in 1296 by Eşrofoğlu Süleiman Bey, son of Eşref, Beyşehir's founder, it has a most striking forest-like interior with 48 closely spaced

Prayer niche in the Eşrefoğlu Camii   *Eflâtun Pınarı sacred spring*

208

pine trunk columns with elaborately carved stalactitic capitals, and a prayer niche with fine tiles. The joinery of the beams supporting the flat wooden roof, enhanced in typical fashion above the centre aisle, is of the highest order. The carving on the staircase pulpit is equally outstanding, as is that on two other pulpits, one large and one small. The founder's türbe (1301) stands beside the east wall.

Next to the Eşrofoğlu mosque is a spacious restored Seljuk bazaar, due to become a museum.

Bedesten

Surroundings

Lake Beyşehir, also called Kireli Gölü after a village which stands a little way back from its north-east shore, is 45km/28 miles long and 25km/15 miles wide, making it the third largest lake in Turkey (roughly the size of Lake Constance). The turquoise blue waters, teeming with carp and other fish, have a slight soda content and so should not be drunk. On the south-west side there are a number of karst chasms into which the lake drains underground. In contrast to the low-lying eastern shore, on the west side rise two massifs, the Dedegöl Dağları (2980m/9780ft) and Anamas Dağ (2992km/9819ft), steep rock walls separating the basins of Lakes Beyşehir and Eğridir. Here, beneath the 2397m/7867ft-high Çiçekdağı, is found the Pınargözü cave (1550m/5087ft up) from which, as at the Kazanbüvet karst spring near Yeşildağ and the Pınarbaşı spring near Adaköy (south-west of the lake), a considerable volume of water flows. There are about 30 islands in the lake, the largest being Mada Adası in the north-west. It was at one time inhabited by settlers from Russia and became known as Kasak Adası (Cossack island).

*Beyşehir Gölü

The rather inaccessible north and west sides of the lake are now a National Park (the Kızıldağ Milli Parkı). Further south only a low sill of land separates Lake Beyşehir from Lake Suğla which geologists assume formed part of a single basin in the late Tertiary.

Above Ulupınar, a village on the south-west side of the Belören/Karaman road about 10km/6 miles east of the small town of Bozkır, lie the ruins of Isauria Vetus, chief town of the Roman province of Isauria and described by Strabo in his time as a well-fortified village. The site, also known as Zengiba Kalesi, was excavated in 1984 by İlhan Temizsoy. Extensive remains were uncovered, including the acropolis wall with an entrance gate to the south and ruined towers once up to 15m/49ft high. On the acropolis are the remains of the agora, an Arch of Hadrian and two churches. Further north stands an octagonal centrally-planned church with an apse and eight pillars. To the north and the south-west are necropolises, their rock tombs handsomely carved with reliefs.

Bozkır,
*Isauria Vetus

Near the village of Çamlık, about 45km/28 miles south of Beyşehir and 9km/6 miles west of Akseki, there is an interesting cave system, unfortunately not easily accessible to the average holidaymaker. A little below the village is the Körükini cave through which the Uzun Su flows for 1200m/¾ mile, widening out at intervals into thirteen small and not so small lakes. It then re-emerges to rush down the Değirmendere (Mill Valley) before disappearing again into the Suluin cave, 300m/328yd long with two more underground lakes. There is another cave (Balat cave) in a side valley a bit lower down on the right, and 6km/4 miles higher up near Hasan Köprüsü are several more large sink-holes.

Çamlık

Eflâtun Pinarı is situated some 4km/2½ miles east of the Beyşehir to Eğridir road, the turn-off being about 15km/9 miles north of Beyşehir. This important Hittite shrine dating from the New Kingdom (1460–1200 B.C.) stands beside a karst spring, its abundant waters forming a pool. The shrine itself consists of a 7m/23ft long altar-like structure of stone blocks, presumed to have come from an earlier complex, decorated on the front with a relief

*Eflâtun Pınarı

depicting deities (left and right) beneath two small winged suns. Below them are figures of several mythical beings and another larger winged sun. There is no agreement among archaeologists as to the significance of the relief. Behind the structure are the base of a lion and lower part of an enthroned god.

Fasılar

At Fasılar, a village about 10km/6 miles east of Beyşehir, a large stone statue, 7.5m/25ft long, lies fallen on the hillside. The village has so far defied classification and experts are yet to agree the exact age of the figure, placing it somewhere between the Old and New Hittite periods. One theory links the figure, assumed to be that of a god or a king, to the shrine at the Eflâtun Pınarı sacred spring 40km/25 miles away. Near the village is a rock tomb with a relief depicting a horse.

Kubadabad

Near Gölyaka, a village on the west side of Lake Beyşehir reached by only moderate roads, are the excavated remains of a Seljuk palace, summer residence of the Sultan Alaeddin Keykubad (1219–36). Remnants of tiles from the walls of this once luxuriously appointed complex, originally consisting of at least sixteen buildings, can be seen in the museum at the Büyük Karatay Medresesi in Konya. The tiles are of considerable art historical interest on account of their portrayal of living creatures, a practice forbidden according to the hadith (the 7th–9th c. corpus of Mohammedan lore and tradition supplementary to the Koran). Despite this prohibition the Seljuk princes apparently continued to adorn their palaces with such images right up to the 14th c. Hundreds of examples of figurative art were recovered from Kubadabad Palace, depicting, for example, Seljuk noblemen, beautiful women with almond-shaped eyes, long hair and small mouths, animals, double-eagles and fabulous and mythical beings. They show clear evidence of Iranian-Central Asian influence, as well as echoing Shamanistic beliefs.

Bilecik   E 3

North-western Anatolian highland
Province: Bilecik
Altitude: 515m/1690ft
Population: 23,000

Situation and Characteristics

The small provincial capital of Bilecik (Ertoğrul), a modern agricultural centre at the foot of the Ahır Dağ north-west of Eskişehir, is now thoroughly eclipsed by its larger industrial neighbours Eskişehir and Bozüyük. It still has some well cared for Ottoman houses set in large gardens, the last surviving remnants of the old town. Knowledge of Bilecik's history is very fragmentary. It was called Agrilium (Agrilion) in antiquity, and under Byzantium was known as Belikoma. Relics of the Greek period are found everywhere and on the market a Roman sarcophagus serves as a fountain trough. The site of the ancient town was a little above the present one.

Sights

Belikoma Kalesi

In the lower town can be seen the remains of Belikoma Kalesi, a Byzantine fortress (now a monastery) which fell to Osman Gazi, son of Ertoğrul and first in line of the Ottoman rulers (1299–1326). Nilphur, a beautiful Greek princess taken captive at the time, later became the wife of Osman's son and successor Orhan. The eight-arch bridge over the Karasu was constructed by the famous Ottoman architect Sinan (1490–1588).

Edebalı Türbesi

The mausoleum of Edebalı, warrior of Islam (Gazi) and comrade-in-arms of Ertoğrul the progenitor of the Ottoman dynasty, occupies a pleasant site below the town, a short distance from the Orhan Camii. It also contains the

A typical nomad settlement awaiting tourists

tombs of several other Ottoman warriors and ladies of rank who played a part in early Ottoman history.

This simple Early Ottoman mosque, a single small domed hall, is situated a little way below the town. Erected in the earliest years of the Ottoman period (13th/14th c.) it continues to have great significance for the Turks. The original minaret is now no more than a stump set on a rock to one side of the mosque, those seen today being added in the 19th c.

Orhan Camii

Surroundings

Having been almost completely redeveloped in the mid 1970s, the mainly industrial Bozüyük's only building of any importance is the Kasım Paşa Camii, erected by Sinan. About 20km/12½ miles east, on the Eskişehir border, lies an early Bronze Age settlement mound, Demircihüyük, finds from which can be seen in the museum in Eskişehir.

Bozüyük

Situated on a hillside at a point where the Karasu, flowing down from Kandilli Dağ, enters the Sakarya, this small town was known in antiquity as Leukai and more recently as Lefke (up until 1921 the population was still predominately Greek). South of the town is a narrow and very beautiful river gorge with rocky walls up to 100m/328ft high, contributing to some spectacular scenery. In the west part of Osmaneli are the well-preserved ruins of a large Byzantine church of indeterminate date (probably Neo-Byzantine) and, not far from it, a building which when in Greek hands was used as a silk-spinning mill, and also the owner's house.

Osmaneli

About 25km/15½ miles south-east of Bilecik, on the old overland route from Eskişehir to İznik, the district town of Söğüt occupies the site of ancient Thebasion. Prior to the Ottoman conquest Söğüt was the seat of the Oğuz

*Söğüt

211

leader Ertoğrul (d. 1289), father of Osman (see Famous People) and therefore progenitor of the Ottoman dynasty. In the mid 13th c. Ertoğrul sided
with the Seljuks against the Mongols, being rewarded by the Sultan Alaeddin Keykubad with the gift of a modest piece of feudal land in the area
bordering Byzantium. From this base he fashioned the beginnings of what
later grew to be the Ottoman Empire.
Ertoğrul's mausoleum, in the Old Ottoman style, endowed in the early
15th c. by Mehmet I and altered several times, stands some 2km/1¼ miles
north of the town. The türbe is surrounded by other family graves, thirteen
in all. Up until the reign of Abdul Hamid II, the spring festival of the formerly
Shiite Oğuz (held on March 9th) regularly brought huge numbers of the
now Sunnite Karakeçil nomads flocking to Söğüt on pilgrimage. Latterly
the Yürük festival took place in autumn. In the town itself stands the
Ertoğrul Gazi Mescidi endowed by Abdul Aziz (1861–76). This small domed
mosque with a low minaret topped by a onion dome is said to stand on the
site of an earlier mosque built by Ertoğrul himself.

Bingöl

See Muş

Birecik   N/O 6

South-eastern Anatolia (Urfa plateau)   See warning page 7
Province: Urfa
Altitude: 450m/1477ft
Population: 26,000

*Situation and
Importance

Birecik, principal town of its district, occupies a picturesque location above
the left bank of the Euphrates at a point where, from time immemorial, the
river has been crossed by a ford. Here, downstream of the cataracts and
foothills of the Taurus, the river also becomes navigable. In the last century
a Colonel Chesney planned a steamship company to ply the Euphrates and
provide a useful transport link betweem Europe and India. The scheme
however came to nothing, in part because the water was too shallow and
the volume irregular. Today a 720m/2363ft long bridge constructed in 1956
spans the river west of the town.

History

The name of this once walled town derives from the Arabic "bira" or
Armenian "birtha" (fort) and so means "little fort". The Romans knew it as
Birtha and the Crusaders as Bile. Captured in 1089 by Baldwin of Bouillon,
Crusader Count of Edessa (see Şanlıurfa), in 1150 it was sold together with
five other fortresses to Byzantium. Ownership changed a number of times
in subsequent centuries. In the 1830s the German H. v. Moltke, military
adviser to the Sultan, visited Birecik on several occasions, describing the
fortifications as the most astonishing structure he had ever seen. In 1838 he
himself was required to draw up plans for the defence of the town. These
were never acted upon however and on August 7th 1839 at Nizip he
witnessed the Turkish defeat at the hands of the Egyptians under İbrahim
Paşa.

Sights

*Birecik Kalesi

The ruins of the citadel, which guarded the Euphrates crossing point at
least from Roman times and was considered unassailable, sit perched on a
narrow isolated limestone outcrop in the midst of the town. According to
an inscription the first refurbishment of the fort, called Beda Castle by the
Turks, was carried out by Elmelik Ezzahir (1183–1216), Prince of Aleppo.

The Mameluke Sultan Baraka Khan (1277–79) and Sultan Ka'it Bay (1482/83) made further alterations. Since then it has been left badly damaged by several earthquakes. In Moltke's time the fortress still had its massive vaulted outer defences, three or four levels, with slits and crenellations. Beyond was a paved slope crowned by the walls and towers of the citadel itself. Behind the 5m/16½ft-thick outer wall were battlemented parapets. Beneath the citadel lies a vast labyrinth of subterranean vaults, and a tunnel (gradient 30°) leading down to a groundwater source and so ensuring the water supply.

Below the town an unmade road runs north along the Euphrates to one of the last refuges and breeding grounds of the hermit ibis, a bald ibis which normally winters in Morocco. It is a species so close to extinction that in 1973 only 25 breeding pairs remained. Prompted by the World Wildlife Fund and with government assistance Turkish conservationists at the sanctuary are now engaged in trying to save it.

Bald Ibis Sanctuary

The hermit ibis, widespread in the Alps as recently as the Middle Ages, had become little more than a creature of legend until its spectacular rediscovery near Birecik in 1839 by the British traveller W. F. Ainthworth. The Turks have long regarded it as almost a sacred bird, since its migration route roughly follows the pilgrim road to Mecca. Of 500 pairs counted in the 1950s most were killed off by agricultural insecticides. Since 1989 there have been no breeding pairs in the wild. None of the birds bred in captivity have yet been successfully released.

Surroundings

On the east bank of the Euphrates opposite Belkis (Zeugma; see below) stands a prehistoric settlement mound, called in earlier times Tell Muşa. It is known to have been already inhabited during the Bronze Age. Also on that side of the river stood the town of Apameia. Excavations carried out by J. Wagner next to the village of Keskince have revealed an acropolis, sections of a town wall, a necropolis, and other finds. Embankment-like structures of stone on both sides of the river suggest there was once a bridge here and indeed according to Pliny and Strabo a pontoon bridge did cross from Apameia on the left bank to Zeugma on the right. It was here in 53 B.C. that Crassus and his Roman legions crossed the river on their way to disastrous defeat at the hands of the Parthians near Carrhae and to Crassus's own death.

Apameia

The Turkish frontier township of Barak, close to the site of ancient Karkamış (Kargamis), sprang up on the right bank of the Euphrates in the late 19th c. as a result of the forcible settlement of the Barak nomads by Cevdet Paşa (1822–95). The ruins of Karkamış lie some 3km/2 miles to the west near the village Cerablus. Because of its position right on the Syrian border visitors to the site require a special permit from the local military and must be accompanied by an escort. The use of cameras is banned.

*Barak (Karkamış)

The earliest reference to Karkamish is as a prosperous trading settlement around the turn of the 18th or 19th c. B.C. After a short period of Hittite rule it then became part of the Hurrian kingdom of Mitanni until finally recovered by the Hittite King Suppiluliuma I (1385–1345 B.C.). He deported some of its inhabitants to Hatti and installed his son as viceroy. The new Hittite dominion soon achieved an extraordinary position in northern Syria and was one of the Late Hittite principalities to survive the collapse of the Empire. It finally fell to the conquering Assyrians under Sargon II (722–705 B.C.). The great battle between the Babylonians under Nebukadnezar and the Egyptians under Necho II, in which the Egyptians were defeated, took place at Karkamish in 605 B.C.

In Greco-Roman times a major military road crossed the Euphrates at this point. With the decline of the Roman Empire the town's fortunes also waned until eventually it disappeared completely, even from memory.

Birecik

The team of archaeologists responsible for excavating the site included for a while T. E. Lawrence ("Lawrence of Arabia"). The finds are now in the Hittite Museum in Ankara.

In the late Hittite period the town consisted of a fortified citadel on the hill by the river, a walled inner town to the south and west, with three gates, and an outer town, also walled. On the citadel hill there was a palace. Stone slabs were used to protect the base of the walls of larger structures and gates. Many of these were carved with reliefs and bore inscriptions in Hittite hieroglyphs. Finds have shown that the area of the later citadel was already settled in the 5th millennium B.C. Most of the major finds, which include chariot scenes, statues and inscriptions, are in the Hittite Museum in Ankara.

*Belkis

The village of Belkis (Balkız) and its prehistoric mound lie on a bend in the Euphrates about 10km/6 miles upstream from Birecik. It was here that Henderson unearthed Greco-Roman remains and artefacts, including mosaic floors depicting, in one instance, Hercules fighting with Centaurs and, in another, Hercules and Venus together with an old man. More recent investigations carried out by J. Wagner have in the last ten years confirmed that this is the site of the once important town of Seleukia.

An acropolis with a temple dedicated to the town's goddess once stood on Belkis Tepesi hüyük (Tell). At the foot of the mound lay the lower town, surrounded by rock tombs. Reliefs from the tombs are built into some of the houses in the village.

Seleukia was founded in about 300 B.C. by Seleukos Nikator I, one of the diadochi, giving him control of a principal Euphrates crossing-point and with it the opportunity to boost state coffers by levying customs dues. At the gathering of leaders in Amisos in 65 B.C. the Romans awarded the town to Kommagene, and then under Augustus to the Roman province of Syria. Various legions (X Fretensis, IV Scythia) were garrisoned there. Roman military power enabled the city to continue to flourish under the Emperors

Rumkale Roman fortress by the Euphrates

Trajan and Septimius Severus, with bridges, roads and tunnels being built to secure the Euphrates frontier against the neighbouring Persians. It was Sassanid incursions however which eventually brought about Seleukia's decline.

Along the old military road on the west side of the Euphrates, between Rumkale and the Karasu bridge, are three Roman pillar tombs from the imperial period. The Hisar tomb (2nd/3rd c. A.D.), southernmost of the three, is a 10m/33ft-high mausoleum on a square base. Pillars at the four corners, articulated with projections, support a now sagging pyramidal roof.

Hisar

The northernmost of the three pillar tombs, at Hasanoğlu, likewise dates from the turn of the 2nd/3rd c. It too stands on a square pedestal higher than a man, with an entrance into the burial chamber.

Hasanoğlu

The third of the three tombs, at Elifköy, has open stonework relieved by large arches and a low doorway. The roof has disappeared.

Elifköy

This arched Roman bridge carried the Roman military road between Zeugma (Belkis) and Samosata on the Euphrates (Samsat) over the Karasu, a western tributary of the Euphrates. It was restored in the Ottoman period. About 2km/1¼ miles from the bridge, in the Karasu gorge, there is a boulder carved with a 10th/9th c. B.C. relief of a god in protective pose armed with a lance.

Karasu Köprüsü

About 36km/22 miles north of Birecik, downstream of the district town of Halfeti, an ancient Roman fortress (Rumkale) perches high above the west bank of the Euphrates on a long and steep rocky spur. It can be reached by taking one of the curious old Euphrates ferries. The site once marked the most easterly point of the Roman Empire. Protected by the fortress the town was until 1921 the last surviving Christian community in Mameluke-controlled Islamic northern Syria.

*Rumkale

Bitlis   S 5

Eastern Anatolia   **See warning page 7**
Province: Bitlis
Altitude: 1550m/5087ft
Population: 38,000

Sandwiched between two massifs, the Muşgüney Dağları (2607m/8556ft) to the west and the Kavuşşahap Dağları (3103m/10,184ft) to the east, Bitlis, capital of its province, hugs the sides of the deep Basor Deresi in the valley of the Bitlis Çayı, a tributary of the Tigris. The population of the surrounding villages is mainly Kurdish, the principal occupation being livestock rearing (sheep and goats) and cultivation of cereals, vegetables and fruit on little irrigated plots of land. The townsfolk are very traditionally minded and show little enthusiasm for modernisation. In addition to its attractive setting Bitlis also boasts an Old Town with numerous charmingly decorated basalt houses, a variety of interesting sights, and a busy bazaar, making it altogether a place worth visiting. There are sulphurous thermal springs below the town on the east bank of the river.

*Situation and Importance

Although the area was certainly settled in the 7th c. B.C. Bitlis itself is said to have been founded in the late 4th c. B.C. by one of Alexander the Great's generals, who named it Balaleson. When or whether it ever belonged to Rome is questionable. The Arabs under the Caliph Omar occupied the town in 641, followed by the Seljuks in the 11th c. and the Mongols in the 13th. Finally, in the 16th c., Selim I claimed the town for the Ottoman Empire. Even so, the local Kurdish princes (of the Rushekid dynasty in the 14th c. for

History

Bitlis: the ruined castle and a shopping street

example) always enjoyed a considerable degree of autonomy in the region. From the 16th c. onwards Bitlis was the capital of a Kurdish beylik.

Sights

Sights

The Alaman Külliyesi, consisting of a hostel (han), medrese, mosque and bath house, was constructed in 1502. As regards the history of Bitlis Kalesi, the massive citadel with its polygonal towers and solid walls, dominating the town, not much is known. Its nucleus appears to be Byzantine. It was enlarged by the Ottomans and at one time contained 300 houses. Part of it was demolished in 1911 to provide stone for building.

The Şerefiye Külliyesi on the market square below the fort was built in 1528/29 under Süleiman the Magnificent. An elaborately carved wooden pulpit graces the mosque. The complex also includes a kitchen for the poor, a Koranic school and the patron's türbe.

The Great Mosque (Ulu Cami) in the town centre was endowed by an Artuk emir in 1126, and according to an inscription was renovated in 1150. Built of rough-hewn basalt it has fifteen bays separated by pointed arches. Be sure to visit the domed minaret next to the prayer house.

Surroundings

*Hizan

The town of Hizan is situated high up in a side valley of the Büyük Dere 50km/30 miles or so east of Bitlis. By hiring a local guide it is possible to visit the medieval – and later Kurdish – fortress at Eski Hizan (10km/6 miles away) and the several ruined 10th and 11th c. monasteries which lie widely scattered in the surrounding area. These include the Monastery of Our Lady of Hzar, a four-hour walk from Nizar Köprüsü (Pira Nizar), the Monastery of the Holy Cross of Hizan (Chinitzor) near Bereket Köyü, and the Monastery of Our Lady of Baritzor with its interesting Göçimen Kilisesi.

Washing clothes by Lake Van

There are a number of caravanserais in the vicinity of Bitlis. Among them are the Alaman Hanı (east side of the Tatvan road), Başhan (in the village of that name) and Papsin Hanı (in the upper Bitlis Çayı valley).

Caravanserais

About 32km/21 miles east of Tatvan, at Reşadiye, there is a small promontory with a little beach, a delightful place to bathe.

Reşadiye

Siirt (provincial capital; population: 67,000) nestles off the beaten track about 100km/60 miles south-west of Bitlis, in the comparatively green countryside between the Botan Çayı and Kezer Çayı on the south-eastern slopes of the Taurus. It has a typically continental climate with cold winters and high snowfall. The main occupation is raising angora goats, from whose wool the famous Siirt blankets are made.

Siirt

The population of Siirt is almost entirely Arab, whereas most of the inhabitants of the surrounding countryside are Kurds. The town's ancient history remains largely shrouded in uncertainty, though in Roman times it stood on the frontier between Rome and Persia. The Arabs captured the town in the 7th c. and under the rule of the Abbasid Caliphs of Baghdad (763–1258) it became an important trade and cultural centre.

Siirt's oldest building, the Hudurul Ahdar Camii (now Cumhuriyet Camii), was probably erected in the 8th c. during the Abbasid period. The Seljuk Kavvam Bath dates from the 11th c. Also of interest are two former Koranic schools, Zinciriye and Mesudiye.

The Great Mosque in Siirt was built with an endowment in 1129 by the Seljuk Sultan Muğizeddin Mahmut. It was restored in the 13th c. The mosque's superb walnut staircase pulpit is in the safekeeping of the Ethnographic Museum in Ankara.

About 6km/4 miles north-east of Siirt lies the little mountain town of Aydınlar ("The Enlightened"; formerly Tillo). In the 18th c. it was the home of the astronomer and sage İbrahim Hakkı whose mausoleum (the İbrahim

Aydınlar

Hakki Türbesi) adorns the town. The scholar came from a village east of Erzurum, having been brought to Tillo by his father as a child to study under a Fakir Ullah. Teacher and pupil endured years of privation before, with the aid of only home-made instruments, İbrahim Hakki succeeded in measuring the precise distance between the Earth and the Moon. His "astrolabium" and other instruments can be seen in a local museum.

Ziyaret

The small village of Ziyaret is situated on a tributary of the Bitlis Çayı about 30km/20 miles north-west of Siirt, at the junction of the main Diyarbakır road. It is a place of pilgrimage for local people attracted not just to its simple domed mosque, but to the square, domed, flat-porched mausoleum of a much revered holy man, Veysel Karani. He is said to have participated in the controversy over the rightful succession to the Prophet, at Siffin during the fourth caliphate (of the Caliph Ali; mid 7th c.). Another account is that, as an old man, he sought out Mohammed in the hope of receiving instruction, but died in the process.

Black Sea Coast   C–R 1–3

Black Sea region
Provinces (from west to east):
Kırklareli, İstanbul, Kocaeli, Sakarya, Bolu, Zonguldak, Kastamonu, Sinop, Samsun, Ordu, Giresun, Trabzon, Rize, Artvin
Total length: 2000km/760 miles

*Coastal landscape
**Bathing beaches

The Turkish Black Sea coast with its rich vegetation will come as a surprise to those who think of Turkey as a hot, dry land. Ridges of mountains with dense pine forests and gentle river valleys, miles of bathing beaches, busy ports and sleepy fishing villages with their typical wooden houses, plus a mild, wet climate in which hazelnuts, maize, rice and tea flourish, are in sharp contrast to the high plateaux of inland Anatolia.

Characteristics

These regions along the Turkish Black Sea coasts (Kara Deniz in Turkish) with their wealth of natural beauties are bordered by the Pontic Mountains which at 4000m/13,000ft dominate the northern Anatolian hinterland. As a result of erosion, however, the coast has fewer bays and inlets than any other part of the Turkish coastline. The climate in the western regions is cooler so that even at the height of summer it never becomes too hot, while the eastern half is very warm and rainy. In Rize, for example, annual precipitation can amount to 2500mm/100in., creating a favourable environment for the area's extensive forests. These northern coastal regions are well worth an extended visit not just for their many bathing resorts, most of them with good sandy beaches, but also for their rich and varied history.

Tea plantations and processing

In the Rize region, tea growing has become an important part of the local economy. In 1938 Mustafa Kemal Atatürk decided to make black tea (çay in Turkish) the national drink instead of expensive imported coffee and now Turkish tea consumption is met by the Black Sea growers. Acid soil, plenty of rain, high humidity (78%), warm summers (35°C/95°F) and mild winters (minimum −8°C/18°F) provide the ideal conditions for tea production. Tea is harvested in April and May.

Myth and history

The coastal strip along the Pontos Euxeinos, the "hospitable sea", has featured prominently in Greek mythology, including the legends of Promotheus, the warlike Amazons and the Argonauts who sailed from Kolchis in the "Argo" in search of the Golden Fleece. From the 7th c. B.C. onwards, Greek colonies have flourished all along the coast and most were founded by Miletus, including Amisos, Kotyora, Kerasus and Trapezous. In 281 B.C. after the death of Antigonos, Mithradetes V founded the kingdom of Pontos, which reached its zenith under Mithradetes Eupator the Great

A tea plantation in the hinterland of Rize

(120–63 B.C.). After the capture of Constantinople by the Crusaders in 1204 the Byzantine dynasty of the Comneni ruled the empire of Trebizond (Trapezous) which extended from Thermodon to Phasis. Trapezous then became the leading commercial city of the ancient world. In 1461, however, Sultan Mehmet II conquered these territories and incorporated them into the Ottoman Empire.

On May 19th 1919 Kemal Paşa (Atatürk) landed at Samsun – an event of decisive importance in modern Turkish history. It marked the beginning of the campaign to free Turkey from foreign occupation, leading to the abolition of the Sultanate and the establishment of the Turkish Republic.

Although the western half of the Black Sea coast between the Bulgarian frontier and Ince Burun, the most northerly point in Asia Minor, is not served by a modern highway, a fine coast road runs east from Sinop (in antiquity the most powerful of the Greek Black Sea colonies) right through to the Turkish-Georgian border. It passes through a series of interesting towns including Samsun, the most important port and commercial centre on the north coast of Turkey, Trabzon (ancient Trabezous and later Trebizond), the tea-producing town of Rize and administrative centre of the mountainous region of Lazistan and the little Turkish port of Hopa just a few miles from the Georgian frontier.

Access

A reasonably regular boat service runs from İstanbul to Zonguldak, Sinop, Samsun, Giresun and Trabzon. In addition, air services connect İstanbul and Ankara with Samsun and Trabzon.

The principal towns along the Black Sea coast are listed below going from east to west.

Western Black Sea coast

A typical fishing village in a bay sheltered to the north by Cape İğneada (lighthouse) lies 15km/9 miles south of the Bulgarian frontier. To the west

İgneada

are the wooded Istranca Hills. Kilyos, a popular seaside resort with a beautiful sandy beach, is 40km/25 miles north of İstanbul.

Bosporus   See entry

Karasu   This small town lies 2km/1¼ miles inland near the mouth of the River Sakarya. Homer and Hesiod called the river Sangarios, after a Phrygian river god, son of Okeanos and Tethys. Long beaches of fine sand line the coast which is attracting more and more tourist development.

Akçakoca   This beautifully-situated little seaside resort has access to a narrow beach
Diospolis   beneath a steep cliff. It occupies the site of the Greek city of Diospolis (or Dia) and to the west of the town is a ruined 14th c. Genoese fortress. The surrounding area is well known for its hazelnut plantations.

Ereğli   This small port with a steelworks lies in a bay to the south of Cape Baba (the
Herakleia Pontike   ancient Acherusia Promontorium) on the site of ancient Herakleia Pontike (Heraclea ad Pontum). According to tradition, the town was founded by Megara in 560 B.C.. There are some fine sandy beaches nearby (Karadeniz Ereglisi, see Zonguldak).

Zonguldak   See entry

*Amasra   This coastal town is situated picturesquely on a peninsula. Its name derives from Amastris, niece of Darius III of Persia (died *c.* 285 B.C.). She was regent of Herakleia and is said to have made plans to build gardens here like those of Semiramis in Babylon. The earlier name of the town was Sesamos. In the 9th c. Amasra was the seat of an archbishop. Now it is a flourishing seaside resort with a fine sandy beach and a small harbour (boat building). The remains of some Roman baths, a theatre and a necropolis have been preserved. The castle dates from the period of 14th c. Genoese rule. Other sights of interest include the Fatih mosque and the local museum.

İnebolu   The principal port on this stretch of slate-covered coast is situated at the mouth of a little river with the same name in a lush garden-like landscape.
*Wooden houses   As well as a ruined castle, the traditional wooden houses are particularly interesting. İnebolu boasts several handsome Pontic-style town houses, some with slate-covered roofs in the traditional style. In antiquity the town was known as Abonouteichos, but was renamed Ionopolis (hence İnebolu) during the period of Roman Imperial rule. Some of the historically important buildings in the old town include Eski Cami, Yen Cami, Küçük Cami and the ruins of a church in the Christian quarter of Erkistos Mahalles. More fine beaches are to be found in the vicinity. Other excellent beaches enhance the neighbouring towns of Gemiciler (10km/6 miles to the east), Özlüce (14km/9 miles to the west), Kayran (24km/15 miles to the west) and Doğnyurt (32km/20 miles to the west) from where boat trips to the Fokkayazı caves leave.

İnce Burun   This cape with a lighthouse, the ancient Syrias Promontorium, is the most northerly point in Turkey.

Eastern Black Sea coast

*Sinop   The provincial capital of Sinop (pop. 26,000) enjoys a charming position on the central section of the Boztepe peninsula. It is both the most northerly point on the Turkish Black Sea coast and also the best protected harbour. It is now a place of little consequence compared with its importance in antiquity when it was a busy commercial city situated at the northern end of important caravan routes from Cappadocia and the lands of the Euphrates. Nowadays, however, communications with the Anatolian Plateau are rendered difficult by the intervening barrier of the West Pontic Mountains. The

The port of Sinop

sandy beaches, with hotels and small airport, to the west of the town are well known. Sinope was an important Black Sea centre in the 8th c. B.C. when it was a Greek colony. In 413 B.C. the Cynic philosopher Diogenes (the one who lived in a tub and not to be confused with Diogenes of Apollonia) was born here.

No buildings survive from the great days of Sinope apart from scanty remains of the citadel, a Temple of Serapis and the town walls near the harbour.

Visitors to the small town of Durağan 133km/82 miles south of Sinop on the River Gökırmak will find a Seljuk caravanserai built in 1266 by Pervane Süleyman (Durak Hanı). A large summer courtyard surrounded by vaulted chambers stands in front of the triple-aisled winter hall which points north. The corners of the complex are fortified with small semi-circular towers and the external walls reinforced with additional rectangular towers.

Durağan

Bafra lies some 25km/15 miles south of the wooded Bafra Burun where the Kızılırmak (Red River), known in antiquity as Halys, flows into the sea. Bafra is noted for its thermal springs, its tobacco and its caviar. Other sights include a 13th c. bath-house and a 15th c. complex consisting of a mosque, mausoleum and medrese. To the east of the town lies the coastal lagoon of Balık Gölü (Fish Lake). Further east along the Gulf of Samsun are large tobacco plantations.

Bafra

Between 310 and 183 B.C. the delta of the old Halys (see Kırşehir) formed the border between Paphlagonia and the Kingdom of Pontos. Now it is the biggest natural wetland area on the Turkish Black Sea coast. The eastern part of the delta is comprised mainly of brackish lakes (Çernek, Gıcı, Paralı, Liman, Balık, Uzungöl, Tatlı Göl) and lagoons with extensive reed beds. This delta where most of the Anatolian bird species are found is used primarily as a winter nesting site for waterfowl. In addition, in an area

Kızılırmak
Deltası

around Balık Gölü and Uzungöl (combined area 1000ha./4sq.miles) lies a riverside forest (1500ha./5½sq. miles) of hornbeam, ash, alder and various species of oak. Sections of the woodland are overrun by climbing plants or covered with thick undergrowth, making an ideal habitat for many woodpecker species. Another phenomenon is the semi-wild dromedary of which there are believed to be about a hundred. Their existence in the area is attributed to the days of the semi-nomadic tribes. The Yürüks, a small tightly-knit tribe from the Adapazarı region, settled here in 1915 in dwellings made from straw and they lived off the land.

Samsun

The provincial capital of Samsun (pop. 31,000,) is the largest city on the north coast and it is also the principal port and commercial centre. Every July it hosts a Trade Fair. The importance of Samsun is due principally to its good communications with the Central Anatolian Plateau and these include a trunk road and a railway line. The coastal plain around Samsun between the Kızılırmak delta to the west and the Yeşilırmak to the east produces tobacco (the best in Turkey), cereals, cotton, poppy seeds and other oil-producing plants. After being processed in the large tobacco and foodstuff factories, they are exported from the port of Samsun. The sandy beaches in the vicinity of the town offer excellent bathing. The site of ancient Amisos, founded in the 7th c. B.C. by Greek settlers from Miletus lay some 3km/2 miles north-west of the present-day Samsun. Later the site was occupied by Athenian settlers and called Peiraieus (Piraeus). The name Samsun first appears in the year 1331. It was here that Mustafa Kemal Paşa, later Atatürk (equestrian statue in the municipal park) landed on May 19th 1919 to begin his fight against the foreign occupying forces. This day is celebrated throughout Turkey as the "Day of Youth".

The hotel in which Atatürk stayed while in Samsun is now the Gazi Museum. The most notable of the town's older mosques are the Pazar Camii or Market Mosque, built by Mongolian governors in the 14th c. and the Great Mosque (Ulu Cami) which dates from the 18th/19th c. The Archaeological Museum exhibits material excavated from the Dündar Tepe, the nearby site of ancient Amisos.

Havza Ladik

Around 80km/50 miles south-west of Samsun a number of other places boast thermal springs. The bath in Havza was mentioned in 1650 by Evliya Celebi and was the Roman town of Thermae. In Havza, like many other

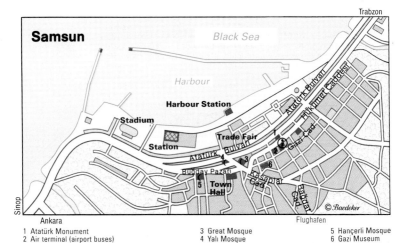

1 Atatürk Monument
2 Air terminal (airport buses)
3 Great Mosque
4 Yalı Mosque
5 Hançerli Mosque
6 Gazi Museum

seaside resorts whose history goes back to ancient times, a bathing business was set up near the 13th c. Seljuk building (two baths). Another
thermal bath can be found in ancient Laodikea (Ladik) alongside the small,
pretty Lake Ladik (Ladik Gölü).

Vezirköprü was named after an old bridge across a tributary of the Kızılırmak. A number of old buildings in the town belonged to the Köprülüs, an
upright and respected family of dignitaries which in the late 17th and 18th c.
produced five Grand Viziers including Mehmet Paşa (the Strict), Ahmet
Paşa and Amcazade Hüseyin Paşa. To the north-east of the town stands
Kapıkaya, a rock with a Paphlagonian monument consisting of four front
pillars. Other similar cave tombs can be found further north along the
Kızılırmak.

Vezirköprü

Çarşamba lies some 30km/19 miles inland on the Yeşilırmak delta. The river
which was known as the Iris in antiquity flows into the sea north-west of the
town at Cape Civa (ancient Ankon). To the east of the cape are numerous
projecting spits of land and coastal lagoons created by an eastward movement of the beaches under the prevailing north-west winds, thus gradually
producing a more regular coastline.

Çarşamba

A little way south of Çalti Burun (ancient Heracleum Promontorium or the
Cape of Hercules) lies this small town on the Terme Çayı, which is probably
the ancient Thermodon.
The ancient town of Themiskyra was situated at the mouth of the river.
Themiskyra was also the name of the plain which according to Strabo
began 60 stadia (10km/7 miles) behind Amisos (Samsun). It extended to the
River Thermodon and was noted for the fertility of its soil.

Terme
Themiskyra

Themiskyra was also believed to be the home of the Amazons, the warlike
man-hating women of Greek mythology who were said to be descended
from the god Ares and the nymph Harmonia. According to the legend, the
women cut off their right breasts to use a bow and arrow better. Amazon in
Greek means without breasts. One of the Labours of Herakles (Hercules)
involved him in going to Themiskyra and taking back to Argos the girdle of
the Amazon queen Hippolyte. When the Greeks came to the area to establish their colonies, they found no Amazons and concluded that Herakles
had either killed them all or driven them away.

Amazons

Ordu (pop. 81,000) occupies the site of ancient Kotyora, an Ionian colony.
Here Xenophon and his Ten Thousand Greeks are said to have embarked
for Sinope in 401 B.C. When King Pharnakes moved families from Kotyora
to occupy Pharnakeia (Giresun), the town started to decline. In the Middle
Ages the area around Ordu belonged to the empire of Trebizond. In 1913
much of town was destroyed by fire.

Ordu
Kotyora

The administrative centre of the province, Giresun (pop. 56,000) lies on a
small rocky peninsula which was once fortified. It is a port exporting wood
and hazelnuts. Notable sights include the tombs of Seyyidi Vakkas and
Osman Aga and an 18th c. church. From the town a wide depression leads
up to a flat-topped conical hill crowned by a Byzantine fortress. Just outside
the harbour is the little island of Giresun Adası (ancient Aretia) where
according to legend the Argonauts landed. The island was uninhabited and
had a temple dedicated to the war god Ares. The ruins of a Byzantine
monastery can be found there.
Giresun occupies the site of ancient Kerasous, founded by Miletus in the
7th c. B.C. Xenophon and his Ten Thousand halted here on their march back
to the sea. The place was later named Pharnakeia after King Pharnakes
(grandfather of Mithradates the Great) who settled families from Kotyora
(Ordu) in the town. During the war with the Romans, Mithradates moved
his harem to Pharnakeia.
The present name of Giresun apparently owes its origins to the Roman
general Lucullus who found a particularly good type of cherry here (Greek

Giresun
Kerasous

= "kerássi", Latin = "cerasus" and Turkish = "kiraz") which he later took back to Rome.

Fener Burnu

The coast road continues east to the small peninsula of Fener Burnu (Cape Yeros), one of the highest capes on the Black Sea coast. In antiquity it was known as Cape Hieron Oros or Holy Mountain. In order to secure the town of Trapezunt, the Byzantine emperor Alexios II built a castle here. Earlier Justinian is said to have founded the St Foca Monastery on the site. The cape has been a well-known landmark to seafarers since the days of the Argonauts.

Akçaabat

The small town of Akçaabat, the ancient Hermonassa or Platana (Pola-thane) is one of the few places along the Black Sea coast where examples of older Greek architecture can still be seen. The Church of St Michael in the west of the town dates from the 13th/14th centuries.

Trabzon

See entry

Sürmene
*Yapukoğlu Konağı

The little town of Sürmene (Hamurgan) is situated some 40km/25 miles east of Trabzon. Known in antiquity as Susarmia or Augustopolis, it lies on the River Kora (Manahoz Deresi) and is best known as the place where Xenophon and his Ten Thousand fell sick after eating wild honey, an event which was confirmed by the local people. In the village of Sürmene Kastil, 5km/3 miles to the west of Sürmene, stands a ruined medieval castle as well as the impressive 18th c. Yapukoğlu Konağı mansion (Derebeyli Kale). It was formerly the seat of the Yapukoğlu family, who lived here as rulers (derebey) of the surrounding region relatively free of interference from the Sublime Porte in İstanbul.

Fetoka
monasteries

A number of monasteries are located in the isolated hilly region behind Sürmene. They lie to the south of Küçükdere and Köprübaşı, both of which are accessible by reasonable roads from Sürmene (20km/12 miles). Until 1923 they were used by Greek monks. Most of these monasteries now have ruined interiors and three of them can only be reached on foot and with the help of a guide: Charveli and Oma monasteries (20km/12 miles south of Köprübaşı on the heights of the upper Manahoz Deresi) and the Seno Monastery near Küçükdere to the south.

Rize

Situated on a narrow coastal strip in a small bay at the foot of the steeply rising Pontic mountain foothills (new town) stands the provincial capital of Rize (pop. 52,000). The port which exports tea and wood, tea production and more recently tourism (excursions into mountainous hinterland and tea plantations) are the main sources of income. In antiquity the town was called Rhizion (Rhizous, Rhition, Rhitium) and was a port for the territory of Kissioi. In medieval times it was known as Risso. In 1461 after Mehmet II captured Trebizond it became part of the Ottoman Empire.
Offering a fine view over the town the ruined castle (Rize Kalesi) with its tea garden dates from the Middle Ages. The view of the town from the Botanical Gardens (Zıraat Bahçesi) is also particularly impressive. The garden itself which can be reached from a steep road near the western entrance to the town has a collection of sub-tropical flora including an informative range of tea plants.

Ayder Kaplıcası

On a plateau about 8km/5 miles south-east of Rize and surrounded by woods lies the town of Ayder with its small thermal spring. To encourage tourists to enjoy the delightful countryside, a visitor centre and a hotel are planned.

Lazistan

South-east of Rize the wild mountainous country of Lazistan (Tatos Dağları) stretches up to the snow-tipped Kaçkar Dağı peaks just under 4000m/13,120ft high. See Facts and Figures: Historical Regions.

Çamburun Plajı

About 11km/7 miles to the east of Rize near the village of Çamburun (Pine Tree Cape), some fine beaches are situated under a steep rocky cliff face.

A farmhouse near Rize

They can be reached by descending 211 steps which have been cut into the rock.

A visit to the small regional centre of Çamlıhemşin 80km/50 miles east of Rize will entail an exhilarating journey through the tea plantations and along the wild Fırtına Çayı valley with its stone bridges and enormous old farmsteads.

Çamlıhemşin

Located on a overhanging rock face the medieval castle of Zilkalesi (Ziykale) lies in the mountainous Üsküt Dağı region 12km/7 miles south-west of Çamlıhemşin high above the Fırtına Deresi valley.

Ziy Kalesi

Hopa is the most easterly Turkish Black Sea port and lies in a wooded setting 8km/5 miles from the Georgian border at Kemalpaşa (hotel).

Hopa

Bodrum

C 6

West coast (Aegean Sea)
Province: Muğla
Altitude: 0–50m/0–165ft
Population: 13,000

The modern town of Bodrum (formerly Budrum), in Caria, lies on the site of the important ancient city of Halikarnassos in a little bay (Bodrum Limanı) on the south-west coast of Asia Minor opposite the Greek island of Kos (Turkish İstanköy Adası). Rising in terraces above the bay – a layout compared by Vitruvius in his "De Architectura" (II, 8) to an amphitheatre – it is an exceedingly picturesque little town. The name Bodrum (= cellar or casemate) may be a corruption of the name of the Crusader castle of St

*Situation

225

The harbour, with the Crusader castle Bodrum Kalesi

Peter (Petronium), built by the Knights of St John, or it may refer to the arcading on the west side of the castle.

In recent years Bodrum has developed into one of the leading holiday centres on the Aegean coast of Turkey. Its great attractions, in addition to its mild climate and delightful situation, are the beautiful bathing beaches and diving grounds in the immediate vicinity, the sheltered harbour (port of call for regular shipping lines and cruise ships), the marina, and the friendly atmosphere of the town. The centre of modern Bodrum with its busy, colourful bazaars is situated at the northern end of the peninsula on which the castle stands.

History of
Halikarnassos

Halikarnassos was founded about 1200 B.C. by Dorian Greeks from Troezen in the eastern Argolid (the area associated with the legends of Theseus and his son Hippolytos). Thanks to its good harbour and the fertile surrounding country Halikarnassos quickly developed into an important commercial city. Originally belonging to the Dorian League of six cities, the Hexapolis, it came under Lydian rule in the reign of Croesus (560–546 B.C.). In 540 it passed, without resistance to the Persians, under whose overlordship the city was ruled by Carian princely families. After the Battle of Mykale (479) Halikarnassos became part of the Athenian Empire. Herodotus (484–425), the "Father of History" and the city's greatest son, was involved in the factional struggles which followed.

In 413 Halikarnassos again fell into Persian hands and, after a brief period of autonomy (*c.* 394–377), remained under Persian rule until Alexander's campaign. After 387, Hekatomnos, Satrap of Mylasa, gained control of the town and made it the chief city of Caria, replacing the more remote Mylasa. His successor Mausolos, one of the most important rulers of this period, established a strong position by skilful statesmanship and war and, follow- ing Hellenistic models, equipped the city with walls, harbours, palaces and temples. Under ancient Carian law women enjoyed great authority as the wives of their brothers, and when Mausolos died he was succeeded by his

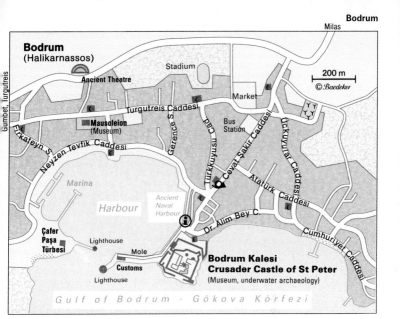

sister-wife Artemisia II (377–353 B.C.), who built the Mausoleion (Mausoleum), one of the Seven Wonders of the Ancient World, in his honour.
In 334 B.C., during Alexander's Persian campaign, the city withstood a long
siege by his general Ptolemaios but was finally taken and destroyed. Its
fortunes only revived again at the time of the Roman Empire. In 1523
Halikarnassos fell to the Ottomans, the castle surrendering without a fight.

Sights

The ancient city was traversed by a main street running from its east end to
the fine Myndos Gate (Gümüşli Kapı) with its tower at the west end. In this
street, in the centre of the town, stood the famous Mausoleion or Mausoleum, which from the time of Augustus became a general term for a large
tomb. Its architect was Pytheos. Under the direction of Satyros the rectangular tower-like structure, 46m/150ft high, was decorated with magnificent
friezes by the most celebrated Greek sculptors of the day. Erected in 351 B.C.
it survived in good condition until the 12th c. A.D. Thereafter it may have
been damaged by earthquakes and was then gradually pulled down, being
finally destroyed in 1552 when the remaining stone was used to strengthen
the castle against Ottoman attack. Dressed stones from the Mausoleum
can be seen in the castle, the town walls, and at the bottom of an old well in
the town. A reconstruction of the monument is planned.

The first reliefs recovered from the Mausoleum were taken to London in
1846; in 1863 C. T. (later Sir Charles) Newton positively identified the site of
the monument and removed much sculpture from the Mausoleion and the
castle to the British Museum. Excavations were carried out by Danish
archaeologists in 1966/67.

Above the Mausoleion, to the north-west, is the ancient theatre, from which
there are extensive views. To the north-east are remains of a Doric stoa

Mausoleion

*Planned
reconstruction*

*Other ancient
remains*

227

(colonnade), and above this the remains of a Temple of Ares (?). Still higher up, outside the town walls to east and west, are various tombs. At the entrance to the harbour fragments of the ancient piers survive. To the east of the naval harbour stood the palace of Mausolos built in the 4th c. B.C. with a lavish use of marble. Along the north side of the harbour was the agora, in which stood a colossal statue of the god Ares.

To the west of the city on the Hill of Kaplan Kalesi, the former acropolis, was the Carian stronghold of Salmakis. The famous spring of that name must have been somewhere below the north side of the hill.

** **Bodrum Kalesi**

Bodrum's principal sight, the Castle of St Peter, now known as Bodrum Kalesi, with its tall, well-preserved towers, was built by the Knights Hospitallers of St John between 1402 and 1437 on the site of the islet of Zephyrion, now joined to the mainland. It replaced an earlier castle built on the site of the first Greek settlement. The Turks erected other buildings within the precincts of the castle, and in the Late Ottoman period it was used as a place of exile. As with the defences of Rhodes, knights of the various nationalities in the Order were entrusted with the defence of particular sections of the walls. The English Tower, having a sculpted lion on its west wall, is also known as the Lion Tower (or "Arslani Kule").

* Museum

The various buildings within the castle, together with the upper and lower wards, have been turned into a very interesting museum, the arrangement of which has not yet been completed.

From the mosque (1723) in the Harbour Square a ramp leads up into the outer ward, on the far side of which is an arched gateway giving access to the lower ward (ticket office). Here there is a Gothic chapel, built by Spanish knights in 1520 and later converted into a mosque. It contains Bronze Age material and the only fragment of a frieze from the Mausoleion still preserved in Bodrum. In the towers of the castle are collections of objects of various kinds and different periods (architectural fragments, sculptures, jewellery, coins, etc.) and other items are displayed in the open.

* Underwater Archeology

The most interesting part of the museum is the section devoted to underwater archaeology. There are original finds and reconstructions of material recovered from wrecks at Yassı,Ada (a short distance west of Bodrum) and Cape Gelidonya (at Finike), displays of equipment used by underwater archaeologists and illustrations of their methods, and a great variety of other objects recovered from the sea.

Bodrum is the Turkish base of the University of Texas Institute of Nautical Archaeology (College Station TX).

Boğazkale (Hattuşaş)   K 3/4

North-eastern Central Anatolia
Province: Corum
Altitude: 1125m/3692ft
Population: about 2500

Situation and
** Importance

The village of Boğazkale (or Boğazköy), starting-out point for exploring the famous ruins of the Hittite capital of Hattuşaş (also Hattusa, Hattusha) as well as the neighbouring rock sanctuary at Yazılıkaya, lies on a bend in the Kızılırmak about 200km/124 miles east of Ankara. It is situated below the sprawling archaeological site, at the upper end of the Budaközü valley where the Zincirli Dağ (1641m/5386ft) and the Akcadağ Tepesi (1689m/5543ft) converge and where the Yazır Deresi and Büyükkaya Deresi, two source streams, join forces to form the Budaközü Dere. On a plateau in between, a kilometre or so south-east of the village and some 90m/300ft higher up, are the ruins of Hattuşaş's lower city, including those of the Great Temple. Limestone outcrops rising abruptly from the plateau and along its flanks made fine natural sites for the acropolis and for various

Hattuşaş

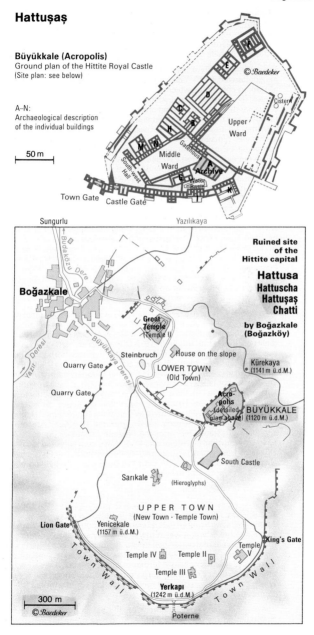

Büyükkale (Acropolis)
Ground plan of the Hittite Royal Castle
(Site plan: see below)

A–N:
Archaeological description
of the individual buildings

50 m

© Baedeker

E

D

C
B

H

M N

South-west
Hall

Middle
Ward

Gatehouse

Upper
Ward

Cistern

Archive

A

Water
Basin

G

I

K

Town Gate   Castle Gate

Sungurlu   Yazılıkaya

**Ruined site
of the
Hittite capital**

**Hattusa
Hattuscha
Hattuşaş
Chatti**

by Boğazkale
(Boğazköy)

Budaközü Dere

Boğazkale

Great
Temple
(Temple I)

Steinbruch   House on the slope

Büyükkaya Deresi

Yazır Deresi

Quarry Gate

Quarry Gate

LOWER TOWN
(Old Town)

Kürekaya
(1141 m ü.d.M.)

Acro-
polis
(detailed
plan above)

BÜYÜKKALE
(1120 m ü.d.M.)

South Castle

Sarıkale   (Hieroglyphs)

U P P E R   T O W N
(New Town · Temple Town)

Lion Gate   Yenicekale
(1157 m ü.d.M.)

Temple IV   Temple II

Temple
V

King's Gate

Temple III

Yerkapı
(1242 m ü.d.M.)

Town Wall

Town Wall

300 m
© Baedeker

Poterne

229

fortifications and towers. The New (upper) City, with three fortresses and numerous temples, stood further to the south, where the far from level plateau, dotted with boulders and broken by summits and ridges, rises to a height of 1242m/4076ft. The huge scale of the city can be judged from the fact that the walls encircling it were once 6km/4 miles long.

History

The acropolis (Büyükkale) is known to have been inhabited in the 3rd millennium B.C. In the 19th c. B.C. Assyrian merchants established the kind of trading colony for which the Assyrians were famous on the northern edge of the pre-Hittite town. At the beginning of the 18th c. B.C. a King Anitta of Kushar (the precise location of which remains unknown) destroyed both the town and the trading settlement. Despite his having also put a curse on it, in the 17th c. B.C. one of his successors moved his capital to Hattuşaş and even styled himself Hattusili (I) accordingly. The next Hittite king, Mursili I, embarked on a wide-ranging and successful series of conquests from which not even Babylon escaped. Following an interim period of reverses and decline, Hittite power expanded once again around 1450 B.C. leading to the creation of the Hittite Empire. Most of the buildings and sculptures seen today date from the heyday of the Empire.

Around 1200 B.C. Hattuşaş and its empire were destroyed by unidentified invaders, possibly the so-called Sea Peoples. Since there is no evidence of any recovery it must be assumed that the entire population of the city was either deported or killed. The ruins stood abandoned for more than two hundred years before Phrygians built a new town on the acropolis.

About 650 B.C. this settlement was in turn partly destroyed. Subsequently there was further building on the acropolis under the Medes, Lydians and Persians. Coins found on the site suggest that, from A.D. 240 to 350, the acropolis may have been in use as a sanctuary. Boğazköy began as an Ottoman village, growing up to the north-west of the ruins in the early 18th c. around the seat of the ruling derebey.

History of the Excavations

The site, the existence of which is referred to in the Old Testament (Genesis 23), was rediscovered in 1834 by the scholar Charles Texier, although he was unable to identify the remains. It was A. H. Sayce who first suggested their possible Hittite origin. In 1882 C. Hamann carried out a survey, and two years later E. Chantre discovered the first cuneiform clay tablets in Accadian and the (then unknown) Hittite language. In 1920, B. Hrozny succeeded in placing Hittite within the Indo-European family of languages. The first systematic excavations were undertaken in 1906/07 and 1911/12, led by H. Winckler, Th. Makridi and O. Puchstein. These brought to light the royal palace archives containing some 2500 cuneiform tablets, enabling the site to be positively identified as that of the Hittite capital Hattuşaş, the name of which was already known from the so-called "Amarna Correspondence" (State Archive of the Pharaoh Echnaton). Since 1977 there have been further investigations by P. Neve concentrating on the upper city, finds from which include 1040 Hittite inscription tablets uncovered on Nişantepe (Medallion Hill). A path has been laid out enabling visitors to make a circular tour of the site.

Sights

Ambarlıkaya

About 300m/328yd east of the Great Temple is a rocky height known as Ambarlıkaya, with a large natural cave on the south-east side. Steps lead up to the summit where a watch-tower probably stood. From here a battlemented parapet of wooden galleried construction, quite separate from the main city wall, went steeply down into the valley between Ambarlıkaya and Büyükkaya (the rocky height further to the north-east). Carried across the intervening 85m/280ft-wide gorge on a wooden bridge the footings of which can still be seen in the rock, it then joined up with the Büyükkaya fortifications on the other side.

*Büyükkale (Acropolis)

The earliest traces of settlement on the acropolis, which stands on a commanding site overlooking the city, go back to the 3rd millennium B.C.

From then onwards it was probably occupied continuously, initially by a chieftain's house and later, from about 1600 B.C., by a citadel-cum-palace which underwent extensive alteration at the time of the New Kingdom (1300 B.C.). During this latter phase the acropolis precincts were enlarged until they occupied more than 3ha/7½ acres. The level of part of the site was also raised to provide foundations for the buildings of the royal palace. The post-Hittite period saw a reversion to a less grandiose residence and correspondingly smaller-scale town. The acropolis hill was re-occupied in the later Phrygian period, being fortified anew in the face of the Cimmerian invasions. It survived as a small fortified town until the collapse of Imperial Rome (3rd/4th c. A.D.).

The defences encircling the citadel, pierced by three gates, reveal two different phases of construction, the south wall being part of the earlier city wall built at the beginning of the 13th c. B.C., the rest some 500 years later. The palace complex was arranged around four courtyards rising in succession to the top of the hill, with colonnades of pillars linking individual buildings, as can be seen from the remains of plinths on the uppermost part of the rock. The second of the four courtyards, surrounded by storerooms, state chancellery, state archive (of clay tablets), scribes' rooms and an audience hall supported by 25 piers, constituted the functional centre of the complex. The royal residence was built around the topmost of the four courtyards, where two barrel-shaped cisterns seen cut in the rock were for drinking water. In the Phrygian period a statue of the Mother/Fertility Goddess Cybele flanked by two little musicians stood in a niche in the court in front of the east gate below the second courtyard.

House on the Slope

Nothing much is known about the function of this building standing southeast of the Great Temple. Being on the route between the temple and the royal citadel it is assumed to be part of a considerably larger complex connected in some way with the temple. Stone socles with cult images carved in relief (now in the İstanbul Museum) were found in its vicinity. The two-storeyed building consisted of a hall measuring 13×17m/43×56ft, an open, columned portal, a wide vestibule, several smaller rooms and a corridor. Underneath were kitchens, storerooms, etc. The upper storey faced uphill towards a pier-bordered square.

*King's Gate

This, the best preserved of all the gates, is situated on the south-east side of the upper city. A ramp leads up through a small, partially enclosed, forecourt to a gate chamber, 6m/20ft wide, with once massive watchtowers. The entrance is guarded by a larger than life-size stone relief of a Hittite god, the original of which is in the Hittite Museum in Ankara. Armed with a battleaxe he is dressed as a warrior in a form of tunic with a broad belt and dagger and a pointed cap adorned with bull's horns.

Lion Basin

Near the main entrance to the temple precinct lie the remains of a 5.8m/19ft-long basin, originally fashioned from a single massive block of limestone but now in four pieces. Carved with crouching lions its function is uncertain.

*Lion Gate

This gate, on the south-west side of the upper city, is the mirror-image of the King's Gate (the east wall of the gate chamber was reconstructed in 1965). Carved in relief on the doorjambs either side are the head and forequarters of a lion, guarding the gate with threateningly open jaws. Hollows in the stonework in front of the lions' paws suggest some form of cult significance. To the left, next to the fallen head of the westerly of the two lions, Hittite hieroglyphs are still faintly discernible in the bright noonday sun.

Museum

On the righthand side of the road leading north out of Boğazköy there is a small museum illustrating the various phases of Hattuşaş's development. The array of items salvaged from the ruins make an interesting complement to the much more comprehensive collection in the Hittite Museum in Ankara.

231

Boğazkale (Hattuşaş)

Hattuşaş: royal castle

Lion Gate

Nişantepe

This rocky platform north-east of Sarıkale was at one time crowned by some fairly substantial structure with a courtyard, of which nothing now remains. On an artificially smooth rock wall below the former entrance gate (excavations in progress) there is a badly weathered but still partly decipherable hieroglyphic inscription. It declares the author to be Suppiluliuma II and the inscription to be a list of his predecessors.

Upper town (Temple town)

As well as encircling the heights of Yenicekale, Sarıkale, Nişantepe and the citadel hill, the walls surrounding the upper town enclose a gently stepped depression on the terrace-like slopes of which the foundations of a considerable number of buildings have been exposed. Initially five of these were identified as temples but, as a result of excavations carried out since 1978, that number has now grown to 25, revealing the area of be a veritable temple town. All exemplify a common overall pattern – an inner court giving access to a suite of cult rooms with a vestibule and main chamber. The vast majority (nineteen in all) seem to be built to a standard design, being similar in all important respects and of a uniformly small size (21.5×26.5m/70×87ft). They also appear to date from a specific architectural period between 1250 and 1220 B.C. The other six are different, being larger and less regular in plan, with more spacious forecourts.

Sarıkale

Sarikale (Yellow Fort), occupying a rocky outcrop between Yenicekale and the acropolis, provides a graphic illustration of the boldness of Hittite rock architecture. It incorporated a temple, a walled cistern and a fortress complex with forecourt, inner courtyard and building wing. The possibility that this rock summit site had some special cult significance attaching to it cannot be ruled out.

**City defences

Fragments of the 3.5km/2 mile-long city defences are still visible in many places. For the most part these took the form of an 8m/26ft-wide cyclopean wall, with massive bastions and posterns protected by towers and gate

Foundations of the cellars

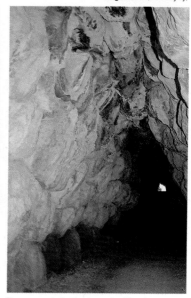

Escape route in the town fortifications

chambers. Clever use was made of the geography of the site by incorporating various rocky outcrops; elsewhere the wall was artificially raised upon great earthen ramparts. At Yerkapı, the most elevated point of the upper city, the rampart is 80m/262ft wide at the base and about 20m/65ft high. All these defence works were completed in two phases in the late 14th and late 13th centuries. During the second phase the wall, previously about 5m/16ft wide, was strengthened by the addition of a another wall set about 4m/13ft in front of the towers of the original one. This new wall was flanked by bastions 6m/19ft wide and 4m/13ft deep, leaving a gap between it and the towers of the main wall. All the walls were built of clay bricks on a foundation of carefully dressed stone. Apart from the Sphinx Gate the design of the gates followed the same pattern – a small, partially enclosed, forecourt in front of the gate, and a gate chamber with parabolic arched entrances front and rear, protected by towers either side.

About 100m/109yd south of the royal citadel (Büyükkale) are what appear to be remnants of a second citadel, strategically placed on a double rock outcrop which drops away steeply on one side. Among the remains are those of a bastion-like defensive wall and houses.

South citadel

The Great Temple and its extensive precinct occupy a 26ha/64 acre site in the Old (lower) City. The precinct is divided into northern and southern sections by a paved street 8m/26ft wide, the northern section containing the temple buildings and associated storerooms, the southern section more storerooms and other chambers. Of the four entrances to the northern section, the one on the south-east side with massive stone thresholds was probably the processional gateway used by the king and his entourage. It leads into a road, 2 to 9m/6½ to 30ft wide, paved with stone slabs and furnished with drains, at the side of which stand monolithic basins, probably holding water for ritual purification (see Lion Basin). Three phases of building have been identified. The temple itself, dedicated to the Weather

*Great Temple (Temple I)

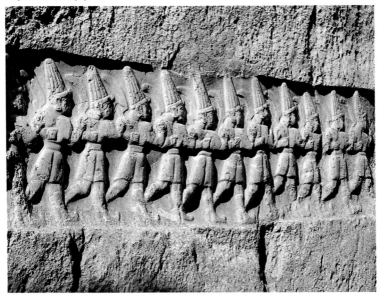

The twelve gods in the Small Chamber of Yazılıkaya

God of Hatti and the Sun Goddess of Arinna, was built under Hattusili III (1275–1250 B.C.) and was the city's holiest shrine. Next came the temple storerooms, where remains of storage jars (pithoi), some with inscriptions, can be seen set in the floor. Last to be completed was the broad paved street. The southern section of the precinct appears unfinished in a number of places.

The temple proper, with a floor area measuring 42×65m/138×213ft, is split into two parts, the first of which comprises an entrance block (vestibule with side loggias, lockable gate chamber and guardrooms), inner court (with stone paving and piered portico to the inner sanctum) and regular-shaped surrounding rooms. Adjoining to the north are the chambers of the inner sanctum, a number of inter-connecting rooms in dark gabbro, of which the most striking is the 75sq.m/800sq.ft cult chamber with windows starting low down in the wall. The temple was probably one-storeyed and like other buildings of this design would have had a flat roof. The walls were half timbered and filled with sun-baked bricks. As well as jars, probably for oil or wine, the adjacent storerooms also housed a large archive of clay tablets.

The southern section of the precinct, situated on the other side of the paved street, was separated from the rest of the lower city by a wall, the entrance being opposite the south gate of the northern section of the precinct. About 100 small and somewhat larger chambers, probably secondary sanctums and workrooms, are grouped along a series passages terminating in dead ends.

Lower city

The majority of the buildings in the lower city surrounding the Great Temple to the south-east of the village of Boğazköy, are either the (earlier) farmstead type or the (later) so-called urban houses with a principal room. Both would have had more than a single storey. The difference between them reflects the evolution of the population, from farmers cultivating land within the city boundaries to townsfolk proper. Below the temple complex are some warehouses dating from the New Kingdom, easily recognised by their large storage jars (pithoi). The impressive "blocks" of housing on the temple precinct's main thoroughfare were probably reserved for persons of privilege, possibly associated with the temple. Since in most cases only the foundations have survived, the houses were almost certainly of clay brick and timber-frame construction resting on rough stone foundations. Dressed stone was mostly only used in gates e.g for thresholds and door-jambs, etc. The wall around the lower city was pierced in several places by unusual and intriguing posterns similar in construction to Yerkapı (eight have been identified), consisting of tunnels with end-gates guarded by towers. Although often referred to as sally-ports, historians are far from agreed on their purpose. The defenceworks, originally constructed towards the end of the Old Hittite period, were altered a number of times in the 14th/13th c. B.C.

The upper (slightly smaller) and lower West Gates gave access from the northernmost corner of the New City to the Budaközü and Yazır Çayı valleys. The gates themselves were similar to the King's and Lion Gates though lacking their decoration and forecourts. West Gates

The rock sanctuary at Yazılıkaya (Inscribed Rock), carved with reliefs which rank among the finest surviving from the Hittite period, evidently had close links with the city temples at Hattuşaş. The shrine, initially established in the 15th c. B.C., lies tucked away 2km/1¼ miles to the north-east, at an altitude of about 1120m/3675ft. It is reached via a long vanished but now reconstructed processional way. ****Yazılıkaya**

The centre-piece of the sanctuary consists of two rock chambers, one large, one small, both formed by natural clefts in the rock of the 12m/39ft-high outcrop. On levelled ground in front are the foundations of several build-ings. Substantial alterations appear to have been made in the 13th c. B.C. under Tuthaliya IV, transforming the cult site into a temple proper for which the two chambers, both open to the sky, served as an inner sanctum. It is clear from the foundations that the temple was subsequently enlarged several times.

On both sides of the large chamber, which is south-west facing and almost 30m/98ft-long, friezes carved along the base of the rock wall depict a procession of gods, predominantly male on the left, female on the right. Among the exceptions are, left side, far end, Ishtar, goddess of love, and two female companions, recognised by their pleated skirts. All are shown advancing towards the narrow north wall where, in the climax to the scene, the two processions meet. Most of the figures have Hittite hieroglyphs above their outstretched hands, making it possible to identify them as divinities of Hurrian origin. Large chamber

The relative importance of each god is reflected in his or her size, position in the order and name. Chief among them, leading the procession, is the weather god Teshup, armed and in Hittite warrior garb, borne aloft on the shoulders of two mountain gods. Facing him at the head of her own procession is Hepat his wife, standing on a panther, its four feet resting on mountain peaks. In the background can be seen the weather god's two sacred bulls. To the left the Hattuşaş weather god with a mace on his shoulder straddles two mountain tops while, on the right, Sharrumma, son of Teshup and Hetap, rides on another panther. The figures above the double eagle are those of the goddess's daughter and granddaughter. While the goddesses in the procession are generally portrayed in near identical fashion, the gods are in many cases individualised, distinguished by their respective attributes and clothing. Of these the most eye-catching are the moon god with the crescent moon above his pointed cap, the sun god with a rounded cap beneath a winged sun-disc, and two bull-headed gods standing Atlas-like on a symbol of earth, holding up the sky.

The most impressive relief of all, on the rear of a rock spur, shows the Hittite King Tuthaliya IV standing on scaly mountain peaks, with a rounded cap,

235

long mantle and crooked sceptre. In his right hand are the combined insignia of his kingly power and rank, a winged sun-disc, conical volute and flower dagger. Despite being Hittite the king would certainly have held the gods of the Hurrian pantheon sacred, not least because his mother (Puduhepa) was in all probability a Hurrian priestess herself. The "assembled" gods are presumed to be those of Hattuşaş's many temples, shown "processing" to the sanctuary at Yazılıkaya (accompanied by the human worshippers) for the spring or new year festival.

Small chamber

The most recent research suggests that the small chamber served both as a funerary temple and, after his death, as a shrine to King Tuthaliya IV. Guarded by a pair of winged demons with lions' heads, the 18m/59ft-long side chamber, varying in width between 2.5 and 4m/8 and 13ft, is entered via a slightly raised passageway leading through a cleft in the rock. The impression conveyed is of entering a narrow gallery, its smooth walls carved with four separate and thematically unconnected reliefs. Immediately inside, near a curve in the east wall, is a repeat of the Tuthaliya IV cartouche from the main chamber. This is followed by the so-called "sword god", a relief of a great sword with a human head for the pommel and four lions for the hilt (possibly based on Nergal, the Mesopotamian god of the underworld).

On the wall opposite are "the Twelve Gods", a simple frieze of stereotyped male divinities similar to those of the processional relief in the large chamber. Finally, on the east wall, is seen the most striking of the four reliefs, showing the god Sharrumma embracing King Tuthaliya. The accompanying inscriptions pay homage to the king as a heroic figure, deified as a mountain god and evidently enjoying divine protection. Some 2m/6½ft from the north wall is a limestone pedestal on which stood a statue of Tuthaliya, erected after the king's death by his son Shuppiluliuma II. Remains of the statue, found in the village of Yekbaz, indicate it was over 3m/10ft tall. The niches in the walls are thought to have been for cremation urns.

**Yerkapı

Yerkapı, the Sphinx Gate, not only pierces the wall of the upper city at its most southerly point but is also positioned on the central axis of the site. The combination of the gate itself, the intriguing postern tunnel 70m/230ft long, the vast incline of the earthen rampart 20m/65ft high, 250m/275yd wide and 80m/262ft across at the base, its outer slopes paved, the staircase ramps either side and the 3m/10ft wide paved pathways, form a marvellously symmetrical ensemble unmatched by any other example of Hittite architecture. The actual gate, set high on top of the huge rampart, was flanked on each side by two substantial towers of dressed stone, and later by an impressive outer wall with six towers. The triangular-sectioned postern tunnel (corbel vaulting) running through the rampart below the gate could be closed off by double gates at both ends. The Sphinx Gate proper had three offset passages of which only the outer was secured by gates. Four sphinxes adorned the gate, two inside and two out. Only one of these winged creatures with the body of a lion and aborescent decoration on the head has survived. Two had their entire trunk carved out of the stone, the others only the forequarters.

At one time the whole structure was thought to have some special military purpose. Now its role is believed to have been purely social and religious.

Bolu

Western Black Sea region
Province: Bolu
Altitude: 725m/2379ft
Population: 51,000

Situation and
Importance

Sandwiched between the densely forested mountains of Bolu Dağ (1829m/6002ft) to the north and the Köroğlu Dağları (2378m/7804ft) to the south, the provincial capital of Bolu is situated in the Bolu Ovası, a small basin west of the Bolu Kargı depression. It is a busy town with timber processing, wool and leather manufacturing industries, and is plentifully supplied with timber from the adjacent mountains and with pastureland for raising livestock. It is also a major source of dairy produce for nearby Ankara and İstanbul, to which cities it is linked by a good fast road, still under construction in places. Bolu in fact has been a thriving commercial centre ever since ancient times and was a halt on the trade route to central Anatolia – coach services between İstanbul and Ankara still break their journey here. The town has a lively market district and a reputation for producing the best cooks in Turkey.

Called Bythnia in antiquity, Bolu was founded by the Bythnian King Prusias I (235–183 B.C.), originally on a site about 4km/2½ miles east of the present town. It was enlarged under Hadrian. Antinoos, the town's most notable citizen in Roman times, was a favourite of Hadrian's and was deified by the emperor after drowning himself in the Nile–a sacrificial suicide intended to influence the gods in favour of Hadrian who had fallen seriously ill. Duly recovered the emperor honoured Antinoos with post-humous deification and his own personal cult. Under Theodosius II (408–450) the town became the capital of the new province of Honorias, and in the Byzantine period was the seat of a metropolitan bishop. Bayazit I (1389–1402) initiated new building during the Ottoman period. In 1668 the town was almost completely destroyed by an earthquake, as a result of which practically nothing from earlier centuries remains.

History

Sights

Among the sights of interest which have survived are the Orta Hamam (baths), thought to have been built in the 14th or 15th c.; a well preserved Ottoman caravanserai, on a hill near the market district north of the town centre; and, in the town centre itself, the Ulu Cami (also called Karadakı Camii, c. 1390) with remains of old inscriptions and antique sculptures.

Surroundings

This small lake (altitude: 1448m/4752ft), about 35km/22 miles south-west of Bolu, was formed by a landslide blocking the valley. It enjoys an idyllic setting amidst fir and pine forests and is a popular recreation area for the people of İstanbul and Ankara, being within easy reach of both. Most of the hotels are fully booked throughout the season, even on weekdays.
The forested countryside around the lake is excellent for hill walking. There are also limited facilities for angling, water- and wintersports.

*Abant Gölü

This Black Sea coastal resort lies 45km/28 miles north of the town of Düzce. Very popular with the Turks, especially those from İstanbul, it is a small modern place without any particular charm. It does however have lovely sandy beaches. About 8km/5 miles further west, in the direction of Karasu, a beach with fine sand, said to be one of best in Turkey, extends between Cape Karaburun and the Melen Çayı.
In the 13th c. Italian merchants from Genoa purchased special Black Sea trading rights from the Byzantines and a Genoese fort in the town dates back to this time. In the 19th c. the town was the seat of a derebey (autono-mous local prince). The surrounding countryside is a mass of hazelnut trees yielding up to 10,000 tonnes of nuts a year, the bulk of which find their way to German chocolate factories.

Akçakoca

Hot springs escaping from faults along the edge of the Bolu basin have transformed this little spot 5km/3 miles south of Bolu into quite a sizeable spa. Treatment for rheumatism and sciatica (hotel).

Büyük Kaplıca

Bolu

Coastal scenery near Akçakoca

Göynük

Göynük, situated about 100km/60 miles south-west of Bolu in the western Köroğlu Dağları, is well worth a visit. In addition to its many old Pontic townhouses and an Ottoman bath house, it boasts the Aksemsettin Mausoleum (1494), tomb of the first hoca (moslem teacher) to summon the faithful to prayer in the Haya Sofya (Hagia Sophia) following the Ottoman conquest of İstanbul in 1453.

*Karadere

Only about 20km/12½ miles north of Bolu a good forestry road leads into one of those remote forested Pontic mountain valleys which tourism has so far left unscathed. There are no villages in the 40km/25 mile-long Karadere valley with its bubbling mountain streams, only a forestry office. This makes a good starting point for hill walks through the jungle-like mixed forests of the valley and surrounding area. Bolu, for example, is over the ridge to the south and can be reached comfortably in a day.

*Köroğlu Dağları

The Köroğlu Dağları, formed by the uplift zone on the southern edge of the great depression marking the main North Anatolian fault, extends for some 400km/248 miles between the Sakarya Nehri in the west and Kızılırmak in the east. The central section of this andesitic range lies immediately south of Bolu, a scenically magnificent and sparsely populated plateau, above which rises Köroğlu Tepesi (2378m/7804ft), the principal summit. Here even in high summer walkers can escape the tourist throng to savour the tranquillity of an unspoilt countryside with a pleasant climate, extensive fir and pine forests, large expanses of summer pasture and picturesque yaylas (Alpine-style summer settlements used by herdsmen). One such village (and police post), Kızgölcük Yaylası, with ancient farmsteads reminiscent of log cabins, is situated about 30km/20 miles south of Bolu on the Seben road.

In the past few years two wintersports areas at altitudes between 1900 and 2350m/6235 and 7712ft have opened in the vicinity of Köroğlu Tepesi, at Kartalkaya and Sarıalan, about 60km/38 miles south-east of Bolu. There are two ski-lifts and a hotel (open only in winter).

A few kilometres north of Düzce, on the east side of the Akçakoca road as it climbs out of the Düzce Ovası, near the village of Konuralp, are the ruins of the Bythnian city of Prusias ad Hypium, founded by Prusias VI. Among the remains are those of a Roman theatre, with the houses of Üskübü rising above the rim of the cavea (auditorium). About 100m/110yds from the theatre are quite substantial remains of a Roman aqueduct, while below the theatre stands part of a gate (the Atkapı or Horse Gate), its massive architrave decorated with a horse in reverse relief. Other ancient fragments are found in the well-house by the mosque and in the little museum – among the exhibits are some very fine sarcophagi with female and animal figures in relief.

The small town of Mudurnu, about 54km/33 miles south-west of Bolu, boasts a long tradition of famous wrestlers, wrestling festivals and related competitions. Also noteworthy are one or two Greek houses in the Pontic style surviving in parts of the Old Town, together with an Old Ottoman bath house and a very beautiful Early Ottoman mosque. In the 16th and 17th centuries Mudurnu was the Turkish Sheffield, famous for its knife-makers; handcrafted metalwork is still a feature of the lively commercial district. – Sarot village about 40km/25 miles north-west of the town has a popular therapeutic spa and there is also a thermal bath in Babas, 5km/3 miles south of the town.

The 2019ha/5000 acre "Seven Lakes National Park" is located about 45km/28 miles north-east of Bolu amidst the lonely forests of the Bolu Dağları. The lakes, three of which dry out in summer, split into two groups on two different levels (780m/2560ft and 880m/2888ft respectively). All have been formed naturally by landslips damming the deep valleys with their steep, easily eroded sides. Surrounded by the native mixed woodland of this valley area, the lakes are reached via forest road from Bolu or Mengen.
Büyük Göl, at 22.5ha/55 acres the biggest of the lakes (maximum depth 15m/49ft) lies together with two smaller ones on the lower level. Of those higher up, Nazlı Göl (16.6ha/41 acres) is the largest. A 26ha/64 acre deer park has been established, principally to protect the now almost extinct maral but also as an added attraction for the mainly Turkish visitors. The lakes are stocked with trout. The dense, natural mixed forest of Cilician fir, Asian beech, oak, rhododendron, fern and wild hemp harbours a variety of flora and fauna typical of the Black Sea region.

Konuralp

*Mudurnu

**Yedigöller Milli Parkı

Bosporus · Boğaziçi   D/E 2/3

Strait between the Black Sea and the
Sea of Marmara
Length: 32km/20 miles
Breadth; 0.66–3.3km/720–3600yd
Depth: 30–120m/100–395ft

Bosporus comes from a Tracian word of unknown origin, interpreted in Greek as meaning "Ford of the Cow", from the legend of Io, who swam across the sea here as a cow. Known in Turkish as Boğaziçi (the Strait), it links the Black Sea with the Sea of Marmara (see entry) and, with the Dardanelles (see Çanakkale), separates Europe from Asia. It is a former river valley (formerly Haliç valley; see İstanbul, Golden Horn) which was drowned by the sea at the end of the Tertiary period.

Characteristics

With the shores rising to heights of up to 200m/650ft, lined with palaces, ruins, villages and gardens, this is one of the most beautiful stretches of scenery in Turkey.

**Scenery

Towards Asia from the Dolmabahça Palace   *The first bridge over the Bosporus*

By boat through the Bosporus

The best way of seeing the Bosporus in all its beauty is to take a trip from İstanbul on one of the coastal boats which ply along its length, calling in alternately at landing-stages on each side and thus affording a constantly changing panorama. The point of departure is just south-east of the Galata Bridge; the ports of call can be seen on the timetables displayed in the waiting room. Not all boats go as far as Rumeli Kavağı, the last station on the European side (1¾–2 hours). At each station there is a ferry to the other side.

European side

İstanbul (*Galata Quay);* then, higher up, the massive square bulk of the Technological University.

* Dolmabahçe, with the large Dolmabahçe Palace.

Beşiktaş; opposite the landing-stage, the *Türbe of Kheireddin Barbarossa.* Beyond this the massive ruins of the *Çırağan Sarayı,* a luxurious palace in the same style as the Dolmabahçe Palace (façade 950m/1040yd long), built by Abdul Aziz in 1874 and burned down in 1910. On the hill above it is the *Yıldız Köşkü* (Yıldız Sarayı), residence of the retiring Sultan Abdul Hamid II.

Suburb of *Ortaköy,* with beautiful gardens; handsome mosque (1870); last view of İstanbul to rear.
Suspension bridge.

Past the little promontory of *Defterdar Burun* and the *Duimi Bank* (navigational light) to the village of *Kuruçeşme* and the Albanian fishing village of *Arnavutköy* on Akıntı Point, where there is always a strong current.

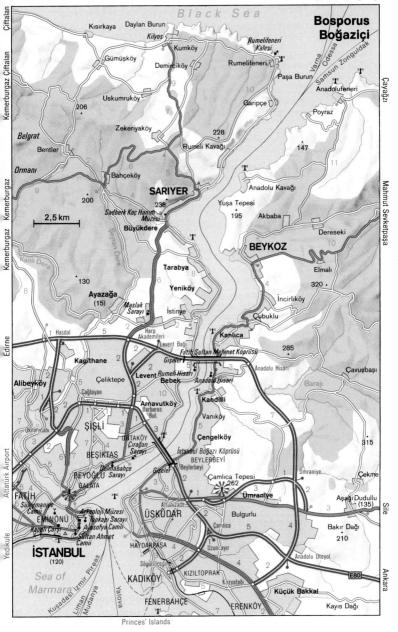

Black Sea

Çiftalan

Kemerburgaz Çiftalan

Kemerburgaz

Kemerburgaz

Belgrat

Bentler

Ormanı

206

2,5 km

130

Edirne

Atatürk Airport

Yedikule

Kısırkaya   Daylan Burun

Kilyos

Kumköy

Gümüşköy   Demirciköy

Uskumruköy

Zekeriyaköy

Bahçeköy

200

SARIYER

236

Sadberk Koç Hanım Müzesi

Büyükdere

Tarabya

Yeniköy

Ayazağa
(15)

Maslak Sarayı

İstinye

Harp Akademileri

Hasdal   Levent Bağı

Kağithane

Çeliktepe   Levent   Rumeli Hisarı

Alibeyköy   Bebek

Çağlayan

Arnavutköy

Barbaros Bul.

Ökmeydanı   ŞİŞLİ

ORTAKÖY
Çırağan Sarayı

BEŞİKTAŞ

Dolmabahçe Sarayı

BEYOĞLU

GALATA

FATİH

Süleymaniye Camii

EMİNÖNÜ

Kapalı Çarşı   Arkeoloji Müzesi
Topkapı Sarayı
Ayasofya Camii

Sultan Ahmet Camii

İSTANBUL
(120)

Sea of Marmara

KADIKÖY

FENERBAHÇE

Princes' Islands

Rumelifeneri Kalesi

Rumelifeneri

Paşa Burun

Garipçe

228

Rumeli Kavağı

Yuşa Tepesi
195

Anadolu Kavağı

Akbaba

147

Varna   Odessa

Samsun Zonguldak

Çavağzı

Anadolufeneri

Poyraz

BEYKOZ

Dereseki

Elmalı

320

İncirliköy

Çubuklu

Kanlıca

Fatih Sultan Mehmet Köprüsü

Gişeler

Anadolu Hisarı

Kandilli

Vaniköy

Çengelköy

İstanbul Boğazı Köprüsü
BEYLERBEYİ
Beylerbeyi

Çamlıca Tepesi
262

ÜSKÜDAR

Bulgurlu

Çamlıca

Altunizade

Uzunçayır

HAYDARPAŞA

Söğütlüçeşme

KIZILTOPRAK

Kozyatağı

285

Anadolu Hisarı

315

Çavuşbaşı

Barajı

Ümraniye

Ümraniye

Çekme

Aşağı Dudullu
(135)

Bakır Dağı
210

Küçük Bakkal

Kayış Dağı

ERENKÖY

Mahmut Şevketpaşa

Sile

Ankara

Anadolu Otoyol

E80

Kuşadası   İzmir   Pireas   Liman   Mudanya   Yalova

Bebek, in a beautiful bay, with villas and waterside houses (yalıs).

Above the cypresses of an old cemetery rise the picturesque wall and towers of * **Rumeli Hisarı** (European Castle), built by Mehmet II in 1452 (well worth a visit; open-air theatre in summer). It commands the narrowest part of the Bosporus (660m/720yd), where the current is at its strongest (Seytan Akıntısı (Satan's Stream); fine * view. Here Darius built a bridge of boats over the Bosporus in 514 B.C. Ahead the Second Bosporus Bridge spans the river.

On a low promontory beyond *Boyacıköyü Emirğan* are the palaces built by the Egyptian Khedive Ismail (d. 1895).

İstinye, with a shipyard.
Yeniköy (last station for most boats), with delightful villas and gardens. In St George's Church is an old icon of the Mother of God Kamariotissa.

Tarabya (*Therapia),* a sizeable township in a little bay, known in antiquity as *Pharmakeios* (Poisoner, after the poison strewn here by Medea in her pursuit of Jason.) Pleasantly cool in summer owing to the wind blowing in from the Black Sea Tarabya has numerous houses, where some of the European diplomatic missions have their summer quarters.

From the little promontory of *Cape Kireç* the Black Sea can be seen in the distance.

Büyükdere, a popular summer resort, with a large park. The bay of Büyüdere (large valley) forms the widest part of the Bosporus (3.3km/2 miles). 10km/6 miles north-west is the *Belgrade Forest* (Belgrat Ormanı), with a number of reservoirs.

Sarıyer, at the mouth of the wooded and well-watered Valley of Roses. There is an interesting museum, *Sadberk Koç Hanım Müzesi* (tiles, porcelain, glass, crystal, silver, costumes, jewellery; documents belonging to the Sadberk Koç family), in the old Azaryan Yalı. From here a bus or dolmuş (communal taxi) can be taken to **Kilyos** (10km/6 miles north), a popular little resort on the Black Sea with a good sandy beach. Then on past the *Dikili* cliffs.

Rumeli Kavaği, the last station on the European side, below a castle built by Murat IV in 1628. On a hill to the north are the ruins of the Byzantine Castle of *İmroz Kalesi,* the walls of which once reached right down to the sea and were continued by a mole, which could be linked by a chain with the mole and walls of Yoroz Kalesi on the Asiatic side.
In summer the boats usually go on (5 minutes) to the resort of **Altınkum** (Golden Sand), with a restaurant on the plateau of an old fortification (view).

The tourist boats continue to the north end of the Bosporus (4.7km/3 miles wide) and turn back when they reach the Black Sea. On both sides bare basalt cliffs rise almost vertically from the sea.

Between Rumeli Kavağı and the promontory of *Garipçe Kalesi* is the little Bay of *Büyük Liman.*

Rumeli Feneri (European Lighthouse), at the northern entrance to the Bosporus, with the village of the same name and an old fortress on the cliffs at the north end of the bay. The dark basalt cliffs to the east are the *Cyanaean Islands* or *Symplegades,* the "clashing rocks" of the Argonaut legend.

Asiatic side

Üsküdar; at the landing-stage, the Mihrimah Mosque.

Kuzguncuk, separated from Üsküdar by a low hill.

Houses on the Asian shore of the Bosporus

Beylerbey, with the *Beylerbey Sarayı,* the most elegant of the Sultans' palaces on the Bosporus, built by Abdul Aziz in 1865; worth a visit.
*First suspension bridge (İstanbul Boğazı Köprüsü) over the Bosporus to Ortaköy (1970–73, clear width 1074m/1175yd, height of piers 165m/540ft).

Past Çengelköy, Kuleli, Vaniköy and **Top Dağı** (Cannon Hill; 130m/427ft); famed for its *view over the whole of the Bosporus, to *Kandilli,* on the promontory opposite Bebek Bay.

Between Kandilli and Anadolu Hisarı is the beautiful Valley of the *Sweet Waters of Asia,* at the mouth of the Göksu (Heavenly Water).
*Second bridge over the Bosporus (Fatih Sultan Mehmet Köprüsü; 1090m/1192yd long, 40m/131ft wide).

*Anadolu Hisarı (Anatolian Castle), also called *Güzel Hisarı* (Beautiful Castle). The picturesque castle from which the place takes its name was built by Bayazit I in 1395 as an advanced post directed against Constantinople.

Kanlıca, on a small promontory. On the shore is the summer palace of Vizier Körprülü (17th c.), built on piles.

Çubuklu, in Beykoz Bay. In Byzantine times there was a monastery of the Akoimetoi (the "Unsleeping Ones") here, in which monks, in successive groups continued in prayer day and night.

At the head of the bay lies *Paşabahçe,* with its beautiful gardens. Near the shore is a Persian-style palace built by Murat III.
Beyond this is **Beykoz,** at the north end of Beykoz Bay.
An hour away to the north is **Yuşa Tepesi** (Joshua's Hill; 195m/640ft), known to the Europeans as the *Giant's Grave,* an important landmark for vessels coming from the Black Sea. The road passes behind the palace of

Mohammed Ali Paşa along the wooded and well-watered Valley of *Hünkâr İskelesi*, once a favoured estate of the Byzantine Emperors and Sultans. On the summit of the hill is a mosque, with the "Giant's Grave" and a *view extending over the whole of the Bosporus (though İstanbul itself is concealed) and part of the Black Sea.

Beyond the conspicuous palace of Mohammed Ali Paşa and the mouth of the Hünkâr İskelesi Valley are the promontory of *Selvi Burun* and the little Bay of *Umur Yeri*.

Anadolu Kavağı, the last station on the Asiatic side, an authentic Turkish village in *Macar Bay,* between two promontories with abandoned forts. On the northern promontory are the picturesque ruins of the Byzantine Castle of *Yoroz Kalesi,* known since the 14th c. as the *Genoese Castle.* In antiquity the promontory and the strait (one of the narrowest points in the Bosporus) were called *Hieron* (Sacred Place), after the Altar of the Twelve Gods and a Temple of Zeus Ourios, granter of fair winds.

Beyond Macar Bay lies the wide *Keçili Bay,* bounded on the north by the *Fil Burun* promontory.

Anadolu Feneri (Anatolian Lighthouse), on a low cape by the village of the same name, situated on the cliff-fringed coast with an old fort.

Then come *Kabakos Bay,* with basalt cliffs in which countless sea-birds nest, and the steep-sided promontory of *Yum Burun,* at the northern entrance to the Bosporus.

Burdur F 6

Western Taurus (Isaurian-Pisidian lake district)
Province: Burdur
Altitude: 852m/2796ft
Population: 56,000

Situation and Characteristics

Burdur, the provincial capital, lies in the approximately 50km/30 mile-long Lake Burdur basin at the tip of a large alluvial fan formed by the Kurna Çayı. In an attempt to halt further erosion in the surrounding countryside a programme of re-afforestation has been launched south-east of Burdur as far as the Çeltikçi pass. The town has little in the way of industry, the tractor plant being the most important.

The lake basin was already settled in Hittite times. After 1600 B.C. the Hittites overran this Arzawan territory on several occasions – one of the sons-in-law of the legendary Hittite ruler Shuppiluliuma I (1370 B.C.) was Arzawan. The name Burdur first appears in use in 1330 when the writer-traveller Ibn Battuta described a castle on a high summit overlooking the little walled town, at that time belonging to the beylik Hamid (Eğridir). Burdur became an Ottoman possession under Bayazit I in 1391. In 1971 it was shaken by a violent earthquake.

Sights

As well as its ethnological section the small regional museum has a collection of mainly neolithic (from Hacılar and Kuruçay Hüyüğü), Pisidian-Lycian and some Roman finds. Also worth seeing are the Seljuk bath house and the early Ottoman Ulu Cami (Great Mosque; 14th c.) built by Dündar Bey.

Surroundings

Ağlasun/
* Sagalassos

About 30km/19 miles east of Burdur (55km/34 miles on the main road), situated at 1650m/5415ft, above the little town of Ağlasun, are the ruins of

the Pisidian border town of Sagalassos (called Budrum by the Turks), said
to date from the 3rd millennium B.C. Arrian mentions that, in around 334
B.C., Alexander the Great had a hard struggle overcoming the pugnacious
Sagalassians. The Romans wrested control of the town from the Seleucid
Antiochos III in 189 B.C.; under Augustus it enjoyed a heyday, to which the
ruins bear ample testimony. The site, comprising a lower and an upper
town, is surrounded by several interesting necropolises (catacombs with
arkosol tombs in the rock faces to the north; a number of sarcophagi on the
slopes to the south; house tombs to the north-east). The temple precinct,
on a plateau, with the Imperial temple of Antoninus Pius, is bordered by
colonnades, as is the processional way leading to the lower agora. Other
ruins include those of the temple of Apollo Clarius (later converted to a
church), a nymphaeum, a therme, an odeion, the upper agora, a large
theatre dating from the 2nd c. and a Doric temple *in antis* next to which
were found slabs decorated with reliefs of dancing girls (now in the local
museum). Near Ağlasun there is a Seljuk caravanserai (Ağlasunhanı).

Lake Burdur (altitude: 845m/2773ft), 35km/22 miles long and 9km/6 miles   *Burdur Gölü
across at its widest, was known in antiquity as Askania Limnae. It lies in a
trough of relatively recent origin, the axis of which runs parallel to the
mountains, with a fault-line close to the lake's southern shore. It is no
surprise therefore that the area is subject to severe earthquakes (e.g. at
Dinar in 1914 and Burdur in 1968). During the last Ice Age the water level
was considerably higher (about 950m/3118ft above sea level) and the lake
much larger, extending south-west into what is now the Lake Yaraslı basin
and draining north-eastwards, via the valley-like watershed of Baradiz,
through the Isparta basin into Lake Eğridir. Clearly the climate has become
more arid since then. Masses of shells found along the old, elevated
shoreline show that mussels were a major ingredient in the diet of the
inhabitants at that time. The Hacılar tombs (see below) are also situated at
the higher level.
In contrast to many of the neighbouring lakes the 200sq.km/77sq.mile
Burdur Gölü has no (karst) drainage system, either above or below ground.
Its waters in consequence are sulphurous and salty, supporting a unique
species of fish (named "Aphanius burduricus" after the lake) and providing
an important habitat for the white-headed duck. Some 11,000 birds, 90% of
the world population of this threatened salt water species, overwinter on
the lake. White storks nest in a village destroyed by an earthquake on the
southern lakeside, and flocks of flamingos sometimes crowd the shores.

Investigation of the prehistoric mound at Hacılar, a village about 12km/   Hacılar
8 miles south-west of Burdur, has shown it to be the site of one of the oldest
human settlements so far discovered. Excavations carried out between
1957 and 1960 exposed nine levels, yielding important, very early finds
from the late neolithic (level six, 5500–5400 B.C.). Below the uppermost
level (a chieftain's and other houses) older fortifications were unearthed,
together with evidence of a Mother-Goddess cult (finds in the Ankara and
Antalya museums).

3km/2 miles west of the main Burdur road about a kilometre north of the   İncir Hanı
town of Bucak lie the ruins of a Seljuk caravanserai, İncir Hanı, endowed by
the Sultan Keyhusrev II in 1239. Only the domed main hall of the former
30×40m/98×130ft han has survived. Now used as a store it has seven
transept-like bays with barrel vaulting over pointed arches, either side of a
tall narrow centre aisle. Next to the shell-shaped arches are small carved
medallions and, above the entrance, a relief of two lions with human heads
inscribed on their backs.

The province of Burdur boasts a total of fourteen lakes, some large, some   Kestel Poljesi
small. Together with the many basin-like depressions found throughout
the region, especially to the south of Burdur, they form a characteristic
feature of the local landscape. Among the most interesting of the karst

phenomena is the so-called Kestel Polje (from Serbo-Croat "polje" meaning valley or basin) to the west of the district town of Bucak. It consists of six large basins – Çeltikçi, Kestel, Zivint, Bozova, Bademağacı and Kızılkaya – linked by gorges or flat sills, the whole system evolving from a tectonic depression formed at least 2 million years ago during the Tertiary. Surface water drains into ponors (swallow holes) situated at or near the foot of the limestone cliffs which everywhere rise steeply from the valley floors. The principal ponors are found north of the village of Boğazköy (in the southern part of the polje) and south of Kestel (in the north). For about four or five months in winter a karst lake forms near Kestel (Kestel Gölü, 843m/2766ft), reverting to marsh in the dry period. The Kestel Polje drains south through a complicated network of underground channels and cave systems, emerging on the far sidze of the Taurus mountains north of Antalya (the Kırkgöz karst springs).

Kremna

Present-day Çamlık or Girme (the ancient Kremna) is situated about 60km/37 miles south-east of Burdur, not far from Bucak. The ruins occupy a plateau commanding splendid views, dropping sheer away on the south side for several hundred metres. In Alexander the Great's time archers were garrisoned in the town; under the Romans it appears to have been largely rebuilt, laid out anew in grid-plan fashion.

Entering the ruins through the great south gate a number of fair-sized buildings are passed before the public buildings are reached – the forum of Longus (with an inscription), the theatre (to the east) with a stoa, a gymnasium (to the north-east), a second agora, 75m/246ft wide (to the south), a colonnaded street and flight of steps beside the south gate, cisterns and a number of (Byzantine) basilicas. Most of these ruins are on the slope of the hill. There are also remains of a substantial number of houses.

*Susuz Han

Also near Bucak is the village of Susuz (meaning "waterless"; 50km/31 miles south-east of Burdur) with a well preserved 13th c. Seljuk cara-

Selelucid caravanserai Susuz Han

vanserai (key in village). Endowed by Bagdatlı Sadik Ağa in 1244/46 the building has a richly ornamented doorway, clustered columns and beautifully decorated side niches in the entrances. The 26×26m/85×85ft hall has a tall dome centrally positioned over the slightly raised roof of the main aisle and the five transept-like bays with their arched windows. Eight not entirely identical towers buttress the external walls. The courtyard has disappeared.

Some 70km/43 miles south-west of Burdur, near Tefenni, there is an interesting Kaya Kabatmanları rock relief of the Pisidian-Lycian horseman-deity Kabaskos (usually identified with Hercules by archaeologists since, like Hercules, he is only ever armed with a club).

Tefenni

Bursa

E 3

Province: Bursa
Altitude: 150–250m/490–820ft
Population: 838,000

The Early Ottoman capital of Bursa, formerly called Broussa and known in antiquity as Prusa, lies about 100km/62 miles south of İstanbul as the crow flies, and some 30km/19 miles inland from the Sea of Marmara. It occupies a limestone terrace on the north-west side of Uludağ, the terrace being dissected by the Gök Dere and the Djilimbos, two mountain streams.

Situation

Blessed with a delightful climate and the loveliest of settings south of the Karadağ coastal uplands, Bursa with its picturesque Old Town and magnificent buildings (mosques and türbes) is one of the highlights of any visit to Turkey. The town also enjoys a long-standing reputation as a spa, the

**The town

Bursa: Osman caravanserai Koza Hanı in the bazaar quarter

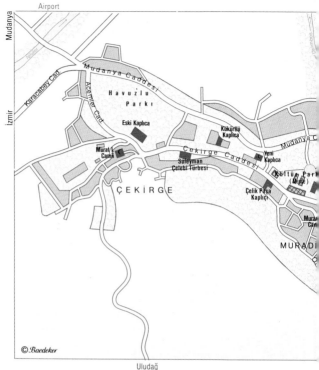

thermal springs in the north-western suburb of Çekirge, popular even in Roman times, attracting large numbers of visitors (modern baths and up-to-date treatment facilities). Agriculture, mainly fruit and vegetable-growing, flourishes in the fertile surrounding countryside; Bursa peaches are renowned throughout Turkey. With its several large textile factories centred around an efficient and productive silk-spinning mill, Bursa, provincial capital and university town (faculty of agriculture), is one of Turkey's most prosperous communities. In recent years a number of metal-working companies have also become established.

History

The town is said to have been founded by King Prusias I of Bythnia in 186 B.C., the first settlement being on the citadel hill. Under Trajan the baths were rebuilt, and a library was established by Pliny the Younger, then governor of Bythnia. In Byzantine times the town's prosperity continued to rely mainly on its thermal springs. After falling into Seljuk hands in 1097, followed by another period of Byzantine rule, Bursa became the first capital of the Ottoman Sultans, a status it retained until 1361. Its great heyday was in the 15th c., which has left many monuments of art and architecture. During the 19th c. it suffered destruction by fire and earthquake.

Sights

*Ulu Cami

The Great Mosque (Ulu Cami) in the city centre was begun in 1379, during the reign of Murat I. It is a typical pillared mosque, very much in the Seljuk

tradition. The entrance on the north side with its two flanking minarets, leads directly into the main hall, its 20 domes supported on twelve pillars linked to pointed arches. The open central dome and the fountain basin below give the hall something of the aspect of an inner courtyard. Round the fountain is the raised platform on which worshippers pray. On the square pillars and the walls are calligraphic inscriptions in the angular Kufic script and the Neshi script. There is a fine cedarwood mimber (pulpit) of about 1400.

The bazaar quarter (Atpazarı) was badly damaged by the 1855 earthquake and a fire in 1957, but has recently been restored. Notable features are the Bedesten (market hall) with its fourteen domes, one of the earliest of its kind (c. 1400), and several hans (caravanserais).

Bazaar quarter

The citadel (hisar), to the west of the city centre, is strategically situated on a small plateau which falls steeply away on the north, east and west sides and on the south side is linked with the Uludağ massif by a lower-lying area with numerous springs. The citadel proper is surrounded by a wall, originally with four gates, which was built in Roman times and several times renovated during the Byzantine and Ottoman periods. Here, too, are the türbes of Sultans Orhan and Osman, which were badly damaged by the 1855 earthquake and rebuilt in the reign of Sultan Abdul Aziz.

Citadel

On the north side of the citadel hill is a terrace (clock-tower) from which there are fine views of the city and surrounding area.

Bursa

*Muradiye Camii

This mosque, just to the west of the city centre, was built by the Sultan Murat II (after whom it is named) in 1447, by which time Bursa had ceased to be the capital of the Ottoman Empire. A forecourt with cypresses and a beautiful fountain leads via a portico, carried on piers and columns, with a doorway and four windows, to the inner hall, its ceiling clad with rare and beautiful tiles.

In the gardens of the mosque are ten polygonal domed türbes, their entrances sheltered under overhanging roofs, belonging to Murat II and members of his family.

*Yeşil Cami

Its sumptuous decoration makes the Green Mosque, a kilometre east of the city centre, one of the great master works of Ottoman religous architecture. It was built by Mehmet I between 1419 and 1423 on the site of an earlier Byzantine church. The original minarets, clad with green tiles, were destroyed in an earthquake in 1855, as was the marble vestibule. The doorway with its stalactitic niche, however, is well preserved. On either side of the entrance to the central hall are beautiful tiled niches, above which are the Sultan's loge and the women's loges, screened by grilles. In the main hall the bases of the walls are covered with the bluish-green tiles from which the mosque gets its name, and above this an inscription around the walls.

Yeşil Türbe

Facing the Green Mosque, rather higher up, is the Green Mausoleum (Yeşil Türbe) of Mehmet I, a domed octagonal building clad externally with the green tiles with which parts of the interior walls are still faced. The missing tiles have been replaced with modern reproductions.

On the octagonal base is Mehmet I's sarcophagus, with superb tile decoration (floral motifs, calligraphic inscriptions).

*Museum of Turkish and Islamic Art

The Museum of Turkish and Islamic Art, in the Green Medrese (Yeşil Medrese, 1414–24), a kilometre east of the city centre, was opened in 1974. It offers a comprehensive survey of the art of the Ottoman period: pearl and ivory articles, intarsia work, manuscripts, decorated book-covers, screens, sections of beautifully decorated wooden ceilings, weapons, tiles from İznik and Kütahya, embroidery, ornaments, fine textiles, superbly wrought articles from tekkes (dervish convents), calligraphy and tombstones.

Archaeological Museum

The Archaeological Museum, originally housed in the Green Medrese, was moved in 1972 to a new building in the Çekirge Park of Culture (2km/ 1¼ miles north-west of the centre). The new museum has four exhibition halls, storerooms, a library and a laboratory.

Atatürk Museum

On the south side of the town is a handsome late 19th c. house in which the "Father of modern Turkey" stayed during his thirteen visits to Bursa between 1923 and 1938. Converted to a museum in 1973 it contains furniture and personal effects belonging to Atatürk and a variety of documentation on his life.

Çekirge
*Thermal baths

In the western suburb of Çekirge are some of the most celebrated sulphurous and chalybeate thermal springs and baths in the East. Known in antiquity as the "royal" springs, they were undoubtedly in use before the Roman Imperial period, but both the Roman and the Byzantine buildings, which were visited by the Empress Theodora among others, have almost completely disappeared. The Old Bath (Eski Kaplıca) was built by Sultan Murat I, using the remains of an earlier building. Close by is his first mosque, Gazi Hunkiar Camii (1365), on a cruciform plan. On the terrace of the mosque is the Türbe of Murat I, who was murdered in 1389 after the Battle of Kosova in Serbia.

The New Bath (Yeni Kaplıca), a master work of architecture with beautiful marble and tile decoration, was built by the Grand Vizier Rüstem Paşa in the 16th c.

Interior of the türbe of Murat I

Exterior of the türbe of Mehmet I

Surroundings

The Uludağ massif (2543m/8344ft) 17km/11 miles south of Bursa, is the most popular and best-equipped winter sports area in Turkey and also, with its forest and Alpine meadows, an excellent holiday area for those seeking rest and relaxation. The massif consists mainly of granites and gneisses, with some metamorphic rocks higher up, and shows signs of glacial action (corries, etc.). It has preserved a very varied flora and fauna. Uludağ offers numerous viewpoints (many reached only by a strenuous walk) from which in good weather the prospect extends to İstanbul and the Bosporus or Black Sea.

**Uludağ
(Mysian or Bythnian Olympus)

A cable car goes up from Bursa to the north-west plateau (1700m/5579ft). There is also a scenic road (bus route) to Büyük Uludağ Oteli.

The port of Yalova (pop. 73,000) occupies a delightful position about 70km/43 miles north of Bursa on the southern shores of the Gulf of İzmit. Ferries run to İstanbul, Kartal and Darıca (passenger ferry terminus in Yalova, car ferry terminus 10km/6 miles further east).

Yalova

A wooded valley a few kilometres south-west of the city centre is the site of Yalova's well known thermal springs (Yalova Kaplıcalar, formerly Kury or, in French, Coury), famous since antiquity, the Pythia of the Argonaut legend and called Soteropolis in Byzantine times. Over the centuries their iron-, carbon- and sulphur-rich waters (65°C/149°F) have brought relief to Greeks and Romans, Byzantine emperors (Constantine the Great, Justinian), the Empress Theodora and a string of Seljuk and Ottoman potentates. Atatürk regularly "took the waters" here as well (Atatürk House). The baths, recently modernised, with new hotels and treatment facilities, are among the most highly regarded in the Near East, particularly for kidney, bladder, rheumatic and nervous complaints.

Yalova
*Thermal baths

Çanakkale

Yenişehir
Süleiman Paşa
Külliyesi

Yenişehir, an unpretentious little town (alt. 230m/755ft; pop. 19,000) in the Yenişehir Ovası, 55km/33 miles east of Bursa, was the Ottoman capital prior to the fall of Bursa. The town has lately become alive again to its history and a number of old Ottoman buildings have been restored, the most interesting being the early 15th c. Süleiman Paşa Külliyesi, originally consisting of a caravanserai, medrese and mosque. Now returned to its former role as a Koranic school, the beautifully restored 27 x 30m/88 x 98ft Süleiman Paşa Medresesi, or "Janissary Barracks" as it is also known, is the centre-piece of the ensemble. Square domed cells, occupied once more by students, surround its rectangular courtyard. The windows, originally arched, have been squared off. Of the south front only the little octagonal mosque adjoining it survives. Immediately to the east of the medrese are remnants of the foundations of the caravanserai, the rest having long since disappeared. Opposite the medrese stands the Sinan Paşa Camii, the mosque belonging to the Külliyesi.

Semaki Evi,
Convent

This restored 16th c. town house in Davutoğlu Sokağı (in the town centre) has been turned into a museum. As well as the old open balcony (now glazed for greater protection) it has a divan room and two living-rooms with painted, ornamented coffered ceilings, chimneys with pointed hoods, and decorated alcove cupboards.
Outside the town, on a long-settled hill in what is now the Baba Sultan Parkı, stand the remains of a convent which, until 1920, belonged to the Kadri dervishes, itinerant monks commonly revered as "saints". One of their number, "Baba Sultan", commandeered the convent mosque for his tomb. Although converted back into a mosque, none of the Moslem faithful will worship there today.

Çanakkale   B 3

Marmara region (Dardanelles)
Province: Çanakkale
Altitude: 0–5m/0–15ft
Population: 54,000

Situation and
Characteristics

Çanakkale is the principal town on the Dardanelles (Çanakkale Boğazı), situated at the narrowest point (1244m/1360yd) of this busy strait. It is the administrative centre of the province of Çanakkale, which broadly corresponds to the ancient Troas, and is the starting-point for visits to Troy (see entry) and to the scene of the fighting during the Dardanelles Campaign of 1915 (see Dardanelles).
Çanakkale (Pottery Castle), so called after the ceramics industry which formerly flourished here, is a relatively recent town with few buildings of any interest, particularly since an earthquake which caused heavy damage in 1912. On the west side of the fairly cramped central area of the town is the harbour, from which there is a ferry service across the Dardanelles to Eceabat on the European side.

Sights

Sultaniye Kale/
Military Museum

The fortress of Sultaniye Kale (Sultan's Castle) on the shores of the strait is the counterpart to the Fortress of Kilitbahir (Key of the Sea; three massive round towers, built in 1454) on the European side. Between them the forts controlled the narrowest point on the Dardanelles. The Sultaniye Kale now houses a Military Museum maintained by the Turkish Navy (guided tours, including English). In addition to guns and other military equipment it has an interesting collection of material concerning the battle for the Dardanelles in 1915. Here, too, is the minelayer "Nusrat", which mounted the successful attack leading finally to the Allied withdrawal.

The Dardanelles, the strait between Europe and Asia

On the southern outskirts of the town (the Troy road, not the bypass) is Çanakkale's new Archaeological Museum, with Hellenistic and Roman material and the rich grave-goods found in the Dardanos Tumulus, 10km/ 6 miles south-west.

Archaeological Museum

**Çanakkale-Boğazı · Dardanelles

The Dardanelles, (the Hellespont of antiquity), which take their name from the ancient Greek city of Dardanos, are the straits between the Gelibolu (Gallipoli) peninsula on the European side and the mainland of Asia Minor. They provide a link between the Aegean (and Mediterranean) and the Sea of Marmara (see entry) and also, by way of the Bosporus (see entry), with the Black Sea. These straits between Europe and Asia have been an important waterway from time immemorial. The excavations at Troy have shown that the Hellespont area (the "sea-coast of Helle", mythical daughter of Athamas, who fell into the sea here when fleeing from her stepmother) was already settled by man about 3000 B.C. In the 13th c. the territory was conquered by Achaeans from Greece. The siege of Troy described in Homer's "Iliad" probably took place during this period.

Situation and Importance

Abydos and Sestos, on opposite sides of the strait, are associated with the story of Hero and Leander, which was recounted by the Greek poet Musaeus (Mousaios; end of 6th c. A.D.?). The handsome youth Leander lived in Abydos and Hero was a priestess in the Temple of Aphrodite in Sestos. Meeting at a Festival of Aphrodite, they fell in love, and thereafter Leander swam across the Hellespont every night to be with his loved one, who lit a beacon on a tower to show him the way. One dark night the beacon was extinguished by a storm and Leander was drowned. When his body was washed ashore the following morning Hero cast herself into the sea to be united with her lover in death.

The legend of Hero and Leander

Çanakkale

As he boasts in "Don Juan", Byron later repeated Leander's feat by swimming from Abydos to Sestos early in May 1810 (it took him 70 minutes).

Physical
Geography

The Dardanelles are 61km/38 miles long, 1.2–1.7km/³⁄₄–1 mile wide and 54–103m/177–338ft deep and were formed by the drowning of a river valley as the land sank during the Pleistocene period. The Sea of Marmara came into being at the same time. Clearly visible raised beaches are evidence of temporary rises in sea level at various times in the past.

The surplus of water from the Black Sea flows through the Bosporus and the Sea of Marmara into the Dardanelles and thence into the Mediterranean. The difference in density between the water of the Black Sea and the Mediterranean resulting from the inflow of great quantities of fresh water into the Black Sea has the effect of producing a strong surface current flowing at a rate of up to 8.3km/5.2 miles an hour from the Sea of Marmara into the Aegean – which makes it difficult for small vessels to enter the Dardanelles. This applies particularly when the so-called Dardanelles wind is blowing from the east-north-east – while at the same time heavier water with a high salt content is flowing back along the bottom into the Sea of Marmara at a slower rate.

The hills of Tertiary limestone and marls which rise to heights of 250–375m/820–1230ft along the shore of the Dardanelles have a certain amount of tree cover. The mild and rainy winter climate favours the growing of olives, which constitute the main source of income for the rural communities.

Gallipoli
Campaign 1915

At the beginning of the First World War the land fortifications (some of which were somewhat antiquated) comprised three defensive cordons. From February 1915 onwards the Allied fleet tried unsuccessfully to force a passage through the straits. Landings on the Gallipoli Peninsula and the Asiatic coast beginning at the end of April 1915 were finally beaten off after bitter trench warfare, so that in December the Allies were forced to abandon the Dardanelles adventure after suffering heavy losses. Mustafa Paşa, later President of the Turkish Republic and better known as Atatürk, distinguished himself during the fighting. (Memorial; a prominent landmark visible for miles around.)

After the First World War the Turks secured, together with recognition of their independence, an acknowledgement of their sovereignty over the straits, which had been occupied for a time by the Allies. Under the Montreux Convention, signed in July 1936, Turkey was granted the right to fortify the straits and to prohibit passage to the ships of belligerent States in the event of war.

At the present time there is an extensive military zone along the Dardanelles, though this does not seriously impede the movement of travellers. Most passenger and cargo ships, however, pass through the strait at night.

Ferries

Ferry services (cars carried) cross the Dardanelles between Gelibolu and Lâpseki and Çanakkale and Eceabat. Roads follow the coast on both sides. There are plans for a bridge from Çanakkale to Kilitbahir.

Sights

Nara

About 8km/5 miles north of Çanakkale is Nara, on Nara Burun, which is believed to occupy the site of ancient Nagara. The cape is the second narrowest point (1450m/1590yd) on the Dardanelles, which here turn south. In ancient times, when this was the narrowest part of the Dardanelles, some 1300m/1420yd wide, it was known as the Heptastadion (Seven Statia) and was crossed by a ferry. It was here that Xerxes, Alexander the Great and the Turks (1356) crossed the straits into Europe.

Lâpseki/
Lampsakos

About 40km/25 miles north-east of Çanakkale on the east side of the Dardanelles, near the entrance to the Sea of Marmara, lies the ancient little port of Lâpseki, situated in the kuşova (Bird Plain) amid vineyards and olive groves. From here there is a ferry (cars carried) to Gelibolu on the Gallipoli Peninsula, on the European side.

Lâpseki occupies the site of ancient Lampsakos, where Aphrodite was said to have given birth to Priapos; and Lampsakos accordingly was the chief centre of the cult of Priapos. When the Phoenicians established a settlement here the place was known as Pityoussa, and according to Strabo was an important town with a good harbour. In 482 B.C. the philosopher Anaxagoras of Klazomenai (b. *c.* 500 B.C.) died in exile here. Lampsakos was also the birthplace of the 4th c. rhetor and historian Anaximenes, who accompanied Alexander the Great on his expedition and was able to save his native town from destruction when Alexander's army passed that way.

A few kilometres south-west of Çanakkale, to the right of the old coast road where it curves beyond the Kepez valley, rises the acropolis hill of ancient Dardanos, today crowned by a memorial to the fallen of the Second World War (Şehitlik Batarya).
A signposted turning barely a kilometre further on (south-west) leads to the Dardanos Tümülüsü, a burial mound situated close to the sea. It was opened up by Rüstem Duyuran in 1959. Beyond an entrance corridor he found a burial chamber with three stone benches (still in situ) and an array of grave-goods, including jewellery, vanitory items, vases, lamps, figures and coins. There were also remains of a musical instrument and inscribed funeral urns (now in the museum in Çanakkale) dating from the 4th c. B.C. well into the Hellenistic period.

Dardanos Tümülüsü

About 30km/19 miles south of Eceabat, near the village of Abide, the Ottoman fortress of Seddülbahir, constructed in 1657, faces Kumkale Fort on the opposite (Asian) shore. Built to guard the southern entrance to the Dardanelles, both forts are now in a restricted military zone. On the east side of the small bay where once the ancient town of Elaios stood, are Turkish and Allied war memorials and cemeteries (1915/16).

Seddülbahir

The ruins of ancient Alexandreia Troas, often just called Troas (present-day Eskiistanbul) occupy a now lonely site 80km/50 miles or so south of Çanak-

Alexandreia Troas

Alexandreia Troas, overgrown Roman ruins near the coast

255

kale near Ezine. An important city at the time of Lysimachos, the massive remains date mainly from the Roman period. (Note the therme with its lovely portal).

**Troy   See entry

Çankırı

See Kastamonu

Cappadocia   I–L 4–6

An ancient region in central Anatolia
Provinces: Aksaray, Kayseri, Kirşehir, Nevşehir, Niğde, Yozgat

Situation and
**Topography

Cappadocia, named after the Cappadocians who settled here *c.* 700 B.C., is generally regarded as the plains and the mountainous region of eastern central Anatolia around the upper and middle reaches of the River Kızılırmak (see Kirşehir). It was here that several ancient highways crossed and different cultures came into contact with each other. It was also the land of the Hittites. The sparsely inhabited landscape of Cappadocia is characterised by red sandstone and salt deposits of the Miocene (Tertiary) period. But the high plains of Bozok Yaylası, the karst regions of Sivas and the pastures of Uzun Yayla are also regarded as Cappadocia. However, the relatively small areas of fertile soil on volcanic tuff is where the population tends to concentrate. This southern part of Cappadocia, the more densely populated, is often spoken of as the heart of the region and yet it lies in the extreme south-western corner. As well as cereals, Cappadocia is best known for potatoes, fruit and wine.

Cave dwellings

Steps to make one dizzy

The origins of this unusual region can be traced to the Tertiary period some 50 million years ago, when craters and chimneys dominated the landscape. Since then, huge quantities of volcanic material have spewed out of the many volcanoes. Forces of erosion have shaped the incredible and unique Cappadocian tuff-coned landscape. For hundreds of years, men and women have dug into the soft but firm tuff to create dwellings, monasteries, churches, even whole troglodyte villages. Ürgüp, Nevşehir and the surrounding area are the main tourist centres.

The history of Cappadocia began in prehistoric times. Hatti culture held sway during the Bronze Age and in about the 2nd millenium B.C., the Hittites settled in the region. Soon the Assyrians had established their trading posts. Phrygians probably ruled Cappadocia from 1250 B.C., but the Lydians were expelled by the middle of the 6th c. B.C. In A.D. 17 the region became a Roman province, trade and military routes were built and urban centres and settlements were encouraged. As Asia Minor came under Christian influence, the first Christian communities appeared in Cappadocia and those persecuted for their religious beliefs elsewhere sought refuge in the region. Cappadocia thus became a melting pot of a variety of ethnic groups, all of which have influenced the culture and religious beliefs. Basilius the Great (329–379) bishop of Caesarea (Kayseri) inspired many religious colonies and for a thousand years an active monastic way of life endured throughout Cappadocia. Invasions first from Turkmenistan and Mongolia and then from Turkey put an end to the movement.

History

From May to November, Robinson Clubs organise balloon trips over Cappadocia.

Tip

Sights

The small town of Avanos on the River Kızılırmak about 13km/8 miles north-west of Ürgüp is said to be of Seljuk origin. It is well known for its pottery, polished onyx and carpet-making. About 7km/4 miles to the east on the southern bank of the Kızılırmak are the remains of Sarıhan, a Seljuk caravanserai made of yellow tuff dating from the 13th c. it has a magnificent gate.

Avanos

To the west of Derinkuyu near a Byzantine church are numerous cave dwellings, some of which are linked by underground passages with Derinkuyu monastery. Rooms with twelve columns and twelve sculptures were dedicated to the apostles.

Ayan

60m/65ft walls of tuff in the village of Çavuşin, about 13km/8 miles north of Ürgüp, conceal numerous cave dwellings. The 5th c. St John's Church with a famous pillared façade (now collapsed) is worth seeking out. The Güvercin Kilisesi Church at the northern end of the village displays some preserved greenish and red-brown frescos. Many other sacred caves are now used as pigeon lofts. A short distance from the village in the nearby valleys, a number of simple flat-roofed chapels can be seen. The best-known is the Haçili Kilise (Church of the Cross) in the Kızılçukur Deresi valley. The 10th c. paintings (Jesus and the four Evangelists) and a large cross in relief are particularly interesting. The Üzümlü Kilise (Church of the Grapes) in the same valley was dedicated to the pillar-saint Niketas. On the ceiling at Üç Haçılı Kilise in Güllüdere valley, three crosses in relief with floral decorations can be seen.

Çavuşin

One of Cappadocia's most interesting troglodyte villages is to be found below the town of Derinkuyu. It probably dates from Hittite times, but evidence from the excavations (e.g. double millstones made of granite) have revealed that the Hittites only used the top storey. So far eight levels have been discovered with dwellings, store-rooms, chapels and parts of

**Derinkuyu

Openings with many corners . . .   *. . . and stepped passages in Derinkuyu*

monasteries, which can be blocked off with stones resembling millstones. The man-made caves are grouped around an 85m/280ft shaft with a cleverly-devised ventilation system comprising 52 vents. The shafts also served as wells.

The underground refuge developed from Roman times to a city 55m/180ft deep and with a total surface area of 4sq.km/1.5sq.miles. Derinkuyu was attacked by Arabs on three occasions. Only the top three levels were used as living accommodation. The lower levels were for emergencies and consisted of chapels and storage areas. Every house had its own kitchen, bedroom, dining room, wine cellar, toilet, weapons store and water cistern (up to 30,000 litres/6,600 gallons), store-rooms and stables. Long underground passages linked the city with other troglodyte communities in the region. The 9km/5½ mile passage to Kaymaklı allows three people to walk together upright. Unfortunately, the air vents have collapsed and this section is no longer accessible.

An underground monastery at Derinkuyu, which was also used as a psychiatric hospital at the same time, was restored by Ayasozori and Ayanarye-ros. The network of rooms contains workshops, holy water containers, medicine chests and a room where the mentally ill were treated (probably with strait-jackets).

At the centre of the complex lies a chapel, constructed of basalt and which is used today as a mosque. It dates from the 16th or 17th c. and contains paintings of Jesus, Mary, angels and saints. Another chapel with a handsome bell-tower houses some notable wooden carvings with some interesting pillars by the entrance.

**Göreme
(National Park)

The famous rock churches of Göreme (or Koroma under Byzantium) lie adjacent to the village of Göreme (formerly Avcılar). Countless rock churches and monasteries can be found within a small area. The frescos have been badly defaced, as until 1964 the chapels were not supervised

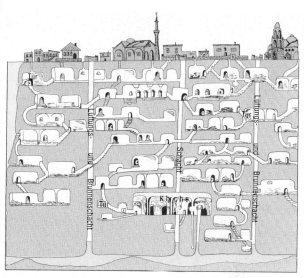

and the value of the frescos was not appreciated. A well-signed round tour
now covers the various sights.

Outside the complex stands the Tokalı Kilise (Church of the Buckle), the
largest church in Göreme, which was restored during the 1960s. Of particular interest are the main nave with barrel arcading 9th c. frescos in a simple,
"provincial" style, the more recent transept with three apses and 11th c.
frescos in "metropolitan" style. The frescos of the twelve apostles, the

Tokalı Kilise

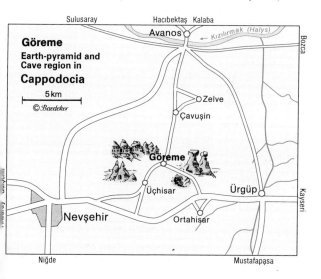

Göreme National park: nunnery . . .   *. . . and Barbara Kilise (church)*

saints and scenes from the life of Jesus (963–969 and 11th c. respectively) are also noteworthy. There is a crypt underneath the nave.

Elmalı Kilise

The Elmalı Kilise (Church with the Apple) is the smallest of the cruciform-domed churches in Göreme (temporarily closed for restoration). It contains some early 11th c. frescos showing the prophets, saints and scenes from the life of Jesus, including Jesus and the world.

Barbara Kilise

In the Barbara Kilise (Barbara Church), it is possible to discern St Barbara alongside Jesus and various other ecclesiastical dignitaries on the preserved ochre frescos. These frescos date from the time after the disputes over Iconoclasm.

In the Yılanlı Kilise (Serpent Church), the Byzantine Emperor Constantine and his wife Helena can be identified and also St George and St Theodore's struggle with the dragon. The legendary figure of Onophirios, a beautiful woman is also interesting. She pleaded with God to protect her from men's advances and her wish was fulfilled. She grew a beard and her beautiful face was disfigured. The fresco shows a half man/half woman figure.

Karanlık Kilise

Karanlık Kilise (Dark Church) forms a part of the monastery and includes a refectory with a double apse and a table and chairs carved from the stone. The 11th c. cruciform dome is borne by four pillars and ranks among the finest in the Göreme valley. The walls and dome are adorned with scenes from the Bible (temporarily closed for restoration).

Carıklı Kilise

The name Carıklı Kilise (Sandal Church) derives from the footprint at the bottom of the Ascension fresco, said to be an exact replica of the same feature in the Church of the Ascension in Jerusalem. The four Evangelists, the nativity and the crucifixion can be identified on the fresco.

Göreme village

Half of the village of Göreme itself consists of cave dwellings. It is here that three deep valleys lined with tuff chimneys meet. In the El Nazar ravine

Fresco in the "Snake Church"   *Rock wall of tufa in Çavuşin*

stand the El Nazar Kilisesi, a chapel now badly damaged after an earth-quake and the Saklı Kilise (Hidden Church) with a nave and three apses. The latter houses some 12th c. frescos depicting Mary and the life of Jesus. In the 12th c. monks from Göreme withdrew here when they were unable to find suitable premises.

In the Kılıclar valley stands Kılıclar Kilisesi (Church of the Sword), where some splendid frescos from the 10th/11th c. may be seen.

Kılıclar Kilisesi

The regional centre of Gülşehir 20km/13 miles north of Nevşehir was known in Hittite times as Zoropassos. The town's modern name derives from its popular rose water (Gülşehir = Rose Town). Well worth a visit is the 17th c. Ottoman complex known as Kurşunlu Külliyesi. It consists of a mosque, medrese (theological college), hamam (Turkish bath), library and a number of fountains.

Gülşehir

To the south of the town lies Acık Sarayı (Open Palace), a multi-storey underground monastery. Instead of frescos, relief designs are the usual form of decoration. Directly adjacent stand two churches, one on top of the other. The upper church Karşı Kilise has some smoke-darkened 13th c. frescos, while below is a small cruciform church.

The small town of Hacibektaş, some 50km/31 miles from Nevşehir was the birthplace of Haci Bektaş Vali, founder of the Bektashi Order of Dervishes. The famous or perhaps notorious janissaries also belonged to this order which combined Shiite, Sunni and Christian values. After 1923 the order was viewed with suspicion, but the founder's mausoleum and monastery are still visited by pilgrims.

Hacibektaş

30km/19 miles east of Ürgüp in the regional centre of İncesu stands the Kara Paşa Külliyesi, a remarkable complex founded by the general Kara Mustafa. Intended as a caravanserai, it comprised a large barracks, a bath, a

İncesu

mosque and a road with a row of shops which is still in use. A number of small stone buildings surround the town and are known as hancık or small caravanserais.

**Kaymaklı

Kaymaklı is situated about 20km/13 miles south of Nevşehir and, like Derinkuyu, stands above an interesting underground city. Discovered in 1964, four levels are open to the public. Here as in most of the other cave dwellings, rooms and passages are kept separate and are equipped with a ventilation system, living quarters, store-rooms and water cisterns. Communication between the living quarters was via a system of small holes in the walls. Above the underground city, some simple graves were recently uncovered on a hill.

Mazıköy

In the Bagirsakderesi valley around the village of Mazıköy many cave churches and chapels have been found together with their tombstones built into the high rock walls. Their façades are adorned with pillars and gables. One rock chapel to the south of the village is well preserved. A variety of different cross motifs which are repeated on the walls can be seen on one of the load-bearing central pillars. Another underground settlement has been discovered near Mazı but it has yet to be excavated.

Mustafapaşa

Until 1923 the village of Mustafapaşa was inhabited only by Greeks and so most of the frescos are Greek. All the old houses have balconies and window ledges carved from local tuff. Most of the homes contain frescos which date from before this period. They depict modern themes and some are well worth inspecting. Beyond the village in Beydere is the Basileios Church, which is noted for its relief carvings. According to an inscription, the decorations date from between 726 and 780, but the paintings are 19th c. The three apse crosses represent Abraham, Isaac and Jacob.

Nar Gölü

About 50km/32 miles south-west of Nevşehir in a valley near the village of Sofular lies Nar Gölü (Pomegranate Lake), a small lake with a water level

Cave church in the underground town of Kaymaklı

some 70m/230ft below the surrounding hills. To the east and south of the lake, water from hot springs is used in the treatment of rheumatism. Numerous rock chapels can be found around the lake, many of which were until recently inaccessible. Their frescos have become darkened by the shepherds' fires.

The history of the modern provincial centre of Nevşehir (pop. 53,000) stretches back into the prehistoric era. The town grew in stature when İbrahim Paşa was the Grand Vizier between 1718 and 1730. He moved his garrison here from Niğde and Yeşilhisar, renamed the town Nevşehir (New Town) and set about building caravanserais, baths, medrese and the Kurşunlu Külliye (1726) with a mosque, hospital, medrese and library. In 1967, the latter became a museum with archaeological and ethnographical exhibits, including manuscripts. The village became a town and the Grand Vizier protected it with a castle. In 1954 Nevşehir became the provincial capital.

Nevşehir

The tiny village of Ortahisar some 10km/6 miles west of Ürgüp lies at the foot of weird pock-marked tuff walls from which countless cave dwellings have been carved. An underground passage supposedly runs to the northeast to the İsa Kalesi fortified rock. Some of the churches in the village were used as barns but the walls are richly decorated with scenes from the Old and New Testament. The frescos at the Üzümlü Kilise (Church of Grapes) demonstrate that local farmers have been producing wine for hundreds of years. Many of the caves are used as intermediate stores for lemons. About 1km/½ mile from the town is the unspoilt Halas Deresi valley with its rock churches and a monastery for Armenian Christians.

Ortahisar

The chapel in Ortaköy some 35km/22 miles south of Ürgüp near Güzelöz dates from the 6th c. and contains paintings from 1293. The chapel is regarded as St George's local church.

Ortaköy

47km/30 miles south of Ürgüp and 20km/13 miles west of Yeşilhisar nestles the blind valley of Soğanlı, cut deep into the tuff. The area is famous for its brightly coloured, hand-made rag dolls which can be seen on sale all over Cappadocia. When in the 8th c. the Arab general Battal Gazi finally conquered this remote valley, he gave it the name Sonakaldi, or "left until last". Large numbers of old dovecotes are to be found in the steep rock walls, many of which belonged to the monasteries. 150 churches have been discovered here, but most of them are now reduced to ruins. The churches, some with fine frescos, are a particular feature of this valley and have been carved out of the tuff chimneys.

Soğanlı Deresi

Üçhisar is situated 13km/8 miles west of Ürgüp and is dominated by a fortified rock, from which many cave dwellings have been carved. The top of the rock affords a fine view of the valley, while to the east of the village İceri Dere offers an impressive view down to Göreme. Many of the old houses in the village still display beautifully sculptured façades but they are increasingly falling into disrepair as the local people move into purpose-built housing.

Üçhisar

Viewed from the east, the regional centre of Ürgüp resembles any one of the old troglodyte communities. Surmounting the tall cave-riddled fortified rock was the 13th c. Seljuk fortress Kadi Kalesi, but it was destroyed in 1954 by a rock fall. As Osiana, a bishop's see, the town enjoyed prosperity in the 10th and 11th c. but no ancient church remains can be seen in the town. There are, however, many attractive old houses on the slopes at the edge of the town, but their residents have moved to the less attractive modern accommodation. Relics from the Seljuk times include the Karamanoğlu Camii (early 13th c.), the Altı Kapı Türbesi, a tomb built by a Seljuk prince for his wife and children and the Nukrettin Mausoleum (1286) for Kiliç Arslan's daughter, which is still a place of pilgrimage. On the same hill stands the Tashın Ağa Kütüphanesi, a library endowed in the 19th c. by one of Ürgüp's rich citizens. The books were transported into the outlying settlements on the back of a donkey. In the garden of the Karamanoğlu Camii stands the

Ürgüp

Çatalhüyük

Tufa pyramids near Zelve

tomb of Sheikh ul-Islam Hayri Efendi, father of a former Turkish Prime Minister S. H. Urgüplü. Ürgüp, whose name derives from "ur kup" meaning "many rocks" has become a typical holiday centre with shops and tourist hotels. The oldest hotel in Cappadocia can be found in Ürgüp – it is 25 years old. Wine production and fruit growing play an important part in the local economy. Situated to the west of the town are the famous rock pyramids of Ürgüp (fine view).

*Zelve

About 15km/9½ miles north-west of Ürgüp between Göreme and Avanos a road leads westwards to the small village of Zelve set in a remote hollow. Two tiny valleys with steep rock sides shelter countless cave dwellings and monasteries. As the valley was and still is threatened by rock falls, the cave-dwellers were moved to a new settlement. The rock mosque with a simple prayer recess and also an interesting minaret made of tuff (formerly the bell-tower) marks the site of the old settlement. One well-known sight is the ruined Üzümlü Kilise, a basilica which dates from the pre-iconoclastic period and contains some interesting grape decorations. Just outside the village is the Valley of the Monks with the classically beautiful tuff pyramids. Simeon's Chimney with its three "protected" tips is probably the best known. A new road leads from here through the Kızıl Wadi (Rock Pyramid) valley to Ürgüp.

Çatalhüyük   H 6

Central Anatolia. Province: Konya
Altitude: 1010m/3315ft. Village: Çatalhüyük near Çumra

Some 18m/59ft high and 12ha/30 acres in area, the Çatalhüyük settlement mound is part of a much larger complex covering a total of 21ha/52 acres, of which only about 5% has so far been excavated. The hüyük is situated on the left bank of the Çarsamba Çayı, in the Konya Ovası, about 10km/6 miles north-east of the little town of Çumra (formerly Çumra İstasyon). The site created headlines in the 1960s following excavations carried out by James Mellaart. He had made a preliminary survey of the mound in 1958, but was later refused permission to excavate further after finds began to surface abroad. The date of the very earliest settlement has been put at 6250 B.C.; traces of fire suggest that the last of the ten settlements uncovered was abandoned around 5400 B.C.

The Çatalhüyük mound is just one of many places on the vast Konya Plain known to have been occupied between the 7th and 3rd millennia B.C. More recent sedimentation has since rendered many hüyüks unrecognisable, and virtually the whole plain has been brought under the plough. The earliest levels at Çatalhüyük now lie buried more than 2m/6½ft below the surface of the surrounding plain.

The dwellings excavated at Çatalhüyük were found to be remarkably similar in construction to traditional buildings still seen today. Only the lay-out of the settlement proved strikingly different. The houses, each roughly 25sq.m/30sq.yd in area, were flat-roofed, with a single living space and a storeroom. In addition to a bench, hearth and oven, the rooms were furnished with platforms, presumably used for working and sleeping on but also for burials. The dead were left in the open outside the settlement until scavenging animals had stripped the skeleton clean. Dressed in their clothes they were then interred beside or under the sleeping platforms, continuing their participation, so to speak, in family life. The settlement had no streets as such, the rectangular houses being close grouped in large blocks with, here and there, a courtyard serving as a latrine and rubbish dump.

The houses were entered by wooden ladder, American pueblo-style via the smoke-hole. The floor was compacted mud, the walls mud-brick with mud, plaster and lime rendering. Reeds were used to strengthen the roof. Sometimes there was a timber frame. Amazingly in view of the vulnerability of mud to weathering, some brickwork is still clearly recognisable. Fire must have fortuitously "baked" the bricks, hardening them and making them more weather resistant.

Çatalhüyük was almost certainly one of the largest New Stone Age settlements, with a population of about 5000 made up of three different ethnic types: Eurafrican (59%), Alpine (24%) and Mediterranean (17%). The men had an average height of 170cm/5ft 9in. and a life expectancy of 34 years, the women 155cm/5ft 1½in. and about 30 years. The economy, though mainly agrarian – wheat, fruit and vegetable cultivation using simple methods of irrigation, stock rearing and some fishing – was also craft based. A wide range of artefacts were produced including obsidian weapons and tools, cult objects, and items for everyday use made from bone, leather, wood and basketwork. This division of labour between farmers and artisans gave the settlement a truly urban character and makes Çatalhüyük one of the world's oldest towns. Its trade links reached as far afield as Cyprus, Syria and Mesopotamia. The settlement had no walls protecting it, which may account for its eventual destruction some 7500 years ago.

Çatalhüyük was evidently also the centre of a religious cult, relics of which can be seen in the Hittite Museum in Ankara though not any longer in situ. Bulls' heads and horns decorated nearly every house, suggesting a vigorous cult of the bull (hence also the name Çatalhüyük, meaning "antler mound"). Clay figurines of obese goddesses would also indicate an active

265

fertility cult, further evidence of which is found in some of the polychrome wall paintings. Other paintings include hunting scenes with men depicted as bulls, rams or bears. A particularly striking picture shows Çatalhüyük itself (in plan) below the outline of an erupting volcano – probably one of the big Central Anatolian volcanos (Karadağ, Hasan Dağ), still active at the time and permanently under the gaze of this Neolithic people.

Cilician Gates

See Tarsus

Çine

See Milas

Çorum   K 3

North-eastern central Anatolia
Province: Çorum
Altitude: 801m/2628ft
Population: 116,000

Situation and Importance

Encircled by wooded hills up to 1500m/4923ft high, this modern provincial capital is situated about 230km/149 miles north-east of Ankara on the edge of the extensive Çorum Çayı basin. As well as being the market town for 100 or more villages scattered across the surrounding countryside (where, in addition to fruit and vegetables, several kinds of cereal are grown), Çorum is also heavily industrialised, the most important of its many industries being copper processing.

History

Excavation has revealed habitation here since at least the 4th millennium. B.C., including throughout the Hittite period (up to 1200 B.C.) and in Phrygian times. The town was Persian (from 546 B.C.) before falling into the hands of the diadochi in the 4th c. After a short spell of Galatian (276 B.C.) and later Roman and Byzantine rule, it was occupied in 1075 by the Danishmendid Ahmet Gazi (who named it Çorum). Control then passed to the Seljuk Kiliç Arslan, the Mongols and the Eretna dynasty, before the town finally came into Ottoman possession in 1393.

Sights

*Çorum Kalesi

The citadel, located in the south-east of the town, is still partly occupied. Numerous pieces of ancient masonry – inscribed gravestones, shafts of columns, architraves, etc. – can be seen incorporated into the lower sections of the limestone wall, e.g. in the protruding gateway with its brick vaulting and ironwork through which "İç Kale" is entered. On the left directly beyond the gate is the citadel mosque (Kale Camii).

Musuem

In addition to its ethnological collection the little museum mainly houses finds from the Hittite, Phrygian and Islamic periods (including a model of Hattuşaş).

Saat Kulesi

The inscription (1894) on this yellow clock- and water-tower in the town centre commemorates its endowment by Yedi Sekiz Hasan Paşa, a native of Çorum working in the Beşiktaş district of İstanbul. Looking like a minaret the tower has a circular lower section on an octagonal base, the upper part above the gallery being four-sided.

Although located some distance away (to the north-west of Kükümet Mey- *Ulu Cami
danı, on the far side of the old business quarter), the 13th c. Ulu Cami, also
known as the Muradi Rabi Camii, is interesting and worth visiting. It was
extensively restored in the 19th c.

Surroundings

Like Yazılıkaya and Hattuşaş, this **Alaca Hüyük
exceptionally interesting archaeological site, halfway between
Boğazkale and Çorum, forms part
of the Tasarı National Park. Alaca
Hüyük's importance lies chiefly in
its finds from the period prior to
the Hittite migrations. Rediscovered by Hamilton in 1836, the
330m/1083ft wide hüyük has since
been researched and excavated
several times; it comprises fourteen different levels representing
four cultures.

Alaca Hüyük was evidently first
occupied in the middle of the 4th
millennium B.C. (early Bronze Age)
and remained so until the collapse
of the Hittite Empire (1200 B.C.).
For a brief period in the 9th and 8th
centuries B.C. it was the site of a
Phrygian settlement.

Visitors are strongly advised to   Museum
make the Alaca Museum their first
stop before touring the site itself,   *Alaça Hüyük: the Sphinx Gate*
commencing with the museum
garden which contains reliefs and other relics from various periods. In the
exhibition hall are (right) finds from the Copper Age (3550–3000 B.C.),
mostly pottery (made without the use of a wheel) and a fascinating
crouched burial complete with grave gifts. Next come Bronze Age items
(3000–2000 B.C.) including beautiful pottery (standards, figurines of deer,
sun-discs, etc.) vividly testifying to the quality of Anatolian Bronze Age
craftsmanship. Information is also provided on the famous "royal tombs"
and the so-called pottery burials – clay pots containing corpses in a
crouched position. Moving on to the Hittites (2000–1200 B.C.), pottery again
takes pride of place, as it does in the Phrygian section (1200–600 B.C.), the
decoration here being red and brown patterns on a white base. There is
also a separate display of more recent craftwork (mainly weaving).

First impressions of the archaeological site can be confusing, but help is   Archaeological
provided in the form of a clearly marked circular walk. The single most   site
spectacular feature is undoubtedly the "Sphinx Gate", in what was the
south inner city wall (nothing remains of the other gates except the postern
underneath the west wall). The two sphinxes flanking the gate show clear
Egyptian influence. On one side is a relief of a goddess seemingly floating
above a double-headed eagle clutching two hares (the significance of
which is unknown). The originals of the reliefs on the adjacent wall (cult and
hunting scenes) are now in the Hittite Museum in Ankara. Two small
forecourts lead to a wide colonnaded street furnished with drains, to the
right of which extends a palace-like building believed by some scholars to
be modelled on the temple at Hattuşaş.

Decorated reliefs on the Sphynx Gate

Most interesting of all, however, are the thirteen royal tombs dating from the 3rd millennium B.C. when the Hatti, a pre-Hittite non-Indo-European people had a major settlement here. Some of the tombs – large rectangular stone-lined pits, originally roofed over with thick planks and then covered – are laid out exactly as they were when first opened. The single and double graves contained a whole array of priceless grave goods (weapons, jewellery and standards from funeral carts) most of which, together with other finds, are in the Hittite Museum in Ankara.

Eski Yapar

During excavation of the Early Bronze Age settlement mound at Eski Yapar (6km/4 miles west of Alaca Hüyük village) in 1967, R. Temicer unearthed an important hoard of jewellery. It too is now in the Hittite Museum in Ankara.

Cemilbey
(Pazarlı)

About 20km/12½ miles from Çorum, near the small town of Cemilbey, lies the Pazarlı archaeological site where, in 1937, H. Kosay uncovered a nobleman's house and fort from the Phrygian period (c. 500 B.C.). Wall paintings, mosaics and other finds from this site, known to have been occupied as early as 3500 B.C., are in the Hittite Museum in Ankara. They include a terracotta plaque showing a row of bulbous-nosed foot-soldiers with drawn swords and circular shields. Not far from the township are the ruins of an old, much altered fortress. Ancient tombs and cisterns are found in the surrounding countryside.

Hacıhamza

The little town of Hacıhamza, about 90km/56 miles north-west of Çorum, boasts a 17th c. caravanserai (c. 1666) endowed by Köprülü Mehmet Paşa. From Hacıhamza upstream almost as far as Osmancık the Kızılırmak valley is awash with rice paddies. Derelict norias – large waterwheels, the traditional method of irrigation along many Anatolian rivers – line the river bank.

Mustafa Çelebi

Deposits from the lime-rich waters of the Karapınar karst spring, which surfaces here in this village near Cemilbey, have built up over millennia into limestone terraces similar to those at Pamukkale.

Dardanelles

See Çanakkale

Denizli

See Pamukkale

Didyma

See Milet

Divriği   O 4

North-west eastern Anatolia
Province: Sivas
Altitude: 1250m/4100ft
Population: 16,000

This district town in the valley of the Çaltı Çayı, a western tributary of the upper Euphrates (Firat Nehri), is the centre of a major iron ore extracting region. The high iron content (50–65%) of the deposits found locally in the mountains makes them the richest in the Near East. The ore is taken to steelworks in Karabük, Ereğli, Yarımca, Samsum and Elazığ for smelting. Though situated in the midst of an infertile mountain landscape Divriği enjoys a favourable climate, with mild winters and rainfall enough to produce lush vegetation. The Old Town below the citadel has some south Pontic Old Ottoman timber frame and mud houses, with simple but very attractive wood carvings and reliefs. |Situation and Importance

In the 9th c. Divriği (or Tephrike as it then was) became a stronghold of the Paulicians, a Christian sect who, fleeing from Byzantine persecution, sought refuge under the protection of the Abbasid emirs of Malatya. The sect first made its appearance in the mid 7th c., militant nonconformists venerating the teachings of St Paul while at the same time rejecting the Eucharist and the symbolism of the Cross. In 872 the Byzantines finally occupied the town and the Paulician leader was murdered. After 1071 the area around Tephrike fell into the hands of the Mengüçoğlu dynasty, who remained in control until 1252. The Mongols dismembered the fortifications and plundered the town. In 1516 Divriği was incorporated into the Ottoman Empire; for a time, ruled by local Kurdish princes, it regained its importance as a regional centre. From the 19th c. onwards the Old Town which Ahmet Süleiman Mengüçoğlu had founded below the citadel was increasingly abandoned in favour of a new settlement a little further west (now the centre of the present town). |History

Sights

This old hospital stands alongside the Great Mosque (Ulu Cami; see below), the two seeming to comprise a single building. They were endowed at the same time by the same patrons and built by the same architects. Note in particular the lavishly ornamented portal and carved interior vaulting. |Ahmet Şah Darüssifası

On the hill above the town are the ruins of a fortress, probably of Byzantine (or perhaps even Paulician) origin, and built in 872. It was restored by the |Divriği Kalesi

269

Mengüçoğlus in 1236 and 1252. Also on the hill is the Şahınşah Mosque (1180). Across the other side of the valley stands the Kestoğan Kalesi.

Mausoleum

The octagonal building (1196) south of the Great Mosque is the tomb of a local prince, the Emir Kemer Ed Din. Adjoining it is a small cemetery. The Kemankes Türbesi on the outskirts of the town dates from 1240. The Sitte Melik Türbesi not far north of the Great Mosque was built, again in 1196, for the patron of the Şahınşah Camii (roof collapsed).

*Ulu Cami

Often described as the "first Baroque work", Divriği's Great Mosque has earned itself a place in architectural history. Standing side-by-side with the Ahmet Şah Darüsifası hospital, a short distance outside the town, the plain-walled complex measuring 64×32m/210×105ft was endowed in 1228 by Ahmet Şah Mengüçoğlu and his wife Turan Malik. Its builders were Hurrem Şah from Ahlat and İbn İbrahim Oğlu from Tiflis. The ensemble as a whole ranks high among the most important early works of Islamic architecture in Anatolia. The three portals, of which the most famous is the main north doorway (one of the other two has been walled up), are exuberantly carved with abstract plant designs revealing Georgian and Armenian influence. The staircase pulpit made in 1240 is one of the most beautiful in the country. The five-bay prayer hall has sixteen pillars carrying stellate vaulting, while above the section containing the prayer niche rises a ribbed dome surmounted by a helm roof. Ahmet Şah Mengüçoğlu's türbe stands next to the mosque.

Caravanserai

About 6km/4 miles west of Divriği, on the old caravan route from Sivas to Divriği and Harput (Elazığ), a few kilometres north of the village of Dumluca, are the ruins of a late 13th c. caravanserai, Dipli Hanı (1292).

Diyarbakır   Q 6

South-eastern Anatolia   **See warning page 7**
Province: Diyarbakır
Altitude: 648m/2127ft
Population: 376,000

Situation and
**Importance

Diyarbakır, one of the most picturesque of all Turkish cities, with a high proportion of its inhabitants Kurds, stands on a pedestal of black basalt on the west bank of the upper Tigris (Dicle Nehri), surrounded by fertile plots of cultivated land. Provincial capital (and unofficial "capital" of Turkish Kurdistan) the city is located in a steppe-like plain, bordered to the south-west by the flat but massive basalt ridge of the Karaca Dağ (1938m/6360ft). Once a staging post on the ancient trade route from the Persian-Arabian Gulf to the Old Syrian Mediterranean ports and, via Byzantium, to the West, Diyarbakır, with its excellently preserved town wall and citadel, its host of lovely medreses and mosques and its winding alleyways is the epitome of an old Anatolian town. For some years now new industries have brought a huge influx of people into Diyarbakır from the surrounding countryside. The walled Old Town is about 1.5km/1 mile across from west to east and a kilometre from north to south.

History

In the 9th c. B.C. Diyarbakır was the chief settlement in the Bit Zamami region, intermittently dependent in subsequent centuries on the Assyrian Empire. Later the city became capital of the Roman province of Mesopotamia. It was here in 115 that Trajan defeated the Parthians. From the 4th to the 7th c. the hard-pressed Byzantines struggled to defend the city against the Sassanids; the emperor Constantius built substantial ramparts to this end in 394, which Justinian strengthened 200 years later. The dark basalt walls led to the city being called "Amida the Black", the Turkish form of which, "Kara Amid", is still used today. In 636 the Arabs captured the town for the Omayyads. They in turn handed it over to the Beni Bakr tribe,

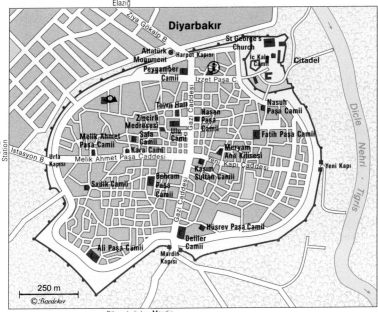

Römerbrücke, Mardin

from whom its present name derives (Diyar-Bakır; land of the Bakr). After a short period of independence, possession changed hands several times before the Seljuks (Ortokids) ravaged the city in 1085. In the final years of the 14th c. the Akkoyunlu Turkomans made it their capital; in 1507 it became Persian and in 1515 it passed to the Ottomans. Located as it is at the very heart of Turkish Kurdistan, Diyarbakır has witnessed and continues to witness bloody confrontations between Turks and Kurds, including full-scale rebellion in 1929.

Sights

The Archaeological Museum, situated in a building in the northern part of town, has displays of finds from various periods; these include Ottoman artefacts excavated in Çayönü and Üçtepe (near Bismil).

Arkeolojik Müzesi

This museum housed in the citadel (open: Wed.–Mon. 9am–noon and 1–5pm) is devoted to the First World War campaigns in southern Anatolia. It focuses particularly on Atatürk who was resident here in 1916 as Commandant of the town.

Atatürk Müzesi

Built in 1572 the Behram Paşa Camii, Diyarbakır's largest mosque, stands in the south-west quadrant of the Old Town, beyond the bazaar quarter with its little shops and open-air market. Its strict observance of architectural canons make the mosque one of the most important in the city. Note the richly ornamented prayer niche.

Behram Paşa
Camii

Also called the Kurşunlu Cami this mosque, located about 300m/330yd south of the citadel, was founded in 1522 by Diyarbakır's Ottoman conqueror Mehmet Paşa. The interior is clad in lovely tiles.

Fatih Paşa Camii

Diyarbakır

Diyarbakır: vegetable market outside the mighty town walls

St George's Church	Now very dilapidated the 4th c. Armenian St George's Church, a cruciform domed basilica with a large colonnade under a wooden roof, is situated inside the citadel.
*Hasan Paşa Hanı	The Hasan Paşa Hanı, across the road from the Ulu Cami and a short distance north-east, is a late 16th c. caravanserai built around a courtyard. The two-storey complex is still in use, divided into shops and lodgings. Calligraphic inscriptions adorn the entrance.
Hüsrev Paşa Camii	This mosque on the southern edge of the Old Town started life as a medrese, endowed between 1521 and 1528 by the city's then governor Hüsrev Paşa. The present prayer hall is the old teaching room. The prayer niche and pulpit are especially fine. The walls are tiled. The minaret was added in 1728.
İç Kale Camii	The small citadel mosque in the southern part of the citadel precinct was built sometime around 1160; it has been restored and altered several times since. Adjoining are a türbe and minaret. The plain base of the minaret suggests Seljuk origin.
Kasım Sultan Camii	Apart from being known by three different names – Kasım Sultan Camii, Kasım Padışah Camii and Şeyh Muattar Camii – the principal feature of this early 16th c. mosque (1512) opposite the post office is its square minaret, standing in the street in front of the mosque on four short columns. Walk round ''the Four-Legged Minaret'' seven times and you will have a wish granted.
Kültür Müzesi	The Kültür Müzesi occupies a very traditional, elegantly furnished house, home of the Turkish writer Cahit Sıtkı Tarancı who died in 1956. In addition to an interesting exhibition of local craftwork, etc., some of the writer's personal effects are on display (open: Tue.–Sun. 9am–noon and 1–5pm).

Nomads at breakfast near Diyarbakır

On the east side of the courtyard of the Ulu Cami an arcade of ancient columns leads via a gate to the Masudiye Medresesi (1198–1223), designed by a Syrian architect for the Ortokid Sultan Sökmen II. The former Koranic and medical school now houses the offices of various religious bodies.
Masudiye Medresesi

This late 16th c. mosque (1591) near the Urfa Gate on the road running east-west across the city has a pretty minaret.
Melik Ahmet Paşa Camii

The Syrian Jacobite Church of the Virgin, in an alleyway north of the Yeni Kapı Caddesi, is of unknown date.
Meryam Ana Kilisesi

Although restored by the Marwanids in 1065 (there is an inscription to this effect on a limestone plaque on the south side) the ten-arched Roman Bridge 3km/2 miles south of the city, already spanned the Tigris in 512, at the time of the Emperor Anastasios I. Downstream from this point the river becomes navigable by keleks (flat bottom craft made from inflated animal skins).
*Roman Köprüsü

This elegant mosque, behind and to the north of the Kara Cami, has an octagonal central bay. Except on feast days, the minaret with its decorative coloured tiling used to be kept in protective drapes to preserve the scent of herbs mixed in with the mortar. The mosque is thought to have been built by Uzun Hasan, the great Akkoyun i.e. "White Sheep" leader (1435–78).
Safa Camii

The walls, built of the dark basalt so characteristic of the area, are 12m/39ft high, up to 5m/16ft thick, and 5.5km/3½ miles long. All but six of the original 78 towers still survive, and four gates, the Harput Kapısı (north), Urfa Kapısı (west), Mardin Kapısı (south) and Yeni Kapı (east). Two of the three arches of the Urfa Kapısı were bricked up in 1183 by the Ortokid ruler Mohammed. Gazi Caddesi, running north through the city to the Harput Kapısı, is the old *cardo maximus* of the Roman town constructed in 363. The Harput Kapısı
**Walls

(or Bab el-Armen, "the Armenian Gate") has a niche on the inner side decorated with reliefs of bulls, birds and lions (probably 10th c.). The gate as a whole is an amalgam of Roman, Arab and Byzantine elements. On the south-west side of the city, the massive Ulu Bardan bastion, 24m/78ft in diameter, built to reinforce a westward-projecting section of the walls, is Byzantine in origin. Further strengthened in 1208 it comprises two casemates, one above the other. At the extreme south-west corner of the wall is another equally massive circular tower and, further east, the Nur Burc tower embellished with reliefs and a Seljuk inscription.
Jutting out abruptly from the south wall beside the Mardin Kapısı is the Kici Burc bastion (1029–37) which has five vaulted rooms.

Ulu Cami	The jewel in Diyarbakır's crown, its Great Mosque, stands on the west side of Ulu Cami Meydanı, in the town centre. Modelled on the Omayyad mosque in Damascus, it was built in the 11th/12th c. and is thought to occupy the site of a 5th c. Christian church. It has been restored several times, in particular following the great fire which resulted from an earthquake in 1115. In the early days a third of the mosque was apparently reserved for Christian use. Above the main courtyard entrance are reliefs of lions and bulls. Ancient columns and capitals are incorporated into the structure of the three-aisle prayer hall with its central crossing as well as into the two-storeyed arcading of the façade. Like the mosque itself the square minaret is Syrian in style.
Zincirli Medresesi	This late 12th c. Koranic school west of the Ulu Cami has student cells grouped around a square courtyard and, on the east side, an iwan. It used to house an archaeological museum.
*Citadel (Kale)	From the Peygamber Camii the İzzet Paşa Caddesi leads east to the citadel gate, flanked by two massive semi-circular towers. Three more gates pierce the 650m/700yd long citadel wall, fortified with sixteen towers, on which Arabs, East Romans, Seljuks and Ottomans have all left their mark. The 40m/131ft high artificial mound on which the citadel stands in the north-east corner of the Old Town, was very probably the site of the original settlement. The arrival in A.D. 363 of thousands of refugees fleeing from the Sassanids, caused the city's expansion westwards.
Ziya Gökalp Müzesi	The house in which the turn-of-the-century Turkish philosopher/sociologist Ziya Gökalp was born and lived, near the Ulu Cami, is now a museum. There is a display of his work and also a library (open: Tue.–Sun. 9am–noon and 1–5pm).

Surroundings

*Çatakköprü	Near Çatakköprü the Malabadi Köprüsü, with a modern bridge beside it, crosses the Batman Suyu, a large tributary of the Tigris. Just upstream the river has been dammed to create the Batman Barajı. The old bridge dates from 1147 and has a span of 35m/115ft.
Çermik	About 90km/60 miles north-west of Diyarbakır the medieval fortress of Çermik Kalesi stands guard over the town of Çermik, to the south of which some very impressive rock formations can be seen in the limestone uplands of the Devkan Tepesi.
Eğil	South-east of Eğil there is an ancient hill fort built sometime in the 1st millennium B.C. It perches on a steep rock, high above the gorge of the upper Tigris. There are also some remains of rock tombs from which passages once led down to the river. If conditions are right late in the day, it is just possible to make out a relief of Assyrian origin on the fortress rock, depicting a god armed with an axe and sword (about 720 B.C.).
Ergani	Ergani, some 55km/34 miles north of Diyarbakır, is situated among the copper-rich "ore mountains". Not surprisingly a strong local tradition of

copper-craft survives in some of the smaller places in the region (such as Maden). When he passed through in 1847, de Hell found the population to be predominantly Christian (three quarters Greek, the rest Armenian).

The road between Ergani and Çermik has several points of interest, chief among which are the thermal springs near Kaplıcarı, an Ortokid bridge near Hauburman, and the cave in which the prophet Ezekiel lived as a hermit (with a church dedicated to the Virgin, a holy place for Muslims as well as Christians).

Kaplıcarı

Lice, a good 90km/60 miles north-east of Diyarbakır, is possibly the site of ancient Legarda. It is dominated by Cepper Kalesi, a medieval fortress.

Lice

The Tigris Tunnel so-called, about 23km/14 miles north-west of Lice on the Bingöl road, is a 750m/820yd long cave through which flows what many consider to be the source of the Tigris, surfacing further west as a rock spring. Above this "source of the Tigris" are two more caves, with rock steps (cut presumably by the Urartians) and a natural rock arch leading to them. At the entrance to the larger cave there is an Assyrian rock relief of King Salmanassar III (858–824 B.C.) and some badly weathered cuneiform text. About 750m/820yd further east at river level two more Assyrian reliefs can be seen on the steep rock face: King Tiglapileser I on the left, King Salmanassar III on the right (only visible in good light).

*Tigris Tunnel

The district town of Silvan (population: 46,000; 100km/62 miles east of Diyarbakır) probably stands on the site of Tigranocerta, the Old Armenian capital. A town called Martyropolis, of which only some walls survive, was founded here in the 5th c. by Bishop Marutha. He was the bishop who persuaded the Sassanids to adopt a more tolerant attitude to Christianity. After a chequered history it became an Ottoman possession in 1515.
The Şelaheddin-i Ayyubi Camii was built by the Sultan Saladin in 1185, incorporating columns from a Byzantine basilica. It has an impressive entrance (rosette frieze; round-arched niche embellished with reliefs).

Silvan

Doğubayazıt

See Ararat

Edirne   B 2

Thrace. Province: Edirne
Altitude: 49m/160ft
Population: 102,000

Once known as Adrianopolis, Edirne, capital of its province, is situated 245km/152 miles north-west of İstanbul at the confluence of the Tunca and Arda with the Meriç (Maritza). It is the second largest city in European Turkey, benefitting from its position as a major road and rail junction close to the Greek and Bulgarian frontiers. It is surrounded by fertile farming country and has recently emerged as an increasingly prosperous industrial town (textiles, leather goods, staple and luxury foods, perfume).
With its endowment of mosques (including the magnificent Selimiye Camii), caravanserais, low timber houses and narrow alleyways, this historic Thracian border town still retains its Old Turkish air.

Situation and *Importance

Edirne was founded around A.D. 125 by the Roman emperor Hadrian (hence Hadrianopolis/Adrianopolis), afterwards being continually fought over on account of its strategic position. From the time of its capture by the Turkish Sultan Murat I, to the fall of Constantinople in 1453, Edirne was the seat of

History

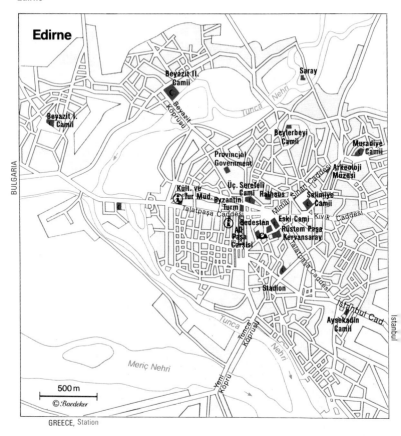

the Turkish rulers. At the end of the 19th c. it became a frontier stronghold and played an important role during the Balkan Wars. In 1989 hundreds of thousands of Bulgarian Turks, fleeing across the Turkish-Bulgarian border, settled in the Edirne-İstanbul area.

Sights

Ali Paşa Çarşısı

This covered bazaar in the Saraçılar Caddesi was built by the famous architect Sinan for Hersekli Ali Paşa, one of Süleiman the Magnificent's viziers. It is constructed on the traditional pattern: a roofed-over street, with rows of shops running parallel, and entrances at the front and sides.

Arkeoloji Müzesi

The archaeological museum, originally housed in the Selimiye Camii medrese but now (since 1971) in a modern building, has collections of pottery, bronze-work, Thracian capitals (8th c. B.C.), glass, and coins from a number of periods. The ethnographic section includes a variety of textiles, rose-water bottles, sewing boxes, cutlery, writing materials, weapons (some with especially fine inlay) and kitchen utensils. Also on display are

Anatolian carpets, prayer rugs from Gördes, Bergama and Kırşehir, and kilims, including Sarkoy and Turkmen kilims.

Now in less exalted use as an antique emporium, the old bedesten in the city centre was built by the Sultan Mehmet I. Fourteen small cupolas adorn the roof of the two-aisle, pillared hall and cluster of little shops.

Bedesten

The 14th c. Bayazit I Camii stands in what is now the suburb of Yıldırım on the western edge of the town. It is built in the (early) Bursa style, laid out in the shape of an inverted "T". A relatively narrow corridor, with domed chambers either side, leads from a narthex-like portico to the domed central space, square in plan, from which barrel-vaulted rooms radiate in the manner of a church.

Bayazit I Camii

Also situated well outside the centre, on the north-west edge of the town, is a mosque considered one of the finest to be built by the great Ottoman architect Hayrettin. The Bayazit II Camii and the other buildings in the complex were erected between 1484 and 1488, loosely modelled on the Sultan Mehmet Fâtih Külliye in İstanbul. The mosque itself has a tall central dome, its loftiness accentuated by the modest height of the nine-domed tabhanes either side and the low porch. The lovely interior is further enhanced by the effect of light from the four-tier arrangement of the windows.

*Bayazit II Camii

Adjacent to the mosque on its south-west side stands a complex of three buildings, the first being a hospital, hexagonal in plan, with a central dome. This is linked by a hall and courtyard to a medrese, the latter entirely classical in conception. North-east of the mosque are two domestic blocks comprising a kitchen for the poor and bakery with storerooms.

The Rüstem Paşa Caravanserai in the south-east corner of the city centre was built by the great Sinan for Rüstem Paşa, Grand Vizier to Süleiman the Magnificent. Completed around 1560 the imposing rectangular, two-storeyed building, with its large inner courtyard and hamam, was restored some years ago and is now a hotel.

Rüstem Paşa Kervanserayı

The turmoil of the 1878 Turko-Russian War left this once magnificent sultan's palace and fortifications on the banks of the Tunca almost completely destroyed, apart from a few fragmentary remains. The first building to occupy the site was a Roman fortress constructed at the time of Hadrian. A pavilion was then erected in the 15th c., probably by the Sultan Murat II. His son, Mehmet II Fâtih, added further buildings until a complete palace precinct took shape.

Saray

The Selimiye Camii, on a hill on the east side of the Old City, was commissioned by the Sultan Selim II and built between 1567 and 1574. It is among the most beautiful buildings of its kind, designed by the great architect Sinan (see Famous People) late in his career when at the pinnacle of his powers. The lesser elements of the complex (arasta, medrese, Koranic school and timekeepers' room) seem to strive upwards towards the mosque itself with its four minarets, each of which has three balconies. The 45m/148ft high dome, 31.3m/102ft in diameter, rests on a circle of eight enormous marble and granite pillars linked by arches.

**Selimiye Camii

The interior of the mosque is magnificent. Granite, porphyry and marble columns support the galleries while the subtle play of light from the skillfully positioned windows creates extraordinary effects as it falls on the stalactitic vaulting and tiled panels. Fine marble plaques, exquisite tiling, gilt calligraphic decoration and generally rich ornamentation add to the splendour of the mihrab, mimber and royal loge in particular. Even the location of the muezzin's tribune is unusual. Raised on twelve small pillars it is placed centrally beneath the dome, enclosing an attractive fountain.

In 1925 the first Museum of Turkish and Islamic Art was established in the former medrese of the Selimiye Camii. The exhibition comprises Ottoman inscriptions, Koranic manuscripts, tiles, embroidery, glass and weapons. A

Museum of Turkish and Islamic Art

Selimiye Camii, masterpiee of the famous architect Sinan

magnificent satin tent in which the Ottoman viziers conducted state affairs has been erected in the main hall. Side rooms contain antique furnishings and household items, also medallions, calligraphy and goblets. In the garden are a number of tombs (15th c. onwards) including that of Siddi Şah Sultan, the wife of Sultan Mehmet the Conqueror.

*Üç Şerefeli
Cami

The "Three Galleried Mosque" on Cumhuriyet Meydanı takes its name from the three (Turkish "uç") galleries (Turkish "şerefe") of its tall south minaret. Founded by Murat II, the 15th c. mosque is transitional from an architectural point of view between the Bursa and later classical styles. It is rectangular in plan, crowned by a vast vaulted central dome on a hexagonal base augmented by four large and three smaller cupolas. The Üç Şerefeli was the first mosque to have an inner courtyard the arcades of which were domed.

The four minarets at the corners of the inner court are all different in design. The tallest, to the south, has three galleries. The "baklavalı minare" (Rhomboid Minaret) has two galleries. The others, one of which is known as the "burmalı minare" (Spiral Minaret), have just one gallery.

Surroundings

About 60km/37 miles east of Edirne lies the provincial town of Kırklareli (pop. 45,000), tucked away at the south-west foot of the Yıldız Dağları (İstranca uplands; about 1000m/3280ft). As well as sunflowers grown for their seeds, livestock are reared in the steppe-like countryside around. In the Byzantine era the town, presumably Roman in origin, achieved a modest degree of prosperity, to which its many Christian churches testify. When the Turks captured the town in 1363 they called it Kırk Kilise (Town of 40 Churches), from which the present name derives.

Kırklareli

The Bayazıt Paşa Camii in the Hatice Hatun district was built by the town's governor Güllâbi Ahmet Paşa at the end of the 16th c. His tomb is found in the mosque garden. The much-restored Büyük Hızır Bey Cami, commissioned by Kösenihalzade Hızır Bey for his son Abdullah Bey and built in 1383, is the oldest mosque in Thrace. Opposite the Ahmet Midhat primary school (İlkokul) stands the Kadi Camii, endowed by Emin Ali Çelebi in 1577.

Several villages in the vicinity of Kırklareli contain rather unusual domed tombs. Examples can be seen in the ancient cemeteries (2nd–4th c. B.C.) near Eriklice, 3km/2 miles north-west of Kırklareli, and at Çadırahlar Tepesi, 3km/2 miles south-east.

Domed tombs

The centre of Lüleburgaz (ancient Arcadiopolis), a town in the Karaağaç Deresi, about 60km/37 miles south-east of Edirne, on the İstanbul road, is graced by the Sokullu Mehmet Paşa Külliyesi, endowed by Sokullu Mehmet Paşa in 1549 and constructed by the Ottoman master builder Sinan. In addition to a mosque the complex comprises a medrese, baths (Çifte Hamam), library and caravanserai (Mimar Sinan Kervansarayı; now just remains). The garden of the mosque contains the 14th c. mausoleum of Zindan Babas, standard bearer to Gazi Evrenos Bey. The name Lüleburgaz derives from the Turkish word "lule" meaning pipe-bowl, for the manufacture of which the town is famous.

Lüleburgaz

Edremit Körfezi

B 4

North-east Aegean. Province: Balıkesir
Length (W–E): 50km/31 miles
Width (N–S): 25km/15½ miles

The southern part of the Troas, in the guise of the Kaz Dağı massif (the ancient Mt Ida; Kırkler Tepesi 1774m/5822ft) fringes the Gulf of Edremit to the south. Towering wall-like above its north shore, the mountains act as a barrier, preventing influxes of cold northern air.

Situation and Characteristics

Sheltered to the south-east by the Madra Dağı (1338m/4391ft) and to the west by the Greek island of Lesbos (Turkish Midilli), the Gulf, named after Edremit, the principal town, enjoys higher spring temperatures and lower rainfall than the windswept Troas, temperatures in summer being every bit as hot. This favourable climate, together with more than 100km/62 miles of equally fine coastline, combine to make the Gulf one of the premier tourist areas in Turkey. Today its character is dominated by the resorts strung like beads along its shores, the main centres being Altınoluk, Edremit–Akçay, Burhaniye–Ören and Ayvalık–Sarmısaklı. Countless hotels of every category cater for holidaymakers from the cities of the Anatolian hinterland (Ankara, Eskişehir, Konya).

Sights

Akçay is an offshoot of Edremit, about 12km/7½ miles further west. It is one of the most popular resorts, recently attracting an increasing number of European holidaymakers. On its west side, beyond the thermal baths (ruins

*Akçay

of a Roman baths) are the rather scant remains of ancient Astyra in the Troas, a colony of ancient Adramittium (Edremit) with a Temple of Artemis Astyrene. Akçay's natural springs (Artemis Sofbanları) offer treatment for gynaecological and other complaints.

Altınoluk

About 26km/16 miles west of Edremit, near Altınoluk, are the sites of two more ancient settlements, Gargara (at the resort itself) and, 215m/700ft above it, the overgrown ruins of Antandros. It was here on Mt Alexandreia (Kaz Dağı/Mt Ida) that Paris, a shepherd on Mount Ida, son of Priam, King of Troy, was judge in the beauty contest between the goddesses Athene, Aphrodite and Hera. Although its origin remains uncertain, the town was probably founded by the Pelasgi. The necropolis, a fortress (Sahinkale) and a few other fragments survive.

*Assos

The ruins of Assos stand on the northern shore of the Gulf of Edremit facing the Greek island of Lesbos (Turkish Midilli). Built on the terraced slopes and summit of a not easily accessible trachyte escarpment between the sea and the Tuzla Dere, this ancient Greek city was once considered the most beautifully situated of any in Europe or Asia. In its heydey it covered an area of 2.5sq.km/1sq.mile, part of which is occupied to-day by the village of Behramkale.

In the 2nd millennium B.C. Assos was the Lelegian capital, later becoming an Aeolian colony. Between 560 and 549 B.C. it belonged to the Lydians and in the 5th c. to the Persians. Aristotle lived in the city from 348 to 345. It was also the birthplace of the Stoic philosopher Cleanthes (c. 331–233 B.C.).

Restored columns in Assos

In A.D. 58 the Apostle Paul visited Assos on his missionary journey south (see Acts of the Apostles 20, 13ff).

Excavation has revealed remains of buildings spanning more than twelve centuries, including the 3km/2 miles of city walls (mainly 4th c. B.C.) which, originally 19m/62ft high, are among the finest examples of Greek military architecture. The principal buildings of the Hellenistic town have also been uncovered and, on the highest point of the acropolis, the foundations of a pre-Hellenistic Temple of Athena (art treasures in İstanbul and Paris) where some attempt at restoration has recently been made.

Be sure to walk to the top of the hill. There is a superb wide-ranging vista, not only across the Gulf to Lesbos but over the hinterland as well.

Kap Baba

Kap Baba, about 30km/18½ miles west of Behramkale (dirt road), is the most westerly point of Asia Minor. On it stands a lighthouse and the village of Babakale. Not far away are the sites of two ancient towns, Polymedion and Hamaxitos. The village of Gülpınar, a few kilometres further north, is close to the site of ancient Chrysa where the Temple of Apollo Smintheos once boasted a statue of Apollo carved by Scopas.

Near the busy port of Ayvalık, about 50km/31 miles south-west of Edremit, the coastline curves around a series of bays backed by pine woods and olive groves, an area of much-frequented beaches and good holiday accommodation. There are also more than 20 offshore islands and islets, the largest of which, Alibey Adası (named after a Turkish general in the War of Liberation) was already settled in antiquity and experienced a golden age under the Romans. Ayvalık itself, which contrary to the Turkish custom faces the sea, was until 1922 a purely Christian (Greek) community. Even today the neo-classical façades of its older houses and the alleys of the Old Town give it a distinctive air. It grew up between the 16th and 18th centuries, becoming a kind of sanctuary for its small Greek population. In 1773 Muslims were actually banned from living there by the Ottoman Sultan Mustafa III. By the beginning of the 19th c. the town had attained a peak of prosperity. In 1821 however the Kydonians siezed two Turkish ships, as a result of which they found themselves expelled, setting fire to the town as they went. In 1827 the Sultan Mahmut II allowed some 18,000 Greeks to return, though without restoring their earlier privileges. The town quickly resumed its role as an important port, reflected in its having as many as five consulates. Its citizens are said to have been accomplished smugglers. Less than a hundred years later the inhabitants again found themselves forced to leave, this time as part of the exchanges of population following the abortive Greek occupation (1919–22). The Greek Christians left behind a great many churches which the Muslims put to use as mosques. The Taksiyarhis Kilisesi, a 19th c. building with a lovely interior, on the northern outskirts of the town, is well worth seeing.

Be sure also to visit two nearby viewpoints on Şeytab Sofrası (Devil's Table) and Tavşankuları (Rabbit's Ear Hill). Both are on the Timerhane peninsula and offer magnificent views across a sea dotted with islets amd islands and the picturesquely indented coastline. There is also a small national park (red and roe deer and partridges). Timarhane was at one time known as "Madhouse Peninsula", the mentally ill being banished there in chains. They are said to have returned completely cured.

Edremit (pop. 30,000), the district town, is situated about 10km/6 miles from the coast at the eastern end of the gulf which bears its name. A short distance to the south, near the village of Kalabak Köyü, are the remains of the earlier Adramittium (Adramittium Thebe; see Ören). Edremit's Seljuk Kurşunlu Cami dates from around 1231 and, together with its türbe (1241), was built by Yusuf Sinan. In the early 14th c. there was a Genoese fortress in the town. The Esnef Rumi Camii was built during the Ottoman period. Today Edremit–Akçay is a popular seaside resort. As well as archaeological finds the town museum has a splendid collection of weapons.

Situated on the coast about 10km/6 miles south-west of Edremit, Ören is a suburb of Burhaniye (which lies just inland). It is one of those well-patronised resorts usually crowded with Turks enjoying their holidays. The long beach has fine sand and is well maintained.

A few kilometres south of Ören (which means "ruined place") is a mound marking the site of the ancient (Lydian) town of Adramyteion, in Strabo's time the Roman port of Pedasus. First settled in 1443 B.C., the town was later destroyed by pirates and between 1093 and 1109 was rebuilt further inland (as Adramittium).

Adramyteion (or Adramittium Thebe further east) is also identified with the Thebe of Homeric legend. According to Homer it was founded by Hercules in honour of his wife Thebe, daughter of Adramys (brother of the Lydian king Croesus). The town, where Hector's wife Andromache had her palace, was sacked by Achilles in the ninth year of the Trojan War. In reality Thebe was probably founded by the Milesians about 600 B.C., growing to be an important trading town on the route between Troy and Pergamum (Bergama). It was already in ruins in Strabo's day.

Eğridir   F 6

Western Taurus (Isaurian-Pisidian lake district)
Province: Isparta
Altitude: 950m/3118ft
Population: 14,500

*Situation and
Characteristics

Few central Anatolian towns can claim so attractive a setting as Eğridir, situated on a promontary in the south-west corner of Eğridir Gölü, at the foot of Davraz Dağ (2635m/8648ft). The town, rich in tradition, has recently witnessed the emergence of a modest inland tourist industry. In addition to fruit, roses are widely cultivated in the surrounding countryside, their petals being used to make rose-water. Fishing is also an important local occupation. The name Eğridir derives from the earlier Greek name Akrotiri. The town's heyday was in the 13th c. when, as part of the Seljuk Sultanate of Rum, it came under the rule of the Hamidoğlu emirs. Persian sources show Eğridir to have been one of the principal towns in the region at that time (Ottoman from the end of the 14th c.).

Sights

Baba Sultan
Türbesi

This simple Seljuk mausoleum stands in a small lakeside park in the northern part of the town.

*Dündar Bey
Medresesi

When first endowed in about 1238 by the Emir Dündar Hamidoğlu, the Dündar Bey Medresesi, a splendid example of Early Seljuk architecture, was clearly intended as a caravanserai. The magnificent ornamented gateway, embellished with the finest of stone carving, originally belonged to another caravanserai, the Eğridir Hanı. Some of the cells around the

Traditional township by the picturesque lake of Eğridir Gölü

arcaded inner courtyard of the now restored building have been turned into shops.

Over the years the ruined Eğridir Hanı, on the slopes of Davraz Dağ 3km/ 2 miles south of the town, has been repeatedly pillaged of its masonry for use in other buildings. Erected betwen 1229 and 1236 it was one of the four largest Seljuk caravanserais in Anatolia.

Eğridir Hanı

The ruined walls of this Seljuk fort rise above the rooftops of the Old Town. The beautiful carvings on the gate originally graced the Eğridir Hanı.

Eğridir Kalesi

First endowed in 1327 by the Emir Hızır Hamidoğlu, the Hızır Bey Camii burned down in 1815 (inscription above the carved wooden door in the portal). It was rebuilt in 1885.

Hızır Bey Camii

Part of Eğridir's old wall still survives, including one of the gates (beside the entrances to the Ulu Cami and Dündar Bey Medresesi).

Kemer Kapısı

East of the town, connected to the mainland by a causeway, are two islands, the larger of which, Niş Adası, is thought to have once been the seat of the Bishop of Limnae. There are the remains of two Byzantine churches.

Niş Adası and Tavşan (or Can) Adası

Eğridir's Ulu Cami, a low, 15th c. building with 48 wooden columns in the style of a "forest mosque", stands immediately adjacent to the Dündar Bey Medresesi.

*Ulu Cami

Surroundings

About 30km/19 miles east of Eğridir, beyond the bridge at the end of the Aksu gorge, are three boulders carved with inscriptions and an animal's head. Near by are two caves, old cult sites of some sort. One half was carefully sealed off some time in antiquity.

Aksu

The Lake Eğridir basin lies at an altitude of 916m/3000ft, being part of the depression zone between the western and central Taurus. With an area of 468sq.km/180sq.miles, Eğridir Gölü is the fourth largest inland lake in Turkey, but with a maximum depth of only 20m/65ft. Completely encircled by mountains – Barla Dağ (2263m/7427ft) and Karakuş Dağ (1995m/6547ft) to the west, Davraz Dağ (2635m/8648ft) to the south, and the summits of Dedogöl Dağ (2388m/7837ft) and Kirisli Dağ (1889m/6199ft) to the east – the lake, its sparkling waters every shade from green to deepest blue, has the air of a huge tarn. The ancient town of Oroanda was probably situated at the north end of the lake.

*Eğridir Gölü

To the south of Eğridir a 2km/1¼ mile-wide longitudinal trench, the continuation of the Eğridir Gölü basin, forms a narrow valley running south for more than 25km/15½ miles to the plane tree fringed Lake Kovada and the Kovada National Park. The terrain at the southern end of Kovada Gölü is heavily karstic, water draining from the lake underground to re-emerge from several karst springs near Gökpınar a little further south. Compounding the already damaging effect of Kovada Gölü's two hydro-electric stations, this water loss poses a considerable threat to the well-being of the Park, to counter which water for the hydro-electric plants is now brought direct from Lake Eğridir by an aqueduct.

*Kovada Milli Parkı

Near Mahmutlar, about 46km/28 miles north-east of Eğridir, south of the district town of Gelendost, the remains of the Seljuk Ertokuş Hanı can be seen standing 100m/110yd or so from the lake shore. It was founded in 1223 by the Atabey Emir Mübarizeddin Ertokuş, an influential functionary of Alaeddin Keykubad. The gateway side of the building is now in very poor

Gelendost

condition. Six rather squat triangular towers on the exterior of the three-bayed, barrel vaulted main hall are of later date. More barrel vaulted rooms lead off the arcades either side of the inner court.

Isparta

Situated at the foot of the 2275m/7466ft high Akdağ on the southern edge of the Isparta basin, the provincial capital of Isparta (pop. 120,000) is famous for its carpets, still sold at a big daily market – though few can nowadays claim to be hand made. The town is also noted for its attar of roses; the small ovens for extracting the rose-oil are a common sight in the countryside around. Süleiman Demirel, a former Turkish Prime Minister, was born in Isparta. Nearby Akdağ shows signs of former glaciation.

Isparta was probably founded by Greeks from Sparta and Greeks continued to inhabit it until 1920. A number of ruined Greek churches can still be seen. The town has been a bishopric ever since the Council of Nicaea (İznik). Once known as Baris, which is the name Ptolemy uses for it, the town came to be called Isparta only in the 14th c. when it was the seat of the Seljuk princes of Hamit. The completely ruined fort almost certainly dates from this time. Described in about 1648 as large and beautiful, by 1706 Isparta had degenerated into a small, unfortified place with miserable houses. In 1889 it was very badly damaged by a violent earthquake.

A number of Isparta's mosques boast 16th and 17th c. tiles; old silver utensils can be seen in some of its churches. The Firdevs Camii is attributed to the Ottoman architect Sinan. The Halil Hamit Paşa Kütüphanesi has a collection of some 14,000 books, amassed in the 18th c. by the library's founder, the Grand Vizier Halil Hamit Paşa after whom it is named. There are also seven old caravanserais in the town dating from the Ottoman period. The museum has an unrivalled collection of coins, as well as fragments of reliefs from sites in the area. There is also a delightful exhibition of local craftwork.

Gölcük

Located about 5km/3 miles south-west of Isparta is a unique geological feature, the Gölcük crater, with a rim rising in places to 1300m/4266ft and a lake one kilometre long and several hundred metres wide. A number of ash and clinker cones, some as much as 100m/330ft high, have been thrown up on the flatter southern rim. On the outside of the crater, slightly below the level of the lake, several springs emerge on the north side. Water from these springs is used for irrigation as well as supplying Isparta.

Elazığ   P 5

Eastern Anatolia (eastern Taurus)   See warning page 7
Province: Elazığ
Altitude: 1020m/3348ft
Population: 212,000

Situation and Importance

Elazığ (Elâzığ) is situated at the foot of the 1724m/5658ft Kartal Tepesi on the northern edge of the Uluova basin. In addition to being a sizeable industrial centre it is a busy market town, serving a large rural area. It has a university, founded in 1966. Much the most important development of recent years however has been the Keban Dam project on the Euphrates, from which the town has benefitted enormously.

History

By Turkish standards Elazığ is still something of a new town. Its story really begins in 1834 when the Ottoman governor Reşid Mehmet Paşa moved his residence from the old hilltop stronghold of Harput to Mazra'a, a village a few miles away on the plain. Faced by rebellious Kurds and the insurgent Mehmet Ali, the Ottoman army then established a headquarters in Mazra'a (the German military adviser H. von Moltke spent some time there in about 1838). In 1862 the Ottoman Sultan Abdul el-Aziz transformed the village into a town, renaming it Mamuret el-Aziz (settlement of el-Aziz) of which

From the rock fortress of Harput there is a fine view

Elazığ is a later corruption. Mazra'a was probably the site of ancient Mazara.

Surroundings

Elazığ's predecessor Harput lies some 6km/4 miles to the north-east at an altitude of 1270m/4168ft, commanding a magnificent view over the plain and the town. Until 1862 Harput (Arabic Khartabirt, Armenian Kharpert, meaning "fortress rock") was itself the provincial centre, with a population of about 20,000. The citadel is almost certainly Urartian in origin, but reconstructed a number of times. Harput may also have been the capital of the ancient region of Sophene Karkathiokerta. It was in several different hands from the 10th c. onwards until conquered by the Ottomans in 1515. Apart from the citadel ruins the building of most interest is the Ulu Cami, founded around 1165. Also dating from the Seljuk period are the ruined Arapbaba Camii and the Alaca Camii, the latter housing a small archaeological collection of mainly Urartian and Roman finds from the surrounding area. The Sarâ Hatun Camii was built in the 15th c. by the Akkoyun Emir Uzun Hasan Bey, in honour of his mother Sara Hatun. There are also three Ottoman caravanserais.

*Harput

Hazar Gölü (altitude: 1248m/4096ft), about 22km/14 miles south of Elazığ, not far from the district town of Sivrice, is the source lake of the Tigris (Dicle Nehri). From the lake the 1900km/1180 mile long river flows for some 523km/325 miles across south-eastern Turkey, reaching the Iraqi frontier south of Cizre.

Hazar Gölü

Completed in 1975 the Keban Barajı (675sq.km/260sq.miles; 30 billion cu.m/39 billion cu.yd) is one of the biggest reservoirs in the world. The most northerly of a whole series of dams built on the Euphrates as part of the

Keban Barajı

285

GAP project, the Barajı collects water from two of the river's great arms, the Murat Nehri and the Karasu. The dam itself is 207m/680ft high and 1100m/1200yd long at the rim.

The Keban Barajı's chief function is to produce electricity (1249 mega-watts). Numerous villages in the Euphrates Valley had to be relocated to enable the dam to be built.

Kömürhan

Constructed in the reign of the Sultan Murat, Kömürhan stands by the Euphrates about 55km/33 miles south-west of Elazığ (to the north of the road). Driving further west, before reaching Kuşsarayı (İzoğlu), the Tomsa fortress can be seen standing guard near the village of Hatip Uşağı. Lower down, to the right of a rock arch, in a spot now flooded by the waters of the Karakaya Barajı, a Urartian cuneiform inscription was discovered on a rock face (by H. von Moltke in 1839). In it Sardur II boasts of his victorious exploits over the King of Melitene (Malatya, 754 B.C.). There are now plans to re-site the inscription elsewhere.

Palu

Above Palu, a town set amid fertile plots on the north bank of the Euphrates (Murat Nehri), a fortress of Urartian origin caps the crest of a steep hillside overlooking the ruins of Eski Palu (Old Palu). There is a staircase tunnel dating from the same period in the north-west side of the hill and, on the west side, an isolated boulder with an inscription by King Menua. Archae-ologists suspect that a Urartian settlement lies hidden beneath the ruins of the old town.

In the form seen today the fortress is attributed to the Genoese. Also on the hill are the remains of two mosques and a church. It was from Palu that H. von Moltke set out on his journey downstream by kelek (a raft made from 60 animal skins) to investigate whether the Euphrates was navigable.

Pınar Tepesi, the hill to the west of the town, has proved a rich source of archaeological finds from the Chalcolithic period (4th millennium B.C. right up to the Middle Ages.

Ephesus   C 6

West coast (Aegean Sea)
Province: İzmir
Altitude: 20–358m/65–1175ft
Town: Selçuk (population: 20,000)

Situation and
**Importance

The remains of the ancient Greek city of Ephesus (Greek Ephesos, Turkish Efes), one of the outstanding classical sites and tourist attractions in Tur-key, lie near Selçuk about 75km/47 miles south of İzmir. Like Miletus, ancient Ephesus lay directly on the sea, and had an important harbour, the main source of its wealth. However, the Little Maeander (Küçuk Menderes), the ancient Kaystros, sediment laden and freqently changing its course, pushed the coastline ever farther away, while the marine currents off the bay built up a spit of land, behind which the ground degenerated into marsh. By Roman times only a tongue-shaped harbour basin could be kept open for shipping. Ephesus was deserted and gradually disappeared under the silt brought down by the river. Any structures remaining above ground were either used as a quarry for building material or burned to provide lime. Investigation of the site began only in the second half of the 19th c. when a British engineer, J. T. Wood, rediscovered and excavated the Artemiseion. The work was then continued between 1896 and 1913 by the Austrian Archaeological Institute. Between 1919 and 1922 Greek archae-ologists investigated the site of the basilica of St John.

History

The earliest inhabitants of this region, the Carians and Lydians, no doubt had a fortified settlement on the hill immediately north of Selçuk, which was directly open to the sea (Sacred Harbour). From the 11th c. B.C. onwards this settlement was occupied and Hellenised by Ionian Greeks.

The reconstructed Temple of Hadrian in the Street of the Curetes

Thanks to its excellent situation on an inlet cutting deep into the land, at the end of a major trade route from the interior, and on a fertile plain, Ephesus developed into a flourishing commercial city.

In about 387 B.C., in order to re-establish the city's link with the sea, King Lysimachos had it moved to the low-lying ground between Mounts Pion and Koressos (now Panayır Dağı and Bülbül Dağı), both of which were brought within the walls of the city.

Under the Roman Empire (1st and 2nd centuries A.D.) it enjoyed a fresh period of prosperity as capital of the Roman province of Asia, becoming the largest city in the East after Alexandria with a population of over 200,000. St Paul preached here on his second missionary journey and later spent three years (55–58) in Ephesus (Acts 18: 19; 19). The city's principal church was later dedicated to St John and became one of the great pilgrimage centres of Asia Minor. In 263 the Goths destroyed the city and the Artemiseion on one of their raiding expeditions.

Under the Eastern Empire, mainly as a result of the steady silting up of its harbour, Ephesus declined in importance and in size. Its circuit of walls was reduced in extent, excluding the Hellenistic agora and giving little protection to the harbour area – though the city was still sufficiently important to be the venue of the Third Ecumenical Council in 431. In the reign of Justinian the population withdrew to the original settlement site on the hill above the Artemiseion.

Ephesus was captured and plundered by the Mongols led by Tamarlane (Timur Lang). Thereafter the last surviving remains of the town were reduced to ruins during the bitter conflicts between the Seljuks and the Ottomans.

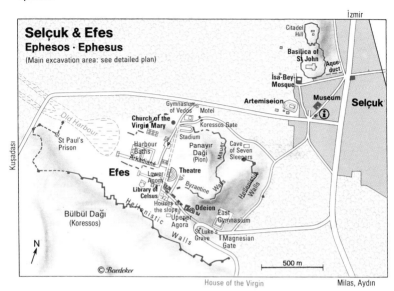

House of the Virgin

Visiting the ruins

Gymnasium of Vedius Stadium

On the slope of the hill to the left is the Gymnasium of Vedius (2nd c. A.D.), the remains of a large rectangular building with an arcaded courtyard, the palaestra (hall for wrestling). The eastern half of the structure, built of brick faced with marble, is better preserved and shows interesting details of the internal arrangement.

Some 100m/110yd south of the Gymnasium of Vedius is the Stadium, which dates from the time of Nero (A.D. 54–68). On the south side the tiers of seating for spectators were hewn out of the hillside; the stone benches are missing. At the semicircular east end was an arena which could be shut off from the main part of the stadium and used, in the absence of a circus, for gladiatorial contests and fights between wild beasts. Between the Gymnasium of Vedius and the Stadium a marble-paved way ran east to the Koressos Gate, of which some remains survive.

200m/220yd along a modern road which runs south from the Gymnasium of Vedius, on the left, are the remains of a Byzantine building. Notable features are the large room with semicircular niches on the south side and the 50m/165ft-long apsed hall on the west side.

Church of the Virgin Mary Theatre Gymnasium

A 100m/110yd or so to the west, to the right of the car park, can be seen a 260m/285yd long complex of remains known as the Church of the Virgin Mary, or the Double Church, or the Council Church. This was the meeting-place of the Third Ecumenical Council in A.D. 431. It was originally a museion (i.e. a centre of research and teaching), a three-aisled hall of the 2nd c. A.D. in which a pillared basilica was inserted in the 4th c.

The new road continues south for another 300m/330yd to the Theatre Gymnasium, a large rectangular structure of the Roman Imperial period with an arcaded courtyard measuring 70m/230ft×30m/100ft on its north side.

Square of Verulanus

Immediately west of the Theatre Gymnasium is a large complex of buildings, the plan of which is not easy to distinguish. Nearest the gymnasium is the Square of Verulanus, a spacious arcaded courtyard for the training of

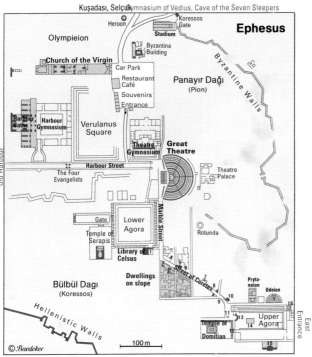

Kuşadası, Selçuk Gymnasium of Vedius, Cave of the Seven Sleepers

Ephesus

1 Market Gate (Gate of
   Macaeus and Mithridates)
2 Byzantine Fountain
3 Octagon
4 Brothel
5 Temple of Hadrian

6 Baths of Scholastica
7 Fountain of Trajan
   (Nymphaeum)
8 Gate of Hercules
9 Hydreion
10 Monument of Memmius

11 Square of Domitian
12 Museum of Inscriptions
13 Fountain of Pollio
14 Temple of Isis
15 Fountain-house
16 Temple of Varius

athletes, and beyond this is the Harbour Gymnasium, which dates from the
Early Empire. This consisted of a number of buildings grouped around a
central courtyard. On the north and south sides of the courtyard were two
magnificent marble halls measuring 16m/52ft×32m/104ft, with columns
and niches for statues. Immediately beyond this were the Great Baths or
Harbour Baths, built in the 2nd c. A.D. and sumptuously rebuilt in the reign
of Constantine the Great (4th c.). These are yet to be completely excavated.

To the west of the baths lay the Old Harbour of Ephesus, now an area of
marshy ground. Immediately south of this group of buildings is the Arkadiane, a fine arcaded street running east from the harbour to the Great
Theatre, which stood facing a long square. The effect of this magnificent
avenue, which was built by Arcadius, the first Eastern Emperor, about A.D.
400 and which is lit at night, was further enhanced by an elaborate gate at
either end.

Arkadiane

The Great Theatre, begun in the reign of Claudius (41–54) and completed in
the reign of Trajan (98–117), is particularly impressive, both for its great size
and for the excellent state of preservation of the orchestra and the stage
buildings. It was here that St Paul preached against the cult of Artemis and

**Great Theatre

Ephesus: façade of the Library of Celsus and the Market Gate

inveighed against the guild of silversmiths responsible for its shrines. The theatre's 3 by 22 tiers of seating, divided into sections by twelve stairways, could accommodate an audience of some 25,000. From the top there is a fine view extending down to the Old Harbour. There were also staircase tunnels leading to the upper tiers. The stage wall, originally three-storeyed and 18m/60ft high but now preserved only to the height of the lowest storey, was elaborately articulated, with columns, niches for statues and richly decorated cornices. In the west terrace wall is a Hellenistic fountain-house in the form of a temple *in antis*, which in spite of its ruinous state is notable for the clarity and simplicity of its structure.

*Lower Agora

South-west of the Great Theatre is the Lower Agora, a spacious square, 116m/127ft each way, from which a colonnaded street leads west. The agora (market square), which has been only partly excavated, was a 3rd c. rebuilding of an earlier structure, to which the use of stone from earlier buildings gives an interesting variety of detail. It was surrounded by a double colonnade housing shops and offices, with a set-back upper storey on the east side.

Serapeion

On the south side of the colonnaded street, which has an elaborate gate at each end, steps lead up to a colonnaded square, on the south side of which is the colossal Serapeion, the temple of the Egyptian god Serapis. Along the 29m/95ft long façade of the temple were monolithic columns 15m/50ft high with Corinthian capitals. The cella was entered through a massive doorway, with doors moving on wheels. In Byzantine times the Serapeion was converted into a Christian basilica.

Marble Street

Along the east side of the Lower Agora the Marble Street leads from the Koressos Gate, but has been excavated only from the Great Theatre south-ward. This fine marble-paved street, once lined with arcades and decorated with statues, continues south to the Library of Celsus. Along the middle can be seen a series of holes through which surface water flowed into drains.

The Marble Street leads from the Great Theatre to the Celsus Library

In a small square lying below street-level is the imposing two-storey façade of the Library of Celsus with its rather crowded columns and prominent cornices (re-erected in 1970–78 by Austrian archaeologists). The library itself, which was entirely faced with coloured marble was of three storeys, with colonnades around the lower two. Along the rear wall was a series of rectangular niches for holding parchment books and scrolls. Below the central niche is a grave-chamber with the Sarcophagus of Titus Julius Celsus Polemaeanus, Governor of the province of Asia, in whose honour his son built the library in the early 2nd c. A.D.

**Library of Celsus

Immediately adjoining the Library of Celsus, at the south-east corner of the Lower Agora, is the Gate of Macaeus and Mithridates, so named in an inscription. It has recently been restored.

Gate of Macaeus and Mithridates

South-east of the Lower Agora the marble-paved street, flanked by numerous impressive public buildings, continues as the Street of the Curetes, climbing uphill towards the Upper Agora. At the point where the Street of the Curetes bends south-east are the bases of the Propylaion, a gate of the 2nd c. A.D. from which a street, continued by a stepped lane, led south to Mount Koressos.

*Street of the Curetes

On the east side of the Propylaion is the Octagon, a monumental tomb with an eight-sided superstructure, surrounded by a Corinthian colonnade, with a stone bench, on a square marble base.

Higher up the slope of the hill a group of terraced buildings are in the course of excavation. On the opposite side of the street is a house which is assumed to have been a brothel.

Beyond this is a small temple, much restored, which an inscription shows was dedicated to the Emperor Hadrian (117–138). Beyond this are the remains of the Baths of Scholastica, once of several storeys, which were originally built in the 2nd c. A.D. and were rebuilt about A.D. 400 by a Christian woman named Scholastica.

Ephesus

Higher up, on the south-western slopes of Mount Pion, can be seen a two-storey rotunda on a square base, with Doric half-columns round the lower storey and free-standing Ionic columns round the upper storey. Probably this, like the Octagon, was a hero's tomb.

Past the Fountain of Trajan (nymphaeum) and the Gate of Hercules, the street bears right to enter the so-called Square of Domitian. Above the square rises the massive substructure of the Temple of Domitian, erected by the province of Asia in honour of the Emperor (A.D. 81–96). In the basement of the temple is the Museum of Inscriptions.

Upper Agora

To the east of the Temple of Domitian extends the Upper Agora, with a Temple of Isis and a hydreion (water-tower) which collected spring water flowing down from the hill. On the north side of the Upper Agora is the site

Prytaneion

of the Prytaneion (council chamber, town hall), located only after a long search. The figures of Artemis which were found here are now in the Archaeological Museum in Selçuk.

*Odeion

Further east is the semicircular structure of the Odeion, built by Publius Vedius Antonius in the 2nd c. A.D. The lower tiers of marble benches are original, the rest are reconstructions. The auditorium of this little theatre or concert hall had seating for an audience of 1400. Since there is no provision for the drainage of rainwater it is assumed that the Odeion was roofed, probably by a wooden structure spanning the 25m/80ft width of the auditorium.

Magnesian Gate

From the Upper Agora the old main street continues east to the eastern entrance to the excavation site, ending outside the enclosure at the three-arched Magnesian Gate, the starting-point of the road to Magnesia on the Maeander (see Menderes). At the bend in the road is the base of a circular Roman structure, wrongly called the Tomb of St Luke, which was converted into a church in Byzantine times by the addition of an apse and a porch.

Eastern Gymnasium

Immediately north of the Magnesium Gate are the imposing ruins of the Eastern Gymnasium (1st–2nd c. A.D.). Like the other three gymnasia in Ephesus, this is a large rectangular building with several magnificent halls and a palaestra. Since many statues of girls were found on the site it is known as the Girls' Gymnasium.

Surroundings

Panayır Dağı
(Pion)

From the Eastern Gymnasium a good road goes north-east up Panayır Dağı (Mount Pion, 155m/510ft), from which there is a fine view of the ancient site set in a semicircle round the hill. A Byzantine wall, some stretches of it well preserved, leads north along the crest of the hill to the Koressos Gate.

Under the north-east side of the hill is the so-called Cave of the Seven Sleepers. According to the legend seven young men of Ephesus were walled up in a cave during the persecution of Christians in the middle of the 2nd c. Falling into a deep sleep they were discovered, alive and well, in the reign of Theodisius II (414–450). After their death, it is said, the Emperor had them buried in the cave and built a pilgrimage church in their honour.

Bülbül Dağı
(Mount Koressos)

To the south-west of the excavated area is the long ridge of Bülbül Dağı (Nightingale Hill 358m/1175ft), known in antiquity as Mount Koressos, which can be climbed either on the east side or by a road ascending from the ancient harbour up the west side of the ridge. Along the ridge extends the Hellenistic town wall of the time of Lysimachos, still retaining some of the battlements.

On a hill above the harbour canal, known in Hellenistic times as Pagos Astyagou, stands a ruined watch-tower, originally on the Hellenistic town walls, which for some unexplained reason is known as St Paul's Prison.

*House of the
Virgin Mary

South-east of Bülbül Dağı, on Ala Dağı (the ancient Mount Solmissos, 420m/1378ft), is a building known as the House of the Virgin Mary (Panaya

Kapula), in which the Virgin is said to have lived and died. The building, the foundations of which date from the 1st c. A.D., was restored in Byzantine times but thereafter was abandoned and fell into disrepair. Its association with the Virgin only dates from the 19th c. following the visions of a German nun, Katharina Emmerich (1774–1824), who gave a precise description of the situation and appearance of a house at Ephesus in which she claimed the Virgin had lived and died. In 1891, on the basis of her account, Lazarists from Smyrna (İzmir) discovered on the south side of Bülbül Dağı the ruins of a small church which had evidently belonged to a monastery, and this is now revered as the Virgin's house.

The pilgrimages which began after the finding of the house continued on an increased scale after the Second World War, and the Feast of the Assumption (August 15th) is celebrated here with particular ceremony. The house, beautifully situated and commanding an extensive view, has also become a major tourist attraction.

The road to the House of the Virgin branches off the main Selçuk-Aydın road. In 4.5km/3 miles it passes close to the Eastern Gymnasium and the Magnesian Gate and then continues for another 3.5km/2 miles round the east side of Bülbül Dağı to the site.

About 15km/9 miles north-east of Ephesus, not far from where the road branches off to Tire near the village of Belevi, are a burial mound (tumulus) and the remains of a monumental structure, evidently unfinished, reminiscent of the Mausoleum at Halikarnassos (see Bodrum). Belevi, possibly dating from the 4th c. B.C. (perhaps Persian), is believed to be the Bonita of antiquity. The tumulus, encircled by a wall of masonry, contains two burial chambers, reached by means of a passageway 20m/65ft long. The burial chambers themselves are carved out of the rock from above. The mausoleum consists of a central burial chamber originally embellished with a sixteen-column peristasis on a three-tiered base (crepidoma). Winged lions and horses adorned the corners of the roof. The sarcophagus found in the mausoleum, carved with reliefs, is on display in the Ephesus Museum. Opposite, on a rock to the west can be seen the medieval Keçi Kalesi (Goat Fort).

Belevi

Selçuk

A short distance from the main square of Selçuk, the lower ward of the citadel is entered through the Byzantine Gate, also called the Gate of Persecution, erected in the 7th c. using fragments of earlier masonry. A few paces beyond this are the remains of the Basilica of St John, which occupied almost the whole breadth of the hill and ranked with Hagia Sophia and the Church of the Holy Apostles (destroyed) in Constantinople as one of the largest Byzantine churches. According to tradition the grave of St John the Divine is under the church. Originally a mausoleum with a domed roof borne on four columns was built over the grave.

*Basilica of St John

The Emperor Justinian (527–565) replaced this church by a monumental three-aisled basilica on a Latin-cross plan, with six domes. Including the narthex at the west end and the arcaded courtyard the new church was 130m/427ft long and 40m/130ft wide. The position of the Saint's tomb was marked by a tiered marbled platform, from which steps led down to the tomb.

After the Seljuks captured Ephesus they converted the church into a mosque (1130). Later it served as a bazaar until it was finally destroyed in an earthquake. In recent times it has been partly restored. A tablet commemorates a visit by Pope Paul VI on June 26th 1967.

To the north of the basilica, on the highest point of the hill stands the Citadel, in an excellent state of preservation. There is no written evidence as to its date, but the style of masonry indicates that it was built in Byzantine times and extended by the Seljuks. The mighty enclosure wall had fifteen

*Citadel

Byzantine Gate . . .   *. . . and St John's Basilica in Sellçuk*

towers, mostly rectangular. Within the walls are several cisterns, a small Seljuk mosque and a Byzantine church.

*İsa Bey Mosque

On the south-west side of the citadel hill is the Great Mosque (also known as the İsa Bey Mosque or Selim Mosque) which dates from Seljuk times. The tall outer walls, 57m/87ft long by 51m/167ft wide, enclose a large arcaded courtyard with the fountain for ritual ablutions and the prayer hall, the central area of which had two domes borne on columns, while the two side wings had flat timber roofs. The large columns of black granite came from the Roman baths at the harbour. The prayer hall was entered from the courtyard with three arches and two side doorways. Above the main entrance, which is richly decorated with inlay work, is an elaborate calligraphic inscription. Dated January 10th 1375 it identifies Ali, son of Mushimish al-Damishki as the architect of the mosque.

Artemiseion

Some 300m/330yd south of the Great Mosque are the sparse remains of the Artemiseion, or Temple of Artemis, once one of the Seven Wonders of the World. The excavations carried out by the Briton J. T. Wood showed that the site was originally occupied by a stone platform on which stood the cult image of the goddess, while under the platform were rooms in which votive offerings were preserved; to the west was another platform. In a later building phase the two platforms were linked with one another, and

Reconstruction of Temple of Artemis

later still a cella measuring 16m/52ft by 31m/102ft was built over them. It is not known whether the cella was surrounded by columns. Finally in the 6th c. B.C. a gigantic marble temple was built, measuring 106m/348ft by 55m/180ft. On 36 of the 127 columns the lower drum of the shaft was embellished with reliefs. The temple was twice restored and rebuilt before finally falling into a state of complete dilapidation in Byzantine times and being used as a quarry for building material.

Columns and marble slabs from the temple can be seen in the Haga Sophia (Ayasofa) in İstanbul and elsewhere. The foundations of the altar, measuring 30m/100ft by 40m/130ft, were discovered in 1965.

In the western part of Selçuk, some 500m/550yd south of the citadel hill, is the recently reorganised Archaeological Museum, with finds from the site of ancient Ephesus, including several statues of Artemis.

Archaeological Museum

*Kuşadası

Situated 17km/10½ miles south of Ephesus on the wide Gulf of Kuşadası, facing the Greek island of Samos (Turkish Sisam; ferry service), Kuşadası (pop. 22,000) is one of the oldest and most popular holiday centres in Turkey. Long sandy beaches (modern holiday villages), the well-equipped "Turban Marina" with 600 berths, and the old harbour (port of call for cruise ships and regular shipping lines) are among the many attractions of this leading resort.

Situation and Importance

The present town was founded in the 13th c. by merchants from Genoa and Venice. Since the harbour of nearby Ephesus (see above) had silted up, the new port was named Scala Nova (in Greek, Neo Ephesos). In the Ottoman period the name of the town was changed to Kuşadası (Bird Island).

The most prominent building in the neighbourhood of the harbour is the Kervanseray (caravanserai or han), a massive battlemented structure 12m/40ft high built by Öküz Mehmet Paşa in 1618. Restored in the 1960s, it has been a hotel (the Club Caravansérail) since 1967. Above the caravanserai, to the south-west, there are still a few 19th c. half-timbered houses in the style typical of the region. Of the old town walls there survives only the south gate.

Caravanserai

A little way west of the harbour a 350m/380yd long causeway leads to the charming island of Güvercin Ada (Pigeon Island; café-restaurant), with a

*Güvercin Ada

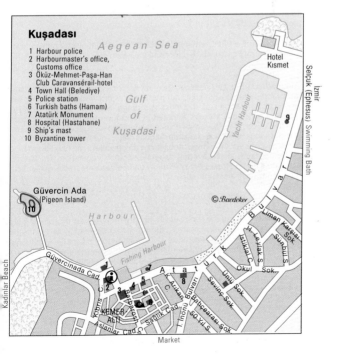

Kuşadası

1 Harbour police
2 Harbourmaster's office, Customs office
3 Öküz-Mehmet-Paşa-Han Club Caravansérail-hotel
4 Town Hall (Belediye)
5 Police station
6 Turkish baths (Hamam)
7 Atatürk Monument
8 Hospital (Hastahane)
9 Ship's mast
10 Byzantine tower

Aegean Sea

Gulf of Kuşadası

Hotel Kısmet

İzmir
Selçuk (Ephesus) Swimming Bath

Yacht Harbour

Güvercin Ada (Pigeon Island)

© Baedeker

Harbour

Kadınlar Beach

Güvercinada Cad.

Fishing Harbour

Atat...

Liman Cad.
Kâhşlar Sok.
Sunbul S.
İstiklal C.
Okul Sok.
Arükan Cad.
Sevinç Sok.
Ünlü Sok.
Babperası Sok.
Saviç Sok.
İnönü Bulvarı
50.Yıl S.

KEMER ALTI
Barbaros Cad.
Kıbrıs Cad.
Aslanlar Cad.
Sağlık Cad.

Market

Kuşadası, one of the oldest holiday resorts in Turkey

tower which is all that remains of a 13th c. Byzantine castle (which later became a pirate's lair). The wall around the island dates only from the early 19th c.

Samsun Dağı
*National Park

The road south from Kuşadası, heading for Söke, soon turns inland and runs south-east through hilly country. To the right (south) can be seen the most westerly outlier of the Messogis range, Samsum Dağı, known in antiquity as Mount Mykale. Situated between the Menderes depression and the Güzelçamlı (Karaova) coastal plain, Samsun Dağı (1237m/4060ft) juts out like a peninsula into the Aegean Sea. Thanks to its marble and chrystalline schists the ridge, notched by steep valleys, has an abundance of springs and so is covered by relatively lush vegetation. On the in-accessible upper slopes, today virtually uninhabited, are traces of fortifica-tions built to protect the adjacent Strait of Samos, and the remains of monasteries. The peninsuala is now a national park the official name of which is the "Dilek Yarımadası Milli Parkı".

Vegetation

Attempts at farming the peninsula in modern times have almost invariably been thwarted, as a result of which the entire 11,000ha/27,200 acre National Park retains its original vegetation. Dense Mediterranean maquis covers up to 60% of the hillsides, in the midst of which grow stands of holm oak (quercus ilex; up to 10m/33ft in height), an evergreen tree with small smooth edged leathery leaves, with furry undersides and shiny dark green tops, a rarity in the eastern Mediterranean. The remainder is tall forest, with plantains, cypresses, laurels, oleander and maple, but with pinus brutia (brutic pine) flourishing in lower-lying areas and pinus nigra (black pine) higher up.

In addition to wild horses and wild boar, porcupines and rock squirrels are among the varied fauna of the Park.

Erdek

See Bandırma

Ereğli (Konya Ereğlisi)   K 6

Central Anatolia
Province: Konya
Altitude: 1020m/3348ft
Population: 74,000

Unlike Karadeniz and Marmara Ereğlisi, Ereğli (Konya Ereğlisi), a country
town lying off the major routes in the steppe country between Konya and
Adana, has no special attractions, only a small museum of local history on
the main street. Although the area around Ereğli was already part of
Lykaonia, in antiquity the town was first called Kybistra and later Herakleia
of Cappadocia. There was a fortress here in Byzantine times, which the
Arabs captured in 806. Being strategically situated near the route through
the Cilician Gates, Haroun al-Rachid and Halif al-Mamum fortified the town
again in the 9th c. For a time Herakleia belonged to Little Armenia (1211)
before being ceded to the Seljuks and then falling to the Mongols. In 1467 it
passed to the Ottomans as part of the Karaman Empire.

Situation and
Characteristics

Sights

Among the few buildings of interest in the town, apart from the Ulu Cami
with its prayer hall embellished with ancient columns, are the Ali Ağa
Mescidi of 1551 and two Ottoman caravanserais.

Surroundings

On either side of the Konya road north-west of the town, in the vicinity of Ak
Göl (altitude: 1005m/3300ft), stretches an area of swamps and small lakes.
During the Ice Age large parts of central Anatolia were covered by vast
freshwater lakes which steadily shrank as the climate became warmer and
drier some 15,000 years ago. Ak Göl (White Lake; usually a stretch of
freshwater 20km/12½ miles long, 8km/5 miles wide and up to 4m/39ft deep)
is a relic of one such Ice Age lake, as are the rest of the swamps around
Ereğli. About 20km/12½ miles west of Ereğli, near Düden Köyü, on the
south side of Ak Göl, there is a small circular lake (Düden Gölü) with
swamps inhabited by countless bird species; Dalmatian and white pelicans, cranes, flamingos, numerous varieties of herons, and white-headed
ducks may all be seen.

Ak Göl

Ak Hüyük (White Mound), a long, narrow travertine ridge 40m/131ft high,
reminiscent of Cihanbeyli, rises on the southern edge of the Ereğli swamps
near the village of Ciller, about 12km/8 miles north of Ereğli. Hot sulphur
springs erupt on the crest.

Ak Hüyük

Çiftehan's Seljuk name (from Çifte Han, meaning "Twin Caravanserais") is
a reminder of the two hans which once stood here on the caravan route
from central Anatolia to Cilicia and Syria some 75km/47 miles east of Ereğli.
Earlier still, as also today, Çiftehan was known primarily as a spa. The hot
springs (altitude: 1020m/3348ft), called Aquae Calidae by the Romans,
were already in use in Hittite and Phrygian times. The baths apparently fell
into disrepair late in the Byzantine era but were restored by the Seljuks.
From this period date two public steam-baths, each divided into separate
sections for men and women. The mineral-rich spring water (temperature

Çiftehan

50°C/122°F) is used to treat rheumatism and skin complaints. In addition to its thermal springs the area around Çiftehan has long been famous for its rock and mineral deposits. That these too were known about in antiquity is shown by a Hittite hieroglyphic inscription found near Bolkar Maden, 15km/9 miles south-west, where there was a silver mine ("maden" being Turkish for mine). 50km/31 miles further north, near Bereketli Madeni (now Çamardi), there are also copper mines.

İvriz   Aydınkent (İvriz) lies about 16km/10 miles south-east of Ereğli in a fertile stretch of valley below Orta Dağ in the foothills of the 3240m/10,634ft high Bolkar Dağı. A little to the south of the village, near where the İvriz is dammed, there is a 10m/33ft high rock face with a Late Hittite-Aramaic relief dating from the second half of the 7th c. B.C. It shows King Warpalawa of Tuwanuwa worshipping the plant god Tarhunt.

Ulukışla   The small town of Ulukışla (Great Barracks) owes its name to the massive Öküz Mehmet Paşa Kervansarayı which, built by Mehmet Paşa between 1566 and 1574, was probably used to garrison troops for a time. The remains of a Seljuk caravanserai, Kamereddin Hanı, can be seen north-west of Ulukışla at Ulukışla Geçidi (altitude: 1467m/4815ft) near Cakmak (Çayhan).

Erzincan   P 4

Eastern Anatolia (northern East Taurus)
Province: Erzincan
Altitude: 1200m/3938ft
Population: 91,000

Situation and Importance   Although with a long history Erzincan, in the north-eastern Taurus, has the look of a new town, its location in the tectonic depression zone of the main north Anatolian fault having repeatedly proved its undoing. Despite being devastated time and again by earthquakes (1471 large areas destroyed, 1667 half the city in ruins, 1782 more than 10,000 inhabitants killed), Erzincan has always been rebuilt. After the severe earthquake of 1939, which cost 15,600 lives and left virtually nothing standing, the city was re-sited a little further to the north. The last severe 'quake occurred in 1991. This too caused great damage and 1000 people lost their lives. Reconstruction is well under way. Erzincan – once known for its silverware – is a road and rail junction with modest food processing (sugar) and textile industries. Because of the altitude cold, snowy winters and cool summers typify the climate of the region.

History   Little information is available about Erzincan's early history. It is situated not far from the Old Armenian city of Erek and claims to be the site of the principal temple of the Old Persian god Anahita (some of whose characteristics are shared by the Greek goddess Artemis). According to tradition the cult statue was taken from the temple by Cleopatra, wife of Tigranes the Great (95–55 B.C.). Until the 12th c. Erzincan seems to have been a town of no great importance. Under the Seljuk Suleiman Kutulmuşoğlu I (1071) it passed to the Mengüçoğlu dynasty and in 1243 was destroyed in the fighting between the Seljuks (Keykusrev II) and Mongols. Between 1916 and 1918 it was under Russian occupation.

Surroundings

*Altıntepe   Altıntepe ("Silver Hill") is one of the most impressive Urartian sites in eastern Anatolia, occupying a prominent position on the plain 20km/12 miles east of Erzincan. A chance find of some bronze objects during the building of the railway in 1938 led to the discovery of the site. Working on

Urartian settlement on the Altintepe

the citadel between 1959 and 1966, Turkish archaeologists identified two levels of Urartian occupation (8/7th c. B.C.), uncovering the foundations of a palace and a square temple, with walls almost 5m/16ft thick, dedicated to the Urartian god Chaldi. Royal tombs containing a large array of funeral gifts (weapons, jewellery, horses' tackle, chariot parts, carved ivory, etc.) were found on the upper slopes of the hill. The complex, encircled by two walls, seems to have been abandoned at about the turn of the 7th and 6th centuries. Little is so far known about its apparently violent end.

The dimensions (14×14m/46×46ft) and construction of the temple foundations (dressed masonry with bastion-like projections at the corners) identify it as a prototype of the Urartian "Susi" temples, with an altar in front of the entrance. Destroyed in the early 7th c. B.C., it also had a colonnaded hall. The palace, adjacent to but not aligned with the temple, dates from the late 7th c. Traces of wall paintings were still visible in the large hall when it was first found but have since completely disappeared.

Kemah

Thought to have been called Ani in earlier times, the fortress and small village of Kemah are situated in the valley of the Firat Nehri west of Erzincan, on the river's southern bank. There are remains of an octagonal fortress dating from the Byzantine period, which was when the name Kemach (or Kamakha) first came into use. Kemah was still walled right up into the 19th c., the citadel being the seat of a local derebey. Relics of an older settlement (Kemah Kalesi) are found on the high rock plateau east of the present village. Ani was the third most important cult centre for the worship of the Old Armenian gods and at the start of the Christian era was the site of a temple-fort belonging to King Aramard. There are two interesting mausoleums, Gazi Türbesi and the octagonal Sultan Melik Türbesi (1191), also the Gülablibey Camii (1192), its roof supported by arches carried on twelve wooden columns.

Erzurum

Kemaliye

The district town of Kemaliye, formerly known as Eğin, was settled originally by Armenian colonists from Waspurakan. Moltke described it in 1838
as one of the most beautiful towns in Asia.

*Tercan

Tercan, another district town, about 95km/57 miles east of Erzincan, used to
be called Mamahatun, after a Seljuk princess of that name, an ally of
Saladin's. Her splendid mausoleum of finely dressed stone, endowed in
1192 by Prince Sesi Muffada ("Cross Eye") of Ahlat (on Lake Van), stands in
an old cemetery east of the town (sarcophagus in the prayer hall/crypt).
Around the türbe are a circular courtyard and wall, the latter with a fine
ornamented portal and eleven niches containing more sarcophagi. Steps
go up to a wall-top walk. Across from the mausoleum, to the west, can be
seen the sturdy outline of the 13th c. Mama Hatun Kervanserayı (Tercan
Hanı), now in process of restoration. The kitchen quarters, guardrooms and
stabling are all clearly recognisable. Keys to both buildings are kept in the
town hall. The staff of the constabulary diagonally opposite the caravanserai are also extremely helpful.

Erzurum   R 4

East Anatolia (northern East Taurus)
Province: Erzurum. Altitude: 1950m/6400ft (citadel hill)
Population: 241,000

Situation and
**Importance

Erzurum claims with every justification to be the economic and cultural
capital of eastern Turkey, with a univeristy founded in 1958. Surrounded by
mountains rising to more than 3000m/10,000ft, snow covered until well
into summer (to the south the 3176m/10,424ft Palandöken Dağları, to the
north Dumlu Dağ, 3169m/10,400ft, and to the north-east the Kargapazarı
Dağları, 3129m/10,269ft), the town lies on the Silk Road from Persia to the
Black Sea. The climate is distinctly continental, with very long very cold
winters and correspondingly short very hot summers. In the last couple of
decades a thriving food processing industry has developed, but the region
generally is one of grassland on which livestock are reared. Such manufacturing industry as the town possesses is of very recent origin. Located
about 40km/25 miles north of Erzerum on Dumlu Dağı is the source of the
Fırat Nehri, or Karasu as it is known, a major northern tributary of the
2800km/1740 mile long Euphrates. The Karasu flows west and then south
for 460km/286 miles before joining forces with the 772km/480 mile long
Murat Nehri near Keban, both rivers now disgorging into the Keban Dam
(see Elazığ).

History

Erzurum's history can be traced with any certainty only from the 4th c. A.D.
at which time it was part of the Old Armenian Empire. When this collapsed
the town found itself cast in the role of easternmost bastion of Byzantium,
coming under seige by the Sassanids. The subsequent armistice left Erzerum in Byzantine hands. In the 5th c. Theodosius II transformed the town
into a frontier fortress and bishopric (held briefly by the Sassanids for four
years from 502). In 632 a special synod was held in Erzerum in an unsuccessful attempt to unite the Orthodox and Armenian Churches. In 655
(until 751) the town was lost to the Arabs, being renamed Karnoy Kalak. It
was so badly damaged in the fighting that the population had to be resettled in Thrace. Later, fleeing from the Seljuks who had been making incursions into the area since 1047, the inhabitants of a town called Arsan(?)
took refuge in Karnoy Kalak, dubbing it Arsan i-Rum (Roman Arsan), from
which the present name Erzerum is derived.
The Mongol invasions in the mid 13th c. brought the town's development
to a temporary halt and for a period in 1400 it was the base from which
Tamerlane mounted his campaigns against Bayazit I. In 1522 it was absorbed into the Ottoman Empire. By now called Erzerum its strategic role as
an eastern frontier town did little to enhance its prosperity. When the

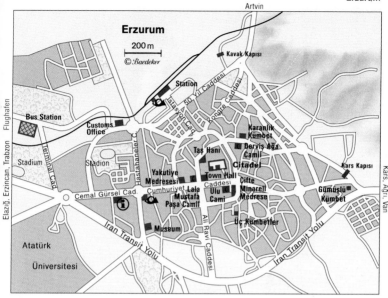

Anatolian railway finally arrived in 1935, Erzurum was little more than a minor station on the line. In 1919 the city was the venue of the first Turkish National Congress, which saw Mustafa Kemal (Atatürk) installed as leader of the national independence movement. Despite many earthquakes (including the severe 'quake in 1939 when about 40,000 people lost their lives), a considerable number of historic buildings have survived.

Sights

Çifte Minareli Medrese   Erzurum
Double Minaret – Koran School

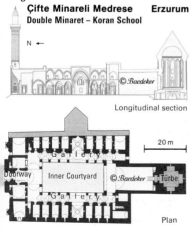

Longitudinal section

Doorway   Inner Courtyard   © Baedeker   Türbe

20 m

Plan

North-west of the Yaku-tiye Medresesi, in a side street off the main thoroughfare, there is a small museum in the house where Atatürk stayed in the summer of 1919 at the time of the first National Congress (memorabilia; open: daily 9am–5pm).

Atatürk Müzesi

Some uncertainty surrounds the date of the Çifte Minareli Medrese, otherwise a typical example of a Seljuk Koranic school. Held by some scholars to have been built by the Seljuk Sultan Alaeddin Keyku-bad II in 1253, more

**Çifte Minareli Medrese

Riding competition in Erzurum

recent research suggests it dates from 1291 at the earliest. The medrese's patron was the Mongol princess Hüdavend Padişah Hatun whose simply decorated türbe can be seen at the rear.

Built of dark volcanic tufa, the medrese now houses a museum. Note the partial relief decoration in the form of ornamental borders, a tree with a double eagle and a vase of leaves. Around the galleried inner court (students' cells) are four iwans linked by arcades.
Two fluted brick minarets flank the exceptionally fine ornamented entrance portal. The princess's türbe is in the form of a twelve-sided drum raised on a square base and capped by a conical roof.

Erzurum Müzesi   Erzurum Museum, in the south-west of the town not far from the Atatürk memorial, has archaeological and ethnographic sections. Both are of interest (open: Thur.–Sun. 8am–noon and 1–5pm).

Gümüşlü Kümbet   As its name implies, the octagonal 13th c. "Silver Mausoleum", situated some 250m/275yd east of the Çifte Minareli Medrese, was once clad in silver (the Russians are said to have stripped it).

Karanlık Kümbet   Decorated with twelve blind arcades the so-called "Dark Mausoleum" (1378) of the Ilkhan Emir Sadrettin Türbeg stands near the Derviş Ağa Camii in the north-east part of the Old Town.

Kongre Salonu   On the north side of the Old Town, 300m/330yd north-east of the Taş Hanı, is the hall where the first Turkish National Congress convened in 1919. Although now a school it is open to visitors (workdays 9am–5pm).

Lala Mustafa Paşa Camii   This little mosque gracing the town centre park was probably designed in 1563 by the famous Ottoman architect Sinan. It was commisioned by the then governor Lala Mustafa Paşa, better known as the conqueror of Cyprus.

The Çifte Minareli Medrese was named after its two minarets

Jewellery can be bought both at the Taş Hanı and in numerous shops around the Georgian Gate Mosque (reached via the road running north from the Çifte Minareli Medrese). Erzerum's small artisan quarter lies to the north-west of the mosque.

Jewellery bazaar

Sections of the basalt city walls can be seen below the citadel hill (remains of a fort); there are more fragments near the stadium.

City walls

About 250m/275yd north-east of the Yakutiye Medresesi, lower down the hill, stands the two-storeyed Rüstem Paşa Kervansarayı, endowed in the 16th c. by Süleiman the Magnificent's Grand Vizier, Rüstem Paşa. It now houses an array of shops and craft workshops where Oltu taş (jet) jewellery is made and sold.

Taş Hanı

The "Three Kümbets", all dating from the 13th or early 14th c., are located in a small park 200m/220yd or so to the rear of the Çifte Minareli Medrese. Much the most splendid of the three is the octagonal Emir Sultan Türbesi, with a conical roof, stalactitic mouldings and handsome reliefs (snake, eagle, rabbits' heads).

Üç Kümbetier

The city's oldest building apart from the Çifte Minareli Medrese is the Ulu Cami, a plain seven-aisle mosque with pillared hall and covered courtyard. Constructed in 1179 it was badly damaged in the 1939 earthquake but has since been carefully and accurately restored.

Ulu Cami

Situated a short distance west of the Lala Mustafa Paşa Camii this delightful medrese and equally delightful tiled minaret were built in about 1308 by the Mongol Prince Uljaitu, whose türbe can be seen at the rear. The main entrance is beautifully decorated with reliefs (tree of life, eagle, lions). The lovely interior is at present barred to visitors while the medrese is turned into a museum.

**Yakutiye Medresesi

303

Erzurum

*Citadel   Erzerum's citadel (wall-top walk) stands guard on its hill in the centre of the Old Town. Originally constructed by the Emperor Theodosius, it was rebuilt by Süleiman the Magnificent in 1555, and at various other times. Inside the walls are a small 12th c. mosque with a conical roof and a free-standing minaret. In the 19th c. the minaret acquired a Neo-Baroque gallery complete with a clock presented by Queen Victoria. Known thereafter as the Saat Kulesi (Clock Tower), the minaret can be climbed.

Surroundings

*Haho (Hahul)   Haho, site of a 10th c. monastery, is reached by an unsurfaced track (9km/5½ miles) branching left off the Artvin road a good 20km/12½ miles north of Tortum. Crossing the Tortum Çayı by a Georgian pointed arch bridge, the track continues west along the Vihik Deresi to the village of Bağbaşı (bear left once in the valley, near Küçük Dereköy). Beyond the village's administrative office, to the north-east and some 300m/985ft further uphill, stands Haho's famous yellow sandstone monastery church. Originally dedicated to the Virgin, it is now in use as a mosque. The monastery itself, of which very little survives, was founded in the 10th c. by the Armenian King David III. Fragments of painting can be seen in the apse which has two side chapels, and some ornate carving still adorns the dome (deer and eagles, lion and bull).

*Öşk   About 24km/15 miles north of Tortum, beyond the Derekapı gorge (on the Tortum Çayı), the ruins of a Georgian fortress, Dikyar Kalesi, can be seen to the right, perched on a rocky outcrop above the village of Uncular. 5km/3 miles further on a turning to the left leads west for another 5km/3 miles to the little village of Çamlıyamaç and the ruined monastery church of Öşk. The huge cruciform church with its dome carried on four free-standing columns, belonged to one of the most important of the region's many monasteries. Note in particular the ornately decorated octagonal column in the south gallery. The church, its façade embellished with delightful reliefs, was erected in 961. Behind it are the sprawling remains of the former monastery.

Oltu   This district town, about 115km/71 miles north-east of Erzurum, grew up on the site of the Old Georgian and Byzantine fortress of Oukhti. Ruins of a church survive from this period. Also of interest are the town's Arslan Paşa Camii of 1664 and the İçkale Camii (inside the fort). The jet for which Oltu is famous, a deep black fossilised resin known as Oltu tas (also called "black diamond"), is found in the vicinity of Oltu Gölü north-east of the town. The deposits lie 150m/500ft below the surface at altitudes between 1800 and 2000m/5900 and 6500ft. The resin is plastic when in situ, hardening through contact with the air, and so is stored underground prior to processing. More than 300 craftsmen produce Oltu taş jewellery in the villages around Oltu alone, carrying on a tradition going back about 250 years.

Palandöken   There is good skiing in the Palandöken Dağları about 4km/2½ miles south of
Dağları   Erzurum. A ski-lift next to the Kayak Evi sports hotel (groups only) on the city's southern outskirts (alt. 2200m/7220ft) ascends to a mountain station at 3050m/10,000ft, just below the 3125m/10,256ft summit. The season runs from December to June (lift in operation Dec.–Apr., weekends and public holidays; otherwise for groups only, by arrangement).

Penek   About 40km/25 miles north-east of Oltu, just before Akşar, a side road heads north for a kilometre or so to the little village of Penek, on the far side of a bridge crossing the Kamlı Su. Penek's round church, badly damaged in the Russo-Turkish War, was probably built in the 7th c. Alterations are known to have been made during the reign of Prince Ardanase (881–923) and under Bishop Kwirike. The centrally-planned church, dedicated to a martyr, has four apses in a quatrefoil arrangement with small chapels in

The cruciform church of Öşk, surrounded by the old monastery ruins

between, and a gallery around the first floor. 2km/1¼ miles further up the valley is another ruined, centrally-planned church, Harap Kilise. An uphill walk of about two hours leads from there to Salomon Kalesi, a severely dilapidated fort with two chapels (remains of wall paintings).

On the way from Erzerum to Tortum (some 52km/30 miles north), the road climbs over the 2120m/6958ft high Güzelyayla Pass. The village of Güzelyayla, to the left on the hillside at the top of the pass, contains an Armenian church (Artsathi), founded in the 5th c. but rebuilt several times. 13km/8 miles beyond Tortum is a crossroads where a minor road branches off east to Oltu, The road in the opposite direction follows a mountain valley westwards to the small village of Tortum Kale where stands another very dilapidated Georgian fort, Tortum Kalesi.

*Tortum

Beyond Tortum, the Tortum Çayı valley extends northwards for about 60km/37 miles to the southern extremity of Tortum Gölü. This 8km/5 mile long lake, a kilometre wide, flanked by steep mountains on either hand, was formed naturally by a gigantic landslip blocking the valley. Probably this happened towards the end of the last Ice Age about 10,000–15,000 years ago; but because there are local villagers who claim to remember their great-grandparents talking about the cataclysmic event, some people believe the lake to be no more then 250 years old.

*Tortum
Şelalesi

At the north end of the lake, just before reaching the hydro-electric station, a little road on the right crosses the lake outflow and bends left to where there is a splendid view of the Tortum Çayı waterfalls, cascading down a 50m/164ft high escarpment to more rapids below. The landslip which created Tortum Gölü was also responsible for four smaller lakelets trapped by the debris. They are full of trout.

Eskişehir   F 4

North-western central Anatolia
Province: Eskişehir
Altitude: 788m/2586ft
Population: 413,000

Situation and Characteristics

Eskişehir lies at the western end of the Eskişehir Ovası, nestling in the large basin which forms the upper Porsuk Çayı valley, below the southernmost chain of Pontic mountains. The town has modern industries, first developed in the 19th c., including Turkey's largest sugar factory and a locomotive engineering plant, This industrial headstart in pre-Republic days has contributed greatly to Eskişehir's prosperity. There are thermal baths in the southern part of the town.

History

Eskişehir is an Ottoman creation. Its predecessor, ancient Dorylaion, occupied a hill about 3km/2 miles north of the present town. Just about the only relic of the ancient city is the name Eskişehir itself, meaning "old town", such few places of interest as there are today being from a much later period. Recent research suggests that Dorylaion was founded by the Phrygians in about 700 B.C.). Despite extensive excavation of the citadel hill (Sar Üyük/Şehir Hüyük; 3km/2 miles north-east of the railway station), virtually nothing has been found. The town is known to have been an important frontier fortress in Byzantine times, several fierce battles being fought in the vicinity. Eventually destroyed and abandoned, Dorylaion was rebuilt on a new site by Manuel I Comnenus (1143–80).

Sights

The Alaeddin Camii, a Seljuk mosque, is thought to have been endowed by the Sultan Alaeddin Keykubad in 1263. The Kurşunlu Külliye, located opposite the Ak Çami in the southern part of the town, is attributed to the celebrated Ottoman architect Sinan. In addition to an early Ottoman "lead mosque" the complex comprises the Kurşunlu Medrese, a kitchen for the poor and a caravanserai.

Surroundings

İnönü

The little town of İnönü, about 36km/22 miles west of Eskişehir, has a 14th c. mosque. Not far from the town are the Tutluca Tepe cave dwellings. The İnönü family – İsmet İnönü was Atatürk's successor as Turkish president – take their name from here.

Karaca Şehir (Dorylaion)

Between 1143 and 1180, after "old" Dorylaion had been abandoned, presumably destroyed in battles between the Seljuks and Byzantium, the Byzantine Emperor Manuel I Comnenus built a new town about 6km/4 miles further to the south-west. Taken by the Ottomans in 1400 and renamed Karaca Hisar, it was sacked by the Mongols in 1402. Afterwards Karaca Hisar became increasingly deserted, the inhabitants dispersing into the surrounding villages. It was one of these villages which grew to become Eskişehir.

Meerschaum Mines

A good 20km/12½ miles east of Eskişehir a minor turning north off the Ankara road leads to the İmişehir meerschaum mines (2km/1¼ miles), Türkmentokat (3km/2 miles) and Karatepe (8km/5 miles). At İmişehir, lumps of meerschaum (magnesium-silicate) are extracted from small pits, the shafts of which go down about 8m/26ft. Once highly prized throughout the world for making tobacco pipes and cases, sales of meerschaum (Turkish "lüle taşı" i.e. pipe-bowl stone) have slumped in recent years. Compared with wooden pipes, meerschaum pipes are light and moisture-absorbent, resulting in a cooler, drier smoke. Compressed meerschaum dust, often seen masquerading as the real thing, is considerably heavier and virtually worthless.

More meerschaum deposits, some of the world's most important at one time, are found near Alpu, 35km/22 miles west of Eskişehir on the Porsuk Çayı.

The district town of Mihalliçik is said to contain the tomb of the Karamanid poet Yunus Emre (1249–1322).

Mihalliçik

The ruins of Pessinus lie about 11km/7 miles south of Sivrihisar, near the village of Ballıhisar. Founded by the Phrygians, Pessinus was later the centre of a powerful theocratic state. It was the capital of the Galatian Tolistoagi (277–244 B.C.) and boasted an important shrine dedicated to the cult of Asia Minor's principal goddess Cybele and her young lover Attis. According to the myth, Attis castrated himself, and eunuch priests played a major role in the cult. After 230 B.C. the Celtic Galatians took over the sanctuary. Right up until the banning of such cults in the reign of Theodosius I (379–395), Roman generals would often patronise this well-known shrine. In 183 B.C. Pessinus became a possession of Pergamum and under the Attalids was endowed with splendid temples and colonnades. After 700 the town fell more and more into ruin. There is now little to see, though the acropolis, some remains of a theatre (to the east beside an ancient drainage ditch), an odeion, a temple of Cybele and a necropolis are still recognisable. Fragments of a processional way lie scattered in the river bed.

*Pessinus

About 30km/19 miles south-east of Eskişehir, the site of the once important Phrygian town of Nakoleia crowns a 120m/394ft hill a short distance south of the district town of Seyitgazi. Surrounded by the buildings of a former Dervish convent are a medrese and türbe, burial place of the legendary Arab warlord and national hero Seyit Gazi, the scourge of Byzantium, whose Arab hordes roamed Asia Minor in the early 8th c. plundering, robbing and killing. Reputedly a giant, his sarcophagus measures more than 4m/13ft in length. Next to it is a white sarcophagus traditionally held to be that of a Byzantine princess who, having fallen in love with Seyit Gazi, accidently caused his death, afterwards taking her own life. In fact he was killed near Afyon in 719 while campaigning against Constantinople, his inamorata apparently dying of grief. In about 1250 Haçi Bektaş, founder of the Bektaç Order of Dervishes, built a Moorish-style convent (enlarged and restored by Selim I in 1510) around the tombs. The mausoleum is still a place of pilgrimage for the Anatolian faithful.

*Seyitgazi

The convent, centre of the politically influential Bektaş Order, was closed on Atatürk's instructions in 1925. There is now a small museum with an interesting and wide-ranging display. At the upper end of the approach to the Battal Bazi Külliyesi stands a large Byzantine church, directly behind which are two mosques and the türbe. Opposite are the monks' quarters with the kitchen, refectory and exercitium rooms.

Situated just off the main Ankara road south-east of Eskişehir (93km/ 58 miles), Sivrihisar occupies a most delightful setting at the foot of a rugged volcanic massif (Çal Dağ). It is built on the site of ancient Justinianopolis, a walled city founded by Justinian around 553. There are a number of Ottoman buildings in the shadow of a ruined Byzantine fort. In 1882 the town's Armenian quarter was burned down, being replaced in part by grid-pattern streets. In the northern part of the town stands a large 19th c. Armenian church (now converted to a power station) with an inscription in Armenian on the façade.

Sivrihisar

The jewel in Sivrihisar's crown, however, is its 13th c. Seljuk mosque (1247) with a timber beam ceiling carried on 62 wooden columns. Based on the plan of an Arab house, with an open, arcaded inner court, this type of mosque (kufa), lacking the usual forecourt and ablutions fountain, is unique to Anatolia. The prayer hall is arranged transversely with the entrance and prayer niche on the longer sides. All the woodwork is

*Kufa-type Mosque

Historic buildings in Seyitgazi

superbly carved. Numerous ancient capitals are incorporated into the building. Colourful paintings with Turkoman tent motifs are another special feature of the mosque. The timberwork and decoration is all fastened without the aid of tenons or glue (kündekari technique). Among other sights of interest in the town is the Gazi Alemşah Türbesi, a typical Seljuk pillar tomb dating from 1308.

A few kilometres north-east of Sivrihisar the Ankara road passes close to Nasrettinhoca, birthplace of the Turkish "Eulenspiegel" (see Famous People).

Fethiye   E 7

South-west coast (Mediterranean)
Province: Muğla
Altitude: 0–50m/0–165ft
Population: 20,000

Situation and Importance

The port of Fethiye, chief town of its district, lies on the Lycian coast some 150km/95 miles south-east of the provincial capital of Muğla. The gulf, dotted with numerous islets, is closed by the little island known since 1936 as Cavaliere, the Island of Knights. The town, previously called Meğri or Makri, was renamed Fethiye when Turkey became a republic, in honour of an airman, Fethi Bey, who crashed here. It was devasted by an earthquake in 1856, and after a further earthquake in 1957 much of it had to be rebuilt. As a result it is now a modern town with a long seafront promenade and a lively bazaar. In recent years, thanks to its sheltered boating harbour and many beautiful beaches Fethiye has developed into a flourishing holiday resort served by the regional airport of Dalaman (about 50km/30 miles north-west).

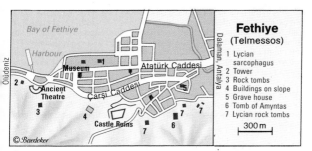

Fethiye occupies the site of ancient Telmessos, an important Lycian city   Telmessos
which was already famed in the time of Croesus for its soothsayers. It is
now difficult after two earthquakes and the subsequent rebuilding to find
any traces of ancient Telmessos in the modern town. The boundaries of the
Hellenistic and Roman towns are no doubt marked out by the almost
vertical rock face to the west, the Roman tombs on the east side of the town
and the Lycian necropolis to the south. The discovery of sarcophagi near
the edge of the modern town indicates the course of the ancient coastline.
On the castle hill, occupied in the Middle Ages by the Knights of St John
and by the Genoese, there are remains of much earlier buildings. The
remains of houses on the north-west side of the hill, with a number of
cisterns and water-supply channels suggest that there was an unwalled
Lycian settlement here, though in a later period the focus of urban life
moved down to the coastal plain. Of the ancient theatre, which was located
and described by the French traveller Charles Texier before the 1856 earthquake , nothing can now be seen but the outline of the cavea (auditorium).

The most striking ancient remains are a number of fine rock tombs of   *Rock tombs
characteristic type, modelled on Lycian timber-built architecture and later
Ionian temple architecture. The main group is in the rock face to the east of
the present built-up area. Particularly notable is the Tomb of Amyntas,
which is dated to the 4th c. B.C.
The little museum in the Town Hall (Belediye) of Fethiye displays material   Museum
from all the main periods of the town's eventful history.

Surroundings

Although now almost completely abandoned, in the 19th c. Levissi (Kaya),   *Kaya
8km/5 miles south of Fethiye, was a town of more than 3000 inhabitants. No   (Levissi)
more than 200 to 300 years old, it stands on the site of ancient Carmylessus.
There was also a settlement here in the Middle Ages (1106), known for its
good harbour. In the 19th c., after neighbouring Makri (Fethiye) had been
devastated, first by the earthquake of 1856 and then by a disasterous fire in
1885, its predominantly Greek inhabitants moved to Levissi where many of
them had summer homes. At the beginning of this century most returned
to Makri. Of those who remained, some left Levissi in 1922 during the
population exchanges and the rest after the 1957 earthquake. The terraces
of large, stone-built, turn-of-the-century European-style houses on the
hillside have a sorry, abandoned air.

Of the many charming bathing-places in the surrounding area the shel-   **Ölüdeniz
tered coastal lagoon of Ölüdeniz (Dead Sea) in Belceğiz Bay (15km/9 miles
south of Fethiye as the crow flies) is undoubtedly the finest, with beaches of
fine sand in an idyllic setting of coastal hills (conservation area). The
growth in tourism has seen this part of the coast become somewhat
overdeveloped in places.

309

Fethiye

Pinara

Pinara, in the hills above the Eşen Ovası south-east of Fethiye, is the site of an exceptionally interesting Lycian necropolis, a honeycomb of more than 900 rock tombs and monolithic house tombs. So inaccessible was the site that the tomb-builders had to be lowered on stages secured with ropes. The monolithic Royal Tomb (with an urban scene in relief inside) is particularly noteworthy, this type of tomb being rare in Lycia. (A local guide should be hired.)

Sidyma

More tombs, also interesting, are found at ancient Sidyma (lower city at 500m/1641ft, acropolis, with small theatre, at 820m/2690ft). The site is about 15km/9 miles south-west of Eşen, near the village of Hisar (gravel road).

*Tlos

The ruins of the ancient city of Tlos are situated in the hills above the Eşen Ovası, about 36km/22 miles east of Fethiye (via Kemer and Yakaköy). Crowning the rounded acropolis hill are the ruins of a Turkish castle, erected over a Lycian fortress. On the east side of the acropolis are remnants of Lycian and Roman walls, with a gate dating from the 2nd c. B.C. Beyond lie the remains of a number of houses, public buildings and other structures from the Lycian, Roman and Byzantine periods. They include cisterns, a stadium, a hall-like edifice (possibly an indoor market), two large baths, an agora, churches, a theatre and a necropolis (Lycian). The Roman town centre (2nd c. B.C.) testifies to the considerable importance of the city in Imperial times. Being tucked away in the mountains the Turkish castle was the stronghold of various "valley princes" (derebeys) and brigands, of whom Kanlı Ali, known as "Bloodthirsty Ali", was the most notorious.

Saklıkent

About 10km/6 miles south of Tlos, a large tributary stream of the Koca Çay emerges from a narrow ravine cut deeply into the karst mountains of the Ak Dağları (karst springs, fish restaurants).

Rock tombs in Pinara resembling honeycombs

Xanthos

At Kınık, some 80km/50 miles south-east of Fethiye, an ancient road leads up to the ruins of Xanthos, rediscovered in the 19th c. by Sir Charles Fellows. Once the capital of the kingdom of Lycia, the city lies in the valley of the River Xanthos (now Eşen Çay), which separates the mountains (Ak Dağ, 3024m/9922ft) from the upland region which falls away towards the coast. Lycia has been called "the oldest republic in the world" – a league of 20 cities governed by a popular assembly and a president. The most notable monuments of Xanthos, its pillar tombs, have no parallel either in Greek or in Oriental art. They first appear in the 6th c. B.C. and disappear from the scene in the middle of the 4th c.

General
*Pillar tombs

In the 7th c. B.C. Xanthos came under the control of the kings of Lydia. In 545 B.C. it was destroyed by the Persians led by Harpagos, and Lycia remained under Persian domination until the end of the 5th c. From the 2nd c. B.C. Xanthos enjoyed a period of renewed prosperity under the Romans.

The road bisects the site from north to south. To the right, inside the walled area, is an inscribed 5.75m/19ft high pillar which recent investigation has shown to be a pillar tomb, originally 9m/30ft high. Round the top was a frieze of warriors, which is now in the Archaeological Museum in İstanbul. The Lycian inscription has not yet been completely deciphered; the Greek inscription extols the exploits of the dead man in Oriental fashion.

Visiting
the site

Immediately south are the Roman agora and two tall pillar tombs. The more northerly of the two is the so-called Harpy Tomb (480 B.C.), a tower-like monolith 5m/16½ft high on a rectangular base. The grave-chamber, with room for a number of urns, was decorated with reliefs (now replaced by casts) depicting two seated figures of women and three standing figures of men being honoured by their relatives, while their souls are being carried off by harpies. This belief in bird-demons which carry the dead up to heaven may be the explanation of the pillar tombs. The pillar tomb to the south is topped by a house-shaped sarcophagus with a pitched roof (probably 4th c. B.C.).

Harpy Tomb

Beyond the Roman theatre and Lycian acropolis, to the left of the road, can be seen the so-called Nereid Monument, an Ionic temple which had rich sculptural decoration (now in the British Museum in London). To the right of the road is the Hellenistic city gate. The city walls, considerable stretches of which are still visible, probably date originally from the 3rd c. B.C.; they were later renewed, incorporating the Roman acropolis, and were again rebuilt in Byzantine times.

*Nereid
Monument
City walls

To the north of the Nereid Monument are the ruins of a Byzantine church, and beyond this, to the east of the north end of the road, the Roman acropolis. On the summit of the hill are the ruins of a large Byzantine monastery. On a spur of rock on the north-east side of the hill is the well-preserved Acropolis Pillar (mid 4th c. B.C.), a limestone monolith 4.75m/16ft high with a three-stage top section. On the top is a band of marble 1.13m/44in high enclosing the 2.28m/7½ft grave-chamber, which is partly hewn from the interior of the pillar. Below the pillar are three rock tombs with splayed window-like façades.
There are also a number of small rock tombs outside the city (Lycian sarcophagi, with high-pitched lids often decorated with reliefs).

Roman acropolis

5km/3 miles south of Xanthos, reached by a side road branching off 1km/ ¾ mile north-west of Kınık, is the Letoon, an important Lycian sanctuary excavated from 1962 onwards. The remains include temples of Leto, Artemis and Apollo and a theatre. A trilingual inscription found here made an important contribution to the decipherment of the Lycian language.

Letoon

*Patara

About 15km/9 miles south of Kınık lie the remains of ancient Patara, once an important city in the Lycian League and later, according to legend, the birthplace of St Nicholas of Myra (see Kaş, Surroundings). There was still a port here in Byzantine times. Outside the area of the city are a Roman and a Lycian necropolis. The city itself is entered through a triple-arched gate of about A.D. 100. The theatre (2nd c. A.D.) is excellently preserved.

Patara has very good sandy beaches, also hotels and a National Park.

Finike

See Kaş

Gaziantep   N 6

Western south-east Anatolia   **See warning page 7**
Province: Gaziantep
Altitude: 800m/2625ft
Population: 628,000

Situation and
Importance

On the east side of the Maraş trench (the northern continuation of the Jordan trench between Antakya and Maraş) a 500m/1640ft high step fault in the form of a wall of intrusive rock with a covering layer of Tertiary limes and marls, marks the boundary of the gently undulating Gaziantep plateau. At the centre lies Gaziantep itself, the provincial capital and economic hub of the region. Sprawled in the shadow of its mighty fortress crowning an enormous hüyük (settlement mound), Gaziantep is a modern industrial city. Around it the countryside is given over predominantly to tobacco growing and groves of fruit and nut trees, pistachio nuts and olives in particular.

History

As the perennially disputed frontier region between Asia Minor and Syria, over which many different armies have fought, the area around Gaziantep has had a chequered history. In the late Hittite period it was the site of an important settlement which fell to the Assyrians during Sargon's reign. Thereafter in antiquity the city was overshadowed by Doliche 10km/6 miles to the north-west (see below), coming to dominate the region only in the Byzantine period. Known by this time as Ayntap (Good Spring), it was held between 1071 and 1098 by the Seljuks who, in place of an earlier fortress built by the Emperor Justinian, constructed the citadel. In 1097 Ayntap was in Crusader hands. It suffered badly during the Egyptian occupation in 1832–40 (Mehmet Ali). From 1918 to 1921 it was under first British and then French military administration, resistance to which earned Antep the honorific title "Gazi" (Gazi Antep, i.e. "Warrior" Antep). There are no notable antiquities in the city.

Sights

Arkeolojik Müze

The archaeological museum in İstasyon Caddesi has finds excavated at Zincirli, Karkamış and Sakçaközü; also an extensive collection of Old Near Eastern cylinder and stamp seals.

Ömerije Camii

This interesting 11th c. mosque is found on Öğuzeli Caddesi, the road out of the city to the south-west.

*Citadel

The well preserved citadel from Seljuk times occupies the site of an earlier Justinian fortress (6th c.) on the northern edge of the Old City. The ancient

Gaziantep: the well-maintained citadel

Tell Halaf (hüyük) on which it stands is known to have been settled as early as about 3500 B.C. The Byzantine fortress, inside the walls of which there were also houses, is said to have been built with the proceeds of sale of a valuable piece of jewellery belonging to the Emperor's sister.

Surroundings

The district town of Araban, on the southern edge of the Altıntaş Ovası, was earlier known as Altıntaş, from a village to the west, Eski Altıntaş, near to which (i.e. south) is located Altıntaş Kalesi, a medieval fortress now in very poor condition.

Araban

About 10km/6 miles north-west of Gaziantep near the village of Dülük are the sparse remains of Gaziantep's ancient rival Doliche, which until 637 far exceeded Gaziantep in importance. The site of a temple to Jupiter Dolichenus, Doliche was later made a bishopric, and gave the surrounding area its name, Teluch. After surrendering to the Arabs without a fight, and despite construction of a frontier fortress during the reign of Haroun el Rachid (786–809), the town ceded its dominancy to Ayntap further to the south-east. There are some rock tombs which are worth seeing.

Doliche

Near the moderately-sized town of Kilis some 53km/32 miles south-west of Gaziantep, stands the medieval fortress of Ravanda Kalesi. In the town itself is the Canbolat Bey Külliyesi with a mosque, türbe, old bath house and monastery.

Kilis

In the vicinity of Sakçagöz, a township about 50km/30 miles west of Gaziantep, there are five old settlement mounds, the smallest of which has already yielded the remains of a palace with an ante-room and defensive wall, as well as portal lions, sphinxes and stone blocks carved with reliefs (8th c. B.C.; now in Ankara). In all, twelve levels of occupation were identified, from

Sakçagöz

Georgia

the Stone Age to the 1st c. Excavation of Karahüyük, about 5km/3 miles to the north-east near the village of Gedikli, has revealed a flourishing Early Bronze Age trading settlement with a wealth of finds dating back to the Chalcolithic period.

Tellbasar Kalesi   Perched on a large settlememt mound about 30km/20 miles south-east of Gaziantep, near the township of Til Bahram, can be seen Turbessel Fort. A gate, fragments of wall, and some fortress buildings have survived.

Georgia

See Artvin

Göreme

See Cappadocia

Gordion   G/H 4

Central Anatolia
Province: Ankara
Altitude: 688m/2258ft
Village: Yassıhüyük (population: about 400)

Situation and   The Gordion archaeological site lies about 100km/62 miles south-west of
*Importance   Ankara and 30km/19 miles north-west of Polatlı. By the time archaeologists led by Rodney S. Young of Pennsylvania University (USA) began work in 1953, the River Sakarya had deposited a layer of sediment several metres thick over the ruins of Gordion's lower town. By 1963 169 bronze vessels and 175 bronze fibulae (ornamental brooches) had been unearthed. There was no trace however of the legendary Phrygian treasure, presumed to have been taken by the Cimmerians.

Myth and history   Excavations at Ahlâtlibel (south of Yassıhüyük) show that the area around Gordion was already settled in the Early Bronze Age (2500 B.C.), while a cemetery discovered beneath the Phrygian necropolis suggests a subsequent Hittite presence. The Phrygians are thought to have been one of the so-called Sea Peoples who overran Asia Minor in about 1200 B.C. in a series of invasions. There are references to them in Assyrian sources from around 1100 B.C. when, as the Mushki or Mosher, they settled on both sides of the Kızılırmak, from where they began to threaten their eastern neighbours. Phrygian finds at Gordion date from the mid 9th c. B.C.

The legend of the founding of the Phrygian dynasty and capital has been preserved in Greek sources. A farmer named Gordius, ploughing his fields, was startled when a myriad of birds flocked around his oxen. Keen to learn the meaning of this omen he set out to consult augurs in a nearby town, meeting a beautiful maiden (later his wife) who told him the birds were a sign of his royal destiny and offered herself for his queen. Gordion then drove his ox-cart to the temple where he was immediately greeted by the people as their ruler, an oracle having prophesied that the first person they saw driving thus to the temple would be their king. The appreciative Gordion set up his ox-cart in the temple, attaching the yoke to the shaft with a long elaborately knotted strap, the legendary Gordion Knot, by cutting which Alexander the Great (see Famous People) was later to make history. The most famous Phrygian ruler was King Midas (see Famous People), the

314

Excavations in the Phrygian capital of Gordion

son of Gordius. When the kingdom was overrun by the Cimmerians (between 700 and 670 B.C.) and the Scythians, he committed suicide.

From the rubble of the kingdom of Phrygia emerged the Lydian Empire (Alyattes 615–560 B.C., and Croesus), under the auspices of which Phrygian culture was, for a period, preserved. In 546 B.C. the Persian Archaemids defeated Croesus and built a new settlement at Gordion. This was destroyed by an earthquake around 400 B.C. Rebuilt yet again the city was so devastated by the Galatians in 278 B.C. that thereafter only a village remained.

The elaborate Gordian knot had no visible end and was considered impossible to unravel. According to legend whoever succeeded would become ruler of Asia Minor. When Alexander the Great set up his winter quarters in Gordion in 334/333 B.C., the ambitious general resolved to fulfil the prophecy. Climbing up to Gordius's ox-cart on the citadel hill, he is said to have cut the knot with his sword. But according to the Greek historian Aristobulos Kaşsandreia (c. 300 B.C.), Alexander removed the peg holding the shaft, so freeing the end of the knot.

Gordian knot

Sights

In the upper town archaeologists have unearthed an imposing city gate from the 8th c. B.C.. Preserved to a height of over 9m/29ft it is a testament to the sophistication of Phrygian stone architecture. Other finds from that epoch include the stone foundations of a palace complex, once supporting walls of mud brick on a timber framework. In three of the four megaron-style buildings, with a hearth, ante-room and principal hall, mosaics of different coloured pebbles were found. A second gate dates from the Persian period. Excavation continues.

Acropolis

*Tumuli
Tomb of Gordios

Beyond the village of Yassıhüyük a number of burial mounds flank both sides of the Polatlı road. The so-called Tomb of Gordios, 53m/174ft high with a diameter of 250m/820ft, facing the site's small museum, is the second largest of its kind in Anatolia (after the 69m/226ft high Tumulus of Alyattes at Bin Tepe near Sardes). Having been erected only at the beginning of the 7th c. B.C. at the earliest, the man-made burial mound can hardly be Gordius's tomb, but more probably that of the legendary Midas. On the south-west side a 70m/230ft long passage leads down to the burial chamber, 39m/130ft below the top of the mound. The 5×6m/16×20ft chamber, concealed beneath a mass of limestone blocks, was originally without an entrance. The wooden beam walls and gable roof have survived. The chamber was protected from robbers by a 3m/10ft thick layer of rubble and against damp by 40m/131ft of clay overlaid with gravel. To the left inside the chamber was a bed on which lay the undamaged skeleton of a man, more than 60 years of age and about 1.6m/5ft 3in. tall, his clothes fastened with well-preserved bronze fibulae (of which a total of 175 were found in the burial chamber). Around the walls stood tables laden with rich grave gifts, few of which were of precious metal despite Midas's reputed love of gold.

The other, smaller mounds contain tombs from the period 725 to 550 B.C. The so-called Child's Tomb to the south-east of the museum yielded some rather special treasures including wooden furniture, ivory reliefs and boxwood carvings.

Gümüşhane   P 3

Black Sea region (central East Pontus)
Province: Gümüşhane
Altitude: 1250m/4100ft
Population: 26,000

Situation and Characteristics

Despite its former standing as a summer resort for the wealthy of Trabzon, Gümüşhane is rather a provincial town. Squeezed into the narrow valley of the upper Harşit Çayı, against a backdrop of impressive East Pontus mountain scenery, it has little scope for development. The economically backward and disadvantaged region in which it lies has one of the highest rates of outward migration of any in Turkey. Gümüşhane is located in the midst of a very old mining district. Its name means "silver works".

History

In the 17th c. Gümüşhane was sited 4km/2½ miles south of the present town, nearer to the silver mines. Marco Polo mentions these mines in his "Travels". Lack of firewood for smelting led to their decline in the early 19th c. In 1837 the town consisted of an (upper) Old Town close to the silver mines, and a newer settlement lower down. By 1870 the mines, which had been worked in the time of the Pontic kings as well as of the Roman and Byzantine emperors, were flooded. The deterioration of the Old Town, laid out like an amphitheatre, was hastened by the Russian occupation of 1915.

Surroundings

Bayburt

The garrison town of Bayburt, about 77km/48 miles south-east of Gümüşhane, has been known by several different names in the course of its history. The Armenian Bagratids called it Paipert and the Ottomans (1361) Baiburt. It was here in 1364 that Alexios III defeated the Mongols and where in 1462 Mehmet the Conqueror confronted the Akkoyun Oğulları. Marco Polo stopped briefly in Bayburt on his journey to China. The town was destroyed in 1825 during the Russian invasion, afterwards being rebuilt. It stands on both sides of the Çoruh Nehri in the shadow of its great fortress,

The garrison town of Bayburt at the foot of its castle hill

likewise partly destroyed in 1829. The main mosque, the Ulu Cami, dates from the 16th c. 20km/12 miles to the south-east there are copper mines on a hillside just south of the little town of Maden.

The north Anatolian section of the Silk Road almost certainly passed through Gümüşhane on its way to Trabzon (Trebizond). Xenophon, too, followed this traditional route, the main long-distance "highway" across central Anatolia to the Pontic coast and the Black Sea. It was not by any means the only route however, there being others of which particular caravans made use. Numerous traces of them remain.
The principal route to Trabzon evidently crossed the Zigana Pass; a second went from Erzincan to Sadek, thence right over the Deveboy Tepesi to Maçka.

Caravan routes

The 2390m/7844ft Kopdağı Pass, about 40km/25 miles south-east of Bayburt on the Erzurum road, was once notorious because whole caravans ran the risk of being snowed under and frozen. It affords a distant view of the eastern Anatolian highlands, a series of magnificent mountain chains reaching in some cases well above 2600m/8500ft: to the south the Kop Dağı (2600m/8500ft), to the south-west the Çoşan Dağları (2963m/9725ft), to the west the Ballıtas Tepesi (2903m/9528ft), and to the south-east the Palandöken Dağları (3176m/10,423ft). Also in view is the Aşkale/Erzurum basin.

Kopdağı Geçidi

From Gümüşhane a road goes via the district town of Kelkit to the village of Sadek (about 90km/55 miles south), which at one time was the summer seat of the Comnene Emperors of Trebizond. Some relics of this period survive. High above the village are the ruins of a fortress. Remains of a Roman aqueduct are found nearby.

Sadek

Above the small town of Torul, once known as Ardasa, the ruins of a medieval fortress, Ardasa Kalesi, perch on a ledge just before the Harşit

Torul

317

gorge. Torul is another place where, prior to 1850, silver mines were still being worked. In the valleys and villages between the Çit Deresi and the İkisu Deresi, south-east of the town, there are numerous churches and monasteries.

*Yağmurdere

About 18km/11 miles south-east of Gümüşhane a narrow road runs north into the remote mountain country of the Kalkanlı Dağları. Driving through this region of impressive scenery and traditional Pontic villages, some quite well preserved churches can be seen, a legacy of the Greeks who formed the majority of the population here until 1924.

*Zigana Geçidi

The 2030m/6662ft Zigana Pass, 63km/39 miles north-west of Gümüşhane, is one of the most spectacular in the Pontus Mountains. Once a crucial north-south "gateway" carrying a considerable traffic, the old route over the pass was very narrow, steep and winding; nowadays there is a new road with a reduced gradient. The old road is still there however, providing breathtaking views of the encircling mountains. The top of the pass marks the boundary between the provinces of Trabzon and Gümüşhane. Further on (45 minute drive) the road crosses another ridge from where, it is said, Xenophon and the Ten Thousand at last caught sight of the sea, 50km/31 miles away, joyfully shouting "thalatta!" (the sea!). A mixture of alpine pasture interspersed with woodland makes the area ideal for hill walking. There is a marked contrast between the firs, beeches, ferns and rhododendrons which grow in the damp northern Pontic climate, and the pines, junipers and oaks of the drier south.

Hakkâri

T 6

South-east Anatolia (Turkish Kurdistan)   **See warning page 7**
Province: Hakkâri
Altitude: 1650m/5415ft
Population: 30,000

Situation and Characteristics

The small provincial capital of Hakkâri lies in the somewhat inaccessible Hakkâri Dağları (High Zap Mountains), 600m/1969ft above the steep-sided gorge of the upper Büyük Zap (Great Zap). Rising 150km/93 miles to the north-east in the mountains on the Iranian frontier, the Zap flows through the heart of untamed Kurdistan to join the Tigris south of Mosul (Iraq). The town and its province are named after a nomadic Kurdish tribe who occupied the area to the south and south-east of Lake Van after the Zengids drove them from Iraq in the 13th c. Large parts of this mountainous region are now in Van Province (see entry). The High Zap Mountains are only thinly, and in the south-east very thinly, populated, the inhabitants of the scattered villages eking out an existence from cereal growing and horticulture. The mountains have plenty to offer climbers; but expeditions to this area on the borders of Iran and Iraq have to be in association with Turkish mountaineering groups (season: June–Sept.).

Warning

The area around Hakkâri is the stronghold of the Kurdish resistance movement. As throughout the whole of the crisis region in south-east Turkey, visitors must expect restrictions on travel, curfews, and frequent military and police checks. Political discussion should be avoided despite the slight easing of tension resulting from the government's sanctioning the use of Kurdish in public.

History

According to Sumerian and Accadian sources the early inhabitants of the area were tribes of semi-nomadic Lullubae who, before being defeated by Naramsis of Accadia, made frequent incursions into Mesopotamia. These were possibly the same semi-nomadic Kurdish hill-people, the "Kardushes", notorious even in Xenophon's day (401 B.C.), whose lifestyle,

Nomadic life in south-east Anatolia

language and culture has remained fundamentally unchanged since Hittite times (as also their predilection for banditry and rebellion). It is thought that the Medes, fleeing to the eastern Taurus in the 7th c. B.C., mixed with the resident Hurrian hill-tribes, nurturing over the centuries, in autonomous family units and tiny feudal states, a form of independence jealously guarded even to the present day. In the 1st millennium B.C. the region was part of the kingdom of Urartu. There then followed periods of Persian, Arab, Seljuk and Turkoman domination before it finally fell to the Ottomans in 1514. In the 19th c. Hakkâri, then a small walled town and known as Culamerik, was the seat of the autonomous Kurdish prince Nurallah Bey. Up until 1921 the Kurds of the Hakkâri region lived side by side with Nestorian Christians, members of a church dissolved by the Patriarchate of Constantinople in the 5th c., whose ancestors fled to Kurdistan and Iraq to avoid persecution. Here Nestorian doctrine survived alongside Islam, Kurds and Christians living for centuries together in peaceful coexistence. After the First World War the Hakkâri Nestorians were forced to flee the country and today the vast majority of inhabitants are Kurds.

Sights

Hakkâri boasts a Seljuk and an Ottoman medrese (16th c.). Towering above the town are the ruins of a fortress, Bava Kalesi.

Surroundings

Up into this century the village of Albayrak, a former monastic settlement 24km/15 miles north-east of Başkale, attracted many Armenian pilgrims to its monastery church, the ruins of which stand on a hill to the west by the   *Albayrak

Barren mountain wasteland east of Zuvari Halil Geçidi

Zap. First mentioned in the 14th c. the medieval building was restored in the 17th c., only for the dome to be badly damaged in 1715. An earth tremor in 1966 brought the ceiling crashing down, making viewing the interior problematic. The external friezes and ornamented portal are still well worth seeing however. Because the church is situated in a military zone near the Iranian border, permission to visit is required from the local police (jandarma).

Başkale

At the time of the Armenian principality of Vaspuragan, Başkale, in south-ern Van Province, was known as Hadamakert. It was the bastion from which the Ardsruni princes held out for a short time against the Bagratids from the north and the Arab Emir Yussuf from the south. Above the town are remains of a Kurdish fort.

Koçanış

To reach the little village of Koçanış, about 20km/12 miles north-east of Hakkâri, over a 3100m/10,175ft-high mountain pass, a 4-wheel drive vehicle is needed; it also involves a walk of about six hours (local guide essential). Up until the First World War Koçanış was the refuge and patriarchal seat of a small Nestorian community. Mar Şalita, a substantially built fortified church, stands at the entrance to the village.

*Tırşın Yaylası

Primitive rock drawings, some possibly dating back to 5500 B.C., can be seen in numerous places on the Tirşin and Gevarik (Gevaruk) plateaux, on the other side of the Van provincial border near Beşbudak (about 100km/ 62 miles north-west of Hakkâri and 30km/19 miles west of the adminis-trative centre of Yalınca; gravel road).

Yanal

The village of Yanal (altitude: 2400m/7877ft) lies about 44km/27 miles north-east of Başkale, not far from the Iranian border. It occupies the site of the old monastic settlement of Edschmiadsin, of which fragmentary traces can still be seen. A short distance outside the village the domed cruciform church of another former monastery (14th c.) stands on a bare hill. The four-concha church, almost certainly the work of the builders responsible for the monastery church at Albayrak, acquired its massive dome in 1681, the earlier dome having been destroyed. The church now serves as a barn.

The town of Yüksekova (High Valley), about 70km/43 miles east of Hakkâri, was already the centre of a highly developed culture (Musassir) when conquered by the Assyrian King Sargon II in 714 B.C., as is evident from the inscriptions and reliefs removed by Sargon for display in his palace in Chorsabad (Iraq). Sadly the originals were lost in the Tigris when on their way to Europe.

Yüksekova

Halikarnassos

See Bodrum

Hattuşaş

See Boğazkale

İskenderun

M 7

South coast (Eastern Mediterranean)
Province: Hatay
Altitude: 0–5m/0–15ft
Population: 156,000

İskenderun, (formerly known as Alexandretta), the most important Turkish Mediterranean port after İzmir, lies on the south side of the Gulf of İskenderun within the wooded foothills of the Amanus range, perhaps on the site of the ancient Alexandria Scabiosa.
The present-day town has little to offer the visitor and is very hot in summer. The harbour, the largest and the best on this stretch of coast, and sheltered by the surrounding hills, handles considerable shipping traffic. Around the harbour, which has a large jetty, are various modern installations (grain-stores, etc.).

Situation and Characteristics

The city of Alexandria, on the Issicus Sinus (Gulf of Issos), was probably founded some time after Alexander the Great's victory in the Battle of Issos (333). The town was intended to be the starting-point of the great caravan routes into Mesopotamia, but after Alexander's death the Seleucids preferred Antiocheia (Antakya) and Seleukeia Piereia. In the 3rd c. the town was destroyed by the Persians. In the 4th c. it was known as Little Alexandria; the epithet Scabiosa reflects the fact that leprosy was prevalent in the area. After a period of decline under the Ottomans at the end of the 19th c., İskenderun expanded from an insignificant harbour into the present town.

History

Surroundings

Belen (pop. 15,000; alt. 500m/1641ft), 14km/9 miles south-east of İskenderun and situated some way up the Topboğazı pass (750m/2461ft), is a summer resort popular with people from İskenderun. Evilya Çelebi's record (1640) shows that even in the 17th c. Arabs and Turks, some of them citizens of Aleppo, used to spend the summer months here. Having been

South-east of İskenderun
Belen

321

İskenderun

from antiquity a staging post on an old trade route, the town boasts the remains of an aqueduct as well a mosque and caravanserai dating from the 16th c.

Güzelyala

The houses of Soğukoluk (now Güzelyala) can be seen across the valley to the south-west of Belen. This elegant summer village with its lovely view over the Gulf of İskenderun, was built in the early 20th c. as a holiday retreat for the rich burghers of Aleppo, Antakya, Reyhanlı, Kırıkhan and İskenderun. Now it enjoys a less salubrious reputation, frequented by the crews of ships lying in the port of İskenderun.

North of İskenderun
Jonah's Pillar

About 10km/6 miles north of the town is Arrian's Pass (Derbent), a narrow passage between the sea and the hills. In medieval times the pass, then probably a frontier and customs post of Little Armenia, was known as Passus Portellae or Portella. On the pass can be seen Jonah's Pillar, a remnant of a Roman building which is variously interpreted as a Seleucid triumphal arch, an obelisk, the remains of a fort and a triumphal arch erected by Pescenius. The 13th c. writer Willebrand of Oldenburg records a legend that Alexander's remains were deposited on this "gate of liberation" so that the kings and princes who had been compelled by Alexander to bow their heads before him should still have him above them in death. According to local seamen the pillar marks the spot where Jonah was cast ashore by the whale.

Sakal Tutan

600m/660yd north-east, higher up (altitude: 91m/300ft), are the remains of an Armenian castle which in medieval times protected the pass and provided accommodation for travellers. Its name of Sakal Tutan (Tearer out of beards) refers to the bandits who lay in wait here to attack and plunder caravans. It has also been known, at different times, as Nigrinum, Neghertz (Middle Castle) and Kalatissia.

Xenophon's Pass

Beyond this, in the narrrow coastal plain of the River Sarısekisu, is Xenophon's Pass (which Xenophon himself calls Karsos), with remains of walls, probably serving some defensive purpose, some 600m/660yd apart.

**Payas/Baliae (Yakacık)

20km/12 miles north of İskenderun is Payas (Yakacık), a beautifully situated little town on a bay north of the promontory of Ras Payas. Its name comes from Arabic bayas (white) – no doubt a reference to the snow-covered peaks of the Amanus. It occupies the site of ancient Baiae, on the Issicus Sinus, a bathing resort much frequented by the Romans; there are remains of baths on the beach. In the Middle Ages it was an important commercial town, but at the end of the 18th c. it fell into the hands of a Turkoman chieftain named Küçük Ali (d. 1808), under whose rule it was ruined and depopulated. Küçük Ali levied tribute on passing caravans and robbed travellers; in 1801 he held the Dutch Consul in Aleppo prisoner for eight months, releasing him only on payment of a ransom of 17,500 piastres. After his death his son Dada Bey persisted in the same practices, but was finally betrayed to the authorities and beheaded at Adana in 1817.

First comes a complex of buildings – a han (caravanserai), a bazaar, a mosque, a medrese and a bath-house – erected in 1574 by Sokollu Mehmet Paşa, one of the most celebrated Grand Viziers of the Ottoman period, during the town's heyday in the reign of Sultan Selim II, son of Süleiman the Great. The han has a large courtyard surrounded by pointed-arched arcading. In front of it is the bazaar, a single-aisled building with a barrel-vaulted roof and a dome. To the south is the mosque, also with a large arcaded court, to the north the bath-house (ruined), with a domed camken (apodyterium) linking the soğukluk (tepidarium) and the domed harara (caldarium).

To the west of this complex, 800m/½ mile from the sea, is a large medieval castle (14th c.) on a polygonal plan. From the interior it is possible to climb up on to the massive walls and towers (fine views).

Issos

The road continues north over the plain. This area close to the coast, extending to the Deli Çayı, is believed to be the scene of the Battle of Issos

322

(333), in which Alexander the Great defeated the Persian King Darius III in a decisive cavalry encounter.

The exact site of the ancient town of Issos has not been established with certainty. It lay at the innermost tip of the Gulf of Issos and in Xenophon's time was a large and flourishing city. It is said to have been renamed Nikopolis (City of Victory) after Alexander's victory.

At Yeşilkent (Erzin), to the right of the main road, lies an extensive area of ruins, formerly thought to be the site of Issos but identified by the Austrian archaeologist Rudolf Heberdey (1864–1936) as the town of Epiphaneia, mentioned by Cicero as the place where he established his camp. According to Appianus, Pompey resettled pirates here, and according to Ammian this was the birthplace of St George, murdered in 361 as Archbishop of Alexandria.

Epiphaneia

From the main road can be seen the 116 surviving arches of a large Late Roman aqueduct which, made from volcanic rock, cross the plain in a gentle curve. The acropolis of the ancient city was probably on the nearby hill. To the south of the hill extends the main part of the city, with the remains of walls (probably belonging to a temple) and a colonnaded street.

The main road then continues over the pass of Toprakkale (see Adana, Surroundings) and joins the road from Adana to Osmaniye.

İslahiye   M 6

South-eastern Anatolia (Maraş trench)   **See warning page 7**
Province: Gaziantep
Altitude: 500m/1641ft
Population: 29,000

İslahiye, a lively and prosperous district town at the foot of the Amanus Mountains is laid out on a completely regular plan. Until a few years ago it was a haven for dealers in contraband (western cigarettes and other goods) smuggled over the nearby Syrian border.

Situation and Characteristics

Lying on the Baghdad railway, İslahiye today makes a good base from which to explore the region's few but very interesting historic sites. In the middle of the last century the Maraş trench, then a marshy area dotted with large lakes, provided winter pasturage for the nomadic tribes. Now intensive agriculture (cotton, wine and cereals) has taken over the vast basin. The Amanus range, running north-south, acts as a climatic divide between the considerably damper Mediterranean regime to the west and the more continental conditions experienced to the east. Due to powerful tectonic forces, earthquakes and volcanic phenomena occur along the edges of the range. The extensive, still fairly fresh, volcanic eruptions at Hassa, south of İslahiye, are a most impressive sight.

From the time of Mahmud II (1808–39), many of the nomadic tribes who had enjoyed considerable autonomy under local derebeys were forcibly resettled. The task of subjugating these fiercely independent beyliks, frequently involved in marauding raids, was entrusted to General Derviş Paşa commanding an elite force known as the "Firka-i İslahiye". In 1866, from a base in İskenderun, they assisted the local police and military to enforce order throughout the region, often only after considerable bloodshed. Kırıkhan, Hassa and İslahiye (named after the Firka-i İslahiye) were all built in the course of this operation, becoming the chief towns of their districts. In about 1880 İslahiye also took the name Niboli, from the fortress, Nibol Kalesi, where in 1864 Hausmann had discovered the remains of Nikopolis.

History

In several surveys of the plain around İslahiye archaeologists have identified more than 40 ancient settlement mounds which, in conjuction with the ceramic finds, implies dense occupation of the area up to the Early Bronze Age. One theory is that this was the flourishing kingdom ruled by Isqippu, "King of the Cedar Mountains" (Amanus = Cedar Mountains), the existence of which is known from cuneiform texts (Gilgamesh Epic).

Surroundings

*Tilmenhüyük

Tilmenhüyük lies on the Yesemek road about 10km/6 miles east of İslahiye, just before the road forks right for Yesemek. The site, located inside a loop in a wide stream, is not easily accessible. Excavation began in 1959, since when foundations of a palace dating from the Old Syrian period (c. 17th c. B.C.) have been uncovered on top of a settlement mound already inhabited from the Early Bronze Age. At that time the area was part of the kingdom of Yamhad.
The Hittite ruler Hattusili is thought to have been responsible for the destruction of the palace, which was replaced on a larger scale in about the 14th c. B.C. The excavated central area, which was probably destroyed and rebuilt a number of times, bears a strong resemblance to the complex on Tell Açana (Alalach) near Reyhanlı. Remains of collapsed Cyclopean walls dating from about 1000 B.C., with the lower part of a gate, can be seen from a distance.

**Yesemek

This most fascinating of ancient sites, a Hittite sculptors' workshop and stone quarry, is well worth visiting. It lies about 35km/22 miles south-east of İslahiye on a road which, asphalted to begin with, runs east before forking south-east and continuing as a dirt road. The site itself spreads over the south-east slope of a little valley south of the village of Yesemek. Turkish archaeologists in charge of the excavations have fenced off the site, setting up a small visitors' park. Although discovered by Luschan in 1890, detailed investigation only began in 1955, being continued in 1958–61.

Hittite stone sculptures near Yesemek

Stone figures can be seen in all different stages of completion, with motifs from the late 2nd and early 1st millennium B.C. At that time the workshop appears to have been supplying all the leading Hittite centres with sphinxes, mountain gods, lions and relief plaques. The most interesting statue yet found is the so-called Bear Man, with a teddy bear-like head.

Situated just 10km/6 miles north of İslahiye, near the village of Zincirli, is the famous site of the Late Hittite city of Sam'al, centre of the Ja'dija kingdom which was conquered by the Assyrians in the reign of Sargon II (722–705 B.C.) Attempting to reassert its independence, Sam'al was finally completely destroyed (650 B.C.) and abandoned. Before excavations could be carried out in 1883 and 1888–1904, a considerable depth of charred ruins had first to be cleared from the site. Founded by the Hittites in the 14th c. B.C., the city was surrounded (by the 9th c. B.C. at the latest) by a double circular wall, 720m/790yd in diameter, with more than 100 towers and three evenly spaced gates. Within the walls were palace-like complexes with Aramaic-style reliefs (in contrast to those on the citadel gates which were Hittite). These reliefs are now in museums in Berlin, Ankara and İstanbul. Among the many other finds were sepulchral stellae, statues, and huge carved lions from gates.

Zincirli

İstanbul   D/E 2/3

Marmara region (Bosporus)
Province: İstanbul
Altitude: 0–125m/0–410ft
Population: 6.8 million

The description of İstanbul has deliberately been kept short, since there is a separate guide to the city in this series.

N.B.

The great city of İstanbul, long known as Constantinople, or in the familiar European form of its Turkish name, as Stamboul, is picturesquely situated on the hills which flank the Bosporus at its junction with the Sea of Marmara. Although it was superseded by Ankara as capital of Turkey in 1923, it still has the largest concentration of population in the country, with a university, a technological university and an academy of art. It is the seat of a Muslim Mufti, Greek and Armenian patriarchs and a Roman Catholic Archbishop. Thanks to its favourable geographic situation, with a magnificent natural harbour – the largest in Turkey – in the Golden Horn, and to its position at the intersection of the land route from the Balkans to the Near Eastern countries with the sea route from the Mediterranean to the Black Sea, İstanbul has been throughout history an important international commercial centre.

Situation and
**Importance

Relentless migration to the city from the countryside keeps the İstanbul conurbation in a perpetual state of rapid growth. To counteract the threat of water, air and soil pollution, the city authorities have drawn up a redevelopment programme, due to be completed by the year 2000 (in association with İstanbul's bid for the Turn-of-the-Century Summer Olympic Games). To ease traffic congestion there are plans to build a metro under the Bosporus and to extend the urban rail network (the Topkapı–Sirkeci line was recently opened) to include more of the outlying districts. Other measures involve the conversion of heating systems from toxic lignite to natural gas and the construction of three sewage treatment plants. (Visitors should be cautious about drinking-water.)

Enviromental
Measures

The city consists of three separate elements – the old Turkish town (Eminönöü, Aksaray, Fatih), in the form of an almost equilateral triangle, which extends from the right bank of the Golden Horn to the Sea of Marmara; linked with the old town by the Galata and Atatürk Bridges, the district of

**Overall view

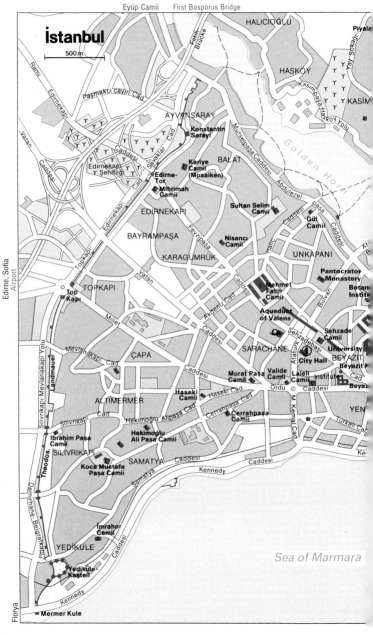

İstanbul

500 m

HALICIOĞLU

Piyala

HASKÖY

KASIM

Rami

Edirnekapı

Paşmakci çayir Cad.

Caddesi

Vatan

Kasımpaşa Haskö Yolu

Golden Horn

AYVANSARAY

Edirnekapı Şehitliği

Caddesi

Savaklar Cad.

Konstantin
Sarayi

Kariye
Camii
(Mosaiken)

BALAT

Mürselpaşa Caddesi

Abdülezel-

paşa

Edirne-
Tor

Mihrimah
Camii

Sultan Selim
Camii

Caddesi

Gül
Camii

Caddesi

EDIRNEKAPI

BAYRAMPAŞA

Edirnekapı

Topkapı

Fevzipaşa

Nisancı
Camii

Atatürk

Caddesi

Edirne, Sofia
Airport

Caddesi

KARAGÜMRÜK

Vatan

Haliç

UNKAPANI

Pantocrator
Monastery

Botan
Institut

TOPKAPI

Top
Kapı

Akdeniz. Cad.

Mehmet
Fatih
Camii

Caddesi

Bulvari

Mille

Aqueduct
of Valens

Caddesi

Şehzadebaşı

Şehzade
Camii

Silivrikapı-Mevlanakapı Yolu

Mevlanakapı Cad.

Landmauer

ÇAPA

Caddesi

SARACHANE

Atatürk

University

BEYAZIT

City Hall

Beyazıt

Murat Paşa
Camii

Valide
Camii

Laleli
Camii

Institut

Beya

Caddesi

Silivrikapı

Cad

Haseki
Camii

Haseki Cad.

Ordu

M. Kemal Cad.

Caddesi

YEN

ALTIMERMER

Hekimoğlu Alipaşa Cad.

Cerrahpaşa Cad.

Cerrahpaşa
Camii

Türkeli Cad

Theodos.

Demirhane-Belgrakapi

İbrahim Paşa
Camii

SILIVRIKAPI

Hekimoğlu
Ali Paşa Camii

SAMATYA

Caddesi

Caddesi

Ke

Koca Mustafa
Paşa Camii

Samatya

Kennedy

İmrahor
Camii

Caddesi

YEDIKULE

Sea of Marmara

Yedikule-
Kasteli

Florya

Kennedy

Mermer Kule

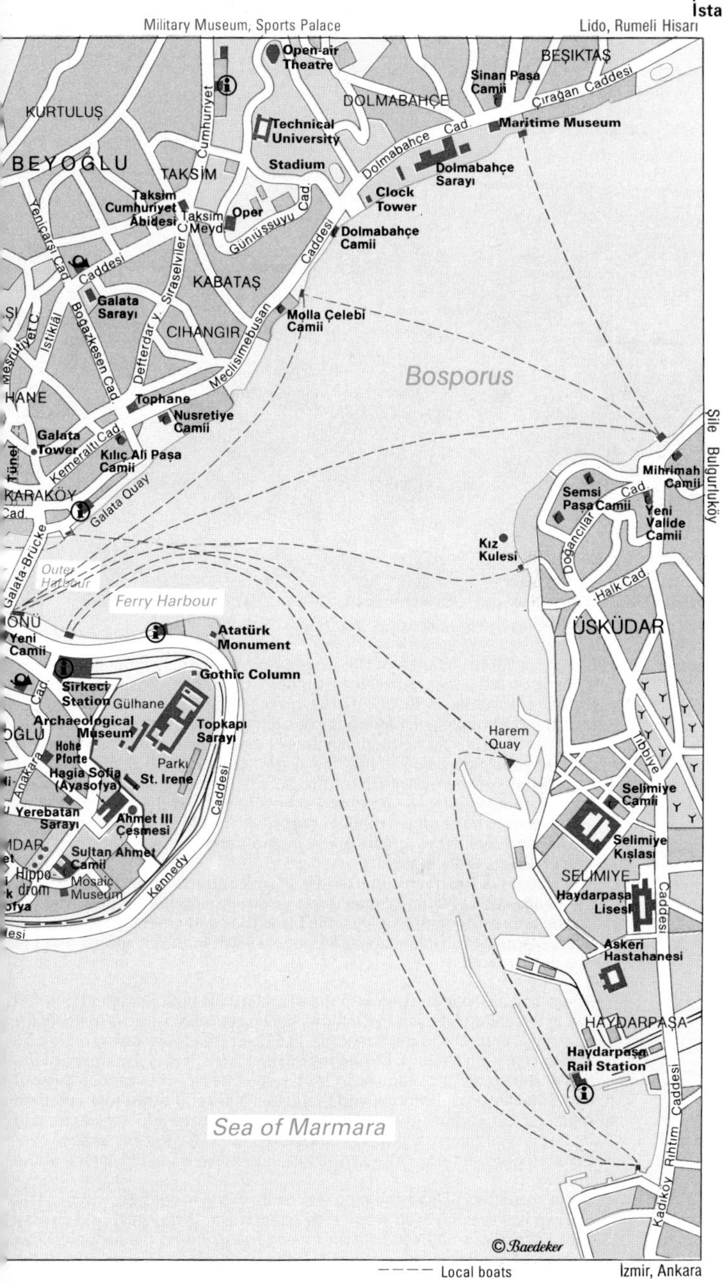

Military Museum, Sports Palace

Lido, Rumeli Hisarı

Open-air Theatre

BEŞİKTAŞ

Sinan Paşa Camii

Çırağan Caddesi

KURTULUŞ

DOLMABAHÇE

Maritime Museum

Technical University

BEYOĞLU

TAKSİM

Stadium

Dolmabahçe Cad

Dolmabahçe Sarayı

Cumhuriyet

Taksim Cumhuriyet Âbidesi

Taksim Meyd.

Oper

Gümüşsuyu Caddesi

Clock Tower

Sıraselviler

Dolmabahçe Camii

KABATAŞ

Galata Sarayı

CİHANGİR

Molla Çelebi Camii

Bosporus

Mesrutiyet C

İstiklal Cad

Boğazkesen Cad

Defterdar y.

Meclismebusan

Yenicarsi Cad

Caddesi

HANE

Tophane

Nusretiye Camii

Galata Tower

Kılıç Ali Paşa Camii

Şile

Bulgurluköy

KARAKÖY

Kemeraltı Cad

Galata Quay

Cad

Mihrimah Camii

Şemsi Paşa Camii

Cad

Yeni Valide Camii

Doğancılar

Galata-Brücke

Outer Harbour

Kız Kulesi

Ferry Harbour

Halk Cad

ÖNÜ

Yeni Camii

Atatürk Monument

ÜSKÜDAR

Gothic Column

Sirkeci Station

Gülhane

OĞLU

Archaeological Museum

Topkapı Sarayı

Parkı

Harem Quay

Anafartalar

Hohe Pforte

Hagia Sofia (Ayasofya)

St. Irene

Tıbbiye

Yerebatan Sarayı

Ahmet III Çeşmesi

Selimiye Camii

DAR

Sultan Ahmet Camii

Hippo drom

Kennedy

Caddesi

Selimiye Kışlası

ofya

Mosaic Museum

SELİMİYE

Haydarpaşa Lisesi

esi

Askeri Hastahanesi

Sea of Marmara

HAYDARPAŞA

Haydarpaşa Rail Station

Kadıköy

Rıhtım Caddesi

© Baedeker

– – – – Local boats

İzmir, Ankara

327

İstanbul

İstanbul: panorama, showing the Blue Mosque and Hagia Sophia

Beyoğlu with its suburbs of Galata and Harbiye, largely inhabited by foreigners, on the slopes between the Golden Horn and the Bosporus; and the district of Üsküdar, with its suburbs, on the Asiatic side of the Bosporus. İstanbul is a unique and unforgettable sight with its towers and its palaces and the numerous domes and minarets of the 35 large and over a hundred smaller mosques rising above the water. Little is left of the colourful Oriental life of the old capital of the Sultans, and the people now wear European dress. Street names and shop signs are in the Latin alphabet; and the old rows of brown timber houses with red roofs and latticed kafes (bow-windows) have given place in the central areas to stone and reinforced-concrete blocks.

The climate of İstanbul is marked by sharp contrasts. In the evening it is frequently cool, even in summer. Among the city's numerous birds visitors will be impressed particularly by the black kites and, on the Bosporus, the black cormorants. Dolphins are a frequent sight in the Bosporus and the Sea of Marmara.

History

About 660 B.C. Dorian Greeks founded on what is now Seraglio Point the city of Byzantion (in Latin Byzantium), which controlled access to the Black Sea at the entrance to the Bosporus. In 513 B.C. the town was captured by the Persian King Darius I. During the 6th and 5th c. it was a member of the first and second Attic Leagues. In 148 B.C. the free city of Byzantion entered into an alliance with Rome, and thereafter it several times lost and then regained its freedom. In A.D. 196 the city was captured and harshly treated by Septimius Severus, but soon recovered. In 324, after his victory over Licinius, Constantine I (306–337) resolved to make a second capital of the Empire.

In the autumn of 326 a beginning was made with the construction of a line of town walls taking in an area which extended far to the west, and on May 11th 330 the new city was solemnly inaugurated, under the name of Nova Roma or New Rome, soon to be changed to Constantinopolis. Like Rome

Gardens outside the Dolmabahçe Palace

A street in the Beyoğlu district

the new city was divided into fourteen regions, and even had its seven hills. After the division of the Empire in 395 Constantinople became the capital of the Eastern Roman Empire. In the reign of Justinian (527–565) who rebuilt the city in greater magnificence after much of it had been reduced to ashes during the Nika Insurrection, it enjoyed its period of greatest splendour. Late Greek and Roman culture developed into the distinctive Byzantine culture, which found expression in the Greek language.

Soon afterwards, however, the Empire was torn by domestic and external conflicts. The city was harried by the Avars and Persians (627) and by the Arabs under the Omayyad caliphs; in 813 and again in 924 it was besieged by the Bulgars; and in 907 and 1048 Russian fleets appeared off Constantinople. Finally came the catastrophe of 1204, when, following disputes over the succession to the Imperial throne, the Crusaders captured the city and founded a Latin Empire.

After the Ottoman conquest of Asia Minor in the 13th c. and the transfer of the capital from Bursa to Edirne (Adrianople) Constantinople was increasingly encircled by Turks. In 1453 Mehmet II Fatih (the Conqueror) took the city, which now became the Ottoman capital under the name of İstanbul. There was a great wave of building by the Sultans and Turkish grandees, particularly by Selim I (1512–20) and Süleiman the Magnificent (1520-66). Many major buildings were also erected in the 17th and 18th c. During the 19th c. Western influences began to make themselves felt in the city's architecture.

After the First World War, in which Turkey had been allied with the Central Powers, İstanbul was occupied by the Allies. In 1922, following Turkey's victory in the War of Independence, Turkish troops re-entered the city. In 1923 the Sultanate and Caliphate were abolished and Turkey became a Republic and its first President, Mustafa Kemal Atatürk, moved the capital to Ankara. In a drastic programme of reform Atatürk banned the fez, the wearing of veils by women, the Order of Dervishes and polygamy and introduced the Latin alphabet, the metric system and regular surnames.

The aspect of İstanbul has since then been increasingly Europeanised by the driving of wide modern streets through the old town, the pulling down of the old wooden houses and their replacement by new blocks of flats and offices, the establishment of a new commercial and business centre north of Taksim Square and the development of whole new districts of the city. İstanbul made a bid to host the 27th Summer Olympic Games in the year 2000.

Beyoğlu

Karaköy Square
Galata Quay

On the southern edge of the district of Galata, at the north end of the Galata Bridge, is busy Karaköy Square. From the south side of the square the Galata Quay runs north-east along the Bosporus. This is the arrival and departure point for both Turkish and foreign shipping lines (Yolcu Salonu).

Grande Rue de
Galata

From Karaköy Square the thoroughfare formerly known as the Grande Rue de Galata runs parallel to the Galata Quay but at some distance from the sea through the Top Hane district, under different names, to the Dolmabahçe Palace.

**Panorama from
Galata Tower

From the north end of the square Yüksek Kaldırım, a steep street lined with shops and with 113 steps on each side, goes up to the Galata Tower (Galata Kulesi), off the street to the left. (The tower can also be reached by following Voyvoda Caddesi and bearing right). The Galata Tower (68m/223ft high), originally built in Byzantine times, was restored in 1423 by the Genoese and again in 1875; it now contains a restaurant and a night-club and affords the best general view of the city. The street continues up to Tunnel Square, with the upper station of the Tünel, an underground funicular, in the main part of Beyoğlu (Lord's Son), and the old district formerly known as Pera. The upper part of Beyoğlu, around Taksim Square, was developed only in the 19th c. in European style; in this area there are numerous hotels, foreign consulates, churches, schools and hospitals.

İstiklâl Caddesi

Now pedestrianised, İstiklâl Caddesi (Independence Street), formerly known as the Grande Rue de Péra, is a busy shopping street with a host of shops and offices and the Galata Sarayı School. It is linked with Taksim Square by the world's oldest underground railway, Tünel, constructed in 1875. A great many churches and consulates are also located here, as too is the bustling Çiçek Pasajı leading off beside the Post Office. The old tram-line has been brought back into service along the whole of its route.
Further west is another busy street, Meşrutiyet Caddesi.

Taksim Square

İstiklâl Caddesi ends in Taksim Square (Taksim Meydanı), with the Monument to the Republic (1928) and the Opera House. On the north side of the square are the gardens of Republic Square (Cumhuriyet Meydanı). From the terrace of the Sheraton Hotel there are fine views.

Cumhuriyet
Caddesi

From Taksim Square İstanbul's most elegant street, Cumhuriyet Caddesi, lined with hotels, shops and offices, goes past the gardens of Republic Square to the northern residential districts of Harbiye and Şişli, with numerous handsome villas belonging to the wealthier citizens of İstanbul. On the east side of Cumhuriyet Caddesi the Republic Square gardens are continued by Maçka Park, in which are the University of Technology, the Hilton Hotel, an open-air theatre, the Palace of Sport and Exhibitions and the Military Museum.

**Dolmabahçe
Palace,
Marine Museum

From the south-east corner of Taksim Square Gümüşsuyu Caddesi runs south and then turns north-east, passing institutes belonging to the University of Technology (on the left) and the Stadium (also on the left) to the Dolmabahçe district, with the Dolmabahçe Palace, a huge edifice in what is called Turkish Renaissance style built by Abdul Mecid in 1854, which was the main residence of the Sultans until 1918 and is now a museum; it is also

Dolmabahçe Palace: decorative fountain and fine staircase

used for important State visits. Also in this district are the clock-tower of the old Dolmabahçe Mosque (1853) and the Maritime Museum (Deniz Müzesi), standing a little to the north-east of the Dolmabahçe Palace at the landing-stage for Besiktas. (Only 1500 visitors a day are admitted to the museum, after which the desk closes; one-hour tours; closed Mon. and Thur.)

From Karaköy Square the Galata Bridge, busy all day with pedestrians and wheeled traffic, crosses the Golden Horn (magnificent views) to the old town of İstanbul. The present bridge (484m/512ft long and 42m/138ft wide; landing-stage used by local steamers) was built in 1992 with German assistance, replacing the old Galata Bridge which burnt down in 1991. Erected by a German firm between 1909 and 1912, the old bridge, resting on 22 pontoons, had a middle section which swung open to allow the passage of large vessels. There are plans to reconstruct the historic Galata Bridge, but no decision has yet been made about a new location for it.

Galata Bridge

The Golden Horn (in Turkish Haliç; boat trip up the Horn recommended), a curving inlet 7km/4½ miles long and up to 40m/130ft deep opening off the Bosporus, is one of the finest natural harbours in the world. It is in fact a drowned river valley, a tributary of the river which once flowed through the Bosporus. The lowest part, below the Galata Bridge, is the Outer Commercial Harbour, with the Galata Quay on the north side and other quays along the south side. Between the Galata Bridge and Atatürk Bridge (1km/¾ mile west) is the Inner Commercial Harbour, to the north the old Naval Harbour. In the Middle Ages the Golden Horn, like the Bosporus, could be closed to shipping by a chain across the mouth.

*Golden Horn

The Old Town

At the south end of the Galata Bridge is Eminönü Square, at the beginning of the oldest part of İstanbul. From here a beautiful seafront road, Florya

Sahil Yolu, encircles Seraglio Point and runs along the Sea of Marmara to Yesilköy.

*Yeni Cami

On the south side of the square stands the large Yeni Cami, the New Mosque of the Sultan's mother, which was begun in 1615, on the model of the Ahmet I Mosque, for Ahmet's mother but completed only in 1663. The interior of the mosque and the adjoining royal apartments are richly decorated with tiles.

*Egytian Bazaar

Immediately west of the Yeni Cami is the Egyptian Bazaar (Mısır Çarşısı), originally intended only for goods from Egypt but now the most important market in the Old Town after the Great Bazaar.

Sublime Porte

From the Yeni Cami a street runs south-east, passing close to Sirkeci Station (İstanbul's main station), to the Sublime Porte, once the seat of the Grand Vizier, later the Foreign Ministry and now the office of the Governor (Valı) of İstanbul province. Opposite it, at the corner of the Seraglio wall, is the Alay Köşkü, from which the Sultan could watch, unobserved, the comings and goings at the Sublime Porte.
A little way south-east is the Soğuk Çeşme Gate, the main entrance to the Seraglio, reached on the street which runs up to the right.
The street ahead passes through Gülhane Park (admission charge) to an outlook terrace, with views of the Bosporus and the Sea of Marmara. To the south, below the Tulip Garden, is the Gothic Column (2nd c. A.D.). Outside the park, near the tip of Seraglio Point, can be seen a bronze statue of Mustafa Kemal Atatürk.

**Topkapı Sarayı

From the Soğuk Çeşme Gate we bear half right to the Topkapı Sarayı (Cannon Gate Palace) or Eski Saray (Old Palace), the old palace-city of the Sultans, built on the Seraglio Point hill, one of the seven hills of New Rome, on the site of the acropolis and the earliest settlement of Byzantion. This great complex of buildings set in gardens (now open to the public) bounded by battlemented walls and towers, consists of a number of buildings outside the main precincts (the Archaeological Museum, the Mint, the church of Hagia Eirene, etc.) and, beyond these, the Inner Seraglio. Mehmet II built a summer palace here in 1468, and this was enlarged by Süleiman the Magnificent into the Sultan's principal residence, occupied by successive Sultan's until Abdul Mecid moved to the Dolmabahçe Palace in 1855.

**Archaeological Museum

On the west side of the Seraglio hill stands the Archaeological Museum (Arkeoloji Müzesi), which contains an important collection of prehistoric Greek, Roman and Byzantine antiquities. Among its principal treasures are sarcophagi of the kings of Sidon from the Royal necropolis of Saida (Sidon, in the Lebanon), including in particular the magnificent Alexander Sarcophagus and the Sarcophagus of the Mourners (with eighteen figures of mourning women) both of the 4th c. B.C.; the Sarcophagus of the Satrap (5th c. B.C.; the Lycian Sarcophagus (c. 400 B.C.); the Sidamara Sarcophagus from Konya (3rd c. A.D.); and some fine funerary stelae and stones with inscriptions.
Opposite the south-west wing of the Archaeological Museum is the Museum of Ancient Oriental Art (Eski Şark Eserleri Müzesi).

In the courtyard of the Archaeological Museum is the graceful Çinili Kösk (Tiled Pavilion), one of the oldest surviving Turkish buildings in İstanbul (1472), in a style which shows Persian influences. It has Turkish ceramic, tile (mainly from İznik, 16th c.) and faience (12th–19th c.) decoration.
Above the Archaeological Museum is the Outer Court of the Seraglio, with the Janissaries' Plane Tree.

Hagia Eirene

On the south-west side of the courtyard stands the reddish domed church of Hagia Eirene (Divine Peace), one of the best-preserved Early Byzantine

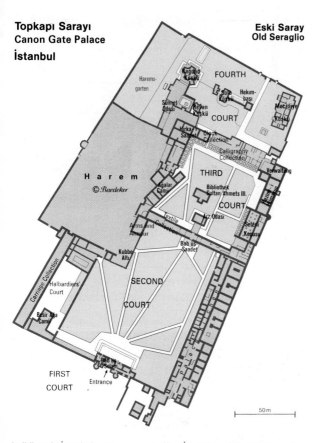

Topkapı Sarayı
Canon Gate Palace
İstanbul

Eski Saray
Old Seraglio

Harems-garten

FOURTH

Bağdad Köşkü

Sofa Köşkü

Hekim-başı

COURT

Mecidiye Köşkü

Sünnet Odası

Revan Köşkü

Hırka Saadet

Clock Collection

Calligraphy Collection

H a r e m

© Baedeker

THIRD

Verwaltung

Ağalar Camii

Bibliothek Sultan Ahmets III.

COURT

Arz Odası

Textile Collection

Seferli Koğuşu

Arms and Armour

Bab üs-Saadet

Kubbe Altı

SECOND

COURT

Carriage Collection

Halbardiers' Court

Beşir Ağa Camii

Bab üs-Selâm

FIRST
COURT

Entrance

50 m

buildings in İstanbul, now a museum (Aya İrini Müzesi). In 381 it was the
meeting-place of the Second Ecumenical Council. During the Turkish period it became an arsenal, and more recently houses an artillery museum.
On the north side of the Outer Court (to the right, the Executioner's Fountain, in front of which dignitaries who had fallen from favour were executed) is the Ort Kapı (Middle Gate; 1524), the entrance to the Inner
Seraglio, the palace-city of the Sultans, which consists of a series of buildings, large and small, laid out round three courtyards. The first of the inner
courtyards, the Court of the Divan, surrounded by colonnades, is the
largest (150m/164yd long) and most impressive. On the right-hand side are
the palace kitchens, topped by 20 dome-like chimneys. With their 24 fire-
places, the kitchens were said to serve up to 20,000 meals a day. They now
house the Porcelain Collection, predominantly consisting of Chinese porcelain and faience (mostly 10th–18th c.), which includes many items of
outstanding quality. On the left-hand side of the courtyard is the Kubbe Altı,
built by Mehmet II, with a tall tower (41.5m/135ft; 16th c., upper part 1819).
This housed the Divan, the council chamber in which the Grand Vizier
received foreign envoys. Adjoining the Kubbe Altı is a collection of Turkish
faience.

**Porcelain
Collection

Chinese porcelain in the former harem kitchen

A room in the harem

Festival hall in the Padidsha

The Bab-üs-Saadet, the Gate of Felicity (to the left, a collection of textiles), leads into the second of the inner courts. Immediately in front of the gate is the Audience Chamber (Arz Odası), a pavilion dating from the time of Süleiman the Magnificent, with a baldachin-like throne in a colonnaded hall. Beyond this is the Library of Ahmet III. On the right-hand side of the court we come to the Treasury (Hazine), with three rooms containing treasures of inestimable value (thrones, rich garments and weapons, precious stones, pearls, vases, clocks, candelabra, writing materials, etc.). Adjoining the Treasury is a collection of splendid costumes worn by the Sultans.

Treasury

On the left-hand side of the court stands the Eunuchs' Mosque (Ağalar Camii), now housing a library (12,000 manuscripts). Beyond this is the Harem (an Arabic word meaning "That which is forbidden"), the women's apartments to which only the Sultan, his blood relatives and the eunuchs had access. Part of the Harem is now open to the public (admission charge; half-hourly tours, 50 people max.). Apart from a few larger rooms, richly appointed, the Harem is a maze of narrow corridors and small – sometimes tiny – rooms, which have preserved little in the way of Oriental splendour. In imperial Turkey men might have up to four legitimate wives at a time; the Sultan was allowed seven. There was no limit on the number of concubines. Since 1926 monogamy has been enforced by law.

*Harem

Beyond the second inner courtyard lies the terraced Tulip Garden. On the uppermost terrace (view) is the Bağdat Köşkü (Baghdad Pavilion), a domed building with magnificent tile decoration erected by Murat IV to commemorate the taking of Baghdad. Adjoining it are the Revan Köşkü (Erevan Pavilion) and the Circumcision Room (Sünnet Odası). Lower down are the Sofa Köşkü (1704, a fine timber building, the Hekim Bası (Surgeon's Tower) and the Mecidiye Köşkü (19th c.), now a restaurant.

Bagdat Köşkü

On the south-west side of the Seraglio walls stands the magnificent Sultan's Gate (Bab-ı Hümayun), facing Hagia Sophia. Outside the gate is the Fountain of Ahmet III (1728).

Sultan's Gate
*Fountain of
Ahmet III

The former church of Hagia Sophia (Holy Wisdom), in Turkish Ayasofya, from the Turkish Conquest until 1935 İstanbul's principal mosque and now a museum, is the supreme achievement of Byzantine architecture and the city's most celebrated monument. The first church on this site, built by Constantine the Great in 326, was burned down and a later church was destroyed during the Nika Insurrection. It was rebuilt on a larger scale in 532–537, during the reign of Justinian, by Anthemios of Tralleis (Aydın) and Isodoros of Miletus, with the avowed intention of surpassing in splendour all the buildings of antiquity. Large numbers of columns were brought to Constantinople from temples in Asia Minor, the Lebanon, Greece and Italy, and the finest marbles and noblest metals were used. It is said that the total cost of the building was 360 hundredweight of gold and that 10,000 workmen were employed in its construction.

**Hagia Sophia
(Ayasofya)
(See plan p. 338)

Hagia Sophia (entrance on south side) is 75m/245ft long, 70m/230ft wide and 58m/190ft high to the top of the dome. In the exonarthex and narthex (outer and inner vestibules) are fine Early Christian mosaics, which were formerly concealed under whitewash but have mostly been exposed since 1931. Particularly fine is the figure of Christ enthroned (9th c.) over the main entrance into the church, the Imperial Doorway. The interior, dominated by the magnificent central dome (diameter 32m/105ft) and lit by countless windows, is of overpowering effect, though its harmonious proportions are somewhat disturbed by the huge circular wooden plaques on the main piers inscribed in gold script with the names of the first four Caliphs and by the mihrab (the niche indicating the direction of Mecca) in the apse.

Outside the south side of the church are five türbes (tombs) of Sultans. To the south-west lies the busy Ayasofya Meydanı (Hagia Sophia Square), on the site of the old Augusteion (Agora), from which there is a fine view of the Blue Mosque.

Türbes

Sultan's throne in the Topkapı Sarayı (see p. 332)

*Cisterns

North-west of the square in Yerebatan Street is the entrance to the Yerebatan Sarayı (Underground Palace), a huge underground cistern (now lit by electricity) built in the time of Justinian (6th c.). It is the largest of İstanbul's cisterns, 140m/150yd long by 70m/75yd across, with 336 columns set in 12 rows.

*Atmeydanı

Adjoining the south-west side of Ayasofya Meydanı extends Atmeydanı (Horse Square), an open space more than 300m/330yd long which occupies part of the site of the ancient Hippodrome, begun by Septimius Severus in 203 and completed by Constantine the Great in 330. This was the centre of Byzantine Court and public life, the scene of splendid games but also of factional conflicts (Nika Insurrection). Between here and the sea-walls on the Sea of Marmara (still largely preserved) were the Roman and Byzantine Imperial palaces with their churches and associated buildings.

Emperor William's Fountain

In the gardens on the north-west side of Atmeydanı can be seen a fountain, rather inappropriate to its surroundings, presented by the German Emperor William II in 1898. Then follow, to the south-west, three ancient monuments: a 20m/65ft high Egyptian obelisk (Dikilitaş; from Heliopolis; reign of Thutmosis III, 1501–1448 b.c.) with Roman reliefs from the time of Theodosius I on the base; the Serpent Column (Burmalı Sütun), the stump (5m/16ft high) of a bronze column bearing a golden tripod on three snakes' heads which was set up at Delphi to commemorate the Greek victory over the Persians in the Battle of Plataea (479 b.c.); and the so-called Colossus, a masonry column of uncertain age with a Greek inscription in the name of Constantine VII Porphyrogenitus.

Obelisk
Serpent Column

Colossus

**Blue Mosque
(Sultan Ahmet
Mosque)
(See plan p. 340)

The south-east side of Atmeydanı is dominated by the Sultan Ahmet Mosque or Blue Mosque with its mighty dome (43m/141ft high, 23.5m/77ft in diameter) and six minarets, built by Sultan Ahmet I in 1609–16. The forecourt, with a beautiful fountain in the centre, is surrounded by colonnades roofed with a series of small domes. The interior (72m/235ft by

64m/210ft), in its lightness, spatial effect and colour, is one of the finest creations of Turkish archtitecture.

On the south-east side of the Blue Mosque is the very fine Mosaic Museum.   Mosaic Museum

South of Atmeydanı, near the Sea of Marmara, stands the Küçük Ayasofya Mosque, the Little Ayasofya. It was originally the church of SS Sergius and Bacchus, built in the reign of Justinian, at the same time as San Vitale in Ravenna. From the north end of Atmeydanı Dian Street (Divanyolu) runs west, following the line of the old main street of the Byzantine city.   Küçük Ayasofya

The second street on the left leads to the Binbirdirek (1001 Columns) Cistern, which dates from the 6th c. (54m/175ft by 56m/185ft; 212 columns). Since 1966 it has been dry.   Binbirdirek Cistern

Farther along Divanyolu, on the second of the seven hills of New Rome (on the right), rises the so-called Burned Column (Çembererlitaş, Hooped Stone), the stump (still 40m/130ft high) of a porphyry column, originally 57m/185ft high, set up by Constantine the Great in his Forum. Until 1105 it bore a bronze statue of Constantine.   *Burned Column

North of the Burned Column, on the east side of the Great Bazaar, we come to the Nuru Osmaniye Mosque, constructed entirely of marble (1748–55).   Nure Osmaniye Mosque

The Great Bazaar (Kapalı Çarşi, covered market) in the depression between the Nure Osmaniye and Bayazit Mosques, is a whole quarter on its own, surrounded by a wall and entered through eleven gates, a maze of vaulted and dimly lit streets and lanes which even after a major fire in 1954 remains one of the great sights of İstanbul. The various trades are still mostly segregated into particular streets or sections of the bazaar.   *Great Bazaar

To the west of the Great Bazaar, on the third of the city's seven hills, Bayazit Square occupies the site of Theodosius I's Forum. On the east side of the square is the Bayazit Mosque or Pigeon Mosque, built in 1498–1505, during the reign of Mehmet II's son Bayazit. The interior, painted in Turkish Rococo style in the 18th c., is a simplified imitation of the Hagia Sophia.
From the south side of the square Ordu Caddesi leads west in the direction of the land walls.   *Bayazit Mosque

On the north side of Bayazit Square stands a large gate, the entrance to the University (İstanbul Üniversitesi; previously the War Ministry, Seras Kerat), on the site of the earliest palace of the Sultans. To the right of the University is the 60m/200ft high Bayazit Tower (Bayazit Kulesi, 1823), now a fire-watch tower; from the top (180 steps) there are superb views of İstanbul, finest at sunset or early in the morning (mostly closed).   University

*View

Below the University to the north, situated on a terrace surrounded by schools, baths, etc., is the Süleiman Mosque (1549–75), built for Süleiman the Magnificent by the great architect Sinan, who, under the influence of Hagia Sophia, carried mosque architecture to its greatest development; after the Selim Mosque in Edirne, the Süleimaniye is his finest achievement. The interior, dominated by its great dome (53m/175ft high, 26.5m/85ft in diameter), is notable for its harmonious proportions and unity of design (on the mihrab wall, beautiful tiles and stained glass). Behind the mosque is the burial ground, with fine türbes (tomb chapels), in particular those of Süleiman and his favourite wife Roxolana.   **Süleiman Mosque

To the west of the mosque, in the street along its outer court, is the Museum of Turkish and Islamic Art (Türk ve İslam Eserleri Müzesi), with both sacred and secular works of art.   Museum of Turkish and Islanic Art

A road north-west under Bayazit Square in a 300m/330yd long tunnel leads into Vezneciler Caddesi (on the left, university buildings) and Şehzadebaşı Caddesi, on the right-hand side of which is the Şehzade Mosque (Prince's   *Şehzade Mosque

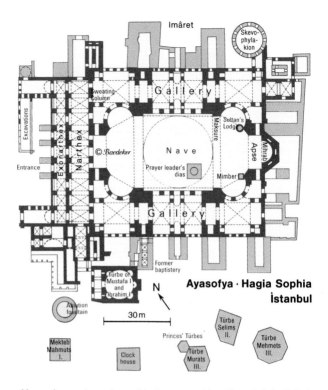

Ayasofya · Hagia Sophia İstanbul

Mosque), an early master work by the great architect Sinan, built in 1543-47 during the reign of Süleiman and Roxolana in memory of their favourite son Mohammed; it has a charmingly decorated interior.

*Aqueduct of Valens

A little way north of the Şehzade Mosque, between the University and the Sultan Mehmet Mosque, can be seen the imposing bulk of the Aqueduct of Valens, built in the reign of Valens (A.D. 368), frequently restored and still in use. The two-storey aqueduct spans the lower ground between the third and the fourth of the city's hills, and at its highest point, half-way along its course, crosses the Atatürk Boulevard, a modern street driven through the centre of the Old Town, including an area devastated by fire.

Municipal Museum

Near by is the Municipal Museum.

Fatih Mosque

West of the aqueduct, on the city's fourth hill, is the Fatih Mosque (Fatih Camii, Sultan Mehmet Camii), built in 1463–71 on the site of the church of the Holy Apostles (founded by Constantine the Great and rebuilt by Justinian) and almost completely rebuilt after an earthquake in 1765. It is the holiest mosque in İstanbul after the Eyüp Mosque. In the first türbe behind the mosque is the Tomb of Sultan Mehmet.

Sultan Selim Mosque

To the north of the Fatih Mosque, on the city's fifth hill, stands the Sultan Selim Mosque (Selimiye; 1520–26), the plainest of İstanbul's royal mosques, built by Süleiman the Magnificent in memory of his warrior father Selim I. From the terrace there is a fine view of the Golden Horn.

İzmir: panorama from the Kadifekale

lined by modern buildings. One part of the city destroyed by the fire is now the Culture Park, home also to the İzmir International Fair. New industrial zones were built in the north, while large residential areas have been developed along the bay's coastline to the south-west of the city and also on the northern side of the Gulf.

Sights

The most important street for tourists is the long Atatürk Caddesi which stretches some 3.5km/2 miles south from the district of Alsancak (landing-stage for passenger ships) at the northern tip of the city. This broad sea-front promenade passes alongside the harbour as far as the old district of Konak and offers a panoramic view of the Gulf of İzmir to the right, while the left-hand side is lined with handsome modern buildings (mainly restaurants).

Atatürk Caddesi ("Kordon")

At No. 248 is the Atatürk Museum with mementos of Atatürk's stay in İzmir. Farther down, standing by itself, is NATO's command headquarters.

Atatürk Museum

About half-way along Atatürk Caddesi is Republic Square (Cumhuriyet Meydanı), with the Independence Monument (İstiklâl Anıtı), an equestrian statue of Atatürk.

Republic Square

The southern part of Atatürk Caddesi leads from Republic Square past the Commercial Harbour (Ticaret Limanı), with the offices of various shipping lines and many banks. At the junction with Gazi Bulvarı is the Stock Exchange.

Commercial Harbour

At the southern end of Atatürk Caddesi lies Konak Meydanı, a long square looking out on to the Gulf of İzmir. The imposing modern Town Hall

Konak Square

345

İzmir

Konak Square: the clock tower . . .　　　*. . . and Konak Mosque*

(Belediye) stands at its north side and at its south side is the Cultural Centre of the Aegean University, a complex of buildings in an unusual architectural style which includes an opera house, an academy of music, exhibition halls and a museum of modern art.

Most of this busy square is occupied by the Central Bus Station. Situated near the Town Hall beside a pedestrian underpass stand the Clock Tower (Saat Kule), an old city landmark, and the little Konak mosque.

*Archaeological Museum

Above Konak Square a little way south-east on the curving main road to the south lies the recently-constructed Archaeological Museum. It contains many interesting finds from ancient Smyrna, Ephesus, Miletus, Sardis, Pergamon, Tralleis (Aydın) and other sites. Among particularly notable exhibits are figures of Poseidon and Demeter (2nd c. A.D.) from the agora at Smyrna, various sarcophagi, a colossal Roman head, a mosaic pavement, fine collections of glass, coins and jewellery and a bronze figure of Demeter from Halikarnassos (Bodrum; 4th c. B.C.).

On the opposite side of the street is the Ethnological Museum, recently installed in an old building. On display are many exhibits of Turkish furniture and traditional handicrafts.

Bazaar

The bazaar is situated to the north-east of Konak Square extends throughout a maze of narrow streets and lanes with innumerable workshops, little shops and stalls, several 18th c. caravanserais (some of them restored) and a number of small mosques dating from Ottoman times. Of particular interest is the well-restored Hisar Mosque (1597).

*Agora

A little way south of Fevzi Paşa Bulvarı in the Basmahane district on the Osmanpaşa Bulvarı are the partly excavated remains of the agora (market), which originally dated from the Greek period but was rebuilt after an earthquake in the 2nd c. A.D. during the reign of Marcus Aurelius. Along the west end of the square which is laid out in gardens, stand thirteen columns

Hagia Sophia, the most celebrated building in İstanbul

At the end of Fevzipaşa Caddesi, in the land walls, is the Edirne Gate (Edirnekapı), which was almost completely destroyed by an earthquake in 1894. Just before the gate, on the sixth and highest of the city's hills (to the left), is the Mihrimah Mosque, built by Sinan in 1556 for the daughter of Süleiman I (numerous windows).

Hagia Sophia, the most celebrated building in İstanbul

Some 300m/330yd north-east stands the beautiful Kariye Camii, originally the church of St Saviour in Chora (in the country), belonging to a monastery which seems to have been in existence before the time of Theodosius II. It is world-famous for its mosaics and frescos of the period of the Palaeologue Renaissance (13th–14th c.). The date of the church and monastery has not been established with certainty. Some authorities believe that the foundation of the church may go back to the 5th c.; but much of the present church was built in the late 11th c. by Maria Dukaina, mother-in-law of the Emperor Alexius Comnenus. Her grandson Isaac Comnenus repaired the church after it had been severly damaged in an earthquake about 1120. The magnificent decoration of the interior dates from the 13th–14th c. The mosaics, preserved almost intact in the two narthexes and fragmentarily in the katholikon (nave), cover a wide range of themes, from the ancestors of Christ to the Last Judgment. In the parekklesion (side aisle), which served as a burial chapel, are a unique series of frescos on the themes of death, resurrection and the life after death.

From outside the Edirne Gate, where is situated İstanbul's largest Muslim cemetery, there is a good general view of the land walls of Constantinople, which extend, excellently preserved for much of the way, for a distance of 6670m/7300yd from the Golden Horn to the Sea of Marmara. With their numerous towers, large and small, they are a superbly impressive sight. The Theodosian walls, which form the main section of the circuit, were built between 413 and 439, and after an earthquake in 447 were developed into a threefold ring of defences some 60m/200ft wide, with a height, from the

Edirne Gate

Mihrimah Mosque

*Kariye Camii

**Mosaics

**Land walls

339

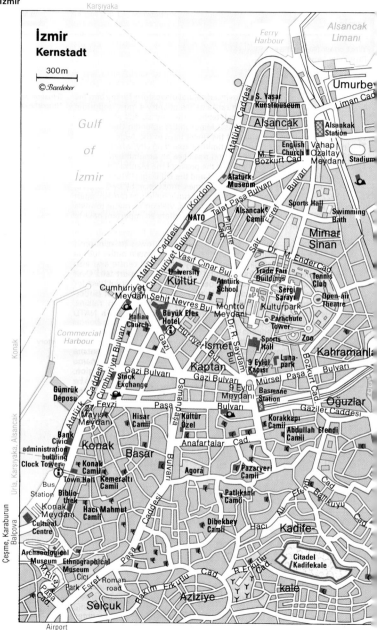

İzmir

İzmir
Kernstadt

300m

© Baedeker

Gulf

of

İzmir

Karşıyaka

Ferry
Harbour

Alsancak
Limanı

Umurbe

Atatürk Caddesi

S. Vaşar
Kunstmuseum

Liman Cad.

Alsancak

Alsankak
Station

English
Church
M. E.
Bozkurt Cad.

Vahap
Ozaltay
Meydanı

Stadium

Bulvarı

Atatürk-
Museum

Talat Paşa Bulvarı

Plevne Cad.

Alsancak
Camii

Sports Hall

Sarı Efesi

Swimming
Bath

Mimar
Sinan

NATO

Atatürk Caddesi (Kordon)

Cumhuriyet Bulvarı

Vasıf Çınar Bul.

Dr. M. Ender Cad.

University
Kültür

Atatürk
School

Trade Fair
Buildings

Tennis
Club

Cumhuriyet
Meydanı

Şehit Nevres Bul.

Montrö
Meydanı

Sergi
Saray

Open-air
Theatre

Cumhuriyet Bulvarı

İtalian
Church

Büyük Efes
Hotel

Gazi

Hürriyet Bul.

Dr. R. Saydam Bul.

Kulturpark

Parachute
Tower

Zoo

İsmet

Sports
Hall

Kahramanl

Commercial
Harbour

Konak

Atatürk Caddesi

Gümrük
Deposu

Stock
Exchange

Gazi Bulvarı

Kaptan

Gazi Bulvarı

Fevzi

Paşa

Mürsel Paşa

9 Eylül
Kapısı

9 Eylül
Meydanı

Luna-
park

Bozkurt

Bulvarı

Basmane
Station

Gaziler Caddesi

Oğuzlar

Mavış
Meydanı

Bank

Hisar
Camii

Osman ağa

Kültür
Özel

Bulvarı

Korakkapı
Camii

Abdullah Efendi
Camii

Civic
administration
building

Konak

Basar

Anafartalar Cad.

Clock Tower

Town Hall

Konak
Camii

Kemeraltı
Camii

Agora

Pazaryeri
Camii

Eşref
Cad.

Balkuyu

Bus
Station

Biblio-
thek

Caddesi

Patlıkanlı
Camii

Ali

Cad.

Konak
Meydanı

Hacı Mahmut
Camii

Cultural
Centre

Dibekbey
Camii

Hacı

Kadife-

Kadife

Archaeological
Museum

M. Rıfat

Ethnographical
Museum

Cici

Park Eşref

Roman
road

Paşa

R. Erkütlü Cad.

Citadel
Kadifekale

kale

Paşa Cad.

Bakım Erkütlü Cad.

Selçuk

Azıziye

Çeşme, Karaburun
Balçova

Urla, Karşıyaka, Alsancak

Konak

Airport

Kuşadası, Selçuk (Ephesus), Pamukkale

344

Sculptures in the Archaeological Museum   *A shady corner on the Kadifekale*

with fine capitals. On the north side is a three-aisled basilica 160m/175yd long with a vaulted roof borne on pillars. The marble figures which were found here are now in the new Archaeological Museum (above). The Kadifekale citadel offers a view of the whole agora, enabling visitors to appreciate the full extent of the site.

900m/1000yd to the south along Esrefpaşa Caddesi, lies a stretch of Roman road (Roma Yolu), which formed part of the old Golden Road (Altin Yol), an important section of the road network built during Roman times. To the west of the Roman road is Cici Park, on the slopes of Değirmen Tepe (Mill Hill; 75m/245ft). On the hill once stood temples of Vesta and Asklepios, but no traces remain. It also marks the spot where a 17km/10 mile Roman aqueduct ended.

Roman road

Kadifekale Hill (Velvet Castle), the ancient Mount Pagus (185m/607ft), on which the acropolis of Lysimachos once stood rises over the east side of the city (access road signposted). The summit, crowned by the remains of a medieval citadel, offers an incomparable panoramic view encompassing the whole city, the Gulf of İzmir and the hills.

Kadifekale
**Panoramic View

The massive, well-preserved walls of the medieval citadel, which originally had 40 towers, incorporate foundations and other masonry from the Lysimachean acropolis as well as work dating from Roman, Byzantine, Genoese and Ottoman periods.

On the slopes of the hill stood the Roman theatre and the stadium (with seating for 20,000 spectators), of which practically no remains survive, although the outline of the stadium can still be traced. According to tradition the Tomb of St Polycarp Bishop of Smyrna who was martyred in A.D. 156 during the persecution of Christians by Mark Aurelius lies above the north side of the stadium.

347

İzmir

Culture Park

In the north-east of the city not far from Basmahane Station, in a district which was burned down in 1922, lies the Culture Park with gardens, a lake, the international fair exhibition halls, a zoo and an amusement park. To the north-east of the Culture Park beyond the railway lines is the large Alsançak Stadium.

Caravan Bridge

South-east of the Culture Park to the east of Basmahane Station, the Kemer Bridge crosses the small River Melez (the ancient Meles), a modern structure on Greek and Roman foundations. It was formerly known as the Caravan Bridge, from the heavy caravan traffic which passed over it on the way to the interior (Manisa, Balıkesir, Sardis).

Diana's Bath

2km/1¼ miles east, outside the suburb of Tepecik, is Diana's Bath (Diana Hamamları), a little lake with eight springs which supply İzmir with water.

A shoeshine boy in İzmir

Surroundings

Balçova

Barely 9km/5½ miles from Konak Square to the south-west of İzmir and beyond extensive residential suburbs lies a major road junction. To the left (700m/765yd) is the spa centre of Balçova with the radioactive Baths of Agamemnon (35–40°C/95–105°F). A cable-car takes the visitor to a panoramic restaurant. Turn right at the road junction for the resort of İnciraltı (2km/1¼ miles).
13km/8 miles beyond the crossroads, the main road which extends west towards Urla and Çeşme reaches another junction.

Teos

In the plain to the south of Sığacık lie the remains of Teos, a member of the Panionic League of cities which was noted as a centre of the cult of Dionysos and the birthplace of the lyric poet Anakreon (c. 540 B.C.). No traces remain of the once-renowned temple built by Hermogenes of Alabanda.

Urla

Situated about 11km/7 miles further along the main road is the town of Urla (pop. 22,000) famous for its magnesium-rich baths. 4km/2½ miles north on an islet linked to the mainland by a causeway near the little town of Urla Iskelesi, birthplace of the philosopher Anaxagoras (c. 500 B.C.), are the remains of ancient town of Klazomenai. A number of Archaic painted clay sarcophagi were found in the grounds of the hospital here.

Çeşme

Rising above the sea and dominated by the walls of a medieval castle, lies the holiday centre of Çeşme which is situated at the tip of the peninsula, 45km/28 miles west of Urla. It takes its name from its thermal springs ("çeşme", spring). The sulphurous water (35–50°C/95–122°F) is recommended for the treatment of rheumatism. From here a ferry service conveys cars to the Greek island of Chios (Sakız in Turkish). The seaside resort of Ilıca (hotels, holiday facilities) is situated 5km/3 miles east of Çeşme, in a bay with a beautiful sandy beach.

Kolophon

South of İzmir lies Cumaovası, home of the city's new "Adnan Menderes" civil airport which was completed in 1987. The road which branches off the main road and passes through the little town, continues south to Değirmendere, close to the site of ancient Kolophon. Kolophon was one of the principal cities of the Panionic League, famed for its wealth and luxury and also noted for the breeding of horses and the production of colophonium, a purified resin harvested from the pine trees growing on the surrounding hills. The site is crossed by the River Avcı Çayı (formerly Ales).

Notion

The city's port of Notion used to stand at the south end of the Ales valley, 12km/7½ miles from Kolophon on a little bay which is now silted up. The remains of the ancient town are on a hill surrounded by walls and towers, from which two promontories project into the sea. On the east side of the site stood a theatre in which more than 20 tiers of seating can still be seen. Nearby are the remains of a temple 12m/40ft long. To the north lies the town's necropolis.

Klaros

Located in a side valley to the east is the site of ancient Klaros, which was celebrated for its cave oracle of Apollo. The site was identified in 1907.

Larissa

The road which leads north-west from İzmir skirts first the beautiful Gulf of İzmir and then passes the remains of ancient Larissa (40km/25 miles). The acropolis was built by Aeolian Greeks in the 6th c. B.C. On a hill to the east is the site of Neon Teichos, a stronghold directed against Larissa which was endowed by the people of Cyme in the 8th c. B.C. The lower town, with polygonal walls, lay under the acropolis.

Foça/Phokaia

Some 2km/1¼ miles further north a side road branches off the main road on the left to the pleasant little port town of Foça (founded 1576) situated on the site of ancient Phokaia (Phocaea) at the northern entrance to the Gulf of İzmir.
Phokaia, the most northerly of the Ionian cities, was founded in the 8th c., probably from Teos. Situated on a promontory projecting into the gulf, the city had two harbours. The Phocaeans were daring seamen who by the 7th c. B.C. were familiar with the coasts of the western Mediterranean, founding Massalia (Marseilles) about 600 B.C. and Alalia (Aleria), on the east of Corsica, about 565 B.C. Many wealthy citizens of Phokaia moved to these new areas when their city fell to the Persians about 540 B.C. The only surviving ancient structures are the foundations of walls. There is also a ruined 15th c. Genoese castle.

Yenifoça

To the north-east on the far side of the promontory (road via Bağlararası) is the little town of Yenifoça with its beach, small harbour and modern tourist developments. Founded at the beginning of the 14th c. it fell to the Turks at the same time as its twin town of Foça, or Focia Nuova as it was once known. In the lonely surrounding area are several attractive bathing beaches.

Çandarlı

On a promontory on the north side of the Gulf of Çandarlı stands the little grain port of Çandarlı, dominated by a restored 13th c. Venetian castle. In antiquity the gulf was known as Sinus Elaiticus, after the city of Elaia, the port for Pergamon. There are still remains of the ancient town walls built by Attalos I. The acropolis was built on an egg-shaped hill.
Çandarlı was traditionally believed to be the site of the Aeolian port of Pitane, founded by the Amazons, which had two harbours, one on each side of the promontory.

Manisa/ Magnesia on the Sipylos

The provincial capital of Manisa (pop. 158,000) lies 40km/25 miles north-east of İzmir at the foot of Manisa Dağı (the ancient Mount Sipylos; 1517m/4977ft), the highest peak in the Manisa range. Manisa has a number of notable mosques but is also worth visiting for its picturesque location on the slopes of a hill. The houses with their typical light-coloured hipped roofs and the minarets which soar up between them make this old Ottoman town into a major attraction. Of the origins of the town, which was known in antiquity as Magnesia on the Sipylos to distinguish it from Magnesia on the Maeander (see Menderes · Maeander), nothing is known. The Akpınar relief (see below) suggests that the region was under the influence of the Hittite Empire after 1400 B.C.

The two principal mosques are the Great Mosque (Ulu Cami), built in 1366, which has antique columns with Byzantine capitals supporting the arcading round its courtyard and the Murat Mosque (Muradiye Camii; 1583–86), now a museum, which is surrounded by an almshouse, a library and a former medrese (theological college).

Near the two mosques stands the Sultan's Mosque (Sultan Camii; 1552), with a medrese and a hospital.

On the hill of Sandık Tepesi, to the south of the town, the walls of the old citadel are still visible. Three circuits of walls can be distinguished. The outermost ring dates from the time of the Byzantine Emperor John III (1222–54). The upper ring must be built on the foundations of the ancient acropolis, of which nothing remains. (3rd c. B.C. statue now in the Archaeological Museum, İstanbul).

The top of the hill offers fine views over the town and the plain of Gediz.

Alexander the Great

Niobe Rock

On the south-western outskirts of the town a crag in the rough shape of a head has been popularly identified as Niobe weeping for her father Tantalus – a legend traditionally set in this area.

*Akpınar relief

On the hillside to the left of the Salihli road 6km/4 miles east of Manisa stands a badly weathered figure of a seated goddess. Referred to by Pausanias as "the oldest sculptured image of the Mother of the gods", the inscriptions date from the period of the Hittite Empire.

Akhisar

To the north-east, 50km/31 miles beyond Manisa lies the town of Akhisar (pop. 74,000) which is situated on the north-eastern edge of the administrative region of the same name (cotton, tobacco and poppy seed plantations). The area is famous for its carpet industry. The small town of Gördes, known in antiquity as Julia Goerdes, lies in the mountain region some 60km/38 miles to the east and is also noted for its carpets. It is here that the term "Gordian knot" originated. The modern settlement of Akhisar (White Hill) grew up on the site of the ancient town of Thyratira which was founded by Seleukos I Nicator on the road from Pergamon to Sardis. Pliny the Younger mentioned the town in his writings under the name of Pelopia. A large Christian community settled here in Early Christian times and is referred to in Revelations (1:11 and 2:18) as the site of one of the churches of the Apocalypse.

İzmit (Kocaeli)   E 3

North-west Anatolia (Marmara region)
Province: Kocaeli
Altitude: 10–110m/32–360ft
Population: 255,000

Situation and Importance

This busy provincial town at the eastern end of the Gulf of İzmit (formerly known as the Gulf of Astakos) is a major industrial centre with factories not only in the immediate vicinity but also in the nearby towns around the Gulf (automobiles, metal-processing, chemicals; Yarımca: ironworks, İpraz oil refinery). The dockyards of Gölcük on the opposite side of the gulf combine with İzmit to create a military base and garrison of considerable importance. As the town lies on one of Turkey's tectonic fault lines, it has often been affected by serious earthquakes and most of the buildings are modern.

Once the residence of emperors Hadrian and Diocletian, the town stands on the site of the Bithynian capital Nikomedeia, which was founded in 264 B.C. by Nikomedes I. A short distance to the north-west stood Astakos or Olbia, a city which was founded by the Megarans and later destroyed by the Thracian Lysimachos. An earthquake obliterated the old settlement in A.D. 358, but magnificent new temples and other public buildings which became famous for their statues adorned the rebuilt Nikomedeia. One life-sized ivory statue of Nikomedes was taken to Rome by Trajan. In 74 B.C., the city fell under Roman influence. Between A.D. 111 and 113, Pliny the Younger became the Roman governor of Bithynia and was resident here. In A.D. 259 after its destruction by the Goths, the city was rebuilt in its original splendour by Diocletian as the capital of his tetrarchy. Under Constantine it rivalled Rome or Alexandria in importance. In 1386 the city became a part of the Ottoman Empire.

History

Sights

The remains of the city walls date from Hellenistic, Roman, Byzantine and Ottoman times. The citadel ruins (acropolis) are of Byzantine origin. The Pertev Paşa Camii Mosque is the work of the famous Ottoman architect Sinan (see Famous People).

Surroundings

The 19th c. provincial town of Adapazarı (pop. 174,000) is situated 20km/12½ miles to the east of İzmit and close to the River Sakarya at the western end of a wide low-lying area (Adapazarı Ovasi). It has assumed increasing economic importance as the centre of north-western Turkey's industrial heartland. The surrounding agricultural land produces potatoes, tobacco and hazelnuts. The town grew out of a weekly market on an uninhabited site ("adapazarı", island market) and there is little of interest in the town. On the southern outskirts of the town the Justinian bridge crosses a now dried-up tributary of the Sakarya (Sangarios in antiquity). Measuring 450m/492yd it dates from Roman times (A.D. 560) and has twelve arches.

Adapazarı

To the north-west of Gevye, about 30km/19 miles to the south of Adapazarı, a well-maintained bridge built in Ottoman times under Sultan Bayazit (1481–1512) crosses the Sakarya. The town itself lies at the northern end of a 30km/19 mile long, intensively-farmed valley, at the heart of which stands the small town of Pamukova, meaning cotton plain.

Gevye

To the south-west of Adapazarı, at an altitude of 40m/131ft, lies the Sapanca Gölü freshwater lake (47sq.m/18sq.miles). The bottom of the lake is 20m/65ft below the level of the Sea of Marmara. It is situated in a low-lying area (Sakarya-Bosporus) which during the Ice Age linked the Black Sea and the Sea of Marmara. Shifts in the earth's crust led to a rise in the level of the surface and the land dried up. By the end of the Pleistocene (Ice Age) period, the Sea of Marmara had flooded the İzmit/Sapanca valley to form a bay into which the Sakarya flowed. The lake slowly silted up and separated from the Gulf, but the River Sakarya continued to flow into the Gulf of İzmit through Lake Sapanca. Finally, deposits from the Sakarya and its tributaries built up in the lake and a new outlet formed to the east, flowing into

Sapanca Gölü

the Sapanca. As a result, the river's course was altered and it now disgorges directly into the Black Sea. Picturesque villages set in extensive fruit orchards can be seen on the south side of the lake, around the town of Sapanca. In the town itself, the Rüstem Paşa Külliyesi Mosque complex is worth a visit.

*Taraklı

About 70km/44 miles south of Adapazarı stands the small, hillside village of Taraklı with its thermal waters. Since 1990 a large part of the town has been subject to a preservation order. There are many two to four storey timbered houses built in Pontic style (e.g. the Town Hall). Other interesting sights include the Yunus Paşa Camii (also known as Kurşunlu Cami, Lead Mosque), which was founded in the centre of the town after a visit by the Grand Vizier Yunus Paşa and was built between 1512 and 1521. After returning from a military campaign in Egypt the general was executed on the orders of Selim I, as he had criticised the sultan.

Gebze

Gebze (pop. 93,000) was known in Byzantine times as Dakibyza. The town which is set back from the northern side of the Gulf of İzmit at the foot of the Gazi Dağı (305m/1000ft) is noted for the splendid Orhan Gazi Camii with its tile decorations and for other Byzantine remains. Also of interest is the dome on the early Ottoman Coban Mustafa Paşa Camii, together with the polygonal türbe (mausoleum) of the founder. To the south of Gebze lay the coastal Bithynian town of Libyssa (ruins near Dif İskelesı), where in 183 B.C. the Punic general Hannibal took poison as he found himself surrounded by the Romans and the Bithynian king Prusias wished to extradite him. An interesting curiosity is to be found in an industrial estate on a small hill beneath some cypress trees. Reputed to be Hannibal's grave, it was magnificently restored by Emperor Septimius Severus (A.D. 193–211), but it is now just a pile of stones. Excavations were carried out in 1906 by Wiegand. The village of Hünkar Çayre was also situated nearby. It was here in 1481 that Sultan Mehmet II the conqueror of Constantinople died.

Hereke

On the northern side of the Gulf of İzmit lies the small town of Hereke (pop. 11,000) in a valley 30km/19 miles west of İzmit. Formerly known as Charax. The town acquired fame when Constantine the Great died in nearby Ankyron castle (now destroyed) in A.D. 337. The main occupations of the local population are wine production and carpet-making, which follows the traditional style of İstanbul and Bursa. Here in 1891 the first factory for the production of finely-woven silk and woollen carpets was established. The carpets produced in Hereke today are made according to the specifications of the Imperial court. The special patterns are skilfully copied from old designs.

İznik   C 6

North-west Anatolia
Province: Bursa
Altitude: 90m/295ft
Population: 17,000

Situation

İznik lies on the intensively cultivated east side of İznik Gölü, a lake (80m/260ft; 303sq.km/117sq.miles; max. depth 75m/260ft) occupying part of a tectonic longitudinal valley which extends from the Gulf of Gemlik into the western Pontic Mountains.

History

İznik occupies the site of ancient Nikaia (Nicaea), founded by Antigonos Alexander the Great's general in the 4th c. B.C. After suffering destruction in a number of earthquakes it was rebuilt by Hadrian and thereafter enjoyed a period of great prosperity. In 325 Nicaea, the see of a bishop, was the meeting-place of the First Ecumenical Council (Council of Nicaea). In 787

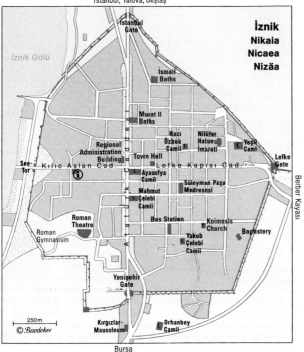

İstanbul, Yalova, Beştaş

İznik
Nikaia
Nicaea
Nizäa

İznik Gölü

İstanbul Gate

İsmail Baths

Murat II Baths

Hacı Özbek Camii
Nilüfer Hatun İmareti
Yeşil Camii

Regional Administration Building
Town Hall
Lefke Kapısı Cad.
Lefke Gate

Kılıç Aslan Cad.

See-Tor

Ayasofya Camii

Süleyman Paşa Medresesi

Mahmut Çelebi Camii

Roman Theatre

Bus Station
Koimesis Church
Baptistery

Roman Gymnasium

Yakub Çelebi Camii

Berber Kayası

Yenişehir Gate

250m
© Baedeker

Kırgızlar-Mausoleum
Orhanbey Camii

Bursa

the Seventh Ecumenical Council which condemned Iconoclasm met in Nicaea.

From 1204 to 1261, when Constantinople was capital of the Latin Empire established by the Crusaders, Nicaea was the seat of the Eastern Emperor and the Orthodox patriarch. In 1331 the town fell to the Ottomans. Under Ottoman rule it became noted for the production of beautiful enamel tiles, after Sultan Selim I brought in craftsmen from Tabriz and Azerbaijan in 1514.

Sights

The outstanding sight in İznik is the imposing circuit of ancient walls, reminiscent of the walls of Constantinople but on a smaller scale. Although partly ruined and overgrown they are still extraordinarily impressive. Little is left of the old Greek walls. Roman rebuilding in the 1st c. A.D. altered the original square plan to a polygon with a total extent of 4427m/4842yd. The towers flanking the gates and the masonry superstructure were added by the Byzantines. The finest section of wall on the west side of the town is built with stone from earlier structures and dates from the reign of Emperor Leo the Isaurian (inscription). Considerable stretches of the wall were built during the Seljuk period. The inner circuit of walls (9m/30ft high and 3.5m/11½ft wide) originally had a battlemented parapet walk. Projecting from the wall are 108 towers with entrances from within the walls.

**Town walls

353

İznik

A photogenic group before the town walls of İznik

*City Gates	On the northern side of the circuit stands the İstanbul Gate, which is like the Lefke Gate in structure. On the inner wall, which is of later construction, are two interesting human masks. The Lefke Gate on the east side was built about A.D. 70 and resembles a Roman triumphal arch. Outside the gate stands an aqueduct which probably dates from the time of Justinian and was later renovated by Sultan Orhan. On the south side of the town is Yenişehir Gate, the oldest parts of which date from the 3rd c. A.D.
*Green Mosque	İznik's finest mosque, the Green Mosque, stands a little north-west of the Lefke Gate. Built between 1384–89, the porch is now glazed and opens on to three arches born on two granite columns. Only a few fragments remain of the original marble screens. The doorway and windows framed in calligraphic inscriptions are particularly notable features.
İmaret (Museum)	Facing the Green Mosque to the west stands the İmaret or Public Kitchen of Nilüfer Hatun, which was built in 1388 by Sultan Orhan's wife. It now houses the municipal museum with Greek and Roman artefacts, tombstones, İznik tiles and inscriptions.
Hagia Sophia	The ruined Church of Hagia Sophia stands in the centre of the town at the intersection of the two main streets which lead to the four old town gates. This was probably the meeting-place of the Seventh Ecumenical Council (787). Built in 1065 to replace an earlier church from the time of Justinian, it comprises a three-aisled basilica with small vaulted chambers on either side of the apse. In the reign of Sultan Orhan it was converted into a mosque and decorated with beautiful tiles.
Roman Theatre	In the south-west of the old town stands the Roman theatre, said to have been built in 112 by Pliny the Younger when he was governor of Bithynia. As there was no natural slope for the theatre's auditorium, the tiers were borne on massive and finely constructed vaulting.

İznik became renowned for its faience

1km/³⁄₄ mile east of Lefke Gate rises the Barber's Rock (Berber Kayası) with the remains of a sarcophagus 4m/13ft long. A magnificent panoramic view of İznik can be enjoyed from the top of the rock.

Barber's Rock

On a hillside 5km/3miles north-west of İznik stands the Obelisk of Cassius (Beştas), a 12m/40ft high funerary monument to C. Cassius Philiscus (2nd c. A.D.).

Obelisk of Cassius

Kahramanmaraş (Maraş)   M 6

South-east Anatolia (Maraş-Valley)   **See warning page 7**
Province: Kahramanmaraş
Altitude: 700m/2296ft
Population: 229,000

The provincial capital of Maraş stands at the southern foot of Maraş Taurus in the foothills of the Maraş mountain chain. The prefix Kahraman means "heroic" and refers to the resistance of the local population to the English and French occupation during the Turkish War of Liberation. Maraş is primarily a market town for local produce, with the main crop being cotton which grows on the plain. The mountainous hinterland, the Maraş-Taurus, has traces of small Ice Age glaciers on its summits and the population is sparse even in the long Betiz and Nuruhak valleys. Before the First World War, many of the villages were settled by Armenians (Süleymanlı = Zeytun). The story of their forcible eviction through Maraş and Aleppo into the desert at Deir es Zor is told in Franz Werfel's "The Forty Days of Musa Dagh". A fierce cold wind sometimes blows through this region. Similar to the Adriatic bora, it occurs when cold and warm Mediterranean air currents meet, bringing bitterly cold storms to the Maraş valley.

Situation and Importance

Assyrian texts refer to the town as the centre of the late Hittite kingdom of Gurgum. Its heyday was around 800 B.C., but it was overrun and destroyed by Sargon II (721–705 B.C.). In the 1st c. under Byzantine rule, when the town was known as Germaniceia, it became a fortress on the Thugur line, the disputed boundary in south-western Anatolia between the Byzantine Empire and Arab khalifs. Around 962 large groups of Armenian refugees, who were fleeing from the Seljuks, settled in the region.
When the Byzantines were defeated by the Arabs, one of the Armenian town governors Philaretes enlisted the support of a Crusader army to

History

establish an independent state. Maraş changed hands a number of times and at one time came under the rule of Dulkadir-Beys, and from 1515 it was a part of the Ottoman Empire. Between 1832 and 1840, İbrahim Paşa brought the town under the control of the Egyptian governor Mehmed Ali.

Sights

Old town and Kapalı Çarşı

The covered bazaar is one of the few attractions in the town and much of its present structure dates from the 17th c. In the remains of the old town below the citadel other sights originate from the 15th/16th c. and include the Ulu Cami from the Dulkadir-Beys times with some valuable wooden carvings and decorations, the Hatuniye Camii founded in memory of Selim I's grandmother, the Taş Han and the Taş Medrese and mausoleum, which all date from the days of the Dulkadiroğulları.

Citadel

The castle of Maraş dominates the old town and much of the land has been given over to gardens and popular cafés. The original building, probably Byzantine, is thought to have been constructed on Hittite remains, but it was altered considerably during Ottoman times. A part of the dilapidated castle is now an archaeological museum with displays of excavated finds from the surrounding area.

Nearby caves

The caves of Döngeli (Döngelı Mağarası) which are only a short distance from Tekir on the road to Göksun have yielded some prehistoric finds. A landslide blocked the Tekir Çayı and now cascades of rock plummet 120m/400ft into a cavern.

Karadeniz Ereğlisi

See Zonguldak

Karaman | 6

Central Anatolia
Province: Karaman
Altitude: 1038m/3404ft
Population: 65,000

Situation and Importance

Known as Laranda until the Middle Ages, Karaman lies in the lowlands of inland Anatolia halfway between Konya and Silifke. Many important buildings remain from the period of its greatest prosperity when it was capital of the Karaman dynasty (Karamanoğulları, 1275–1466) which ruled Konya for many years, succumbing eventually to Mehmet II. In 1190 Frederick I (Barbarossa) Holy Roman Emperor stayed here before crossing the Taurus Mountains on the Third Crusade.

History

Historical research suggests that Hittite Landa, an important commercial centre and garrison town c. 1300 B.C., preceded the Laranda that one of Alexander the Great's generals laid waste. Later, under Byzantium Laranda remained a garrison town against Arab incursions. Apart from a short period of occupation under Barbarossa and six years of Armenian rule, Karaman stayed under Seljuk control from the 12th c. In 1220 the famous mystic Celâleddin Rumi (see Mevlana under Famous People) sought refuge here from Afghanistan with his parents, until his father was summoned to Konya to become a theological professor. As the Seljuks' influence waned, the beylik of Karaman's fortunes improved. The first ruler Kerimüddin-Karaman a Türkmen timber merchant from the region around

Mut and Ermenek took up residence in Laranda from 1255 to 1320, giving his name to the region. Before long the Karamans had occupied the Seljuk heartlands and in 1320 even moved the capital to Konya to claim and exhibit the Rumi-Seljuk's inheritance. However, the life-style of the Karamans was not the usual, refined Persian-Seljuk way in most beyliks, but the more austere ways of a nomadic existence. The Karaman ruler Mehmet Bey insisted on the use of Turkish instead of Persian as the language of the court and officialdom. Science and art were encouraged and Karaman retained the same status as Konya. The stable Karaman state was able to resist Ottoman pressure until 1466.

Sights

About 1371 Alaeddin Bey Karamanoğlu endowed a monastery and a mosque for Mevlana's mother Mümine Hatun, where her tomb now lies. The adjacent Süleyman Bey Hamami (baths) were built in 1358.

Ak Tekke

This polygonal domed sarcophagus with a handsomely decorated portal contains the remains of the important Karaman prince, who was also the son-in-law of the Ottoman sultan Murat I.

Alaeddin Bey
Türbesi

This theological college which is known as either the Nefise Hatun or Nefise Sultan Medresesi was built in 1387 by Nefise, the wife of Karamanoğlu Alaeddin Bey. Note the imposing entrance porch of black and white marble. At the time, it was one of the most distinguished universities in the Muslim world. The founder's mausoleum can be found in the domed winter quarters, which is itself flanked by domed sections.

Hatuniye
Medresesi

In the 12th c. the Seljuks built the huge Karaman castle on the foundations of what was probably a Hittite site. It has been restored a number of times

* Karaman Kalesi

Karaman Kalesi – a ruined 12th c. castle

and is now in good condition. A stage for folk concerts.has been constructed within the castle. In the mid-1970s one of the few preserved old town centres typical of central Anatolia could be seen around the castle. The houses consisted of single- or two-storey flat-roofed constructions made of clay similar to those seen in Konya, but all but one of the old houses have since been demolished.

*Karamanoğlu
Külliyesi

This complex founded in 1433 and consists of a small mosque, a fountain in Seljuk style, a medrese (İbrahim Bey İmaret), a printing press and İbrahim Bey's türbe with a pyramid roof. The Koran school building is of particular interest as it picks up the compact Seljuk style of the 13th c. Nestling against an open entrance hall stands a minaret with enamel tile decorations.

Yunus Emre
Camii

Behind the Hatuniye Medresesi stands a well-managed museum housing collections from Çanhasan dating from Neolithic times to the present day. The Yunus Emre Camii the oldest building from the Karaman era (1349) contains the tomb of Yunus Emre (c. 1280–1321), who is regarded as the most important exponent of Turkish literature with prose and poetry written in a language accessible to the common man.

Surroundings

Alaçatı

On the eastern side of the village of Alaçatı, 13km/8 miles east of Karaman stands a 5m/16ft hillock, where in 1961 British archaeologists started to unearth the remains of dwellings dating from the 5th c. B.C. As in Çatalhüyük, the houses here have an entrance in the roof.

*Alahan

Some 60km/39 miles south of Karaman a track snakes its way 1200m/3900ft up to the Alahan Monastery (magnificent view!). The 5th c. complex consists of two churches and a chapel. At the beginning of the 1960s work began on the western church (Church of the Evangelists) to restore the main walls, including the monumental church portal and the relief stonework with symbols of the Evangelists. The resulting church was much smaller and had only a single nave. The eastern church with its three porches ornamented with vine tendrils and fish remains as an impressive domed basilica, whose style characterises the transition from late Greco-Roman to Byzantine ecclesiastical architecture. The arcades in the nave are borne by Corinthian columns.

**Binbir Kilise
(Değle)

Barely 25km/16 miles north of Karaman a metalled road branches off the route to Hotamiş up to the brim of the Kara Dağ volcano (2288m/7500ft) and to the village of Madenşehri (Madenşehir) 8km/5 miles further east. At the entrance to the village stands a large ruined church with some old frescos. The village of Değle can be found higher up about 5km/3 miles to the west on a continuation of the metalled road (keep left). It stands on a hill at the end of a track on the right-hand side of the road. Now almost abandoned, the village is the centre of Binbir Kilise which includes the remains of some well-maintained Byzantine churches and mausoleums. The complex enjoyed prosperity between the 3rd and 8th c. but in the 11th c. was destroyed by the Seljuks. About 50 church ruins remain and they have given some insight into the history of church architecture. The basilica are particularly interesting. They are constructed of ashlar and unlike most churches of Asia Minor do not have flat roofs, but are vaulted throughout because of the shortage of timber in central Anatolia. To the north-east can be found more ruined churches and monasteries dating from the 9th and 10th c. On the Mahliç Tepesi the principal summit of the Kara Dağ range at a height of 2771m/9088ft stand the remains of a 9th c. Byzantine monastery and a Hittite sacred grotto with hieroglyphics, copies of which may be seen in the museum at Karaman. Another of the Hittite's sacred sites lies on the western slopes of the Kara Dağ on Kızıl Dağ.

Ermenek

Ermenek lies on a direct route via Mut 150km/94 miles south-west of Karaman but on roads of variable quality. Here stood the ancient town of

Germanikopolis which was founded in the 1st c. B.C. by Antiochos IV and was the first centre of the later Karaman emirates. The architectural styles here also demonstrate the close links between the Karamans and the Seljuks, who used the Arab Kuf style for their mosques. All the mosques are pillared, have no courtyard and are set transversely to the wall showing the direction of Mecca. Examples in Ermenek include Ulu Cami (1302) Akca Mescit (1300), Sipas Camii (1306) and Meydan Camii (1436). A further interesting mosque complex can be found at the 12th c. Sarı Hatun Camii. Of particular interest are the diagonal-cut carvings on the staircase.

The so-called Yabangülü Saklı or "hidden churches" can be found in the area around the village of Güldere 40km/25 miles south-east on the Gödet Çayı pass. Several smallish, but still quite spacious cave churches are "hidden" in raised positions on one rock.

Güldere

To the west some distance from the road to Konya, 20km/12½ miles north-west of Karaman stands the village of Kâzim Karabekir – carpet-weaving village with unusually constructed houses. In contrast to the normal clay brick constructions typical of central Anatolia, almost all the houses in this village are built with flat limestone slabs. There are two interesting mosques in the village.

Kâzim Karabekir

The remains of three Seljuk caravanserais can be found in the region around Karaman: at Gaferyat Hanı, 15km/9½ miles north-west of Karaman in the village of İlisira, at Kozak Hanı, south-west of the road to Silifke and the Sartavul Hanı, founded by Alaeddin Kaykobad in the 13th c., which lies some 20km/12½ miles south of Karaman, to the east of the Silifke road.

Caravanserais

The small town of Mut 75km/47 miles south of Karaman was formerly known as Ninica Claudiopolis which was founded by Marcus Aurelius Polemo. There are few ancient remains with only the tower of the once Byzantium-controlled citadel still standing. Try to visit the 14th c. Lal Ağa Camii with a central dome, a large front porch and annexes that create a side-aisle effect.

Mut

The landscape close to the 1600m/5248ft Sertavul Pass to the south of Karaman differs from the other mountain passes in the Taurus region because it is relatively flat. It changes in character as the pass extends further south into the deep valley around Mut. The mainly treeless terrain is often devoid of grass but the plains are covered with cushion plants. The karst landscape is dotted with limestone rocks and riddled with countless sinkholes. It was this mountain pass that Barbarossa crossed before he drowned in the bath in Kalykadnos.

Sertavul Geçidi

Near the village of Yeşildere some 30km/19 miles south of Karaman lies one of the oldest Early Christian monasteries. The countless rooms, tunnel-like passages and galleries are reached via a remarkable staircase.

Yeşildere

Kars

T 3

North-east Anatolia
Province: Kars
Altitude: 1750m/5740ft
Population: 80,000

North-east of Aras Nehri (Araxes) beyond the Kura pass and near the Turkish-Georgian border stretches the biggest and highest lava plateau in Anatolia. Predominantly basalt and andesite but also tuff, pitchstone and volcanic rock, the impressive, monotonous landscape consists mainly of grazing pastures, with cattle and sheep farming the primary occupation of the local population. The high steppes of Kars and Ardahan, (up to

Situation and Importance

2500m/8200ft) are dominated in places by volcanoes and divided into four sections by deep hollows. In one of these valleys between the Ardahan and Kars Yaylası lies the provincial capital of Kars, which was settled by Turks before 130 B.C., but there are many reminders particularly in the architecture of the period of Russian domination before the First World War. The new town is laid out in a chequerboard pattern and many of the houses display the colonial style typical of many Russian cities such as St Petersburg.

The modern town centre was planned after 1877 during the Russian occupation. There is still a community of Protestant Germans in the village of Karacaören only a short distance from Kars. They were brought here by the Tsars over a hundred years ago. With little industry to speak of, the region is best known for the manufacture of hand-woven carpets displaying eagle and shield motifs. Many of the local cheese factories owe their origins to the Volga German settlers who moved here in the 19th c.

History	The history of Kars is closely linked with the fate of Armenia. Ashot the Iron Man (914–918) expelled the Moslem emirs and opened the way for his brother Abbas I to establish a Bagratid kingdom with Kars as the capital. The town remained the royal seat under the rival Mushegh (962–984) and his successors Abbas and Gagik, when Ashot III (The Merciful, 952–977) moved the capital to Ani. The collapse of Armenia into a number of principalities occurred at around the same time. In 1050 Kars fell to Byzantium, but in 1064 the Seljuk Alp Arslan won control. The majority of the Armenian population fled south to Cilicia. From 1205 to 1585 under Georgian rule Kars enjoyed a degree of prosperity, before falling to the Ottomans. The Kars and Ardahan region belonged to Russia in 1807, 1854–56 (Crimean War) and again from 1873 to 1921.

Sights

Old town	The old town is said to have been enclosed by a 27km/17 mile wall with 220 towers. At the moment the only remains lie in a neglected part of the town with three preserved towers: Su Kapısı (Water Gate) or Çeribaşi Kapı in the west, Kağizman Kapısı in the middle and Behram Kapısı or Bayram Paşa Kapısı in the east.
Beşik Camii	The Beşik Camii (Cradle Mosque) below the castle was built in 1045 by the Bagratids and is used today as a warehouse.
Beylerbey Saray	The ruined Governor's Palace in the lower castle is also known as Paşa Sarayı. It was built in 1579 by Lala Mustafa Paşa.
Celal Baba Türbesi	The tomb of the local saint Celal Baba who perished in the Mongol invasion of 1239 is open to visitors on Thursdays.
Evliya Camii	This rather nondescript building was constructed in 1589 when the town underwent restoration. It was destroyed in 1604 and again in 1626 during an attack by Safavids. It was then renovated and covered with a mud roof. In the garden stands the türbe of St Evliya.
Ilbeyoğlu Hamami	These Turkish baths with 18th c. reliefs and ornaments are still in use. With the long balcony overlooking the river they are also known as the Balkonlu Hamam.
*Kümbet Camii	This mosque which was until recently Kars museum was built under the Bagratid Abas I (of Ani) 930–937 as the Church of the Apostles, but became a mosque in 1664. When the town was under Russian control it became a church again until 1921. The tall drum is embellished with reliefs of the Twelve Apostles.
Müze	The new museum can be found in a road which forks off the road to Ani (Ani Yolu) in the north-east of the town. Finds from the Bronze Age to the present day are on display. An annex also houses an ethnography depart-

Kars: the Osman citadel dominates the Old Town

ment. Of special interest are the panels of a carved, Armenian church door and a Russian church bell which dates from the time of Tsar Nicholas II.

An Armenian castle and later an Ottoman citadel dominates the old town. It stands on Urartian foundations and was altered around the middle of the 12th c. by the Saltukoğulları and then rebuilt on the orders of Sultan Murat III after it was completely destroyed by the Mongol Timur in 1386. The castle site is unchanged since the 19th c. Crimean War. Visits can be arranged at certain times.

*Narın Kalesi

According to an inscription on the gate, this mosque was built by the provincial governor Seyyid Yusuf Paşa. A wooden minaret was later replaced by one made of stone.

Yusuf Paşa Camii

Surroundings

The regional centre of Ardahan is situated some 95km/60 miles north-west of Kars. It lies in the Ardahan valley below the Yalnızçam Dağları and it is reached by crossing the 2640m/8660ft Çam Geçidi in the heart of Turkish Georgia (see Artvin). Ardahan is dominated by a huge fortress with square towers (up to 12m/40ft high). The present fortress was built by Selim I. Ardahan formed a part of the Russian Empire from 1873 to 1921.

Ardahan

Stone Age cave drawings of deer can be seen in the village of Çamuşlu, some 65km/40 miles south of Kars.

Çamuşlu

About 90km/57 miles north of Kars lies the small town of Çıldır. In a long valley about 14km/8 miles further along the Aktaş Gölü road (the last 4km/2½ miles have to be covered on foot) stands a medieval castle. Known as Şeytan Kalesi (Devil's Mountain) or more correctly Rabat Kalesi mean-

Çıldır

361

	ing "fortified monastery", it perches at a dizzy height on a rocky peak. Because of the proximity to the Armenian-Turkish border visitors require a special pass from the military.
*Çıldır Gölü	The extensive Lake Çıldır (130m/426ft deep; 128sq.km/79sq.miles) is a natural lake. It was at one time linked with the Çıldır basin until a 1.5km/1 mile wide and 14km/9 mile long stream of lava from the Papa Dağı (2900m/9512ft) split it into two sections. Close to the north-western tip of the lake near the village of Gölebelen stands a domed basilica which is now used as a mosque. Further south near Peresin and only accessible by a cross-country vehicle lie the ruins of a double church and nearby an interesting Kurdish cemetery. The remains of a church and castle can also be seen on an island known as Agenkale in the middle of the lake.
Kecivan	The old Armenian town of Artageyra lies about 65km/40 miles south-west of Kars. Some Seljuk remains include a mausoleum (kümbet) with relief carvings on the entrance.
Sarıkamış	This garrison town and regional centre of Sarıkamış lies about 80km/50 miles south-west of Kars. Until the First World War it was a border town for Tsarist Russia. A small skiing centre with a lift is situated nearby.

Kaş   E 7

	South-west coast (Mediterranean) Province: Antalya Altitude: 0–50m/0–165ft Population: 5000
Situation and Importance	The idyllic little port of Kaş stands in a small bay near the southern tip of Lycia. The most easterly of the Greek islands Kastellorizo (Megisti; Turkish Meis) lies just offshore. The houses line the slopes surrounding the main ancient harbour, which is protected by a breakwater. A marina is under construction.
*Holiday resort	Thanks to its beautiful setting and the sailing facilities it offers, Kaş has become a popular tourist resort with hotels, guest-houses and a good camp-site. Boat trips are available to the many fascinating places along the coastline of tiny coves and bays as well as the Greek island of Kastellorizo (Meis).

Sights

The present town occupies the site of ancient Antiphellos (Lycian Habesa) and serves as the port for the Pınarbeşi hinterland and Phellos which lies opposite on a steep-sided hill. The principal sights are a Lycian sarcophagus in the centre of the little town, a well-preserved ancient theatre on the west side of town (with a fine view over the bay to the island of Kastellorizo), the remains of the ancient town walls near the shore and Lycian rock tombs to the north-east.

Surroundings

Bronze Age shipwreck	Off the promontory of Ulu Burun to south of Kaş a shipwreck dating from 14th/13th c. B.C. was found in 1984 by Turkish and American underwater archaeologists. Some valuable bronze artefacts were recovered.
**Kekova and the Yavu mountain region	The coastline between Kaş and Kale has a wealth of historic sites. No less than seventeen large-scale settlements have been discovered in the mountain region of Yavu, along the southern section of the coast and the offshore

island of Kekova. The historical names for many of these sites are not yet known. Many interesting remains including ancient farmsteads, sarcophagi, Lycian fortresses and fortified settlements are often hidden away in the undergrowth, but the local people usually know their whereabouts.

The fishing village of Üçağız, originally Tristoma, lies in Tristomas Bay and well sheltered from the open sea. The bay is situated to the west of Kaş next to the ancient settlement of Teimiussa, which as early as 4th c. B.C. was under the command of the Lycian ruler Perikles von Limyra. As well as a few relics on the acropolis, a settlement in the east and a 50m/164ft harbour wall (outside the village under water), there are also two burial grounds one to the north and one to the east. Many of the graves which include family tombs and sarcophagi belong to citizens of Myra and Kyaneai.

On the eastern peninsula of Tristomas Bay, a medieval castle looks down over the tiny village of Kaleüçağız. The site of ancient Simena dating from the 4th c. B.C. usually has to be reached by boat. The castle was built on the foundations of an ancient citadel. Part of the village can be found inside the castle walls alongside the remains of a temple. Below the fortifications stands a seven-tiered theatre with space for 300 seats – an indication that the settlement was not a large one. To the west is the town and in the water on the shore line below lie the well-maintained ruins of the Titus Baths (A.D. 79–81).
Further west can be found a necropolis which contains mostly Roman sarcophagi in the Lycian style. More sarcophagi and remains are to be seen underwater.

At the extreme south-eastern tip of the Yavu mountain region, the ancient River Andrakos meets the plain of Kale (Demre/Myra). At this point a wide marshy valley extends out on both sides of the river between the mountain region and the coastal hills of Myra and Andriake. The name of Antiochos III was linked with the town of Andriake as early as 197 B.C.
The ancient harbour is now marshland. The Andrakos flows down from its source in the karst rock passing an ancient water-mill and divides the town into north and south. The north town is mainly sand dunes with a still recognisable ruined church. Several buildings in the south town are in good condition including a warehouse, harbour wall, granarium (grain store), temple, market-place, parts of the harbour road, residences, water tanks, a number of churches and chapels. A wall surrounded the whole town and an aqueduct supplied water from the karst spring.
Outside the walls an extensive necropolis lies on the northern slopes behind the nymphaeum. In the south-western corner two watch towers stand on either side of a protective wall.

Some 7km/4½ miles east of Yavu behind the village of Gölbaşı, a metalled road leads north up to the ancient town of Trysa. Located at the northern end of the acropolis stands a heroon, a 4th c. B.C. shrine of an important Trysan dynast and the site's best-known relic. The famous 20m/65ft long and 3m/10ft wide heroon frieze, showing 600 figures, was taken from inside the enclosure and can now be seen in the Kunsthistorisches Museum in Vienna.

Due north of the coast road above the harbour and village of Yavu, the steep cliff of Kyaneai rises up. This Lycian town a large settlement even in the 4th c. B.C. was the see of a bishop. Three towers surmount the town walls. Interesting sights within the town include a number of sarcophagi, several rock tombs, the enormous town wall, the remains of buildings, market-place, water tanks on the acropolis and a large theatre at the foot of a gentle incline with 25 rows of seating (superb view).

50km/31 miles east of Kaş at the mouth of the Demre Dere (Myros in antiquity) lies a wide coastal plain, now an area of plastic-covered green-

Teimiussa

*Simena

Andriake

Trysa

Kyaneai

*Myra

houses where vegetables, particularly aubergines and tomatoes, are cultivated. The little town of Kale (Demre) occupies the site of the important Lycian town of Myra, which was visited by the Apostle Paul on his first journey to Rome in A.D. 61. In the 3rd c. St Nicholas became Bishop of Myra. Theodosius II made Myra the capital of Lycia.

At the foot of the acropolis, some impressive remains can be seen. Mostly hewn from the rock, the large theatre and many Lycian rock tombs, some of them dating from the 4th c., are particularly interesting.

Basilica of
St Nicholas

In Kale stands the early medieval domed Basilica of St Nicholas. Apart from minor restoration work, the church has been preserved in its original 11th c. form. Built into the sides of the nave are 2nd and 3rd c. sarcophagi. Remains of frescos can be seen in the apse and at certain points on the wall.

*Mediterranean
coast

The coast road between Finike and Kale (29km/18 miles) follows the coastline at some points, passing picturesque rocky coves with tempting places to bathe in crystal-clear water. The port of Finike (formerly Phoinika) with a population of 20,000 has little to offer tourists other than many miles of beautiful beaches with fine sand on the shores of the bay. The coast road east to the industrial town of Kumluca is currently being improved to motorway standard.

Statue of St Nicholas

Limyra

10km/6 miles north-east of Finike near the village of Zengerler at the foot of Mount Tocat stands the ancient town of Limyra (5th c. B.C.), one of the oldest settlements in Lycia.
On the hill to the north of the site an upper and a lower acropolis can be seen with remains of a Byzantine church and a Roman theatre on the latter. On the crag to the south stands the so-called Heroon of Perikles (c. 370 B.C.) hewn from the rock in the form of a temple. Other notable features are the Tomb of Gaius Caesar (d. A.D. 4), the tall Sarcophagus of Katabura, the Tomb of Tebersele (both 4th c.) and three large groups of Lycian rock tombs.

*Arykanda

30km/19 miles north of Finike the ruined town of Arykanda lies on the slopes of the Akdağ. Much of the 5th c. remains are arranged on terraces overlooking the River Arykandos which cascades down the valley and through the village of Başgöz (fish restaurants and trout farming). The citizens of Arykanda (Akalanda in Byzantine times) are thought to have had an extravagant lifestyle.
The stadium on the highest terrace is comparatively small (80 × 16sq.m/87 × 19sq.yd). It dates originally from Hellenistic times but was restored by

Lycian rock tombs . . .

. . . and entrance to the tombs in Myra

A picturesque rocky bay . . .

. . . on the south coast

the Romans. Below the stadium lies a small Greek theatre with 20 rows of
seating. It is almost intact, having been partially restored by the Romans.
Some inscriptions are visible on the top row. On the lowest terrace stands
the odeion containing a 75m/246ft long and 8m/26ft wide stoa with a
mosaic floor. Stretching out in front is the market-place with a gallery to the
south and west sides. It is presumed that a temple occupied the centre of
the market-place. To the west of the ruined town lies the bouleuterion. A
stoa (destroyed in late antiquity) stands in front and a row of seats carved
out of the rock is still visible.

Baths

The baths which lie to the south of the necropolis are certainly among the
best preserved buildings as they remain almost intact to roof level. A
semi-circular viewing room provides a splendid view into the Arykandos
valley. The hypocaust system in the frigidarium and caldarium is still in fine
condition. To the west of the baths in an annex to the complex stands a
gymnasium with school-rooms on the northern side. The baths are easily
accessible from here. Similarly a door opened from the adjacent palaestra
to the baths. Spring water (Başgöz Pınarı) still flows into the town through
rock canals supported with masonry. There are two necropoles, one to the
east and one to the west of the ruined city, where some interesting sarcophagi, huge tombs and small temples with relief designs can be seen. Near
the western burial ground lie some pre-Christian rock tombs.

Elmalı

The regional centre of Elmalı (pop. 12,000) on the edge of the Elmalı Ovası
offers some relief from the heat of summer as it stands at an altitude of
1200m/3936ft in the Taurus mountains surrounded by cedar and pine
forests. Until the 1950s the valley lay under large, shallow karst lakes, but
these have since been drained (Karagöl, Avlan Gölü), although the outline
of the water levels can still be discerned. A typical example of a drained
karst lake and drainage channel are to be found at Düden Mağarası about
15km/9 miles south of the town below the road to Finike.
In Beyler and many other villages in the Elmalı Ovası on the road to Kaş
ancient wooden grain-stores of varying sizes can be seen. The construction
methods used are reflected in the many Lycian rock tombs. Clearly a
centuries-old building tradition was preserved as it passed down the
generations.
In the 1960s American archaeologists found the remains of an early Bronze
Age settlement at Karataş-Semayük 5km/3 miles north-east of Elmalı. Finds
included a walled Megaran-type building with an oval courtyard.
Not far from Karagöl (see above) and to the south-west of Elmalı, excavations at Kızılbel and Karaburun exposed some 6–5th c. B.C. wall paintings,
depicting images from Greek mythology, the Land of the Dead and hunting
scenes. They have been skilfully restored.

Kastamonu I 2

North Anatolia
Province: Kastamonu
Altitude: 798m/2617ft
Population: 52,000

Situation and
Importance

The province of Kastamonu lies in that area of northern Turkey where the
Pontic Mountains flatten out. The peaks rarely exceed 2500m/8000ft. The
population is distributed more densely in the wider valleys of the region
between the coastal mountains in the north and the mountain range to the
south which acts as a barrier. This gently undulating high plateau is broken
up by rivers some of which have carved deep valleys in the rock. Time
seems to have stood still in the attractive Pontic town of Kastamonu which
lies in the Gökırmak valley. Timber façades, bay windows and roofs which
are usually flat characterise many of the large well-preserved town houses
two or sometimes three storeys high, which rise up both sides of the

valley's terraced slopes. Despite its proximity to Turkey's populous north-western corner, Kastamonu and the surroundings are underdeveloped in economic terms as well as being poorly served by the transport network. Only after Turkey became a republic did the links with the outside start to improve. Nevertheless, the first grammar school was established here in 1885 and it is still in existence. The small mining town of Küre supplies many of the local shops with copperware.

According to one theory, Kastamonu is a juxtaposition of Gas Kumana (Land of the Gasgas) – the Gasgas lived here under the Hittites c. 1300 B.C., but Castra Comneni (Castle of the Comnenes) is a more likely derivation.

Before the Comnenes built their castle in the 12th c. and established their dominance, the town was occupied by the Seljuks (11th c.) and soon after by the Danishmends. Despite many attempts by Byzantium to reconquer the town, towards the end of the 12th c. Castamon fell to the İsfeniyaroğulları. Süleyman (1300–39) the second ruler used the town as a base to subjugate Paphlagonia. The Ottomans seized control for a short period, but the rebuilt town became the seat of the İsfeniyaroğulları until 1459, as Timur returned the regional princes to power. The town finally fell to the Ottomans.

History

Sights

The ceiling of the famous mosque (1273) is borne by 40 wooden pillars and is of the early "Wood Mosque" type. The founder's mausoleum can be seen inside the mosque.

*Atabey Camii

This late Seljuk/early Ottoman bath house in the town's main square was recently excavated and restored.

Cemaleddin Firenkşah Hamami

Panorama of Kastamonu

Kastamonu

Ev Kayası
The locals refer to this Phrygian tomb as the Rock House. Situated to the south of the town and a short distance from the Ismail Bey Külliyesı, the tomb shows a male figure flanked by horses.

Ismail Bey Külliyesı
This complex was built *c.* 1454 by the last İsfeniyaroğlu Ismael Bey (1443–61) and includes a mosque (reminiscent of the early Sultan's Mosque in Bursa; remarkable porch), bath, paupers' kitchen, caravanserai, theological college and mausoleum for the dynasts. The former Koran school is now used as a free lodging house for older men.

Kale
Kastamonu castle, situated on a rock 112m/367ft above the town, dates from the time of the Byzantine Comnenes (11th/12th c.). Large sections of the inner castle and wall are well preserved (fine view).

Karanlık Bedesten
This covered bazaar was built in the 15th c. and is now used for the sale of ropes and rope-making equipment.

Caravanserais
Several Ottoman caravanserais can be found in the town but are now put to a different use.

Kastamonu Müzesi
It was here on August 25th 1925 on the terrace of the town's museum (interesting ethnological section) that Atatürk announced in a famous speech that the fez was to be banned and Western-style hats were to be introduced for all Turks. The speech was interpreted to indicate closer ties with Europe and a break between church and state (open: Tue.–Sun. 9am–noon, 2–5pm).

Nasrulla Camii
This nine-domed mosque was endowed by the town's judge Nasrulla Bey in 1506. It has been rebuilt on several occasions and the rectangular prayer room and the two ceremonial washing fountains at the front are of special interest.

Yakub Ağa Külliyesı
This complex consisting of a mosque with a central dome, richly ornamented porch, carved door and twelve-roomed medrese of irregular construction was built in 1547 on the orders of Süleyman the Magnificent's master cook Yacub Ağa.

Yilanlı Darüşşifası
This small integrated mosque with a fine entrance porch was originally built as a sanatorium for the mentally ill and dates from 1271. A number of tombs from the Esfendiyaroğlu era can be seen on the ground floor.

Surroundings

Abana
The fishing village of Abana is a popular resort for local people. There are some fine sandy beaches near İlişi and Hacı Veli rock.

Çankırı
Away from the main roads and without any major industry Çankırı (pop. 46,000) enjoys the unhurried life of a provincial town. In Hellenistic times Gangre, as it was then known, was the capital of Paphlagonia. As the empire collapsed it became a garrison town. In the 11th c. it was occupied by an Ogusan army, but retaken by John II of the Comnenes in 1135. It later fell to the Beys (Emirs) of Candar/İsfendiyar (Kastamonu). The Ottomans finally seized power in 1495. At the beginning of the 20th c. an earthquake destroyed a large part of the town.
The famous Ottoman architect Sinan built the large mosque in the centre of the town between 1522 and 1528. Previously restored, it suffered serious damage in the earthquake and the rubble was cleared away in 1936. The Seljuk-style Taş Mescidi medrese endowed in 1235 by Atabeg Cemal-Eddin Ferruk was turned into a hospital by Alaeddin Kaykobad. In the same complex stands the founder's mausoleum. The staircase and gate have been restored, but they and the porch decorations are still good examples of Seljuk architecture.

The ruined fortress which has undergone a number of restorations stands on a hill overlooking the town and is clearly of Byzantine origins, although it stands on Roman remains. Some cave tombs can be found at the foot of the castle mound.

Cide lies 185km/114 miles north-west of Kastamonu, 2km/1¼ miles from the coast and is a little-known and rarely visited Black Sea town. It can only be reached via some very tortuous country roads. The surrounding mountainous region of Küre Dağları is dotted with medieval castles. Pebble and sandy beaches can be found in the neighbouring coastal villages. Sakallı and Urlu are situated to the east at a distance of some 15km/9½ miles and 28km/17 miles respectively. In the west Akbayır and İlyazbey (Fakaz) are 45km/28 miles away. Most of the villages in this remote part of Pontus contain examples of traditional wooden houses and their roofs are made from large sheets of slate.

Cide

A mountain road leads to the entrance of the İlgaz Dağı National Park which lies about 40km/25 miles south of Kastamonu. The thickly wooded İlgaz Dağları mountain range and the deep Devez Çayı valley are favourite haunts for hunters and walkers who enjoy remote landscapes.

İlgaz Dağı
Milli Parkı

Some 45km/28 miles north-east of Kastamonu and to the north-west of the village of Donalar stands a Phrygian gabled rock tomb known as the "Rock Gate". Fronted by pillars with some extensive Achaemenid (Persian)/Greek decorations depicting fables, wild animals and a double eagle, the tomb dates from the 5th c. B.C.

Kale Kapı

Few visitors have previously ventured as far as the unusual Mahmut Bey Camii in the village of Kasaba. Situated about 17km/10 miles north-west of Kastamonu off the road to Daday near Göcen, it is by far the finest "Wood Mosque" in Anatolia. Facing the village school, it is noted for its interior, door, calligraphy and brightly-coloured paintings in which dark red predominates. It was built in 1366 in traditional Seljuk style with a five- aisled wooden beam ceiling (central beam wider and higher) borne by planed wooden pillars hence "Wood Mosque" and a two-storey gallery.

*Kasaba

Situated some 110km/68 miles east of Kastamonu, Safranbolu or Saffron Town is regarded as a gem among the small towns of Pontus. The old town houses are better preserved than those in Kastamonu thanks to UNESCO funds. The impressive sights to be found in this picturesque village include the Pontic houses (probably 19th c. Greek), the network of vine-covered alleys in the centre and the Ottoman caravanserai (Cinci Hanı).

*Safranbolu

The Mencilis caves and underground river lie about 6km/4 miles north-west of the town near the village of Bulak. They are not open to tourists.

Mencilis
Magarası

Known in antiquity as Pompeiopolis, Taşköprü lies some 45km/28 miles north-east of Kastamonu. At the entrance to the village a 150m/500ft wide arched bridge, probably of Ottoman construction, crosses the River Gökırmak (Blue River). Several Roman cave tombs can be found in the vicinity.

Taşköprü

Kaunos

See Marmaris (Surroundings)

Kayseri
L 5

Central Anatolia (Cappadocia). Province: Kayseri
Altitude: 1054m/3457ft. Population: 416,000

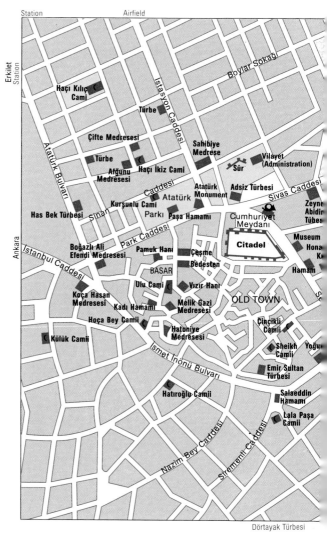

Station   Airfield

Erkilet Station

Boylar Sokağı

Haçı Kılıç Cami

Türbe

İstasyon Caddesi

Çifte Medresesi

Atatürk Bulvarı

Türbe

Afğunu Medresesi

Haçı İkiz Cami

Sahibiye Medrese

Vilayet (Administration)

Sûr

Caddesi

Atatürk Monument

Adsiz Türbesi

Sivas Caddesi

Kurşunlu Cami

Atatürk Parkı

Sinan

Paşa Hamamı

Cumhuriyet Meydanı

Zeyne Abidir Tübes

Has Bek Türbesi

Ankara

İstanbul Caddesi

Park Caddesi

Boğazlı Ali Efendi Medresesi

Pamuk Hanı

Çeşme

Bedesten

Citadel

Museum

Hona K

Hamam

BASAR

Ulu Cami

Vızır Hanı

OLD TOWN

Koça Hasan Medresesi

Kadı Hamamı

Melik Gazi Medresesi

Hoça Bey Camii

Hatuniye Medresesi

Çinçikli Camii

Külük Camii

İsmet İnönü Bulvarı

Sheikh Camii

Yoğu

Emir Sultan Türbesi

Salaeddin Hamamı

Hatıroğlu Camii

Lala Paşa Camii

Nazım Bey Caddesi

Stremanır Caddesi

Dörtayak Türbesi

Situation and
**Importance

The provincial capital of Kayseri which stands at the northern foot of the Erciyes Dağı volcano and at the eastern end of the Kayseri Ovası must surely be one of the most rewarding destinations in Turkey. Although the city itself is an important industrial centre and at first sight has little to offer the tourist, the magnificent mountain backdrop, the picturesque old town (part of which has been preserved) and the wealth of interesting monuments has helped to raise the city's tourist profile in recent years – despite

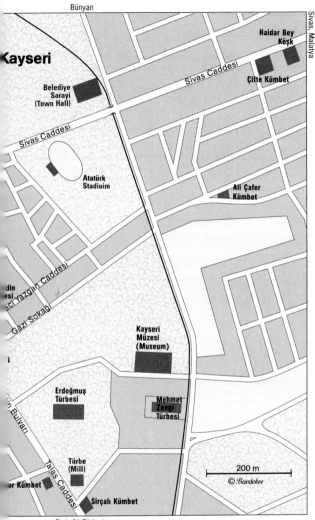

Emir Ali Türbesi
Hisarçık, Talas, Develi

or because of its proximity to the spectacular tuff chimney landscape of Cappadocia.

Visitors are recommended to include in their itinerary the remains of the old town, particularly around the citadel south of the Cumhuriyet Meydanı. It is in this relatively small quarter of the town that the many Seljuk and Ottoman buildings can be found.

Kayseri has always been an important crossroads and also a central market town for inland Anatolia. In recent decades with its modern city centre it has been able to make major strides towards industrialisation. It has also an important carpet-making industry.

History

Until the 4th c. the site of the modern city was covered with salt lakes and malaria-infested swamps, some of which were not finally drained until the last century. The first settlement was established c. 150 B.C. but in 77 B.C. the town was overrun by the Armenian Tigranes, who forced the inhabitants to leave for Tigranocerta (Silvan) in northern Mesopotamia. Only when the latter had been captured by Pompeius were the deported population able to return to Eusebeia. In 41 B.C. the last king of Cappadocia Aruhelanus died to be replaced by the Roman Antonius. In 17 B.C., Tiberius, who later became Roman emperor, named the town Caesarea. When Cappadocia was partitioned under Emperor Valens, Caesarea became the provincial capital.

According to the first letter of the apostle Paul in which he addresses "the strangers scattered throughout Pontus, Galatia, Cappadocia, Asia and Bithynia" (1 Peter 1:1), Christianity was well received by the townspeople and by the beginning of the 3rd c., Caesarea was playing an important part in the advancement of Christian theological thinking.

At the heart of the town stands a monastery which was founded in the 4th c. The new town was growing rapidly while the old buildings were decaying although some remains are still visible. After a disturbed period, in 1077 the town fell to Byzantium. In 1082 the Danishmends took control and then during the First Crusade (1096–99) the Crusader Godfrey of Bouillon occupied the town, which enjoyed great prosperity from the middle of the 12th c. under the Seljuks. After a number of assaults it was overrun by the Mongols. After a period of Ottoman rule, in 1401 the Mongolian hordes under Timur recaptured the town, but by 1468 it had reverted to the Ottomans. Many years of peace allowed Kayseri to grow in importance as a provincial centre. Around 1900 work started on the new town north of the citadel.

Sights

**Bazaar area and Kapalı Çarşı

Compared to the covered bazaar in İstanbul, the Kapalı Çarşı at Kayseri certainly looks provincial and yet it is a typical example of traditional Turkish basalt structures. When the current restoration work is finished, it promises to become an impressive sight. The absence of the typical "tourist shops" in the bazaar may well strike the visitor – Kayseri's bazaar is primarily a shopping centre for the local people. The best way to view the bazaar is from the İstanbul Caddesi. Opposite the Kurşunlu Cami, an opening in the old city wall leads into the old town passing the daily yoghurt market which is certainly worth a visit. A few yards further on opposite the Pamuk Çeşmesi stands an Ottoman caravanserai, which can be identified by the balls of sheep's wool hanging outside. Diagonally opposite next to a small mosque stands the main building of the traditional bazaar, which gives access to the domed square bedesten (late 18th c.), the covered part of the bazaar.

A short distance to the south a narrow alley leads to the square in front of the Ulu Cami where to the south-west stand four historic buildings: Melik Gazi Medresesi, Hatuniye Medresesi (see below), Kadi Hamamı and Hoca Bey Camii (both Ottoman).

To the north-east on the left of the southern entrance to the covered bazaar and opposite the Ulu Cami stands the late 18th c. Vezir Hanı caravanserai, one of Kayseri's most interesting sights. Before passing through the arcade with the pointed arch to the large courtyard and fountain, first cross another small older caravanserai, where sheepskins and carpets are sold in bulk. A stroll through the rest of the adjoining, renovated but still traditional-style bazaar will reveal how oriental Islamic markets are laid out

Erciyes Dağı, the "local mountain" of Kayseri

in sections for each trade. Beyond the covered bazaar past the streets of modern shops and to the east stands the southern entrance to the citadel.

The Twin Koran School behind the Kurşunlu Cami is a much restored building combining a hospital and a school which dates from 1206–08. The right-hand building houses one of the first medical schools in Anatolia.

Çifte Medresesi

The offices of Kayseri's preservation society are located in the restored palace of an old and wealthy family. It dates from the 15th c. and was rebuilt in the 18th c.

Gümgüboğlu Konaği

To the north on the right, behind the Kurşunlu Cami on İstasyon Caddesi stands the Hacı Kilic Camii and Koran school which were built in 1249 under Abdül Gazi a Seljuk vizier. Some handsomely wrought designs can be seen on the portals.

Hacı Kilic Camii ve Medresesi

One of the most opulent complexes in the town is the Hunat Hatun which lies to the north-east of the citadel. It consists of a mosque with a mausoleum of the founder, a medrese which now houses an ethnographical museum, a paupers' kitchen, a fountain and a bath, all decorated in grandest Seljuk style (open: Tue.–Sun. 8.30am–noon, 1–5.30pm). Mahperi (Honat) Hatun built the complex in 1237 and was responsible for founding numerous caravanserais.

*Honat Hatun Külliyesi (Museum in the Medrese)

The old town is situated to the south of the citadel and was originally surrounded by a wall which still partly visible. Within the walls lie the İç Kale (inner castle), some important mosques, caravanserais, the business quarter and covered bazaar (see above). The citadel was extensively rebuilt by the Seljuks (1210–26) on the foundations of Justinian's 6th c. structure. It was subsequently used as a barracks by the Ottomans (1466). The inner castle has been restored recently and a small area has been set aside for

Kayseri Kalesi (citadel and old town)

Portal of the Honat-Hatun complex

Döner Kümbet, richly decorated mausoleum

tourists to buy souvenirs. Access to the turreted battlements is restricted for safety reasons, but a key may be obtained from the police station in the castle. The view from the walls encompasses the surrounding quarters and the rest of the town. Nineteen towers can be counted on the citadel but there must be 30 in the whole complex. Yoğun Burç (Wide Tower) built in 1212 on the eastern tip of the old town walls is of special interest. The citadel's inner castle and Ok Deposu (Arrow Store) were built by Alaeddin Kaykobad in 1224.

*Döner Kümbet Mausoleum

Kayseri can justifiably be described as the city of mausoleums as there are so many of them. The appearance and origins of these tombs owe a great deal to the central Asian funeral tents in which the mummified body was left to lie in state for several months before it was interred. Among the most interesting türbe and kümbet in Kayseri is the so-called Döner Kümbet situated on the road to Talas about 1km/½ mile south of the citadel. This richly decorated structure with a pointed roof was built in 1267 for the Seljuk princess Şah Cihan Hatun. The origin of the irksome inscription "Revolving Tomb" is unknown.

Three other türbe can be found nearby: Sırçalı Kümbet, Emir Ali Türbesi and a türbe of unknown origin. The Sırçalı Mausoleum originates from an Uigur named Eretna. Near Cumhuriyet Meydanı on Sivas Caddesi stands the Zeynel Abidin Türbesi and further out of town on the road to Sivas, the Çifte Kümbet (Twin Vault Mausoleum) can be found. It was constructed for one of Alaeddin Kaykobad's wives in 1247. One rather unusual construction is the Köşk Medresesi, also known as the Köşk Kümbet. Located near the Archaeological Museum the mausoleum is surrounded by a turreted wall and was built by Eretna in 1339.

Arkeoloji Müzesi (Kayseri Müzesi)

The Archaeological Museum with its interesting displays is situated in the south-east of the city near Talas Caddesi (open: Tue.–Sun. 9am–noon, 1.30–5.30pm). The Kayseri Müzesi lies opposite the Mehmet Zengi Türbesi

and houses finds from Kültepe, Göllüdağ and Malatya as well as Roman
and Byzantine Caesarea.

This mosque which stands on İstasyon Caddesi has a magnificent porch
and was built in 1267 on the orders of Keyhusrev III. It houses a collection of
Turkish and Islamic art.

Sahibiye
Medresesi

The Grand Mosque can be found directly behind the covered bazaar in a
small square which contains a fountain for ritual washing. Started in 1136,
it was rebuilt in 1189. Dominated by a huge minaret, the mosque roof is
supported by four rows of pillars and crowned with a raised dome above
the central crossing.

Ulu Cami

Near the Grand Mosque to the south stands the Melik Gazi Medresesi
(1432). A little further on is the more important Hatuniye Medresesi (c.
1430). The pillars in the porch are embellished with Ionian and Corinthian
capitals. Both edifices were built under the Karamans.

Surroundings

The small town of Bünyan about 40km/25 miles north-east of Kayseri is well
known for its hand-woven carpets, which are often made according to
traditional designs by homeworkers. Some attractive waterfalls can be
found on the Bünyanıhamit.

Bünyan

The regional centre of Develi 45km/28 miles south of Kayseri at the foot of
the Erciyes Dağı was formed from an amalgamation of three communities
in the 19th c.: Everek (Christian population, bazaar and administrative
centre), Ağostan and Fenisse. The old town of Yukarı Develi lies to the south
on the hillside. The medieval castle ruins of Develi Kalesi overlooks the

Develi

Sahibiye Medresesi   *Ulu Cami*

Armenian quarter of the town from a rocky outcrop. Some of the town's interesting sights include the late 13th c. Ulu Cami (Develi Cami, Sivaşı Hatun Camii, Seljuk graves in the cemetery), the Seyit Şerif Türbesi (1276) and the ruins of the Church of St Kosmas and Damian in the old Christian quarter.

The peaks of the Erciyes Dağı, Ala Dağı and Tahtalı Dağları remain covered in snow until late spring and form both a picturesque backdrop to the Sultan's Marshes and a birds' paradise with reeded shallows and floating reed islands. When an Ice Age lake dried up near the marshlands mud-flats formed which, as a consequence of artificial drainage, often dried out completely in the summer months, thus restricting the habitats of much wetland wild-life. A number of initiatives have persuaded the authorities to turn the Sultan's Marshes to the south-west into a nature reserve. The local inhabitants use the reeds as roof thatch and for the manufacture of matting.

*Erciyes Dağı

Kayseri's famous volcanic peak ancient Ergaeus Mons dominates the foot-hills and plains. Reaching a height of 3917m/12,847ft, it is the highest mountain in central Anatolia. It is believed to have last erupted in antiquity. Strabo described it as an active volcano in the 1st c. A.D.

Some distance to the east lies Koç Dağı, which separated from the Erciyes Dağı in the early Tertiary era (26 million years ago). The highlands are used today as summer grazing pastures. Kayseri's new ski centre can be reached via the Talas Caddesi. After 2km/1¼ miles fork off to Kayakevi and the centre can be found in a broad valley behind the village of Hisarcık on a 2150m/7052ft pass. During the summer months expeditions to the top of the volcano begin from here (guide recommended).

Firaktın

12km/7½ miles east of Develi just before the village of Firaktın stands a Hittite rock carving showing King Hattusilis and Queen Puduchepas.

Hanyeri
(Gezbili, Gökbel)

A rocky crag with a Hittite stone carving which dates from 13th c. B.C. stands due north on the road from Develi to Tufanbeyli at a bend in the road just before the village of Hanyeri. The carving depicts an armed prince wor-shipping a bull in the company of two mountain gods.

İmamkulu

About 45km/28 miles from Develi a road forks to the north to İmamkulu. A Hittite stone relief from the 14th/13th c. B.C. can be found on the slopes of a rocky crag just before the village about 250m/275yd to the east of the road behind a farm. The carving depicts the goddess of love Ishtar and a warrior with a yoke of oxen motif (weather god).

Karatay Hanı

About 44km/28 miles east of Kayseri lies the village of Karadağı which is dominated by the caravan staging post founded by Alaeddin Kaykobad in 1240.

**Kültepe
(Karum-Kaneş)

The famous Hittite hill settlement at Kültepe is to be found to the north-east of Kayseri near the village of Karahüyük. The excavations here have un-covered an extensive site which comprises two towns and is regarded as the most important Bronze Age site in Turkey (open: Tue.–Sun 9am–noon, 1–5pm). In the 19th and 18th c. B.C. Karum became a trading colony for the Assyrians in Anatolia. In two of the four layers of ruins, 12,000 cuneiform scripts were found. According to the interpretations, the first trading centre (1950–1850 B.C.) was destroyed by fire and accommodation in the nearby town of Kanes was extended. The rulers of the colony lived outside the settlement in a palace on a nearby hill. In 1790 B.C. this settlement also suffered a violent end. Phrygians are known to have built a fortress on the site after 1200 B.C. and established the principality of Tabal (c. 8th c. B.C.). The excavations cover the 18m/60ft hill with Kaneş measuring 250,000sq.m/300,000sq.yd and the trading colony of Karum below extend-ing to 700,000sq.m/833,000sq.yd. The foundations of the crowded living accommodation, ruined temples and the palace can still be distinguished. Many of the finds can be seen in the museums of Ankara and Kayseri.

On the old Seljuk trading route between Sivas, Kayseri and Konya, a number of staging posts were endowed by the sultan himself. The Sultanhanı, about 50km/30 miles north-east of Kayseri near a village of the same name, is one of these Seljuk caravanserais. In many ways it resembles the Sultanhanı west of Aksaray on the road to Konya (see Konya). After the 1950 earthquake, the structure was completely restored and represents a typical example of Seljuk secular architecture. The key may be obtained in the village.

*Sultanhanı

One of the favourite haunts for the citizens of Kayseri during the summer is the town of Talas, some 10km/6½ miles to the south- east. A little further south stood the old centre of Zincidere (Roman Flaviana), the seat of the Archbishop of Caesarea. Two rock chapels and a troglodyte church have been preserved.

Talas

Kırklareli

See Edirne

Kırşehir

K 4

Central Anatolia. Province: Kırşehir
Altitude: 978m/3207ft. Population: 75,000

In a small valley between extensive agricultural land at the south-western edge of the Bozok plain (Bozok Yaylesi) and 20km/12½ miles from the River Kızılırmak lies the prosperous provincial capital of Kırşehir. Nearby thermal springs have led to the development of tourist spas, e.g. Karakurt (15km/9½ miles) and Terme (12km/7½ miles). The town acquired its charter in Byzantine times under Justinian and it was originally called Justinianopolis or Mokyssos. The Seljuks recognised its importance as a trading centre and it was known as Gülşehir (Rose Town). The name Kırşehir was first encountered in the 14th c. when it became a centre for the politically influential religious Ahi brotherhood (Akhiyyet) which grew out of a craft guild. They remained a powerful force until the 18th c.

Situation and History

Sights

Two Ottoman caravanserais can be seen in the commercial centre of the town: the Kasaplar Çarşısı Hanı (meat market) and the Saraçlar Çarşısı (leather market).

Caravanserais

Three mausoleums are of interest: Beneath the Ahi Avran Türbesi lie the remains of the influential Ahi sect's founder Ahi Avran (1236–1329). The Aşik Paşa Veli Türbesi with its splendid portal is a memorial to the 13th c. poet (Love Pasha). It is situated in the north-east adjacent to the trunk road. To the south-east of the Nureddin Cacabey Medresesi stands the octagonal Melik Gazi Türbesi with a round conical roof.

Mausoleums

Built in the early 12th c. as a Seljuk theological school and observatory, the complex is now surrounded by a wall. It stands on the market-place at the foot of the slope between the town centre and trunk road. It was later converted into a mosque.

Nureddin Cacabey Medresesi

Surroundings

The Seljuk caravanserai Çamalak Hanı is situated in Çamalak some 70km/43 miles from Kırşehir on the old caravan route to Zile which crosses the Bozok Yaylası.

Çamalak

Kesik Köprü Hanı

This caravanserai with its handsome portal and tall central aisle stands by the destroyed Seljuk bridge across the River Kızılırmak some 300m/325yd from the northern bank. The site is about 17km/10 miles south of Kırşehir and was founded in 1263 by the governor of Kırşehir, Nureddin Cibrail Ben Cece Bey. It is also known as Cacabey Hanı.

Kızılırmak
(Halys)

The River Kızılırmak or Halys in antiquity (probably after the salt spring in the river's upper reaches) is 1355km/840 miles long and after the Euphrates ranks as Turkey's most important river and the longest in Asia Minor. Its source is located to the east of Sivas from where it crosses the karst lowlands of Zara and Sivas. A large bend, the Halys bend, takes the river through Cappadocia south-west as far as Kayseri, then north-west to Kırıkkale and finally to the north-east where after a zigzag route across the Pontic mountains it flows into the Black Sea at the Bafra Ovası delta between Sinop and Samsun. It owes its modern name, meaning red river (kızıl, red), to the red clay which colours the waters as they pass through Cappadocia.

The Halys never had any strategic value as a transport artery but was often used to define borders. In the war between the last king of Lydia Croesus (*c.* 560–546 B.C.) and the founder of the ancient Persian empire Kyros (*c.* 559–529 B.C.), an ambiguous oracle spoken to Croesus made the river famous: "If you cross the Halys, you will destroy a large empire!". At Pteria in 546 B.C. Croesus was defeated by Kyros II. Several dam projects (Hırfanlı Barajı, Keşikköprü and Altınkaya Barajı) have recently been completed along the Kızılırmak to supply Turkey not just with water but also with hydro-electric power.

Hırfanlı Barajı

The Kızılırmak dam at Hırfanlı 80km/50 miles west of Kırşehir was completed in 1959. It required 6,000 million cubic m/212,000 million cubic ft ballast and a surface area of 263sq.km/100sq.miles to create the second-largest artificial lake in Turkey after the GAP Euphrates dam project.

Knidos

See Marmaris

Konya   H 6

Central Anatolia
Province: Konya
Altitude: 1016m/3332ft
Population: 509,000

Situation and
**Importance

This famous oasis bordering the mountains and a former capital of the Seljuk Empire lies at the heart of the Anatolian steppes. Major irrigation projects have created fertile land around the city and produce includes fruit, vegetables and sugar beet. Wheat is the main crop and rearing livestock also plays an important part in the local economy, in particular Anatolian fat-rump sheep. As early as the 13th c. Konya was making carpets. It was the first carpet-making centre in the Islamic world and even Marco Polo enthused over the quality of the product. Konyan carpets with their pastel shades and floral patterns are today regarded as the finest in Turkey.

The busy market town which stands at a major crossroads and also on the Baghdad railway line has become one of the most important industrial centres of central Anatolia. The town has been a national place of pilgrimage (Mevlana) for many hundreds of years and despite economic progress, the population remains steeped in the old traditions. With its strong oriental links, the lively bazaar and important buildings, Konya is well worth a visit.

Konya: Alaeddin Camii on the citadel hill

The citadel in the town centre would appear to have been settled since the   History
Anatolian Copper Age (3500–3000 B.C.) and the Phrygians are thought to
have established the first settlement. Konya's old name was Ikoneum
(Iconium), which according to a legend of Perseus and Medusa dates from
this period. Under Roman rule Iconium belonged to a number of different
provinces. It was one of the first towns to adopt Christianity and Barnabas
and Paul both stayed in the town (Acts 14:1). The latter met Thekla (later St
Thekla) the merchant's daughter here. The Seljuks were responsible for
advancing the city's fortunes. In the course of the 9th c. this Turkish tribe
advanced from the Aral Sea to make Ikoneum the capital of their empire
which was soon to embrace a large part of Asia Minor. Despite some fierce
struggles Konya sought greater cultural independence from Byzantium.
The Crusades also impinged on Konya. On May 26th 1190 during the Third
Crusade Frederick "Barbarossa" captured the town and his son Frederick
took control of the whole city apart from the castle. Konya enjoyed a period
of great prosperity under the well-known sultan Alaeddin Kaykobad (1219–
37) who had learnt something of western culture in Constantinople. In 1221
Konya's fortifications were rebuilt using ancient building materials. 108
towers endowed by the empire's wealthy benefactors reinforced the wall
only a few fragments of which remain today. A series of magnificent
mosques, medrese and caravanserais were constructed in the town. Alaeddin's court became a centre for scientists, poets (preferably Persian) and
artists who were responsible for the Byzantine and Persian buildings and
enamel tiles. But the decline began under the sultan's son who had his
father murdered and in 1307 the last Seljuk ruler was killed by the Mongols.
In 1320 the now powerful emir from the neighbouring principality (see
Karaman) made Konya his capital and the tradition of glittering architectural showpieces received new impetus. The Ottoman interregnum (Bayazit I
from 1397) ended the rule of the Mongol Timur in favour of the Karamans,
before Konya finally succumbed to the Ottomans in 1466. After a long
peaceful phase the city was occupied for at time by the rebellious Egyptian
viceroy Mehmet Ali. Konya is the seventh largest city in Turkey.

Sights

The former citadel on the western side of the city is now mainly a park   Alaeddin Tepesi
(Alaeddin Parkı with monuments to the fallen). At the foot of the incline
Alaeddin Kaykobad's palace and the remains of the old city wall can be
seen although the latter are covered for protection. The city wall was
removed at the beginning of the 20th c. to make way for modernisation of
the city centre. Some painted sections from the inner fortress of the Seljuk
sultan's palace were still standing in 1860 but now only part of a pavilion on
one the fortified towers remains (marble portal with inscriptions dating
from 1221; round-arched gallery with pillars).
The Alaeddin Camii (1221) is no longer accessible as a result of severe
earthquake damage but restoration work is planned. It was built as a

379

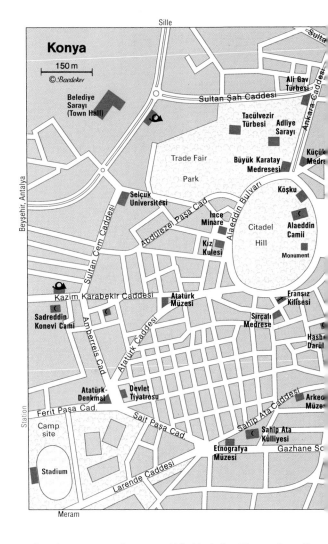

Konya

150 m

© Baedeker

Sille

Sulta

Belediye
Sarayı
(Town Hall)

Sultan Şah Caddesi

Ali Gav
Türbesi

Tacülvezir
Türbesi

Adliye
Sarayı

Küçük
Medr

Trade Fair

Büyük Karatay
Medresesi

Park

Köşku

Selçuk
Universitesi

İnce
Minare

Citadel

Hill

Alaeddin
Camii

Kız
Kulesi

Monument

Kazim Karabekir Caddesi

Atatürk
Müzesi

Fransız
Kilisesi

Sırçalı
Medrese

Sadreddin
Konevi Cami

Hasb
Darül

Atatürk-
Denkmal

Devlet
Tiyatrosu

Arkeo
Müze

Ferit Paşa Cad.

Camp
site

Sahip Ata
Külliyesi

Etnografya
Müzesi

Gazhane So

Stadium

Meram

Beyşehir, Antalya

Sultan Cem Caddesi

Abdülezel Paşa Cad

Alaeddin Bulvarı

Ankara Caddesi

Amberreis Cad.

Atatürk Caddesi

Sahip Ata Caddesi

Sait Paşa Cad.

Larende Caddesi

Station

pillared mosque according to an old Arabic design. The wooden ceiling
was supported by 42 antique columns ("Wood Mosque"). In the centre
alongside a prayer niche and an old pulpit lies a türbe faced with blue
enamel tiles in which rest the Seljuk sultan Mesut, Kılıç Arslan IV and
Keyhusrev I with a number of their relatives. A decagonal pyramid roof
covers the mausoleum and the tomb of Kılıç Arslan II which occupies the
forecourt.

*Arkeoloji Müzesi   South of the Sırçalı Medrese at the edge of the old town stands the Archae-
ological Museum which houses a comprehensive display of architectural

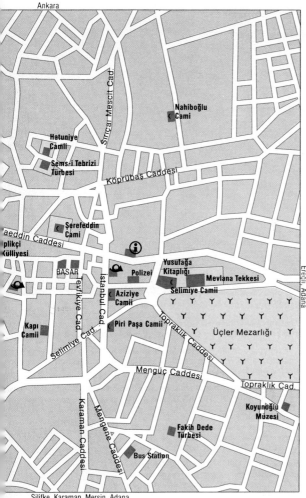

Ankara

Nahiboğlu
Cami

Hatuniye
Camii

Sırçalı Mescit Cad.

Şems-i Tebrizi
Türbesi

Köprübaş Caddesi

Şerefeddin
Cami

'aeddin Caddesi

plikçi
Külliyesi

Yusufağa
Kitaplığı

BASAR

Polizei

Mevlana Tekkesi

İstanbul Cad.

Tevfikiye Cad.

Aziziye
Camii

Selimiye Camii

Kapı
Camii

Selimiye Cad.

Piri Paşa Camii

Topraklık Caddesi

Üçler Mezarlığı

Ereğli, Adana

Mengüç Caddesi

Topraklık Cad.

Karaman Caddesi

Koyunoğlu
Müzesi

Mengene Caddesi

Fakih Dede
Türbesi

Bus Station

Silifke, Karaman, Mersin, Adana

exhibits, stelae, statuettes from the various eras, but mainly fantastically decorated Roman sarcophagi (open: Tue.–Sun. 9am–5.30pm).

On Kasım Karabekir Caddesi in the direction of Meram stands the governor's residence which dates from the early 20th c. and was presented to Atatürk in 1928. A museum displaying the papers and personal belongings of the country's first president has occupied the house since 1964.

Atatürk Müzesi

First built in 1676 by court adviser Mustafa Paşa and later rebuilt after a fire (1867–74), this fancifully designed mosque can be found beside the bazaar.

Aziziye Camii

Konya

Konya: Hercules sarcophagus in the Archeological Museum

The Baroque-influenced Rococo mosque with twin minarets also possesses a Rococo prayer niche. The brightly painted interior is quite striking.

Etnografya Müzesi

The rehoused Ethnographical Museum stands in Sahip Ata Caddesi and displays crafts, costumes, jewellery and household goods from Konya and the surrounding region.

Hasbey
Darülhüffazı

To the south-east of the citadel near Sırçalı Medrese, the Karaman dynasty built a hospital. It was also used as a medrese but today is a home for men who recite the Koran. The west façade is covered with ornate marble slabs and the prayer niche is decorated with enamel tiles. Underneath the building lies a crypt.

*Ince Minare
Medresesi veya
Camii

Between 1260 and 1265 the Vizier Sahip Ata endowed this building which was designed by Keluk Ibn Abdullah. The once-slim minaret finished with enamel tiles and bricks was struck by lightning in 1901. The richly sculpted Baroque decorations on the side of the portal are of special interest. The Koran school is now a museum housing selected wooden and stone sculptures including animal reliefs from the old city walls.

İplikçi Külliyesi

Only the mosque remains of the complex which stood in Alaeddin Caddesi to the east of the old citadel. It was built in 1201 by Sultan Rükneddin Süleymanşah and Alaeddin Kaykobad I.

İplikçi Mosque means the "yarn-makers mosque" as the site was initially endowed by a family of yarn manufacturers. Sometimes also known as the Altan Baba Mosque, it was renovated in 1932. The square mosque with two oval and one round dome stands on twelve huge "elephant's foot" columns and has a richly decorated prayer niche made from marble. The minaret is in need of repair. For a while (1953–59) the site was used as a museum for classical art. Very little is left of the medrese apart from the remains of a dome near the mosque. Mevlana Celaleddin Rumi and his father taught here.

To the south-west behind the bazaar in the Odun Pazarı quarter stood one of Konya's old gates and the İhyaiyye Camii or Kapi Camii (Tower Mosque) is named after it. The building was constructed in 1658, it fell into disrepair and in 1811 Konya's Mufti (spiritual leader) Esenlerlizade Seyid Abdurrahman commissioned a new mosque. A fire destroyed the mosque and adjoining shops but it was rebuilt the following year. The roof of the eight-domed mosque, one of the oldest Ottoman mosques in Konya, is supported by ten pillars.

Kapı Camii

To the north of the citadel on the Ankara Caddesi stands a theological college with a superb marble gate. It was founded in 1251 by Karatay. The building is now an impressive museum of Seljuk enamel tiles (open: Tue.–Sun. 9am–5.30pm). The pupils' cells can still be identified around the courtyard. The mosque is attached to the college on the right-hand side. Its internal walls are completely covered in blue tiles. On the left in one room with brick vaulting lies the tomb of the Vizier Celaleddin Karatay (temporarily closed for renovation).

Karatay Medresesi

In Topraklık Caddesi stands the old home of Ahmet Izzet Koyunoğlu, a member of one of the oldest Konyan families, in which the owner has set up a small museum. In 1983 it was moved to new premises (open: Tue.–Sun. 9am–noon, 1.30–5.30pm). The exhibits include an assortment of items from the Koyunoğlu private collection (minerals, fossils, birds, archaeological finds and ethnography section, carpets from the region and 20,000 books). A preservation order protects the old building from demolition.

Koyunoğlu Müzesi

In the east of the old town stands the famous green conical roof which covers the tomb of the philosopher and theologist Mevlana Celaleddin (see

**Mevlana Tekkesi

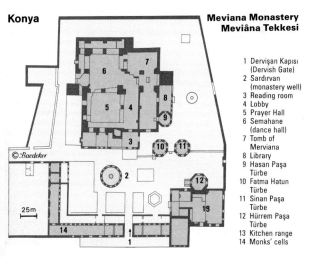

Konya

**Meviana Monastery
Meviâna Tekkesi**

1 Dervişan Kapısı (Dervish Gate)
2 Sardırvan (monastery well)
3 Reading room
4 Lobby
5 Prayer Hall
6 Semahane (dance hall)
7 Tomb of Merviana
8 Library
9 Hasan Paşa Türbe
10 Fatma Hatun Türbe
11 Sinan Paşa Türbe
12 Hürrem Paşa Türbe
13 Kitchen range
14 Monks' cells

© Baedeker

25m

Konya

Mevlana Monastery of the Dervish order   *A stringed instrument, in the monastery*

Famous People and Karaman). The roof has become a symbol of the town and the mausoleum is visited not only by tourists but also by countless Turkish pilgrims, who come to pay their respects to one of the country's greatest mystics. Anatolian villagers come in their thousands to pray at the tomb of the man Mevlana Celaleddin who was for many more than a philosopher and saint. His words are not just engraved on his own mausoleum but also on the tombstones of believers: "Do not seek our tombs on this earth – our tombs are in the hearts of the enlightened".

The monastery, whose present layout dates from the 16th c., is entered through a gate and an impressive garden of fountains, trees and tombstones (open: Tue.–Sun. 9.30am–6.30pm). Inside can be found not just Mevlana's sarcophagus, but that of his wife Kerra Hatun, his children Melike Hatun and Müzafferüddin Emir Ali Çelebi, plus the tombs of six dervishes, the so-called "Soldiers of Horasan", who came to Konya from Balkh with Mevlana. In addition the large complex houses a huge collection of artefacts belonging to the Mevlana Order, valuable carpets, metal and wooden objets d'art, musical instruments and books, most of which can be found in the former dance-hall, the monk's cells and the mosque. The grounds of the complex contain a bright blue marble fountain (1512) and more mausoleums. The museum itself has an ethnography section and also a library with over 1700 manuscripts and 500 books. Linked directly to the Mevlana Monastery is Selimiye Camii, a huge domed mosque with an open porch and a multicoloured heavenly staircase. Commissioned by Selim II it was built between 1566 and 1574 and marks the climax of Ottoman church architecture.

*Selimiye Camii

Sadreddin Konevi Camii

This mosque stands only a short distance from the road to Meram in the Sadreddin quarter and was built in 1274 in honour of the mystic Sadreddin Konevi. Restoration work was completed in 1899. Apart from the prayer niche, the mosque dates from Ottoman times. The prayer room is entered

384

through a hall with a wooden ceiling and a door leads from here into the old library. The mystic's türbe was built in the domed style of the Seljuks together with a marble coffin and marble pillars. It can be found in the adjoining cemetery.

This complex of mosque, türbe, dervish monastery and baths stands on the corner of Larende Caddesi and Ressam Sami Sokağı and was built between 1258 and 1283. The portal and minaret are beautifully decorated and the prayer niche displays blue enamel tiles. Baths for men and women have recently been restored.

Sahip Ata Külliyesi

This mausoleum and mosque are dedicated to the dervish Şems from Tabriz who was a close companion of Mevlana. It is situated to the north behind the Şerefeddin Camii.

Şems-i Tebrizi Türbesi

Opposite the main post office on Alaeddin Bulvarı to the east of the citadel stands this large mosque built in classical Ottoman style, although it had originally been constructed by Şerefeddin Mesud by the middle of the 13th c. It was restored, but fell into such a state of disrepair that in 1636 it had to be completely rebuilt on the foundations by Memi Bey. Some of the old Seljuk enamel tiles can still be recognised on the external façade. The main entrance is decorated with stalactite vaulting. The dome of the prayer room is supported by six pillars.

Şerefeddin Camii

To the south of the old citadel stand the school of jurisprudence and the theological college which was built by Bedreddin Musli in 1242 with a summer courtyard, tiled decorations and an ornate stalactite portal. It houses a collection of Islamic tombstones as well as some Hittite funerary urns (opening times: daily from 9am, Mon. and Tue. from 12.30pm).

Sırçalı Medrese

The Yusufağa library next to the Selimiye Camii was endowed in 1795 by the chief courtier to Selim III's mother Yusuf Ağa. It contains 2917 manuscripts and 7759 books.

Yusufağa Kitaplığı

Surroundings

In Cihanbeyli a salt town about 100km/62 miles north of Konya, a road forks off to the national salt works 23km/14 miles away at Yavşan Tuzlası by the Tuz Gölü. The management will usually permit a guide to accompany visitors around the extensive complex on the lake. Another smaller private salt works is situated by Bulak Gölü some 15km/9 miles to the south.

*Cihanbeyli *Salt works*

The regional centre of Çumra is an important station on the İstanbul to Baghdad railway and also lies at the heart of the 50,000ha/123,5000 acre Çumra irrigation zone in the Konya Ovası. This irrigated area, the first such enterprise in the Middle East, was established by a German company before the First World War. The town grew up after 1912 around the once uninhabited station of İçeri Çumra which is situated a little further to the west when political refugees from the Balkan wars began to arrive. Nearby are the neolithic excavations of Çatalhüyük (see entry).

Çumra

130km/80 miles south of Konya lies the regional centre of Hadım. A passable road runs eastwards for 39km/24 miles to a spot known as Yerköprü (bridge) near the administrative centre of Aladağ. Near Yerköprü and a small hydro-electric power station the powerful karst spring of the Karasu, a tributary of the Göksu Nehri (Kalykadnos), has formed a natural calcareous tuff barrage in the valley of the main river and this causes the Göksu Nehri to disappear underground into a 500m/600yd long cave. Of special interest are the 20m/65ft waterfalls at the entrance and exit to the cave through which the stream rushes from the travertine bridge into a small lake formed by the Göksu Nehri.

Hadım

Konya

Taşkent

Only 12km/7 miles south of Hadım, the picturesque town of Taşkent with its traditional, flat-roofed houses clings like an amphitheatre to the vertical rocks and overhangs from a dizzying height the deep valley cut by a tributary of the upper Göksu Nehri.

Hatunsaray

A road leads 34km/21 miles south-west of Konya to the village of Hatunsaray on the Kavak Deresi. It is the ancient town of Lystra, home of Timothy and a disciple of the apostle Paul. The latter cured a lame man there and was then almost stoned to death (Acts 14: 8–20). Only a few remains of Lystra are preserved but they include a Temple of Zeus.

Horozlu Han

Close to the northern edge of Konya opposite the fork to Aksaray lies an attractive caravanserai which was restored in 1956 and includes a raised nave and ten transepts, strong semi-circular supporting pillars, central brick dome with an octagonal drum and narrow windows.

İlgın

The small town of İlgın lies on the road to Afyon some 85km/53 miles north-west of Konya near the ancient site of Tyriaion where, according to Xenophon, the Persian king Kyros stopped for three days to muster his troops. In 1576 Mustafa Paşa built the Pir Husein Bey Camii for Murat II, following the same plans as for the Ayasofya (Hagia Sophia) in İstanbul. Some sulphur baths rebuilt by Alaeddin on the Byzantine ruins can be seen to the west of the town on a hill.

Kadın Hanı

About 61km/38 miles north-west of Konya stands the town of Kadinhani (women's caravanserai), a Seljuk caravanserai that dates from 1223. It was endowed by a woman named Raziye Hatun Bt. Mahmut. The three-aisled hall (inscription above the doorway) has only three windows and the decorations on the façade include a sarcophagus with a relief of two women.

Karapınar

Karapınar (formerly Sultaniye) lies on the road to Adana, some 90km/56 miles east of Konya. It has developed from an old winter settlement for the semi-nomads of central Anatolia and was also a staging post for pilgrims on their way to Mecca. In 1766 Carsten Niebuhr described the town as poorly built comprising a caravanserai, two rows of shops and a superb mosque with two minarets. 5km/3 miles east of the town behind a roadside service area on the slopes leading to the Karacadağ volcanic mountain range are a number of interesting phenomena deposited by Tertiary volcanic activity in the steppes. Directly behind the service area the terrain opens out into a huge steep-sided volcanic crater or caldera. The water of the Gölü crater or Acı Göl is salty (65g per litre) and lies at 35m/115ft below the normal water level.

2km/1¼ miles south of the service area in the middle of a number of small lava ash chimneys lies the impressive Meke Gölü (Tuzla Göl) a huge oval crater (800×500m/2650×1650ft) carved from black volcanic ash. Emerging from the inside of the water-filled crater is an imposing 50m/165ft black ash volcano with a 25m/80ft deep crater. The water has a high sulphur dioxide content (150g per litre).

The Meke Dağı volcano 10km/7 miles south-west of the Meke Gölü stands 1265m/6840ft above sea level. The very steep sides (250m/820ft) dominate the surrounding landscape and the crater itself is some 100m/330ft in diameter. To the west between Meke Gölü and Meke Dağı some crescent-shaped island sand dunes up to 8m/25ft high have formed in the middle of an Ice Age lake.

Meram

Meram 8km/5 miles from the town centre was well known to the Seljuks because of its springs and luxuriant vegetation. Wealthy Konyalı had their summer residences here and the governor of the town owned a castle in the town. His poetry anthology (Divan) contains poems in praise of Meram. Here also Mevlana wrote a large part of his work "Mesnevi", stories and mystical thoughts written in verses (six volumes). The old gardens are a popular haunt for the townsfolk during the evening.

Aci Göl crater lake, near Karapınar

Near the village of Kızö-
ren and 75km/46 north-
east of Konya to the north
of the road to Aksaray
stands the old village
of Obruk. Abandoned
several decades ago, it
has been rebuilt further
north. This nondescript
old village is in fact the
site of a large dilapidated
13th c. Seljuk caravanse-
rai, situated near the village mosque. An ex-
tensive cemetery lies

*Obruk

In section diagram:
Sinkhole
Abandoned village of Obruk
145 m
Obruk
Section through the giant sink-hole near Kızören
Representation according to Erol

opposite the caravanserai, mosque and the few houses which remain from
this once large winter village.
Other traces of the previous settlement can be found in front of the cemetery and around the edge of a giant sinkhole (Obruk), which lies due east
behind the caravanserai and extends some 170m/550ft into the limestone.
The oval sinkhole some 200–230m/650–750ft wide is filled with water to a
depth of 145m/475ft. The water from this freshwater lake which is linked to
the underground karst spring of Taspınar on the edge of the Tuz Gölü
30km/19 miles to the north comes from underground sources and is used
for irrigation and drinking. In the middle of the plateau (Obruk Yaylası)
25km/16 miles south-east of Obruk (Kızören) and south of the village of
Çukurkuyu as many as 20 giant sinkholes can be found in fairly close
proximity. With a diameter of 502m/1646ft, they range in depth from
50m/165ft to 120m/395ft; however most of them are dry.

İlica Yatlası, a sink-hole near Konya

Sadeddin Hanı

About 20km/12½ miles north-east of Konya stands the magnificent cara-vanserai of Sadeddin Köpek (Zazadin Hanı) which was built between 1235 and 1236. To the left on the wide southern side, alongside the imposing marble and limestone court entrance, stands the hall with a tall narrow nave, six transepts and a ruined dome. Thirteen towers secure the com-plex's long courtyard. A staircase leads to the mosque above the entrance. Unlike the main entrance the winter hall is decorated.

°Sille

The town of Sille near Meram (see above) and the reservoir 9km/5½ miles from the town centre have become the Konyans' second-favourite destina-tion for excursions. Formerly a Greek settlement it is now a centre for carpet-weaving. St Helena's, one of Sille's two Byzantine churches, is said to be the oldest church in the world but only the foundations remain. Mevlana is said to have withdrawn here to meditate. In the late Byzantine Archangelos Church, examples of works by younger, Baroque-influenced painters from the early 18th and 19th c. can be found.

°Tuz Gölü

Tuz Gölü with an area of 1500sq.km/580sq.miles and the second largest of Turkey's inland lakes lies about 100km/62 miles north-east of Konya in the heart of the Anatolian highlands at an altitude of 905m/2968ft. Lying amid the treeless cereal-producing steppes, this salt lake occupies the major part of the Tuz Gölü basin. The lake is no deeper than 2m/6ft, but its surface area can change quite considerably depending on seasonal variations in rain-fall. In the summer months it can often dry up completely as temperatures of 40°C/104°F cause evaporation on a massive scale. Often a 30cm/12in. deposit of almost pure cooking salt remains. Salt has been collected from here by even the very earliest settlers. The two nationalised salt works at Cihanbeyli and Şereflikoçhisar produce 150,000t/147,630 tonnes which make up about a quarter of Turkey's total salt production and supply the country's own needs. Layers of salt and deposits from the early Tertiary period can often be found on the edges of the salt lake and these provide evidence that the high salt content of 23% (a near saturated salt mixture in which the salt crystallises in the solution) is not primarily due to the internal drainage of the lake but to the high salt content of the subsoil.

It is possible to demonstrate that the water level during the Ice Age, or more precisely the so-called Pluvial period, was much higher than it is now and that the lake probably contained fresh water, as at that time the water drained to the north-east into the River Kızılırmak. The lake has been shrinking for about 15,000 years.

Konya Ereğlisi

See Ereğli

Kütahya   E 4

Western Anatolian Mountains
Province: Kütahya
Altitude: 949m/3112ft
Population: 131,000

The provincial town of Kütahya occupies a position on the plain at the foot of the Yellice Dağı where the River Porsuk Çayı flows. The town is overlooked by a magnificent, medieval castle with many towers. It is also famous as a pottery manufacturing centre, supplying the home market with beautifully decorated plates painted in traditional patterns. In contrast to the tile production of the 16th c. examples of which can be found in Turkey's many sacred buildings, the emphasis here has been and remains on the production by hand of ornamental plates and pottery.

Situation and Importance

* Glazed earthenware

A Kütahaya jug

Temple of Zeus in Çavdarhisar

Today's potters produce bright colourful pieces which are distinct from the really valuable, more soberly painted works of the older artisans. Replicas of the latter are available but can be quite expensive. The town is an important carpet-weaving centre and many of the factories are run as co-operatives.

History

The history of Kütahya goes back to Phrygian times. Alexander the Great stopped in the town while marching to Gordion and it was here that the Byzantine emperor Romanus Diogenes had his eyes gouged out. In 1071 the town was captured by the Seljuks before falling to the Crusaders. It was won back in 1096. Members of the Germiyanoğlu family, a Kurdish/Turkish dynasty, later built the fortress as it now appears, before the Ottomans took control under Mehmet II. The Mongol Timur used Kütahya as a headquarters. After Selim I conquered Persia in 1514, the forced resettlement of Azerbaijani artisans to Kütahya and İznik resulted in the creation of the now famous glazed earthenware industry in which the workers followed Persian designs.

Sights

İshak Fatih Külliyesi

The İshak Fatih Camii dates from 1434 and the adjoining İshak Fatih Medresesi a famous theological college from 1440.

Kilise

The Orthodox church was built by Polish and Hungarian refugees who lived here in the middle of the 19th c.

Kütahya Kalesi

Within the handsome 14th c. fortress stands the Kale-i Bala Camii (1375) and also an old medrese.

*Ulu Camii

In the lower town stands the recently restored Grand Mosque. Dating from 1411 it was started by Bayazit I before 1400 and then finished by Mehmet II. The Ottoman architect probably replaced the original oak supports for the roof with 57 marble pillars from Aezani. Next door stands the old library (Kütüphane).

Vecidiye Medresesi

Umur Bey Bin Savat founded this theological college, observatory and institute of natural science and mathematics c. 1314. It now serves as a Museum of Handicrafts with exhibits of glazed earthenware, embroidery and weaving (open: Tue.– Sun. 9.30am–noon and 1.30–5pm).

Surroundings

**Çavdarhisar

At the western end of Çavdarhisar some 60km/37 miles south of Kütahya stand the remains of a well-preserved Ionic Temple of Zeus with columns (8×15). Measuring 33×37m/108×121ft and built without mortar from white-veined marble, it can be found inside other ruins of the ancient town. The remains of the construction stand on an eleven-stepped 2.90m/9½ft podium above underground tunnel vaulting with windows dedicated to the Cybele cult. It was badly damaged in the earthquake of 1970. Other buildings to the north include a stadium, theatre and on the far side of the river a circular building which was the old food market (macellum). 10km/7 miles to the west Stemnos (Steunos), the cave sanctuary of Cybele the mother of the gods, can only be reached by a cross-country vehicle.

Gediz

In 1970 80% of the small town of Gediz was destroyed by an earthquake measuring 6.3 on the 10-point Richter scale. The main quake occurred at 11pm on March 28th and lasted 20–30 seconds followed by a month of aftershocks. The damage was considerable. 3,500 houses were destroyed and 17,000 damaged in some way. The earthquake claimed 1,100 victims and 80,000 were left homeless. Hot springs (which have subsequently subsided) and small lakes developed. After the disaster the government built a new town 7km/4½ miles from the original Gediz. Some of the remains including an old bridge have been re-used. Even after the earthquake many of the original timbered houses give the town a distinctive style.

50km/31 miles west of Kütahya lies the ancient town of Tavşanlı with a notable 12th c. Seljuk mosque. 18km/11½ miles to the north in a side valley of the Koca Çay stands a Phrygian rock monument Dikilitaş, a huge volcanic partly smoothed rock with geometric designs. | Tavşanlı

A number of thermal baths can be found in the region around Kütahya. The spa town of İlıca is the most modern and is situated 30km/19 miles north of the town. Better known are the baths near Yoncalı some 17km/10 miles to the west. The temperature of the radioactive spring water ranges between 42–56°C/107°–132°F. | Yoncalı Kaplıcalari

Kusadaşı

See Ephesus, Surroundings

Magnesia on the Maeander

See Menderes

Malatya   O 5

Eastern Anatolia
Province: Malatya
Altitude: 980m/3214ft
Population: 277,000

The provincial capital of Malatya lies in the middle of the south-east Anatolian highlands (Eastern Taurus) at the south-eastern edge of a fertile plain crossed by the River Euphrates. The modern market town and industrial centre is only 150 years old. For many centuries during the summer the population of today's Eski Malatya (Old Malatya) plied between the town and the well-irrigated garden suburb of Aspuzu in the foothills of the Bozdağ, but in the winter of 1838/9 Ottoman troops (who had been engaged in the battles with Mehmet I the rebellious Ottoman governor of Egypt) were billeted in the town. In the circumstances the local population preferred to spend the winter in Aspuzu and this new settlement became new Malatya. Consequently the town possesses few buildings of historical interest. | Situation and Importance

The oldest settlement Milidia is mentioned in some 18th c. B.C. cuneiform scripts and is said by the Roman historian Pliny the Younger to have been founded by the legendary Assyrian queen Semiramis. It lies 8km/5 miles north-east of modern Malatya (see Arslantepe). More precise information dates from the first half of the 1st millennium B.C. when the late Hittite capital Milid came under Assyrian influence.
By A.D. 70 the Greek town of Melitene, modern Eski Malatya (see below), 5km/3 miles to the north was emerging. The town had become famous as an important crossroads and as headquarters of the Roman "Legio XII Fulminata", whose fame and reputation derive from a legend. According to this legend, in response to the prayers of the Christian soldiers lightning struck the legion's opponents. Emperor Trajan raised Melitene's status and | History

in Byzantine times Justinian built a wall around the town. Main roads were constructed to Tephrike (Divriği) and to Samosata on the Euphrates (Samsat). In 575 Melitene was the scene of a Byzantine victory over the Persian Chosroes I, who burnt the city to the ground before fleeing.

After an uncertain period between the 7th and 10th c. Malatya belonged to a number of fortified towns along the so-called Thugur line between Syria and Armenia, the disputed border between Byzantium and the Caliphate. Several conflicts (751, 837, 841) led to the destruction and subsequent rebuilding of the city.

Around the middle of the 9th c. the Paulicans a militant religious movement found refuge with the emir in the town, which was at that time under Arab occupation. In 934 Melitene came under Byzantium rule until 1071 when the Seljuks captured the town and installed an Armenian as the provincial governor, but he then sought political independence. Crusaders occupied the town for a short time but in 1106 it was recaptured by the Seljuks and then fell to the Danishmend dynasty. From 1168 it reverted to Seljuk rule, although between 1235 and 1395 it had to face attacks from the Mongols. Selim I took Melitene with Eastern Anatolia for the Ottoman Empire.

Surroundings

Afşin

About 132km/81 miles west of Malatya near Elbistan stands the ancient town of Arabissos (later known as Eshab-i Kehf/Eshabkehf). Lying to the west of nearby Afşin, it developed around the crossroads of two main routes: from Caesarea (Kayseri) to Antiocheia (Antakya) and Cilicia to Militene (Eski Malatya). A series of Roman milestones has been discovered near Kurt Tepesi. Also of interest is the complex which dates from the Seljuk period (1215–33) and consists of a mosque, caravanserai and monastery (ribat). The ruined caravanserai is made up of an asymmetrical, four-aisled winter hall with two separate sections. The mosque which is

Children studying the Koran . . .   *. . . and a lorry-driver*

attached to the sloping west front is domed at the rear (prayer niche). The three-aisled prayer hall has a flat roof and nearby the monastery section with its maze of rooms, three-aisled hall and typical Seljuk pointed-arch portal lies to the south towards the slope.

More Roman ruins (Castaballa) can be found about 15km/9½ miles to the north-east near Percenik. In the same region, a little further north-west, the village of Tanir contains some Roman mosaics. Due north of Afşin (21km/13 miles) on the old route to Kayseri stands the Seljuk Kuru Han and another 5km/3 miles to the north near Karakol the Seljuk castle of Hurman Kalesi simultaneously controlled three mountain passes.

Arslantepe lies 8km/5 miles to the north of the town near the village of Orduzu on the remains of a 16th c. Ottoman palace. Excavations are still taking place on the site but finds so far include remains of pre-historic origin and relics from Hittite, late Hittite and Assyrian settlements. The ruins of a late Hittite palace with a large entrance have been unearthed. Stone slabs with relief carvings and monumental lion portals have been discovered. There is evidence to suggest that some of the slabs date from the time of the Hittite Empire. Remains of a later palace are from the time when Milid formed a part of the Assyrian Empire. Its decline in the early 7th c. B.C. was brought about by the Cimmerians. Finds from the excavations are on display in the Hittite Museum in Ankara.

Arslantepe

Darende is dominated by the medieval castle of Senkbar Kalesi. As recently as 1840, 40 houses inside the castle were inhabited. It is known that the remaining houses were abandoned in 1890. Clearly the earlier settlement is very old. A Hittite stele of Sarruma the god of children has been found there.

Darende

The regional centre of Elbistan (pop. 49,000) some 126km/78 miles west of Malatya is overlooked by the medieval fortifications of Kız Kalesi (5km/3 miles to the west). The castle marks the position of former Elbistan – Kara Elbistan or secret Elbistan. Finds here include a stone bowl belonging to a cult of sun-worshippers and figures of the goddess Anahita (probably the same as Cybele) dating from Hittite times. The Ulu Cami in the town provides the earliest example of a mosque with a central dome and four adjoining half-domes. It dates from the Beylik period c. 1500.

Elbistan

Just 5km/3 miles to the north-west on the Elbistan plain, in a hill near Karahüyük archaeologists have unearthed the remains of a Hittite settlement. Some of the interesting finds include a terracotta horse's head from a drinking horn (1200 B.C.) and a memorial stele to a late Hittite prince. The stone which resembles a menhir displays a hieroglyphic inscription on three sides and can now be seen in Ankara's Hittite Museum.

Karahüyük

The ruins of Eski Malatya 12km/7½ miles north-east of modern Malatya lie on the old road to Erzincan and Sivas. The course of the road had to be moved to the west to make way for the Keban reservoir. The village now surrounded by poplars and fruit orchards nestles inside the ruins of old Malatya. Ruins of what was probably a Byzantine wall, an irregular trapezium with four gates, defensive ditches and tower bastions are still preserved and are best seen on the southern side. A little further along the old Sivas road stand two türbe with small cemeteries. The Ulu Cami, which is partly buried, was built in 1247 by Hüsrev on the foundations of an older 7th c. mosque. The latter was destroyed by the Byzantines and then rebuilt in 765 by Al-Mansur. To reach the rear of the mosque pass through the galleried inner courtyard and the divan decorated with glazed tiles into the domed prayer room. The Yeni Cami (1307) like the Ulu Cami dates from Seljuk times. In the north-east of the town stands the Mustafa Paşa Hanı, a well-preserved Ottoman caravanserai. It was founded by Mustafa Paşa one of the Ottoman Murat IV's generals between 1623 and 1640.

Eski Malatya

Manisa

Hekimhan

About 80km/50 miles north-west of Malatya in the small village of Hekim-han stands the Seljuk Hekim Hanı caravanserai (hekim, doctor). This complex was founded by Alaeddin Kaykobad I's doctor Ebu Salim Ben Ebil-Hasan el-Şammas from Malatya. It consists of a square summer courtyard and a three-aisled winter hall. It was last restored in 1660.

Boğazören

7km/4½ miles north of Hekimhan about 3km/2 miles east of the road to Kangal and Sivas is the village of Şirzi, where a Hittite mining settlement lies hidden. 500m/550yd outside the village about 400m/440yd south of the access road stands a huge rocky crag which displays a Hittite hieroglyphic inscription and which the local people call yazılıtaş (inscribed stone). It is clearly a mining inscription similar to one found at Bolkar Madeni (Konya Ereğlisi/Çiftehan).

Manisa

See İzmir

Maras

See Kahramanmaraş

Mardin   Q 6

South-east Anatolia   See warning page 7
Province: Mardin
Altitude: 935–1325m/3066–4346ft
Population: 53,000

Situation and
*Town

The provincial town of Mardin which lies on a picturesque site at the foot of a steeply sloping rocky plateau, offers a tremendous view to the south over the extensive cultivated plains of northern Syria. This is the seat of the Patriarch of the United Syrian Christians (Jacobites) of Tur Abdin (see Surroundings). Many of the grand stone houses reflect the town's strong agricultural traditions and the style is clearly influenced by Arabic architecture. Cereal growing is important in the region and there are also a number of olive groves. Extensive vineyards and fruit orchards flourish in the hinterland (Tur Abdin).

History

Little is known of the town's history before the spread of Islam. In 640 the town came under the control of the Omayyad caliphs from Damascus and a century later fell to the Abbasid dynasty of Baghdad. Before the Seljuk era a Kurdish dynasty held sway (1100) but then eight years later the Artukids from Turkmenistan became masters over Mardin and remained in control until 1260. In 1516 Mardin fell to the Ottomans until the renegade Egyptian governor Mehmet Ali supported two Kurdish uprisings (1832 and 1840) against the Sublime Porte but they were brutally put down by Reşid Paşa.

Sights

Bishop's Palace

Mardin is the official seat of one of the metropolitans of the Syrian Orthodox church, whose adherents follow the thinking of its first and most important teacher Jacob Baradai (490–578). He spent 35 years as an itinerant monk in Syria. His followers, also known as Jacobites, split from the Byzantine church which in 451 at the Council of Chalcedon (Kadıöy near İstanbul) rejected monophysitism, the belief that Christ has a god-like nature and was never a human being.

The Koran school complex, the best preserved building in Mardin can be seen on the eastern side of the town centre above the main street. Founded in 1385 by İsa Bey the decorations on the portal are of special interest. The complex comprising a domed mosque, a mausoleum and two inner court-yards is being restored but it can still be visited. Part of the building is used as a boarding school and part as museum where the rarest exhibit is a Seljuk door-knocker from the Ulu Cami at Cizre.

*İsa Bey Külliyesi

This complex in the west of the town consists of a theological college and domed mosque. It was founded by the Akkoyun Oğulları in the 15th c.

Kasım Bey Külliyesi

The Latifiye Mosque which stands on the town's main road was built in 1371 and has a fine portal. The minaret was added in 1845.

Latifiye Camii

Mardin castle or Telhan Kalesi towers above the town on a rocky crag, near a radar station belonging to the US army (access forbidden). Many assai-lants have tried in vain to conquer this castle but now a steep path leads up from the Sultan İsa Medresesi. Dating from Roman times, it had been extended by the 15th c. so that all the inhabitants of the town could seek refuge there in the event of an impending attack. A relief carving of two magnificent lions can be seen on the gateway.

Mardin Kalesi

To the west above the Sultan İsa Medresesi was another Koran school which used to house an archaeological museum. Only the ethnography section remains.

Sinciriye Medresesi

The large mosque in the centre of the town was built in the 11th c. by the Artukids, but it was reconstructed in 1176. The building suffered badly during a Kurdish uprising in 1832 and it has been partially restored. Be-neath a prism-shaped stone dome supported by pillars lies a prayer room which is divided in three sections. Only the three simple entrance doors remain from the original building.

Ulu Cami

Surroundings

On the edge of the desert close to the Syrian border lies Ceylanpınar D.Ü.Ç state farm where in the middle of the steppe landscape wheat is grown on a large scale. The region was also home to the ahu or goitred gazelle, a species which was at one time threatened with extinction, but now lives on protected reserves.

Ceylanpınar

This Jacobite monastery is situated about 7km/4 miles east of Mardin. The Patriarch of the Jacobites has resided here almost uninterrupted since 1160, when he and his followers were driven out of Antioch (Antakya). The well-tended site surrounded by a high wall is also a boys' boarding school. Dedicated to Ananias the monastery contains three churches which adjoin the rear façade of the arcaded courtyard: the 6th c. St Mary's Church, the Ananias Church which was founded by Anastasios I (491–518), a rectan-gular building (with a pyramid roof and a bell-tower which was added later) and the memorial chapel with a crypt for the Jacobite patriarchs.

*Deir az-Zafaran

An old bridge dominates the town of Hasankeyf 110km/68 miles north-east of Mardin. It crosses the Tigris which narrows at this point. The town was established as Cephe (Kiphas) by the Romans as a border post against the Persians. Under Byzantium it became an important bishop's see. The town's prosperity ended when it fell to the Artukids and Ayyubids and later a Mongol invasion. Four arches remain from the old bridge which was restored in the 12th c. On a rock overlooking the bridge lie the remains of the Artukid palace, which can be reached via a steep flight of steps through three gateways. The palace also 12th c. was known as the "Castle of the Forgotten" as nobody dared to mention its real name for fear of death. The Parthian king Arshak was incarcerated by the Romans and was tied with silver chains to the stuffed corpse of his general Varsak until he died.

*Hasankeyf

Village life, near Mardin

Outside the town stands 15th c. Zeynel Bey Türbesi a cylindrical building constructed out of natural and blue bricks in a herringbone pattern. As a dam is being built in the Tigris valley (İlısu Barajı), in 1994 part of the town is set to disappear under water.

İstilil

92km/57 south-east of Mardin and 17km/10 miles north of Nusaybin lies the village of İstilil and the remains of the ancient settlement of Dara. The town was expanded under Justinian in the 6th c., but it declined in the 7th c. after suffering a defeat by the Arabs. Remains of the town wall and part of an old flight of locks have been preserved. The water comes from a powerful karst spring (worth a visit) which supplies water to the Çaçak Çayı near Şeyhmehmet in the north of the valley.

Kızıltepe

The regional centre of Kızıltepe (pop. 41,000) made the headlines in the early 1980s when a blood feud led to violence. It is situated some 20km/12 miles south-west of Mardin. In 1766 it was the seat of a provincial governor. In 1840 it was scarcely more than a village and did not become an administrative centre again until 1945. The Ulu Cami with its magnificent portal and impressive prayer niche date from the town's heyday in the 13th c.

Nusaybin

The border town of Nusaybin (pop. 45,000) on the Çaçak Çayı is situated 83km/51 miles south-east of Mardin. It lies only 5km/3 miles from an old settlement of Nasibina which is mentioned in Assyrian texts dating from the 1st millennium B.C. The results of the excavation of the Girnavaz settlement which began in 1982 show that the site was inhabited at the beginning of the 3rd millennium. B.C. In 68 B.C. Roman Lucullus captured the town for a short period, but it finally fell in A.D. 115. In 363 the Christian population was forced to move to Amida (Diyarbakır) after a peace treaty was agreed between Byzantium and the Persians. The famous theological college of the Syrian Ephraim was closed and moved to Urfa. It was forced to close there too probably as a result of accusations of heresy associated with its adherence to Nestorian teachings. The Nestorians reject the belief that Mary was the mother of God, only the mother of Jesus. The flourishing town was destroyed in 1260 by the Mongol hordes, but came under Ottoman control in 1515. The town received a boost when it became the border station for the Baghdad railway. One interesting church can be found in the town, namely the 4th c. Mar Jakub Kilisesi which is a square building with a pyramid roof, apse and double-aisled narthex. It was enlarged in 759 and restored in 1872.

By the time of the Seljuks Nusaybin had become a dilapidated town and Ibn Battuta described it as a virtual ruin. When the town ceased to be a garrison before 1540, it became no more than a village. Only when Hafız Paşa marked out the location of a new bazaar in 1837 did Nusaybin begin to recover and by 1870 it became an administrative centre again.

The surrounding area contains a number of interesting Christian monasteries. The Mar Augen Monastery can be reached on foot (6km/4 miles) from the village of Girmeli, itself 20km/12 miles east of Nusaybin. In the Middle Ages, it was home to several hundred Nestorian monks and then Jacobites. Ruined walls, churches, towers and a cloister can be seen in the complex which remained under Nestorian control until 1505.

Tur Abdin
Jacobites

"Mountain of the Servants of God" is the name that is sometimes given to this highland region (900–1400m/2950–4590ft) east of Mardin. It is bordered to the east and north by the Tigris, in the west by the Mazdağı-Kerbe and to the south lie the Syrian plains. Between the 4th c. and the Arabic conquest countless monasteries were established here and the Tur Abdin developed into a centre for the Syrian Jacobites. In the Middle Ages the area was divided into four bishoprics with more than 80 monasteries. The decline began with the Crusaders whose pillaging raids extended into the prosperous villages of Tur Abdin. In the First World War, most of the Christian minorities were expelled after the French emerged as the Jacobites' protectors. In the 1970s more Christians emigrated. Now about 25,000 Syrian Orthodox Christians (Jacobites) live here, some of whom speak Aramaic, the language of Christ, although a modern Aramaic dialect known as Türöyö is more likely to be heard. Only six of the monasteries are now used by monks.

Yeziden (Alevites)

Another minority group lives on the Tur Abdin. The Yeziden (or Alevites) are regarded with mistrust by the Turks because of their liberal interpretation of the Koran and their refusal to pray in mosques. None of the Yeziden villages has a mosque and the Turks regard them as devil-worshippers. Their religion is an amalgamation of Islamic, Persian and Christian elements.

*Midyat

Midyat is the geographical and administrative centre of Tur Abdin. It lies 60km/37 miles to the east of Mardin and consists of two quarters some 3km/2 miles apart. The western quarter is inhabited predominantly by Moslems, while the eastern part with its churches is clearly Christian. Many of the large multi-storey town houses resemble those in Mardin with façades of finely carved stone. The old church Mar Philoxenos became known as Mar Aznoyo after its restoration, while in the Mar Barsaume the metropolitan himself conducts the services. Midyat is a centre for silversmiths and many workshops and small shops selling their jewellery (telkari) can be found in the town.

Monasteries

Midyat is the ideal place from which to visit the monasteries. 15km/9 miles east of Midyat near Arnas stands the Mar Kyriakos Monastery. The church on the northern side of a galleried courtyard was restored in the 19th c. The choir is said to date from the 8th c. Near to the village of Keferzi about 7km/4 miles south-east of Arnas stands the monastic church of Mar Azaziel. It contains an iconostasis with acanthus capitals on columns which support an architrave.

The small village of Anıtlı is situated 10km/7 miles south-west of İzbirak and is noted for the domed church of El Hadra (St Mary's). Of interest are the decorated external walls and the relief work on the narthex doors (c. 700).

An improvised raft on the Tigris

A beautifully decorated façade in Midyat

25km/16 miles south of Midyat on the road to Cizre, at a junction 3km/ 2 miles before the village of Yayvantepe, a metalled road leads off to the north towards the Mar Gabriel Monastery (about 2km/1¼ miles). This 5th c. monastery complex consists of several churches and memorial chambers. Its name derives from Bishop Gabriel (593–667) who is said to have revived the dead. The Gabriel Church with the wing of the choir as the narthex, a transverse nave, central apse and two annexes is situated behind the entrance on the right. To the west stands St Mary's. The memorial chambers to Egyptian monks and 40 martyrs can be found on the north side of the inner courtyard. The Empress Theodora is thought to have endowed the rectangular dome structure with an octagonal interior.

*Mar Gabriel Monastery

100km/62 miles west of Mardin lies the regional centre of Viranşehir, meaning ruined town (pop. 45,000). A relatively modern town, until 1883 it consisted of a small bazaar and an administrative building for the local council which lay within the ruins of Antoniopolis (Konstantina). It is now a progressive town with a modern hotel alongside the ruins of the ancient settlement. The ancient town of Antoniopolis (Maximilianopolis) was laid waste by the Persians at the beginning of the 4th c. Restored by Maxentius, it was destroyed by an earthquake c. 350 and rebuilt as a Roman castle with a double wall and then called Constantina (Tela). By 1644 it lay in ruins again. Under İbrahim Paşa the son of the rebellious Egyptian governor Mehmed Ali, the old castle became a winter residence (1833–40) and was known as Yenişehir (New Town). In 1908 an uprising by Kurds and Turks almost completely destroyed the town.

Viranşehir

Marmara, Sea of

B–E 2/3

Marmara region
11,500sq.km/4440sq.mile inland sea between Thrace and Asia Minor

The Sea of Marmara separates European Turkey from Asia Minor. In antiquity it was known as Propontis. 280km/173 miles long and 80km/50 miles wide, it extends from the Bosporus to the Dardanelles and links the Black Sea with the Aegean Sea. Tectonic movement in the Early Quaternary period created a rift valley with large parts of the old land surface ending up only 200m/650ft under water. The deepest water is to be found in an underwater trough which extends 1300m/4250ft below the surface and which follows the line of a broken shelf into the Gulf of İzmit (İzmit Körfezi). This rift valley is part of the long North Anatolian fault line, which is responsible for making the Sea of Marmara and northern Anatolia an area where earthquakes are frequent.

Situation and Origins

The southern coast in particular consists of bays, peninsulas and low-lying lakeland and these troughs and ridges include the Gulf of Gemlik, Erdek, Bandırma, Kapıdağ peninsula and Samanlı Dağ. Most of the protected ports such as İzmit, Gemlik, Bandırma and Mudanya are situated along this part of the coastline. The northern coastline on the other hand is relatively straight, there are few natural harbours and what were once high mountains are now islands. Close to İstanbul in the east lie the Princes' Islands (see İstanbul). In the south-west a number of small islands are clustered around the island of Marmara and the Kapıdağ peninsula, which in antiquity was an island.

Coasts

The summer climate in the Marmara region has many attractions as it stays relatively cool in high summer with frequent northerly and north-westerly winds (meltem) and also cooling currents from the Black Sea. In winter, however, the Sea of Marmara is subject to cold and stormy weather, but the olive groves in the region rarely fall victim to sudden frosts.

Climate

In the last ten years the northern coastline of the Sea of Marmara has become very popular with holidaymakers from the major Turkish cities.

Resorts on the north coast

Holiday villages, chalets and apartment blocks line the coast between Tekirdağ and the western outskirts of İstanbul and also for 100km/60 miles on the eastern side of the Bosphorus. With building work continuing unabated, almost the whole length of coast is now devoted to tourism, but the western section and the area between Marmara Ereğlisi and Kumburgaz are most affected. The sandy beaches south-west of Tekirdağ remain as yet untouched with the exception of the Barbaros and Kumbağ regions (10km/7 miles) and, after the coast-road was extended, Şarköy (55km/34 miles).

Tekirdağ

The provincial town of Tekirdağ (pop. 63,000) is a busy place on the northern coast of the Sea of Marmara with a small commercial port. Previously known as Rodosto, it was called Bisanthe in antiquity and later Rhaidestos. The Turkish name Tekir Dağ (Slate Mountain) refers to the İsıklar Dağı range of slate mountains which line the coast to the south-west. Tekirdağ was the birthplace of the Turkish poet Namık Kemal (see Famous People).

The Phrygians set out across the Sea of Marmara from Tekirdağ in their conquest of Asia Minor. For many years the town was under control of the Thracians who gave their name to the whole region. In 46 B.C., the Romans under Vespasian occupied Tekirdağ and the rest of Thrace but the town continued to play an important part during Byzantine times.

The birthplace of the Hungarian prince Rakóczi has been converted into a small museum and the Damat Rüstem Paşa complex which comprises a mosque and bedesten (covered bazaar) was built about 1565 by the famous architect Sinan.

Çorlu

The regional centre of Çorlu (pop. 59,000) is a picturesque town set on a hillside some 36km/22 miles north-east of İstanbul on the main transit route from İstanbul to Bulgaria and beyond. The famous Roman road known as the Via Egnatia which linked İstanbul with the Adriatic coast passed through Çorlu and the Roman bridge behind the town was a part of the road.

Marmaris   E 5

South-west coast (Mediterranean)
Province: Muğla
Altitude: 0–50m/0–164ft
Population: 10,000

Position of the
holiday resort

The port town of Marmaris lies 60km/37 miles south of the provincial capital Muğla at the head of Marmaris Bay, an inlet sheltered from the sea by a number of rocky islets. Owing to its beautiful situation in lush green surroundings and pine woods, its sheltered harbour and long beautiful beaches around the shores of the bay, Marmaris has developed into a popular holiday resort with modern hotels, guest-houses and holiday homes, some of which are a long way from the town. It is easily accessible via the regional airport at Dalaman 100km/60 miles to the east.

History

The modern town's predecessor was Physkos, a dependency of Rhodes. A few traces of the old Hellenistic town can be detected on the Hill of Asartepe outside the built-up area. During the 14th c. under the Seljuks, Marmaris was ruled by the Emirs of the Menteşe dynasty from Milas and then later incorporated into the Ottoman Empire. Many of the present inhabitants are the descendants of Turks from Crete.

*Old Town

The half-timbered houses of the old town huddle round a medieval castle on a peninsula projecting into a bay. At the foot of the hill lies the well-equipped harbour with berths for yachts, landing-stages for car ferries to Rhodes, boat trips to Kaunos in the Dalyan delta, Datça Knidos or Bodrum. Restaurants, cafés and the tourist information bureau can also be found in this quarter. There is a lively bazaar in the old town.

Surroundings

Copper market in Muğla

The main trunk road from Marmaris to İzmir passes well to the west of Muğla, so many travellers miss this picturesque town (pop. 36,000) with its steep alleys and delightful bazaar. The sparkling white houses in the old quarter are noted for their huge overhanging roofs and must rank as the finest in Turkey. The town lies to the north-east of the fertile Muğla Ovası basin on the edge of the İkizce Dağı. Muğla is overlooked to the north by a medieval castle and the 800m/2625ft acropolis of the ancient Carian town of Mobolla.

For a superb view of the town and the surrounding region leave Muğla to the east along an old winding track which is generally not suitable for motor vehicles. The road ascends first to a plateau and then beyond to Kale (Kale Tavas) passing through some impressive, secluded mountain woodland. Sights of interest here include relics dating from the town's Islamic past and in particular from the Mentese emirs who once resided in Muğla. Worth seeking out are the Şey Camii, the Üçerenler Camii (Mosque of the Three Saints) and the oldest building in Muğla the Ulu Camii which was founded in 1344 by İbrahim Bey Menteşeoğlu. Most inhabitants live off the land or work in the nearby opencast brown coal mine at Yatağan 25km/16 miles to the north-west.

*Muğla

Near the village of Dalyan some 30km/20 miles east of Marmaris as the crow flies lies the site of ancient Kaunos. The road to the site runs north to Gökova at the head of the long Gulf of Gökova and then east via Köyceğiz. The Köyceğiz lagoon is linked to the open sea by the River Dalyan.

Roughly half-way between the lagoon and the sea is the village of Dalyan, where a boat plies across the channel, flowing here through a marshy plain, to the monumental rock tombs of Kaunos on the west side. The 4th c. B.C. tombs hewn from the steep rock face can be seen from a considerable distance. Investigations of the site by Turkish archaeologists since 1960 have suggested a dating in the first millennium B.C.

Kaunos
**Dalyan Delta

In the 1980s Turkish and German environmental groups succeeded in preventing the construction of a luxury hotel in Dalyan Bay which was to be paid for with German development aid. This area is one of the last breeding grounds in the Mediterranean for the loggerhead turtle (caretta caretta) and it has since been designated as a protected area by the Turkish government. Nevertheless, in high season thousands of tourists still descend on the area by boat and by bus and their presence alone is endangering the existence of these rare creatures. It is therefore advisable to avoid the area.

Note

On the ancient site of Stadeia and in Datça Bay 80km/50 miles west of Marmaris lies the growing holiday resort of Datça (marina). It can be reached either by boat or on a winding hill road which runs along the narrow Reşadiye Peninsula known in ancient times as Cnidian Chersones. Both sides of this road offer beautiful views over the sea and the splendid bathing beaches with their adjacent campsites.

A regular car ferry service to Bodrum (Halikarnassos) operates from the port of Körmen on the peninsula 10km/6 miles north-west of Datça (see Bodrum).

Datça

The rock tombs of Kaunos, most easily reached by water

*Knidos

Position and
Importance

35km/22 miles beyond Datça on a poor unsurfaced track at the western tip
of the peninsula is the site of ancient Knidos. It is preferable, however, to
make this trip by boat. The peninsula which rises to a height of
1175m/3855ft (Boz Dağı) was known as the Cnidian Chersones or Dorian
Promontory (Reşadiye Yarımadası in Turkish). The western tip of the peninsula Cape Triopion, now Deveboynu Burun, falls steeply down to the sea.
Originally an island, in classical times it was linked to the mainland by a
narrow strip of land. Ancient Knidos, famous for its scholarship and art,
was built on the island but later also expanded on to the slopes of the
mainland. The first excavations were carried out by the British archaeologist Sir Charles Newton in 1857–58.

Ancient Knidos (Cnidus or Gnidus in Latin) was probably founded in the
7th c. by Laconians (Lacedaemonians) from the south-eastern Peloppon-
nese and rapidly developed into an important centre for shipping, trade
and crafts e.g. pottery. On Cape Triopion once stood a Temple of Apollo
(not yet located), the Shrine of the Hexapolis, a league of six Dorian cities
comprising Knidos, Kos, Halikarnassos, Lindos, Ialysos and Kameiros. The
last three were all on the island of Rhodes. The city continued to flourish
when it became part of the Athenian Empire. Like Kos it had a famous
medical school. Later it became a Spartan base but was liberated by the
Athenian general Konon in 394 b.c. Works of art which date from this time
include the Cnidian Aphrodite, Praxiteles' most famous work and now on
view in the Louvre and also the figure of Demeter which is now in the British
Museum.

Harbours

Knidos had two excellent harbours, one on either side of the narrow strip of
land linking the former island with the mainland. The Great Harbour to the
south had an entrance 145m/160yd wide between two massive moles. In
the north-west the smaller harbour, formerly a naval harbour, had an

Turtles in Dalyan Bay

entrance only 24m/26yd wide protected by a fine round tower. On the former island only the remains of the town walls and ancient terracing can still be seen.

The part of the town built on the mainland at a date which cannot be established with any certainty had a regular street layout, although – as at Priene – the rising ground made terracing necessary. Running along the crest of the ridge above the theatre and the steep slopes above is a long stretch of the town wall. It extends from the old naval harbour to the acropolis (285m/935ft) and, with the walls and towers surviving almost intact, creates one of the finest examples of Hellenistic fortifications. The ascent is fairly strenuous.

* Town walls

6km/4 miles south-east of Knidos on the Aslancı Burun or Lion Cape (accessible only by boat) is the ruined Lion Monument commemorating the victory won in 394 b.c. by Konon. 90 Athenian and Persian vessels defeated 85 vessels commanded by the Spartan general Persandros. The monument was a cenotaph, an empty tomb erected in memory of those who died far from home, and similar in appearance to the Mausoleion of Halikarnassos (see Bodrum). A square base articulated by Doric half-columns supports a stepped pyramid on which a lion stood guard. The lion was sent to the British Museum by Newton.

Lion Monument

Menderes · Maeander

C–E5/6

Aegean region. Three rivers in western Anatolia
Küçük Menderes (Little Maeander). Length: 175km/108 miles
Büyük Menderes (Great Maeander). Length: 584km/362 miles
Küçük Menderes (Skamander; Sarımsaklı since 1987)
Length: 124km/77 miles

Menderes · Maeander

The first two of the rivers mentioned above flow through the deep, broad, long and extremely fertile rift valley in the 150×100km/90×60 mile Menderes massif, one of the oldest mountain ranges in the middle and southern section of the Turkish Aegean region. The third river irrigates the western part of the Biga peninsula in north-western Anatolia but all three rivers are characterised by a favourable climate, dense population and intense agricultural exploitation (cotton) in an extensive and well-irrigated area. They were of particular importance for many of the ancient towns.

Küçük Menderes
The Küçük Menderes of today is the ancient Kaystros. The source of this 175km/108 mile long river is to be found north of Kıraz on the Bozdağı (2159m/7080ft) about 80km/50 miles east of İzmir. It winds its way down to the 25km/16 mile wide and 80km/50 mile long Küçük Menderes depression disgorging into the silted, marshy delta of the Gulf of Kusadası not far from the ancient town of Ephesus. The decline of Ephesus as a port was due largely to the river mouth which had become choked with sand.

Büyük Menderes
The Büyük Menderes is the ancient Maiandros (Maeander). This river over 500km/310 miles in length flows from a powerful karst spring near Dinar and another source south-west of Afyon ("Sağ Menderes", Right Maeander). The two streams converge south of Çivril, hurry through the mountain region of Çal and then follow a course of tiny loops (hence the term "meander") from Sarayköy through the 200km/120 mile long and up to 20km/12 mile wide Great Maeander valley, where the section to the east of Denizli is known as the Çürüksu Ovası. A very marshy and rapidly growing delta south of Kuşadası marks the spot where the river flows into the Gulf of Miletus.

The river's sedimentation has made the ancient Greek ports of Miletus, Priene and Herakleia into inland towns and cut off a part of the old bay to form Bafa Gölü (Herakleia Lake).

In the Meander Plain

The Sarımsaklı of today was also officially known as the Küçük Menderes until 1987 (in antiquity as the Skamander). It rises on the Biga peninsula some 80km/50 miles south-east of Çanakkale on the Öldüren Dağı in the Ida Mountains (Kaz Dağı 1774m/5810ft) and flows on through the fertile but in places marshy lowlands of Ezine/Bayramiç and Truva (plain and battlefield of Troy). These coastal towns also fell victim to sedimentation. The Sarımsaklı flows into the Aegean by the south-west entrance to Dardanelles near Kumkale.

The remains of ancient Magnesia lie on the northern edge of the wide alluvial plain of the Maeander (Büyük Menderes) 25km/15 miles inland from Kuşadası as the crow flies. The site can be reached from the main İzmir to Milas road by bearing right at a fork just beyond Ortaklar, 95km/60 miles south-east of İzmir. The ancient city lies only a short distance further along this road. Although it is not signposted, the site can easily be recognised by the extensive remains of walls on either side of the road.

The site was occupied by the Magnetes from very early times. They are a people whose origins and character were the subject of many later legends. About 650 B.C. a town which had been established further downstream at the confluence of the Lethaios and the Maeander by settlers from Magnesia in Thessaly was destroyed by the Cimmerians. The town was later rebuilt by the Milesians and then in 530 B.C. captured by the Persians. About 400 B.C. the Spartan general Thibron compelled the Magnesians to leave their town, which was unfortified and subject to flooding, and to move upstream to the present site at the foot of Mount Thorax.It only began to prosper under the Seleukids. From the time of Sulla (84 B.C.) the town was independent but an ally of Rome. The excavations carried out by Texier in 1842–43 and Humann in 1891–93 have since been overlaid with soil deposited during the winter floods and overgrown by vegetation so that more recent Turkish researchers have had difficulty tracing the layout of the old town. Some of the finds from the 19th c. excavations are to be seen in the Pergamon Museum in Berlin.

The first remains to be seen, the foundations of a Roman barracks, lie to the east on the other side of the road and railway line. The remains of a 7th c. Byzantine wall which re-used earlier masonry can be seen on both sides of the road.
Further on to the west lie the remains of the once-celebrated Temple of Artemis Leukophryene, an Ionic temple (a pseudo-dipteros with a double-width gallery) built by Hermogenes of Alabanda at the end of the 3rd c. B.C. One of the largest examples in Asia Minor, it had an Amazon frieze, regarded as one of the most extensive relief compositions of ancient times. Parts of the frieze are to be found in the Paris Louvre, Berlin and İstanbul. To the west of the temple lies the site of the Ionic propylon which linked the sacred precinct with the agora. To the south is a ruined Byzantine church. Other sights include the remains of the Roman gymnasium, the stadium, town walls and the necropoles. The theatre which was excavated by a German archaeologist had become overgrown but has now been cleared and restored.

Sarımsaklı

History

Excavations

Mersin

See Tarsus

Midas Şehri (Yazılıkaya)   F 4

Central Anatolia. Province: Eskişehir
Altitude: 1100m/3608ft. Population: 160

Midas Şehri (Yazılıkaya)

Situation and
**Importance

The small village of Yazılıaya or "inscribed rock" and the ancient site of Midas Şehri (Midas Town) and Midas Tomb are situated 100km/62 miles south of Eskişehir at the northern foot of the Oluk Dağı (1713m/5618ft) in the headwaters of the Sakarya Nehri. It can be reached either from the regional centres of Çifteler or Seyitgazi in the north or Afyon and Kümbet. The region contains many interesting rock monuments from the last Phrygian period which date from the 6th c. B.C. but some believe them to be even older. The houses only rarely have flat roofs but have been carved to create façades which were combined with the usual wooden constructions. The Phrygian monuments are characterised by a flat geometrical design around the edging or else cover larger surfaces like a carpet. Only rarely are figured motifs found. Frequently occupying a central position is a door which leads either to a burial chamber or to a niche where an image of a deity would be placed during devotions.

*Midas' Tomb

The so-called Midas' Tomb discovered in the 19th c. is not in fact a tomb at all but a sacred site with a niche and some ancient Phrygian inscriptions which have as yet to be fully deciphered but include the name "Mida", hence the belief that the site contains Midas' tomb (see A to Z Gordion and Famous People). The 16m/52ft wide and 17m/55ft tall façade with elaborate geometrical patterns is situated on the north-west side of the acropolis in Midas Şehri. The shrine which is dedicated to the earth and mother goddess Cybele bears the name "Mida". Her statue would be placed on a niche during ceremonies. Some 200m/215yd to the south-west stands another incomplete façade and in the east below the acropolis some more smaller tombs. On the north-west slope of the acropolis stands an impressive 10m/32ft wide and 7m/23ft tall Küçük Yazılıkaya sacred monument with some splendid decorations.

"Midas Town"

The original name for this Phrygian metropolis at Yazılıkaya is not known so it was named after its one-time ruler Midas. "Midas Town" dates from 1000 B.C. and the 600×200m/1975×650ft acropolis, which is linked in the north to a lower town, probably from around the 7th c. B.C. The once-walled plateau contained houses and larger public buildings with sacred altars and terracotta friezes. Of special interest are the cisterns which can be reached by a number of stairways. At the summit of the acropolis stands a stone throne with a large Phrygian inscription. The local people believe it to be Midas' seat, but it was probably for a deity to be displayed during sacred devotions. On the northern side some Hittite relief carvings can be found from which it can be ascertained that the site was occupied in pre-Phrygian times. The most recent building is a 3rd c. B.C. Hellenistic shrine on the north-west side of the acropolis. A number of indications including a Latin inscription in one of the tombs point to the occupation of the site well into Roman times. It was destroyed and finally abandoned in the 3rd c. A.D.

Surroundings

Bahşiş

South of Kırka at the end of a rough track about 12km/7 miles south-west of Yazılıkaya lies the Caucasian village of Gökbahçe (Bahsayis or Bahşiş). In a gorge behind the village school a shrine has been carved out of the rock.

Cukurca

The village of Cukurca (Gügürça or Burhaniye) is situated 2km/1¼ miles north of Yazılıkaya. Alongside a number of burial caves is a typical cave tomb in the shape of a temple with pediment and columns – what the local Turks call "gerdekkaya" (bridal chamber rock). A magnificent coffered ceiling with beams has been faithfully carved from the rock. Some 500m/540yd south of the village stands a simple 8m/26ft high pedimented Arezastis shrine with lines of inscriptions and rectangular ornaments.

*Kümbet

In the tiny village of Kümbet 15km/9 miles east of Yazılıkaya stands a pedimented monument from Roman times with carved lions in front of an urn and other smaller animals. Two more shrines can also be seen close to the mosque. The one at the rear has a pointed canopy above a rock throne.

Geometric decoration on Phrygian monuments

The Seljuk türbe opposite, like many of the village houses, incorporates some ancient stones (old cemetery).

Milas

South-west Anatolia (Menteşe Highlands)
Province: Muğla
Altitude: 46m/150ft
Population: 24,000

This ancient Carian town nestles beneath the Sodra Dağı (565m/1850ft) at the western edge of the Milas valley and is well known today, as it was in antiquity for grapes, olives and figs. The town, which is also noted for its carpet-weaving, was not on a major traffic route but the arrival of tourism in Bodrum and Marmaris has raised its profile. It is, nevertheless, one of the lesser known of Turkey's historical sites, primarily because there are so many other places of cultural and historic interest in the surrounding mountains and the coastal region of the old Turkish Menteşe principality. The cobbled alleys, red, overhanging tiled roofs and the handsome old town houses with their small bay windows are, however, a delight.

Situation and Importance

Ancient Mylasa was probably founded by Mylasos of the Aiolos tribe as the capital of Inner Caria. By the time of Herodotus (484–425 B.C.) it had achieved fame under the tyrant Oliatos. Milas was the home town of the later Carian king Mausolos. During Roman times and until the 3rd c. it minted its own coins. While under Byzantium the town was a bishop's see and a provincial centre. It enjoyed prosperity in the 13th c. as centre of the Menteşe beylik (from 1291) before falling to the Ottomans in 1390. Unfortunately the town was accidentally bombed by the British in 1943.

History

Milas

Sights

Baltalı Kapı

Only a Corinthian round-arched gateway between the remains of a wall are left from the white marble temple and secular buildings in the north of the town. The double axe (Labrys, Balta) of the Carian Zeus can be seen on the keystone of the vaulting.

** Beçinkalesi

The 14th c. fortifications also known as Peçin Kalesi lie 5km/3 miles to the south of the town. The site of the Menteşe emirs' castle which dates from Turkman times is particularly striking. There are also relics which go back via the Hellenistic period to the Bronze Age. The impressive fortress site contains not just the castle but many other sacred and secular buildings including mosques, baths and caravanserais. Many researchers have thus concluded that the site on the hill preceded the modern site at Milas, possibly even that of ancient Mylasa.
Opposite the castle halfway up the rock face lies the Berber İni rock tomb (barbarian's cave) or Berber Yatağı (barbarian's bed) in the shape of a Doric anta temple with two rooms and a false door.

* Gümüşkesen

The Gümüşkesen (silver box) mausoleum stands on a plinth of stone blocks to the west of the town near Gümüşlük. The pyramid roof is supported by twelve pillars. Its construction resembles that of the famous mausoleum of Mausolos in Bodrum (see Bodrum).

Ulu Cami

The Grand Mosque which dates from the second half of the 14th c. (1370 or 1378?) is typical of the Menteşe emirs' prosperity. Carved stones from earlier buildings were incorporated into the structure, including a double axe on the right side of the façade and some Greek inscriptions. Byzantine influence is evident from the rather cumbersome interior.

Gümüşkesen Mausoleum

Town gate in Herakleia on Latmian Gulf

Surroundings

Çine (formerly Kıroba), hemmed in by the mountain ridges of the eastern
(Topçambabadağ 1792m/5875ft) and western (Teke Dağ 1276m/4185ft)
Menteşe highlands, is a regional centre barely 60km/37 miles north-east of
Milas. Agricultural land predominates in the lowlands of the Büyük Menderes valley with the cultivation of Mediterranean fruit and vegetables.
This region was densely populated in the past and many ancient remains
can be found. About 7km/4 miles to the south-west near Araphisar and its
ruined castle the important ancient site of Alabanda lies on the left bank of
the Çine Çayı (Marsyas in antiquity). This free town which prospered in
Roman times was also known as Antiocheia and became famous for its
wealth. Its most famous citizen was the rhetorician Apollonios. It is also
well known for "alabandicus", a black to purple-red marble used in the
production of glass as it melts when heated. Some of the ruins lie near the
village of Araphisar but they extend from the Çine Çayı south to the col
between two hills separated by the Kemer Deresi.

According to legend the town was founded by King Kar. He called his son   History
Alabandos and the town Alabanda after a successful cavalry battle (Carian
"ala", horse and "banda", victory). The town enjoyed its greatest prosperity in the middle of the 4th c. B.C. under King Mausolos (see Bodrum). Upon
the death of Ada, Mausolos' sister (see Karpuzlu) who was made queen of
Caria by Alexander, Alabanda became the Carian capital. It attracted fame
as the source of a precious stone similar to garnet.

Sights

The 36×26m/39×28yd bouleuterion (meeting place) stands on the plain at
the northern edge of the town. Two flights of steps lead to the rear seats. To
the south of the bouleuterion stands the 80×120m/87×130yd agora
(market-place) which at one time was bordered by double-aisled colonnades. On the hill to the east, the remains of the acropolis walls and towers
can be found, while on the slope of the acropolis lies the 85m/92yd wide
theatre auditorium. Part of the supporting walls and the two entrances are
preserved. The famous frieze found on the Temple of Apollo Isotimus
showing an Amazonian battle is now on display in an İstanbul museum.
South-east of the agora among some Byzantine ruins can be seen the
foundations of an Ionic pseudo-dipteros mentioned by Vitruv. West of the
Temple of Apollo lie the remains of a large baths complex and another
temple.
Excavations on the western hillside in 1904/05 exposed the remains of a
Doric Temple of Artemis (?) with eleven by six columns. Still recognisable is
the town wall which measures between 2.5 and 3m/8 and 11ft wide.
Remains of projections and towers can be seen along its length. Some
simple stone sarcophagi can be found on the outskirts of the town. Many of
the tombs bear inscriptions stating the profession of the deceased. In the
Kemer Deresi valley the remains of an aqueduct are visible.

Near to Çine some 30m/100ft high Byzantine, painted rock carvings were   Rock carvings
recently discovered. The ten figures (each 2sq.m/7sq.ft) from the life of
Christ probably date from the 9th c. and include Christ with Bible and cross,
John the Baptist, Mary with infant, Mary with her parents, archangel and
angels.

At the eastern end of the Selemiye valley 12km/7 miles north-west of Milas   ** Euromos
near the village of Kızılcakuyu (Ayaklı) lies the ruined town of Euromos.
Covering an area of 2sq.km/³⁄₄ sq. mile, the remains include one of the best
preserved temples in Asia Minor, the Roman Temple of Zeus Lepsynos
which lies close to the town walls. Constructed on the foundations of an
older Hellenistic building, the temple measures 15 by 17m/16 by 19yd.
Sixteen of the 66 Corinthian pillars are standing and some of the beams are

Milas

Picturesque rocky shore of the Bafa Gölü lake

still in place. There are many examples of the double axe symbol of Zeus to be seen. One or two clues suggest that the temple was never finished. Large parts of the ruined town to the north of the temple are overgrown with shrubs and grass including walls, theatre and agora. A huge round tower overlooks the remains of the wall. Excavations by Turkish archaeologists are planned.

Güllük

This attractive coastal town in the delightful Güllük Bay 25km/16 miles south-west of Milas has in recent years become a popular resort catering mainly for local people. The ruins of Iasos can be reached by boat from here as the overland route from Euromos to the site is very poor. The region around Güllük has seen little development. The silting up of the River Değirmenderesi (Sarı Çayı) has created marshy terrain and an ideal habitat for birds. Mosquitoes are in abundance too but the release of certain species of fish may well see an end to them.

**Herakleia under Latmos

Herakleia can be reached by an 11km/7 mile long unmetalled road which forks northwards off the main İzmir to Muğla trunk road and ends at Kapıkırı. The ruined town lies on the north-east shore of the beautiful Bafa Gölü which was once the innermost southern tip of the Latmian Gulf but was then cut off from the sea by sediment brought down by the Maeander (Büyük Menderes). Consequently the lake is slightly salty and has an abundance of fish.

The extensive remains combine with the rugged heights of Mount Latmos in the background to create one of the most picturesque spots in western Asia Minor. It only enjoyed a brief period of prosperity in Hellenistic times. In the early Christian period the town and surrounding region were a favourite haunt of monks and hermits. The Seljuks, however, drove the Christians out of the area c. 1080, completing the process about 1300. Excavations were begun here before the First World War.

The city area is entered through the East Gate with a well-preserved arch in cut stone, one of the earliest of its kind. A peninsula with numerous tombs and a Byzantine castle which used to be the bishop's seat extends to the south and offers a fine view. On the way to the West Gate the visitor passes a magnificent rock shrine (with a four-columned porch) dedicated to the local hero Endymion, the agora now partly covered with soil and the tall Temple of Athena which is well-preserved but minus roof and porch. Beyond some rough and rocky ground and the West Gate lie the remains of the town wall and some old harbour defences.

Ruined town

The town walls, some 6m/20ft high and with an average thickness of 2.25m/7½ft although in places up to 3.20m/10½ft, are preserved at some points to the height of the parapet and as such create one of the best surviving examples of ancient fortifications. Two stretches of the wall which originally had a total of 65 towers meet high up on the hill, extending in total to 4.5km/2¾ miles in length. At one time the upper section of the walls enclosed a second acropolis. From the highest point, however, the walls continued further, enclosing a third acropolis (350m/1150ft) as the city originally stretched further east making the total perimeter 6.5km/4 miles.

*Town walls

A visit to the monasteries and caves on 1367m/4480ft Mount Latmos (in Turkish Beş Parmak Dağı, Five Finger Mountain) is a strenuous expedition. The principal monastery Stylos (Arabavlu) dates from the 10th c. and is dedicated to St Paul. It is an eleven-hour walk from Herakleia through wild terrain. In 1079 St Christodulos left this monastery and in 1088 founded another on the Greek island of Patmos. The Latmos caves contain some notable 12th and 13th c. wall paintings. According to Strabo in a cave south-west of Herakleia lies the Tomb of Endymion, the handsome youth who won the love of the moon goddess Selene and was condemned to eternal sleep.

Mount Latmos

Some 20km/12 miles west of Milas near the village of Kıyıkışlacık (Kuren) and close to a fine beach lies the ancient site of Iasos. A boat trip from Güllük is recommended. In recent years Italian researchers have carried out a number of excavations here. The prosperous Carian town of Iasos traded with the Minoans and Mycenaeans and attracted settlers from Miletus. Remains on the small peninsula include Roman tombs, the old town hall (bouleuterion) near the agora, a Hellenistic theatre, a church and dwellings. A huge late 5th c. wall more than 2km/1¼ miles in length extends westwards over a mountain ridge.

Other sights
Iasos

The ancient settlement of Alinda is situated a good 30km/20 miles to the west of Çine. Ada the sister of King Mausolos (see Bodrum) withdrew here after a dispute over the succession with Mausolos, brother Pixadoras and sister Artemisia. She extended this typical Carian hill settlement with a variety of defensive fortifications. Alexander the Great made preparations to capture Halikarnassos from Alinda where he lived in close friendship with Ada after she had handed over the towns of Alabanda (see Çine) and Alinda in 334 B.C. without a struggle. He later installed her as queen of Caria after she provided Carian troops for his battle against Halikarnassos.

Her palace was probably situated on the acropolis above the town centre where the dwellings were supplied with running water from cisterns. As well as a 30m/100ft wide agora which was once surrounded by a colonnade, the well-preserved remains include a business quarter, a Hellenistic theatre (35 rows, two entrances and a 5m/5½yd wide stage) and a three-storied market building (100m/110yd long and 15m/50ft high) comprising shops with store-rooms in the basement and pillared halls as warehouses on the first floor. The town is surrounded by the remains of a strong 4th c. B.C. wall made from stone blocks. A two-storey tower which overlooks the theatre forms a part of the wall with access via a tunnel.

Karpuzlu
(Alinda)

Miletus

Koca Kavak

About 40km/25 miles east of Muğla lies Yatağan (Bozüyük, Ahirkale), the old town of Astragon. Heading towards Çine 15km/9 miles to the north before the 416m/1365ft Gökbel pass near Koca Kavak stands the imposing "Ince Kemer Taş" – a vast limestone landscape set back about 1km/½ mile to the east of the road. This 20m/65ft high, wall of rock with a smooth surface turns out on closer inspection to be an ancient carving of a warrior. At the foot of the rock images of saints can be seen. Nearby an bridge with many arches carries an ancient pathway over the Çine Çayı.

*Labranda

The ancient site of Labranda lies some 15km/9 miles north-west of Milas near the village of Türbe on the Koca Yayla, one of the foothills to the south of the Latmos Mountains. The principal shrine of the Carians is situated on four man-made terraces and was named after "labrys", the double axe. These excavations have been carried out by the Swedish university of Lund. A cobbled Sacred Way connected it with Mylasa. According to legend, the famous Temple of the Carian Zeus (5th c. B.C.) contained a pond with fish which bore golden necklaces and rings. Other buildings in the town included a Roman bath complex with an adjoining Ionic house, an early Christian church, a Roman well-house, several shops, three remarkable androns (meeting-places and shrines for men) and so-called wash houses (Shrine of the Fish Oracle) with seven monolithic granite columns (south-east). The remains of a porch (stoa) are of special interest. Above the temple stands the entrance to a burial ground which contains five magnificent sarcophagi. On the slopes above lie the remains of a stadium.

Stratonikeia

37km/23 miles along the route from Milas to Muğla via Yatağan, the road passes near the village of Eskihisar (opencast brown coal mine) and the site of ancient Stratonikeia which was badly damaged by an earthquake in 1958. Among the ruins can be found the remains of the town hall, a well-preserved theatre for 10,000 spectators and the Temple of Serapis (2nd/3rd c. B.C.). This Hellenistic town was founded by Seleukos I in 282 B.C. and was named after his wife Stratonike. A museum is situated near the school close to the entrance to the village. The site is directly adjacent to the opencast mine.

Miletus

West coast (Aegean Sea)
Province: Aydın
Altitude: 2–63m/7–205ft
Place: Yeniköy

Situation and
**Importance

The remains of the celebrated ancient commercial city of Miletus (Miletos), the largest of the Ionian cities, lie by the little village of Balat near Yeniköy in a narrow bend on the Büyük Menderes (ancient Maeander) some 150km/95 miles from İzmir. In ancient times this region was known as Caria. Until the 5th c. B.C. the city stood on a peninsula projecting into the Latmian Gulf and had four harbours which shipped locally-made textiles and Pontic corn. Subsequently silt deposited by the Maeander filled the whole of the Latmian Gulf and pushed the coastline 10km/6 miles away from the city, which then slowly declined and was eventually abandoned. The remains, now isolated in the alluvial plain, still bear witness to the greatness of this one-time economic, cultural and political centre and are certainly one of the most interesting archaeological sites in Turkey. During the rainy season the ground is frequently marshy. German archaeologists started excavations here in 1899.

History

Miletus is thought to have been founded by settlers from Crete, where there was a city of the same name. The first site adjoined the Theatre Harbour but then in the 11th c. B.C. Ionians under the leadership of Neleus relocated the town on Kalabak Tepe further south. With a favourable sit-

412

uation on a peninsula in the Latmian Gulf and at the meeting-place of several important trade routes, it soon became the principal port for the territories in the hinterland. Miletus reached its period of greatest prosperity at the end of the 7th c. B.C. under a tyrant named Thrasybulos, a friend of the Corinthian Prince Periander. The city began to mint coins and the alphabet was perfected. The death of Thrasybulos was followed by long and bloody civil wars and the city's power and trade declined.

The city which had been completely destroyed was rebuilt about 480 B.C. in accordance with Hippodamian principles on a new site to the north-east of its previous position. In 479 it shook off Persian control and became a member of the Athenian maritime league known as the Confederacy of Delos. Art and industry flourished again and Milesian beds, chairs and textiles were widely renowned. The Milesians themselves became notorious for good-living and effeminacy. Soon after 200 B.C. Miletus became an ally of Rome and went on to enjoy a further period of prosperity as the huge theatre and other important ruins testify.

Under Byzantine rule Miletus became the see of a bishop and later of an archbishop. A castle was built above the theatre. A document issued by the Monastery of St John on Patmos in 1212 refers to the castle as "Kastrion Palation". Feuds between the Ottomans, Byzantines and Venetians together with the steady retreat of the coastline which increasingly hampered its maritime trade led inevitably to its decline.

Miletus was the birthplace of several notable figures of the ancient world. Among the best known are the great philosopher Thales (c. 625–545 B.C.), Anaximander, Anaximenes and a certain Kadmos to whom the first historical records in prose are attributed. Hecataios (c. 500 B.C.) was a distinguished historian and Timotheus a noted poet and musician from the first half of the 4th c. B.C. Hippodamos was a famous town-planner who designed the gridiron layouts of Piraeus, Thourioi in southern Italy and Rhodes and is also said to be responsible for the regular plan of his native city. The celebrated Aspasia, the witty hetaira (courtesan) who was a companion of Pericles, is said to have been a native of Miletus c. 470 B.C.

Famous Milesians

*The site

The layout of the site is difficult to follow since few remains of the ancient city are preserved. The practice of laying out a town on a strict rectangular grid probably originated in Miletus. The principle was consistently applied in the rebuilding of the city in the 4th c. B.C., probably under the direction of the great architect and town planner Hippodamos.

The best-preserved and therefore most prominent structure in the ancient city is the Roman theatre which with its 140m/460ft long façade and a circuit of almost 500m/1640ft round the semi-circular auditorium is a visible symbol of the city's former greatness and also reminiscent of some of the greatest Roman buildings in Italy. Greeks, Romans and Byzantines all played their part in its construction. An earlier Greek theatre was replaced in Trajan's time (2nd c. A.D.) by a Roman theatre which was enlarged in the 3rd and 4th c. giving it a total capacity of 25,000 spectators. The theatre was lavishly decorated with a facing of multi-coloured marble. The seating in white, the 34m/112ft orchestra and the stage itself were all finished in marble. In the middle of the lowest tier of seating stood the Imperial box, with a canopy borne on columns. The stage had three rows of columns in red, black and white marble and was decorated with numerous statues. The acoustics were said to be excellent.

**Theatre

On the hill 32m/105ft above the theatre lies a ruined Byzantine castle built of plundered masonry. It was linked to the town walls which used to pass near the stage but have since been removed. The castle offers a splendid view of the whole site.

*Byzantine castle

413

Miletus

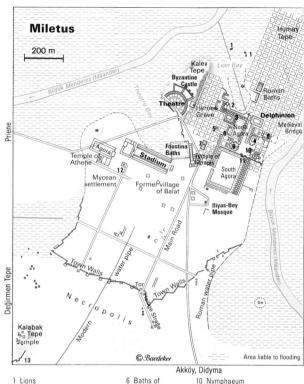

Miletus

1 Lions
2 Harbour monument
3 Hellenist Harbour Hall
4 Hellenist Gymnasion
5 Byzantine Church of St Michael
6 Baths of Vergilius Capito
7 Palästra
8 Prytaneion
9 Buleuterion
10 Nymphaeum
11 Market Gate (original in Berlin)
12 Temple of Eumenes II
13 Town walls of ancient Miletus

Theatre Harbour
Lion's Bay

The peninsula on which the town was situated – less than 1km/1100yd wide at its broadest point – had two inlets on the north side so that a harbour lay on both sides of the theatre. The Theatre Harbour was situated on the shores where the Cretan settlers had established themselves. The Lion's Bay is to the north-east and can be clearly distinguished when the river floods. This bay cut deeply into the peninsula and was flanked by two massive marble lions, the city's heraldic symbols. Across the head of the bay ran the 160m/175yd long harbour colonnade. In the angle between two colonnades stood the Harbour Monument erected at the time of Augustus; the plinth can still be seen.

Delphinion
Harbour Gate

At the south-east end of the harbour colonnade was the Delphinion, the city's principal shrine, parts of which date from the Archaic, Hellenistic and Roman periods. It was dedicated to Apollo Delphinios, protector of ships and harbours. Between the harbour colonnade and the Delphinion stood the Harbour Gate with sixteen columns. It gave access to a 30m/32yd wide colonnaded street running south-west for some 200m/220yd.

Miletus: the ancient theatre, overlooked by a Byzantine castle

In the angle between this street and the harbour colonnade lay the northern agora (90×43m/98×47yd), surrounded by two-storey colonnades. The colonnades on both sides of the street housed shops. Numerous stone bases, presumably for statues, were found in the agora.

On the left-hand side of the street on a six-stepped base stood a 140m/155yd Ionic colonnade presented to the city by Cn. Vergilius Capito c. A.D. 50. The rear wall has been rebuilt.

Northern agora
Ionic colonnade

Behind this colonnade (to the south of Delphinion) lay the Baths of Vergilius Capito which date from the time of the Emperor Claudius (A.D. 41–54), the walls of which are still standing. The baths, originally faced with marble, consisted of a palaestra 38m/125ft square surrounded by two-storey colonnades, in front of which was a semi-circular swimming pool. Also beyond the Ionic colonnade, immediately south-west of the Baths of Vergilius Capito was a gymnasium c. 150 B.C.

Baths of
Vergilius Capito

The end of the Ionic colonnade and the gymnasium form the north-east side of a square which is surrounded by the remains of a number of major public buildings. On the south-east side was a nymphaeum, a shrine of the fountain deities, dating from the reign of Titus (A.D. 79–80). The three-storey reservoir (20m/65ft wide) was fed by an aqueduct which also supplied the baths. To its right was a marble Temple of Asklepios (Aeskulapius). The foundations of the temple were later used in the construction of an early Byzantine basilica.

Nymphaeum
Temple of
Asklepios

On the opposite side of the square lie the remains of the bouleuterion (council chamber), a building 35m/115ft wide erected between 175 and 164 B.C. by two Milesians, Tinarchos and Herakleidos for their patron King Antiochos IV Epiphanes of Syria. The 35m/114ft wide interior of the chamber resembles a theatre. The orchestra had a diameter of 8m/26ft and the

Bouleuterion

auditorium, divided into four sections by stairways could seat about 5000 people.

Market Gate
Southern agora

From the little square between the nymphaeum and the bouleuterion a magnificent gateway 29m/95ft wide with three openings led into the southern agora. The gateway (c. 165 B.C.) is now on display in the Pergamon Museum in Berlin, while the southern agora was similar in layout to the northern agora. This colonnaded square (196.5m×164m/215×180yd), the largest known Greek agora, was built in several stages and completed about the middle of the 2nd c. B.C.

Baths of Faustina
Stadium

To the west of the southern agora were the Baths of Faustina of which considerable remains survive. They are named after the Empress Faustina wife of Antonius Pius in whose reign (c. A.D. 150) they were built.
West of the Baths of Faustina is an area now occupied by modern building where the large Roman stadium once stood. Some of the remains survive. It was over 230m/250yd long and 74m/80yd wide and the track between three water-clocks at each end measured 185m/200yd. Adjoining the stadium on what used to be a peninsula stood a third agora probably dating from Roman times.

Gate to the
Sacred Way

An ancient main road some 4.30m/14ft wide linked Lions' Bay with the gate in the south which gave access to the Sacred Way to Didyma. Under the street ran a drain 1.5m/5ft wide and 2m/6½ft deep joined by side drains 0.60m/2ft deep from the buildings on either side, thereby creating a drainage system similar to that of a modern town.
The gate to the Sacred Way was a Trajanic restoration. On the left-hand side of the passage, an inscription in the name of Trajan recorded the beginning of the work on the road in A.D. 100. Substantial remains of the Hellenistic gate and also of the Greek gate which preceded it have been unearthed. They were a part of the 2m/6ft thick town walls which were stormed by Alexander the Great in 334 B.C. On either side of the gate rose the massive Hellenistic town walls, renovated by Trajan, which were 5–10m/16–33ft thick.

Necropolis

To the south of the town walls lay a large necropolis, remains of which extend over a considerable area. These burial grounds extend south-west from the gate for a distance of some 800m/880yd and was part of the Archaic settlement of Miletus. Its acropolis formed part of the 63m/207ft Kalabak Tepe (Cup Hill) some 1.5km/1 mile from the theatre. The seashore lay barely 100-m/110yd from the foot of the hill.
On the south side of Kalabak Tepe a section of the town wall some 3–4m/10–13ft thick and originally over 12m/40ft high has been uncovered. The pottery finds have enabled the archaeologists to date the remains to c. 650 B.C. A north-east and a south-west gate, another smaller gate and a tower have also been found in this section.

Museum

On the road running south from the theatre is the site museum housing artefacts recovered in recent excavations, including structural fragments and pottery, etc. In front of the theatre is a stall selling refreshments.

Didyma

Situation and
Importance

Didyma is linked with Miletus 20km/12 miles to the north by the Sacred Way, parts of which are still traceable. According to an inscription on the last milestone, it was built in A.D. 101 in the reign of Trajan. Situated behind the resort of Didim Plajı (Altınkum Plajı) 4km/2½ miles from the Aegean coast, the ruined site of Didyma was once the greatest Greek oracular sanctuary in Asia Minor and its main features include the remains of a huge Temple of Apollo. Within the site stands the village of Yeni Hisar (New Castle) which was partly abandoned after the Greek withdrawal in 1923. The remaining inhabitants were later moved to Altınkum so that the site could be excavated unhindered.

Head of Medusa

Even before the coming of the Greeks and the foundation of Miletus, a Carian oracular shrine had existed here above a crack in the earth's surface. The Ionians who settled in this area in the 10th c. B.C. dedicated the shrine to Apollo Philesios and thereafter the shrine enjoyed considerable prestige, even rivalling Delphi. The original sanctuary was destroyed in 494 B.C. by Darius' Persians. After Alexander the Great's victory over the Persians the temple known as the Didymaion was rebuilt on an even grander scale. It was begun about 300 B.C. by Paionios of Ephesus and Daphnes of Miletus after the completion of the Temple of Artemis in Ephesus. The new temple was planned on such a grandiose scale, however, that in spite of financial support from the Roman emperors and other benefactors, it was never finished. According to Strabo, the building was never roofed because of its size.

A number of modifications were later undertaken but it was destroyed by a severe earthquake in 1446. Excavations have been carried out since the middle of the 19th c. by British, French and German archaeologists and in 1985 a sacred area (Temenos) was uncovered.

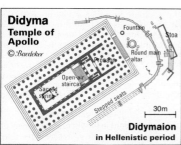

The huge Temple of Apollo or Didymaion has been well-excavated and partially restored. It stood on a north-east/south-west axis and was originally surrounded by a sacred grove. At the north-east end lay a semi-circular partly-raised terrace dating from the Archaic period, on which stood a portico, other buildings and various votive offerings. Four 2.50m/8ft wide flights of steps led down to the cella of the temple.

Outside the north-east end of the temple stands the main altar, similar to the one at Olympia in the Peloponnese. Within a low parapet was a conical structure built up from ashes mixed with the blood of sacrificial animals. To the north of the altar are bases for votive statues and a well dating from the Hellenistic period. Seven tiers of seating for spectators at the Didyma games run alongside the south-east side of the temple at a distance of 15m/50ft. The temple itself measured 108m/356ft long and 50m/165ft across. The unusual column bases dating from the time of Caligula (A.D. 37–41) are arranged in matching pairs. The corner columns on the east front had figural capitals from the 2nd c. A.D. each with two bulls' heads, a bust of a god and a griffin. Foliage ornaments and Medusa heads alternated on the frieze.

The temple consisted of a forecourt, a small antechamber and the cella or main chamber. The 11m/36ft walls of the pronaos (forecourt) are still standing but the original fine coffered ceiling has been lost. The cella could be reached either through two small doors and vaulted passages directly into the cella or through the main doorway into the small antechamber or

the chresmographeion where the priests revealed and interpreted the pronouncements of the oracle. The ceiling here was borne by two Ionic columns, making 122 columns in all.
From the antechamber, three doors opened on to a flight of steps 16m/52ft wide leading into the cella 5.50m/18ft lower down. The sacred spring, at which the priestess put the questions to the oracle, and a sacred olive tree stood at the far end of the cella and the cult statue of Apollo was located by the end wall in a special room. Surrounding the temple lay gymnasia, baths and hostels for pilgrims. Further excavations are necessary to determine the precise dimensions.

*View
A fine view extends northwards to Karakuyu Bay, former site of the Milesian port of Teichioussa, eastwards to the hills of Caria and southwards to the Bodrum peninsula and the Greek island of Kos.

Didim Plajı
This lively resort with its numerous hotels, guesthouses and apartment blocks lies about 4km/2½ miles to the south. More holiday accommodation can be found further to the east in the Akbük Limanı Bay.

Muş
R 5

Eastern Anatolia (Turkish Kurdistan)
Province: Muş
Altitude: 1500m/4920ft. Population: 42,000

See warning page 7

Situation and General Information
The town of Muş lies at the southern end of a valley beneath the 2646m/8678ft Karaçavus Dağı. The valley itself, 20km/12 miles wide and 60km/37 miles long, is intensively farmed for sugar beet, tobacco and cereals and is irrigated not only by the Murat Nehri, one of the sources of the Euphrates, but also by the Karasu, one of its tributaries. In earlier times the settlement which was dominated by a castle and extended over the lower slopes of the mountain, but the old town was destroyed by a severe earthquake in 1966. It was rebuilt in a safer position, but many of the older buildings in the town had been badly damaged in skirmishes during the Russian occupation.

History
The settlement was established by Armenians in the 6th c. as the capital of the Taron kingdom. After a period of Byzantine rule, it was conquered by the Seljuks in the Battle of Malazgirt (1071). In 1260 Muş was destroyed by the Mongol hordes and in 1515 was captured by the Ottomans. During the First World War, it was occupied by the Russians until 1917.

Sights

As well as the old town beneath the fortified hilltop, the Seljuk Arsanlı Han caravanserai and the Yıldızlı Han (Star caravanserai) are worth a visit. Only the elaborately decorated portal remains of the latter. Other places of interest include the Seljuk Hacı Şeref Camii with a minaret of coloured stonework and the Ulu Cami, the oldest mosque in the town, which has been restored on a number of occasions. Dating from Seljuk times, several Ottoman features are visible.

Surroundings

Bingöl
About 100km/62 miles to the east of Muş, the town of Bingöl (pop. 42,000; 1125m/3690ft) stands above a widening in the Bayram Deresi valley (Bingöl Ovası) and not far from where the river flows into the Murat (Euphrates).

Mountainous landscape around the Çobantaş Pass

This provincial capital which is inhabited predominantly by Kurds was known as Çevlik (or Çabakçur in old Armenian?) Severe earthquakes in 1966 and 1971 caused considerable damage to the relatively low-lying old town and it has now been rebuilt at a higher level. Only the medieval fortifications have been preserved. Since the town was destroyed the number of alcohol outlets in the town has been drastically reduced, as the natural disaster was seen as a reminder from heaven that Islamic teaching bans the consumption of alcohol.

The 3250m/10660ft Bingöl Dağ is a broad volcanic mountain range to the north-east of Bingöl and the ridge marks the boundary between the provinces of Muş and Erzurum. Ice-holes, evidence of Ice Age glaciation can be found in the countless lakes of the highlands ("bingöl", thousand lakes) and it is a magnificent area for walkers. The nomadic Beritan tribe use the Bingöl Dağları plateaux as summer grazing pastures. A minibus covers the 30km/19 mile journey from Karlıova to Zarovan Yaylası (Yaylası pastures) via Karapınar, from where a walk to the summit of Bingöl Dağ will take 3½ hours. Fantastic sunrises in July make the trip worthwhile.

Bingöl Dağları

The Kayalıdere Kalesi, ruins of Urartian fortifications which were built as defences against the Assyrians, can be seen on a steeply rising hillside on the northern bank of the Murat Nehri 45km/28 miles north of Muş and about 8km/5 miles east of Tepeköy (Hızırköyü). In 1965 Turkish and British archaeologists started excavations inside the upper and lower fortification. Finds have included stelae foundations and also a temple with tower, courtyard, store-rooms, rock staircases and rock tombs (six chambers).

Kayalıdere Kalesi

At weekends in the winter months a ski-lift operates on the 1800m/5900ft Kurucu pass 27km/17 miles west of Bingöl.

Kurucu Geçidi

The small town of Malazgirt (Manzikert in old Armenian) lies 120km/75 miles north-east of Muş on the upper reaches of the Murat Nehri. It was

Malazgirt

Transporting livestock in Bingöl

here in 1071 that the Seljuk Alp Arslan defeated the Byzantine Romanos IV Diogenes. Victory was decisive and the Byzantine leader was captured. As a result, Turkman tribes were able to penetrate Asia Minor and the Seljuks extended their empire into central Anatolia. This historic event holds great significance for the Turks is commemorated every year at the site of the battle.

Around 726, when the town was in fact under Arab rule, a Christian Council was held here at which the Armenians with their Monophysite beliefs (Christ has a god-like nature and was never a human being) split from the orthodox Byzantine church (Christ is a human as well as a god-like being). In the 9th c. the town became the centre of an Arab emirate and Christians were allowed to worship unhindered. Large parts of the town wall and its towers are still preserved and the walls of the old town houses contain countless plundered Armenian remains.

Surb Karapet
Surb Salah

A short distance from the village of Çengeli (Çangilli) near Ziyaret and about 25km/16 miles north-west of Muş lie the foundations and two vaults from the Monastery of Surb Karapet (Çengeli Kilisesi, Çanlı Kilise). John the Baptist is said to be buried in this 5th c. five-aisled church with five irregular-shaped chapels added to the east side. The addition of the bell-tower was made 300 years later. The site has frequently fallen victim to Kurdish pillagers. It was most recently restored in the 17th c., but since then builders have repeatedly used the monastery as a quarry.

4km/2½ miles from Surb Karapet near the village of Çengeli can be seen three ruined churches which were built by Gregory the Illuminator in the 4th c. on the foundations of a heathen temple. At that time the three churches Ashtishat (Church of Mary and Christ), Karapet (Church of St John) and Matnavank (Church of the Apostles) formed the Armenian religious centre and were the seat of an Armenian patriarch or catholicos.

Myra

See Kaş, surroundings

Nazilli   D 6

Western Anatolia (Menderes valley)
Province: Aydın
Altitude: 87m/285ft
Population: 80,000

Nazilli, halfway between Kuşadası and Pamukkale, was probably founded in Seljuk times *c.* 1176 by Emir Yazır the leader of an Ogusan tribe. In Ottoman times the village was first known as Cuma Yeri (Friday Square) or Pazarköy (Weekday Market). The town was only later referred to as Nazlıköy. According to legend, the son of Aydın's provincial governor fell in love with a young woman from Pazarköy but was rejected by the girl's father. The young man later named the town Nazlı İli (Nazlı's Home) after his loved one. Evliya Çelebi mentions the town as Nazlu. By the 19th c. (1836) Nazilli consisted of two settlements: the larger one Aşaği Nazilli or Büyük Nazilli (Lower or Great Nazilli) was the seat of an Aga and stood on the edge of the Maeander plain, while by today's main road on the slopes of the valley 2km/1¼ miles further north lay the smaller settlement of Nazilli Pazarı or Yukarı Nazilli (Nazilli Market or Upper Nazilli) which had a huge bazaar.

Situation and Place-names

North of Nazilli on the road to Ödemis, about 1km/½ mile from Bozyurt, lie the remains of Mastaura, the early settlement of Nazilli. The ruins include a theatre, polygonal stones in the bed of the Mastaura Çayı, remains of a vault and a castle but little is known of the town's history.

Mastaura

Surroundings

The town of Başalan (formerly Çiftlik Köyü) is situated in the valley of Vandalas Çayı (formerly Dandalas Çağğ, Morsynos or Orsinos in antiquity) on the route from Nazilli to Aphrodisias (see entry). On the foothills to the north between Morsynos and the Maeander (see entry), where even in ancient times a bridge crossed the river, lie the remains of Antiochia, a town on the Maeander. The town was founded by Antiochos I Soter in honour of his mother on the site of two settlements which Pliny referred to as Symaithos and Kranaos. The site is signposted from Başalan and from the main road between Nazilli and Kuyucak.

Başalan/ Antiochia on the Maeander

North-west of the regional centre of Sultanhisar 14km/9 miles west of Nazilli lies the ruined site of Nysa, which probably developed from three towns founded either by the Spartan leaders Athymbros, Athymbrados and Hydrelos or by the Cretan Athymbros under its original name of Akara (see below). The town prospered under the Roman Empire and was described in some detail by the geographer and historian Strabo (XIV, 1,43ff) from Amasya who studied grammar and rhetoric here between 50 and 45 B.C.

Nysa enjoys a superb location on the lower slopes of the Malkac Dağı (Mesogis), split in two by the Tekkecik Çayı and protected by the steep Beylik Deresi gorge in the east and the Asar Deresi in the west.

To find the site of Nysa, first of all follow the traces of an ancient paved track which climbs out of Sultanhisar towards the eastern side of the town. After a short distance a piece of the old fortified Byzantine walls with some encased marble pillar drums will be found. Higher up on the right lie the remains of the agora, recognisable from the numerous pillar stumps.

*Nysa (Sultanhisar)

The site

Nazilli

The Roman theatre of Nysa

Opposite the north-west corner to the left of the path and in the middle of a cluster of olive trees stands the bouleuterion which consists of a large council chamber (20×23m/22×25yd) with five well-preserved rows of seats. To the south-west close to the gorge which separates the east and west town stands a large ancient Greek building (40×50m/43×55yd) with stone blocks up to 4.5m/5yd long in the north side and two beautiful gate pillars in the south-east corner. Further up the valley a stadium was built at the foot of the gorge with rows of seats cut into the steep hillside. The stream was bridged for the race track as at Pergamon. Higher up, a bridge crosses the gorge.

Theatre

To the rear by a bend in the valley the gorge is bridged again by a 115m/125yd long tunnel, 10m/11yd high and 9m/10yd wide and this creates space for the 35-row theatre. Most of the south-facing auditorium is cut out of the sloping sides of the gorge. The front length measures 110m/120yd with proskenion and paraskenia constructed from enormous stone blocks. The top of the theatre offers a superb view over the Maeander plain with the Madran Baba Dağı forming a backdrop to the south. Above the theatre a large water cistern can be found. A narrow path leads from the theatre through the west town to the village of İletmes (Erekmes) which lies at the end of the gorge. This route passes Roman and Byzantine buildings including what is reckoned to be the finest library in Asia Minor after Ephesus and, between the town and the necropoles, a church from whose west side a Sacred Way to Akaraka (see below) begins.

Gymnasium

The large 30×95m/33×104yd gymnasium can be reached from above the steep slope on the third lowest terrace. The stonework some 3m/10ft wide and 5m/16ft high is of Roman-Byzantine origin and in the middle of the north side stands a well-preserved propylon and a cistern.

Barely 1½km/1 mile from both Nysa and Salavatlı, a village a short distance
to the west of Sultanhisar, the site of the ancient village of Acharaka
(Akaraka) can be found. Linked with Nysa by a Sacred Way, it was home to
the Nysean Shrine to Pluto and Persephone with a dream oracle and
sulphur springs. The remains of the marble temple lie well to the east of the
village. Lined with a double row of vaulted tombs of which some remains
are preserved, a sacred path led from the necropolis on the west side of
Nysa to this plutonium.

Salavatlı
(Akaraka)

To the south of Nazilli about 40km/25 miles along the eastern side of the
Akçay (Harpassos) valley near the village of Yakızent (İnebolu) lie the ruins
of the ancient town of Neapolis (İnebolu Kalesi, Arpaş Kalesi). It was here in
229/228 B.C. that the Seleukid prince Antiochos of Attalos was defeated by
troops from Pergamon, leading to the fall of Asia Minor to the Attalids.

Yakızent

Nemrut Dağı

See Adıyaman, Surroundings
See Ahlat, Surroundings

Nevşehir

See Cappadocia

Niğde   K 6

Central Anatolia. Province: Niğde
Altitude: 1230m/4034ft. Population: 55,000

The provincial capital of Niğde lies in a mountain pass region on the
south-east edge of the Lycaonian steppe between the Melendiz Dağları
volcanic massif (2935m/9626ft) in the north-west and the Çamardı Taurus
foothills (Pozantı Dağı 2689m/8819ft) in the south-east. The railway follows
the same route through Niğde as an ancient road which led from Cilicia to
Caesarea (Kayseri) and Sebaste (Sivas). For many hundreds of years the
town has benefited from the traffic which this important trade route has
brought. Like Bor, Niğde is well known for its carpet-weaving.

Situation and
Importance

The region around Niğde was inhabited as early as 3000 B.C. In the 1st
millennium B.C. the town was known as Nahita, later as Nakita and then
Nigdah. It first acquired importance in the 7th/8th c. B.C. as a border town
between the Assyrians in the south-east and the Phrygians in the north-
west. The first recorded reference to Niğde was around 1188. Several
church ruins from Byzantine times can be seen. The Seljuks built fortifications and many other important buildings, thereby enhancing the town's
prosperity.

History

The town's fortunes faded, when in 1720 the Grand Vizier İbrahim Paşa
transferred all administrative functions from Niğde (which had become a
part of the Ottoman Empire in 1470) to Nevşehir, a town he had founded. In
1864/65 the Ottomans initiated a series of administrative reforms (Tan-
zimat) and it became capital of the eponymous province.

Sights

The "White Koran School" with an open eyvan used as a lecture hall dates
from the 15th c. and now serves as an Archaeological Museum housing

Ak Medrese

423

artefacts from Roman and Byzantine times. It was founded by Alaeddin Bey in 1409 at the time of the Karamans. Other exhibits include finds from the Stone and Bronze Ages, Hittite writing and a relief from Tyana. To the west on the Ankara Yolu stands an interesting ceremonial washing fountain (Şadırvan Çeşmesi).

*Alaeddin Camii

Lying to the south of the castle is the three-aisled Alaeddin mosque, a fine Seljuk construction dating from 1223. Like other buildings from this era it resembles many similar complexes in Konya. The most striking features include three domes, a finely carved doorway and a squat but still well-proportioned minaret. Opposite stands a small fountain known as Hatıroğlu Çeşmesi from 1267. Concealed in the ornamentation above the typically Seljuk portal is a woman's face. This is unusual as Islamic art forbids the representation of human forms.

Bedesten

Beneath the citadel directly adjacent to the Sungur Bey Camii stands the bazaar (bedesten). The main 80m/87yd thoroughfare which harks back to the town's former role as an important commercial centre is covered by pointed tunnel vaulting dating from the 17th c.

Caravanserai

The "Yellow Caravanserai" (Sarı Han) in Niğde was endowed in 1357 in the time of the Ertenoğullari or Karamans by El-Hacı Muhammed Ben Ahmet Fakıh. There are two other Ottoman caravanserais in the town: Baş Han (Main Caravanserai) and Paşa Hanı from the late 18th c.

Mausoleums

Three türbe can be seen in the north-west corner of the town near the high school campus. The finest was built for Sultan Rükneddin's daughter Hudavend Hatun in 1312. Bird-like figures with women's faces and a variety of animal and floral designs adorn the spandrels of this octagonal mausoleum which bears all the hallmarks of Seljuk architectural style. The Gündoğdu türbesi stands opposite alongside the Fatma Hanım türbe c. 1600. Further to the north the Dört Ayak Camii and adjoining mausoleum date from the first half of the 14th c.

Paşa Külliyesi

This complex consisting of a mosque, caravanserai and bath dates from Ottoman times (late 18th c.) and is situated in the northern part of the inner town near the post office and town hall.

Sungur Bey Camii

In 1335 the town's governor Seyfeddin Sungur – head of a Mongol tribe – commissioned this mosque and mausoleum which can be found to the south of the bedesten. The flat tiled roof and minaret in Gothic style are particularly fine. After a fire in the 18th c. the interior was altered (second row of pillars). Other features include some fine masonry work on the portal, a large rosette above the north entrance and outside a ceremonial washing fountain borne by six columns.

Citadel mound

The picturesque old town can be clearly seen about 500m/550yd to the west of the main trunk road. To reach the citadel follow the route from İstasyon Caddesi (Station Road) past a park, round the citadel mound and up to the market-place. The citadel was built in the time of Alaeddin Kaykobad (1219–37) on a man-made hill. Restored in 1470, the large octagonal Seljuk tower and the clock tower on the west side are of particular interest. The foundations of one house on the mound revealed an inscription about Saruvana of Nahita, a contemporary of King Urballa of Tyana. The latter is best-known as an opponent of the Assyrian Tiglath-Pileser III (738 B.C.). To the south of the citadel stands the Hanım Camii, a small mosque of more recent construction.

Surroundings

Bor

Bor, or Poros in antiquity, is a carpet-weaving town, lying some 15km/9 miles south of Niğde in the fertile Bor Ovası plain. Split in half by the

Human Çayı, the plain is surrounded by steep-sided tuff rocks. During Byzantine times Poros came to replace the ancient town of Tyana. Around 1205, it is thought that the Seljuks founded a small Islamic settlement here and surrounded it with a clay brick wall (now ruined). It was here that 100 mortars produced gunpowder for the Ottoman troops using the saltpetre deposits in Kemerhisar (see below). Places of interest in the town include the oldest mosque, Sarı Cami (Yellow Mosque; 1205), the Ottoman Kale Camii (Castle Mosque; 1629) and the Seljuk caravanserai Bor Hanı.

Barely 10km/7 miles north-east of Niğde lies the town of Gümüş where a gorge separates Eski Gümüşler and Yeni Gümüşler. The former's man-made rock caves are reminiscent of the Cappadocian Zelve canyon. Some well-preserved frescos which date from the 11th c. can be found in a rock church in the northern part of the town. The church with an inner courtyard was formerly used as stables and its original function may well have been as a fortified church or a retreat, while the frescos show Mary with child between the Archangels Gabriel and Michael, the Annunciation and the birth of Jesus. The dome of the square church rests on four pillars. The central apse on the east side shows a three-part fresco with Jesus, the Archangel Gabriel, Mary, the four Evangelists with symbols, the Apostles and the Early Fathers.

*Eski Gümüş

Kemerhisar (formerly Kilisehisar) lies 25km/16 miles south of Niğde and is scattered over three hills on the site of the ancient town of Tyana. Semiramis the legendary queen of Assyria and founder of the Hanging Gardens of Babylon is thought to have been instrumental in establishing Tyana, which existed here from 1200 B.C. as a late Hittite principality, named Tuhana after the decline of the Hittite Empire. In the second half of the 8th c. B.C. one of the rulers was Varpavalas whose stele can be seen in an İstanbul museum. Ancient remains on the site include a Doric marble pillar on the "Hill of Semiramis" and fifteen linked tuff and marble arches ("kemer", arches) of a Roman aqueduct. A path leads from the south of the site to the Baths of Kemerhisar (Kemerhisar İçmesi) which is mentioned in ancient writings. The warm water (15°C/60°F) containing sodium hydrogen carbonate, magnesium carbonate and salt was drunk for its healing powers. The site also comprises a bathing pool.

Kemerhisar

Pamukkale (Hierapolis)

E 6

Western Anatolia (Interior)
Province: Denizli. Nearest town: Denizli
Altitude: 350m/1150ft

The ancient site of Hierapolis, now known as Pamukkale (Cotton Castle) after the famous calcareous terraces, offers a superb view over the valley of the Büyük Menderes and the Aksu. It lies on the borders of Caria, Lydia and Phrygia some 20km/12 miles north of Denizli on a plateau of chalky deposits nearly 3km/2 miles long, up to 300m/330yd wide and about 160m/525ft above the Lykos valley. Gleaming white limestone deposits, flanked by oleanders as they cascade down the steep hillside like a petrified waterfall, the inviting warm water baths and the remains of the ancient city of Hierapolis combine to create one of Turkey's most fascinating sights. The first archaeological investigation was carried out in 1887 under the leadership of Carl Humann. Further excavations were undertaken by an Italian team from 1957 onwards.

Situation and
**Landscape

The calcareous deposits (travertine) come from a number of warm water springs (34–35°C/93–95°F) which contain large quantities of dissolved calcium bicarbonate. When the water reaches the surface, the calcium bicarbonate breaks down into carbon dioxide, water and calcium carbonate. The

*Limestone
terraces

Pamukkale (Hierapolis)

latter is deposited in the form of a hard greyish-white layer. These deposits gradually fill up, sometimes even raise the water channel, so that the water flow disperses in all directions and the deposits produce a series of fan-like formations with small dips and terraces. In the same way that stalactites form in limestone caves, the deposits grow on the steep slopes eventually taking on the appearance of cotton wool. Calcareous deposits can be found wherever water emerges from karst rock, e.g. Lake Plitwitz in Croatia and near Antalya in Turkey. The thermal spring water, which in addition to chalk and carbon dioxide, contains sulphuric acid, sodium chloride, iron and magnesium, has long been valued for its healing powers and thus revered as a shrine.

As the springs now supply the nearby hotels and their swimming pools, insufficient water permeates the terraces and consequently the deposits are hardly increasing in size. In order to ensure the continuation of this unusual natural phenomenon, the hotels are due to be demolished in the near future and a bypass road built.

Hot spring pool

The main outlet for the spring water today is near the Pamukkale Motel (no group tours) and a number of antique columns are submerged in the bathing pool where water at a temperature of 38°C/100°F circulates. The spring with a flow of 200–250 litre/44–55 gallons per second has covered the whole of the lower town with a chalky coating and numerous earthquakes have caused this layer to crack and split open.

*Hierapolis

A town was founded here by King Eumenes II of Pergamon soon after 190 B.C. Intended as a rival to Laodikeia (see below), the new settlement was a fortified military colony. It may have been named after Hiera ("Hierapolis", city of Hiera), wife of Telephos, the mythical ancestor of the Pergamenes. The first town was destroyed by an earthquake in A.D. 60 and now only the scanty ruins of a theatre are visible. A new town was built on a site to the south. The city enjoyed its greatest prosperity around the 2nd and 3rd c. but most of the ruins date from later. The existence of a large Jewish community in Hierapolis led to the early arrival of Christianity (Colossians 4:13). In A.D. 80 the Apostle Philip was martyred here and later a church, perhaps the basilica outside the north gate, was dedicated to him. Hierapolis became the see of a bishop and a metropolitan but its main function was as a spa. With the coming of the Seljuks (1094) it gradually decayed and was abandoned. A severe earthquake in 1354 also affected Laodikeia.

Importance

Like Laodikeia, Hierapolis owed its prosperity to various branches of the wool industry including shearers, spinners, weavers, dyers and dealers. Their products were exported as far afield as Italy. The city was also a much-frequented spa where dazzling festivals and games were held to entertain visitors.

Temple of Apollo/ Plutonium

The Plutonium, a cave beneath the Temple of Apollo, was a source of poisonous gas, probably carbon dioxide. The temple with a 20×15m/65× 50ft podium and a flight of stairs to a pillared porch was built in the 3rd c. from plundered materials. An annexe concealed the entrance to the underworld, the Plutonium. The priests of Cybele, who were venerated here long before Apollo, the city's principal god, were in charge of the cave and it was their practice to bring in birds and sometimes even bigger animals who were killed by the rising gas. The priests were unharmed, their heads being above the level of the gas. The cave is no longer in existence and the temple has collapsed.

Castle

The road which winds its way up from the plain to the plateau affords superb views of the terraces of calcareous deposits. Nearby are the remains of an 11th/12th c. castle, whose name Pamukkale meaning Cotton Castle was extended to refer to the whole terrace and the site of ancient Hierapolis. There are fine views of the limestone terraces cascading down the steep slope.

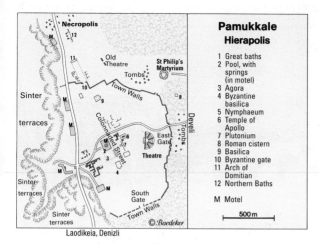

Pamukkale Hierapolis

1 Great baths
2 Pool, with springs (in motel)
3 Agora
4 Byzantine basilica
5 Nymphaeum
6 Temple of Apollo
7 Plutonium
8 Roman cistern
9 Basilica
10 Byzantine gate
11 Arch of Domitian
12 Northern Baths

M Motel

500 m

Laodikeia, Denizli

The ruins of the Great Baths, now a museum, stand further east and their marble-faced walls and vaultings are reminiscent of the great buildings of Rome. A large colonnaded courtyard used for exercises and games extends beyond the baths.

Baths

The remains of a colonnaded street run parallel to the limestone terraces for a distance of about 1200m/1300yd. The street extends from the north gate past a Byzantine church and the barely recognisable site of the agora as far as the south gate. 13.5m/45ft wide, it was lined on both sides by 6m/20ft deep covered walks for shops to open off the street. The street extended outside the north and south gates for a distance of 160m/175yd in each direction as far as the round towers. The gates themselves which were only 3m/10ft wide and equipped with niches for statues were similar in form to the Roman gate in the north-west.

Colonnaded street

Beyond both the north and south gates lie necropoles. The northern cemetery ranks as one of the largest and best-preserved examples in Anatolia with 1200 tombs including Hellenistic tumuli, Roman sarcophagi, burial chambers, temples to the dead and complete burial grounds from Early Christian times. Over 300 inscriptions describe the cemetery's development and the origins of the dead.

*Necropolis Town walls

About 150m/165yd east of the theatre substantial remains of the old town walls can be seen and behind them lie more burial grounds. Outside the walls stands a Roman cistern which supplied the town with drinking water via two aqueducts.

On a sloping expanse of land 500 m/550yd north-east of the theatre stands the octagonal martyrium of the Apostle Philip. It was built on the spot where the saint and his children were martyred. The 60×63m/65×69yd church dates from the 5th c. and lies at the meeting point of several lines of guest rooms.

Martyrium of St Philip

On a slope some 300m/330yd east of the spring a little higher than the Temple of Apollo stands the theatre. This well-preserved building has a façade over 100m/130yd long. The auditorium, entered by two broad vaulted passages, contained an Imperial box, two tiers of seating each with 26 rows separated halfway up by a gangway and was divided into sections

Theatre

Pamukkale (Hierapolis)

The ancient main street of Hierapolis

by eight stairways. A Dionysos relief has been returned to its original position between the doors. The orchestra and two-storey stage building which had five doors was a mass of rubble consisting of fragments and reliefs but it is undergoing restoration. The theatre was built in the reign of Septimius Severus *c.* 200 B.C.

Surroundings

Akhan

On the road from Denizli to Dinar (8km/5 miles) stands a Seljuk caravanserai which was founded in 1253 by Emir Karasungur. The marble-faced east façade gives the complex its name ("akhan", white caravanserai). Other features include an arcaded courtyard and a triple-aisled winter hall.

Çardak

Between the town of Çardak and the railway line, 55km/34 miles east of Denizli at the western tip of the large Lake Acıgöl, stands the well-preserved Çardak Hanı. This Seljuk caravanserai with five aisles, each with two massive towers (one with five and one with three sides), was endowed in 1230 by Raşideddin İyaz, a general of the sultan Alaeddin Kaykobad. Above the porch an inscription is flanked by two lions. Known in antiquity as Anaua Limne, Lake Acıgöl (836m/2742ft) covers an area of 1153sq.km/445sq.miles but can often dry up in the summer months.

Çivril

About 10km/7 miles south of the regional centre of Çivril on the Beyşesultan Tepesi, the archaeologists Lloyd and Mellaart (see Çatalhüyük) unearthed a prehistoric settlement. The excavations took place between 1954 and 1959 and the finds are now on display in an Ankara museum. Evidence of settlement here exist from the Chalcolithic times (4500 B.C.) until the

The "petrified waterfall" of Pamukkale, sinter formations now endangered ▶

Pamukkale (Hierapolis)

A circular tomb in the necropolis

early Bronze Age (1250 B.C.) and again 400 years later until Byzantine times. For the Stone Age alone, 21 layers have been found within 11m/36ft of sediment. In layer V (1900 B.C.), the remains of a palace reminiscent of Knossos were found. It was destroyed in the 18th C. B.C. by the Hittite Labarna. Within four Bronze Age layers were found the traces of a shrine with sacrificial vessels, a blood altar, a phallic symbol and statuettes of Cybele. To one side the tomb of an important Islamic figure can be seen.

Denizli

The provincial capital of Denizli is situated about 20km/12 miles south of Pamukkale above the fertile Çürüksu valley (Aksu Deresi, Lykos in antiquity, Maeander Minor in the Middle Ages) and lies at the foot of the block-shaped Honaz Dağ (Kadmos 2571m/8432ft). The town probably grew up in the early 14th C. in what is now the bazaar district as a replacement for Laodikeia and it was known originally as Ladik or Lazik, but later assumed the name of the abundant Denizli spring ("denizli", with the sea). Ibn Battuta described the town as a fine commercial centre with seven

A sarcophagus by the roadside

Danger of collapse!

430

mosques, baths and bazaars as well as a resident prince. Denizli has twice been destroyed by earthquakes – once at the beginning of the 18th c. and again in 1899. There are no buildings of any historical interest in this thoroughly modern town.

More hot springs (Kızılpınar 55°C/131°F) bubble from the chalk-coated rocks on the same plateau only 5km/3 miles west of Pamukkale near the village of Karahayıt. The presence of various other oxides, e.g. iron oxide, tinges the calcium carbonate with a variety of colours. A small bathing pool is situated beneath the springs.

Karahayıt

Take a side road to reach the village of Honaz which lies a good 20km/12 miles east of Denizli beneath the Honaz Dağ. A short distance to the north, the River Lykos cuts through a limestone plateau partly in an underground channel and partly in a 4km/2½ mile long gorge (Boğaz Kesen). The scanty remains of the once great Phrygian city of Kolossai lie beyond the gorge. They are referred to by Herodotus (Bk 7: 30) and in the time of Xenophon (Anabasis Bk 1: 2,6) Kolossai was still a place of some consequence, but became increasingly overshadowed by Laodikeia and Hierapolis. Its name has remained familiar because of Paul's epistle to the Christian community here. 4km/2½ miles to the south the hillside town of Chinai (Honaz) with its patron saint Michael was of more importance in Byzantine times

Kolossai (Honaz)

The ruined site of ancient Laodikeia (Laodicea) which is situated about 5km/3 miles north of Denizli is referred to by local people as Eskihisar or "Old Castle". The town, built on the site of an earlier settlement known originally as Diospolis and later as Rhoas, was founded by Antiochos II of Syria (261–246 B.C.), who named it after his sister Laodike. The city subsequently became the part of the kingdom of Pergamon, probably after the Treaty of Apameia in 188 B.C. and thereafter passed into Roman hands. Its commercial activities and especially its wool and textile industries made it one of the wealthiest cities in Asia Minor (Revelations 3:17). After a devastating earthquake in A.D. 60, the citizens rebuilt the city out of their own resources. It was home to one of the oldest Christian communities and ranked among the Seven Churches of Asia (Revelations 1:11;3:14; Colossians 4:13ff). After its conquest by the Seljuks in the late 11th c., the city fell into decay and in the 13th c. the remaining inhabitants abandoned the site and moved to Ladik (Denizli).

*Laodikeia

The scanty remains of Laodikeia are scattered over an undulating plateau (1sq.km/0.4sq. miles) which is crossed by the road from Eskihisar to Goncalı. Three gates allowed entry through the walls and the ruins of an ancient bridge are visible below the north-west gate. A short distance beyond the walls lies a necropolis. This gate to Ephesus, triple arched and flanked by towers, was devoted to the Emperor Domitian (A.D. 81–96). On the south-west side stand a number of buildings built under Vespasian (A.D. 69–79) including a stadium (350×60m/380×65yd) and a large building known as the Palati which was either a gymnasium or a bath-house. An aqueduct bringing water from the spring of Baş Pınar (beside the old administrative offices in Denizli) ended in a 5m/16ft high water-tower from which water was distributed to the various parts of the city.

The site

To the north-east an odeion stands on a hillside terrace. In the middle of the hill to the left lie the remains of a Roman nymphaeum which was excavated in 1962/63 by French archaeologists. A square water pool with a semi-circular fountain and a number of chambers is flanked on two sides by pillars. The complex was later used as a chapel. Close by the remains of a larger Ionic temple can be seen and on the north-eastern edge of the plateau lie the scanty remains of a large theatre. Further north there is a smaller and better preserved theatre. The acropolis at the northern tip is relatively small.

The town of Sarayköy at the western edge of the Hierapolis valley is probably old Karura (Kyorara) which lay on the border between Phrygia

Sarayköy

and Caria. It became known for its hot springs by the Maeander and its Herophilian medical school. Herophilus (4th c. B.C.) was regarded as the most important doctor of antiquity after Hippocrates. He was one of the first doctors to dissect the human body.

Pergamon

C 4

West coast (Aegean Sea). Province: İzmir
Altitude: 50–333m/165–1095ft. Population of Bergama: 39,000

Situation and
**Topography

The site of the celebrated ancient city of Pergamon is more or less the same as the modern Turkish town of Bergama, which is situated some 90km/56 miles north of İzmir in the old region of Mysia. The remains of the Roman city are for the most part beneath the modern town, while the Greek city with the imposing ruins of its royal stronghold occupies a magnificently impressive location on the summit and along the terraced slopes of the hill which rises above Bergama to the east. To the east of the hill flows the Kestel Çayı (Ketios in antiquity) and to the west the Bergama Çayı (Selinus).

*Bergama

Although Bergama cannot claim the same importance as ancient Pergamon in its role as capital and commercial centre of a great kingdom, it is

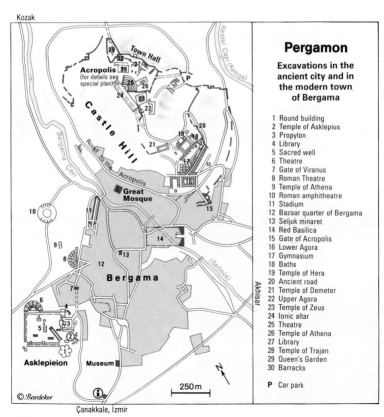

Pergamon

Excavations in the ancient city and in the modern town of Bergama

1 Round building
2 Temple of Asklepius
3 Propylon
4 Library
5 Sacred well
6 Theatre
7 Gate of Viranus
8 Roman Theatre
9 Temple of Athena
10 Roman amphitheatre
11 Stadium
12 Bazaar quarter of Bergama
13 Seljuk minaret
14 Red Basilica
15 Gate of Acropolis
16 Lower Agora
17 Gymnasium
18 Baths
19 Temple of Hera
20 Ancient road
21 Temple of Demeter
22 Upper Agora
23 Temple of Zeus
24 Ionic altar
25 Theatre
26 Temple of Athena
27 Library
28 Temple of Trajan
29 Queen's Garden
30 Barracks

P Car park

© Baedeker

250 m

Çanakkale, İzmir

nevertheless a busy modern town with carpet-weaving, textiles and leather-working industries. Cotton, tobacco and vines flourish in the subtropical climate of the fertile surrounding area.

The Archaeological Museum lies on the main road and houses a large collection of material from the Stone Age to Byzantine times as well as an ethnographic department.

Follow the main road in a north-easterly direction through the busy streets of Bergama to the massive brick-built ruins of the Red Basilica (Temple of Serapis; "kızı avlu", red courtyard). It was originally built by Hadrian (A.D. 117–138) as a temple, probably dedicated to Serapis but converted into a church in Byzantine times and dedicated to the Apostle John. The building takes its name from the red-brick walls.

*Red Basilica (Kızıl Avlu)

The interior of the Red Basilica was divided into three aisles by two rows of columns. The central aisle ended in a semi-circular apse, under which was a crypt. Above the lateral aisles were galleries. After the destruction of the basilica by the Arabs in the early 8th c., a smaller church was built within the ruins.

From the 5th to the early 3rd c. B.C., Pergamon was a small fortified settlement on the summit of a hill, and may well have belonged in its early days to large Persian landowners. The Pontian Philhetairos (283–263) established himself as the ruler of the independent state of Pergamon. It was subsequently defended by Eumenes I (263–241) and Attalos I (241–197) against the Syrian kings and the Galatians, a Celtic people who had made their way into Asia Minor. Attalos I was responsible for the circuit of walls built half-way down the hill.

History of Pergamon

During the reign of Eumenes II (179–159) an alliance with Rome brought the Attalid dynasty to its peak and a new ring of walls was built around the foot of the hill. One of the most famous achievements was the creation of the

The town of Bergama with the Red Basilica

Pergamon

Statue of Nike in Archaeological Museum   *View from the Red Basilica*

library which came to possess 200,000 volumes. These later went to enrich Mark Antony's rival library in Alexandria.

Pergamon is credited with the invention of parchment. Learning flourished and there was a great flowering of sculpture and painting. Christianity gained a foothold and Pergamon is listed as one of the Seven Churches of Asia (Revelations 1:11 and 2:12ff). When insecurity increased in the second half of the 2nd c., a new wall was built round the hill at a higher level than that built by Eumenes II.

In Byzantine times another wall was built higher up the hill, enclosing a still smaller area, to provide protection against Arab invasions (7th c.) and also the Seljuks and Ottomans in later years.

The Pergamon region was occupied by the Ottomans in the 14th c. and thereafter the city on the hill was abandoned and fell into decay, while the new town of Bergama grew up on the south side of the hill.

Excavations

The Department of Antiquities of the Berlin Museums supported the work of the German engineer Carl Humann, who with the assistance of A. Conze began research on the site in 1878 and continued until 1886. The German archaeologists W. Dörpfeld and E. Boehringer continued the work in the 20th c. and excavations are still in progress.

Sites

Lower Agora

The first site of interest is the Lower Agora, built by Eumenes II at the beginning of the 2nd c. B.C. to supplement the existing Upper Agora. The 80×50m/260×165ft paved square was surrounded by two-storey colonnades from where the merchants offered their wares.

Gymnasium

Around the market-place stood the odeion, stadium and a gymnasium built on three terraces. On the lowest terrace was the children's gymnasium – the gymnasium of the "paides", i.e. children aged between six and nine

Temple of Trajan on the acropolis

years. Above this was the gymnasium for the "ephebes" (between ten and fifteen) and on the highest terrace, the largest and finest of the three, the gymnasium for the "neoi" (young men over 16). To the north-east stood the Roman baths lavishly decorated with marble cladding.

Half-way along the ancient track which winds its way up to the acropolis in a wide S-shaped curve lie the remains of the Sanctuary of Demeter. Motorists should follow the road round the acropolis to the car park (4km/2½ miles). Built in the 3rd c. on a site which was then outside the acropolis and protected by strong walls, it is thought to be one of the oldest structures in Pergamon. The entrance to the sacred precinct containing the remains of the temple is marked by a propylon (gateway) with two columns. It was here that the Eleusinian mysteries were celebrated.

Sanctuary of Demeter

From the Sanctuary of Demeter, the road climbs up in a wide right-hand curve to the acropolis, where the terraces are laid out in an arc round the theatre on the south side of the hill. The road arrives first at the colonnaded Upper Agora (84×44m/275×145ft). A small Temple of Dionysos used to stand on the west side.

**Acropolis

Above the agora lies a trapeziform terrace with massive retaining walls, once occupied by Pergamon's celebrated Altar of Zeus. Only the foundations remain of this altar which was built between 180–160 B.C. by Eumenes II. A full-scale reconstruction of the altar with part of the original frieze has been on display in the Pergamon Museum in Berlin since 1902. The frieze round the podium is a vigorous representation of the battle between the gods and giants, symbolising the victory of Greek civilisation over the Barbarians and no doubt reflecting Pergamene pride in the successful defeat of the Galatians.

Terrace of the Altar of Zeus

To the north of the altar within the acropolis walls are a number of other terraces. This area is entered through the citadel gate. Along the north wall are the scanty remains of several palaces, most notably that of Eumenes II.

Pergamon

Library

*Temple of
Trajan

On the terrace to the west of the citadel gate stood the Temple of Athena, a Doric temple dating from the 4th c. Adjoining the north colonnade of the Temple of Athena stood the famous library built about 170 B.C. With its 200,000 volumes ("volumes" in the sense of folded sheets of parchment rather than the older parchment rolls) it was one of the largest libraries in the Ancient World. The collection was later presented to Cleopatra by Antony and carried off to Alexandria. The main hall of the library contained a copy of Phidias' "Athena Parthenos".

To the west of the library the Temple of Trajan stood on a colonnaded terrace 100 × 70m/330 × 230ft which is currently undergoing restoration. A peripteral Corinthian temple (9×6 columns) of white marble, it was built in the reign of Trajan but later was destroyed in an

Pergamon Acropolis

Arsenal
Palace I (Barracks)
Palace II
Palace III
Trajaneum
Palace IV
Dionysos Temple
Library
Palace V
Rotunda
Group VI
Theatre
Temple of Athena
Castle Gate
Ruler's cult precinct
Great Altar (foundation)
Upper Market
Acropolis

50 m

© Baedeker

Upper Town of Pergamon

earthquake. From the front of the terrace there is a magnificent view of the lower terraces of the acropolis, the theatre, the town of Bergama and the hills beyond the alluvial plain of the Bergama Çayı.

*Theatre

Temple of
Dionysos

The most striking feature on the acropolis is the theatre. Set on the steep south-west slope of the hill, it is reached by a narrow flight of steps from the Temple of Athena. The theatre, which was built in the time of the Pergamene kings could accommodate some 15,000 spectators on its 80 rows. Along the outside of the 216m/710ft long upper terrace was a colonnade. At the north-west corner of the theatre terrace stood a prostyle Ionic temple, probably dedicated to Dionysos, the mythical ancestor of the Pergamene royal house. After its destruction in the 3rd c. A.D. it was rebuilt by Caracalla.

*The Asklepieion

On the western outskirts of Bergama, in a military area with restrictions on photography, lies the ruined site of the Asklepieion which was dedicated to Asklepios (Aesculapius) the god of healing. It ranked with Epidauros and Kos as one of the most celebrated places of healing in the Ancient World and was probably founded in the 4th c. B.C. The sanctuary flourished particularly in Roman times when the famous doctor Galen (A.D. 129–199) worked here. The Emperor Caracalla was one of many who came to the Asklepieion in search of a cure. Treatment methods included suggestion and "incubation" in which patients were treated on the basis of dream interpretation.

The "Sacred Way" to the Asklepieion

The north gallery in the Asklepieion

Description of
the site

From the Sacred Way cross a colonnaded forecourt in the middle of which stands the Altar of Asklepios, a stone bearing the Aesculapian snake and then pass through a large propylon (gateway) into the Sacred Precinct. The northern colonnade, relatively well-preserved with seventeen columns still in place, leads from the Library to the Theatre set on the slope of the hill. It has been restored and is used for the annual Bergama Festival when classical plays are performed.

A Sacred Well with pool and the incubation rooms were situated in the square which was originally paved with flagstones. The Sacred Precinct was linked by a tunnel to a two-storey round building just beyond known as the Temple of Telesphoros. The basement was used for water therapy and incubation. To the north beside the propylon stands the Temple of Asklepios a 20m/65ft high building with a domed roof. Patients had to visit the temple before leaving the sanctuary.

Between Asklepieion and the Bergama Çayı is the Roman city, a site which has only been partially explored. It is covered with silt deposited by the river and a part of the site has been built over.

Perge

See Antalya

Priene   C 6

West coast (Aegean Sea). Province: Aydın
Altitude: 36–130m/120–425ft. Nearest town: Güllübahçe

*Situation and
Importance

The remains of the ancient city of Priene lie opposite Miletus and 130km/80 miles south of İzmir along a lonely rock terrace on the Milesian peninsula, below the south side of a 371m/1217ft high marble crag. To the south extends the wide alluvial plain of the Büyük Menderes (Greater Maeander) created by the silting up of the Latmian Gulf, which in ancient times reached far inland. The terrace must have seemed an attractive site for a city while the crag above it, protected by a sheer drop of almost 200m/650ft, was ideal for the acropolis and seen from the plain must have had the same kind of picturesque aspect as Assisi has today. But even as a ruin, Priene is still worth a visit not just for the beauty of its setting, but for the total picture it offers of a Hellenistic country town with 4000–5000 inhabitants.

History

Priene, a Carian name, was a member of the Panionic League. After submitting to King Ardys of Lydia, it became a stronghold of Lydian power in this region and under the leadership of Bias one of the Seven Sages (c. 625–540 B.C.), it grew and prospered. About 545 B.C. it was taken by Cyrus' Persians. As one of the smaller cities, it was in constant conflict with its more powerful neighbours – Samos, Miletus and Magnesia on the Maeander. Later Priene was incorporated into the Athenian Empire and in 442 B.C. Athens handed it over to Miletus.

The site of Ionian Priene is not known. It probably lies deep under the alluvial plain of the Maeander. It certainly did not occupy the site of the new Priene which Athens founded in the middle of the 4th c. B.C. as a rival to Miletus and which Alexander the Great helped to complete after 334 B.C. The principal temple was dedicated to Athena by Alexander himself. Under Turkish rule from the end of the 13th c. Priene, now called Samsun Kalesi, declined and decayed.

Excavations

Systematic excavations were begun in 1895 by Carl Humann for the Imperial Museums in Berlin. After his death Theodor Wiegand continued the work which was completed in 1898. Important finds from the site can be seen in the British Museum, the Louvre, the Pergamon Museum in Berlin and also in İstanbul.

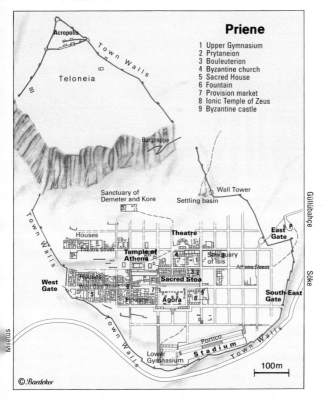

Priene

1 Upper Gymnasium
2 Prytaneion
3 Bouleuterion
4 Byzantine church
5 Sacred House
6 Fountain
7 Provision market
8 Ionic Temple of Zeus
9 Byzantine castle

© Baedeker

The *Site

The finely coursed town walls (2m/6½ft thick) extend on both right and left for 2.5km/1½ miles up the citadel. Apart from the walls themselves there are practically no ancient remains on the summit. A rough footpath leads up from the lower town to the acropolis, the place of refuge in emergencies.

Town walls
Layout

The lower town was laid out according to Hippodamian principles with streets intersecting at right angles to create some 80 rectangular blocks. The main streets which ran along an east–west axis were 5–6m/16–20ft wide. Two of these roads led to the main east and west gates, another to a subsidiary gate which gave access to a spring.
From the car park at the end of the Güllübahçe (district of Söke), the entrance to the ruined site is through the east gate. Continue westwards across the town to the west gate. Immediately to the right is the gate-keeper's lodge, consisting of a single room and a porch. Just beyond stands the Sanctuary of Cybele with a sacrificial pit. The Sacred House may have been a dynastic shrine.

Lower town

From this point up to the agora, the main street is flanked on both sides by private houses, of interest as they date from the 4th c. B.C. and give an idea of what a classical dwelling was like.

The main street continues through a cutting in the rock passes the small meat and vegetable market on the right (30×16m/98×52ft) and leads to the

Agora
Sacred Stoa

439

Priene

Priene: Temple of Athene at the foot of the acropolis

large Agora (128×95m/140×105yd), all the more impressive in such a relatively small town. An Altar of Zeus would probably have stood in the centre of the square which would have been the scene for festivals and sacrifices.

On the north side of the street on a seven-stepped base stood a double-aisled roofed colonnade or stoa (150 B.C.) with an outer row of Doric columns and an inner row of Ionic columns. It was here that the town's political business was conducted. The better preserved west wall is to be found in the Pergamon Museum in Berlin. A series of larger rooms, probably the offices of the city officials can be found to the rear of the stoa. The Bouleuterion and the Prytaneion are situated at the east end of the Sacred Stoa.

* Bouleuterion
Prytaneion

The Bouleuterion, the chamber for the people's assembly and city council, met here. Thanks to its sheltered position beneath a steep slope it remains one of the best-preserved buildings in Priene. Constructed about 200 B.C., it resembles a small theatre. In the centre of a small square is an altar decorated with reliefs and on three sides are thirteen rows of seating with room for 640 people, accessible by a number of stairways.

The Prytaneion (offices of the civic authorities), a courtyard with rooms opening off it, was altered in Roman times. A marble table and a water-basin can be seen in the courtyard and in one of the rooms stands a large hearth, perhaps the civic hearth with an eternal flame.

An Ionic Temple of Zeus occupied a position on the east side of the agora, but it was destroyed by the construction of a Byzantine castle.

* Temple of
Athena

The city's principal sanctuary the Temple of Athena is situated at the western end of "Athena Street" above the Bouleuterion. According to an inscription on one of the pillars in the entrance hall, now in the British Museum, the temple was dedicated to Athena Polias by Alexander the Great in 334 B.C. Built by Pytheos, architect of the Mausoleion at Halikarnas-

440

sos, it was an Ionic peripteral of six by eleven columns, five of which have been restored. The cult image, almost 7m/23ft high, was a copy of Phidias' "Athena Parthenos". Outside the entrance at the east end was a large altar with figures in high relief between Ionic columns and further east an entrance gateway dates from Roman times. Part of the south wall is intact up to a height of 4.5m/15ft.

On the right of the street which leads west from the East Gate above the Sanctuary of Isis lies a well-preserved example of a 3rd c. B.C. theatre. Only eight rows of seating have been excavated in the auditorium. The city's principal Byzantine church can be reached through the middle of the stage building.

Theatre

Near the church is a path which runs up to the Sanctuary of Demeter and Kore. Of the two statues which once stood outside the entrance one can now be seen in a Berlin museum. The sanctuary itself, a temple *in antis* of unusual form and fitted with wooden roof-trusses, is badly damaged. To the left of the temple is a sacrificial pit.

Sanctuary of Demeter and Kore

To the east of the Temple of Demeter adjoining a tower on the town walls is a settling basin which was constructed in such a way that the water could be purified without interrupting supplies. The water was brought from Mount Mykale. From here it is possible to climb up the steps to the summit of the hill or descend to the East Gate.

Water supply

Princes' Islands

See İstanbul

Rize

See Black Sea Coast

Samsun

See Black Sea Coast

Şanlıurfa (Urfa)   O 6

South-east Anatolia
Province: Urfa
Altitude: 550m/1804ft
Population: 279,000

See warning page 7

The town is situated on the north-western edge of the Harran Ovası not far from the Turkish-Syrian border. Many researchers regard the town as one of the oldest in history. Sumerians and Hittites called it Urshu and the Babylonians called it Hurri (caves) from the caves in the citadel hill. The Greeks christened it Orhai and from the time of the Macedonians to the Middle Ages the place was called Edessa and then Urfa, a corruption of Orhai. During the French occupation of the region in the Turkish War of Independence, the town put up staunch resistance and since 1983 "şanlı" (famous) has been prefixed to the name in recognition of its bravery. Urfa is an important regional and commercial centre for the predominantly agricultural area. When the "Urfa Tunnel" is completed as part of the GAP

Situation

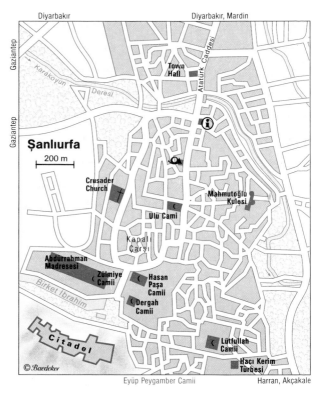

Diyarbakır   Diyarbakır, Mardin

Gaziantep

Gaziantep

Karakoyun Deresi

Town Hall

Ataturk Caddesi

Şanlıurfa

200 m

Crusader Church

Mahmutoğlu Kulesi

Ulu Cami

Kapalı Çarşı

Abdürrahman Madresesi

Zülmiye Camii

Hasan Paşa Camii

Dergah Camii

Birket İbrahim

Lütfullah Camii

Citadel

Hacı Kerim Türbesi

© Baedeker

Eyüp Peygamber Camii   Harran, Akçakale

Euphrates project (South-east Anatolian Project; see Facts and Figures: Topography), an additional 6910sq.km/2667sq.miles of land will be irrigated and the Harran Ovası is likely to become one of the most favourable agricultural areas in Turkey, similar to Adana in the Çukurova.

*Townscape

Modern Urfa is a fascinating mixture of the traditional and the contemporary with Arabic, Kurdish and Turkish features. In the bazaar and old town, oriental influences predominate. Hectic commercial activity and high summer temperatures characterise the town.

Climate

As early as March, the average daytime temperature can reach 29°C/84°F and in November 31°C/87°F is not unusual. In July and August, the thermometer at midday can sometimes reach 45°C/113°F. During these months rainfall averages are as low as in Antalya.

History

Sumerian, Akkadian and Hittite texts all make references to Urshu as an important centre for the Hurrians. By the 18th c. B.C. these Indo-Iranians had penetrated as far as Syria and were trying to bring Hittite expansion to a halt. About 1370 B.C. the Hittites destroyed the town which was later to become a part of the kingdom of Karkamiş or more precisely, the Assyrian vassal state of Haddatu. Abraham is said to have been born in the town and spent some time here on his way from Ur to Canaan. As he was revered as a prophet and founding father by Jews, Moslems and Christians, Urfa has been a traditional destination for pilgrimages.

The town precincts of Urfa, with the Hali Rahman Camii in the foreground

In the 4th c. B.C. Seleukos I "re-founded" Orhai as the capital of his eastern Hellenistic Empire, settling Macedonian veterans here who named the town Edessa after their home province.

In the 4th c. A.D. Ephraim of Nisibis (Nusaybin) established the "Persian Academy" here. Together with a similar academy in Nisibis, it became a focus for Hellenistic learning, but Emperor Zeno (see Facts and Figures: Historical Regions, Isauria) closed it down. When the Roman provincial ruler Abgar the Great (A.D. 9–46) was converted to Christianity, after a miracle when Christ's handkerchief cured him of a skin ailment, Edessa soon became receptive to Christian teaching. Before the town was plundered by the Sassanids (502–505), the bones of St Thomas had been buried here. Under Justinian, Edessa became a centre for Monophysite Christians.

In 1098, the Crusaders under Baldwin de Bouillon captured the town and founded the flourishing Christian state of Edessa which survived for nearly 50 years. In 1144 Arabs conquered the town and some of the inhabitants were deported, enslaved and later killed. The town was completely destroyed.

Sights

Exhibits at the museum which is situated on the north-western edge of the old town include finds from Urfa, Sultantepe and Harran. Also on display is a 3rd c. Syrian mosaic from a cave in the citadel hill.

Archaeological Museum

Sometimes known as the Yeşil Kilise, the mosque and Koran school (c. 1211), situated beneath the citadel, now occupy the site of the old St Mary's Church. It is thought that the minaret dates from the time of the Omayyads around the 8th c.

Hali Rahman Medresesi

To the south of the medresesi lies the Birket İbrahim, Abraham's Pool or sometimes Halil Rahman Gölü. It is linked with other ponds in an adjoining

**Birket İbrahim

Şanlıurfa (Urfa)

park and fed by water from the so-called Spring of Roha at the foot of the citadel. A legend surrounds the "holy" fish which can be found in the pool and are fed by visitors. On his way from Ur to Canaan in the 18th/19th c. B.C. when many nomadic tribes were heading west from Mesopotamia, Abraham stopped in Urfa. The cruel King Nimrod wanted to burn him at the stake because of his monotheistic beliefs, but God intervened to save him and a violent storm swept him and the embers into the air. He landed comparatively gently in a specially-created pool together with the ashes and glowing embers. These turned into holy carp whose descendants are now fed chick peas and lettuce leaves by visitors.

Hasan Paşa Camii

Due east of the Birket İbrahim stands the Hasan Paşa Camii. It was formerly the site of a synagogue and later a Roman tetrapylon.

Abdürrahman Medresesi and Zülmiye Camii

To the north of the carp pool the skyline is dominated by the extensive 17th c. Abdürrahman Medresesi complex and the Zülmiye Camii (1736). The three-domed mosque with its slender minaret is also known as Ahmet Paşa, Ridvaniye or Zulumiye Camii. It is thought to occupy the position of the former Church of St Thomas.

* Dergah Camii

The Dergah Camii (or Dersa Cami) with its large inner courtyard is hidden away to the south-east behind the Hasan Paşa Camii directly beneath the citadel. It is noted for its Hermitage of the Prophet Abraham (Makram İbrahim) and the curative powers of its spring water. Once a year the faithful gather here to seek blessings for their pilgrimage to Mecca. This site was previously occupied by the Byzantine Church of the Redeemer.

Eyüp Peygamber Camii

To the south-east of the citadel at the far end of the town stand the tomb and mosque of the prophet Eyüb, who corresponds with the Old Testament Job. A staircase leads to a rock chamber (hermitage).

** Kapalı Çarşı

Between the Ulu Camii and Hasan Paşa Camii to the south-east of the main street lies the lively business quarter and a special attraction for visitors. It

"Sacred" fish swim in "Abraham's Pool"

consists of a covered bazaar still without any facilities for tourism. An Ottoman caravanserai with an inner courtyard ought not to be missed. The colourful tea-room (Çayhane) is a popular haunt of the locals (mainly men).

The only preserved church is found west of the Ulu Cami and dates from Edessa's Christian heyday. It is currently being restored, having been used as a prison.

Crusader Church

To the east of the old town near the Harran road, modest remains of the old town wall (Mahmutoğlu Kulesi) are still visible. The course of the wall has scarcely changed since Roman times. Whenever the town's river, known as Karakoyun Deresi (Skirtos in antiquity, later Daisan), burst its banks, large parts of the town's fortifications disappeared under water, so in Byzantine times it was re-routed. Barrages have been constructed from large stone slabs in the north and east of the town and they have prevented further flooding.

Town walls

The 12th c. Grand Mosque was erected on the site of the former Church of St Stephen. A synagogue is believed to have preceded the church. One interesting feature is the octagonal minaret in the west of the complex. It would probably have been retained from the church which was built at the time of Justinian. The prayer rooms are laid out as a cross vault and above the prayer niche is a small, simple dome. The mosque was commissioned by Nur Eddin, son and successor to the Seljuk governor of Mosul, Imad Eddin Zengi, founder of the Zengi dynasty.

*Ulu Cami

The remains of the 300m/984ft long and 80m/262ft wide fortress in the foothills of the Top Dağı dominate the south-west of the town. The hill is known by the locals as Nimrud Kürsesi (Nimrud's Pulpit) and whole colonies of hermit ibises nest on the steep rock faces. A 12m/40ft man-made ditch separates the castle from the hinterland. It was probably here that the Hurrians established themselves and it was also the winter palace of the Abgars (Abgar IX 179–244). Two 15m/50ft high pillars with Corinthian capitals provide evidence of the latter's presence. The Crusaders were the last settlers to make alterations. The external wall still has three gates, while inside the ruins of 25 fortified towers can be seen.

*Citadel

Surroundings

The old centre of the lower Harran Ovası, ancient Harran (Akkadian "charranu", road) where Abraham is said to have lived, is now called Altınbaşak. The village 50km/31 miles south of Urfa is not only famous for its ancient history, although until recently it was not that spectacular, but rather for some quite distinctive Syrian influences which manifest themselves in the style of the houses, the clothing of the women and the faces of the people. The impact of Arab settlement is more obvious here than anywhere else in Turkey. Harran's ancient past provides some fascinating links with the present.

**Harran

Foremost is the settlement hill at Harran with evidence of 3rd millennium B.C. habitation. Excavations are still taking place on a mound near the hill where the town is located and there is a possibility that an older acropolis will be found underneath. The badly decayed town walls, the course of which is still easy to trace, encompassed the major part of the old town; the cratered and undulating terrain is typical of an abandoned town. A similar landscape is evident in the abandoned old town of Van. The ring of walls is broken by seven gates, of which five can still be identified: the Aleppo Gate in the west which according to an inscription was restored by Saladin in 1192, the Lions' Gate in the north, the Mosul Gate in the west, the Raqqa Gate in the south and the Roman Gate (Bab ar-Rum). The south-east of the site is overlooked by the impressive remains of the citadel. Once a three-

The Site

storey structure, it was restored by the Fatimids in 1032. Three polygonal fortified towers can still be identified and it is assumed that they occupy the site of the moon temple for which Harran was once so famous. Others have suggested that this shrine was situated near or even under the Ulu Cami, whose striking but few remains dominate the north-east of the site. The large square site was once a mosque which was built by the Omayyads. It was extended in 830 and restored in Saladin's time between 1174 and 1184.

History

Harran receives a mention in the Old Testament (Genesis 11:31 and 12) as the place where Abraham and his tribe stayed for several years on his journey from Ur to Canaan. Harran must have existed at that time c. 18th c. B.C. Excavations have confirmed that the site was settled in the 3rd millennium B.C. and clay tablets dating from the 18th c. B.C. mention the town and other neighbouring settlements which frequently bear the names of Abraham's relatives (Genesis 11:10–31): Harran (Abraham's brother), Peleg (Serug's grandfather), Serug (Abraham's great-grandfather), Nahor (Abraham's grandfather or brother), Terach (Abraham's father).

In subsequent years Harran became a centre for sun and moon worshippers. A double temple to Sin ("shahr" = "moon") and Shamash (sun) dates from the 16th c. B.C. Domination by different nations (Mitanni Empire c. 1400 and the 13th c. Assyrian Empire) did little to change Harran's status as a moon-worshipping centre. The Babylonians (Nabonid 556–539 B.C.) also encouraged the Sin cult. Even the successors to Alexander the Great and the Romans revered the moon god. The town was known in those days as Karrai and later Carrhae. In 53 B.C., the Parthian Orodes II annihilated the army of Crassus here. In Harran in A.D. 217 Caracalla was murdered on the way from the temple to the ruler's palace and in 296/297, the Sassanids defeated the Roman army under the leadership of Galerius. It was 382 before all heathen shrines were destroyed by Theodosius the Great and that included the Sin Temple at Harran (Charrae). The Omayyad caliph Marvan II resided in Harran from 744 to 750 and he is thought to have established the Ulu Cami and the oldest Islamic university. A Mongol invasion in 1260 destroyed the town and it did not recover until the Ottomans gained control in 1516. Sabians worshipped astral bodies at a shrine in neighbouring Sumatar (now Sumatar Harabesi; see below) until the early Middle Ages (12th c. records mention a Sin Temple).

**Trulli houses

After its decline Harran never became a centre of habitation again but gradually a hamlet called Altınbaşak grew up at the foot of the "tell" (inhabited hill). Beehive-shaped "trulli" houses in the north Syrian style with their domed roofs made from crushed clay recall the old Harran and are also somewhat reminiscent of southern Italy. This type of house is far better suited to the climatic conditions than the modern concrete structures which are increasingly replacing the traditional dwellings. Nevertheless the latter are subject to preservation orders.

Sultantepe

About 15km/9 miles south of Urfa on the east side of the road to Harran a massive hill rises up from the plain. It conceals the tiny village of Sultantepe. Excavations on the hill have unearthed remains of a 8th/7th c. B.C. Assyrian settlement (citadel). Discoveries include countless clay tablets forming a library of epic poems, including parts of the Epic of Gilgamesh, prayers, letters, texts relating to mathematics, astronomy, astrology and medicine and an exercise book belonging to an 8th c. B.C. scholar. The writings ended two years after the destruction of Nineveh. Some of the finds are on display in an Ankara museum.

Sumatar Harabesi

This impressive ancient site of the pre-Christian Sabian sect is only accessible by a cross-country vehicle and lies almost 60km/37 miles south-east of Urfa. Sumatar can be reached either via Sultantepe from where it is 10km/7miles further east or 15km/9 miles to the south of Çamlıdere (Mecrihan on the road to Mardin). The remaining journey of 30km/19 miles follows an east-south-east direction through the rocky Tektek mountain range. Use a local guide from Sumatar if possible and head for Sumatar Harabesi or Eski Sumatar, a watering place near Yağmuralan (Yağmurlu).

Altogether there are eight groups of ruins set in a semi-circle at a distance of 400–800m/435–875yd around a rocky crag. Six of the ruins consist of underground chambers and the remaining two caves contain reliefs and inscriptions. The hill in the centre, also with sculptures and inscriptions, is clearly the focal point of this mysterious Sabian temple to the heavens. The Sabians were a Bedouin sect who believed in human sacrifices. Despite their "godless and barbaric rites", they were accepted by medieval Arabs as a religious community. The hill was thought to be a shrine to the sun god Helios, known to the Sabians as Marilaha and who was worshipped in the form of a stone monument (Betyl). The surrounding buildings are assumed to be shrines to the moon god Sin, the principal shrine in Harran, and the five planet gods of Mercury, Venus, Saturn, Jupiter and Mars. The Sabians believed that the heavenly bodies directed destiny. Some elements of Babylonian astrology were incorporated into their beliefs.

Sabian sect

Sardis   D 5

Western Anatolia (Interior)
Province: Manisa
Place: Sartmustafa

The site of the ancient Lydian capital Sardis, once celebrated for its prover-bial wealth and for its Sanctuary of Artemis, lies some 100km/60 miles east of İzmir near the little village of Sartmustafa on the edge of the Gediz (Hermos) valley, a tributary of the Sart Çayı (ancient Paktolos). The Lydian and Greek city lay on the west side of a steeply scarped acropolis some 200m/650ft high, while the later Roman town laid out in the form of a semi-circle occupied a lower terrace below the north side of the hill. The oldest part of the town can be found on the acropolis. Excavations and restoration work have been carried out by a team of American archaeologists.

Situation

The development of Sardis (Sardeis) was closely dependent on the emer-gence and growth of the Lydian Empire. It is not yet established, however, whether the Lydians, a Semitic people whose rulers claimed descent from the Assyrian sun god, founded the town themselves or whether they conquered and incorporated an already existing Maeonian settlement. The town enjoyed great prosperity from the reign of King Gyges (c. 685 B.C.) to that of Kroisos (Croesus; 560–546 B.C.) thanks to its location at the end of an ancient trade route, exploitation of gold deposits from the River Paktolos and busy trade with the Orient. In 546 B.C. Sardis was conquered by the Persians under Cyrus and until 499 B.C. was the seat of a Persian satrap. From here the great Royal Road of the Persian kings ran from Ankyra (Ankara) to Susa with posting stations at four-hourly intervals.
The city enjoyed a further period of prosperity under Roman rule. It was ravaged by an earthquake in A.D. 17 but was rebuilt by Tiberius. Christianity came to Sardis at an early stage, no doubt through the missionary activity of Paul. It is mentioned in Revelations (1:11 and 3:4) as one of the Seven Churches of Asia.
Towards the end of the 11th c. Sardis passed to Seljuk rule. Thereafter it declined rapidly until it was burnt to the ground by the Mongols of Tamer-lane (Timur-Leng) in 1402. The present village of Sartmustafa was not established until the beginning of the 20th c.

History

On a low hill within the Lydian and Greek city are the remains of the celebrated Temple of Artemis built by King Kroisos (Croesus) of Lydia in the 6th c. B.C. It was destroyed by the Greeks in 498 and later rebuilt in the reign of Alexander the Great. The temple is unusually large, measuring

The site
*Temple of Artemis

447

Sardis

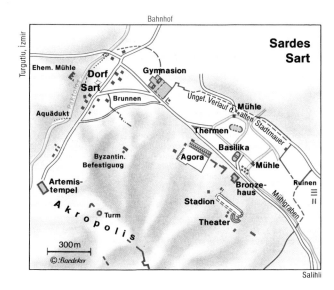

100×48m/330×155ft. Along each long side stood 20 Ionic columns with eight more at the each end. The temple itself was divided into two parts by a transverse wall. A Lydian inscription with an Aramaic translation which was found nearby provided the key to decoding the Lydian language. On the south-east side of the temple can be seen the ruins of a Byzantine chapel dating from the 8th c. A necropolis from the Lydian period is situated near the temple.

°View from the acropolis

As a result of weathering and rain-water erosion practically nothing has survived on the acropolis apart from the scanty remains of walls on the south and east sides. There are some superb views from the top of the acropolis.

°Roman city Gymnasium

A few houses, a theatre (fine view from the top) and a stadium measuring 230×45m/250×50yd are all that remain of the Roman city. They are all thought to date from after the great earthquake (A.D. 17).

North-east of Sartmustafa on the road to Salihli, archaeologists unearthed a 2nd c. A.D. gymnasium. To the south-east, they found other buildings including a synagogue and Byzantine shops and, some 650m/710yd to the east of the gymnasium, baths. The so-called "Bronze House" lies a little way north of the stadium.

Necropolis

Some 10km/6 miles north west of Sartmustafa stands another large necropolis. Here scattered over an undulating plateau ("bin tepe", thousand hills) lie more than 60 conical burial mounds of varying size. Among them is an unusually large mound 69m/225ft high, traditionally believed to be the tomb of Kroisos' father, Alyattes, which is described by Herodotus (Bk 1, ch. 93).

Surroundings

°Bozdağ

Barely 30km/19 miles south of Sardis lies the village of Bozdağ (1100m/3608ft), which is reached by a picturesque mountain road. It lies

448

Sardis: remains of the famous Temple of Artemis

below the 2159m/7081ft high Kırklar Tepe on a pass in the Boz Dağları mountain range from which the village derives its name. This 100km/70 mile long plateau-style mountain ridge which is enclosed by the valleys of the Gediz Nehri and the Küçük Menderes Nehri lies to the east of İzmir. Known as Tmolos in antiquity, since Seljuk times local people have sought refuge here from the nearby lowlands during the hot summer months. Summer resorts, such as Bozdağ itself, have gradually grown into year-round settlements. Livestock are reared and the farmers grow fruit, cereals and potatoes, in contrast to the vines, fruit, olives and cotton cultivated on the coastal plains. Many rural villages and mountain settlements in Turkey are decaying as the population migrates to the cities, but in Bozdağ during the summer all the accommodation is occupied by local people. However, in spring when the fruit trees blossom and during the late autumn Bozdağ is an ideal spot. Visitors will discover an impressive, peaceful, wooded landscape with many comfortable places to spend the night between Bozdağ and Tekeköy and near Gölcük (by the lake; see below). The village of Bozdağ itself can be reached from Ödemiş or Birgi via a picturesque mountain pass but the town itself has little to offer in the way of historical sights other than a very old Ottoman cemetery at the south-eastern exit.

80km/50 miles away on the north-eastern side of the Bozdağları in the middle of some extensive vineyards lies the town of Alaşehir. The surrounding area is reminiscent of Tuscany. The "Bright Town" now occupies the spot where King Attalos II Philadelphos founded the town of Philadelphia (later Neokaisereia) as a frontier fortress. It is mentioned in Revelations (1:11 and 3:7) as one of the Seven Churches of Asia and was the last Byzantine outpost in Asia Minor before succumbing to Bayazit I in 1390. Substantial remains of the medieval town walls can still be seen and there are some sulphur baths close by.

Alaşehir

A good 10km/7 miles south of the Bozdağ pass, the old town of Birgi spreads up both sides of a deep valley cut by a stream. The town was

*Birgi

probably constructed in the 14th c. with building materials plundered from the ruins of Pyrgium (or Dio Hieron) of which nothing now remains. In the middle of the 14th c. Ibn Battuta described "Birgui" as the summer residence of Prince Mohammed, but the most impressive sights in the town today are the magnificent 18th and 19th c. houses. The Çakirağa Konağı, a particularly handsome large town house in the traditional style is currently being expertly restored and in the near future it will be opened to visitors as a "show house". The town centre set on a hill is dominated by the five-aisled Ulu Cami (1312), an early Seljuk mosque in the kufa style with a rectangular, transverse prayer room, a flat wooden roof and plain rows of columns ("Wood Mosque"). The pulpit staircase displays some tasteful carvings which demonstrate the "kündekari" technique.

*Gölcük

This small, peaceful town, Torrhebia in antiquity, (1030m/3378ft) on the northern bank of Lake Gölcük is a typical summer village for the more prosperous town-dwellers and farmers from the lowlands and makes a good starting point for walks in the mountains or to the remains of ancient Hypaepa near Datbey lower down towards the south-west. Most of the lavish summer villas are clustered around the west and north banks of the lake (rowing boats) inside a ring of magnificent pine forests. The lake was created by a landslide which blocked off the valley to the north.

Ödemiş

The town of Ödemiş (pop. 47,000) was founded in late Ottoman times and developed from the splendid Kabazakaloğulları property, constructed at the end of the 13th c., which is situated nearby to the south beneath the ruins of Roman Hypaepa. The lively market town contains many fine 19th c. town houses. Much of its wealth derives from mining deposits of antimony, mercury and copper.

Tire

The administrative centre of Tire 60km/37 miles south of Bozdağ occupies a site close to old Teira (north-east on a hill; Torrebia or Arkadiopolis in antiquity) which was relinquished in favour of Tire after the Turkish conquest. In 1308 Ephesians settled in Teira and during the Middle Ages the town was an important caravan stop. The remains of five caravanserais from the Ottoman years can still be seen in the town: Bakır Han, Dellaloğlu Hanı, Kulu Hanı, Lüftü Paşa Hanı and Savran Hanı. The most interesting of these buildings, a large two-storey complex with an arcaded inner courtyard, is situated south of the railway station diagonally opposite the eight-domed central bazaar. Around 1453 Mehmet II (the Conqueror) forced 65,000 inhabitants of Tire to migrate to Constantinople and the old capital of the Kaystros valley (Little Maeander, Küçük Menderes) suffered badly as a result.

Siirt

See Bitlis

Side   G 7

South coast (Eastern Mediterranean)
Province: Antalya. Altitude: 0–15m/0–50ft
Nearest town: Selimiye (pop. 4000)

Situation and Importance

The remains of the once important Hellenistic city of Side lie about half-way between Antalya and Alanya on a rocky peninsula in the Gulf of Antalya. The peninsula reaches its highest point a little way inland at the bare limestone crag of Ak Dağı, while on either side of this point, lines of hotels overlook the broad and long sandy beaches of the gulf. In the heart of the ancient city, now much overgrown and covered by drifting sand, lies the

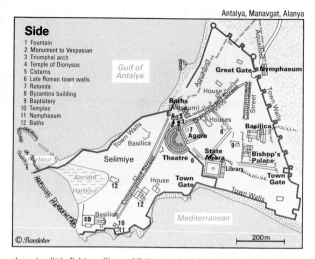

Side

1 Fountain
2 Monument to Vespasian
3 Triumphal arch
4 Temple of Dionysos
5 Cisterns
6 Late Roman town walls
7 Rotunda
8 Byzantine building
9 Baptistery
10 Temples
11 Nymphaeum
12 Baths

Antalya, Manavgat, Alanya

Gulf of Antalya

Great Gate · Nymphaeum

House Street

Baths (Museum)

Houses

Agora

Basilica

Selimiye

Theatre

State Agora

Bishop's Palace

Library

Town Gate

Town Gate

Harbour

Basilica

Ancient Harbour

House

Town Walls

Town Walls

Mediterranean

© Baedeker

200m

charming little fishing village of Selimiye which has developed into a busy holiday resort. Many of the inhabitants are the descendants of Cretans who settled here about 1900. The little town amid the ruins has grown into one of the most important resorts on the Turkish Riviera and boasts numerous hotels and clubs as well as splendid beaches including the Sorgun Plajı.

*Seaside resort

There was already a settlement on the Side peninsula by 1000 B.C. In the 7th or 6th c. B.C. Greek settlers from the city of Kyme on the west coast of Asia Minor established a colony here and built a harbour. After a period when it was a pirates' lair and a slave market Side developed in Roman times into an important and prosperous commercial centre. As at Perge and other ancient coastal cities, coastal currents gradually caused the harbour to silt up. This, combined with the collapse of Roman rule led to the decay of the city and it was finally abandoned between the 7th and 9th c.

History

Along the east of the peninsula extend the Byzantine town walls, once reinforced by towers. Outside the North Gate or Great Gate (which was originally several storeys high) is a nymphaeum (2nd c. B.C.) fed by an aqueduct coming in from the north. From the Great Gate two colonnaded streets laid in Roman times ran through the town, one leading due south, the other south-west. After 350m/380yd the latter meets up with the square agora, which was surrounded by colonnades housing shops. At the west corner the foundations of a small round Corinthian temple are clearly discernible. Two Roman peristyle houses (2nd–1st c. B.C.) with mosaics can be found some 30m/35yd north of the agora.
Along the south-west side of the agora stands the Theatre, the largest in Pamphylia. It could accommodate an audience of 15,000 in its 49 rows of seating. Although several of the supporting arches have collapsed, bringing down part of the auditorium, this is still a remarkable example of Roman architectural skill.

*The site

Facing the north-west side of the agora stand the imposing Agora Baths, which now house an interesting museum containing the finest of the statues, reliefs, sarcophagi, urns, etc. recovered during the 20 year Turkish excavation campaign (1946–67). The exhibits are displayed in the various restored rooms of the baths and in the garden.
Items of particular interest in the frigidarium are two Roman altars, a Hittite column base, a Roman sundial and a carving of weapons from the East

*Agora Baths (Museum)

451

Side

Side: the largest ancient theatre in Pamphylia

Gate; in the caldarium figures of girls and women including the Three
Graces; in the large tepidarium a magnificent sarcophagus with a frieze of
Eroses, statues of Hercules (with the apple of the Hesperides in his hand),
Hermes and the Emperor Licinius; in the small tepidarium a large statue of
Nike, goddess of victory and in the palaestra garden architectural frag-
ments, reliefs, Medusa heads, etc.

Other buildings

South-west of the Agora Baths stands a triumphal arch, a monument to the
Emperor Vespasian and a number of fountains, notably one known as the
Fountain of the Three Basins.

From the theatre the colonnaded street continues south-west across the
peninsula, passing through the village of Selimiye with a wide choice of
restaurants and souvenir shops and ending at a semi-circular temple by the
sea dedicated to the moon god Men. West of here at the tip of the peninsula
lie the remains of the city's two principal temples, probably dedicated to
Athena and Apollo; adjoining to the east are the ruins of a Byzantine
basilica.

At the south-west end of the peninsula is the ancient harbour, now largely
silted up. Its outline is marked by the steep scarp of the coastal rocks.
Following this scarp to the north-east the remains of some Byzantine baths
are visible. In the eastern part of the city the State Agora is situated. Its east
side is occupied by an imposing building, originally two-storied, which is
thought to be the library. In a columned niche, still *in situ*, is a figure of
Nemesis, goddess of fate.

Byzantine
churches

Between the State Agora and the eastern town wall the extensive ruins of
the Byzantine bishop's palace, principal and baptistery can be found. These
early Christian buildings date from the 5th and 10th c.

Surroundings

8km/5 miles north-east of Side, a little way in from the coast, lies the town of Manavgat on the river of the same name (Melas in antiquity). It rises in the Seytan range (Seytan Dağları) of the Taurus. The beautiful Manavgat Falls (Şelalesi) can be reached 5km/3 miles upstream via an access road. The area is laid out as a garden and visitors can make their way on various paths and gangways to the immediate vicinity of the falls, the roar of which can be heard a long way away.

Manavgat waterfalls

A mile or two north-west of the waterfalls at the point where the track crosses the Naras Çayı, a Seljuk arched bridge over the Manavgat Çayı leads downstream. It was built on Roman foundations.

Naras Köprüsü

About 5km/3 miles further north above the village of Bucak Şeyler, which can be reached from Side via the Manavgat Şelalesi amid an area of pine forest, lie the fine remains of the Seleukid town of Seuleukeia in Pamphylia. Little is known of its history and its exact identity is still not certain despite the existing remains. Excavations in the 1970s unearthed a large baths complex, a well-preserved agora with store-rooms, colonnades and rows of shops, a Byzantine church, a heroon, an odeion and a mosaic of Orpheus.

Seleukeia in Pamphylia

Akseki is situated about 80km/50 miles beyond the junction of the eastward coast road and the road to Konya. Between Akseki and Aydınkent (İbradi), near the village of Ürümlü and 500m/545yd on foot to the west of the Manavgat Çayı lies the Düdensuyu Mağarasgı cave complex.
There are a number of underground lakes here, one of which (100m/325ft long) can be crossed by a natural bridge. At the moment only the first of the lakes can be visited (with a guide). The caves can be reached more directly with a cross-country vehicle via a scenic route from Manavgat and Dikmen.

Akseki/ Düdensuyu Mağarası

Manavgat Waterfalls near Side

Side

Cevizlik

Düdencik Mağarası, the deepest cave network in Turkey (330m/1082ft) can be found in the upper valley of the Manavgat Çayı close to the town of Cevizli (1050m/3444ft; pop. 4000). One underground river which dries up during the summer months emerges as a karst spring near Pamukluk Köprüsü close to the source of the Manavgat Çayı.

*Aspendos

The site of Aspendos, in antiquity probably the most important city in Pamphylia and now notable particularly for its splendidly pre-served theatre, lies some 50km/30 miles east of Antalya and 15km/9 miles from the coast. It is situated near the village of Belkıs in the alluvial plain of the River Köprüırmağı (ancient Eurymedon), which is navigable in the lower reaches.

Aspendos was founded by the Greeks – according to tradition by the legendary Mopsos about 1000 B.C. As with other neighbouring towns such as Perge and Side, it enjoyed its most prosperous pe-riod under the Romans and as with those cities, its eventual de-cline was due to the silt-ing up of its harbour and the centralising policy of the Byzantine Empire.

**Theatre

The outstanding feature of Aspendos is the theatre in the lower town, the best preserved and one of the largest in Asia Minor. Built in the 2nd c. A.D. by Crespinus Arruntianus and Auspicatus Titianus, the theatre has seating for an audience of between 15,000 and 20,000. It has recently been restored and is now used for music and drama festivals. The semi-circular audi-torium, divided into two sections by a broad passage half-way up, has 20 tiers of seating with ten staircases in the lower half and nineteen tiers with 21 staircases in the upper part. Round the top runs a barrel-vaulted colon-nade. At either end of the stage are vaulted passages giving access to the orchestra. The two-storey stage wall was articulated by slender double columns with Ionic capitals on the lower order and Corinthian capitals on the upper one. The double column flanking the central entrance to the stage had a common broken pediment. The stage itself had a wooden roof suspended by ropes and the auditorium too was probably covered by an awning.

Acropolis

Immediately above the lower town rises the 40m/131ft acropolis hill. Be-yond the remains of a small temple and the agora stands the nymphaeum (fountain shrine), once a monumental structure articulated by double columns but now represented only by a wall 32m/105ft long with ten niches for statues. Adjoining this on the north are the foundations of another building, probably the bouleuterion or council chamber.

Aqueduct

To the north of the acropolis hill can be seen remains of an ancient aque-duct and two linked water towers.

Aspendos: orchestra of the theatre . . .

. . . and ruins in the upper town

The theatre in Aspendos is well maintained

Köprülü Kanyon Near the fork off the road to Beşkonak, 10km/7 miles east of Aspendos, a long Seljuk hump-back bridge with Roman foundations crosses the Köprülü İrmak. 46km/29 miles further north behind the village of Alabalık near Beşkonak, the river narrows, marking the point where the mountainous and impressive Köprülü Kanyon (Bridge Gorge) National Park begins. Behind some small fish restaurants a track leads off to Selge (within the park) across a Roman bridge which spans the gorge. Remains of an ancient cobbled road can be found on the road from here to Selge.

*Selge High up in the Taurus Mountains about 60km/37 miles north of Aspendos lies the village of Altınkaya Köyü (Zerk; 1050m/3444ft) and the ruins of Selge. The road via Beşkonak beyond Alabalık is very poor, but quite an experience. It is said that the town was founded by Kalchas, the blind prophet of the Trojan War, and the rest of his army from Troy. Until Roman times the remote location of the settlement served to protect the town's inhabitants from foreign rule. Yet trade flourished thanks to some good relations with the towns of Pamphylia and other regions of Asia Minor and the Pisidian town of Selge enjoyed great prosperity during Imperial Roman times. The extensive ruins contain many interesting remains, but the principal sights are the Roman theatre with a Greek auditorium (10,000 seats) and the adjacent stadium. Some distance to the south-west on a mound lie the remains of a Temple of Zeus and a Temple of Artemis and just beyond a cistern-like round vessel for the town's water supply. About 500m/550yd to the east on another hillock stands the agora, at one time surrounded on three sides with rows of shops and from which a colonnaded street runs to the north. The remains of a triple-aisled basilica and a hall 120m/394ft long can be found nearby. The course of a town wall with a gate can be clearly discerned.

Siirt

See Bitlis

Silifke   I 7

South coast (Eastern Mediterranean)
Province: İçel
Altitude: 50m/164/ft
Population: 47,000

Situation Silifke (formerly Selefke) lies about 10km/6 miles from the Mediterranean on the right bank of the Göksu Nehri. It occupies the site of ancient Seuleukeia Tracheia, one of the cities founded by Seleukos Nikator (312–281 B.C.) and an important road junction in "Rough" Cilicia. The town which flourished up to the end of the Imperial Roman period was also famous for its oracle of Apollo.

Sights

The remains of the Konak which dates from the Roman period are visible. Inside is a collection of architectural material (inscriptions, statues, fragments, etc.). The ruins of the Crusader Castle of Camardesium, successor to the acropolis, can be seen on the hill to the west. An ancient necropolis with many sarcophagi and rock tombs lies on the southern slope and on the neighbouring hill.

Surroundings

Göksu Nehri The Göksu Nehri (Blue Water), the sources of which originate in the mighty
(Saleph) Ak Dağı range to the north-west, acquired some notoriety as it was here on

June 10th 1190 that Emperor Frederick Barbarossa was drowned while on the march during the Third Crusade. A memorial stone was erected in 1970 on the road to Konya. The predominantly westerly direction of the wind is causing the river delta to extend southwards in a long narrow sand spit, creating areas of marsh, small lakes and coastal lagoons.

A good half-hour's walk to the south of Silifke along a stepped footpath hewn from the soft local rock lies Meriamlık. It is situated on a hill projecting to the east and was one of the most frequented places of pilgrimage during the Early Christian period. St Thekla, a pupil of the Apostle Paul, was said to have lived in a cave here and to have disappeared into the earth to escape her oppressors. Of the numerous churches, monasteries and other sacred buildings, only the apse of the great columned basilica at the southern end of the plateau remains above ground. This huge structure (90×37m/ 295×120ft) with forecourt, narthex, three aisles and sacristies in addition to the apse was built by the Emperor Zeno (474–491) on the site of an earlier basilica. Below the church are the sacred caves, reconstructed in the 2nd c. to form a three-aisled crypt; they are still visited by pilgrims.

*Meriamlık
(Aya Tekla)*

About 7km/4 miles north of Silifke, the road to Uzuncaburç passes a number of 2nd and 3rd c. tombs in different styles. There are three basic architectural styles: towers, temples and houses: the square towers are mostly simple and relatively slender, the temple tombs are so called because of their Corinthian columns, while the plain house-tombs have a rather squat appearance. The last two often display sculptures of the deceased on the gabled wall. These tombs are a part of the necropolis of the ancient Roman town of Imbriogon, dating from the 2nd/3rd c.

Demirçili

Visible some 30km/20 miles north of Silifke to the right of the old road to Karaman and situated in the rolling uplands of the Southern Taurus at 1100m/3640ft are the well-preserved remains of ancient Olba known in

***Olba
Diocaesarea
(Uzuncaburç)*

Diocaesarea: columns of the Temple of Zeus

457

Turkish as Uzuncaburç. To the north stands the five-storey tower ("uzunca-burç", high tower; *c.* 200 B.C.), to the south are the remains of dwelling houses and beyond a colonnaded street running from east to west dates from the Hellenistic and Roman periods. At the east end of the street are the theatre (165/164 B.C.) and a Byzantine church. Further west on the south side of the colonnaded street stands a Temple of Zeus built soon after 300 B.C. with 6 by 12 Early Corinthian columns 30 of which are still standing (four with capitals). A road crosses from here to the north and at 70m/75yd a well-preserved Roman gate with three passages. At the west end of the colonnaded street is the Tychaion, a 1st c. B.C. temple with an unusual ground plan. All but one of the six front pillars are still in situ. 110m/120yd to the south of the Temple of Zeus stands another large public building (*c.* A.D. 200) which contained a colonnaded hall on its upper floor.

From the high tower a paved ancient road lined by cemeteries runs east to another historic site in the Ura Basin (975m/3200ft), the residential part of Olba which has numerous remains of churches, houses, tombs, a water tower and a large aqueduct built in the reign of Emperor Pertinax.

*Narlıkuyu

6km north of Susanoğlu lies the small coastal town of Narlıkuyu (pomegranate fountain) with the remains of ancient baths and a finely coloured 4th c. mosaic on display in a small covered museum. The mosaic represents the "Three Graces" with the goddesses Aglaia (Grace), Euphrosyne (Merriment) and Thalia (Charm). According to the inscription it was presented by the governor of the Princes' Islands, Poimenios, who controlled the flow of water from the spring and built a bath here. Another inscription reads: "Whoever drinks this water will become wise and live long, the ugly will become beautiful."

*Corycian Caves
Cennet ve
Cehennem

A side road on the left (3km/2 miles) goes up to the two Corycian Caves or in Turkish Cennet ve Cehennem (Heaven and Hell) with a chapel and various ancient remains. The two huge, collapsed sink-holes (obruk) are sited above a cave system with an underground lake that extends under the sea in the Bay of Narlıkuyu emerging as a karst spring. When the sea is calm, the flow of water can be seen from the surface. While the round 120m/393ft Cehennem (Hell) cave 75m/80yd further east is not accessible, steps lead down to the larger Cennet (Heaven) cave which is 100m/325ft wide and 550m/1800ft long. What is initially an open pit leads to a deeper cave at the rear. Known as the Typhon Cave (300m/984ft long and 75m/246ft high), the 5th c. Chapel of St Mary stands at the edge, guarding the entrance to the underworld where the monster Typhon with a hundred dragon heads and snake feet lived.

Korykos
*Kızkalesi

4km/2½ miles north-east of Narlıkuyu the massive remains of the citadel of ancient Korykos face the picturesque island fortress of Kızkalesi (Maiden's Castle). During the Middle Ages this fortified islet became one of the most notorious pirates' lairs on the coasts of the Mediterranean. The present name derives from an old legend. A sultan was told by a soothsayer that his daughter would die of a snakebite, whereupon he built a castle, hoping that the sturdy walls would protect her. The prophecy was fulfilled however,

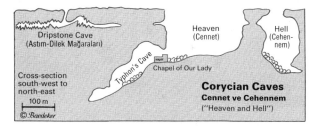

Cross-section
south-west to
north-east
100 m
© Baedeker

Dripstone Cave
(Astım-Dilek Mağaraları)

Typhon's Cave

Chapel of Our Lady

Heaven
(Cennet)

Hell
(Cehen-
nem)

Corycian Caves
Cennet ve Cehennem
("Heaven and Hell")

The island stronghold called "Maiden's Castle" (Kiskalesi)

when he himself sent her a basket of fruit and she was bitten by a snake concealed inside.

4km/2½ miles further north lies Ayaş with the widely scattered remains of ancient Elaiusa-Sebaste. Partly covered by drifting sand, there are remains of a five-aisled basilica on the mainland and various ruined parts of the city including a temple, theatre, grain-stores, etc. In a wide arc around the city lie several necropolises with house-tombs and sarcophagi.

Ayaş
Elaiusa-Sebaste

Above the Cennet ve Cehennem Caves some 3km/2 miles from Kızkalesi in the direction of Hüseyinler some interesting rock tombs and carvings with human figures can be seen.

Adamkayalar

About 40km/25 miles north-east of Silifke a side road forks off to the left to the ruined site of ancient Kanytelleis (3km/2 miles). It was discovered by Langlois in 1852 and lies around a deep sink-hole (obruk) which it is possible to descend by a narrow footpath. The ruins of many of the town's sacred and secular buildings can still be seen, including five churches (two large 8th/9th c. basilica). On the south side stands a huge Hellenistic tower, which the priestly prince Teukros of Olba Diocaesarea (Uzuncaburç) built around 200 B.C. in honour of Zeus Olbios who was revered in Olba. Extensive necropoles with sarcophagi, temple tombs and house-tombs can be found around the town.
Several decades ago the town was settled by the Yürüks (a nomadic or semi-nomadic tribe), whose simple dwellings and cemetery can be found inside the ruined site.

*Kanlıdivane

About 20km/12 miles west of Silifke beside the large bay of Taşucu (Boğsak Körfezi) stands the octagonal castle of Liman Kalesi. Cisterns and dwellings can be found hidden behind the walls. At the beginning of the 19th c. it was almost certainly used as a pirates' lair.

Liman Kalesi

Sinop   See Black Sea Coast

Sivas   M/N 4

North-eastern central Anatolia
Province: Sivas
Altitude: 1275m/4182ft
Population: 219,000

Situation and
Importance

Despite the existence of several interesting old buildings, Sivas is not an
attractive town, having suffered badly from rebuilding work. Situated on
the north-western edge of a broad alluvial plain crossed by the River
Kızılırmak, it is an important road and railway junction. Cotton and metal-
working are the main sources of employment.

History

Little is known of the town's early history. Excavations have unearthed the
remains of a Hittite settlement. The town grew under Pompeius with the
name of Megalopolis. The Emperor Justinian built strong walls and elevated it to capital of Armenia Prima province, although the young Christian
community here was then subjected to persecution by the Romans. The
town came to prominence in this context when in A.D. 320–340 soldiers from
the 12th "Fulminata" legion were driven naked into the ice-cold Kızılırmak
because of their beliefs. The "40 martyrs of Sebastea" thus became a part
of religious history with March 10th as the anniversary. Sivas experienced
a revival under the Seljuks in the 12th/13th c. When the Mongols invaded
around 1400, Sivas enjoyed the protection of a strong wall, but nevertheless Timur-Leng succeeded in taking the town after an eighteen-day
siege. Christians (Greeks and Armenians) were murdered or sold as slaves.
It was many years before Sivas recovered from this blow. In 1808, there
were 16,000 inhabitants but trade and commerce did not equal the levels

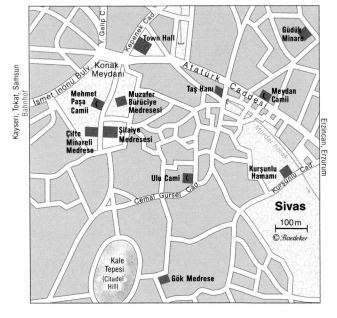

achieved during the city's heyday. However the foundation of the Turkish
Republic gave Sivas a place in history as Mustafa Kemal Paşa (Atatürk)
summoned the National Congress of the Freedom Movement (September
4th–11th 1919) here to call for national unity.

Sights

The remains of the Çifte Minareli Medrese (1271) on Konak Meydanı in the
town centre are of architectural interest. It is named after the twin minarets
("çift", double). Only the front of the building with its decorative portal and
the two minarets remain. The foundations are visible behind the portal in
the park.

*Çifte Minareli
Medrese

At the southern end of the town by the junction of the road to Kangal and
Darende, an old dog-leg bridge ("eğri", buckled) with eighteen arches
crosses the Kızılırmak.

Eğri Köprü

Directly below and to the east of the citadel lies Gök Medrese with its
famous doorway. This former theological school (now closed for reno-
vation work) was endowed by the Vizier Sahip Ata (Fahreddin Ali Ben
Hussein) in 1272. It was designed by the Greek architect Koloyan from
Konya. With its distinctive Turkish blue tiles it is known as the Blue
Medrese.

Gök Medrese

The rectangular portal area with its stalactiform entrance niche and ornamental border is dominated by two minarets which display some characteristic Seljuk features: deep relief palmettes, starred and scripted
decorations, channelled shafts and pedestals decorated with stalactiform
patterns. At the corners of the entrance wall stand round columns with
honeycomb motifs.
The inner courtyard is surrounded on three sides by a two-storey building
with cells for the scholars. There is an eyvan (lecture hall) with barrel
vaulting on both side walls and on the rear wall.

Sivas: Çifte Minareli Medrese

Portal of the Şifaiye Medresesi

461

Sivas

Güdük Minare	To the east of the Atatürk Caddesi behind the Meydan Camii stands a tomb to Sheik Hassan (1347) which looks like a cropped minaret (Güdük Minare). This unusually shaped building with a tiled upper section which changes from a triangular to a cylindrical form is built on a stone plinth.
Kale Tepesi	To the east of the station rises the citadel hill on which a two-tiered castle once stood. The hill is now laid out with an attractive garden which offers a fine view over the town. The Castle Mosque (Kale Camii) from Ottoman times is also situated here.
Mehmet Paša Camii	The domed Ottoman mosque commissioned by Mehmet Paşa (*c.* 1580) dominates the park near Konak Meydanı.
*Muzafer Bürüciye Medresesi	The Muzafer Bürüciye Medresesi located a short distance from the Çifte Minareli Medrese and to the north-east of the small park by Konak Meydanı has recently become a museum. Built by the Mongol Muzafer in 1271, the interior conceals another mosque and the founder's mausoleum. The magnificent Seljuk façade is particularly impressive.
*Şifaiye Medresesi	Directly opposite the Çifte Minareli Medrese stands the Şifaiye Medresesi complex (Dar üş-Şifa), initially endowed as a hospital by the Seljuk Izettin Kaikavus I in 1217. The façade is decorated with a glazed earthenware mosaic. The founder's türbe can be found in the right eyvan of the courtyard.
Taş Hans	At the junction of Atatürk Caddesi and Nalbantlar Başi Caddesi, the remains of the old bazaar can be seen. Behind a small textile and leather bazaar stands the Ottoman Taş Hanı caravanserai which was built by the town's governor in 1573.
Ulu Cami	The Grand Mosque situated to the south of the Şifaiye Medresesi north-east of the citadel hill is of interest. The plain pillared mosque is thought to date from about 1100. A staircase leads down to the extensive forecourt. The flat roof of the prayer room is borne by 50 squat, rectangular pillars which create an awe-inspiring impression. The slightly crooked minaret dates from the 13th c.

Surroundings

Bedohtun	The remains of this Byzantine hermitage can be found in the mountains of the Yıldız Dağı, 120km/74 miles north-west of Sivas. They lie on a slope facing the Yıldız Dağı volcano (2537m/8321ft) above the Bedohtunyazı valley.
Boğaz Köprü	10km/7 miles east of Sivas beneath and to the south of the Seyfibeli mountain pass (road to Erzincan; 1300m/4264ft), a now ruined "gorge bridge" with seven pointed arches crossed the Kızılırmak.
Gemerek	About 10km/7 miles west of the regional centre of Gemerek and about 115km/71 miles south-west of Sivas on the Kayseri road the Şahrukköprü crosses the Kızılırmak just south of the village of Karaözü. Nearby is the Şahruk Köprüsü Hanı which is thought to be of Seljuk origins. An old route across the Bozok Yaylası to Yozgat and Kırşehir starts here.
*Karst region around Sivas, Hafik and Zara	Tertiary Era limestone extends underground between Sivas in the west and the regional centre of İmranlı in the east and a karst landscape dominates the upper Kızılırmak for a distance of 100km/62 miles, extending 10–20km/6–12 miles on both sides. The river has cut its way through the layers of gypsum to create this wide valley and for over 100km/62 miles it flows mainly through red sandstone, gypsum and marl. There are many tributaries which give the water a permanently dull red colour, hence the name

Kızılırmak ("red river"). The high levels of sodium and potassium compounds also give the water a bitter taste. The higher gypsum plateaux at about 1550–1650m/5000–5500ft are riddled with a dense network of dolines. The slopes close to the river abound with 50–100m/165ft–325ft wide and 30m/100ft deep funnels and craters with swallow holes (ponors). Uvalas and tiny poljes with shallow lakes and marshes have been created from larger dolines merging together.

Near the village of Hanlı a short distance to the south-west of the administrative centre of Kayadibi (50km/31 miles south-west of Sivas) stands the Seljuk caravanserai known as Latif Hanı. | Hanlı

About 11km/7 miles north-east of Kangal (90km/56 miles south-west of Sivas) lie the Kavak thermal baths with a medicinal spring and an abundance of fish (Balıklı Kaplıca). | Kangal

This many-arched "mutilated" bridge about 8km/5 miles to the west of Sivas crosses the Kızılırmak before the river cuts through to the south. It marks the point where the old caravan route headed across the karst Yassıbel pass (1570m/5150ft) to Kayseri. | Kesik Köprü

80km/50 miles south-west of Sivas the road to Kayseri passes the regional centre of Şarkişla, which has become famous as the birthplace and home of the greatest Turkish popular poet of modern times Aşık Veysel (1894–1971). He was born near the town to a poor peasant family and is also buried here. He was left blind at an early age, but still mastered the "saz", an Anatolian stringed instrument. He composed and wrote the lyrics of songs which had an element of social comment and which reflected his own background and the world of the poor Anatolian farmer. | Şarkişla

On the Çermik Suyu some 18km/11 miles north-east of Sivas lies the small resort of Soğukçermik, with a thermal bath, an indoor pool, and a hotel. | Soğukçermik

Formerly known as Yenihan after a 14th c. caravanserai (restored in the 17th c. but now ruined) the town lies about 70km/43 miles west of Sivas. The single rooms of the old three-aisled caravanserai can still be seen in the central aisle with colonnaded halls along both side aisles. According to an inscription on the neighbouring mosque it was built by Abu Sayıd Bahadur Khan.
Another caravanserai (Saray Hanı) can be found 20km/12 miles to the south of the town on the Sivas road. | Yıldızeli

Sultanhanı

See Aksaray

Tarsus | K 7

South coast (Eastern Mediterranean)
Province: İçel
Altitude: 0–15m/0–50ft
Population: 191,000

The city of Tarsus on the Tarsus Çayı stands in the hot Cilician Plain at the foot of the Taurus and is one of the few towns in the eastern Mediterranean which can trace its history back without interruption for 3000 years.
Its importance in ancient times depended on its position at the southern end of the celebrated pass through the Taurus known as the Cilician Gate and on a lagoon beside the Mediterranean. Since then the lagoon has silted | Situation and Importance

up and the coastline has moved away from the town destroying its maritime trade, while the main road from Ankara through the Cilician Gate to Syria passes some distance away. Tarsus is now a commercial and market centre (cotton exports) but it has no features of any special interest to tourists.

History

Marayas statue

Excavations on the Gözlü Kale have brought to light occupation levels extending from about 5000 B.C. into Roman times. The town walls were built in the 3rd millennium B.C. Accounts by the Greek general and historian Xenophon (430–354 B.C.) indicate that Tarsus, then a flourishing city, was plundered by Cyrus' forces. During the Third Syrian War (246 B.C.) it was conquered by Egypt. In 64 B.C. it became a part of the Roman Empire and was made capital of the province of Cilicia. A 9th c. B.C. statue is on display in İstanbul's Archaeological Museum. The university and the school of philosophy in particular vied with the great schools of Athens and Alexandria. The Apostle Paul the son of a tentmaker was born in Tarsus during the last century B.C. but there was no appreciable Christian community there until the end of 4th c. A.D.

After the occupation of Syria by the Arabs, Cilicia became a frontier area and the decline of Tarsus began. About the middle of the 11th c. the town was captured by the Seljuks, but in 1097 they were dislodged by the Crusaders who returned the town to the Byzantines. During the 13th and 14th c. the Armenians who had been driven out of eastern Asia Minor by the Seljuks established a kingdom here. With the conquest of the town by the Ottomans in 1515 its political importance came to an end. Thereafter it lived on as a place of little consequence having lost its function not only as the chief town of the region and but also as a port.

Sights

Kleopatra Kapısı

Its great ancient buildings, in particular those from the city's heyday in the early years of Christianity have been almost totally lost. The ancient city lies buried 6–7m/20–23ft below the alluvial plain of the Tarsus Çayı and little excavation has so far been carried out.
A town gate from the Roman period is described as Cleopatra's Gate. Remains of a stoa and a Roman theatre have been found south-east of the present town.

Tomb of
Sardanapalus

Near the town on the right bank of the Tarsus Çayı stands a massive structure 5–6m/16–20ft high known as Donuk Taş or the Tomb of Sardanapalus after the legendary founder of Tarsus. It is probably the substructure of a huge temple dating from the Imperial Roman period.

Surroundings

*Cilician Gates

Just over 50km/30 miles north of Tarsus the valley of the Tarsus Çayı narrows into the defile now called Gülek Boğazı but famed in ancient times as the Cilician Gates (Latin "Pylae Ciliciae") – a rocky gorge several hundred metres high but barely 20m/65ft wide through which the river rushes. The ancient road which frequently featured in history was used by such notable figures as Semiramis, Xerxes, Darius, Cyrus the Younger, Alexander the Great, Haroun al-Rashid and Geoffrey de Bouillon. It followed the east side of the gorge, partly hewn from the rock face and partly borne on projecting beams. A modern road has been blasted out of the cliffs and the new trunk road by-passes the gorge to the west. The old road is now in poor condition. Immediately south of the Cilician Gates rise the fortress-like crag of Gülek Kale Dağı with the ruined castle of Assa Kaliba crowning the hill 600m/2000ft higher up.

Çamlıyayla

A narrow country road 65km/40 mile long links Tarsus with the popular summer resort of Çamlıyayla (1200–1300m/3900–4250ft). Even a hundred years ago this attractive town was inhabited only in the summer providing refuge from the sweltering heat. One 19th c. traveller described it as a large village (''Namrun, consisting of a scattering of Swiss-style wood cabins). Çamlıyayla (wooded pasture) is not just the centre of the settlement beneath the Namrun castle (Lampron), but an expanse of land measuring 25sq.km/9sq.miles dotted with summer houses.

Çamlıyayla (formerly Namrun) is dominated by the castle of Namrunkalesi (formerly Lampron), the ancestral home of the Armenian Hetumids, who replaced the Rupenids as the kings of Armenia Minor (see Armenia). The castle set on a steeply sloping rock plateau consists of a higher and lower fortress and the remains of a large residential settlement. Apart from the fortifications with a keep and four towers, the inhabitant's way of safeguarding the water supply is of interest: a water tunnel links the keep with a spring and a bath. The castle itself with its huge walls occupies a position on the northern corner of the plateau and contains five rooms, the large east room being the most striking. The castle offers a magnificent view over the Taurus mountains.

*Namrunkalesi
(Lampron)

Mersin (pop. 421,000), an important port and capital of the province of İçel, lies 30km/19 miles north-west of Tarsus and is only 150 years old. Parts of the town were built from the ruins of Soloi. The Atatürk recreation park is worth a visit.

Mersin
(İçel)

The village of Viranşehir is situated 14km/9 miles south-west of Mersin and lies close to the remains of the ancient port of Soloi. The town was founded about 700 B.C. as a Rhodian colony but was later captured by Alexander the Great. During the subsequent struggle between the Ptolemies and Seleucids the town was destroyed several times. In the 3rd c. it was the birthplace

Soloi
Pompeiopolis

View of Çamıyayla from the Namrunkalesi

of the Stoic philosopher Chrysippos and the mathematician and astronomer Aratos who wrote a didactic poem on the constellations ("Phainomena"). In 91 B.C. the town was destroyed by King Tigranes of Armenia (95–60 B.C.) and also during the wars against the Mediterranean pirates.

After defeating the pirates Pompey settled them in Soloi, rebuilt the town and called it Pompeiopolis. Thereafter it developed into a flourishing commercial centre. In A.D. 527 or 528 it was destroyed by an earthquake.

Since the site was used as a source of building material for the construction of Mersin there are few remains of the ancient city to be seen. The main feature is a colonnaded street 450m/490yd long running north-west from the harbour through the centre of the site. Other features which can be identified are a gate in the town walls of which only the foundations survive, an almost completely destroyed theatre probably built against an artificial hill on the north-east side of the town, an aqueduct outside the town and the harbour wall which ends in a semi-circle. The harbour itself is almost totally silted up. To judge by the capitals of the colonnaded street, it was begun in the middle of the 2nd c. A.D.

Tekirdağ

See Marmara, Sea of

Tokat   M 3

Central South Pontus
Province: Tokat
Altitude: 623m/2043ft
Population: 83,000

Situation and
*Importance

The main road from Sivas to Samsun passes through the town of Tokat, which is dominated by a small medieval castle and lies at the eastern end of the fertile Tokat-Turhal Ovası close to the confluence of the Tokay Suyu and the upper reaches of the Yeşilırmak. Since the Middle Ages Tokat has benefited from its situation at the junction of two trade routes: one from Mesopotamia to the Black Sea and the other from Persia, and India (silk!), to İzmir (Smyrna) on the Aegean Sea, from where goods were shipped to Europe. Although several of the town's historic buildings have been destroyed or have disappeared, many still remain and a few have been splendidly restored. Most of the old buildings are located on the two main axes: the north–south through route from Sivas to Amasya by the Meydan (main square, near the museum) and on the east-west Sulu Sokak either side of Cumhuriyet Meydanı (Republic Square near the Town Hall) and further to the east.

Since the 17th c. the town's principal trades have included copper beating, batik printing, weaving and silkworm rearing. The textile printers use traditional skills to produce attractive hand-printed linens with patterns based on old motifs. Over 1000 families, mainly in the rural communities of Niksar, Almus and Cat, make silk and wool carpets under state control using the famous Hereke method. Since 1982 Afghan refugees have been producing wool and silk carpets using traditional patterns from their homeland.

History

Unlike the nearby ancient Commana Pontica (see Gümenek), Tokat developed from the medieval town of Eugocia (Dazimon) after the earlier heathen Hittite settlements declined as Christianity spread. In 1631 there were twelve churches in the town, one of which was said to have been built by

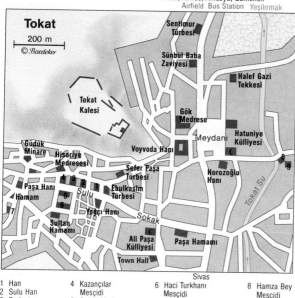

Niksar, Almus, Amasya, Gümenek
Airfield Bus Station Yeşilırmak

Tokat
200 m
© *Baedeker*

Sentimur Türbesi
Sünbül Baba Zaviyesi
Halef Gazi Tekkesi
Tokat Kalesi
Gök Medrese
Meydanı
Hatuniye Külliyesi
Güdük Minare
Hisariye Medresesi
Voyvoda Hanı
Sefer Paşa Türbesi
Norozoğlu Hanı
Paşa Hanı
Hamam
Ebulkasım Türbesi
Sulu Sokak
Yağcı Hanı
Sultan Hamamı
Ali Paşa Külliyesi
Paşa Hamamı
Town Hall
Sivas
Tokat Su

1 Han	4 Kazançılar	6 Haci Turkhanı	8 Hamza Bey
2 Sulu Han	Mesçidi	Mesçidi	Mesçidi
3 Bedesten	5 Çukur Medrese	7 Tatar Haci Mesçidi	9 Sezaı Evi

Justinian (527–565). After Arab incursions *c.* 1071 the region fell to the founder of the Rum Seljuk dynasty, Qutulmusch Sultan Süleyman I. In 1074 the castle was captured by the Danishmend Melik Ahmet Gazi. The Ottomans took the town temporarily in 1380 but only gained full control in the late 15th c. Before the days of the republic there was a large contingent of Armenian Christians in the town but they were expelled after 1923.

Sights

The complex around the Cumhuriyet Meydanı was built by Ali Paşa between 1565 and 1572 during the reign of Selim II. It consists of a mosque, a Koran school and a bath (to the east on the other side of the road). The prayer niche and heavenly staircase are made from yellow and blue marble. The founder's mausoleum lies to the east of the mosque in the cemetery garden.

Ali Paşa Külliyesi

The covered bazaar was built in the 15th/16th c. on the north side of the Sulu Sokak and modelled on similar bazaars in Aleppo and Bursa. It is currently being used as a store and is slowly decaying.

Bedesten

To the east of the Latifoğlu Konağı and behind the clock tower on the other side of the Tokat Çayı (immediately to the right of the small bridge), Bey Sokağı ascends into the old quarter. Over recent years the whole street has been fully restored. The houses are not museums but are occupied and in daily use – one as a school for the blind. In the upper section of the street on the right stands an original timber-framed mosque, Yolbaşı Camii (1922), which has an unusual minaret.
Some other fine 19th c. town houses can be seen in the Müftü Mahallesi (Madğağın Celel'in Evi) and Aksu Mahallesi (Maaz Gürkan Evi) quarters.

*Bey Sokağı

Tokat

Gazioğlu Caravanserai, still in use

Çukur Medrese	Also known as Yağıbaşan Medresesi, the theological school on the south side of Sulu Sokak dates from Danishmend times (1152) and was later restored by the Seljuk sultan Izzettin Kaikâ'ûs.
Ebulkasim Türbesi	Sometimes known as the Ali Tusi Türbesi, this mausoleum on the north side of the Sulu Sokak contains the remains of Ebulkasim Bin Ali El Tusi Kendisi, a Sultan vizier.
Garipler Camii	One of Tokat's oldest mosques, the Garipler Camii in the Pazarcık quarter of the town, was built in 1074 by the Danishmends.
°Gazioğlu İşhanı	Probably of Armenian origin, this caravanserai with a large inner courtyard was sometimes called Vergilioğlu Hanı. It was built in the 19th c. and is situated in Boya Hane Sokağı north of the Sulu Sokak, beneath the castle. It is now used as a centre for batik printing and may be visited.
Gök Medrese	In use now as an archaeological museum, this so-called Blue Koran School with a fine doorway was built between 1271 and 1277 as a hospital (Muhineddin Pervane Şifanesi) but was converted into a theological college in 1811. The restored building houses a small but significant collection of icons which date from the town's Armenian period. Archaeological finds and exhibits of ethnographic interest are on display in the former scholar's cells which surround the arcaded courtyard with its decoration of blue tiles.
Hacı Turhan Mescidi	The small mosque of Hacı Turhan (1478) can be found in a road which runs parallel to the Sulu Sokak opposite the Sultan Hamamı.
Halef Gazi Tekkesi	This small dervish monastery in a side alley north of the Meydan dates from 1292. Features of interest include a vaulted prayer room, two mausoleums and seven visitors' rooms.
Hatuniye Külliyesi	This complex of domed mosque (Meydan Camii) and medrese to the east of the Meydan was founded in 1485 by Sultan Bayazit II in honour of his

Decorative furniture in the old Ottoman house Latifoğlu Konağı

mother Gülbahar Hatun. The ancient columns and some other building materials were plundered from Commana Pontica.

This early Ottoman home is a masterpiece of Baroque architecture. The two-storey building has been restored and converted into a small museum. It is well worth a visit as much of the furniture in the kitchen, study, visitors' rooms with bath and toilet, bedroom, master's room and harem is original.

*Latifoğlu Konağı

This mausoleum (1314) is situated to the west of the road to Amasya just north of the Meydan.

Nureddin İbn Sentimur Türbesi

The "General's Bath" at the south-western end of Sulu Sokak is said to date from 1425 and it was thought to have been built by Yürgüc Paşa a vizier of Mehmet I.

Paşa Hamamı

This caravanserai situated in the district of İvaz Paşa on the Sulu Sokak was built about 1752. The main doorway is decorated with a relief of animals and cypresses. Only the façade side remains. A dwelling and a large, productive fruit orchard can be found inside.

Paşa Hanı

Tokat's clock tower was built in 1902. The tapering octagonal tower on a square base comprises four storeys separated by ledges.

Saat Kulesi

This mausoleum on Gazi Osman Paşa Caddesi is one of the most important structures of the Ilkhan period (1314).

Sentimur Türbesi

Situated just north of the Gök Medrese on the road to Amasya this dervish monastery and mausoleum date from Seljuk times (1292).

Sünbül Baba Zaviyesi

When precisely this caravanserai north of the Sulu Sokak was built is not known, but the open courtyard is similar to Ottoman style. The two-storey building has been faithfully restored.

Sulu Han

Tokat

Tokat Kalesi   The castle, remains of the wall and the 28 towers were built on Hittite
                    foundations probably during Byzantine times by the former inhabitants of
                    Commana Pontica when they moved to Tokat. It was captured by the
                    Danishmend Gümüştekin in 1074, extended during the Seljuk period and
                    has been restored on a number of occasions subsequently. The castle
                    contains a small mosque, store-rooms, a governor's residence and accom-
                    modation for soldiers. 362 steps hewn from the rock link the town with the
                    castle site.

*Voyvoda Hanı   Sometimes known as Taş Hanı, this two-storey caravanserai (1630/31)
                    situated by the Meydan near Gök Medrese consists of 32 rooms, a small
                    prayer room and an extensive inner courtyard.

Surroundings

Akça   10km/7 miles to the west of the regional centre of Erbaa (pop. 29,000), close
*Silahter Ömer   to the border of the neighbouring Amasya province and about 70km/43
Paşa Camii   miles north of Tokat lies the tiny village of Akça and its mosque (Silahter
                   Ömer Paşa Camii). The interior of this 18th c. mosque has been beautifully
                   painted. Some 15km/9 miles north-west of the town near the village of Kale,
                   the remains of a castle with some interesting underground passages can
                   be found. The site was formerly known as Magnopolis (Eupatoria).
                   The Pontic fortress of Kainokhorion (also Mahalic Kalesi) lies some
                   35km/22 miles north of Erbaa near the village of Ahretköy but it can only be
                   reached along some poor roads. It was here that Mithradetes VI Eupator
                   sought protection in 70 B.C. The most interesting sight in the Erbaa region is
                   without doubt Horoztepe, a short distance to the south. Valuable finds from
                   the Hittite era have been unearthed here including cult rattles, banners and
                   mother figures. These are now displayed in an Ankara museum.

Alanköy   20km/12 miles south of Tokat in the village of Alan stands a caravanserai
                   (1239) endowed by Mahperi Hatun, the mother of Kaichosrev II.

Almus   The more modern regional centre of Almus lies 36km/22 miles east of Tokat
                   beside the Almus dam, which forms a barrier across the Yeşilırmak. The
                   medieval castle of Akıncı Kalesi can be found to the north-east near the
                   village of Aksaray ("White Castle").

Camlıbel   Several older caravanserais lie beyond the Kızılnış Geçidi (1750m/5740ft)
                   and can be found near the village of Camlıbel in the Çekerek valley 60km/37
                   miles south of Tokat. They form part of a series of caravanserais which
                   were built c. 1238 on the trade route from Sivas to Amasya.

Dazya   Dazya Hanı at the southern edge of the Galut valley east of Turhal was built
                   in 1238/39 by Kaichosrev II. The remains can be found near the village
                   mosque.

Gümenek   10km/7 miles north-east of Tokat the scanty remains of Tokat's prede-
(Commana   cessor, Commana Pontica are visible. Excavated finds are housed in
Pontica)   Tokat's museum. On one hill lie the relics of a Pontic Ma-Artemis temple.
                   The town was the centre of a cult which revered the "Great Anatolian
                   Earth-mother" (Cybele), who was known here as Ma. The senior priests
                   ruled like princes, organising orgiastic feasts, fairs and temple prostitution,
                   but with the spread of Christianity the appeal of this type of worship waned.
                   The inhabitants moved away to settle in Dazimon (Tokat) and Commana
                   Pontica started to decay. All that remains is a tiny village whose name is a
                   distortion of the earlier settlement (Gümenek). Nearby a Seljuk bridge
                   dating from 1250 crosses the Yeşilırmak. It is said that it took only two days
                   to build.

Horostepe   On a steep hill near the village of Keslik about 9km/5 miles south of Tokat
                   the remains of a medieval citadel can be seen. It has been identified as

Dadasa, one of the fortresses built to defend the Pontic Empire. Two rock tombs and a rock tunnel have been preserved.

Niksar, a regional centre (pop. 29,000), lies 57km/35 miles north-east of Tokat on the slopes above the Niksar valley. In Roman times it was known as Neocaesarea and also as the Pontic kings' famous fortress Cabeira. Mithradates VI Eupator had a hunting lodge here. The Byzantines and Ottomans transformed the castle into its present structure. The remains stand above the lively old town on a rocky ledge. The castle complex consists of a medrese (1158) and a türbe. The single storey medrese with a self-contained hall was badly damaged in the earthquakes of 1939 and 1942. It was in Niksar in 71 B.C. that Lucullus won an important victory over the Pontic rulers. Seven years later the fortress fell to Pompey.
The town's prosperity returned after 1071 when the Danishmends established their court here. The founder of the dynasty Melik Gazi is buried in the town. In the district of Bengiler stands a mausoleum with the remains of Bedrettin Şah, one of Kılıç Arslan II's generals.

Niksar
(Neocaesarea)

Another interesting collection of tombstones contains that of a woman named Külah (1220), the Kırk Kızlar Türbesi with arabesque decorations and the Seljuk Akyapı Kümbeti which lies alongside the Melik Gazi Türbesi and dates from the 13th c. Another Seljuk caravanserai (1224) can be found in the town. Niksar was the birthplace of Gregorius Thaumaturgos (212). To the church fathers he was known as Pontic Gregorius and became the first bishop of Neocaesarea. In Christian times the town was designated as a metropolis and in 314 it was the venue for a Christian Council.
Some 2km/1¾ miles outside Niksar lie the Ayvas mineral water springs. The waters from this source are well known throughout Turkey and are said to be effective against kidney-, bladder- and gall-stones, arteriosclerosis and high blood pressure.

There are three interesting buildings in the small town of Pazar which is situated about 30km/19 miles west of Tokat: the Mahperi Hatun Hanı, its adjoining bridge over the Yeşilırmak at the eastern entrance to the town and a mosque.

*Pazar

The thermal baths of Çermik (50°C/122°F) are situated about 90km/56 miles north-east of Tokat and the water is used in the treatment of rheumatism and skin complaints. A little further up and to the west in a wooded depression lies Zimav Gölü (Zünnav Gölü), a lake with a plentiful supply of fish.

Reşadiye Çermik
Kaplıcası

The residents of Sulusaray (Water Castle) a tiny village on the Çekerek İrmağı, some 70km/43 miles south-west of Tokat, live on top of the remains of the ancient settlement of Sebastopolis. There is scarcely a building in the place which does not contain some stonework salvaged from the ruins. It is intended to re-settle the population on a new site so that the excavations which were started in 1987 can be completed in full. The finds show that the town was important from Hellenistic through to Byzantine times. Those excavations that have already taken place give a good overview of the town. It was encircled by a 17m/55ft high wall with semi-circular towers. In the north-east the remains of an ancient temple are visible. The floor is covered with multi-coloured marble tiles and its semi-circular east apse indicates that it later became a church. In the east the remains of a bathing complex with a stone basin and supporting pillars have been discovered. The water for the baths was channelled here from the sulphurous thermal spring about 3km/2 miles to the south-west. Some of the most interesting finds including lion statues, fragments of pillars and friezes, stelae with inscriptions and epitaphs are on display in an open-air museum.

Sulusaray
(Sebastopolis)

On a rock above the regional centre of Turhal (pop. 60,000) 45km/28 miles west of Tokat, stands the town's old fortress, which like other castles in the

Turhal

region were constructed to defend the Pontic kingdom. It was altered in 1068 and again in Ottoman times. Other interesting buildings in the town include the Ulu Cami (1453), the Kesikbaş Cami near the Yeşılırmak bridge, the Mehmet Dede Türbesi (1312) and the Ahi Yusuf Türbesi (1324).

*Yalınyazı
(Maşat Hüyük)

The settlement hill of Maşat Hüyük rises above the western side of Yalınyazı, a village some 30km/19 miles to the south of Zile. A Hittite prince built a palace here on a natural chalk crag. The remains of the town's brick wall and pithoi (storage jars) are still visible. Ask at the village police station for further information. At that time the town was an important frontier post against the Kashkas, marauding semi-nomads from Pontus who sometimes launched raids into Anatolia. Excavations in 1943 and 1973 unearthed some interesting clay tablets which revealed correspondence with the capital Hattuşaş. It would seem that the palace complex set on a hill, partially flattened by manual labour, consisted of a courtyard enclosed by a colonnade of pillars. About 40 rooms were grouped around the courtyard within a space of about 8000sq.m/9520sq.yd. From the three settlement levels within the site, archaeologists have deduced that the palace was burnt to the ground after an attack by Kashkas c. 1400 B.C. It was subsequently rebuilt and then destroyed again c. 1300 and was laid waste again at the end of the 13th c. In the 6th c. the place was finally abandoned. The village of Maşat is a gem in itself – a village typical of north-central Anatolia with half-timbered houses in an almost urban style.

Zile

Zile was an important frontier defence against the semi-nomadic Kashkas and owes its name to the Hittites. It achieved fame in 47 B.C. after the battle between Caesar and the Pontic king Pharnakes who had been installed as provincial governor of Pontus but soon rebelled against Roman rule. The battle raged for only five hours and Caesar quickly prevailed. His brief but now famous report to the Senate when he returned to Rome reflected the short time it had taken to see off his opponent: "Veni, vidi, vici!" ("I came, I saw, I conquered"). Zile is also well known for its handsome Pontic-style town houses. A number of historic buildings in the town are worth viewing. The remains of a Roman theatre are visible to the east of the citadel hill, together with some rock tombs. Two Ottoman baths, the Yeni Hamam and the Çifte Hamam, date from the 16th and 17th c. and the Hasan Ağa Medresesi was built in 1497. The Boyacı Hasan Ağa Camii with its stalactiform prayer niche dates from 1479 and the Şeyh Musa Fakih Türbesi is also very old – with 1106 or 1305 given as possible dates.

Trabzon

North coast (Black Sea)
Province: Trabzon
Altitude: 0–36m/0–120ft
Population: 150,000

Situation and Importance

The port town and provincial capital of Trabzon (ancient Trapezunt) is the most important town on the eastern Black Sea coast and the third largest of the Turkish Black Sea towns after Samsun and Zonguldak. It has a technical university. The coastal scenery is particularly beautiful with the steeply scarped peaks of the Eastern Pontic Mountains bordering a narrow coastal strip. The highest peak Tatos Dağı (3937m/12,917ft) lies 100km/60 miles to the east of Trabzon. The climate in winter is mild but often oppressively close in summer – ideal conditions for a luxuriant subtropical vegetation. No other part of Turkey enjoys similar conditions. The road from Trabzon over the Gümüşhane pass (Zigana pass 2030m/6660ft) through the Pontic Mountains to the Eastern Anatolian Plain has been a major factor in the development of the port.

History

Trabzon took its Greek name of Trapezous from the shape of its flat-topped acropolis (Greek "trapeza", table). According to Xenophon in the 5th c. it

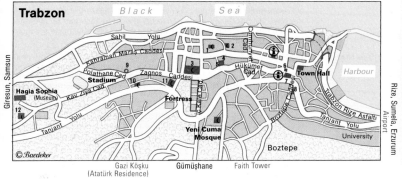

1 Pazar Kapı Mosque
2 Bazaar Mosque
3 Orttahisar (Fatih) Mosque
  (Panagia Chrysokephalos)

4 St Basil's Church
  (Büyük Ayvasıl Kilise)
5 St Anne's Church
  (Küçük Ayvasıl Kilise)

6 Atatürk Monument
7 Air terminal
  (airport buses)
8 Bus station

9 Fountain
10 Pir Ahmet Mausoleum
11 Gülbahar Hatun Mosque
12 Yeni Fatih Mosque

was founded perhaps as early as the 8th c. B.C. by settlers from the Greek colony of Sinope and it soon developed into a flourishing city. It lay at the end of a caravan route which was used to carry Persian goods to the Black Sea for onward transport to the Mediterranean. This was also the route by which Xenophon and his Ten Thousand found their way back to Trapezous after serving in Cyrus the Younger's campaign against Artaxerxes II. During the war between King Mithradetes Eupator of Pontus and the Roman general Lucullus (c. 70 B.C.) the city remained neutral and was spared the ravages of war. It remained a free city after Rome gained control of Asia Minor. In A.D. 260 Trapezous was captured by the Ostrogoths and in Byzantine times it was the seat of a provincial governor but Seljuk attempts to take the town did not succeed. After the capture of Constantinople by the Crusaders in 1204 Alexius Comnenus V proclaimed himself emperor and made Trapezous capital of the reduced Greek Empire of the Comneni. After the re-establishment of the Byzantine Empire in Constantinople the emperor granted Trapezous its independence. In 1461 it fell to the Ottomans under Sultan Mehmet II.

In recent decades Trabzon has shared in the general economic upturn of eastern Turkey and the harbour has been extended to enable it to handle vessels with a deeper draught.

Sights

Trabzon consists of three districts built on low hill ridges – the commercial district or İskander Pass immediately west of the harbour, the Cumhuriyet quarter adjoining it to the north-west and an old quarter of irregular streets and wooden houses further west.

Town centre

The triple-aisled St Anne's Church is situated in the İskander Pass quarter ("Küçük Ayvasıl Kilise", small Armenian Church). Nearby is St Basil's Church ("Büyük Ayvasıl Kilise", large Armenian Church). Both churches date from the 8th c.

Armenian churches

The Cumhuriyet quarter begins beyond the Tabakhane Deresi (fine views from the viaduct) at the old citadel hill. The most notable building in this district is the Orthisar Camii or Fatih Camii, originally a 13th c. Byzantine church known as the Panagia Chrysokephalos (Church of the Virgin with the Golden Head), a name which derives from the gilded dome above the

*Ortahisar Mosque

473

crossing. It has a Latin cross plan with a nave flanked by lower aisles and cut by the transept. The galleries over the aisles which are marked off from the nave by triforia were the gynaecea, the areas reserved for women. Outside the main doorway stand a fountain and a marble basin for ritual washing (şadirvan).

*Hagia Sophia

Some 3km/2 miles west of the harbour charmingly situated on a hill near the coast is the Church of Hagia Sophia (Ayasofya), probably built by Emperor Alexius Comnenus immediately after his arrival in Trabzon from Constantinople in 1204. It was converted into a mosque in Ottoman times and is now a museum.

Like other Byzantine churches in Trabzon, Hagia Sophia has a cruciform plan with a nave flanked by aisles and a transept with wall-paintings. Over the crossing is a dome. Along the base of the south doorway is a frieze depicting the story of Adam in a style which shows a clear Eastern influence.

Boztepe

On the north side of the 244m/800ft Boztepe hill (fine views) stands the monastic Church of Panagia Theoskepastos, built in the 13th c. on the site of an ancient temple (ancient frescos).

Surroundings

Hezit llys

The former Monastery of St George in Peristera can be reached from the village of Esiroğlu (Yesiroğlu in the Maçka valley) which lies 28km/17 miles south of Trabzon. A local guide is advisable and the walk will take at least three hours. This monastery and look-out post for Trabzon was built in the reign of Justinian (532). A famous collection of manuscripts was destroyed by a fire in 1906 and in 1923 the monks had to abandon the monastery.

Kaymaklı

About 5km/3 miles south of Trabzon a steep track off the main Erzurum road leads to the Monastery of Kaymaklı, where Armenian monks lived

Hagio Sophia in Trabzon

Sumela Monastery

until 1923. The two-storey building with an arcaded façade stands along-side the ruins of a bell-tower. In the vicinity two chapels can be found: one (1424) is now used as a hay barn and the other (1622) contains the remains of some paintings.

Kücük Konak, a village 46km/29 miles south of Trabzon, is the starting point for a 10km/7 mile walk to the Vazelon Monastery (St John of Vazelon) which is set on a rock high above the Değirmendere valley. It is one of the most important Pontic monasteries and was used by Justinian as a look-out post to warn of attacks from hostile mountain tribes. The monastery was linked with Trapezunt by a cobbled road (King's Road). The main building which has been altered many times stands in front of a cave. The nearby Chapel of St John (John the Baptist) which was built by Manuel III in 1410 contains the remains of some paintings.

Kiremitli

Some 70km/45 miles south of Trabzon in the Altındere Vadisi Milli Parkı (Gülden Valley National Park) the Meryam Ana Manastiri (St Mary's Mon-astery) clings to a rock high above the Altındere. During the summer months visitors are admitted each day at 9am, 11am, 2pm and 4pm. There are two ways to get there. One very steep track leads directly up from the car park, while another longer, more leisurely route initially follows the valley upwards, but then at the first bend to the left a path runs back almost parallel to the monastery. The old Greek name for the monastery was Hagia Maria tou Mela (St Mary from the Black Mountains). 67 steps lead to the inner courtyard well back behind the entrance doorway. Directly above the precipice are the main living quarters and the old library while beneath a rock face several other monastery buildings huddle around the courtyard including the painted cave chapel. The monastery in its present form with cells for 75 monks, a refectory, visitors' house and fountain (miracle-working water) dates from 1860.

**Sumela Monastery

According to legend, the monastery was founded in the 5th c. by two Greek monks (Barnabas and Sophronios) who had intended it to house an icon (Mary) painted by St Luke. They claim the site, a spring on the rock face appeared to them in a dream. When the monastery was destroyed in the 12th c. this icon was said to have survived all attempts to destroy it.

The Sumela Monastery remained a popular place of pilgrimage until the 19th c. In 1923 the monks abandoned the burnt out monastery and buried the relics of the cross and St Luke's icon in the monastery's Chapel of St Barbara. The monk's successors now live some 100km/70 miles west of Salonica in Greece. In 1931 the icon, the relics of the cross and Abbot Fazelon's four-volumed gospel book (644) written on gazelle skins were taken to the Benaki Museum in Athens.

The main road from Trabzon to Erzurum and Erzincan, runs south-west through the Eastern Pontic Mountains and climbs the 2030m/6660ft Zigana pass. It was perhaps on a mound near here (about an hour's walk) that Xenophon and his Ten Thousand caught their first glimpses of the Black Sea ("Thalatta!").

Zigana pass

Troy   B 4

West coast (Aegean Sea)
Province: Çanakkale
Altitude: 8–40m/25–130ft
Region: Hisarlık

Troy – originally Troia, Turkish Hisarlık (settlement hill with castle), ancient Greek Ilios or Ilion, Latin Ilium – is the excavated site of the chief town of the ancient Troad, made famous by Homer's "Iliad" and occupies a 40m/130ft high hill a little to the south of the point where the Dardanelles merges with the Aegean. This wedge-shaped foothill lies in an area of high ground

Situation and
**Importance

Troy

Nine periods in the
settlement-hill of Hisarlık

Ilios
Ilion
Ilium
Truva

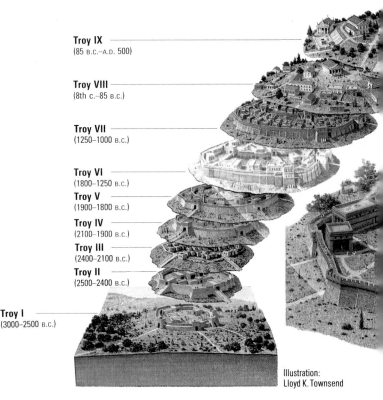

Troy IX
(85 B.C.–A.D. 500)

Troy VIII
(8th c.–85 B.C.)

Troy VII
(1250–1000 B.C.)

Troy VI
(1800–1250 B.C.)

Troy V
(1900–1800 B.C.)

Troy IV
(2100–1900 B.C.)

Troy III
(2400–2100 B.C.)

Troy II
(2500–2400 B.C.)

Troy I
(3000–2500 B.C.)

Illustration:
Lloyd K. Townsend

which broadens out towards the east and rises steeply to the alluvial plain
of the Küçük Menderes (the Scamander of the Greeks) and the Dümrek Çayı
(ancient Simois).

The hill rising out of the surrounding plain offered a good strategic site for a
fortress, far enough away from the sea to be safe from surprise attacks but
near enough to be able to keep a watch on the Dardanelles. The acropolis
was certainly the only building on the hill with the rest of the town extending over the flat terrain below. This location contributed to the settlement's
early prosperity but also exposed it to repeated attacks and frequent destruction. Consequently there are no buildings left standing on the site; all
that the visitor will see are the excavators' trenches and the settlement
levels they have unearthed. What is visible is extraordinarily impressive
both as a revelation of history reaching back 5000 years and as a demon-
stration of what and how archaeologists are able to unravel the mysteries
of the past.

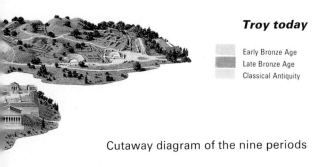

Troy today

- Early Bronze Age
- Late Bronze Age
- Classical Antiquity

Cutaway diagram of the nine periods

Homeric Ilios

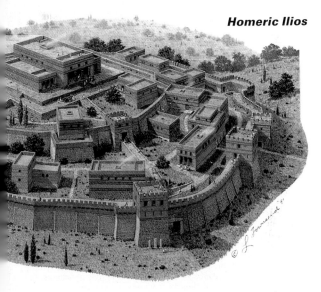

To get to this rather remote site, take a bus or car to Çanakkale from İstanbul via Tekirdağ and the Dardanelles ferry (380km/235 miles) or via Bursa, Bandırma (580km/360 miles); from Çanakkale by minibus or long-distance bus to Edremit/İzmir, alight at the fork to Troy and take a taxi (5km/3 miles).

The journey

Troy I to Troy IX

Excavations have shown that there was a fortified settlement of large, long houses on the rocky hill of Hisarlık some 5000 years ago.

Troy I
10 levels
(3000–2500 B.C.)

About the middle of the 3rd millennium the Troy I settlement was extended towards the south-west. An area of 8000sq.m/9500sq.yd was surrounded by a fortified wall which was rebuilt three times. To the south-west stood a huge entrance of stone blocks. In the centre of the circuit of walls stood the palace of the ruler. In the upper section of Troy II (i.e. the "Burnt Town")

Troy II
7 levels
(2500–2400 B.C.)

477

Schliemann found what he called the Treasure of Priam (gold and silver vessels, gold jewellery, etc.). This treasure has been dated to around 2400 B.C. and is linked with the fire. Schliemann was convinced until shortly before his death that this was Homer's Troy.

Troy III–V
13 levels
(2400–1800 B.C.)

The fire mentioned above which destroyed Troy II left a 2m/6½ft thick layer of rubble and ashes. Later settlers dwelt in primitive huts, living from hunting and little is known about them. Some vessels with depictions of human faces and thin goblets with opposing handles have come to light. The last layer here indicates that this settlement was also destroyed by fire.

Troy VI
8 levels
"Homer's Troy"
(1800–1250 B.C.)

It is the new town's huge walls of large smooth-faced irregular blocks which form the most impressive of Troy's remains. In the years between the 15th and 13th c. B.C., the town enjoyed its greatest period of prosperity. The area (200×300m/220×330yd) was surrounded by a wall once 10m/33ft high. Inside the walls the foundations of a number of palaces have been preserved. No trace has yet been found of a lower town in the plain below. The cemetery which contains the funerary urns with the ashes of the dead is situated some 500m/550yd to the south.

Troy VIIa
(c. 1250–1180 B.C.)

The town seems to have been rebuilt soon after an earthquake. The inhabitants' way of life remained unchanged. A century later the town was destroyed again.

Troy VIIb
(c. 1180–1000 B.C.)

After the destruction of Troy VIIa the site was occupied by settlers from the Balkans. It is thought that the last people to settle here during this period were the Dardanians who gave their name to the Dardanelles.

Troy VIII
(8th c.–85 B.C.)

After an interruption the site became a Greek colony. c. 730 B.C. Homer described the events of the Trojan War which is dated at sometime in the 13th c. B.C. Since then Troy has been regarded as a "sacred site".
In 652 B.C. the Cimmerians after defeating King Gyges of Lydia, moved into Troad but without displacing the Greeks. In 547 B.C. King Cyrus of Persia incorporated Troy into the Persian satrapy of Phrygia.
In 334 B.C. Alexander the Great crossed the Dardanelles and took Troy where he offered a sacrifice to Athene Ilios. About 300 B.C. Lysimachos built a harbour for the town at the mouth of the Scamander and replaced the old Temple of Athena by a splendid new one in marble. At least by the time of this construction work, the main buildings from the periods of Troy VII and Troy VI on the surface of the hill had been levelled. Between A.D. 278 and 270 the town was held by the Galatians, a Celtic people.

Troy IX
(85 B.C. to
A.D. 500)

Whereas the importance of Troy had hitherto depended on its Temple of Athena, which was ranked equal in status to the Temple of Artemis, it now enjoyed Roman favour as the city of Aeneas – Rome seeing itself as the political heir to Troy.
There was now a period of great building activity.
Until the incursion of the Goths about A.D. 262 Troy flourished and this prosperity continued into Early Byzantine times. Constantine the Great even contemplated making Troy his capital. With the recognition of Christianity as the State religion, however, the old temples fell into ruin and Troy's glory rapidly faded. In the Middle Ages Troy still had a fortress and until the 13th c. it was the see of a bishop, but after its conquest by the Ottomans in 1306 the town rapidly decayed. The ruins were used by the Turks as a source of building stone for their homes and tomb stelae. Grass grew over the site and Troy fell into oblivion.

History of the
excavations

The first Westerner to visit Troy seems to have been a French government official named Pierre Belon (1547). In 1610 an Englishman named George Sandys looked for the ruins of Troy. Between 1781 and 1791 Count Choiseul-Gouffier and a French archaeologist named Lechevalier explored the

Troad and identified Homer's Troy on the hill of Balıdağ at Pınarbaşı, 8km/5 miles southeast of Hisarlık. Helmuth von Moltke, then a captain in the Prussian army also saw Pınarbaşı as the site of Troy. From 1859 onwards Frank Calvert an Englishman who owned part of the hill of Hisarlık carried out excavations there. In 1868 Heinrich Schliemann (1822–90) a German businessman who had made a fortune in St Petersburg came to Troad to look for Troy. After a brief exploratory excavation on Pınarbaşı which yielded only a thin layer of rubble he turned his attention to Hisarlık. Thereafter in a series of excavation campaigns between 1870 and 1890 he was proved correct and felt able to defend his case against the passionately held views of other archaeologists. Until 1882, it is true, his

Trojan Horse

excavations showed little concern with exact observation or the conservation of remains. Much evidence was destroyed for ever, particularly by the broad trench which he drove across the site from north to south. Thereafter, with the collaboration of the German archaeologist Wilhelm Dörpfeld (1853–1940), the work was carried out much more scientifically.

Fate intervened to prevent Schliemann from reaping the full rewards of his excavations. After discovering on June 14th 1873 the so-called "Treasure of Priam" which was shipped to Germany in dramatic circumstances (recently discovered in Moscow's Pushkin Museum), he proclaimed Troy II to be the city of Priam. It was only his 1890 excavations and Dörpfeld's excavations of 1893–94 after Schliemann's death which suggested that Troy VI should be assigned to the rather uncertain Mycenaean period.

Excavation was continued in 1932–38 by Carl W. Blegen of Cincinatti University. According to legend Troy fell after Greek soldiers emerged from within a hollow horse dedicated to the earthquake god Poseidon; consequently scholars such as Schachermeyr have identified Troy VI as the city of Priam. Other researchers regard Troy VIIa as the more likely level. Since 1988 the German archaeologist Professor Manfred Korfmann from Tübingen University has been continuing the work of Schliemann, Dörpfeld and Blegen. Excavations have been continuing on Beşiktepe and in Beşik Bay west of Troy near Yeniköy, already identified as a port for Troy (1982–87). More recently the area south of the hill, the lower town, has been under the archaeologists' spotlight.

After an interval of 50 years research in and around Troy has been restarted under the direction of Professor Manfred Korfmann from the Institute of Prehistory at the University of Tübingen. The latest findings are published in the journal "Studia Troica". The official guide to the excavations is available at the site and in İstanbul's Archaeological Museum.

Information

*Tour of the site (see Plans on pages 480 and 481)

Visitors to the site follow a recommended route which comprises twelve information points. Information Point 1 is the starting point of the tour, from where a flight of steps leads to Information Point 2 on the wall which encompasses the area of the Roman Temple.

Information Point 1

This point offers a view over the whole site. The East Wall, a part of the hill's defences in Troy VI, consisted of an embanked substructure some 6m/20ft high, 5m/16ft thick and exposed on the outside. On top of this, 1m/40in. above the ground-level of the settlement, was a vertical superstructure of flat rectangular stones, almost regularly dressed. The surface has been rebuilt with clay bricks.

Information Point 2

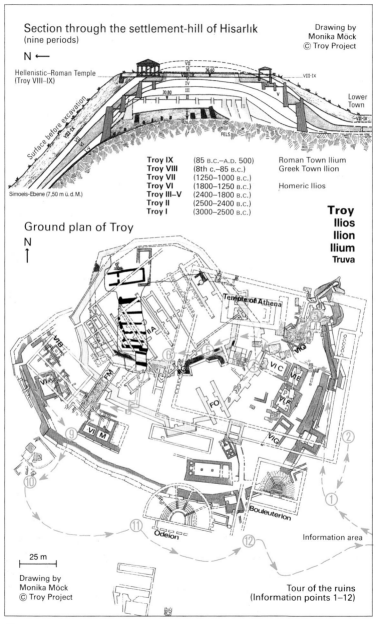

Section through the settlement-hill of Hisarlık
(nine periods)

N ←

Drawing by
Monika Möck
© Troy Project

Hellenistic–Roman Temple
(Troy VIII–IX)

Surface before excavation

Lower
Town

Simoeis-Ebene (7,50 m ü.d.M.)

Troy IX (85 B.C.–A.D. 500)	Roman Town Ilium
Troy VIII (8th c.–85 B.C.)	Greek Town Ilion
Troy VII (1250–1000 B.C.)	
Troy VI (1800–1250 B.C.)	Homeric Ilios
Troy III–V (2400–1800 B.C.)	
Troy II (2500–2400 B.C.)	**Troy**
Troy I (3000–2500 B.C.)	**Ilios**

Ilion
Ilium
Truva

Ground plan of Troy

N ↑

Temple of Athena

Bouleuterion

Odeion

Information area

25 m

Drawing by
Monika Möck
© Troy Project

Tour of the ruins
(Information points 1–12)

The South-East Tower was originally two-storeyed. One of the characteristic features of the wall, the vertical offsets, can be seen in this area.
They are spaced out at regular 9–10m/30–33ft intervals.

Beyond the wall and the tower, large houses of the Mycenaean settlement
are visible: first House VI G, then to the north-east away from the wall
House VI F and further north Houses VI E and VI C. The houses of Troy VI
were built round the hill on a number of concentric terraces with almost
certainly the king's palace on the highest point.
Building VI F had pillars suggesting a second floor. Passing through the
gate it will be clear that House VI E was particularly well built. It needs to be
remembered that at the time these grandiose buildings were built, iron or
steel had not been discovered. The quality of the stonemasonry is therefore
all the more impressive.

The wall projecting from the East Gate is overlaid with a Roman wall of
dressed stone which bore the columns at the east end of the temple. The
defensive wall from the south helped to form a curving passage some
10m/33ft long and 1.80m/6ft wide.

South-East Tower

Mycenaean
houses
Troy VI

East Gate

Aerial view of the ruins of the Castle of Troy with marked points 1–12.
Photo: H. G. Jansen – Project Troia

Troy

From one of more than 20 limestone altars which surrounded the Temple of Athena, it is possible to see the massive tower of the North-East Gate in the Mycenaean walls.

Information Point 3
North-East Bastion

The 8m/26ft high substructure of fine dressed stone with a receding embankment once bore a clay brick superstructure giving the gate a commanding height. Within the gate is a square well hewn from the rock and descending to a considerable depth. It remained in use for a long period. In the Troy VIII period a flight of steps was constructed on the north side of the tower leading down to another well outside the tower. The great retaining wall to the south-east dates from the Roman period. In the background, the auditorium of the Greek and Roman theatre can be seen with the Dümrek Çayı plain (Simois) beyond.

Information Point 4
Altars and Temple of Athena

Only the altars and mounds give any indication of the existence of the Temple of Athena. It has to be imagined lying to the west and north of the altars. The magnificent new temple which had been promised by Alexander the Great was built by Lysimachos but little survives. Columns, parts of the coffered ceiling, as well as other marble fragments from the temple built by Augustus, "strayed" into the levels of Troy II during the course of the excavations.

These fragments were gathered together there by the researchers so that they could discover more information on the construction of the temple.

View

From these heights there is a fine view over the Dardanelles, European Turkey and the Menderes (Skamander) river plain. In the foreground lie remains of the "Burnt Town" (Troy II), which Schliemann believed was the city of Priam.

Information Point 5
Fortified wall

At Information Point 5 stands a cross-section of Troy I's fortifications with a tower-like projection behind which the then South Gate was situated. The gateway was only 2m/6ft wide. Troy I was built directly on to the rock floor and layers 4m/13ft deep would suggest that this period endured for many years (c. 3000 to 2500 B.C.). Troy I covered the smallest surface area and in the course of time this settlement spread out to the south.

Further finds from Troy I can be found at Information Point 7. Immediately above the tower stands a small propylon from Troy III. Its massive 3m/10ft long and 1.10m/3½ft wide stone threshold is still in place.

Information Point 6
Palace

The propylon was the entrance to a group of buildings in the centre of Troy II citadel which were probably occupied by the city's ruler. The dwellings of the ruler and his family led off a gravelled courtyard. The main building directly opposite the propylon known as the Megaron consisted of a porch and a main hall with a hearth in the middle. The structure of the walls (1.44m/4ft 9in.) can be clearly seen here, but the height cannot be ascertained. It would have had a flat roof with an opening over the hearth. To the right was a smaller building with a porch, main room and rear chamber. On either side were buildings of a similar type opening off the courtyard but they were all destroyed by fire, leaving a 2m/6½ft thick layer of stone and ash (Schliemann's "Burnt Town"). Many interesting finds have been unearthed in this level (see Information Point 7).

The Troy II era (c. 2500 B.C.) was characterised by major cultural and technological changes: a stratified society as witnessed by these buildings with the forerunner to the Greek temple ("megaron", porch and main room), the mixture of copper and tin to make bronze as well as the invention of the potter's wheel. So impressed was Schliemann by the astonishing finds, he believed that he had found the "Treasure of Priam" but he was wrong by at least 1000 years.

Northern Schliemann excavations

The great north–south trench which Schliemann drove across the site passes between the first and second groups of Troy II houses and it is possible to see house walls and parts of ancient settlements, made from stones bound together with earth mortar. The restored supporting wall on the east side which is made from air-dried clay bricks marks the limit of the long, spacious buildings. A wooden bridge crossing the three ring walls of Troy II leads past the base of the ramp to Information Point 8.

Information Point 7
Schliemann's trench

From the corner of House M6 A a stone ramp to the Gate FM can be seen at a lower level. It leads from a lower settlement area (discovered in 1992) up to the inner citadel hill. The pre-historic citadel of Troy II which was destroyed by fire was at first thought by Schliemann to be the citadel of Priam. It had a circumference of some 300m/330yd and is now almost completely exposed. The layers of rubble range from a thickness of 1m/40in. to 2m/80in.

Information Point 8
Prehistoric settlement

The citadel's ring of walls stretches out on both sides of the ramp. It consists of a substructure 1m/3ft to 4m/13ft high made from roughly hewn limestone and earth mortar and has recently been restored (1992). It now resembles the condition it was in before the first excavations about 100 years earlier.

Ramp

Some 6m/20ft north-west of the ramp Schliemann found the so-called "Treasure of Priam" built into a cavity in the brick superstructure of the ring wall. It later found its way into the Museum of Prehistory in Berlin but disappeared at the end of the Second World War. It was recently discovered in the Pushkin Museum in Moscow. Similar finds of jewellery, vessels, weapons and tools made of gold, silver, electron (an alloy of gold and silver) and bronze have been made elsewhere in the Troy II level ("Burnt Town") and also in the layer of fire debris in Troy III.
The remains of Troy III, IV, V are of little to interest the ordinary visitor. The

Treasure of Priam

Troy

Recently restored stone ramp

citadel's principal monuments from Troy VI have been preserved and of Troy VII some wall remains survive, chiefly those between the citadel wall of Troy VI and the first terrace walls. The two walls belong to quite different periods. First the walls and houses of Troy VI were repaired by simple country-dwellers who still used "Mycenaean" pottery. They built their own smaller houses (similar in plan to Troy VI) against the inside of the citadel walls.

Facing the northern corner of VI A, the remains of similar but larger houses (VI B) have been found. It is at this point that the "Mycenaean" wall which at one time had encircled the whole citadel (about 540m/590yd in length) ceases, although about two-thirds of the full length still remains. At a much lower level the huge foundations of the western corner of the citadel are visible, but its north side and a part of the west wall have disappeared.

**Information
Point 9**
Kitchen building
Palace VI M

The preserved remains of Troy VII's wall are visible on the way to Information Point 9 above the fortifications for Troy VI. Inside the ring wall stands the impressive 27m/30yd long supporting wall for House VI M which certainly formed a part of Troy VI's citadel.

This large building of the Mycenaean period on a 4m/13ft high terrace is known as the Kitchen Building on the basis of the large pithois (storage vessels) and other objects found in one of the rooms. A flight of steps inside led to a second floor.

**Information
Point 10**
Shrine

The shrine altars in the south-west show that soon after the Greek settlement and continuing well into the Roman phase, cult rituals took place outside the wall of "Sacred Ilios". The latest excavations reveal that the marble altar higher up dates from the time of Augustus, when the whole site of Ilios was renovated. A tribune and more shrines are situated beyond. The large supporting wall and the older altars lower down all originated in Hellenistic times (Troy VII).

At the edge of the former agora stood the odeion a small theatre for musical performances and a little further east the bouleuterion, the Roman town hall. The odeion consists of a semi-circular orchestra which is separated from the skene or the stage building. The rows of seating are divided into wedge-shaped blocks. Some of the fragments belonging to the odeion are gathered together nearby.

Information Point 11
Odeion and bouleuterion

The bouleuterion about 70m/75yd away was built above Troy VI's fortified wall. The interior was surrounded by a wall on all sides, enabling the city fathers to conduct their business uninterrupted.

The South Gate was probably the main entrance to the town, but only the paved roadway to the right of the tower (1.30m/50in. wide) remains. A covered water channel can be seen in the middle. To the left behind the South Tower, a pillar marks the location of the "Pillar House", which with a surface area of 27×12.5m/29×13yd was one of the largest houses of Troy VI. Set in front of the tower are two vertical stones, no doubt serving some cult purpose.

Information Point 12
South Gate

The lower town (not open to visitors) situated on the plateau to the south below the citadel hill was, according to the latest excavations, inhabited towards the end of the 2nd millennium B.C. (Troy VI/VII). Traces of an enclosing wall have been found and some historians have recently suggested that this settlement and its citadel constituted an important seat of power and a commercial centre, but excavations are in progress at the moment. The area of the lower town on the plateau to the south and east of the hill has so far been little explored, but a small township was established here in the Hellenistic period and then expanded in Roman times, particularly in the reign of Augustus. It was planned and laid out in traditional style with a ring wall which totalled 3.5km/2 miles in length and was 2.50m/8ft thick. The large theatre to the north-east belonged to this settlement.

Lower town

Tunceli

P 4

Eastern Anatolia
Province: Tunceli
Altitude: 1020m/3345ft
Population: 25,000

See warning page 7

In one of the most underdeveloped but also one of the most attractive regions of eastern Turkey lies the provincial town of Tunceli, a settlement on the southern edge of an impressive mountainous region. Town names which have frequently changed point to years of political upheavals.

Hemmed in by the paths of the Peri Suyu in the east, the Firat Nehri to the west and the north and the Murat Nehri in the south, all sources of the Euphrates, the triangular region thus created which forms the "wild" Tunceli highlands is characterised by two very different types of mountains. The northern Munzur range of steep limestone peaks with deep folds, a part of the Eastern Taurus, creates a wall which separates the major seismic fault-line of northern Anatolia from the Tunceli highlands proper to the south. The climate in this natural barrier of peaks over 3000m/9850ft high is harsh with severe winters and cool summers, but the wooded slopes at the heart of eastern Anatolia, nevertheless, make ideal walking country.

* The highlands of Tunceli

In the southern highlands the winter is milder. It is here that the mainly Kurdish speaking population, densely spread throughout a region on average 2000m/6500ft above sea level in a network of farms and hamlets, expresses its culture. The farmers make the most of the plentiful rainfall in this region, which has been settled from early times. As well as Kurds and at one time Armenians, another minority, the Alevite Zazas or Kızılbaş (red heads, on account of the traditional red headgear) have predominated in this disputed territory.

485

Tunceli

Tunceli became the provincial capital in 1950 and like the earlier village of Mamiki, it has little of interest to offer visitors. The region acquired notoriety as a result of local squabbles among the predominantly Kurdish population and these led increasingly to changes in the regional administration. In 1938 under Seyyid Riza the inhabitants of Dersim (now Hozat 50km/31 miles east of Tunceli) used terrorism to protest against military conscription and taxation demands. After atrocities on both sides, enforced resettlement followed and the region is now dotted with abandoned villages, some of which go back to the "resettlement" of Armenians in 1915/16. The main victims, however, were the Zaza ethnic minority, known throughout the land as "devil worshippers" – Alevites who had resided in the Tunceli region in large numbers since at least the 16th c.

Alevites

In the history of Islam, the Alevite sect can be traced back to a 12th c. Persian-Shiite movement known as the Messianic Revolution. It was named after its leader Ali, one of Mohammed's sons-in-law who was murdered in a mosque. The followers of Ali (often Kurds) were subject to systematic persecution by the Ottoman Empire and were forced to keep their beliefs secret and stopped worshipping at the mosque.

With time some questionable practices came to replace traditional Islamic principles, leading sometimes to a complete abandonment of the faith. The Alevites more relaxed stance towards the Islamic taboos such as women wearing the veil, alcohol, fasting and ceremonial rites encouraged the dissemination of wild rumours and untruths. It was claimed the Alevites took part in orgies, worshipped the devil and had breath smelling like animals. For most Sunni Turks this was sufficient justification to discriminate against the Alevites. The latter became generally identified with the Kurds, who are now more likely to express their dissidence by associating with the political left and often seem to be the victims of police violence.

Surroundings

Çemişkezek

The small town of Çemişkezek can be reached via reasonable roads and lies about 110km/70 miles west of Tunceli by the Tahar Çayı. The dervish cells hewn from the rocks and the Ulu Cami are worth visiting.

Mazgirt

Mazgirt is a small town dominated by a medieval castle about 30km/19 miles south-east of Tunceli. The Etli Sultan Türbesi and the adjoining mosque are of interest. It was in Mazgirt that a column displaying some Assyrian cuneiform writing was found. The thermal baths at Bağin, formerly Castrum Palios, to the east of Mazgirt can be reached by making a detour via Palu and Karakoçan (105km/65 miles) or taking the poor road through Darıkent (35km/22 miles).

Nazimiye

The Dereova Şelalesi close to Dereova (Hakis) and the Karagöl Şelalesi are both impressive waterfalls and can be found near Nazimiye, about 35km/22 miles north-east of Tunceli.

Ovacık

The original place-name for Ovacık (small valley) was Maraşalçakmak (marshal's pipe). In 1878 the town became a regional centre, but it was abandoned in 1916. In 1925 it was re-settled and in 1938 the village of Ovacık became an administrative centre for the region.

**Munzur Vadisi Milli Parkı

The green Ovacık valley lies at the eastern edge of the Munzur Vadisi Milli National Park and is an ideal starting point for mountain walkers and is attractive to fishermen. Like the whole mountain range, the Munzur National Park consists of tracts of untouched land. The chain of mountains has many peaks over 3000m/10,000ft and extends for 100km/62 miles but it is nevertheless good walking territory as the valley is already 1500–2000m/5000–6500ft above sea level.

The ruined Castle of Pertek

This wet region contains a number of small circular hollows (cirques) which were formed from the mountain glaciers (Ice Age). Water gushed from springs, often in the form of waterfalls, down into the deep valleys. The best time to visit the park is from the middle of June to the end of September, but there are no tourist facilities available yet. Ask the National Park and Forestry Authorities for further information.

Pertek

The small town of Pertek dominated by its medieval castle ruins can be reached either directly from Tunceli (about 45km/28 miles to the south-west) or north from Elazığ by ferry across the Keban Dam Lake (16km/10 miles by road to the landing stage).
An interesting 18th c. caravanserai can be seen in the town and at the foot of the castle hill two old mosques: Bay Sunğur Camii (1560) and Çelebi Ali Camii.
A medieval fortification known as Pertek Kalesi (1367) crowns a hill on an island in the middle of the Keban Lake. With access by boat it was built to guard what was once a crossing point of the Euphrates (Murat Nehri) and was mentioned by the German traveller von Moltke who journeyed by raft from Palu to the south in 1838.

Ürgüp

See Cappadocia

Urfa

See Şanlıurfa

Eastern Anatolia   See warning page 7
Province: Van
Altitude: 1750m/5740ft. Population: 154,000

Van Gölü   Inland lake
Province: Van, Bitlis. Altitude: 1646m/5400ft
Area: 3765sq.km/1453sq.miles
Depth: about 400m/1300ft (exact depth not known)

Measuring 80km/50 miles long, 40km/25 miles wide and with an area of
3765sq.km/1453sq.miles Lake Van is the largest lake in Turkey and seven
times bigger than Lake Geneva. Its catchment area extends over
16,000sq.km/6080sq.miles and its deepest point has not yet been established. It is believed to be about 400m/1300ft, but even close to the bank
depths of more than 250m/820ft have been measured. The water is rich in
natural sodas (13%) and consequently there is little underwater life. Lake
Van has no outflow as it is surrounded on all sides by mountains: to the
south by the Eastern Taurus Bitlis massif (İhtiyarşahap Dağları
3634m/11,919ft, Çadır Dağı or Artos 3537m/11,600ft), to the east by single
peaks such as the Çomaklıbaba Dağı (2602m/8534ft) or Erkdağı or Erekdağı
(3204m/10,500ft), to the west and north largely by volcanic mountains such
as Süphan Dağı (4058m/13,300ft), Nemrut Dağı (2828m/9275ft) and Ala
Dağlar (3510m/11,500ft). It is known that in earlier times Lake Van was a
freshwater lake which was drained by the Murat Nehri, one of the sources
of the Euphrates.
In the Quaternary Period, the era between the two Ice Ages, volcanic rock
(andesite) from the Nemrut Dağı blocked the outlet near Tatvan in the
so-called Rahva plain. Thereafter, on account of the surrounding mountains, there was no way out for the lake's water even at its highest level
(80m/260ft higher than now) during the third Pleistocene Era. The Assyrians called Lake Van the "Upper Lake" or "Sea of the Nairi lands" (Surging
Sea). Three times a day a ferry for cars and lorries crosses the lake from Van
İskelesi to Tatvan. Departure times depend on the rail service from Tatvan
to Van which also uses the ferry. The line then continues to the Iranian
border (mainly goods traffic, journey time six hours, buses about two
hours).

Van   The earliest excavations in Van began in 1827 and were important in
Excavations   unravelling the mysteries of Urartian civilisation and language. İstanbul
University conducted further excavations in 1959/1960 and established a
"Centre for Historical and Archaeological Research of Van" in 1967.

History   About 840 B.C. the Urartian ruler Sardur I built a citadel and the town of
Tushpa, the capital of his empire, on the rocky outcrop. To the west of the
modern town this later became Van fortress (Van Kalesi). The region was
inhabited in the 3rd millennium B.C. by the Hurrians, regarded as the
ancestors of the Urartians and also as the first tribe to create a political and
cultural entity in eastern Anatolia. Assyrians attacked the east of the Hurrian lands, forcing the natives to emigrate to the north and into the Van
region where they formed separate small kingdoms. The oldest Urartian
kingdom, called "Bianli" (people of Bian), had two capitals under King
Aramu in the still unidentified places of Sugunia and later Arzashgun
(probably to the south and north-west of Lake Van respectively). Sardur I is
regarded as the founder of the empire when he established a new capital of
Tushpa (Van Kalesi) by Lake Van in 840 B.C. The kingdom of Bian was later of
course to become Van.

Even when the Urartian Empire (Biani Empire) was at its greatest, it had no
access to the sea. Under Ishpuini (830–810 B.C.) new buildings were erected

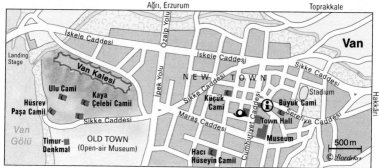

Tatvan, Bitlis

in Tushpa and the town enjoyed a measure of prosperity. His son Menua, other children and grandchildren concerned themselves with irrigating the farmland and then with building a defensive system based on warning beacons located at a number of fortresses within sight of each other. Ishpuini's grandson Sardur II was responsible for creating cultural centres such as the great open-air Temple of Tushpa, but in 743 B.C., territory in northern Syria was lost to the Assyrians. Further defeats to the Assyrians continued under his son Rusa I (735–714 B.C.) and were warning signs to the Urartian Empire. Nomadic threats from steppe tribes such as the Cimmerians and later the Scythians heralded the end of the empire, finally brought to an end by the Medes in 590 B.C.

Before the Armenian king Tigranes the Great (95–54 B.C.) extended Van as the centre of his empire, the fortress belonged to the Persian satrapy of Armenia and then after Alexander the Great to the kingdom of Pontus. The Armenian Reshtuni dynasty lasted until an Arab raid in 634. In 1071 Van fell to the Marvanid dynasty and then to the Karakoyun Oğulları ("Black Rams"). The ensuing dispute between the Ottomans and the Persians ended in favour of the Ottomans but the old Ottoman town beneath the citadel was destroyed when Russian troops withdrew in 1917.

More recent history

Sights

In a side street of the modern town to the east of Cumhuriyet Caddesi lies Van Museum, which despite its limited size is well worth a visit. Most exhibits, some on display in the front garden, were unearthed at Urartian sites. On the first floor is an ethnographic section.

Archaeological Museum

The view from the citadel rock over the ruined old town is impressive. The town walls which can easily be identified extended as far as Lake Van. The area destroyed during the Russian troops' withdrawal was eventually abandoned in favour of the new town to the east. The site is now an open-air museum and part of the national park designated by UNESCO as the "Citadel and Old Town of Van". Restoration work and excavations are currently in progress as the old town contains many important monuments from the Islamic period despite all the destruction.

*Old town

In the old town area two Armenian churches, Surb Paulus (c. 960) and Surb Petrus (badly damaged) are secreted close together behind the remains of the so-called Twin Church.

Çifte Kilise

489

Van Castle dominates the surrounding landscape

Çifte Kümbet

The Twin Mausoleums in the old cemetery to the south outside the old town are situated opposite the former Orta Kapı. The two domed tombstones with columned supports are reminiscent of nomadic tent life and date from the 18th c. although the tradition of open türbes continues. Both mausoleums commemorate governors of Van province: Demirpaşa (1789) lies in the eastern tomb, while Ahmet Paşa (1796) lies in the other one. A walk through the historic cemetery can prove difficult but it contains old sarcophagi and gravestones with Kufic inscriptions and embellishments.

Hüsrev Paşa Camii (Kurşunlu Cami)

To the south-west close to the old city wall and Orta Kapı (Middle Gate) stands the still well-maintained single-domed mosque which was endowed by Koca Hüsrev Paşa. According to the inscription above the doorway, it was built in 1567. Evliya Çelebi reported that the dome was covered with lead plates in the 17th c., hence its other name of "Kurşunlu Cami" or "Lead Mosque". The walls of the prayer room were tiled to a height of 2m/6½ft in the 16th c. It also suffered badly when the Russian troops were withdrawn but it was faithfully restored in 1968.

Clearly other buildings formed a part of the complex including a bath mentioned by Katip Çelebi in the 17th c. None of the remains, however, can be discerned. By the east wall a simple but elegant octagonal mausoleum contains the remains of the founder. The roof made from stone blocks tapers to a cone and the door and window surrounds are decorated with patterns of rosettes, palms and geometrical figures.

Kaya Çelebi Camii

To the east of the Kurşunlu Cami stands the mosque which was endowed in the 16th c. by Kaya Çelebizade Koçi Bey. The huge dome above the prayer room is dotted with small window openings and supporting projections. The pillars which flank the window openings are deliberately simple and the porch topped by a number of domes extends into the main hall.

Also known as Tebriz Kapi Camii, this mosque stands close to the earlier city gate to Tabriz in the eastern quarter of the old town. It was probably built in the 13th and 14th c. and also housed a Koran school. The minaret made from bricks arranged in a diamond pattern is decorated with a geometric design of dark-blue tiles.

Kızıl Cami

The Grand Mosque, praised by Evliya Çelebi in the 17th c., is situated some way to the west almost directly beneath the citadel's rock wall. It was probably built in the 11th or 12th c. but was rebuilt between 1389 and 1400. The dome collapsed during an earthquake in 1648 and the mosque was further damaged between 1915 and 1917 during the Russian occupation. Despite some initial work to clear away the rubble at the beginning of the 1970s, only the shell and a part of the minaret remain of the once impressively decorated prayer room. The Seljuk Kiliç Arslan built a 1000 step stairway leading up to the citadel 90m/295ft higher up but this is now closed.

Ulu Cami

The increasing flow of tourists, the growing cost of running repairs and the need to protect the famous fortress at Van have forced the Turkish authorities to make changes to the open site designated by UNESCO as the "Historic National Park, Citadel and Old Town of Van".

**Van Kalesi

The Urartian citadel only occupied the western part of the hill. Broad, sometimes unfinished trenches in the rock were cut by the Urartians to the east and west of the fortress to secure the flanks. The step-like recesses with their supporting wall ("bin merdivenler", thousand steps or "seytan medivenleri", devil's steps) which are still visible help to give some idea of the rock's huge proportions. The castle was extended by the Seljuks and Ottomans to its current dimensions. The less secure, but not so steep north side was strengthened at the same time by several enormous limestone walls built on stone foundations and with round towers which can still be recognised. In 1387 the Mongol Timur-Leng badly damaged the citadel after a 20 day siege. Both Akkoyun rulers and the Ottomans made significant attempts to restore it and also added at the same time, close to the hill, a water tower, various store-rooms, a barracks, a mosque with a minaret still in situ and a medrese.

Tushpa

The vertical descent on the south front of the citadel rock contains various rock burial chambers of Urartian rulers. To the south beneath the centre of the castle, stone steps lead from the summit plateau to the burial chamber of King Sardur, the builder and to the rock tomb of King Menua. The tombs which are all built to the same plan consist of an entrance hall which gives access to the plundered burial chambers alongside or behind one another. The remarkable rectangular cavities in the walls with holes in the middle probably accommodated so-called "knob-tiles" (zigati) which were attached as decorations. On the south-east wall of the rock face lies another burial chamber with a small door. Inside, a 1m/3ft high platform with 78 cavities runs along the wall. They were built to hold the urns of the deceased and the holes helped to keep the containers upright.

*Rock tombs

The most interesting of the tombs can be reached from the north-west peak of the citadel. The rock faces on the south-west side, before the entrance to the burial chamber of King Ardisti I, are covered with Urartian cuneiform texts describing the deeds of the deceased. These texts are known as the "Horhor Inscriptions".
On an inaccessible middle section of the south rock another cuneiform inscription can be found in a rectangular rock niche. It dates from the Persian king Xerxes and is written in three languages: ancient Persian, Elamitic and Babylonian.

Two large niches in the rock each with hemispherical vaulting, a broad platform, a sacrificial altar and cuneiform inscriptions mark the tomb of King Sardur II at the north-east end of the citadel rock. This sacred site is

Analı Kız

known to the native population as "Analı Kız" (Daughter with Mother). Every Thursday the local people visit the spot, bring sacrificial offerings and request the fulfilment of secret wishes by sliding down the existing "blood channels" to appease the sacrificial victim. This sacred site, also known in local parlance as the "Treasure Gate", came into being under Sardur II in honour of the principal god Haldi.

*Sardur Burcu
(Madır Burcu)

On the north-eastern side under the citadel rock the remains of the impressive harbour walls acquired the name "Sardur's Castle" in ignorance of their true function. At Tushpa, as at several other places around Lake Van, Sardur had a solid mole built of black basalt blocks which were quarried from Alniunu near Gümüsdere 17km/10 miles to the south.

Surroundings

**Ahtamar Adası

The Armenian church ruins are probably the most popular place for tourists in the Van region. They lie on the largest of Lake Van's islands Ahtamar Adası, situated 40km/25 miles west of Van and 2.5km/1½ miles from the south shores of the lake. Boats leave from a jetty directly opposite the island. Little remains of this once important Armenian town.

The remains of a monastery complex are still visible in the vicinity of the church which the monk Manuel founded between 915 and 921. It is thought that here stood the royal palace apparently with gilded domes and throne and the last seat of the rulers of Vaspuragan. Also said to have been lavishly decorated with gold were the relief carvings on the external walls of the old monastery church, which as the last but still very interesting relic dominates the island. Clearly the figures at one time had jewels for at least the eyes as particles of a glass-based adhesive have been found. In contrast to the white-washed frescos inside the four-conch principal Church of the

Fishing in Lake Van

Holy Cross which date from 921 and are the oldest known examples of Armenian frescos, the reliefs on the external wall (restored in 1963) of the 1316 annexe (chapel) provide the real attraction. Situated to the north-east, this wall was extended to the west with a porch in 1763 and by a bell-tower to the south in 1900. The reliefs beneath the roof ledge depict such well-known themes as Adam and Eve, the Angels, David and Goliath, Abraham and Isaac, Jonah and the Whale, Jesus the Child, Christ, King Gagik with a model of the church, human faces amid vines, animal figures, the heads of the Evangelists – all intertwined with more animals and vines. An Armenian cemetery with some interesting gravestones can be found in the vicinity of the church.

To find the "Red Monastery" of Kamrak Vank follow the main road 65km/ **Altinsaç**
40 miles west of Van and then fork off 7km/4 miles west of Gevaş to the village of Göründü (10km/6 miles). The monastery lies a further three hours' walk beyond Göründü in the mountains. A local guide is recommended. The site can also be reached from the village of Altinsaç on the southern shores of Lake Van. The two preserved cruciform churches with simple domes probably date from around the 12th c.

On the road to Özalp, near the village of Dereüstü some 16km/10 miles **Anzaf Kalesi**
north-east of Van, the remains of the upper and lower Anzaf castles can be seen. In Urartian times both castles controlled the trade route to Persia. The lower square fortress with four thick semi-circular towers on the north side of the road was built by King Ishpuini, while the upper castle 800m/½ mile to the south-east, also with Cyclopean walls, was the work of his son Menua. The high castle walls and some typically Urartian stone markings can still be seen.

A little to the north-west of Müküs at almost 1900m/6200ft above sea level **Aparank Manastiri**
stands the Kurdish village of Aparank (Vatas). Allow ten hours for the journey with guide and mule. Of the five Armenian churches and a 17th c.

An isolated cemetery by the seashore

monastery in the village, the oldest building is the Church of St John (943–952) with a central dome and three apses. In 1664 another church was built to serve as the main church for the community, but it is now used as a barn.

Wschny

More Armenian church ruins can be seen in the Narlıca Deresi between Bahçesaray and Çatak at the village of Wschny. The Church of St Mary (Church of the Mother of God) with its central dome, one long main transept and a short one is of interest as are the unusual conical roof above a round drum and the former village church nearby.

Çaldıran

The small garrison town of Çaldıran which lies 120km/75 miles north-east of Van is dominated by the ruins of an Urartian fortress. The place is situated on the north-western edge of a wide plain where in 1514 Selim I defeated the Safavid ruler Ismael I.

Çarpanak Adası

North-west of Van and about 100 minutes away by boat the island of Çarpanak lies opposite the Cape of Çitören. Here too can be found the remains of an Armenian church. It was initially built as a square structure with a central dome but later converted to a long triple-naved building. Light and dark volcanic rock from Ahlat was used in its construction. The main portal on the narrow side is particularly impressive displaying decorations in geometric, cruciform and stalactiform patterns.

*Çavuştepe

About 24km/15 miles south-east of Van in the Hosap Suyu valley the impressive remains of the Urartian castle and seat of King Sardur II (764–735 B.C.) stand on an isolated ridge. These remains, including the walls and the palace complex with an Urartian "king's toilet", give visitors some notion of Urartian architectural style, although many structures were affected by alterations made in the Middle Ages. The site also offers a superb view over the Gürpınar plain.

The site consists of an upper and lower castle within which lie the remains of a Temple of Chaldi (with porch, column pedestal and an inscription about the artificial irrigation of the surrounding plains), citadel walls, 7th c. B.C. workshops, store-rooms and cellar with pithois (storage vessels), cisterns, kitchen, palace with throne room, harem and colonnaded halls. Şardurihinili was destroyed by the Scythians in the 7th c.

Deveboynu Yarımadası

The remains of three Armenian monasteries can be found close to the shores of the Deveboynu peninsula about 70km/43 miles west of Van. The site can best be reached by boat from the jetty opposite the island of Ahtamar. At the tip of the peninsula stands the Monastery of the Resurrec-

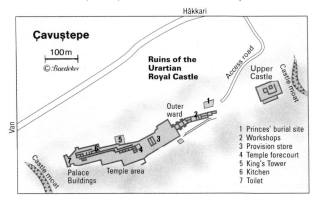

Çavuştepe

100m
© Baedeker

Hâkkari

Ruins of the Urartian Royal Castle

Access road

Upper Castle

Castle moat

Outer ward

Van

Castle moat

Palace Buildings   Temple area

1 Princes' burial site
2 Workshops
3 Provision store
4 Temple forecourt
5 King's Tower
6 Kitchen
7 Toilet

tion with the remains of frescos which date from before the 13th c. Further inland is the 10th c. Monastery of St Mary (Monastery of the Mother of God) and nearby the badly damaged Monastery of the Miracle of Chakhur. At a secluded spot some distance further inland near the village of Mezir (about 3 hours away) is the Monastery of St Thomas where the holy relics of St Thomas are said to have been kept. As well as a number of monastery buildings, the Church of St Thomas stands within the walled site.

The sacred rock niche of Hazine Piri (also known as Hazine Kapısı) can be found near the village of Elmalık some 12km/7 miles south of Van. It is thought to be the oldest sacred niche of this type in the Van region.
The Urartian castle known as Zivistan Kalesi is also to be found in the village. It consists of an upper and lower fortress. The upper site has been destroyed, but considerable remains of the lower site can still be seen.

Elmalık

The regional centre of Erciş (pop. 37,000) lies a good 115km/70 miles north of Van. Known to be well-established as early as the 11th c., in Armenian times it was called Agantz and was one of the most important towns of that period. In 996 David of Taik annexed Erciş and Manzikert (Malazkirt) to the Armenian province of Karin (Erzurum), in 1055 it fell to the Seljuks and in the 14th c. to the Turkmans, whose princes resided here from time to time. Around 1840, a catastrophic flood occurred when the level of Lake Van rose forcing the inhabitants around the lake (Agantz) to move to new homes, the villages of Plohur, Gazımbağ and Çelebibağ. Some of the old town is still under water or else in the marshy terrain near Eski Erciş Kalesi.

Erciş

One remaining feature of the old town is a simple domed tomb, the Yar Ali Türbesi (also known as the Hargin Türbesi or Kadem Hatun Paşa Türbesi). It almost certainly dates from the days of the Karakoyun dynasty and can be found in an historic cemetery about 3km/2 miles south-east of the town on the road to Van. Most of the other tombs have been destroyed.

The remains of an Urartian harbour made from black basalt blocks can be seen about 20km/12 miles east of Erciş close to the point where the River Deliçay flows into Lake Van. It is thought that a castle once stood here but no traces remain.

Deliçay

About 40km/25 miles off the eastern shores of Lake Van lies a small island where the ruins of a medieval Armenian monastery can be found. Opposite the mainland a little further south stand the ruins of the Arab castle of Amik Kalesi.

Gadir Adası (Adır Adası)

The regional centre of Gevaş is situated on the road to Tatvan almost 40km/25 miles south-west of Van. The remains of Vastabkalesi, an Armenian castle can be seen on the edge of the town, while in the town itself to the south-east of the citadel stands the extensive İzdisar Camii.

**Gevaş
*Domed tomb**

The mosque of the provincial governor of Van, İzzeddin Şir Beş, has the rooms of an old Koran school in the forecourt. To the north of the town on the road to Tatvan lies an Islamic cemetery with a polygonal mausoleum and some other interesting tombstones and pyramid-shaped sarcophagi. The richly decorated domed tomb with a pyramid roof dates from 1358.

On the slopes to the east side of Gümüşdere, a town about 17km/10 miles south of Van, lies an open-air workshop used by the stonemasons of Alniunu, an Urartian town whose name can be found inscribed on the harbour mole at Tushpa. Like the Hittite quarries at Yesemek (see İslahiye), examples of half-worked stone blocks can be seen. They were clearly intended as the pedestals for sacred sites and were used on the citadel at Tushpa (Van). Unfortunately a lime kiln in the vicinity destroyed a number of the stone blocks.

Gümüşdere

The village of Güzelsu lies beneath the Hoşap Kalesi about 60km/37 miles south-east of Van on the way to Başkale. It was built in 1643 by the local

***Hoşap**

Van

Horsemen in the wasteland

Kurdish prince Sarı Süleyman on the ruins of its 14th c. Seljuk predecessor. The massive construction on and around a steep-sided rock was used in antiquity as a watchtower to survey the military road from Van along the Çuh pass to northern Persia.

The complex of several storeys contains three baths, two mosques, a medrese, a well, cisterns, prison and 360 rooms spread over several floors – all of which can be reached by passing through an impressive entrance hall with inscriptions and a lion relief and mounting some steep steps. The citadel which is itself surrounded by huge stone walls is reinforced by a town wall with equally thick walls and four towers. The wall surrounded the town of Hoşap to the north, where today some of the houses are made from sun-dried bricks. A Kurdish-Ottoman bridge over the Hoşap Suyu links the castle to the old military road, which at this point passes through a narrow gap in the rock. The Kurdish fortress Mahmudiye Kalesi takes its name from the local dynasty.

Kalecik

About 15km/9 miles to the north of Van on the road to Erciş lies the village of Kalecik, where the ruins of an Urartian castle known today as Kalecik Kalesi can be seen on a small rock. It was built by King Ishpuini to protect Tushpa against attacks from the north.

Kavenli and Kavuncu

Two Urartian castles known as Kavenli and Kavuncu are situated 6km/4 miles and 7km/4½ miles respectively east of Van on the western slopes of the Erek Dağı. The function of these two fortresses was primarily to protect the Urartian capital, but they were also used as stores for agricultural produce.

Muradiye

Despite its remote location the region around the small town of Muradiye 90km/56 miles north-east of Van can offer visitors both historical interest and some delightful landscapes. At the north end of the settlement, the ruins of the former seat of a Kurdish bey (1840) stand on a rock. The castle was built by the Urartians to protect the plain. In the 9th c. an Arab colony (Bergri) grew up here after Arab incursions but it was not mentioned as a town in its own right until 1021. The Persian shah Ismail I rebuilt the fortress at the turn of the 15th/16th c.

The area to the north of Muradiye is characterised by a wide volcanic expanse of basalt. Through a narrow gorge, water breaks out of the volcanic ridge of Gönderme (Gönderme Boğazı) at Caldıran. It then rushes down the valley over the volcanic rock until 8km/5 miles north of Muradiye near the village of Degerbilir it plunges into a deep, narrow gorge as a wide and impressive waterfall.
*Bendimahi Şelalesi

The remains of a well-preserved fortress wall sometimes as high as 8m/26ft and flanking fortified towers rise above the village of Uluşar which is situated 20km/12 miles south-east of Muradiye.
Körzüt Kalesi

Little is left of the monastery of Narek Vank near the village of Narek (now known as Yemişlik) about 60km/37 miles south-west of Van. The magnificent complex once stood on a hill roughly to the south of the road to Tatvan in the upper Narek Deresi but it has been dismantled and many examples of plundered building materials can be seen in the village houses.
Narek

Drive south-west along the coast road from Van to Bitlis via Gümüşdere and fork to the east after 31km/19 miles beyond the bridge over the Hoşap Suyu (Dönemeç Çayı) and follow the Hoşap Suyu upstream. On the left hand side of the road the line of a large irrigation canal becomes clearly visible along the slope of one of the western Erek Dağı foothills. This canal stretches 51km/32 miles and is known as the Semiramis Canal (Şamran Kanalı), although it is mistakenly attributed to the Assyrian king Semiramis. It was in fact built by the Urartian king Menua to irrigate the plain of Van and the town of Tushpa.
Şamran Kanalı

In various places blocks with cuneiform inscriptions concerning the builder can be found. Constructed c. 800 B.C. in the area around Van, the canal runs between the old road and the new road to Gümüşdere and then flows into the Kurubaş Deresi. Numerous water channels which today run through the plain to the south of Van old town are a part of this irrigation system and the canal is still supplied with water from springs in the Hoşap valley.

German (1899) and American (1937) scientists carried out investigations on Tilkittepe near the village of Ayaspınar not far from Gümüşdere and came across a settlement which about 7000 years ago had been used as a trading station for obsidian. This volcanic rock was hewn from the Nemrut Dağı, processed and sold to Mesopotamia.
Tilkittepe

On the southern foothills of the Zimzim massif (Akkerpi Dağı) on the north side of Van lies the other later capital of the Urartian Empire. Known as Rusahinili, it was founded by Rusa II. The king needed to secure the water supply to the new town, so he constructed a dam to create the so-called "Broad Lake" (Geniş Göl) in the Erek Dağı and the Sıhke ponds beneath Rusahinili. After some minor work, both still serve the purpose for which they were intended – the irrigation of orchards, vineyards and vegetable gardens. Excavations have revealed painted sun-dried bricks of foundation walls, a Temple of Chaldi and a palace as well as store-rooms, castle remains, cisterns, floor mosaics and cuneiform texts. Most finds are displayed in museums in Van, Ankara and İstanbul.
Toprakkale

The Armenian monastery site of Varak Vank which the Patriarch Anania Moks I founded between 943 and 967 can be found on the south-west slopes of the Şuşanis Dağı near the village of Yedikilise (seven churches) and 15km/9 miles south-east of Van. It consists of buildings from five different periods including a Church of St Mary as well as three chapels. Most of the buildings have been incorporated into a farmhouse or are badly
*Yedikilise

decayed. In the 10th c. Yedikilise, which also included the churches of Surb Paulos and Surb Petros, was the seat of the Patriarch of Moks, accommodated up to 300 monks and is also supposed to have been in possession of a Relic of the Cross.

The best preserved building is the cruciform domed Church of St Mary which displays some fine decorations and 11th c. paintings. It was built before the Armenian king Senekerim exchanged territory with Byzantium. In the 17th c. a square front church with eight shallow domes (frescos and decorations) was added, followed by a pillared porch. On the north and south side, three chapels adjoin the main church.

*Yedisalkım

About 76km/47 miles south-east of Van on the Boset Tepesi (3684m/12,080ft) a gorge about 9km/5 mile long and 100–150m/110–160yd deep cuts through rock at a height of 2500m/8200ft. Over 60 caves have been found in the area of the gorge and paintings, some of dancing female figures, have been discovered in four of them. One of the caves is known as the Kızların Mağarası (Maiden's Cave). Other animal paintings include depictions of mountain goats and deer. Altogether there are about 150 drawings but many are covered in soot. In prehistoric times the caves were obviously used for pagan rites. The flat-topped Başet Dağı (3684m/12,080ft) towers above the west of the valley. The mountain is regarded as sacred by the local population and certain cults still conduct their rituals here.

Van Gölü · Lake Van

See Van

Xanthos

See Fethiye

Yozgat
K 4

Central Anatolia
Province: Yozgat
Altitude: 1310m/4267ft
Population: 51,000

Situation

In nomadic societies early settlements in the form of semi-permanent villages often proved to be the first step towards a fixed, often much bigger settlement. It was in this way that in 1746 the Turkman leader Ahmet Paşa of the Çapanoğulları family founded a village and his residence amid the summer pastures of Ekred-i-Lek on the high plains of the Bozok Yaylası. Although the residence burnt down in 1822, with the arrival of Greek and Armenian settlers Ahmet Paşa's son Süleyman Bey quickly transformed the village into a thriving centre. By 1836 a town had become established on the site of the modern provincial capital of Yozgat. Some of the building material for the town had come from nearby Tavium. By 1858 the population had grown to 15,000 and in the locality at that time the Turkman Çapanoğulları dynasty was more important than the Ottoman rulers. In view of the town's relatively short history there are few historical remains.

Sights

The ethnographic collection at Yozgat was housed in the 19th c. Nizamoğlu Palace. The Çapanoğlu Mustafa Paşa Camii was founded in 1779 by Mustafa Çapanoğlu, extended in 1795 and restored in 1900. Directly adjacent to the Mustafa Paşa Camii stands the Süleyman Paşa Camii, another endowed mosque of the Çapanoğlu dynasty dating from the 18th c. The Clock Tower (Saat Kulesi) documents the special position of the town in the 19th c. The Tunusoğlu Hanı is an Ottoman caravanserai.

In the middle of the otherwise desolate steppe landscape, natural wood-land flourishes to the south of Yozgat on the Çingıraklı Tepesi (1676m/5497ft) and it has become a recreation area. A 7km/4 mile long access road winds its way up to a small, long-established hotel. The wood-land has been designated as a national park and is home for an extensive range of flora and fauna.

Yozgat Çamlığı Milli Parkı

Surroundings

The Sümrük Sivrisi settlement hill near the village of Alişar about 60km/ 37 miles south-east of Yozgat and 20km/12 miles south of Sorgun was excavated by American archaeologists between 1927 and 1932. Evidence was found of habitation here from the 4th millennium B.C. to Phrygian times and finds included a Chalcolithic village with rectangular houses, which had been walled in during the Early Bronze Age (2500 B.C.), an Assyrian trading centre which met a violent end (cuneiform texts) and perhaps the Hittite provincial town of Ankuva.
Remains of a Phrygian fortress have been found in the most recent settle-ment level. Very little of interest can be seen on the site as all the important finds have been taken to the Ethnographic Museum or the Hittite Museum in Ankara.

Alişar

At the south-west corner of a hilly ridge 10km/7 miles south-west of Sorgun and 35km/22 miles east of Yozgat, the remains of a Late Hittite fortress have been excavated. It is not clear whether it was built by the native Luvers as a defence against the Phrygians or by the Phrygians themselves. The site is called Kaykavus Harabesi or Kaykavus Kalesi and is situated on the west side near the village of Şahmuratlı.

Kerkenes

Zonguldak   G 2

Western Black Sea region
Province: Zonguldak
Altitude: 5m/16ft
Population: 120,000

The Zonguldak mountains 800m/2620ft high and 50km/32 miles long are situated to the north-east of the lower Pontic mountains of Bolu and Akçakoca and extend along the coast from the mouth of the ancient Filyos (Yenice İrmağı). Seams of coal rise to the surface and an important coal-mining industry has grown up in the deep mountain valleys. The absence of work-place safety regulations means that Zonguldak mine counts as one of the most dangerous mines in the world. The last serious mining disaster occurred in March 1992.
Until 1850 Zonguldak was a small village but the coal fields, the steelworks in neighbouring Karabük (with a rail link for transporting coal) and Karade-niz Ereğli and the resulting expansion of the original 1899 harbour have transformed the place into the second-largest town on the Black Sea coast. Nestling in the steep wooded areas to the west and east of the town are the mining communities of Kozlu, Kilimli and Çatalağzi. The name Zonguldak derives from "zongalık" meaning reeded marshland. The small port of Sandaraca stood here in antiquity. In the Hittite times it was known as Palla.

Situation

The coastal region to the east of Zonguldak beyond the Yenice İrmağı offers fine sandy beaches with Karpuz and İnkum (İnkumu) 70km/43 miles to the east worth a special mention. Other excellent beaches can be found near Kuzlu (e.g. İliksu) 18km/11 miles west of the town.

Surroundings

*Amasra

This coastal resort with an old town is located in a picturesque spot on a peninsula 60km/37 miles north-east of Zonguldak. Established in the 6th c. B.C. by Milesian colonists during the 3rd c. B.C. renamed Amastris after a niece of Darius III of Persia. She became the regent of Herakleia Pontike (Karadeniz Ereğlisi) upon her marriage to Lysimachos the king of Thrace. It is said that she planned to lay out hanging gardens here like those of Semiramis in Babylon.

After its destruction, it was rebuilt by the Byzantines, but in the 14th c. it fell to Genoese trading companies who extended the citadel. Mehmet II (the Conqueror) acquired Amastris for the Ottomans in 1485. A local museum displays finds of historical interest.

The town is a popular seaside resort for nearby city dwellers and the preferred home of wealthy families connected with the Zonguldak mining industry. More recently the steelworks has also grown in importance. Little remains of the old town apart from the ruins of a Roman theatre and baths. A castle on a narrow strip of land protected the old town and peninsula, which is still linked to an offshore island by a Roman bridge and an ancient tunnel. Within the fortress site near the West Gate stands the Kilise Mescidi, a small church mosque which served as the chapel for the castle commander. Parts of an ancient cemetery extend above the western beaches (Büyük Liman; 500m/550yd) and below what was once the acropolis.

In some fields about 2km/1¼ miles inland stands a well-preserved Roman store-house over 100m/110yd long.

Bartın

The busy administrative town of Bartın (pop. 25,000) on the Kocağrmak 70km/43 miles east of Zonguldak is the former Parthenios. Traditional wooden houses help to give the town a pleasant atmosphere.

To the north-west near the towns of İnkum, Mugadar and Güzelcihisar (Hisar), other attractive beaches can be found but unfortunately some are not easy to reach.

Çatalağazı

The longest caves in Turkey are situated just a few kilometres to the south-west of Çatalağazı, a small coastal town about 20km/12 miles east of Trabzon. The entrance, Kızılelma Mağarası, can be found by the border with the neighbouring district of Gelik, while the northern exit 10km/6 miles to the north is known as Cumayanı-Mağarası. Because of the long underground siphon within the watercourse, it is not possible to pass through the cave network from one end to the other.

Near the exit the cave opens out into a large cavern with travertine terraces and basins similar to those at Pamukkale. The cavern is open to the public.

Çayğrköy

The village of Çayğr (pop. 1648 in 1985) lies 10km/6 miles past the village of Güdüllü on the road from Çaycuma to Zonguldak. The 1km/½ mile long Çayğrköy Mağarası can be found close to the village. The cave was surveyed by a Swedish explorer in 1951 and there are plans to open it up to the public.

Karadeniz Ereğlisi

Situated around 50km/30 miles to the south-west of Zonguldak, at first sight there seems to be little of interest for visitors to the coal port and industrial town of Ereğlisi (formerly Herakleia Pontike; pop. 55,000) with steelworks and coalfields to the south and dominated by a ruined Genoese fortress. The old town nestling below, however, has much to commend it. About 558 B.C. the town was founded by colonists from Megara. For a short time it came under Lysimachos and then became a part of the Pontic Empire. The Romans destroyed the town in the war with Mithradates as the townsfolk took sides against the Roman army. It was rebuilt as a Roman garrison. Until 1922 Karadeniz was almost entirely Greek. Few ancient remains can be seen today.

The Caves of Hercules lie north-west of Ereğli in the valley of ancient
Acheron about 100m/110yd upstream. According to Xenophon in his "Anabasis", it was here that Hercules, hero and demigod, descended into the
underworld and brought out Cerberus the three-headed dog which
guarded the entrance to Hades.

Plundered ancient stones can be seen at the entrance to the cave. The
valley which leads to the mouth of the cave is known in local parlance as the
"Valley of the Infidels". This description harks back to Byzantine times
when a Christian resurrection cult used the caves and a floor mosaic in the
first cave provides some evidence of their existence. The actual entrance to
the underworld was believed to be in the second cave as a narrow staircase
leads down from there into a dark chamber 50m/55yd wide. There is an
underwater lake and also traces of painting and other workings.

A 1km/½ mile long cave known as Gökgöl Mağarası can be found near the
mining town of Üzülmez just a few kilometres south-east of Zonguldak. An
underground river flows through the cave and it is not yet open to the
public.

Practical Information

Accommodation

See Camping, Hotels, Youth Accommodation

Air Transport

The national airline, Türk Hava Yollan (THY; Turkish Airlines), İstanbul Airlines and a large number of foreign carriers operate international flights in and out of Turkey (see Getting to Turkey).

Turkey's main airport is İstanbul's Atatürk Airport at Yeşilköy, about 25km/15 miles out of town; tel. (0–212) 573 29 20, 248 26 31, 246 40 17 and 247 13 38. There is a bus service at regular intervals between the airport and the THY terminal in the city centre (Şişhane, Meşrutiyet Caddesi 26).

The following places also have international airports:
Adana: Şakirpaşa; tel. (0–322) 435 91 86 and 4 35 92 06
Ankara: Esenboğa; tel. (0–312) 312 60 26 and 312 28 20/427 (international flights), tel. (0–312) 398 101 00 (internal flights)
Antalya; tel. (0–242) 330 32 21 and 330 32 30
Dalaman; tel. (0–252) 692 58 99
İzmir: Adnan Menderes Airport; tel. (0–232) 251 11 79 and 251 26 26/10 78–11 00 (international flights); tel. (0–232) 251 25 25 (internal flights). Trains run relatively cheaply from the airport every hour into İzmir's Alsan-çak station, near the large hotels.
Trabzon; tel. (0–462) 325 67 38

THY and THT, the domestic airline, also operate internal flights to: Batman, Bursa, Denizli, Diyarbakır, Elazığ, Erzurum, Kars, Kayseri, Konya, Malatya, Muş, Samsun, Sinop, Şanlıurfa and Van.

Airlines

Offices abroad:
American Express Tower Suite 1602, 388 George St., NSW 2000, Sydney, Australia; tel. 2332 105–2211 711
c/o Aer Lingus, Dublin Airport, Dublin, Eire; tel. (3531) 37 00 11
c/o South African Airways, P.O. Box 7778, Johannesburg, South Africa; tel. (713) 22 06
11–12 Hanover Street, London W1R 9HF, United Kingdom; tel. (071) 499 44 99
Suite 3, Lancaster Buildings, 65/77 Deansgate, Manchester, United Kingdom
5230 Pacific Concourse Drive, Suite 200, Los Angeles, USA; tel. (304) 643 45 95
821 UN Plaza, 4th Floor, New York, NY 10017, USA; tel. (1–212) 986 50 50

Offices in Turkey:
Atatürk Blv. 167/A, Ankara; tel. (0–312) 312 49 00
THY A.O. Rez., İstanbul; tel.(0–212) 574 82 00 (25 lines) and 248 26 31
THY also has representatives at all Turkish airports.

◀ *Yachts in Antalya Harbour*

Air Transport

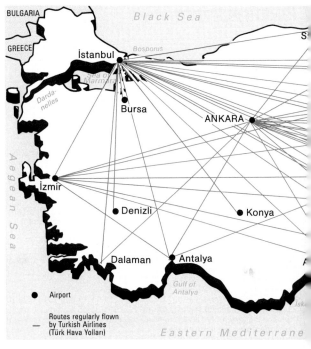

Airport

Routes regularly flown
— by Turkish Airlines
(Türk Hava Yolları)

THT Airlines	Ankara: THY A.O. Rez.; tel. (0–312) 309 04 00 İstanbul: THY A.O. Rez.; tel. (0–212) 574 82 00 THT also has offices in all the other major towns and desks at the main airports.
İstanbul Airlines	Atatürk Bulvarı 83–5, TR-Kizilay/Ankara; tel. (0–312) 432 22 34 and 431 09 20/21 Esenboğa Airport; tel. (0–312) 398 04 21/22 İncirli Caddesi 50, TR-İstanbul-Bakirköy; tel. (0–212) 543 62 58/59 Cumhuriyet Caddesi 111, TR-İstanbul-Elmadağ; tel. (0–212) 231 75 26/27 Atatürk Airport, Yeşilköy; tel. (0–212) 573 40 93, 574 04 56 and 573 20 74 (international flights) and 574 42 71 (internal flights) Gasiosmanpaşa Caddesi 2/E, TR-İzmir-Alsançak; tel. (9–51) 89 05 41/42 Adnan Menderes Airport; tel. (9–51) 51 30 65 Also offices in Adana, Antalya, Dalaman, Marmaris and Trabzon.
Air Canada	Hilton Hotel, Harbiye Cumhuriyet Caddesi 10, İstanbul; tel. (0–212) 212 251 61 30
Air New Zealand	10 Cumhuriyet Caddesi, Harbiye, İstanbul; tel. (0–212) 212–234 13 00
American Airlines	Ticaret Sanayı A.Ş., Taksim 800900 İstanbul; tel. (0–212) 212–237 20 03

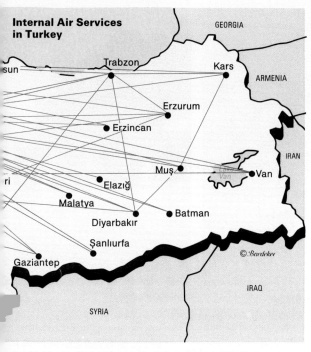

Internal Air Services in Turkey

Cumhuriyet Caddesi 10, İstanbul; tel. (0–212) 146 40 17/147 13 38   British Airways
Yasar Holding, Şehit Fethi Bey Caddesi 120, İzmir;
tel. (0–232) 13 92 59, 14 17 88, 12 22 00

TGI Travel Service, Cumhuriyet Caddesi 155–151, Elmadağ, İstanbul;   QANTAS
tel. (0–212) 212–240 50 32

Milta Turizm, Cumhuriyet Caddesi 151–13 İstanbul;   TWA
tel. (0–212) 212–234 53 27

Beaches

Turkey's coastline, full of bays and inlets, guarantees a wonderful holiday
by the sea, with a choice of sandy or pebble-strewn beaches, most of them
in settings of great natural beauty.
The season for swimming is from early April to late October in the southern
Aegean and the Mediterranean, and from June to September in the Black
Sea, northern Aegean and Sea of Marmara. You can also swim in the sea in
winter in southern Turkey at resorts such as Antalya, Alanya and Dalaman,
and Side and Kemer.

Turkish beaches are public and open to all. Hoteliers usually try to keep the
beach clean in front of their hotels but the weather and tides can bring in
tar, rubbish and other pollutants, so take something to wear on your feet
when swimming, especially if the beach is likely to be stony.

Hotels provide simple wooden sunbeds, usually without charge, but you   Facilities
pay for the covers to go on them. Water sports equipment tends to be the

Beaches

Beaches in historic settings

Alanya and Antalya

province of private operators on the beach rather than hotels, and outside the peak season the supply of sailboats, surf boards, etc. is more limited.

Nudity

Swimming and sunbathing in the nude is definitely against the strict moral code of Islam, and this usually applies to being topless as well. Ignoring this code can lead to arrest.

Bathing beaches
Black Sea coast

The places worth recommending as you move westward along the Black Sea coast include Kilyos, on the western part of the Bosporus, which has miles of beaches of fine sand and is a favourite with the people of İstanbul; Şile, which has a sandy beach on the eastern part of the Bosporus; Karasu, the little town with another long beach of fine sand at the mouth of the Sakarya, and on a wooded coastline with a number of lakes further inland; then Akçakoca with a particularly lovely beach 8km/5 miles further west; Abana to the north-east with a long sandy beach; the little port of İnebolu with its scenic beach; Ayancık in its forest setting with a beach stretching for 10km/6 miles; the old port of Samsun; Çamlık with a particularly good bathing beach of fine sand; and the little ports of Ordu, Giresun, Trabzon and Rize, all with bathing beaches and on a superb mountainous coastline.

Sea of Marmara

Most of the best developed bathing beaches are in western Turkey. The main ones on the Sea of Marmara are: Büyük Ada, one of the Prince's Islands; Yalova on the south coast with a very fine sandy beach and a spa some 20km/12½ miles inland; Gemlik, a popular resort in a beautiful setting, but with a rather stony beach; Tirilye; Eşkel with a sheltered beach of fine sand; the little port of Bandırma with a flat but exposed sandy beach; the lovely little peninsula town of Erdek; Tatlısu with a sheltered sandy beach; the islands of Avşar and Marmara, both with fine beaches; and, on the north coast, Tekirdağ and Silivri, the latter with a long sandy beach.

Aegean coast

Bathing beaches on the Aegean coast include Çanakkale at the narrowest point of the Dardanelles, with beaches at Çamlık Intepe (thermal springs);

the islands of İmroz and Bozcaada south of the Dardanelles, along the Gulf of Edremit, Aklıtınoluk on the north side, Ören, near Burhaniye, at the head of the gulf, and Ayvalık on the south side with many small offshore islands and pine woods close to the beach. The best beaches around İzmir are between Yenifoça and Foça (quiet little coves) and at the west end of the Çeşme Peninsula, especially near Ilıca. Kuşadası (Ephesus) has long stretches of beach, with a number of holiday villages, then come Altınkum south of Didyma, Bodrum (Halicarnassus) with several beautiful coves and good diving waters, the sheltered Bay of Marmaris, and Fethiye, with good beaches on the adjoining coastline, the islands in the bay and the lovely Ölüdeniz lagoon.

Tourism has grown considerably along the Mediterranean coast, especially around the Gulf of Antalya with its magnificent mountain backdrop, because of the long beaches along the western shore between Antalya and Çamyuva and Kemer. Farther east Manavgat (Side) and Alanya have also become popular with holidaymakers, but the stretch from Alanya to Silifke is less developed although this part of the coast, extending beyond Silifke to Mersin, also has its attractions.

Mediterranean coast

Buses

Buses (otobüs) are far and away Turkey's most important form of public transport since train services are relatively limited. Bus lines of various kinds operate between all the major towns and cities, and also effect transfers between the main airports and city centres (see Air Travel). The buses themselves are for the most part clean, modern – many of them brought in second-hand from Western Europe – and reasonably comfortable, if frequently rather overcrowded.

The fares are relatively low, and anyone planning to tour Turkey by bus is also bound to find opportunities for getting to know the local people, although to get the best out of a journey a seat by the window is essential. Tickets should be bought in good time from the special kiosks (information in the hotels).

Fares

Larger places usually have one or more bus stations (otagar, garaj) for the long-distance routes. These are often on the edge of town in the larger cities. The following is a selection of bus stations and the telephone numbers of their information offices:

Bus stations

Ankara: tel. (0–3124) 310 47 47; Antalya: tel. (0–242) 241 62 31; Aydin: tel. (0–256) 225 73 11; Bursa: tel. (0–224) 214 60 72 and 214 31 22; İstanbul: Topkapı tel. (0–212) 582 10 10 and 582 09 61, Trakya tel. (0–212) 577 56 17, Harem tel. (0–216) 333 37 63, International tel. (0–212) 558 61 40; İzmir: Halkapınar: tel. (0–232) 486 22 66 and 486 22 63; Kayseri: tel. (0–352) 336 43 73; Kuşadası: tel. (0–256) 614 39 81; Mersin: tel. (0–324) 233 78 24; Muğla: tel. (0–252) 214 18 46/218; Nevşehir: (0–384) 213 40 25; Trabzon: tel. (0–462) 325 23 43

Bosfor Turizm, İstanbul-Taksim: tel. (0–212) 504 80 39;
Ulusoy Turizm, İstanbul-Topkapı: tel. (0–212) 582 36 36/7;
Varan Turizm: tel. (0–212) 151 74 74

Bus company central offices

See also Getting to Turkey

Business Hours

Since Kemal Atatürk's secular reforms Turkey, unlike other Muslim countries, has its day of rest on Sundays rather than Fridays.

Banks	See Currency
Government and other offices	Mon.–Fri. 8.30am–12.30pm and 1.30–5.30pm
Museums	See entry
Post offices	See Post
Shops	Mon.–Sat. 9.30am–1pm and 2–7pm

Shops in the bazaars and small retailers, especially food stores, often stay open during lunchtime and well into the evening. Shops (and museums) are closed on some days during religious festivals such as Ramadan (three days) and the Holy Days of Sacrifice (four days).

Camping and Caravanning

With 116 registered campsites Turkey still has relatively few compared with Europe and North America, but the network is steadily expanding. Most are concentrated along the Aegean and the Mediterranean, with far fewer on the Black Sea.

Experienced campers will find a uniquely Turkish flavour about these campsites, especially the Government-run ones established around the National Parks (see entry) and other conservation areas.

Campsites are usually on the main roads and close to towns and holiday resorts. For detailed information check with the Tourist Information Centres (see Information).

Opening times   Campsites are normally open from April/May through to October, although some stay open all year round.

Facilities   Although many campsites have guesthouses as well and some even have their own private beach, facilities can be limited so that they really only lend themselves to a shorter stay. There are often problems with poor access roads, shortages of drinking water and proper sanitation, not to mention the all-pervading dust. Recommended sites include those operated by BP Mocamps.

Warning   There is no general ban on camping away from the organised sites or spending the night on parking areas by the roadside, etc. but for safety reasons it is as well to use the registered campsites.

Motorhomes   See Car Rental under Motoring

Car ferries

International car ferry services

Italy–Turkey (April to November)

Venice–İzmir (both ways)	once a week	Turkish Maritime Lines
Venice–Antalya/Marmaris (both ways)	once a week	Turkish Maritime Lines
Venice–Marmaris (both ways)	once a week	Turkish Maritime Lines
Venice–Çeşme (both ways)	once a week	Turkish Maritime Lines

Italy–Greece–Turkey

Ancona–Patras– Heraklion (Crete)–Kuşadası (both ways)	once a week	Minoan Lines

Greece–Turkey

Patras–Heraklion (Crete)–Kuşadası (both ways)	once a week	Minoan Lines

See also Coastal Shipping.

If you plan to take a caravan or motorhome on the ferry check beforehand with the ferry company or the travel agent making the booking as to the maximum permissible size of vehicle and trailer. — Caravans

The following addresses for the ferry companies and their agents should be able to supply you with the further information you may need on car ferries.

Central Office: Rıhtım Caddesi, Karaköy, İstanbul; tel. (0–212) 245 53 66, 249 18 96, (res.) 249 92 22, 244 74 54, (inf.) 244 02 07
Harbourmaster, Karaköy; tel. (0–212) 244 25 02–244 02 07 — Turkish Maritime Lines (TDI – Türkiye Denizcilik İşletmeleri)

Agents in United Kingdom: London Sunquest Holidays Ltd., 9 Grand Parade, Green Lanes, London N4 1JX; tel. (081) 800 54 55/800 80 30

Central Office: 64b, Kifissias Ave., Maroussi, Athens, Greece 15125; tel. (91) 689 83 40
Agents in Kuşadası: Haci Feyzullah Mah. (Liman) Kibris Caddesi 2/1; tel. (0–256) 614 12 79 — Minoan Lines

---

Car Rental

See Motoring

Coastal Shipping Services

Throughout the year the State shipping line, Turkish Maritime Lines (Türkiye Denizcilik İşletmeleri; TDI), operates regular passenger services – some of which take cars – along the Mediterranean, Marmara and Black Sea coasts. They have agents in all their Turkish ports where timetables and ticket prices can be obtained (see also Car Ferries). — Turkish Maritime Lines (Türkiye Denizcilik İşletmeleri TDI)

There are connections from İstanbul with the Black Sea ports of Sinop, Samsun, Ordu, Giresun and Trabzon. — Black Sea coast

Around the Sea of Marmara car ferries run between İstanbul and Mudanya and Bandırma, and from Kartal, 20 mins east of İstanbul on the Asian side, and Danca (south-east of Kartal) to Yalova. — Sea of Marmara

Marmara and Bosporus boats depart from Eminönü quay in İstanbul and minicruises begin in Kabataş.

Catamaran sea-buses (Deniz Otobüsleri) are a quicker but rather more expensive way of getting from İstanbul to Yalova, Çınarçık and the islands of Büyükada, Marmara and Avşa. — Sea-bus service

509

Information from the sea-bus central office in İstanbul; tel. (0–216) 362 94 44 (2 lines) and 380 28 22 (3 lines).

Dardanelles

Car ferries operate across the Dardanelles between Eceabat and Çanakkale and between Gelibolu and Lâpseki.

Aegean and Mediterranean coasts

Ports along the Aegean west coast and the Mediterranean south coast are Dikili, İzmir (also direct service to İstanbul), Kuşadası, Bodrum, Marmaris, Taşycy/Silifke and Mersin.
Car ferries also operate from Kabatepe to the island of Gökçeada and from Odunluk to the island of Bozcaada.
Another car ferry on the Aegean south-west coast sails from the port of Bodrum to the ferry terminal at Körmen, not far from Datça on the Reşadiye peninsula.

Cruises, Yachts

See Sport

International ferries

See Car Ferries, Getting to Turkey

Consulates

See Diplomatic Representation

Currency

The unit of currency is the Turkish lira (TL, also known as the Turkish pound and originally subdivided into 100 kuruş or 4000 paras). Banknotes currently in circulation are for 1000, 5000, 10,000, 20,000, 50,000, 100,000 and 250,000 TL; coins are for 50, 100, 500, 1000 and 2500 TL.
Because of the high rate of inflation, currently at around 70%, you should check with the banks on the very latest exchange rates.

Banks

Open Mon.–Fri. 8.30am–noon and 1.30–5pm.
On weekends and public holidays you can change money at the international airports (see Air Transport) and İstanbul's Sirkeci Station.

Changing money

Given the weakness of Turkey's currency it pays to change money in the country rather than before you leave, but then only in banks or official exchange bureaus such as those in the larger hotels. Changing money anywhere else is illegal and you also run the risk of getting counterfeit bills in return!
Keep the receipts for these transactions since you may have to produce them when converting TL back into your own currency and when you have to prove at the frontier that goods purchased in Turkey have been paid for with money that has been exchanged legally.

Import and export of currency

There are no limits on the import and export of foreign currency, but not more than £3,300/US\$5000 worth of Turkish currency may be brought in or taken out.
The locals in the tourist resorts quite often like to be paid in a hard currency, so it is worth carrying a few pounds or dollars in small denomations to avoid having to change larger ones. But do remember not to change money illegally.

Eurocheques

Eurocheques can be cashed, on production of a Eurocard, in tourist information centres and, in the large towns, in the main banks but not the smaller branches. The same applies to the usual travellers' cheques.
Ordinary cheques will take longer since it may take several days to check with the bank of origin.

In the main towns and tourist centres the Turks are becoming increasingly used to accepting credit cards such as American Express, Eurocard/Master-card, Visa/Bank Americard, Diners Club, etc. for payment for goods and services.

Credit cards

Customs Regulations

A verbal declaration is all that is required on entry into Turkey but items of value, including portable TV sets, camcorders and jewellery worth over £10,000/15,000 US dollars, have to be entered in your passport and will be checked again when you leave.

On entry

Duty-free you can take in personal effects, camping and sports gear, spare parts for the car (to be entered in passport), a camera and 10 rolls of film, a cine-camera and 10 films, tape-recorder, record-player, transistor radio, walkman, portable typewriter, 3 musical instruments, 200 cigarettes and 50 cigars or 200g tobacco, 1.5kg coffee, 500g tea, 5 litres spirits, 5 120ml bottles of perfume and presents up to the value of £200/330 US$. You need special permission to take in knives of any kind, including those for camping, etc.

Drugs are illegal in Turkey so don't import them, deal in them or use them when you're there – the penalties are very severe!

Souvenirs can be exported from Turkey free of duty up to a total value of £600/900 US$.

On exit

Valuable items, including personal effects, can only be taken out if they were already entered in the owner's passport or you can show they were bought with currency which had been legally exchanged (see Currency). New carpets must be accompanied by a receipt and old carpets, copper articles and pistols also require a certificate from a museum directorate as well.

The export of antiques and weapons is prohibited.

Minerals may only be exported with a special permit from MTA, the General Directorate of Mining Exploration and Research; tel. (0–312) 287 34 30.

For persons over 15 the allowances are 500g coffee or 200g powdered coffee and 100g tea or 40g teabags, 50g perfume and 0.25 litre toilet water and for persons over 17, 1 litre spirits with more than 22% alcohol or 2 litres spirits with less than 22% alcohol or 2 litres sparking wine and 2 litres table wine and 200 cigarettes or 100 cigarillos or 50 cigars or 250g tobacco.

Re-entry to
EC countries

For countries outside the European Union the allowances are as follows: Australia 250 cigarettes or 50 cigars or 250g tobacco, 1 litre spirits or 1 litre wine; Canada 200 cigarettes and 50 cigars and 900g tobacco, 1.1 litres spirits or wine; New Zealand 200 cigarettes or 50 cigars or 250g tobacco, 1.1 litres spirits and 4.5 litres wine; South Africa 400 cigarettes and 50 cigars and 250g tobacco, 1 litre spirits and 2 litres wine; USA 200 cigarettes and 100 cigars and a reasonable quantity of tobacco, 1 litre spirits or 1 litre wine.

Re-entry to
non-EC countries

See Sport

Private yachts

See entry

Travel Documents

Diplomatic Representation

Embassy: Nene Hatun Caddesi 83, Gaziosmanpaşa, Ankara; tel. (0–312) 436 12 40
Consulate L Etiler, Tepecik Yolu Üzeri 58, İstanbul; tel. (0–212) 257 70 50

Australia

Embassy: Nene Hatun Caddesi 75, Gaziosmanpaşa, Ankara; tel. (0–312) 436 12 75/79

Canada

	Consulate: Büyükdere Caddesi, Bengün Han 107, Kat. 3 Gayrettepe, İstanbul; tel. (0–212) 272 51 74
Eire	Consulate: Honorary Consul-General Mr Ferruh Verdi, Cumhuriyet Caddesi, Pegasus Evi 26a, Harbiye, İstanbul; tel. (0–212) 246 60 25
United Kingdom	Embassy: Şehit Ersan Caddesi 46a, Çankaya, Ankara; tel. (0–312) 427 43 10/15 Consulates: Kazin Özalp Cadessi 149/A, Antalya; tel. (0–242) 241 18 15 Meşrutiyet Caddesi 34, Beyoğlu/Tepebaşı, İstanbul; tel. (0–212) 244 75 40 1442 Sokak 49, P.K. 300, Alsancak, İzmir; tel. (0–232) 421 17 95
USA	Embassy: Atatürk Bulvarı 110, Kavaklıdere, Ankara; tel. (0–312) 426 54 70 Consulates: Atatürk Caddesi, Vali Yolu, Adana; tel. (0–322) 234 21 45 Meşrutiyet Caddesi 104–108, Tepebaşı, Beyoğlu, İstanbul; tel. (0–212) 251 36 02 Atatürk Caddesi 92, Alsancak, İzmir; tel. (0–232) 484 94 26

Electricity

Turkey has 220–volt 50 cycles AC. You can use most European standard plugs but North American ones are likely to need an adaptor.
Power failures are quite common.

Emergency Services

Emergency calls nationwide	General emergency: tel. 155/077 Medical emergency: tel. 112/077 Fire brigade: tel. 110/000 Police: 155
Tourist Police	In all the main towns the Tourist Police can be contacted by telephone in an emergency.
Pharmacies	For information about the availability of doctors (doktor, hekim) and pharmacies (eczane) telephone 118.
Breakdown service	See Motoring

Events

The following list covers a number of festivals, fairs and other special events. For information about the precise dates check with the tourist information centres (see Information). For public holidays see separate entry.

January	Selçuk: camel wrestling
March	Çanakkale: 1915 sea victory celebrations İstanbul: International Film Festival
April	Ankara: International Children's Day (children's festival; April 23rd) Ankara: International Arts Festival Manisa: Mesir (traditional festival) Sultanhisar: International Nysa Culture and Arts Festival
April/May	Selçuk: Ephesus International Festival of Culture and Tourism

Emirgân: Tulip Festival	May
Eskişehir: Yunus Emre Culture and Art Week	
Giresun: Aksu Culture and Art Festival	
Marmaris: International Yachting Festival	
Silifke: International Music and Folklore Festival	
Ankara: International Asia-Europe Biennale (1994)	May/June
Aksaray: Atatürk Culture Festival	June
Alanya: Tourism Festival	
Artvin: Kafkasör Culture and Art Festival	
Bergama: Bergama Festival	
Çeşme: International Pop-music Contest	
Edirne: traditional greased wrestling at Kırkpınpar	
Marmaris: Marmaris Festival	
Safranbolu: Architectural Treasures and Folklore Week	
Amasya: Ihlara Tourism and Art Week	June/July
Bursa: International Arts Festival	
İstanbul: International Culture and Arts Festival	
Akşehir: Nasreddin Hoca Festival	July
Black Sea region: ceremonial cattle drive up to the Alpine pastures at Kadirga, Sis Dağı and Hidirnebi, followed by celebrations	
Çorum: Hittite Festival	
Foça: Music, Folklore and Watersports Festival	
İskenderun: Tourism and Culture Festival	
Kütahya: Pottery Festival	
Erzurum: International Commemoration Festival of Congress	July/ August
Avanos: Craft and Tourism Festival	August
Bolu: Mengen Chefs Festival	
Çanakkale: Troy Festival	
Hacıbektaş: Hacı Bektaş Veli Commemoration Festival	
Samsun: International Folk Dance Festival	
İzmir: International Fair	August/ September
Ayder (Black Sea): Alpine pasture cattle drive with beautifully decorated cattle	September
Antalya: Altın Portakal (international film competition)	
Eskşehir: Beyaz Altın International Meerschaum White Gold Festival	
Göreme: tourist festival	
Kemer: carnival	
Mersin: Art and Culture Festival	
Söğüt: Ertuğrul Gazi (remembrance celebrations)	
Ürgüp: International Grape Harvest Festival	
Antalya: Akdeniz (music festival) Mersin: International Fair	September/ October
Safranbolu: Folklore Week	
Bozburun: International Gullet Festival	October
Kırşehir: Ahi Trades Festival	
Demre, Antalya: International St Nicholas Symposium	December
Konya: Mevlana commemoration ceremony, dervishes dancing to reed pipes (ney)	

Food and Drink

Turkish or Ottoman cuisine is among the best in the world and has dishes to suit even the most jaded Western palate. It uses good, fresh ingredients   **Food**

Food and Drink

prepared in delicious combinations according to recipes refined over the centuries. A meal in a proper Turkish restaurant (see Restaurants) is something to linger over so allow plenty of time. Food tends to be served warm rather than piping hot, and you can usually choose from a wide range of meze for starters, washed down with rakı, followed by a main course of meat or fish, accompanied by beer or one of the very acceptable local wines, ending up with a mouthwatering dessert and of course Turkish coffee.

Breakfast

Breakfast usually consists of bread, butter, feta cheese, tomatoes, cucumber, olives, jam, honey, tea and/or (instant) coffee. The better hotels (see entry) provide a buffet with plenty of choice.

Rakı

Rakı, the national drink, is an aniseed liqueur, 45% proof, which can be drunk neat or with water which it turns milky-white, hence the name "lion's milk". You can drink rakı any time but traditionally it's the typical pre-dinner aperitif and the accompaniment to starters and fish dishes.

Meze for starters

Favourite starters include various kinds of dolma, i.e. stuffed vegetables with a filling of rice or minced meat, such as biber dolması (stuffed peppers), kabak dolması (stuffed squash), lahana dolması (stuffed cabbage leaves), yaprak dolması (stuffed vineleaves) and domates dolması (stuffed tomatoes). Also on the menu are zeytin (olives), tarama (fish roe creamed with oil and lemon juice), beyaz peynir (goat's cheese), kabak kızartması (thinly sliced fried zuccini/courgettes dressed with yoghurt and vinegar), and patlıcan kızartması (fried eggplant/aubergines) as well as various dips and pide (unleavened pitta-type bread or pizza).

Soups

Among the popular soups are düğün çorbası (wedding soup, lamb broth with lemon juice and a beaten egg), işkembe çobası (mutton tripe soup), yayla soup (rice soup thickened with whipped yoghurt and eggyolk, flavoured with mint leaves), and tarhana soup (a thick soup of yoghurt, tomatoes, peppers and onions).

Main course

The main course will usually be something with lamb or mutton or, near the coast, fish or seafood. Turks do not eat pork because it is against their religion, and beef is relatively rare because few cattle are raised for their meat, which makes it expensive. On the other hand, there is plenty of chicken.
Turkey's best-known speciality is probably the kebab, pieces of meat grilled on a skewer. Şiş kebap is diced shoulder of lamb grilled between pieces of onion, tomato and peppers and served with rice. Döner kebap is lamb or mutton grilled on a vertical spit then thinly sliced as it cooks. Güvec is meat casseroled with rice, vegetables, peppers and tomatoes, kuzu kapama is braised lamb with onions, kuzu dolması is roast lamb stuffed with rice, sultanas and pinenuts, comlek kebabı is mutton steamed with vegetables, and kuzu or koyun külbastısı is a spit-roast joint of lamb or mutton. A favourite chicken dish is çerkez tavuğu, Circassian chicken, served in a thick sauce of paprika and walnuts.
Local restaurants tend to specialise in either meat or fish. Needless to say, surrounded as it is on three sides by water, Turkey has some very tasty fresh fish to offer, ranging from swordfish, bluefish, turbot and tunny to sardines and anchovies, a particular speciality of the Black Sea. Seafood is good too, in season, but tends to be more expensive.

Accompaniments

Pilav, Turkish rice, is usually delicious, as is bulgur pilavı, cracked wheat pilaf. Rice and vegetables often come after the main course. One of the most popular accompaniments is cacık, yoghurt prepared with cucumber, olive oil, dill, salt and garlic. Other side-dishes include piyaz (haricot beans and onion salad), taze fasulya (green beens), zeytinyağlı fasulya (beans in olive oil), and many more.

Dessert

Anyone with a very sweet tooth will enjoy the typical Turkish desserts (deser) and sweetmeats, of which lokum, or Turkish delight, is only one.

Fish market in İstanbul

Equally famous is baklava, flaky pastry filled with almonds, hazelnuts and pistachios and soaked with honey. Other specialities are kabaktatlısı, pumpkin slices boiled in milk and sprinkled with grated nuts, and güllac, waffles dipped in milk filled with grated almonds, while milk puddings, mualabe, are also delicious with a dusting of pistachio or chocolate.

Turkey also has wonderful fresh fruit, and is famous for its strawberries from the Bosporus, figs and grapes from İzmir, peaches from Bursa, apricots from Eastern Anatolia, cherries from Giresun, citrus fruit from the Mediterranean, and pears from around Ankara, while melons of all kinds are found throughout the country.

Street vendors are everywhere, selling dried fruit, hazelnuts, pistachios, sunflower seeds, etc. In summer you can get all kinds of fruit, especially melons, but also corn on the cob, twists of sesame seed bread, fried fish and işkembe çorbası, the mutton tripe soup. Water, lemonade and, in winter, çay, the national beverage of hot sweet tea, are all sold on the street, but be careful of the water or lemonade. Hot chestnuts are another cold weather favourite.

Snacks on the street

Alkollü İçkiler – spirits; besides rakı Turkey also produces its own local brandy and gin.

Ayran – slightly salted goat's milk yoghurt blended with water.

Bira – Turkish beer, good quality and fairly light. Efes is a popular local brew. Lagers and other European beers are also available, brewed here under licence.

Çay – tea, the national beverage, is drunk without milk and often prepared and served straight from the samovar. In summer everyone flocks to the outdoor tea-houses (çayhane) to enjoy drinking tea in the gardens.

Kahve – Turkish coffee is relatively expensive but in good coffee-houses individually prepared. A heaped coffee spoon of very dark roast ground coffee beans is placed in a little copper pot and the desired amount of sugar

Drinks

515

The diversity of Turkish cuisine . . .

. . . and typical Turkish desserts

is added. The Turks prefer their coffee very sweet (çok şekerli) but you can also have it slightly sweetened (az şekerli), sweet (orta şekerli) or with no sugar at all (sade). This is all stirred together with some water, boiled up on an open flame as more water is added, allowed to bubble up several times and then served.

In many of the more traditional coffee houses, still largely all-male pre-serves, you can see the men smoking the Turkish version of the hookah or water pipe, here called the nargile. Another popular coffee-house pastime is a game of tavla, the local form of backgammon.

Madensuyu – carbonated mineral water; bottled water is good value and can be recommended; tap water is heavily chlorinated.

Meyanşerbeti – sherbet

Meyva suyu – fruit juice; there is a wonderful selection of fruit juices since juice is produced from nearly all the different kinds of fruit in Turkey.

Rakı – the anisette liqueur which turns milky-white when water is added, hence the name "lion's milk", and drunk as an aperitif or with starters and fish dishes.

Şarap – wine; Turkey produces its own wine, some of it very good indeed.

Getting to Turkey

By air

The best way to get to Turkey for a short visit is by air. Turkish Airlines (THY) and British Airways operate daily flights from London Heathrow to İstan-bul, while THY also operate regular flights to Ankara, İzmir, Antalya, Adana, Trabzon and Dalaman from many of the world's other major cities. Amer-ican Airlines flies the New York–İstanbul route daily via Paris and Geneva. In fact most international airlines schedule connecting flights to Turkey's international airports and a number of operators provide charter flights as well, especially during the holiday season.

A number of Mediterranean cruises (see Sport) have ports of call along the Turkish coast, with İstanbul, Çanakkale, İzmir, Kuşadası, Bodrum, Marmaris and Antalya among the most popular.

By sea

If you have enough time and want to take a car there are car ferries from the Italian Adriatic ports of Venice and Ancona to İstanbul and İzmir respectively (see Car Ferries, Coastal Shipping). Check with a travel agent for further details.
You can also get to Turkey from Northern Cyprus and from some of the Greek islands but the Greeks charge quite a high departure tax.

In the light of the situation in former Yugoslavia the overland route to Turkey through this part of the Balkans is certainly not to be recommended. The longer way round, the northern route eventually passing through Hungary, Rumania and Bulgaria, has little to recommend it either. Not only will you have to contend with long waits at frontiers and filling stations, fuel shortages and bad roads full of potholes, but, and this is more serious, you cannot count on getting proper medical or technical assistance in the event of an accident or a breakdown. In any case you should check with one of the motoring organisations on the very latest situation.
The best route from Northern Europe – London to İstanbul is about 3000km/1850 miles by road – is undoubtedly the southern one, via Belgium, Germany, Austria then Italy and a ferry to Greece or direct to Turkey.

By car

There are regular coach services between Turkey and Austria, France, Germany,Italy, the Netherlands, Switzerland and Greece, as well as Iraq, Iran, Jordan, Saudi Arabia, Kuwait and Syria. They are usually operated by Turkish companies such as Bosfor Turizm, Varan Turizm and Ulusoy Turizm, working in conjunction with another European operator. Olympic Bus (Russell Square, London) also runs a service to İstanbul via Thessalonika. Since the journey to Turkey is such a long run – Munich to İstanbul by express coach takes about 40 hours – you would be well advised to choose the most comfortable vehicle possible, or opt for one of the coach trips organised by a tour operator where your accommodation, etc. are all provided.

By bus

Owing to the situation in the Balkans there are at present no direct sleeper services from Munich or Vienna but İstanbul can still be reached from Greece and Bulgaria. The fares are relatively inexpensive, with reductions for students and young people under 26, but the journey is not particularly comfortable.
The Orient Express, which once used to go as far as İstanbul, now only runs from London to Venice, where you can join a cruise ship or take a ferry; it is now known as the Venice Simplon Orient Express (VSOE, Jean-Paul & Edith Diner, Chemin des Grives, CH–1261 Le Vaud, Switzerland; tel. (022) 366 42 30).

By rail

Hotels

The building boom since the mid-Eighties has seen the number of beds in Turkey's holiday areas soar from barely 60,000 to 250,000.

The best-known areas for Alpine-style holidays, with high mountain pastures and the associated annual festivals (see Events), include those on the Black Sea such as Ayder by Rize, Kadırga by Trabzon, and Kümbet by Giresun. Information about these holidays can be obtained from the tourist offices listed in the section on Information.

Alpine-style holidays

The big hotels and holiday villages have night clubs or similar establishments, with belly dancers, folk dancing, etc., as well as bars and discos.

Night life

Hotels

Many holiday resorts have their own casinos. You will be required to show your passport for purposes of identification.

Holiday villages

Holiday villages such as those run by Club Aldiana, Club Méditerranée, Robinson and Sunsail Clubs are very popular thanks mainly to their wide range of sporting facilities; they are listed according to location.

Classifications

The following list gives the official categories for hotels (oteli) and other types of accommodation:

*****	luxury hotel
****	1st class hotel
***	2nd class hotel
**	3rd class hotel
*	4th class hotel
Ö	Özel: private
(i.e. not state-run)	
M	1st class motel
M2	2nd class motel
APRT	holiday apartments
O	hostel, inn
P	guesthouse
S	spa
TKA	1st class holiday village
TKB	2nd class holiday village

Prices

Although most accommodation in Turkey is subject to state control the authorities in question will not commit themselves on prices for short or longer term stays. Because of Turkey's high rate of inflation indications of price are often given in German marks (DM) or US dollars.

Generally speaking, prices as a whole tend to be well below the levels of those of the more highly developed countries. This particularly applies to accommodation in the lower categories, but the level of comfort they offer also varies accordingly.

Room reservations

If you have not booked your holiday in Turkey in advance and are travelling independently it is essential, at least in the peak season, to book your accommodation directly with the place concerned and to make the room reservation as far ahead as possible.

b. = number of beds
r. = number of rooms
Bul. = Bulvarı (boulevard)
Cad. = Caddesi (street)
Kat. = Bina katı (floor)
Mev. = Mevki (square)
Mey. = Meydan (square)
Sok. = Sokak (street, alley)

List of hotels (a selection)

Abant

*****Abant Palace, Abant Gölü Kenarı
***Turban-Abant, Abant Gölü Kenarı

Adana

*****Büyük Sürmeli, Özler Cad., Kuruköprü, 329 b.; Seyhan, Turhan Cemal Beriker Bul. 30, 300 b.
****Adana Sürmeli, İnönü Cad. 151, 252 b.; İnci, Kurtuluş Cad. 40, 185 b.; Zaimoğlu, Özler Cad. 72, Kuruköprü, 156 b.
***Sedef, Turhan Cemal Beriker Bul. 203

**Ağba, Abidinpaşa Cad. 1; Cavuşoğlu, Ziyapaşa Bul. 115; Hosta, Bakıyurdu Cad. 3, Kurkuköprü; İpek Palas, İnönü Cad. 103; Koza, Özler Cad. 103
Raşit Ener Turistik Tesisleri (M1), İskenderun Yolu Girne Bul.

**Bozdoğan, Atatürk Bul., 105 b.; Serdaroğlu, Turgutreis Cad. 20   Adıyaman

**Ece, Ordu Bul. 2, 78 b.; Oruçoğlu, Bankalar Cad. 3, 112 b.   Afyon
Güzelköy Turistik Tesisleri (M2) on the Afyon–İzmir road (20km/12½ miles)

***Sim-Er Turistik Tesisleri (M2), Iran Transit Yolu   Agri
**İsfahan, Emniyet Cad. 26; İshakpaşa, Emniyet Cad. 9

***Ahlat, Zübeydehanım Cad.   Ahlat

**Sumela, İnönü Cad.   Akçaabat

***Akçakoca, Ereğli Cad.   Akçakoca
*Yeni Çınar, Tevfik İleri Cad.

**Güneş Otel II, Buruncuk Mev., Altınoluk   Akçay
Eren (M1), Çayağazı Cad., Altınoluk
Turban Akçay Tatil Köyü (TK2)

***Tütün, Devlet Karayolu, 21. Sok. 68   Akhisar

**Vadi, Ankara Cad. 17, 74 b.   Aksaray
Orhan Ağaçli Turistik Tesisleri (M1), on the Ankara–Adana road
TMT Tatil Köyü (TK1), Akçebük

*****Ananas, Cikcikli Köyü; Elit Hotel Doğanay, Gerperlit Mev. Konakli,   Alanya
210 b.; Serapsu, Konakli Köyü, 447 b.
****Alantur, Dimçayı Mev.; Handullah Paşa Turistik Tesisleri, Konakli, 1100
b.; Jasmin, Avşallar; Obaköy Banana, Göl Mev., Gazipaşa Cad., 362 b.
Özkaymak Resort, İncekum Mev. Avşallar, 800 b.; Syedra Princess, Kuyu-
cak Mev., Mahmutlar, 254 b.; Sunshine, Çamyolu Köyü; Top, Beyyaylası
Mev., Avşallar, 430 b.
***Akropol, Çamyolu Köyü; Alaaddin, Saray Mah.; Alanya Büyük, Güller-
pınar Mah.; Alara, Yeşil Köyü; Albayrak, Oba Göl Mev.; Anilgan, Keykubat
Cad. 79, 110 b.; Annabella, İncekum Avşallar, 160 b.; Aytap, Keykubat Cad.
155; Aytur, Keykubat Cad.; Azak, Atatürk Cad.; Banana, Cikcikli Köyü; Blue
Sky Bayırlı, İskele Cad. 66; Boulevard, Keykubat Cad. 39, 196 b.; Club
Santana, Mahmutlar Mev.; Club Titan, Kargıcık Köyü, Mev.; De-Ha, Mah-
mutlar Kasabası; Doğanay, Gerpelit Mev. Konaklı; Eftalia Aytur, Keykubat
Cad. 101; Gardenia, Güzelyalı Cad.; Grand Atila, Oba Kasabası Göl Mev.;
Kaptan, İskele Cad. 70; Kösedere, Fiğlu Mev. Türkler Köyü; Krizantem,
Obagöl Mev.; Melani, Göl Mev. Obayolu Üzeri: Obaköyü, Gazipaşa C. Göl
Mev.; Panorama, Keykubat Cad. 52; Saphir, Konakli, 244 b.; Serda, Telatiye
Mev., Konakli, 236 b.; Sus, Mahmutlar Kasabası, Örenönü Mev.; Tulp,
Mahmutlar Kasabası, 120 b.; Turintaş, İskele–Konaklı; Turtaş, Konaklı
Köyü; Vikingen, Konaklı Köyü; Yalihan, Avşallar İncekum, 250 b.
**Akşam Güneşi, Keykubat Cad. 40; Alaiye, Atatürk Cad. 228; Alangün,
Atatürk Cad. 262; Aspendos, İncekum, Avşallar Mev., 388 b.; Atilla, Keyku-
bat Cad. 1; Ahlap, Keykubat Cad. 155; Blue Sky Bayırlı, İskele Cad. 66;
Bulut, Keykubat Cad. 61; Gallion, Atatürk Cad. 123, 106 b.; Ladin, Keykubat
Cad. Karasaz Mev., 88 b.; Yeni Otel International, Güllerpınarı Mah. 97.;
Bedestan Oteli (Ö), Cami Önü Mev., Hisariçi Köyü
Club Aquarius (TK1), Alanya Tatil Köyü, Konaklı Mev., 448 b.

*Dönmez, Hükümet Cad. 49   Aliağa
Afacan (M2), Şakran Köyü

Hotels

Sheraton Hotel in Ankara

Hotel Mustafa in Ürgüp

Amasra	Only Aile Pansiyonu (P), Çamlı Sok.
Amasya	**Turban, Helkis Mah.
Anamur	**Anahan, Tahsin Soylu Cad. 109 Karan (M2), Bozdoğan Köyü
Ankara	*****Büyük Ankara, Atatürk Bul. 183, Kavaklıdere, 402 b.; Hilton, Tahran Cad. 12, Kavaklıdere, 670 b.; Merit Altinel, Gazi Mustafa Kemal Bul. 151, Tandoğan, 176 r.; Sheraton, Noktalı Sok. Gaziosmanpaşa, 622 b. ****Ankara Dedeman, Büklüm Sok. 1; Best, Atatürk Bul. 195, Kavaklıdere; Bilkent, 1. Cad. Lodumlu Köyü; Büyük Sürmeli, Cihan Sok. 6.; İçkale, Gazi Mustafa Kemal Bul. 89, Maltepe, 238 b.; Kent, Mithat Paşa Cad. 4; Stad, İstilal Cad. 20 ***Alfin, Menekşe Sok. 11; Altınışık, Necatibey Cad. 46; Apaydın, Bayındır Sok. 8; Büyük Erşan, Selanik Cad. 74. Kızılay, 155 b.; Elit Olgunlar Sok. 10; Etap Mola, Atatürk Bul. 80; Evkuran, Dr Media Eldem Sok. 40, Kızılay; Eyüboğlu, Karanfil Sok. 73; Karyağdi, Sanayi Cad., Kuruçesme S. 4, Opera Meydani, 40 b.; Keykan Çakmak Sok. 12; Metropol, Olgunlar Sok. 5 Bakan-liklar, 68 b.; Seğmen, Büklüm Sok., Kavaklıdere; Tunalı, Tunalıhilmi Cad. 19; Turist, Çankiri Cad. 37, Ulus, 236 b.; Yeni, Sanayi Cad. 5 **Akman, İtfaiye Mey.; Barınak, Onur Sok. 25, Maltepe; Başyazıcı, Çankırı Cad. 27, Ulus; Canbek, Soğukkuyu Sok. 8, Ulus; Ercan, Denizciler Cad. 36; Güleryüz, Sanayi Cad. 37, Ulus; Karyağdı, Sanayi Cad., Kuruçeşme Sok. 4; Melodi, Karanfil Sok. 10, Kızılay; Örnek, Gülseren Sok. 4, Anıteppe; Sultan; Bayındır Sok. 35 Ömür (M2), 9km/5½ miles outside İstanbul Mege Center (Ö) Tahran Cad. 5
Antakya	****Büyük Antakya, Atatürk Cad. 8, Antakya/Hatay, 144 b.

520

*****Antalya Dedeman, Lara Yolu; Club Sera, Lara Yolu, 1020 b.; Falez,   **Antalya**
Falez Mev., Konyaaltı; Ofo, Lara Yolu, 300 b.; Sheraton Voyager, 100 Yil Bul.
409 b.; Talya, Fevzi Çakmak Cad. 30
****Kişlahan, Kazim Özalp Cad. 55, 232 b.
***Antares, Lara Cad. 1537. Sok. 16; Atan Lara Cad., 117; Baymurat, Lara
Cad., Barınaklar, 1537. Sok. 16; Bilgehan, Kazim Özalp Cad. 194, 306 b.;
İsinda, Altinkum Mev. 4801 Sok. 30, Konyaalti, 60 b.; Lara, Lara Yolu;
Merve, Cumhuriyet Cad. 24. Sok. 2, 90 b.; Mithat, Fatih Cad. 591, Sok. 47;
Olbia, Konyaalti Mev. Aldeniz Bul. 1, 160 b.; Princess, Karpuzkaldiran, 228
b.; Start, Ali Çetinkaya Cad. 19; Susanne, Akdeniz Bul. 4804. Sok. 6; Tigris,
Çağlayan Mh. 2054. Sk. 23, Lara, 100 b.
**A. Erdem, Konyaaltı; Damla, Kenan Evren Bul., 124. Sok. 8; Güleryüz,
Tınaztepe Cad. 8; Kozan, 1312. Sok. 6; Maraton, Lara Yolu 162; Merve,
Cumhuriyet Cad. 24. Sok. 2; Orsa, Tınaztepe Cad. 7; Özkavak, Yeşiltepe
Mah. Ziya Gökalp Cad. 6, 84 b.; Pinus, Lara Cad., 1505. Sok. 9; Şengüller, Ali
Çetinkaya Cad. 26; Uno, Lara Yolu Üzeri 243, 45 b.; Yayla, Ali Çetinkaya Cad.
12, 78 b.
Abad Pansiyon (Ö), Hesapçi Sok. 52; Altun III Pansiyon (Ö), Kaleiçi 10;
Aspen (Ö), Kılıçaslan Mah. Kaleiçi; Frankfurt Pansiyon (Ö), Hıdırlık Sok. 17;
Leta Pansiyon (Ö), Atatürk Cad., Kaleiçi Mev.; Marina (Ö), Mermerli Sok. 15,
Kaleiçi; Özgurbet Pansiyon (Ö), Liman Cad., 4706. Sok. 2, Konyaaltı; Turban
Adalya (Ö), Kaleiçi Yat Limanı, 58 b.; Tuvana (Ö), Tuzcular Mah. Karanlık
Sok. 18

Karahan, İnönü Cad.   **Artvin

****Holiday in İstanbul, Sahil Yolu Bakirköy   **Ataköy**

***Altınyazı, Göreme Yolu; Kotaş, Yeni Mahalle   **Avanos**
**Venessa, Köprübaşi Mev.; Zelve, Atatürk Cad.

****Turtay, on the Aydın–Muğla road (3km/1½ miles)   **Aydın**
*Baltacı, Gazi Bul. 3, Sok. 17.; Orhan,Gazi Bul. 63

Asase Eden B., Behramkale–Kadırga Köyü   **Ayvacık
Behram (Ö), Behramkal Köyü

*****Grand Temizel Oteli, Sarımsaklı Mev.   **Ayvalık**
***Washington, Tuzla Mev.
**Ankara, Sarımsaklı Mev.; Billurcu, Sarımsakli Mev.; Büyük Berk, Sarım-
sakli Mev.; Sonay, Sarımsakli Mev.; Zeytinki, Sarımsakli Mev.
Camp (M1), Orta Çamlık 115

İmanoğlu, Örücüler Cad. 12; Kervansaray, Istasyon Mey., 78 b.   **Balıkesir

***Eken, Soğuksu Cad. 11   **Bandırma**
**Asuhan, Atatürk Cad. 253

Bartur, Tuzcular Köyü, Dörtyol Mev.   **Bartın

***İlihan, Diyarbakır Cad. 75   **Batman**

See Kemer, below   **Beldibi**

Kamelya, Girne Cad. 2; Seyran, Girne Cad. 7   **Belen

Bergama İskender, İzmir Cad., Ilica Önü   **Bergama
Tusan Bergama (M2), on the Bergama–İzmir road, Çatı Mev.

Beşikdüzü Tur-tes, Sahil Cad. 1   **Beşikdüzü

*Bey-Tur, Irfan Gümüşsel Cad. 47   **Beypazarı**

Büyük Bingöl, Genç Cad.   **Bingöl

Hotels

Birecik Mirkelam (M2), Karşiyaka, Köprübaşı

Bodrum *****Cesars, Okaliptus Sok. 4
****Javelin, Yahşi Mev., Kargı Köyü
***Atrium, Omurca Mah. Fabrika Sok. 21, 120 b.; Ban-Tur, Rasattepe Sok. 1; Blue Oteli, Neyzen Teyfik Cad. 226; Catamaran, Yalimevkii–Gündoğan, 70 b.; Club Hotel Flora, Gümbet Mev. Eski Çeşme Mah, 110 b.; Club Petunya, Yahşi Yalısı; Ece Resort, Gölköy, 70 b.; Ersan, İçmeler Mev., Kızılağaç Köyü; Gloria, Geriş Mev./Yalikavak, 154 b.; Halfmoon, Bitez Yalısı; Manastır, Bariş Sitesi Mev.; Myndonos, Caferpaşa Cad. 1; Napa, Zeki Müren Cad. 168; Naz, Dr Mümtaz Ataman Cad.; Samara, Kaynar Mev., 108 b.; Şamdan, Yalikavak, 111 b.; Torba Han, Sahilyolu 23, Torba, 130 b.
**Ayaz, Gümbet; Babana, Gölköy Yalı Mev., 82 b.; Baraz, Cumhuriyet Cad. 76; Bergamut, Aratepe Mev. Yalıkavak; Club Amerisa, Bitez Yalısı; Gala, Neyzen Tevik Cad. 224; Gözen, Cumhuriyet Cad. 18; Padesa Gardens, Gümbet; Parıltı, Ortakent Yahşi Yalısı; Sami, Gümbet; Sport, Eski Çeşme Mah., Gümbet Mev.; Taraça, Eski Çeşme Mah., Gümbet Mev.
Halikarnas (Ö), Cumhuriyet Cad. 184

Holiday Villages Club Arcadia (NUR-Touristic); Ora Tatil Köyü (TK1), Kaynar Mev., Milas Karayolu (7km/4½ miles); Sunsail Club Yedi Bükü, 7km/4½ miles outside Bodrum, 80 b.; TMT Tatil Köyü (TK1), Akçabük; Torba Tatil Köyü (TK1), Torba Mev., Kızılağaç Köyü.

Bolu ***Bolu Termal, Karacasu Köyü, 145 b.; Köroğlu, Belediye Meydanı Bolu, 110 b.; Koru, Ömerler Köyü, Bakırlı Mev.
**Yurdaer, Belediye Meydanı, 100 b.
Çizmeci (M2), Kılıçaslan Köyü Mev.; Emniyet (M2), Ayrılık Çeşmesi Mev.

Bor *Tyana, Hükümet Mey. 18

Bozöyük **Taşkın, İsmet İnönü Cad. 145

Bulancak Gedikali, Turistik Tesisleri Oteli, Maden Köyü

Burdur *Burdur, Gazi Cad.

Burhaniye ***Urut, Hürriyet Mey. 14
Efem Tatil Köyü (TK2), Ören–Burhaniye; Klüp Orient Tatil Köyü (TK2), Ören; Turban Tatil Köyü (TK2), Burhaniye–Ören

Bursa *****Almira, Ulubatlı Hasan Bul.; Çelik Palas (S), Çekirge Cad. 79, 359 b.; K.S. Termal (S), Çekirge Mey.
****Anatolia (S), Zübeyde Hanım Cad., Çekirge; Dilmen (S), 1st Murat Cad. 20; Kervansary, Fevzi Çakmak Cad. 29; Selimhan, Fevzi Çakmak Cad. 29
***Büyük Yıldız, Uludağ Cad. 24; Gönlüferah (S), 1st Murat Cad. 6; Kırcı, Çekirge Cad. 21; Kent, Atatürk Cad. 119
**Akdoğan, 1st Murat Cad. 1; Büyük Yıldız II (S), Selvinaz Sok. 1, Çekirge; Dikmen, Maksem Cad. 78; Diyar, Çekirge Cad. 47

Büyükada *Splendid, 23 Nisan Cad. 71

Çanakkale ****Akol, Kayserili Ahmet Paşa Cad., 300 b.
**Anafartalar, Kayserili Ahmet Paşa Cad., 148 b.; Bakir, Yalı Cad. 12
Büyük Truva, Yalıboyu

Çandarlı Kibele Pansiyon (P), Talatemmi Cad. 3

Çankırı ***Büyük Çankırı, Abdüllhalit Mah.

Çeşme ****Boyalik, Boyalık Mev., 420 b.; Turban Çeşme (S), Ilıca Mev.
***Arinnanda, Ilıca, 116 b.; Çeşme Ladin, Dalyan Köy Mev. Petek Sitesi Karşisi, 142 b.; Delmar (S), İzmir Cad. 154; Hora, İzmir Cad. PTT Yanı 150, Ilıca, 104 b.; İnkim, İzmir Cad. PTT Karşısı; Kardiya, Çiftlik Köyü Mev.

**Rıdvan, Cumhuriyet Meydanı; Turban Ilıca, Dereboyu Mev. Boyalık;
Yurna, Ilıca Mah. İzmir Cad. 31021; Z, PTT Arkası, Ilıca
Kanuni Kervansaray (Ö), Çeşme Kalesi Yanı
Altınyunus Tatil Köyü (TK1), Boyalık Mev.

**Kadıoğlu, Yenidörtyol Civarı   Cizre

***Turban, Çepri Mah.   Çorum
**Kolagası, İnönü Cad. 97

****Garden Beach Hotel Sarigerme, 8km/5 miles north of Dalaman Air-   Dalaman
port, right on the sandy beach, 550 b.
***Dalaman Park, Dalaman Havaalani Yolu, 120 b.
In Ortaca, 16km/10 miles from Dalaman Airport
****İberotel Sarigerme Park, Ortaca Postahanesı P.K. 1, 750 b.

**Mare, Yanıkharman Mev.   Datça
Club Datça Tatil Köyü (TK2), İskele Mev.
At Perili, 15km/9½ miles out of Datça fishing port
Sunsail Club Perili, 80 b.

***Palaz, Çarşı Kayalık Cad.   Denizli
**Altıntur, Oğuzhan Cad. 1; Arar, Delikliçınar Mey.; Aygören, Cumhuriyet
Cad. 26; Ben-Hur, 632. Sok. 13; Halley, Cumhuriyet Cad.; Keskinkaya,
İstasyon Cad. 83; Kuyumcu, Atatürk Bul. 136; Laodikya, Otogar Arkası;
Park, Atatürk Bul. 104; Seza, Halk Cad. 6

*****May (Akbük), Atanaj, Deresi Mev.   Didim
***Golden Sand, Altınkum; Holiday, Altınkum; Saadet, Altınkum Yenihi-
sar; Tuntaş, Altınkum Gevrek Mev., Yenihisar
**Budak, Çağlar Sitesi, 10. Sok. 7; Gökkuşaği, Gevrek Mev.; Markizet, Yeni
Hisar Karakoyu Mev.; Yıldırım, Altınkum Mah. Diniz Sok 23

**Perla, Şehit Sami Akbulut Cad, 97   Dikili

****Demir, İzzetpaşa Cad. 4   Diyarbakır
**Diyarbakır Büyük, İnönü Cad., Yoğurtçu Sok. 4; Kristalim, Ziya Gökalp
Bul.; Turistik, Ziya Gökalp Bul. 7
Deliller Büyük Kervansaray (Ö), Gazi Cad., Mardinkapı

**Kutlubay, Atatürk Cad. 39   Dörtyol

**Çobantur, E–80 Karayolu Çoban Mev.   Düzce

**Balta, Talatpaşa Asfaltı 97, 165 b.; Şaban Açikgöz, Tahmus Sok. 9   Edirne
Fifi (M2), E–80 Karayolu

***Canan, Yeşilada Mah. 15; Eğirdir, Kuzey Sahil Yolu 2   Eğridir

**Beritan, Hürriyet Cad. 24, 125 b.; Büyük Elaziğ, Harput Cad. 9   Elazığ

Turban Elmadağ Dağ Evi (O), Yakupabdal Köyü   Elmadağ

***Toronto II., Çuğra Mev.   Erdek
**Arteka, Ali Haydar Sahil Parkı 216, Çuğra, 74 b.; Ciciler, Kumluyuvalı Cad.
146; Gülplaj, Kumluyuvalı Cad. 76; Kirtay, Tatlisu Köyü, 130 b.; Pınar,
Mangırcı Mev.; Yücel, Çuğra Mev. 90

**Yaka, Kızkalesi Mev.   Erdemli

**Roma, Ordu Cad. 102. Sok. 1, 60 b.   Erzincan

***Büyük Erzurum, Ali Ravi Cad. 5;   Erzurum
**Oral, Terminal Cad. 3, 180 b.; Sefer, İstasyon Cad.

Hotels

Eskişehir ***Büyük Otel, 27 Mayıs Cad. 40
**Dural, Yunusemre Cad. 97; Emek, Otogar Yanı; Has Termal (S), Hamam
Yolu Cad. 7; Porsuk, Yunusemre Cad. 103

Fatsa Dolunay (M2) on the road between Samsun and Trabzon

Fethiye ****Aries Club Hotel, Çaliş Mev., 350 b.; Pirlanta, 1st Karagözler Mev. P.K.
20, 150 b.
**Dedeoğlu, İskele Mey.; Dostlar, Dolgu Sahası; Ein Rose, İnkilap Cad.;
Malhun, Çalış Plajı; Meri, Ölüdeniz; Prenses, Karagözler Mah.; Vizon, Hastahane Sok. PTT Santral Yanı

Holiday villages Club Aldiana, 600 b.; Letoonia Holiday Village, P.O. Box 63, 1502 b.;
Robinson Club Lykia, Ölüdeniz Kidirak Mev., 1350 b.

Finike Anadolu, Kum Mah., 28 r.

Foça **Hanedan, Büyükdeniz Mev.
(near İzmir) Karaçam (Ö), Sahil Cad.

Holiday village Club Méditerranée–Foça Tatil Köyü (TK1)

Gaziantep **Kaleli, Hürriyet Cad., Güzelce Sok. 50
*Alfin, Hürriyet Cad. 27; Miramar, Hürriyet Cad. 24

Gebze **Club Atabay Oteli, Eskihisar
*Doğus, Eskhisar Köyü

Gelibolu ***Boncuk, Sütlüce Köyü

Gemlik **Atamar (S), Kumla Yolu Hasanağa Mev.

Gerede ***Esentepe Turistik Tesisleri, Esentepe Mev.

Gerze Gerze Köşkburnu Turistik Tesisleri (M2), Köskburnu Mev.

Giresun ***Kit-Tur, Arifbey Cad. 2
**Çarıkçi, Osmanağa Cad. 6; Giresun, Atatürk Bul. 103

Gölcük *Coskun, Amiral Sağlam Cad. 83
Astakoz (M2), Değirmendere, Müzviran Mev., Karayolu Üstü

Gönen ***Yıldız Kaplıca (S), Kaplıcalar Sahası

Güllük **Kont Oteli, P.K. 18; Sürücü, Atatürk Anıtı Karşısı

Gülşehir *Gülşehir Belediye, Kızılırmak Cad.

Gümüldür **Paşa, Özdere Köyü
Turban Gümüldür Tatil Köyü (TK1), Gelinos Mev., Dayanıklı Köyü

Hacıbetaş *Village House, Karsıhamam Mev.

Hakkari *Mustafa Ümit, Altay Cad.

Hatay ***Büyük Antakya, Atatürk Cad. 8; Defay, Defne Cad.
Hidro, Karyer Mah.

Havsa Dereli (M2), Necatiye Köyü

Haymana *Cimcime, Kemalpaşa Cad; Saraçoğlu, Hama Sok. 4

Hopa *Cihan, Ortahopa Cad. 7

*****Nunamar, İçmeler
***Alinda, Musayeri Mev.; Mar-Bas, İçmeler Köyü; Martı II, İçmeler Köyü
Mev.
**Alınorfe, İçmeler Köyü, 69, Sok. 7; Berkit, İçmeler; Kanarya, Kumlu,
Örencik Mev.; Oylum, İçmeler; Piccolo, İçmeler; Rally, Kenan Evren Bul.
22; Sarba, İçmeler; Yavuz II, Kumluörek Mevkii; Wite Haleyes, İçmeler
Martı Tatil Köyü (TK1), İçmeler Köyü

İçmeler

**Parlar, Irfan Cad. 39, 83 b.

İğdir

****Alaaddin II, Avşallar İncekum Mev.
***İncekum, Avşallar
**Aspendos, Avşallar; Yalıhan, Avşallar Köyü

İncekum

***Arsuz, on the Arsuz–İskenderun route
**Alpaydin, Şehit Pamir Cad. 48; Bahadırlı, Pr. Muammer Aksoy Cad. 31;
Cabiroğlu, Ulucami Cad. 16; Hataylı, Osmangazi Cfad. 2nd İnciler, Raifpaşa
Cad., 105 Sok. 10

İskenderun

****Büyük Isparta, K. Kapi Mey., 126 b.
**Artan, Cengiz topel Cad., Mustantık Sok. 12/B; Bolat, Demirel Bul. 87

Isparta

*****Büyük Sürmeli, Saatçibayırı Sok. 3, Gayrettepe; Büyük Tarabya, Kefe-
liköy Cad. Tarabya, 525 b.; Çirağan Palace Hotel Kempinski, Çirağan Cad.
84, Beşiktaş, 672 b.; Divan, Cumhuriyet Cad. 2; Hilton, Cumhuriyet Cad.,
Harbiye, 500 r.; Holiday Inn, Sahil Yolu, Bakırköy, Ataköy, 219 b.;İstanbul
Dedeman, Yıldız Posta Cad. 50, Esentepe; İstanbul Mövenpick, Büyükdere
Cad. Üçyol Mev., 49 Maslak, 610 b.; Ramada, Ordu Cad. 226, Lalelı, 551 b.;
Sheraton, Taksim Park, Taksim, 854 b.; Swissôtel İstanbul – The Bosporus,
Bayildim Cad. 2 Macka, Beşiktaş, 1185 b.; The Marmara, Taksim Mey. 395 r.
****Dilson, Sıraselviler Cad. 49, Taksim; Etap, Meşrutiyet Cad., Tepebaşı;
Eysan, Rıhtım Cad., Kadıköy, 125 b.; Fuar, Namık Kemal Cad. 26, Aksaray;
Grand Hotel Haliç, Şişhane, Refik Saydam Cad. 153, 180 b.; Güneş, Nadide
Cad. Günay Sok. 10, Merter, 180 b.; Hidiv Kasri (view of the Bosporus) in the
suburb of Çubuklu, 15 r.; İstanbul Parksa (Hilton), Beyıldım Cad. 12, 123 r.;
Kalyon, Sahil Yolu, Sultanahmet; Maçka, Eytam Cad. 35, Tesvikiye, 368 b.;
Keban, Sıraselviler Cad. 51/A, Taksim; Merter Günes, Güney Sok. 10, Mer-
ter, Bakırköy; Olcay, Millet Cad. 187, Topkapı; Perapalas, Meşrutiyet Cad.
98, Beyoğlu; Sport, Sekbanbaşı Sok. 6, Beyazıt, 250 b.; The President,
Tıyatro Cad. 25, Beyazıt, 323 b.
***Aden, Osmanağa Mah., Yoğurtçu Sükrü Sok. 42, Kadiköy, 152 b.;
Akgün, Ordu Cad., Haznedar Sok. 6; Arman, Manastırlı Rıfat Sok., Fatih;
Bale, Refik Saydam Cad., Akarca Yolu 55; Baron, Büyük Tulumba Çikmazı
Sok. 12, Beyazıt, 212 b.; Benler, Ordu Cad., Ağaçeşme Sok. 11, Beyazıt;
Berr, Akdeniz Cad. 78, Fatih; Carlton, Fevziye Cad. 25, Şehzadebaşı; Cihan-
gir, Aslanyatağı Sok. 33, Cihangir, 106 b; Epos, İstanbul Cad., Havlucular
Sok. 3, Bakırköy; Erboy, Ebussuud Cad. 32, Sirkeci; Eysan, Rıhtım Cad.,
Misak-I Milli Sok. 1/3, Kadiköy; Ferhat, Binbir Direk Mah. Terzihane Sok. 9,
Sultanahmet, 130 b.; Gold, Şair Haşmet Sok 11, Laleli, Gönen, Fethi Bey
Cad. Zeynep Kamil 54–56, Lali, 130 b.; Grand Salman, Laleli Cad. 10,
Aksaray; Grand Star, Sıraselviler Cad. 79, Beyoğlu; Grand Washington II,
Gençtürk Cad. Ağa Yokusu 7, Laleli; Gülsoy, Mithat Paşa Cad. 5, Beyazıt;
Harem, Ambar Sok. 2, Selimiye-Usküdar; İkbal, Koska Cad. 45, Laleli, 300
b.; Intersport, Sekbanbaşı Sok. 6, Beyazıt; Kaya, Millet Cad. 86, Fındıklı-
zade; Keçik, Fetibey Cad. 18, Laleli; Kilim, Millet Cad. 85, Fındıkzade, 14 b.;
Konak, Cumhuriyet Cad., Nisbet Sok. 7, Elmadağ; Kuran, Güvenlik Cad. 1,
Laleli; Monaco, Fitnat Sok. 28; Niza Park, Kore Şehitler Cad., Mithat
Uluünlü Sok. 19/1, Zincirlikuyu, 88 b.; Pen, Ankara Cad. 258, Pendik; Piyer-
loti, Piyerloti Cad. 5, Sultanahmet, 72 b.; Prestige, Koska Cad. 8; Royal,
Aksaray Cad. 16, Laleli, 202 b.; Şahinler, Koska Cad. 10, Laleli, 220 b.;
Suadiye, Plaj Yolu 51, Suadiye; Sultan, Gençtürk Cad. 29, Laleli; Manastırlı
Rıfat Sok. 33, Aksaray; Topkapı, Oğuzhan Cad. 20, Fındıklızade, 90 b.;

İstanbul

Hotels

Tozbey, Şair Haşmet Sok. 33, Lalei; Usta, Topçu Cad. 19, Taksim, 125 b.; Uyan, Utangaç Sok. 25, Sultanahmet, 34 b.; Washington, Gençtürk Cad. 12, Laleli; Yüksel, Mesihpaşa Cad. 81, Laleli; Zürih, Harkizadeler Sok. 37, Laleli **Alfa, Op. Raifbey Sok. 40, Şişli; Bebek, Cevdetpaşa Cad. 113–115, Bebek, 95 b.; Bern, Muratpaşa Cad. 16, Aksaray; Opera, İnönü Cad. 38, Taksim; Yenişehir Palas, Meşrutiyet Cad. Tepebaşı
Motel Londra Camping (M2), Londra Asfaltı, Süt Sanayi Karşısı, Bakırköy, 60 b; Yeşilköy (M1), Havan Sok. 4, Yeşilköy
Hidiv Kasrı (Ö). Çubuklu Beykoz; Sokullupaşa (Ö), Mehmetpaşa Sok. 3, Sultanahmet; Splendid, 23 Nisan Cad. 71, Büyükada; Sümengen (Ö), Mimarmehmetağa Cad., Tafdif Sok. 21, Sultanahmet; Yeşilev (Ö), Kabasakal Sok. 5, Sultanahmet; Kariye (Ö), Kariye Camii Sok., 27 b.
Ataköy Tatil Köyü (TK1), Sahil Yolu Ataköy
At Yeşilköy Airport
****Çinar, Fenermevkii, Yeşilköy, 372 b.

İzmir

*****Büyük Efes, Gaziosmanpaşa Bul. 1. 885.; Grand Plaza, Saka-rya Cad. 156, 300 b.; Hilton, Gaziosmanpaşa Bul. 138, 381 r.
****Etap, Cumhuriyet Bul. 138; Sevranoğlu Turistik Tesisleri, Mithat Paşa Cad. 128
***Anba, Cumhuriyet Bul. 124, 96 b.; Atlantis, Gazi Pul. 128, Basmane; Balçova Kaplıca (S), Vali Hüseyin Öğütçen Cad. 2, Balçova, 400 b.; Ege Güneşi, Fatih Cad. 69, Çamdibi; Hisar, Fevzipaşa Bul. 153, 138 b.; İzmirim, Gaziler Cad. 284, Yenişehir; İzmir Palas, Vasıf Çinar Bul. 2, Alsancak, 296 b.; Karaca, 1379. Sok. 55, Alsancak, Kilim, Kazı, Dirik Cad. 1; Karşıyaka, Anadolu Cad. 691, Karşiyaka; Kocaman, Gaziler Cad., 1195. Sok. 2, Yenişehir, 160 b.; Marıa, Vali Kazım Dirik Cad. 7, Paşaport; Rantha, Mürselpaşa Bul. 2, Basmane; Yumukoğlu, Şair Eşref Bul. 10
**Billur, Anafartalar Cad. 783, Basmane, 121 b.; Ege Çinar, 9 Eylül Mey. 2, Basmane, 70 b.; Kaya, Gaziosmanpaşa Bul. 45; Zeybek, 1368 Sok. 5, Basmane

İzmit/Kocaeli

***Altınnal, Alemdar Cad. 7
**Asya, Ankara Cad. 3

Kadirli

**Sülemiş, Turistik Tesisleri, Cemal Paşa Mah.

Kahraman Maraş

**Belli, Trabzon Cad. 10; Kazancı, Kıbrıs Mey. Civarı

Kâhta

Nemrut Tur (M2), on the Adıyaman–Kâhta road; Zeus (M2), Nemrut Dağı Karadut Köyü

Kalkan

***Enerhan, Kalamar Yolu; Pirat, Kalkan Marinası
**Kalamar Turistik Tesisleri

Karaman

*Nas, İsmetpaşa Cad. 2

Karamürsel

Kırahmetoğlu Turistik Tesisleri (M1) on the Karamürsel–Yalova road; Şirin Kaptan Turistik Tesisleri (M2), Kavak Mev.

Kars

**Güngören, Halitpaşa Mah., Millet Sok. 2

Kas

****Aqua-Park, Çukurbağ Yarımadası, 271 b.
***Ada Apartments, Çukurbağ Adası, 18 APRT, 72 b.; Club Hotel Phellos, Doğruyol Sok, 200 b.; Ekici, Hükümet Konağı Yanı, 168 b.
**Kekova, Milli Güvenlik Caddesi 2; Mimosa, Elmalı Cad.; Oryant, Elmalı Cad. 7

Kayseri

**Çaparı, Donanma Cad. 12; Hattat, Camli Kebir Cad. 1; Konfor, Atatürk Bul. 5, 85 b.; Köseoğlu, Talas Cad. 22; Titiz, Marif Caddesi 7; Turan, Turan Cad. 8

Kemer

*****Art, Kızıltepe Mev., 712 b.; Göynük Sultan/Saray, Göynük Mev., 1000

b.; Grand Phaselis, Tekirova; Kırış World Magic, P.K. 99, 900 b.; Princess, Tekirova, 700 b.; Ramada Renaissance Resort, P.O. Box 654, 657 b.; Türkiz, Yalı Cad. 3
****Bilkent Paradise, Kızıltepe Mev.; Otem, Yat Limanı Karşısı; Palmiye, Tekerlek Tepe Mev.; Pegasos Princes, Deniz Cad., 114 b.; Nona, Deniz Cad., 125 b.; Roman Centrum Apart., Liman Cad., 252 b.
Club Med Palmiye Hotel, Tekerlektepe Mev.; 544 b.
***Dragos, Deniz Cad.; Golden Lotus, Tekirova; Ifa Beach, Tekirova; Korient, İskele Cad. 1; Olimpos, Kemer; Pegases, Deniz Cad. 39; Roman Plaza, Deniz Cad., 268 b.
**Ambassador, Liman Cad. 10, 62 b.; Daallar Adonis, Karayer Mev., 60 b.; Dragos, Deniz Cad.; Elegance, Karayer Mev. 202, Sok. 5, 40 b.; Hasan Şeker, Kemer; Kemer Doruk, Liman Caddesi 19; Roman Beach, Deniz Cad. 33, 40 b.
Bonn (Ö), Deniz Cad.; Nona (Ö), Deniz Cad. 1

Çamyuva Tatil Köyü (TK1), Çamyuva Köyü; Club Alda, Beldibi, 900 b.; Club Aldiana Milta Tatil Köyü (TK1), Kızıltepe Mev., 750 b.; Club Méditerranée Kemer Holiday Village, Akdeniz Turistik Tes. A.S. 1200 b.; Club Méditerranée Palmiye Holiday Village, Tekerlektepe Mev., 1010 b.; Club Turtle's Marco Polo, Çamyuva, 937 b.; Eldorador Tatil Köyü (TK1), Kemer; Hydros Village Tatil Köyü (TK1), Kemer; Kemer Holiday Club, Göynük, 600 b.; Kemer Tatil Köyü (TK1), Kemer; Kimeros Tatil Köyü (TK1), Kızıltepe Mev.; Milta Tatil Köyü (TK1), Kızıltepe Mev.; Novotel Ağamarine Tatil Köyü (TK1), Beldibi; Palmariva Tatil Köyü (TK1), Tekirova; Robinson Club Çamyuva, 780 b.; Salima Tatil Köyü (TK1), Beldibi, Kızıltepe Mev.; Simena Ceytur Ceylan Tatil Köyü (TK1), Çamyuva; Şampiyon Tatil Köyü (TK1), Beldibi; Ulusoy Tatil Köyü (TK1), Güynük Mev. **Holiday villages**

***Yener, Demirciler Cad. 18 **Keşan**

***Terme (S), Kaplıca, Kuşdili, Mah. Terme Cad., 264 b. **Kırşehir**

***Cam, Milli Park İçi **Kızılcahamam**

***Balıkçilar, Mevlana Karşısı, 102 b.; Dergah, Mevlana Cad. 19; Selçuk, Alaaddin Cad., 158 b. **Konya**
**Konya, Mevlanda Alanı; Özkaymak Park, Otogar Karşısı; Sema 21, Mevlana Cad. 15, 72 b.; Sifa, Mevlana Cad. 11, 65 b.; Touristic, Mevlana Alanı, 104 b.; Yeni Sema, Yeni Meram Yolu, 128 b.; Zafer, Saitpaşa Cad., Kemah Sok. 11

*****Ra, Sarıgerme **Köycegiz**
****Sarıgerme Park
**Kaunos, Topel Cad. 37; Özay, Ulucamii Mah.

***Marin, Silivri Yolu (6km/3½ miles) **Kumburğaz**

Kilyos Kale, Kale Cad. 78 **Kumköy
*Turban Kilyos, Kilyos

*****Club Ephesus Princess, Pamucak Mev., 55 b.; Fantasia, Söke Yolu (5km/3 miles), 624 b.; Imbat, Kadılar Denizi, Hacı Feyzullarh Mah., Mev., 650 b.; Onur, Yavansu Mev., 660 b. **Kuşadası**
****Adakule Bayraklıdede, Mev., 550 b.; Batıhan, Ilıca Mev., P.O. Box 130, 310 b.;
***Hotel Club Adkeniz, Karaova Mev., 1030 b.; Asena, Kadınlar Denizi; Atınç, Atatürk Bul.; Barbados, Kadınlar Denizi; Club Akdeniz, Karaova Mev.; Club Pıgale Hotel, Kemerönü Mev., 232 b.; Derici, Atatürk Bul. 40; Kısmet, Akyar Mev.; Martı, Kadınlar Denizi; Minay, Alitepe Sitesi Arkası, Kadınlar Denizi, 120 b.; Özçelik, Yat Limanı Karşısı; Pagos, Çevre Yolu Üzeri; Santur, C. Tarhan Bul.; Sözer Biraderler, Atatürk Bul.; Surtel, Atatürk Bul. 20; Talat, Camıatık Mah. Kanarya Sok. 8, 66 b.; Tusan, 31'ler Plaj Mev.

Hotels

**Akman, İstiklal Cad. 13; Alp, Yat Limanı Karşısı; Altümsek, Güvenevler 1; Aydın, İnönü Bul. 14; Barbados, Köyaltı Mev., Güzel Çamlık Köyü; Club Hotel Solara, Güzelçamlı Köyü, 216 b.; Efe, Güvercinada Cad. 37, 89 b.; Eke, Yat Limanı; Minik, Cephane Sok. 8; Nilay, Candar Tarhan Bul., Cemali Dağyaran Sok. 10; Ölmez, Kemerönü Mev., 130 b.; Royal, Söke Yolu Üzeri, Kirazlı Yol Ayrımı; Stella, Bezirgan Sok. 44; Turkad, Kadılar Denizi, 104 b.; Mehmetpaşa Kervansarayı (Ö), Atatürk Bul. 1

Holiday villages   Club Méditerranée Kuşadası Holiday Village (TK1), Akdeniz Turistik Tesisleri A.Ş, Arslanburnu Mev., 1180 b.; Kuş-Tur Tatil Köyü (TK1), 31'ler Plaj Mev., 1007 b.; Ömer Tatil Köyü (TK2), Yavansu Mev.

Kütahya   ***Erbaylar, Afyon Cad. 16, 84 b.
*Gönen, Menderes Cad., 102 b.

Lüleburgaz   **Yaman, İstanbul Asfalti Civarı

Malatya   **Malatya Büyük, Yeni Cami Karşıl, Zafer İşhanı 1

Manavgat   *****Asteria, Side; Cesars, Kumköyü; Grand Prestige Side, Titreyengöl Mev., P.K. 84, Sorgun, 750 b.; Kaya, P.K. 26, 635 b.; Novatel Turkuaz, Sorgun-Acısu Mev.; Saray Regency, Titreyengöl Mevkii, P.K. 34, 310 b.
****Belinda, Titreyengöl, 280 b.; Excelsior Conrinthia, Titreyengöl, 310 b.; Iberotel Side Palace, P.K. 57, 562 b.; Linda, Titreyengöl Mev.; Süral, Tilkiler Mev. Çolaklı Köyü; Terrace, Kumköy Mev.
***Ark, Çolaklı, 42 b.; Defne, Side Köyü; Hotel Club Golf, P.K. 4, Titreyengöl, 160 b.; Side Büyük, Bingeşik Mevkii P.K. 90, 300 b.; Tayyar Bey, Gündoğdu Mevki

Holiday villages   Club Aldiana Tatil Köyü (TK1), 630 b.; Club Ali Bey, 528 r.; Robinson Club Pamfilya (TK1), Acısu Mev., Side, 823 b.; Sidelya Tatil Köyü (TK1), Çolaklı Köyü; Turtel Tatil Köyü (TK1), Selimiye Köyü

Manisa   **Arma, Doğu Cad. 14

Marmaris   *****Altınyunus Turistik Tesisleri, İçmeler Köyü, 706 b.; Nuna-mar, İçmeler, 320 b.; Elegance, Uzunyalı Cad. 130, 205 r.
****Pineta, Kenan Evren Bul., Şirinyer, 360 b.; Turunç, Turunç Köyü, 512 b.
***Alinda, İçmeler; Blubays, Kenan Evren Bul.; Blue Rainbow, İçmeler; Emre, Siteler Mah. Kenan Evren Bul. 4, 192 b.; Havaii, Çıldır Mev.; Kalemci, Kemal Elgin Bul., Dergahcivarı Mev.; Karacan, Kenan Evren Bul.; Ketenci, Kemeraltı Mah. 9; Lidya, Siteler Mah. 130; Mavi, Atatürk Cad. 72, 126 b.; Mar-Bas, İçmeler Köyü; Martı II, İçmeler Köyü; Nergis, Kemal Elgin Bul.; Otel 47, Atatürk Cad. 10; Öz-Çan, Turunç Köyü; Selen, Kemal Elgin Bul.; Siesta, 68 Sokak. 4, 72 b.; Yavuz, Atatürk Cad. 10

Holiday villages   Halıcı Tatil Köyü (TK2); Iberotel Marmaris Park, Pamucak Mevkii P.K. 129, İçmeler, 402 b.; Marti Holiday Village, P.K. 5, İçmeler, 582 b.; Mordeniz Tatil Köyü (TK1), Pamucak Mev., İçmeler; Robinson Club Maris; Turban Marmaris Tatil Köyü (TK1)
Bei Orhaniye, in the Bay of Keci, just 45 min. west of Marmaris Sunsail Club Orhaniye, 45 b.

Mersin/İçel   *****Hilton, Adnan Menderes Bul., 273 b.; Ramada, Kuvayı Mıllıye Cad., 498 b.
****Gondol, Gazı Mustafa Kemal Bul. 20, 160 b.; Atlıhan, İstiklal Cad. 168.; Mersin, Camii Şerif Mahallesi, 10th Sok. 2
***Club Solı Hotel, Gırıt Mevkii Mezıtlı, 191 b.; Aloğlu, Mustafa Kemal Bul. 2; Nobel, İstiklal Cad. 101–74
**Aktas, İstiklal Cad. 152; Bayraklı, Mersin'li Ahmet Cad., 7th Otogar Karşısı; Damlaca, Fasılkayabalı Cad. 6; Derman, İstiklal Cad., İleri İlkokul Yanı; Ezgi, Yeni Otogar İçi; Hayat, İstiklal Cad. 88; Hosta, Fasılkayabalı Cad. 4;

Ocak, İstiklal Cad. 48; Özdemir, 252th Sok. 12; Sargın, Fasılkaya Cad. 10;
Toros, Atatürk Cad. 33

***Club Soli, Mezitli; Sahil Martı, Mezitli   **Mezitli**

Hülya Beldesi (P), Karaburun Ardıç Mev.; Rüya Beldesi (P), Ardiç Mev. **Mordoğan**

Köksal, Güzelyalı Mah.   **Mudanya

***Petur, Marmaris Bul. 27   **Muğla**
*Özalp, Recai Gürel Cad. 5

*Hande, Lalaşahin Mah., Hamam Sok. 11   **Mustafa Kemal
Paşa**

Ticaret Odası, Hürriyet Cad.   **Nazilli

****Altınöz, Ragıp Üner Cad.; Nevşehir Dedeman, Ürgüp Yolu (2km/1 mile) **Nevşehir**
***Kavas, Ürgüp Yolu Üzeri; Şehir Palas, Belediye Cad.
**Epok, Hükümet Cad. 39; Orsan Kapadokya, Kayseri Cad. 15; Uçhisar,
Aksaray Cad. 35

Robinson Lodge, Kapadokya   Holiday village

*Nizip Belediye, Atatürk Bul. 28   **Nizip**

Nezirhan (M2), Girmeli Köyü Mev.   **Nusaybin**

*Çaykent, Sahil Cad. 52   **Of**

See Fethiye, above   **Ölüdeniz**

***Belde, Kirazlimanı Mah., 126 b.   **Ordu**
**Turist, Atatürk Bul. 134.
Denizcan (M2), Güzelyalı Mah.

See Dalaman, above   **Ortaca**

Tekinoğlu (P), Yeşilyazı Cad. 20   **Ovacik**

***Ergür, Karahayıt, 332 b.; Pam, Karahayit Köyü; Tusan, 94 b. **Pamukkale**

Koru, 260 b.; Palmiye, 120 b.   Motels

Club Hierapolis Tatil Köyü (TK1–K), Karahayit, 456 b.   Holiday village

***Pen, Ankara Cad. 258   **Pendik**
Doğa Güneş, Güzelyalı, Batı Sahili Yolu 33

*Vona, Aktaş Mev.   **Perşembe**

*Toros, Atatürk Cad. 101; Tuğrul Palas, Dinar Cad. 58   **Pozantı**

Keleş, Palandöken Cad. 2   **Rize

Uz, Misaki Milli Mah., Arpa Hacı Sok.   **Safranbolu

***Akyar, Atatürk Bul. 75; Baltürk, Ankara Cad. 53   **Sakarya**

Alkent Tesisleri (M2), on the İzmir–Ankara route, Taytan Köyü **Salihli**

Hotels

A holiday village for the well-to-do: Hierapolis Spa Hotel (Pamukkale)

Samsun	****Turban Büyük Samsun, Atatürk Bul. ***Yafeya, Cumhuriyet Mey. **Vidinli, Kazımpaşa Cad. 4
Sandıklı	*Kaplıca (K), Hüdai Kaplıcaları; Tuğrul Palas, Dinar Cad. 58
Şanlıurfa	***Harran, Atatürk Bul. **Köran, İpekyolu Cad. 13/A; Turban Urfa, Köprübaşı Cad. 74
Sapanca	***Sapanca Vakıf, Rüstempaşa Mah., Kumbaz Sok. 10 Saraçoğlu Turistik Tesisleri (M1), Sapanca Gölü Kenarı
Sarayköy	***Sıla, İstanbul Yolu
Selçuk	****Tamsa Pamucak, Pamucak Sahili **Ak, Kuşadası Cad. 14; Atadan, Atatürk Cad. 6; Bayern, Atatürk Mah., Kubulay Sok. 45; Cenka, Kubilay Cad. 24–26; Mekan, Atatürk Mah. 1, Spor Sok. 11; Victoria, Cengiz Topel Cad. 4 *Kalehan II, Atatürk Cad. 49; Katibim, Atatürk Cad. 5 Tusan Efes (M1), Efes Yolu 38; Kale Han (M2), Atatürk Cad. 49
Side	*****Asteria, Side; Cesars, Kumköyü ****Terrace, Kumköy Mev. ***Defne, Side Köyü; Golf, Tityereyengöl Mev. **Cennet, Side Köyü.; Club Bella I, Bingeşik Mev. *Karaelmas, Bingeşik Köyp Turtel Tatil Köyü (TK1), Selimiye Köyü 7km/4½ miles outside Side, 65km/40 miles from Antalya ***Excelsior Corinthia, 151 r. Club Aldiana Side: see Manavgat, above
Siirt	**Erdef, Cumhuriyet Cad. 9

**Değirmen, Play Yolu 24   Şile
Kumbaba Oberj (O)

*****Klassis, Kargakuma Mev., 710 b.   Silivri
**Blanche Marmara, Karayolu Üzeri, Selimpaşa Köyü; Sel, Ayazma Mev.
Selimpaşa Köyü

**Melia Kasım, Gazi Cad. 49   Sinop

**Köşk, Atatürk Cad. 11; Madımak, Eski Belediye Sok. 4   Sivas
*Sultan, Belediye Sok. 16

**Saraçoğlu Muzaffer Turistik Tesisleri, on the Amasya–Samsun route   Suluova

Hitit (M2), on the Amasya–Samsun road   Sungurlu

****Altınorfoz, Kuruçay Mev. Atakent, 236 b.; Ertur, Kuru Cam Mev.,   Taşucu/Silifke
Atakent
***Taştur, Taşucu, 108 b.
**Olba, Sahil Cad.
*Korikos, Kızkales Mev.
Tolya Moteli Susamoğlu (M2), Mah., 5th Sok. 6, Atakent.

*Huzur, Cumhuriyet Cad.   Tavşanlı/Kütahya

*Yat, Yalı Cad. 8   Tekirdağ
Miltur Turistik Tesisleri (M1), Kumbağ Köyü

****Tokat, Demir Köprü Mev., 120 b.   Tokat
*Plevne, Gaziosmanpaşa Bul. 83; Turist Cumhuriyet Mey.

Avşar (M1), Dağarlı Köyü, Avşar Mev.   Tosya/Kastamonu

**Özgür, Atatürk Alanı 29   Trabzon
*Horon, Sıran Mağazaları 125

*Alabalık, Kışla Cad.   Tunceli
***Club Armany, Akyarlar Kemer Mev.; Faye, Akyarlar Köyü, Palamut
Mev.; Mut, Domalan Mev.

**Duygulu, on the Bodrum–Turgutreis road; Gizem, Abide Cad. 11; Opal,   Turgutreis/Bodrum
Damalan Mev.; Simin, Akyarlar Köyü, Akçabük Mev.
*Özünal, Abide Cad. 24; Sami, Gümbet Mev.

***Robinson Club Kapadokya, Ürgüp Yolu Uçhisar Yolkavsaği   Uçhisar
Kaya (M1)

****Grand Yazıcı Oberj, 1st Gelişim Bölgesi   Uludağ/Bursa
***Alkoçlar Oberj, Milli Park; Yazıcı Oberj, Oteller Mev.
**Fahri, 1st Gelişim Bölgesi; Panorama, 1st Gelişim Bölgesi; Turistik Ulu-
dağ, 1st Gelişim Bölgesi

*Çiftehan (S), Çiftehan Kaplıcaları   Ulukışla

*Kumsal, Gölevi Köyü   Ünye

****Dinler, Ürgüp, 344 b.; Mustafa, Tuzyolu, 204 b.; Perissia, Kayser Cad.,   Ürgüp
462 b.
***Taşsaray, Mustafa Paşa Cad. 10, 218 b.; Yeni Yükseller, Kayseri Yolu
Ortahisar Köyü
**Boytas Tepe, Teslimiye Tepesi
Boytaş (M1), Kayseri Yolu; Turban Ürgüp (M1)
Alfina (O), Karağendere Mah. 25

Hotels

Hotel bar in Ürgüp, in the style of a nomad parlour

Urla/İskele	Nebioğlu Tatil Köyü (TK2) Yutur Pansiyon (P), 43. Sok. İskele Mev. 22, İskele Mah.
Uşak	***Şahlan I (S), İsmet Paşa Cad. 39/A **Ağaoğlu, İsmetpaşa Cad. 62; Onarslan, Evren Bul. 3; Şahlan II, Uzuncarşı Fabrikalar Sok.
Uzunköprü	*Ergene, Cumhuriyet Mey. 20
Vakfıkebir	***Büyük Liman Tesisleri, Sahıl Cad., 105 b. **Vakfıkebir, Sahil Cad. 6
Van	***Akdamar, Kazi Karabekir Cad. 56; Büyük Urartu, Hastane Sok. 60; Necdet Şahin, İrfan Başbug Cad. 30 **Büyük Asur, Cumhuriyet Cad. 126/1 *Çaldıran, Sıhke Cad.; Güzel Paris, İrfan Baştuğ Cad. 20; Tekin, Kücük Cami Cıvarı
Yalova	**Önder Şeref, Yalı Cad. 19; Gökçedere, Gökçeder Köyü *Ülke, Yalı Cad.; Ferah, Gökçedere Köyü Turban Yalova Termal (Ö)
Yeşilköy/İstanbul	See İstanbul, above
Yozgat	**Yılmaz, Ankara Cad. 14
Yumurtalık	**Öztur, Atatürk Cad. 31
Zonguldak	**Konak, Nizam Cad. 8 *Ay, Gazipaşa Cad. 61; Otel 67, Fevzipaşa Cad. 1

Information

Turkish Tourism and Information Office
170–173 Piccadilly (1st floor), London W1V 9DD;
tel. (071) 734 86 81, 734 86 82, 355 42 07, 408 20 21

Office of the Culture and Information Attaché
Turkish Consulate-General,
821 United Nations Plaza, New York NY 10017;
tel. (212) 986 50 50

Culture and Tourism Office, Turkish Embassy,
2010 Massachusetts Avenue NW, Washington DC 20036;
tel. (202) 833 84 11, 429 98 44

Turizm Bakanlığı (Ministry for Tourism)
İsmet İnönü Bulvarı 5, Bahcelievler, Ankara;
tel. (0–312) 212 83 00

Adana (main office): Atatürk Caddesi 13; tel. (0–322) 359 19 94; airport:
Şakirpaşa, Hava Limanı; tel. (0–322) 352 67 90
Adiyaman: Atatürk Bulvarı 184; tel. (0–416) 216 10 08
Afyon: Dumlupınar Mah., Ordu Bulvarı 22, 1st floor; tel. (9–491) 3 54 47
Agri: Cumhuriyet İlkokulu arkası, Sağlik Eğitim Merkezi eski binası; tel.
    (0–472) 215 37 30
Akçakoca: Cumhuriyet Meydanı; tel. (9–46 14) 45 54 and 38 15
Akçay: Edremit Caddesi, Karabudak Apt. 20; tel. (0–266) 384 11 13
Aksaray: Ankara Caddesi, Dinçer Apt. 2/2; tel. (0–382) 212 46 88
Alanya: Çarşi Mah., Kalearkası Cad., Damıataş Yanı; tel. (0–242) 513 12 40
    and 513 54 36
Amasya: Mehmrypaşa Mah., Mustafa Kemal Bulvarı 27;
    tel. (0–358) 218 50 02 and 218 74 27)
Anamur: Atatürk Bulvarı 64; tel. (0–324) 814 35 29
Ankara: (central office) Gazi Mustafa Kemal Bulvarı 121, Tandoğan; tel.
    (0–312) 229 26 61 and 229 36 61; also G.M.K. Bulvarı 33, Demirtepe; tel.
    (0–312) 231 73 80/95 and at Esenboğa Airport (Esenboğa Hava Limanı);
    tel. (0–312) 398 03 48 and 398 00 00/15 78
Tourist information can also be obtained in Ankara by calling freephone
    900 44 70 90
Antakya: Atatürk Bulvarı, Vali Ürgen Alanı 47, Hatay; tel. (9–891) 1 26 36 and
    3 57 40
Antalya: (main office) Selçuk Mah,, Mermerli Sokak, Ahiyusuf Cami Yanı,
Kaleiçi; tel. (0–242) 247 05 41, 247 50 42 and 242 18 33; also Cumhuriyet
Caddesi, THY Yanı, Özel İdare İşhanı; tel. (0–242) 241 17 47
Artvin: Turizm Danışma Müdürlüğü; tel. (0–466) 212 27 38
Aydın: Yeni Dörtyol Mevkii; tel. (0–256) 225 41 45 and 212 62 26
Ayvalık: Yat Limanı Karşisi; tel. (0–266) 312 21 22
Avanos; Kenan Evran Caddesi, Heykel yanı; tel. (0–384) 511 43 60
Balıkesir: Dumlupınar Mah., Anafartalar Caddesi, Sayar İşhanı 42; tel.
    (0–266) 241 18 20
Bartın: Hükümet Konaği; tel. (0–378) 227 61 17
Batman: Ziya Gökalp Mah., Kültür Merkezi Bürosu; tel. (0–488) 212 07 18
Bayburt: İleri Caddesi 2; tel. (0–458) 211 49 95
Bergama: Zafer Mah., İzmir Caddesi 54; tel. (0–232) 633 18 62
Bilecik: Vilayet Binası; tel. (0–228) 212 19 78 and 212 39 41
Bingöl: İl Halk Kütüphanesi; tel. (0–426) 213 34 60
Bitlis: İl Halk Kütüphanes Meydanı, 2nd floor; tel. (0–434) 226 53 05
Bodrum: 12 Eylül Meydanı; tel. (0–252) 316 10 91
Bolu: Eski İstanbul Caddesi 2; tel. (0–374) 212 22 54, 212 39 45 and 215 54 79
Burdur: Cumhuriyet Meydanı, Kültür Sarayı, 2nd floor;
    tel. (0–248) 233 50 94 and 233 10 78

Information

Burhaniye: Ören Polis Karakolu Yanı; tel. (0–266) 42 28 70
Bursa: (main office) Fevzi Çakmak Caddesi, Fomara Han, 6th floor; tel. (0–224) 254 22 74 and 253 04 11; also Ulucami Parkı, Altgeçit 1; tel. (0–224) 221 23 59
Çanakkale: (main office) Hükümet Konağı, 1st floor; tel. (0–286) 217 50 12 and 217 37 91; also İskele Meydanı 67; tel. (0–286) 211 11 87
Çankırı: Cumhuriyet Man., 60 Yıl İşhanı; tel. (0–376) 213 40 47
Çeşme: İskele Meydanı 8; tel. (0–232) 712 66 53
Çorum: Yeni Hükümet Konağı 8, A Blok, 4th floor; tel. (0–364) 213 77 17, 213 85 02
Dalaman: at Dalaman Airport (Hava Limanı); tel. (0–252) 692 52 20
Datça: Hükümet Binası, tel. (0–252) 712 35 46 and 712 31 63
Denizli: (main office) Atatürk Caddesi 8, 2nd floor; tel. (0–258) 264 39 71 and 264 76 21; also at the station (gar) İstasyon Caddesi; tel. (0–258) 268 28 20
Diyarbakır: (main office) Kültür Sarayı, 6th floor; tel. (0–412) 221 78 40 and 223 26 35; also Lise Caddesi, Onur Apt. Altı 24/A; tel. (0–412) 221 21 73
Edirne: (main office) Talat Paşa Asfaltı 76/1; tel. (0–284) 225 52 60 and 212 14 90; also Hürriyet Meydanı 17; tel. (0–284) 212 15 18
Edremit: Edremit Caddesi 20; tel. (9–671) 4 11 13
Eğirdir: 1 Sahil Yolu 13; tel. (0–246) 312 20 98 and 311 43 88
Elazığ: (main office) Hükümet Konağı, 2nd floor: tel. (0–424) 122 21 59 and 236 58 54
Erdek: Hükümet Caddesi, 1st Sokak 2, Şeref Apt., tel. (0–266) 835 11 69
Erzincan: Vilayet Binası, 5th floor; tel. (0–446) 223 06 75 and 223 37 92
Erzurum: Cemal Gürsel Caddesi 9/A; tel. (0–442) 218 56 97, 218 91 2790 73
Eskşehir: Vilayet Binası, 1st floor; tel. (0–222) 230 38 65 and 230 17 52
Fethiye: İskele Meydanı 1; tel. (0–252) 614 15 27
Foça: Atatürk Mah., Foça Girisi 1; tel. (0–232) 812 12 22
Gaziantep: Hürriyet Caddesi, Güzelce Sokak 28/A; tel. (0–342) 230 59 69 and 231 68 29
Giresum: (main office) Şeyh Keramettin Mah., H Avni Öğütcü Sokak 11, Özel İdare İşhanı, 2nd floor; tel. (0–454) 212 31 90
Gümüşhane: Hükümet Konağı; tel. (0–456) 213 34 72
Gürbulak Hudut Kapısı (border crossing); tel. (0–472) 321 20 09
Hacıbektaş: Nevşehir Caddesi 44; tel. (0–384) 441 36 87
Hakkari: İstiklal Caddesi 3/20–21; tel. (0–438) 211 65 09
Hatay: see Antakya
İçel: see Mersin, below
İpsala: İpsala Hudut Kapısı (border crossing); tel. (0–284) 616 15 77
Isparta: Hükümet Konağı, 2nd floor; tel. (0–246) 218 44 38 and 212 10 64
İskenderun: Atatürk Bulvarı 99/B; tel. (0–326) 614 16 20 and 613 28 79
İstanbul: (main office) Beyoğlu, Meşrutiyet Cad. 57/6; tel. (0–212) 68 75, 243 34 72, 243 37 31 and 243 29 28, Harbiye: Hilton Oteli Girişi (Hilton entrance); tel. (0–212) 233 05 92; Karaköy: Limanı Yolcu Salonu (Maritime Station); tel. (0–212) 249 57 76; Sultanahmet Meydanı; tel. (0–212) 518 18 02; also at Atatürk Airport (Atatürk Hava Limanı), Yeşilköy; tel. (0–212) 573 73 99 and 573 41 36
İzmir (main office): Atatürk Caddesi 418, Alsancak; tel. (0–232) 4 22 02 07/8, 421 68 41 and 422 10 22; also Gazi Osman Paşa Bulvarı 1/D, Büyük Efes Oteli; tel. (0–232) 489 92 78 and 484 21 47; also at Alsancak Airport; tel. (0–232) 463 16 00/263, and at Adnan Menderes Airport (Adnan Mendres Hava Limanı); tel. (0–236) 251 26 26/10 85 and 251 19 50
İzmit/Kocaeli: Ömerağa Mah., Ankara Caddesi 2; tel. (0–262) 321 56 63 and 321 23 48
İznik: Belediye Paşajı 130/131; tel. (0–224) 757 19 33
Kahramanmaraş: Azerbaycan Caddesi, Yeşiltepe Sokak, Gölkan Apt. 2/2, tel. (0–344) 212 65 90 and 213 30 55
Kahta: Mustafa Kemal Bulvarı, Nemrut Dağı Milli Park Md. Hizmet Binası; tel. (0–416) 725 50 07
Kapıkule: Kapıkule Hudut Kapısı (border crossing), Turing Tesisleri; tel. (0–284) 238 20 19

Karaman: Eski Buğday Pazarı, Şimşek Apt., C Blok, 2nd floor, No 39; tel. (0–338) 212 67 41
Kars: Ortakapı Mah., Ordu Cad. 241; tel. (0–474) 223 27 24 and 223 35 68
Kaş: Cumhuriyet Meydanı 6; tel. (0–242) 836 12 38
Kastamonu: Cumhuriyet Caddesi 22/3; tel. (0–366) 214 61 59
Kayseri: Kağnı Pazarı 61; tel. (0–353) 231 92 95, 231 11 90 and 232 88 71
Kemer: Belediye Binası; tel. (0–242) 814 15 36 and 814 15 37
Kırklareli: Vilyet Binası; tel. (0–228) 214 16 12, 214 18 42 and 214 15 22
Kırşehir: Cumhuriyet Meydanı, Aşık Paşa Caddesi; tel. (0–386) 213 14 16
Konya: Mevlâna Caddesi 21; tel. (0–332) 351 10 74 and 350 64 89
Köyceğiz: Atatürk Kordonu 1; tel. (0–252) 262 47 03
Kuşadası: Liman Caddesi; tel. (0–256) 614 11 03 and 614 62 95
Kütahya: Azarbeycan Parkı İçi; tel. (0–274) 223 24 33
Malatya: İnönü Cad., Tütünbank Üstü, 2nd floor; tel. (0–422) 323 30 25
Manisa: Doğu Caddesi 14/3; tel. (0–236) 231 25 41 and 232 74 23
Maraş: see Kahramanmaraş, above
Mardin: Meydanbaşı Caddesi, İl Halk Kütüphanesi; tel. (0–482) 212 58 45
Marmaris: İskele Meydanı 92; tel. (0–252) 412 10 35 and 412 72 77
Mersin: Yeni Mah., İnönü Bulvarı, Liman Girişi; tel. (0–324) 231 27 10 and 231 12 65; also İsmet İnönü Bulvarı 5/1; tel. (0–324) 231 63 58
Muğla: (main office) Emir Beyazıt Mah., Marmaris Bulvarı 24/1; tel. (0–252) 214 12 61 and 214 12 44
Muş: Hükümet Konağı; tel. (0–436) 212 38 49
Nevşehir: Atatürk Bulvarı, Hastane Yanı; tel. (0–384) 213 11 37
Niğde: İstiklal Caddesi, Vakıf İshanı 1/D: tel. (0–388) 232 33 93
Ordu: (main office) Vilayet Binası, A Blok, 1st floor; tel. (0–452) 223 16 07 and 223 29 22; also Sahil Caddesi, Belediye Binası altı; tel. (0–452) 223 16 08
Pamukkale: Örenyeri; tel. (0–258) 272 20 77
Pergamon: see Bergama, above
Rize: Müftü Mah. Özel İdare Kültür Sitesi, 3rd floor; tel. (0–464) 213 04 07 and 213 04 08
Safranbolu: Arasta Çarşısı 7; tel. (0–372) 712 38 63
Sakarya/Adapazarı: Çark Caddesi 56/1; tel. (0–264) 273 98 44 and 274 28 04
Samsun: 19 Mayıs Mah. Talimhane Caddesi 6; tel. (0–362) 415 28 87 and 431 12 28
Şanlıurfa: Yusufpaşa Mah., Asfalt Caddesi 3/D; tel. (0–414) 215 76 10 and 215 24 67
Sarp: Hopa Kaymakamlığı; tel. (0–466) 371 51 72
Selçuk: Atatürk Mah., Agora Çarşısı 35; tel. (0–232) 892 69 45
Side: Side Yolu Üzeri; tel. (0–242) 753 12 65
Siirt: Atatürk Bulvarı, Özel İşhanı, 5th floor; tel. (0–484) 223 57 90 and 223 44 36
Silifke: Atatürk Caddesi 2/1; tel. (0–324) 714 11 51
Sinop: (main office) Hükümet Konağı; tel. (0–368) 261 52 07
Şirnak: Milli Eğitim Müdürlügü Hizmet Binası, 2nd floor; tel. (0–486) 216 17 08
Sivas: Hükümet Konağı, Zemin Kat, 3–4–6; tel. (0–346 221 35 35, 221 31 35 and 222 22 52
Tatvan: Denizcilik Oteli Yanı, Kütüphane Binası; tel. (0–434) 827 63 00 and 827 63 01
Tekirdağ: (main office) Hürriyet Mah., Rüstem Paşa Caddesi 33–35; tel. (0–282) 261 43 46: also Atatürk Bulvarı, İskele Yanı 65; tel. (0–282) 261 20 83 and 261 16 98
Tokat: Vilayet Binası, 3rd floor; tel. (0–356) 214 37 53 and 214 86 24
Trabzon: (main office) Vilayet Binası, 4th floor; tel. (0–462) 223 58 33 and 223 58 18; also Atatürk Alanı, Park Köşesi; tel. (0–462) 321 46 59
Tunceli: Hükümet Konağı; tel. (0–428) 212 31 05
Ünye: Belediye Binası; tel. (0–462) 323 49 52

Ürgüp: Kayseri Caddesi 37; tel. (0–384) 341 40 59
Uşak: Belediye İşhanı, 1st floor, No 110/112; tel. (0–276) 223 15 70 and
223 38 71
Van: Cumhuriyet Caddesi 19; tel. (0–432) 216 20 18 and 216 36 75
Yalova: İskele Meydanı 5; tel. (0–216) 814 21 08
Yozgat: Özel İdare Binası, 3rd floor; tel. (0–354) 212 64 23, 212 91 64 and
212 75 69
Zonguldak: Hükümet Konağı, 5th floor; tel. (0–372) 253 88 27 and 253 48 57

Insurance

General

Visitors are strongly advised to ensure that they have adequate holiday
insurance, including cover against illness, accident, etc., loss or damage to
luggage loss of currency and jewellery and, particularly if a package holiday has been booked, cancellation insurance.
Arrangements can be made through a travel agent or an insurance company. Many companies operating package holidays now include insurance
as part of the deal.

Vehicles

Visitors travelling by car should ensure that their insurance is comprehensive and covers use of the vehicle in Turkey

See also Travel Documents.

Language

The official and the spoken language of Turkey is Turkish, the most west-
ernly member of the Turco-Tataric language family. It is believed to have
been originally related to the Ural-Altaic languages, a non-Indo European
family of languages. The origins of Turkish can be traced back to the 12th c.
In subsequent centuries it adopted many loan words and grammatical
features from Persian and Arabic, and it was only from the 19th c. onwards
that systematic attempts were made to eradicate these elements. On the
other hand, many words of European and particularly of French origin have
been adopted, mainly in the field of technology.
Turkish is an agglutinative language, quite different from any European
language, in which words are built up by the addition of one or more
suffixes to the root. Another distinctive feature is vowel harmony, which
means that all the vowels in a word must be either front vowels (e, i, ö, ü) or
back vowels (a, ı, o, u), the various suffixes being modified to match the
vowels of the root; there are some exceptions to this rule, mainly in words
of Arabic or other non-Turkish origin.
One common suffix is the -i (modified to -ı, -u or -ü), or after a vowel -si (-sı,
-su, -sü), used in nouns modified by other nouns or possessives. Thus *cami*
is a mosque, but when modified by a noun it becomes *camii* (e.g. Sultan
Ahmet Camii); when modified by an adjective it takes no suffix (Ulu Cami,
the Great Mosque).
The Latin alphabet was introduced in 1928, replacing the Arabic script
previously in use. Some additional diacritic marks were added; the most
notable feature is the dotless i (ı), to be distinguished from the ordinary i
(which retains its dot in the capital).

Turkish	Pronunciation
a	*a*
b	*b*
c	*j*

Turkish	Pronunciation
ç	*ch* as in "church"
d	*d*
e	*e*
f	*f*
g	*g* (hard, as in "gag")
ğ	(barely perceptible; lengthens preceding vowel)
h	*h* (emphatically pronounced, approaching *ch* in "loch")
ı	a dark *uh* sound
i	*i*
j	*zh* as in "pleasure"
k	*k*
l	*l*
m	*m*
n	*n*
o	*o*
ö	*eu*, as in French "deux"
p	*p*
r	*r*
s	*s*
ş	*sh*
t	*t*
u	*u*
ü	as in French "une"
v	*v*
y	*y*, as in "yet"
z	*z*

Do you speak English?	Ingilizce biliyor musununz?	Some useful words and expressions
yes	evet	
no	hayır, yok, değil	
please	lütfen	
thank you	teşekkür ederim	
excuse me	affedersiniz	
good morning	gün aydın	
good day	iyi günler	
good evening	akşamınızhayırli olsun	
good night	geceniz hayırlı olsun	
goodbye	Allah ısmarladık	
Mr	bay	
Mrs, lady	bayan, hanım, kadın	
Miss, young lady	bayan, kücük hanım	
where is . . .?	nerededir . . .?	
when?	ne zaman?	
open	açık	
right	sağ	
left	sola, solda	
straight ahead	doğruca doğru	
what time is it?	saat kaç?	

0 sıfır	20 yirmi	Numbers
1 bir	21 yirmi bir	
2 iki	30 otuz	
3 üc	40 kırk	
4 dört	50 elli	
5 beş	60 altmiş	
6 altı	70 yetmiş	
7 yedi	80 seksen	
8 sekiz	90 doksan	
9 dokuz	100 yüz	

Language

Turkish	Pronunciation
10 on	200 iki yüz
11 on bir	1000 bin

Topographical terms

Turkish	Pronunciation
ada	island
bahçe	garden
bedesten	market hall
bulvar	avenue, boulevard
burun	cape
cadde	street
cami	mosque
çarşi	bazaar, market
çay	stream
çeşme	(drinking) fountain
dağ	mountain
deniz	sea
dere	valley, stream
geçit	pass
göl	lake
hamam	bath-house
han	inn, caravanserai
harabe	ruin
hisar	castle, fortress
imaret	public kitchen (attached to a mosque)
ırmak	river
iskele	landing-stage
kale	fortress
kapı	gate
kaplıca	(medecinal bath)
kaya	rock
kervansaray	caravanserai
kilise	church
köprü	bridge
körfez	gulf
köşk	pavilion, kiosk
köy	village
kule	tower
külliye	mosque complex
kütüphane	library
liman	harbour
medrese	theological college
mektep	primary school
meydan	museum
müze	museum
oda	room
orman	forest, wood
plaj	beach
şadırvan	ablution fountain
sahil	shore, coast
saray	palace
sebil	fountain-house
sokak	street
şose	street, avenue
su	water
tekke	dervish convent
tepe	hill
türbe	tomb
vadi	valley
yalı	mansion on the Bosporus
yarımada	peninsula
yıkıntı	ruin
yol	road

Medical Assistance

There are hospitals (hastahane) in all the provincial cities where medical care is always available. Many Turkish doctors have trained abroad and therefore speak at least one foreign language.
Ankara, İstanbul and Gaziantep also have some foreign hospitals as well:

American Hospital, Balgat Amerikan Tesisleri, Ankara;   Ankara
   tel. (0–312) 425 99 45/32 54

German Hospital (Alman Hastanesi), Sıraselviler Caddesi 119, İstanbul-   İstanbul
   Taksim; tel. (0–212) 251 71 00
International Hospital, İstanbul Caddesi 28, İstanbul-Yeşilköy; tel. (0–212)
   574 78 02
Amiral Bristol Hospital, Güzelbahçe Sokak, İstanbul-Nisantası; tel. (0–212)
   231 40 50
French Lape Hospital (Hôpital Français), Şişli; tel. (0–212) 246 10 20
Italian Hospital (Ospedale Italiano), Defterdar Yokuşu 17, İstanbul-
   Tophane; tel. (0–212) 249 97 51
St George's Hospital (Sen Jerj Hastanesi), Bereketzade Sokak 5/7, İstanbul-
   Karaköy; tel. (0–212) 243 25 90/91

American Hospital, Tepebaşı Mah., Yüksek Sokak 3/A, Gaziantep;   Gaziantep
   tel. (0–342) 231 10 69 and 231 34 20

No vaccinations are required but check with your doctor or travel clinic   Health care
before you go about preventitive measures – you should seriously consider protecting yourself against malaria and hepatitis.

Tel. 155   Emergency
                                       number

Tel. 112 (see also Emergency Services)   Emergency doctor

Call 118 or information about the availability of doctors (doktor, hekim) and   Pharmacies
pharmacies (eczane). Pharmacies and clinics run by the Turkish equivalent
of the Red Cross carry the sign of the red crescent. Medicines are not
expensive but if you are likely to need much of a particular product bring a
supply with you.

In most cases it is advisable to take out additional short-term health and   Health insurance
accident insurance to cover the cost of, for example, being flown home in
an emergency.

Motoring

International car rental firms have desks or offices in the main centres for   Car rental
tourism and at airports as well as in some of the big hotels. Local firms also
provide transport for hire, including jeeps, convertibles, motorbikes,
mountain bikes, etc., and at cheaper rates than the better known names,
but the vehicles they supply are often not up to the same standard.

To rent a car a driver must normally be over 21 and have held a driving
licence for at least two years. Insurance and free mileage are usually
included.

To rent a car in the peak holiday season it is wise to book it before leaving
home, either with the hire company direct or through a travel agent.

The following firms operate a computerised service through which book-   Where to book
ings can be made before leaving home. The addresses and phone numbers

Motoring

Distance
Chart in
Kilometres

	Adana	Afyon	Aksaray	Amasya	Ankara	Antakya	Antalya	Bitlis	Bolu	Burdur	Bursa	Çanakkale	Denizli	Diyarbakır	Edirne	Erzincan	Erzurum	İstanbul	İzmir	Kahramanmaraş
Adana	•	573	265	640	489	190	553	735	677	670	831	1101	766	526	1166	748	831	939	898	18
Afyon	573	•	363	592	257	763	287	1308	423	165	275	528	219	1099	684	945	1137	457	325	7
Aksaray	265	363	•	433	224	455	559	689	412	460	594	864	556	783	901	618	810	674	688	4
Amasya	640	592	433	•	335	805	879	833	490	757	681	951	811	701	898	366	558	671	917	6
Ankara	489	257	224	335	•	679	544	1106	192	422	380	650	476	921	681	688	880	454	582	6
Antakya	190	763	455	805	679	•	743	723	867	860	1021	1291	956	514	1356	762	819	1129	1088	1
Antalya	553	287	559	879	544	743	•	1288	690	122	542	727	238	1079	950	1177	1369	724	469	7
Bitlis	735	1308	689	833	1106	723	1288	•	1242	1405	1486	1756	1501	209	1731	467	344	1504	1633	5
Bolu	677	423	412	490	192	867	690	1242	•	568	272	542	618	1110	489	775	967	262	594	7
Burdur	670	165	460	757	422	860	122	1405	568	•	420	605	168	1196	828	1078	1270	602	382	8
Bursa	831	275	594	681	380	1021	542	1486	272	420	•	270	444	1301	470	1047	1239	243	322	9
Çanakkale	1101	528	864	951	650	1291	727	1756	542	605	270	•	503	1571	223	1317	1509	325	316	12
Denizli	766	219	556	811	476	956	238	1501	618	168	444	503	•	1292	726	1164	1356	652	231	9
Diyarbakır	526	1099	783	701	921	514	1079	209	1110	1196	1301	1571	1292	•	1599	406	324	1372	1424	3
Edirne	1166	684	901	898	681	1356	950	1731	489	828	470	223	726	1599	•	1264	1456	227	539	12
Erzincan	748	945	618	366	688	762	1177	467	775	1078	1047	1317	1164	406	1264	•	192	1037	1270	5
Erzurum	831	1137	810	558	880	819	1369	344	967	1270	1239	1509	1356	324	1456	192	•	1229	1462	6
İstanbul	939	457	674	671	454	1129	724	1504	262	602	243	325	652	1372	227	1037	1229	•	565	1
İzmir	898	325	688	917	582	1088	469	1633	594	382	322	316	231	1424	539	1270	1462	565	•	1
Kahramanmaraş	187	760	452	630	602	175	740	573	794	857	982	1252	953	364	1283	587	644	1056	1085	•
Karaman	291	331	212	625	790	481	518	1026	552	421	589	859	520	817	998	757	949	771	656	4
Kars	1037	1343	1016	764	1086	1025	1575	430	1173	1476	1445	1715	1562	530	1662	398	206	1435	1668	8
Kastamonu	705	499	466	281	242	895	786	1100	244	664	516	786	718	982	733	633	825	506	824	
Kayseri	331	540	177	344	316	461	736	791	508	637	696	966	733	606	997	441	633	770	865	
Konya	356	223	146	579	258	546	413	1091	446	316	481	751	415	882	890	764	956	663	548	
Kütahya	670	97	460	645	310	860	364	1405	326	242	178	431	292	1196	587	998	1190	360	334	
Malatya	410	894	531	468	670	398	963	437	862	991	1050	1320	1087	252	1351	364	421	1124	1219	
Mardin	530	1103	795	797	1005	518	1083	282	1197	1200	1361	1631	1296	96	1686	502	420	1459	1428	
Mersin	69	565	258	633	482	259	484	804	670	606	823	1093	722	595	1159	765	900	932	890	
Muş	766	1250	887	752	1025	754	1319	85	1161	1347	1405	1675	1443	259	1650	386	263	1423	1575	
Nevşehir	282	438	75	358	276	472	634	893	468	535	656	926	631	708	957	543	735	730	763	
Niğde	205	472	121	435	345	395	668	917	533	569	715	985	665	731	1022	567	759	795	797	
Rize	1048	1096	980	552	839	1082	1383	696	893	1261	1165	1435	1315	682	1382	320	358	1155	1421	
Samsun	745	674	538	130	417	910	961	911	471	839	743	1013	893	818	960	444	636	733	999	
Şanlıurfa	345	918	610	718	820	333	898	390	1012	1015	1176	1446	1111	181	1501	587	505	1274	1243	
Sinop	878	691	658	263	434	1043	978	1069	436	856	708	978	910	964	925	602	794	698	1016	
Sivas	501	698	371	221	441	593	930	665	630	831	821	1091	917	480	1119	247	439	892	1023	
Tokat	608	656	409	114	399	700	943	772	523	821	779	1049	875	587	1012	305	497	785	981	
Trabzon	972	1020	842	476	763	1006	1307	644	817	1185	1089	1359	1239	624	1306	244	300	1079	1345	
Van	905	1473	1110	973	1248	893	1458	170	1382	1570	1628	1898	1666	379	1871	607	415	1644	1798	
Yozgat	486	474	279	197	217	655	761	889	409	639	597	867	693	704	898	471	663	671	799	
Zonguldak	753	494	488	485	268	943	761	1318	160	649	343	613	689	1186	560	851	1043	333	665	

	Kayseri	Konya	Kütahya	Malatya	Mardin	Mersin	Muş	Nevşehir	Niğde	Rize	Samsun	Şanlıurfa	Sinop	Sivas	Tokat	Trabzon	Van	Yozgat	Zonguldak	
05	331	356	670	410	530	69	766	282	205	1048	745	345	878	501	608	972	905	486	753	Adana
99	540	223	97	894	1103	565	1250	438	472	1096	674	918	691	698	656	1020	1473	474	494	Afyon
66	177	146	460	531	795	258	887	75	121	980	538	610	658	371	409	842	1110	279	488	Aksaray
61	344	579	645	468	797	633	752	358	435	552	130	718	263	221	114	476	973	197	485	Amasya
42	316	258	310	670	1005	482	1025	276	345	839	417	820	434	441	399	763	1248	217	268	Ankara
05	461	546	860	398	518	259	754	472	395	1082	910	333	1043	593	700	1006	893	655	943	Antakya
06	736	413	364	963	1083	484	1319	634	668	1383	961	898	978	930	943	1307	1458	761	761	Antalya
00	791	1091	1405	437	282	804	85	893	917	696	911	390	1069	665	772	644	170	889	1318	Bitlis
44	508	446	326	862	1197	670	1161	468	533	893	471	1012	436	630	523	817	1382	409	160	Bolu
54	637	316	242	991	1200	606	1347	535	569	1261	839	1015	856	831	821	1185	1570	639	639	Burdur
16	696	481	178	1050	1361	823	1405	656	715	1165	743	1167	708	821	779	1089	1628	597	343	Bursa
6	966	751	431	1320	1631	1093	1675	926	985	1435	1013	1446	978	1091	1049	1359	1898	867	613	Çanakkale
8	733	415	292	1087	1296	722	1443	631	665	1315	893	1111	910	917	875	1239	1666	693	689	Denizli
2	606	882	1196	252	96	595	259	708	731	682	818	181	964	480	587	624	379	704	1186	Diyarbakır
3	997	890	587	1351	1686	1159	1650	957	1022	1382	960	1501	925	1119	1012	1306	1871	898	560	Edirne
3	441	764	998	364	502	765	386	543	567	320	444	587	602	247	305	244	607	471	851	Erzincan
5	633	956	1190	421	420	900	263	735	759	308	636	505	794	439	497	300	415	663	1043	Erzurum
6	770	663	360	1124	1459	932	1423	730	795	1155	733	1274	698	892	785	1079	1644	671	333	İstanbul
4	865	548	334	1219	1428	890	1575	763	797	1421	999	1243	1016	1023	981	1345	1798	799	665	İzmir
9	286	543	857	223	403	256	579	388	392	907	735	218	968	418	525	831	743	480	487	Kahramanmaraş
6	316	114	428	670	821	234	1026	267	190	1057	730	636	798	510	601	981	1196	471	628	Karaman
1	839	1162	1396	627	626	1106	349	941	965	358	780	711	948	645	703	434	451	869	1249	Kars
	463	500	552	749	1078	698	1019	423	500	732	310	967	192	502	395	656	1240	326	265	Kastamonu
	●	323	626	354	689	324	710	102	126	741	449	504	582	194	301	665	933	194	584	Kayseri
)	323	●	320	677	886	348	1033	221	255	1064	675	701	692	517	555	988	1256	425	522	Konya
2	626	320	●	980	1200	662	1335	535	569	1149	727	1015	744	751	709	1073	1558	527	397	Kütahya
3	354	677	980	●	348	479	356	456	480	684	585	268	731	247	354	608	579	471	938	Malatya
3	689	886	1200	348	●	599	355	791	735	778	914	185	1060	576	683	720	452	800	1273	Mardin
3	324	348	662	479	599	●	835	275	198	1065	738	414	871	518	609	989	974	479	746	Mersin
3	710	1033	1335	356	355	835	●	812	836	615	830	440	988	584	691	563	227	808	1237	Muş
3	102	221	535	456	791	275	812	●	77	843	463	606	596	296	334	767	1035	204	544	Nevşehir
3	126	255	569	480	735	198	836	77	●	867	540	550	673	320	411	791	1059	281	690	Niğde
3	741	1064	1149	684	778	1065	615	843	867	●	422	863	590	547	517	76	767	701	969	Rize
7	449	675	727	585	914	738	830	463	540	422	●	835	168	338	231	346	1051	279	547	Samsun
7	504	701	1015	268	185	414	440	606	550	863	835	●	981	497	604	805	560	698	1088	Şanlıurfa
2	582	692	744	731	1060	871	988	596	673	590	168	981	●	484	377	514	1209	412	457	Sinop
1	194	517	751	247	576	518	584	296	320	547	338	497	484	●	107	471	807	224	706	Sivas
3	301	555	709	354	683	609	691	334	411	517	231	604	377	107	●	441	912	206	599	Tokat
3	665	988	1073	608	720	989	563	767	791	76	346	805	514	471	441	●	715	625	893	Trabzon
3	933	1256	1558	579	452	974	227	1035	1059	767	1051	560	1209	807	912	715	●	1031	1485	Van
1	194	425	527	471	800	479	808	204	281	701	279	698	412	224	206	625	1031	●	485	Yozgat
	584	522	397	938	1273	746	1237	544	609	969	547	1088	457	706	599	893	1485	485	●	Zonguldak

Distance Chart in Kilometres

listed below are those of their offices in İstanbul and at Atatürk Airport where bookings can be made in Turkey.

Avis	Kadıkoy Bağdat Caddesi, Alağeyik Sok. 196/4, Selamicesme, İstanbul; tel. (0–212) 355 36 65 Atatürk Airport (Yeşilköy); tel. (0–212) 573 44 03 and (0–212) 573 14 52 Hilton Oteli; tel. (0–212) 248 77 52
Europcar	Cumhuriyet Caddesi 47/2, İstanbul-Taksim; tel. (0–212) 254 77 88 Kadıköy Bağdat Caddesi 222, Ciftehavuzlar, İstanbul; tel. (0–212) 360 33 33 Atatürk Airport (Yeşilköy); tel. (0–212) 573 70 24 and 574 19 08
Hertz	Cumhuriyet Caddesi 295, İstanbul-Harbiye; tel. (0–212) 141 53 23 Atatürk Airport (Yeşilköy); tel. (0–212) 573 59 87
Sixt/Budget	İnönü Caddesi 33/1, Gümüşsuyu, İstanbul-Taksim; tel. (0–212) 143 03 43 Atatürk Airport (Yeşilköy); tel. (0–212) 574 16 35 and 574 60 10

Roads

Turkey has quite a good road network which it is constantly adding to and improving. All the main roads – about 40,000km/25,000 miles of them – are tarmac but relatively few stretches rank as motorways. Most of these are around the conurbations of İstanbul, İzmir, Adana and Ankara. There are also many roads only surfaced with gravel chippings. These are suitable to drive on in summer but can present problems at other times of the year. Roadworks are frequent and often involve long detours. If touring away from the main highways a good sturdy vehicle is necessary.

Road numbering

Although most Turkish roads are numbered they are not always systematically signed, and this particularly applies to the E-numbered European routes across Asia Minor. The numbering for these has recently been revised, the new numbers appearing only in the very latest road-maps. In fact the main cross-country E routes follow the ring road round İstanbul

Turkish . . .   *. . . roads*

over the Bosporus bridge into Asia Minor and onto the E80, the İstanbul–Ankara motorway. From Ankara to Adana and Iraq you take the E90 as far as Gaziantep and then turn onto the local 850 to get to Syria and Lebanon. In more general terms, although Turkey has less signing of places, distances, detours, etc. than Western Europe it will be relatively easy to get your bearings provided you pay careful attention.

A good main road runs along the whole of Turkey's Aegean and Mediterranean coastline, but places on the western Black Sea coast as far as Sinop can often only be reached from the İstanbul–Samsun road further inland.

Coast roads

In Turkey vehicles travel on the right and overtake on the left.
Two warning triangles must be carried to place behind and in front of the vehicle in the event of a breakdown and a supply of spare bulbs for front and rear lights should also be carried.
The wearing of seat belts is compulsory.
There is a total ban on drinking and driving.
Speed limits are 50kph/31mph in built-up areas (40kph/25mph for cars with trailers) and 90kph/56mph elsewhere (70kph/44mph for motorcycles and cars with trailers).

Traffic regulations

Road signs follow the usual international pattern (yellow shields denote sites of archaeological or historical interest), but there are also some written in Turkish:

Road signs

Bozuk yol	Poor road surface
Dikkat	Caution
Dur	Stop
Düşüt banket	Unstable verge
Park yapılmaz	No parking
Şehir merkezi	City centre
Tamirat	Roadworks in progress
Viraj	Bend
Yavaş	Slow down

Turkish drivers tend to be none too careful about traffic discipline. Although they are not unduly aggressive at the wheel, lorries and buses in particular can be guilty of some risky overtaking and of a tendency to stop without warning on open roads to pick up prospective passengers.

Standard of driving

The possibility of encountering farm machinery or some of the many straying livestock means you also need to take special care when driving on country roads. Driving at night can be hazardous as well on account of the number of vehicles driving with poor lights or no lights at all, and the sudden changes in road surface, not to mention the potholes.

In the event of an accident always notify the police immediately even if no-one is injured, since by law there has to be a police report. If your vehicle is a total write-off or has to stay in Turkey for repairs for longer than three months you must notify the appropriate customs office so that the entry for the vehicle in your passport can be altered accordingly (see Travel Documents).

Accidents

If your vehicle is stolen you must get a certificate to that effect from the provincial governer (vali), so that the entry in your passport can be cancelled when you leave Turkey.

Vehicle theft

There are filling/gas stations at regular intervals along the main highways. These stay open 24 hours a day and usually have their own repair shop and restaurant as well.
If travelling away from the main roads you should carry a spare can full of fuel and top it up again as soon as possible if you have to use any.

Fuel/gas

Museums

Ordinary leaded petrol (benzin, 91 octane), super leaded petrol (super, 95 octane) and diesel (motorin), as well as engine oil (motor yağı) are available. Motoring organizations can supply a list of filling stations carrying unleaded petrol (kurşunsuz benzin).

TTOK: Turkish
Automobile Club

Türkiye Turing va Otomobil Kurumu (TTOK)
Halaskargazi Caddesi 364, TR–80222 Şişli İstanbul;
tel. (0–212) 231 46 31/36

Garages,
repair shops

There are garages and repair shops on the main highways and the edge of towns, but since it can take time to get spare parts for some makes of car it is as well to carry a supply of spares.

Breakdown
patrols

"Turing Servisi" operates breakdown patrols on the Edirne–İstanbul–Ankara and İzmir–Ankara main trunk roads.

Breakdown
service

For assistance with breakdowns telephone the following numbers at the times mentioned:
May–November Mon.–Sat. 9am–6pm
December–April Mon.–Fri. 9am–5pm

İstanbul; tel. (0–212) 146 70 90
İzmir; tel. (0–232) 421 71 49
Ankara; tel. (0–312) 131 76 48

The charge will be according to the distance travelled.

Emergency calls

See Emergency Services

Museums

The major museums are covered in the A to Z section under the headings for where they are located.

Opening times

Museums are usually open between 9am and 4.30pm and closed on Mondays. Major exceptions in İstanbul are Dolmabahçe Sarayı, where the palace is closed all day Thursday as well as Monday, and Topkapı, which is closed on Tuesdays. Since closing over lunchtimes and the timing of late visiting hours can vary enormously you should check beforehand on the spot or at tourist information centres (see Information).

Necropolis of Hieropolis (Pamukkale)

Museums are also closed for a number of days in connection with some religious festivals (Ramadan three days and Holy Days of Sacrifice four days).

If you intend to film or take pictures at some archaeological sites or museums you will have to pay an additional fee. If the pictures are for publication or of objects which have not been cleared for copyright you need to get a special permit from the General Directorate of Antiquities and Museums in İstanbul.

Filming and photography

National Parks

Turkey has a large number of national parks designed to protect the indigenous flora and fauna, to conserve archaeological sites and national monuments and to honour the fallen.

In Trabzon province (highway 885)
Lovely mountain scenery rich in flora and fauna, Sumela monastery; cafés, picnic sites, post office

Altındere

Afyon and Kütahya provinces
Monuments to the fallen in the Turkish War of Independence; flora in abundance; open air museum, picnic site
May–October

Başkomutan Park

Çorum province 181km/112 miles east of Ankara towards Samsun, then south for 23km/14 miles; Alaca Hüyük is 36km/22 miles north-east of Boğazkale
Excavations of Hittite remains; rich in fauna and flora; camping, picnic sites, restaurant

Boğazkale/ Alacahüyük

Cave dwellings . . .

. . . and a rural scene near Göreme

545

National Parks

Daylan	Muğla province, just east of Marmaris Beach used for breeding by loggerhead turtles
Dilek Yarımadası	Aydın province, on the E87, 28km/17 miles east of Kuşadası Peninsula with Mount Samsun; Mediterranean seals and sea turtles, Anatolian cheetah, wild horses Picnic and camp sites, hiking, climbing, water sports April–December
Gelibolu Yarımadası	Gallipoli peninsula north-west of Çanakkale History park dedicated to the fallen of the First World War (Australian, British, French. New Zealand and Turkish war memorials) Information stands at the Kilitbahir and Kabatepe entrances; beaches, campsite, hotel, motel, restaurants
Göreme	Nevşehir province Fascinating landscape of rock cones and fairy chimneys, underground cities, cave dwellings and Seljuk and Byzantine rock churches; traditional villages, open air museum Camping, hotels, shopping centres; all year round
Güllük Dağı/ Termessos	Antalya province (E87) Rugged countryside, flora and wildlife, open air museum Picnic site, restaurant, campsite April–October
Ilgaz Dağı	Kastamonu province, between Ankara and Kastamonu Flora and wildlife in a beautiful mountain settting; picnic site May–September
Karatepe- Aslantaş	Adana province, Ceyhan valley (E90 or highway 825) Hittite and Roman remains; hills and valleys Picnic and camp sites; April–November
Kızıl Dağ	Between Isparta and Konya (highway 330) Beautiful park of cedars on the northern edge of Lake Beyşehir Picnic and camp sites; May–October
Köprülü Canyon	Antalya province (E87) Deep river canyon (14km/8 miles long), Roman bridge, woods; site of ancient Selge, open air museum Picnic and camp sites, fishing, restaurants; April–October
Kovada Gölü	Isparta province, just south-east of Isparta Karst scenery, lake, rich in flora and wildlife Picnic and camp site, fishing, water sports, climbing May–September
Kuşcenneti Bird Paradise	Balıkesir province, north-east of Balıkesir, highway 565 Bird reserve (over 200 species) near Lake Manyas Museum and tower hides; most interesting March–October
Munzur Vadisi	Tunceli province Trout-streams and variety of wildlife plus flora; camping, picnicking, fishing May–September
Nemrut Dağı	86km/53 miles north-east of Adıyaman in northern Mesopotamia Colossi of ancient gods on the summit of Nemrut Dağı (2150m/7056ft) including the 30ft-high statue of Antiochus I, King of Commagene 69–34 B.C. Vehicles to get there can be hired in Adıyaman or Kâhta; overnight accommodation or camping

Antalya province	Olympus
Ruins of Phaselis and Olympus, wooded mountains	Beydağları
Museum, post office, restaurants, picnic and camp site, motels, beach	
Manisa province	Sipil Dağı
Thermal springs, interesting flora and wildlife	
Picnic and camp site, walking and climbing	
April–November	
Ankara province, on the E80 near Kızılcahamam	Soğuksu
Forested mountain plateau with thermal springs	
Picnic and camp site, hotel and restaurant, climbing	
April–October	
South of Bursa	Uludağ
Ancient Mysian Olympus (1800–1900m/5908–6236ft); forests and lakes;	
variety of flora and wildlife; campsite, walks and picnics June–September	
Winter sports centre with skilifts, hotels, chalets, restaurants, post office	
December–April	
Bolu province, E80 or highway 750	Yedigöller
"Seven Lakes", full of fish, surrounded by forests, museum, wildlife exhibition	
Picnic and camp site, chalet accommodation, restaurants	
April–October	
Yozgat province, E88 between Ankara and Sivas	Yozgat Çamlığı
Forests rich in flora and wildlife; camping and picnic site	
April–October	

Opening Times

See Business Hours

Post

Turkish post offices are identified by the letters PTT in black on a yellow background. Mailboxes on the street are also yellow. The large main post offices are open Monday to Saturday from 8am to midnight and Sundays from 9am to 7pm. Counters at the smaller post offices usually observe the same hours as government offices (see Business Hours).

Post offices, PTT

Stamps currently cost 3000 TL for letters to Europe up to 20g and 5000 TL up to 50g, while postcards cost 2500 TL. There is also an Express Post Service (Acele Posta Servisi).
Philatelists will find a large selection to choose from.

Cost of stamps

Letters for collection must be sent to the head post office (merkez postane) of the place in question marked "postrestant". You will need to show your passport when collecting them.

Post restante/ General delivery

Post offices will also change money at the current rate as well as cashing postal cheques and all kinds of travellers' cheques. See Currency for further details.

Changing money

Telegrams can be sent from the telegram offices (telgrafhane).

Telegrams

Public Holidays

Public holidays

The official public holidays when banks, etc. are closed are:
January 1st (New Year's Day)
April 23rd (National Independence and Children's Day)
May 19th (Atatürk Commemoration and Youth and Sports Day, usually extended to two or three days)
August 30th (Victory Day, celebrating Turkey's 1922 War of Independence from Greece)
October 29th (Republic Day, anniversary of the declaration of the Republic in 1923)

Religious festivals

Ramazan (Ramadan): Muslim month of fasting and prayer, based on the Islamic lunar calendar and beginning eleven days earlier every year, with a holiday on the 24th day.

Şeker Bayramı (Sugar Holy Days): three-day holiday following the end of Ramadan.

Kurban Baramı (Holy Days of Sacrifice): four-day holiday around the date of Mohammed's birth, when sheep are sacrificed and distributed to the poor. This festival also occurs ten days earlier every year.

Shops and museums close for the three Sugar Holy Days and for the four Holy Days of Sacrifice. Local beautyspots and attractions get very crowded around these times, making it hard to find accommodation or to board public transport.

Following Atatürk's secular reforms Turkey observes Sunday as the weekly day of rest rather than Friday as is usually the case in Muslim countries.

Day of rest

Radio and Television

TRT – Türkiye Radyo Televizyon Kurumu
(Turkish Radio and Television Corporation)
Nevzat Tandoğan Caddesi 2, Kavaklıdere, Ankara
tel. (0–312) 428 22 30

TRT

Turkish Radio's Third Programme (TRT3) broadcasts three-minute bulletins daily in English, French and German on FM at 9am, 10am and noon, and 2, 5, 7 and 10pm. The Voice of Turkey broadcasts daily for tourists on shortwave from 7.30am to 12.45pm and 6.30 to 10pm.

Radio broadcasts in English

Turkish television's international channel (chanel 2) also broadcasts the news in English after the evening News at Ten.

TV news in English

Railways

Turkey has an extensive rail network connecting most major cities and operated by Turkish State Railways (Türkiye Cumhuriyeti Devlet Demiryolları, TCDD: for information call 9–4/309 05 55 in Ankara and 9–1/348 80 20 in İstanbul). Some trains have couchettes, sleeping cars, restaurants

TCDD logo

Network of the Turkish Railways and Long-distance Buses

© Baedeker

and 1st and 2nd class lounge cars. Because of a shortage of rolling stock the trains on the relatively small number of main routes tend to be over-crowded and consequently less well looked-after.
Other options are to travel by coach or by boat (see Buses, Coastal Shipping).

Fares	Fares are cheap and based on distance and the nature of the service. There are reductions for return tickets and travel by groups of more than 24. Details about special reduced fare schemes such as "Euro Domino" for students and young people under 26 can be found in the "Youth Tourism" leaflet published in English by the Ministry of Tourism in Ankara (see Youth Accommodation).
Distances and time taken on selected routes	İstanbul–Ankara/Central Turkey: 667km/414 miles, 7½ hrs (a new fast track is planned for express trains travelling at speeds of 250km/155 miles an hour which will reduce the time taken to 2 hrs.)
	Ankara–Zonguldak/Black Sea coast: 486km/302 miles, 11 hrs
	Ankara–İzmir/Western Turkey: 824km/512 miles, 13½ hrs
	Ankara–Adana/Southern Turkey: 674km/419 miles, 13½ hrs
	(Antalya is not on the rail network)
Steam trains	Steam trains operate on regular tours in Western Turkey between İzmir and Aydın. They can also be chartered for tours by large groups anywhere in Turkey.
	For further details contact the Tourist Offices listed under Information.
Stations	İstanbul has two railway stations, one on the European side and one on the Asian side:
	Sirkeci İstasyonu; tel. (0–212) 527 00 50/51 and 520 65 75 (for westbound trains to European destinations)
	Haydarpaşa İstasyonu; tel. (0–216) 336 04 75 and 348 80 20 (for destinations inside Turkey and further east)
İzmir city/airport rail link	An hourly rail link operates between İzmir's Alsancak railway station; tel. (0–232) 421 01 14 and 33 58 97–336 and Adnan Menderes airport (see Air Transport) and only costs a fraction of the price of a taxi.

Restaurants

As well as the restaurants in the better hotels (see Hotels) which usually serve Turkish and international food, there is also a good range of restau-rants and other eating places in the all the main towns and tourist centres serving the delicious dishes for which Turkey is justly famous (see Food and Drink) in addition, more recently, to other specialities from the Far East and elsewhere.
Throughout Turkey and along all the main roads you will come across "lokantas", the simple traditional eating places where you can often select your meal simply by pointing to what you want in the kitchen.

Categories	The following selection of established restaurants gives an indication of the standard you can expect based on the official Turkish categories. Top restaurants are starred with an asterisk (*) while the numbers in brackets refer to the standards, namely:
	(1) = above average
	(2) = average

Restaurants (selection)

Adana	Daylan (2), Atatürk Cad. 89, İncirlik; Nihat Lokantası (2), Sivil Hava Mey-danı; Topaşlar Din. Tes. (2ú, Alpu Köyü Mevkii Pozantı; Yaşar Pelit (2), Sekerpınarı Mevkii Pozantı

A table traditionally laid

Pancar (2), Saraylar Mevkii, Çakirköyü; Varan Tesisleri (2), Akoren Köyü Sincanlı	**Afyon**
Vadibaşi, Ihlara Vadisi Girşi	**Aksaray**
Shangai (2) Atatürk Cad. 155	**Alanya**

İnci, Gazipaşa Cad.; Meram, Gazipaşa Cad.; Ta-mara, Saray M.; Yönet, Gazipaşa Cad.

Maden Otelcilik Turizm (2), Dere M MKC 5; Saraçoğlu Muzaffer Turistik **Amasya** Tesisleri (2), Saraçoğlu Muzaffer Tur. Tes., Suluova

*Washington, Bayındır S. 22/A, Kızılay **Ankara**
Çengiz Kaan (1), Büyükesat M. Çankaya; China Town (1), Köroğlu S. 19
G.O.P.; Kuğu (1), Gaziosmanpaşa M. Fabrika Cad. 90, Gölbaşi
Akman et Locantası (2), Opera Meydanı Tavus S. 4, Ulus; Atatürk Buz Pateni
Lokantası (2), Kurtuluş Parkı İçi; Aysa Turistik Tesisleri (2), 2km/1 mile out of
Gölbaşı; Biz Lokantası (2), Hatir S. 4, Çankaya; Çamalti Lokantası, at km 104
on the Ankara–İstanbul road, Kizilca Hamam; Chez Le Belge (2), Konya
Asfaltı Üzeri 86; Çin Lokantası, Çankaya Cad. 24/1, Çankaya; Demet Cafe
Restoran (2), İvedik Cad. 370/A, Demetevler Park, İçi; Hyde Park Lok. (2),
Nenehatun Cad. 56/1, Çankaya; Italyan, (2), Hoşdere Cad. 200/B; Kanyon
(2), Hoşdere Cad. 193/A, Çankaya; Merkez Lokantası (2), Çiftik Cad. 72/A,
Çiftik; Milka (2), Atatürk Bul. 185; Panorama (2), Çankaya Cad. 28/A; Pena
(2), Bestekar S. 88/B. Kavadiklere; Piknik Rub (2), İnkilap S. 7, Kızılay; Pizza
Ekspres Lokantası (2), Köroğlu S. 48/A G.O.P.; Pizza Pino Lokantası (2),
Tunali Hilmi Cad. 111/B, Kavaklidere; Varan Lokantası (2), Eskişehir
Karayolu Üzeri–Söğütözü; Villa (2), Boğaz S. 13, Kavaklidere; Yahya (2),
Filistin S. 28 G.O.P.; Yakamoz (2), Köroğlu Cad. 38/B G.O.P.

Orkinos Bar (1), Kaleiçi Eğlence Merk.; Yat (1), Kaleiçi Eğlence Merkezi. **Antalya**
Riza (2), Demircikara M.; Yelken 2 (2), Eski Devlet Hast.; Yörükoğlu (2), İçi
Parkı

Restaurants

Cafés: Anfi, Kaleiçi Yatlımanı, İskele, Kaleiçi Yat Limanı

Aydın Cappello (2), Akyar Mevkii Türkmen M

Balıkesir Duman (2), Çayağzi Köyü, Erdek; "E" (2), Altınnal Sahil Sitesi, Altınova/ Ayvalık; Sengün (2) Atatürk Parkı

Bergama Bergama Restaurant, Cumhuriyet Cad.

Bodrum Aktur (2), Bitez Kabakum; Amphora (2), Neyzen Tevfik Cad. 164; Günsu TurcTes (2), Cumhuriyet Cad. 98; Han (2), Kale Cad. 29; Maşa (2) Cumhuriyet Cad.

Bolu Filiz (1), Ec5, Karayolu Üzeri Bolu
İdris (2), Belediye Meydanı; Varan (2), Karayolu Üzeri Kaynaşlı–Düzce

Bursa Çamurlu, Kükürtlü Çekirge Cad.; Gümüsraket (1), Eski Mudanya Yolu; Oda (1), Organize Sanayi Bölgesi 1. Cad.; Sönmez (1), Yükseller Mevkii Altınceylan (2), Kültürpark; Denizatı, İskele Mey. 1; Papağan (2), 1. Murat Cad. 15 Çekirge; Yeşim Turistik Tesisleri (2), Cumalıkızık Köyü Karapinar Meydanı

Çanakkale Helen (2), Tevfikiye Köyü

Çeşme Tetamur (1), Paşalimanı Mevkii

Dalyan Antik Hotel Restaurant

Datça Vido 2 (2), Emecik Köyü Çiftlik Mevkii

Diyarbakır Erdil 2000 (2), Ofis Gevran Cad.

Edirne BP Kervansaray (2), Ayşekadin; Fifi (2); Kervan Hotel Rest. (2); Park Hotel Rest. (2), Maarif Cad.

Elazığ Altınşiş (2), Gazi Cad. 50'ler Çarşısı; Cardik (2), İnönü Cad. 38/B.

Erzincan Erkont (2), Erzincan/Refahiye Karayolu, at km 13

Erzurum Güzelyurt (2), Cumhuriyet Cad. 54; Tufan (2), Cumhuriyet Cad.

Eskişehir Dorlion (1), Ankara Asfaltı
Aytaç Turistik Tesisleri (2), Hamamderesi Mevkii Sakarıllıca Köy; Emeğim (2), Cumhuriyet Cad.; Gür (2), Altın Sk. 11; Regüratör (2), Dsi. Regüratöru Karacaşehir; Sönmez Tesisleri (2), Honudiye M. Altun S. 11

Gaziantep Kervantep (1), Hürriyet Cad.
Bebek (2), Suburcu Cd. 11/F

Hatay Saray Lokantası (2), Atatürk Bul. 57

Isparta Anıl (2), İstiklal M. Muhtesyol S.; Eğirdir (2), Cami M

İstanbul *Abdullah, Koru Cad. 11, Emirgan; *Asitane (Hotel Kariye), Kariye Camu Sok. 18 (old Ottoman court cuisine); *Betyi, Orman S., Florya; *Borsa Lokantarı, İstiklal Cad. 87–89, Beyoğlu; *China Town, Cevdet Paşa Cad. Bebek; *Hıdiv Kasrı (half an hour's drive from the centre of İstanbul, on the same side as the Adriatic, in a restored castle; also garden setting; *view of the Bosporus), Çubuklu; *Le Chalet, Yeniköy Cad. Postaci Halil S., Tarabya; *Ocakbaşi, in the Ramada Renaissance Hotel, Ordu Cad. 226, Laleli; *Ottoman restaurant in the Çirağan Palace Hotel Kempinski, Çirağan Cad. 84, Beşiktaş; *Plaza, Bronz S., Maçka; *S. Rest., Bebek Cad., Arnavutköy; *Urcan Balik Lokantası (fish and seafood) at Sariyer port and fish market

China Place (1), Keçiburnu Ca. 19/7, Tarabya; Çiçek Paşaji (1; here lots of restaurants offer a wide variety of starters, fish and meat dishes), İstaklal Cad.; Darüzziyafe (1; no alcohol), Sifahane Cad. 6, Süleymaniye; Flora (1), Vali Konağı C. 9, Harbiye; Gelik (1), Demirhans S., Zeytinburnu; Le Premier (1), Köyü M., Yeşliköy; 29 (1), Nisbetye Cad. 9, Etiler; Piyer Loti (1), Divanyolu; Rejans (Russian restaurant, meeting place for artists), Olivya Geçidi 15, at the top of İstiklal Cad. 244, Galatasaray; Sandal (1), Çapariz Sok. 13/A; Seoul (1) Nisbetiye Cad. 41, Etiler; Sarnic Lokantası (1), Soğukçesme Sok., Sultanahmet; Süreyya (1), Vezirköprü S., Arnavutköy; Uludağ et Rest. (1), İstanbul Cad. 12, Florya; Zya (1), M. Kemal Öke Cad. 21, Nişantaşı; Ziye Turistik Tesisleri (1), Muallim Naci Cad., Ortaköy

Aşrom 2 (2), Çamlıca Cad. 28, Üsküdar; Bab Cafeteria (2), Yeşilçam S. 24, Bey.; Dilhayat (2), Dilhayat S. 7, Etiler; Dörtler et Rest. (2), Kasaplar Çarşisi 6, Bostanci; Dört Mevsim (2), İstiklal Cad. 509, Bey.; Façyo (2), Kireçburnu Cad. 13, Tarabya; Florya Kosova et Rest. (2), Florya; Fondüe (2), Yeniköy Cad. 30, Tarabya; Hacı Abdullar (2), Sakızaäcı Cad. 19; Hacıbaba (2), İstiklal Cad. 49, Taksim; Hanedan (2), Çiğdem S. 27, Beşikt.; Havuzlu Beyaz Köşk (2), Şemsettin Günaltay Cad. 130/2, Erenköy; İlyas (2), Halaskargazi Cad. 306, Şişli; Karides (2), Kennedy Cad. 90, Yenikapı; Klüp Reşat (2), Plaj Yolu 20, Suadiye; Konyau Cafeteria (2), M. Kemalettin Cad. 5, Sirkeci; Köşem Bistro (2), Kefeliköy Cad. 72, Tarabya; Leylak (2), Kalamiş Cad. 83, Fener; Liman (2), Rıhtım Cad., Karaköy; Markiz (2), İstiklal Cad. 362; M.G. Wine Bar Restaur. (2), Halkalı Yolu 3, Bakirköy; Neptün (2), Gülistan Cad. 1, Büyükada; Osmanlı Hünkar (2), Sakizağaci Cad. 29, Beyoğly; Palet 1 (2), Cad. 110, Tarabya; Palet 2 (2), Yeniköy Cad. 80, Tarabya; Palet 3 (2), Kefeliköy Cad. 74, Tarabya; Pandrosa (2), Cumhuriyet Cad. 6, Taksim; Pizza Prima (2), Halaskargazi C. 40, Şişli; Pizza Teras (2), Bağdat C. 294, Caddebostan; Pub Sempati (2), Halaskargazi Cad. 27/16 Pangaltı; Rosa (2), Cumhuriyet Cad. 75, Elmadağ; Şamdan (2), M. Kemal Öke Cad. 18, Şişli; Şamdan 2 (2), Nisbetiye Cad. 30, Etiler; Sanatevi (2), Sıraselv. Cad. 69/1, Taksim; Swiss Pub (2), Cumhuriyet Cad. 14, Elmadağ; The Amorcorde (2), Bağdat C. 208, Kadiköy; Vin Tavuk (2), Bağdat C. 263, Kadiköy; Yumeya (2), Cumhuriyet Cad. Beyoğlu

Café Opera (2), Bağdat Cad. 315, Erenköy; German Café (2), Teccedüt S. 66/68, Aksaray

*Park, Kültürpark — **İzmir**
Çin (1), 1379 Sok. Efes İşhani 57/A; Crystal (1), Kıbrıs Şehitleri Cad. 70/A, Alsancak, Deuxmegots (1), Atatürk Cad. 148; Golden Restaurant (1), Atatürk Cad. 314/A, Alsancak; İkizler (1), 163 Sok. 1, Bornova; Park Cafe Restaurant (1), Şehit Fethibey Cad. 118A; Yangec (1), Cumhuriyet Bul. 236; Yeni Kordelya (1), Atatürk Cad. 148/A

Cafe Plaza Restaur. (2), Mustafa Bay Cad. 3/A; Civan (2), 3 Beylar C. 850 Sok. 9/A, Konak; Denizkızı (2), Hüseyhin Ögütcen Cad. 29/A, Bal Çova; L'Aventure (2), Atatürk Cad. 150/A, Kordonboyu; Kordon Palet (2), Atatürk Cad. 79, Alsancak; MercŞan (2), Mustafa Kemal Cad. 112; Palet (2), Yalı Cad. 294, Karşıyaka; Pizza Hut (2), Şehit Nevres Bul. 5/A, Alsancak, and Atatürk Cad. 140/1; Smyrna (2), Mithatpaşa Cad. 888/A Göztepe; Usas (2), Adnan Menderes, Havalimanı; Venedik (2), 1382 Sok. 10/A–B, Alsancak; Yeni Karadeniz (2), Sahil Evleri, Narlıdere

Classic (2), Bayrak Çarşısı Dut Sok. 22, Bayramoğlu Gabze; La Villa (2), — **İzmit**
Bayramoğlu Sahil Sitesi

Ekol (1), Sivas Cad. Tuna Kavşağı — **Kayseri**
Osman Yıldız (2), Kumarlı Mevkii Çirkolan Köyü Kayseri

Günübirlik Turistik Tesisleri (2); Mavi Akdeniz (2) — **Kemer**

Erdal (2), Çamdaki M. Büyük Mandira Babaeski; Kongarlar (2), İstanbul — **Kırklareli**
Cad., Lüleburgaz; Üysallar (2), Gündogdu M. Ec., 5 Karayolu Üzeri Lüleburgaz

553

Carpets

Turkey has long been famous for its hand-knotted Anatolian carpets. Back in the 13th c. Marco Polo was already remarking on the beauty of the carpets which adorned the palaces of the Sultans, and Konya, which under the Seljuks became the first of the country's centres for knotted carpets, still produces large and medium-sized geometric-patterned knotted-pile rugs today.

Turkey is also a leading producer of prayer rugs. The basic design represents the mihrab, the niche in the mosque showing the direction of Mecca, so that the faithful during their five-times daily prayers can lay their rug on the ground with the top of the mihrab indicating the direction in which they should pray. An ewer (ibrik) serves as a reminder of the ritual washing of hands before prayer. Mosques are also carpeted with their own prayer rugs. Saphs, or family prayer rugs, can have between five and seven prayer compartments, each in a different colour but usually on an ivory ground. Since the Koran forbids the depiction of living creatures, the motifs are primarily geometric or architectural (e.g. mihrab, dwelling) with the influence of carpet-makers from Persia reflected in the use of medallions and floral patterns such as the "tulip ladik", a stylized row of tulips above the mihrab and named after Ladık in Central Anatolia.

Anatolian carpets are made using the Turkish or Ghiordes knot, which gets its name from the town of Gordion, probably in connection with the legendary Gordian knot (see A to Z, Gordion). Unlike the Persian or Senneh knot, made by passing the thread under one warp-thread and then round over the next, the Turkish knot is made by looping the knot round two warp-threads and bringing the ends of yarn, the pile, out between them.

Until the discovery of aniline dyes in 1865 only vegetable dye-stuffs were used, with their formula a closely-guarded family secret. The old dyes have kept their lustrous colours for centuries. Chief among them are red, symbolising wealth and good fortune, and blue, for nobility and splendour, with the individual colours clearly defined and none of the intermediate shades of the Persian rugs.

The Yürüks, the Kurdish nomads in the remote mountains of Eastern Turkey, still use plant dyes for their soft rugs, made entirely of sheep's wool. With their long pile, as protection from the cold, and fewer knots, these rugs are less hardwearing. The semi-nomadic herders from around Bergama also knot pure wool rugs, using largely Caucasian designs on a red ground and featuring a leaf-pattern border with swastikas, a motif found only in their work. Their carpets are nearly all square in shape, often 2m×2m/6½ft×6½ft, and they make virtually no prayer rugs.

Uşak in western Turkey was one of Asia Minor's most famous regions for knotted carpets in the 16th and 17th c. Their "Transylvanian" Oushak carpets got their name from the Persian-style rugs found in many churches in that part of what is now Rumania. Since they were used for altars and hence got very little wear they have remained in an excellent state of preservation.

The richly traditional rugs still made today in Milas hark back in simplified form to those of the Ottoman court. Mostly in plant-dyed pastel shades, especially yellow, they are worked in geometric designs. Kula, north of Milas, has been making "mezarlı", the carpets used in burials, since the 17th c. Since the older ivory and blue Kulas, traditionally depicting a tree of life with a house or tomb, are particularly sought after, pale dyes are used to give them an antique look.

More modern carpets have less of a reputation as the process has been speeded up to meet the demands of the export trade and designs have been imported from different provinces. Since the older traditional carpets are still popular collectors' pieces there is a tendency to satisfy the growing demand by artificially ageing the new ones. Some workshops, as used to be the case with those of Panderma (Bandırma), spread new rugs out to be bleached by the sun. Others soak them in chlorine, despite the fact this destroys the fibres and actually shortens the life of

the carpet, so if a rug smells of chlorine its colouring has been tampered with. Another trick is to fake wear of the carpet with iron filings or brick dust. Genuine old prayer rugs will only show signs of wear in the places where the believer has touched them with his knees, hands and forehead. Nowadays Panderma carpets are made in Kayseri. Here, like the original Pandermas, they produce copies of the ancient Persian and Anatolian rugs, some of them pure silk and high quality, while others are made from "floş", silk leftovers or a mixture of silk and cotton or artificial fibres.

Government support is helping traditional carpet-weaving qualities and designs to make a comeback. Nowadays almost exclusively for export, the workshops of Hereke are turning out valuable silk carpets – on an ivory ground but on red and blue as well – with between one and five million knots to the

Carpet knotting

square metre. Now run on a commercial basis, the factory here was originally established for the court of Sultan Abdül Hamid in 1844 and produced carpets of the finest materials, with Persian floral designs, for the palace and high dignitaries. Colourful flat weave kelims with their bright zigzag patterns on a dark background are also very widespread as wall-hangings and floor-coverings. Kiz kelims – made as gifts by the bride (kız = maiden) – from Konya are particularly fine.

Whatever happens don't let yourself be led astray by the fine words and persuasive sales technique of the carpet merchant. What you're offered in the tourist traps may well be over advertised and overpriced so be sure to bargain. Remember that genuinely antique carpets have to be cleared for export and don't take anything at face value.

Shopping and Souvenirs

Konya	Hasabahçe (2), Meram Yeniyol; Hoşseda (2) Anit Alani; Metin (2), Cumhuriyet Alani 42
Malatya	Melita (2), Atatürk Cad. Turfanda İşhani 180
Manisa	Erdil Tur. Tesisleri (2), Burçak Ovası M. Ankara İzmir Karoyolu, km 6
Marmaris	*Joy, Musa Yeri Mevkii, İcmeler Bamboo (2), Atatürk Cad. 9/10; Cafe Serenat (2), Kemeraltı M. Hacı Sabri S.; Club House (2), Orhaniye Köyü; Mangal (2), Hacı Sabri Sok. İçmeler; Tilla (2), Atatürk Cad.
Mersin/İçel	Babil (1), Azmak Mev. Devrim S., Mezitli; Piknik (1), İnönü Cad. 58, Silifke Intermot (2), Bosak Köyü, Taşucu
Muğla	Paşa (2), Salihpaşalar Köyü
Side/Manavgat	Bademalti, Liman Cad.; China, Liman Cad. 93; Kalamar Restaurant I, Liman Cad.; Şarapsı Han, Liman Cad., İskele; Toros Restaurant in the Toros Motel
Söke/Aydın	Şengün (2), Didim Play Sitesi

Shopping and Souvenirs

Bazaars

Many things are cheaper in Turkey than in Great Britain or America, but if you want to be sure of getting a bargain check local prices before leaving home. The fact that the various craftsmen tend to be grouped together according to product in their own particular streets and alleys makes it easier to compare quality and prices. Household wares, for example, are attractive and good value, as are the handbeaten copper vessels found everywhere.

Foreign visitors usually have high hopes of Turkish bazaars as places with a particularly wide range of national specialities, and this is certainly true of Kapalı Çarşı, the great bazaar in İstanbul between the Nuruosmaniye and Beyazıt mosques – an exotic treasure trove of about 4000 stalls in some 90 streets. Elsewhere, however, you may find the

A jeweller's shop in Kayseri

bazaars rather disappointing – even the bazaar at İzmir. The fact is that generally speaking a local bazaar, although a colourful spectacle, basically caters for the needs of local people and is unlikely to provide little out of the ordinary for the collector of more valuable souvenirs.

The larger cities have modern shopping centres, such as Galleria and Perpa in İstanbul, and Atakule and Karum in Ankara, with plenty of boutiques; particularly attractive are magnificent silk kaftans, embroidered with silk thread and gold leaf, and with belt and footwear to match.

Traditional arts and handicrafts can be found in state shopping centres such as those at Göreme or İstanbul's Topkapı Palace, or in the many workshops producing handbeaten and very decorative copper and brass wares (vases, braziers, plates and richly patterned candlesticks), or those making hand-knotted rugs and flatwoven kelims (see also *Baedeker Special*, Carpets).

İstanbul, İznik and Kütahya are all centres for glassware and pottery, including tiles and beautiful handpainted ceramics. Bileci, Söğüt, Nevşehir and Hacıbektaş are famous for earthenware pots, vases and the like. Also popular as souvenirs are the small wooden boxes inlaid with silver or mother of pearl. Jewelry is another favourite, and there is a wide choice of gold, silver and precious stones made up into necklaces, bracelets, earrings and tiepins, although you should insist on a guarantee of authenticity. One national speciality is the nargile, the Turkish version of the waterpipe which comes in many different shapes and sizes.

Meerschaum, mined around Eskişehir, is widespread in the form of pipes and smoker's accessories, as are embossed wares in non-ferrous metals. Textiles, such as headscarves and Turkish towels, as well as colourful mohair blankets and leatherwear, especially jackets, but also gloves, bags, belts, shoes, etc., are among the many other bargains worth considering, and village workshops in particular are full of beautiful crochetwork and embroidery.

Clever copies of internationally famous names – from designer clothing to perfume and cosmetics – are touted for sale throughout the country but

Shops and boutiques

Popular souvenirs

Beware of imitations

Turkish souvenirs

557

especially in places frequented by tourists, so if you pay a high price for anything check first that it is genuine.

Tourist touts

Visitors not travelling with an organised tour will find themselves the target of persistent locals wanting to act as guides. Since they usually speak English it is all too easy to accept their offer, but the tour usually finishes in a shop where visitors will be pressurised to buy rugs, jewellery or some other kind of souvenir – and will have to be very firm indeed to leave without buying anything

Food and drink

Sweetmeats and candied fruits such as Turkish delight (lokum) and marrons glacés, and bottles of rakı, the national drink, also make good souvenirs of a trip to Turkey.

Antiques

The export of genuine antiques and antiquities is forbidden by law and subject to very severe penalties, so avoid the temptation. If you are planning to take out any carpets or precious metals you must be able to prove that they were purchased with legally exchanged currency, so keep the exchange receipts to show on departure (see Currency).

Spas

Turkey has over a thousand thermal springs, and some of the spas with the appropriate facilities are listed below, with the water temperatures in brackets.

Balçova

10km/6 miles west of İzmir
For rheumatism, gynaecological conditions
Facilities: Ege University treatment centre; Turkey's largest indoor thermal pool (62°C/143°F)

Balıklı
(Yılanlı) Çermik

Sivas province, 12km/7 miles north-east of Kangal
For rheumatism, psoriasis, gynaecological conditions
Facilities: thermal basin (35°C/95°F); accommodation

Bolu

On the E80 between Ankara and İstanbul, 4km/2 miles south of Bolu
For rheumatism, respiratory passages, kidney disease, neuralgia, circulatory and respiratory disorders, gynaecological conditions
Facilities: thermal baths (44°C/112°F)

Bursa

South of İstanbul
For rheumatism, gynaecological conditions, dermatological and metabolic disorders
Facilities: cures in hotels under medical supervision (47–78°C/116–172°F)

Çeşme

On national road 300, west of İzmir (7km/4 miles east of Çeşme)
For rheumatism, gynaecological conditions, dermatological and metabolic disorders
Facilities: accommodation (42–55°C/108–131°F)

Gönen

Balıkesir province
For rheumatism, urinary and nervous complaints
Facilities: treatment centre (78–82°C/172–180°F)

Harlek

27km/17 miles north-east of Küthaya on the road to Eskişehir
For rheumatism, psychological and metabolic disorders, diseases of the urinary tract
Facilities: bathing and drinking cures (25–43°C/77–109°F)

Afyon province, 10km/6 miles south-west of Sankıklı
For rheumatism, gynaecological conditions, skin, circulatory and digestive
system disorders
Facilities: small treatment centre (60–70°C/140–158°F)

Hüdayi

Konya province
For rheumatism, gynaecological conditions, dermatological, urinary, cir-
culatory and heart disorders, glandular and digestive complaints
Facilities: good treatment centre, basic accommodation

Ilgın

At 975m/3200ft on the E89 86km/53 miles north-west of Ankara
For rheumatism, neuralgia, gynaecological conditions, circulatory and di-
gestive disorders
Facilities: bathing and drinking cures (37–47°C/99–117°F)

Kızılcahamam

Denizli province 20km/12 miles north-east of Denizli
For heart and circulatory complaints, rheumatism, digestive, gall bladder
and kidney diseases
Facilities: accommodation (33–56°C/91–133°F)

Pamukkale
and Karahayıt

33km/21 miles north of Eskişehir near the town of Sarıcakaya
For sciatica and rheumatism, skin and metabolic disorders
Facilities: medicinal spring (35°C/95°F)

Sakar

İstanbul province, springs 11km/7 miles south-west of Yalova
For rheumatism, gynaecological conditions, urinary and nervous com-
plaints, control of cholesterol and lipid levels
Facilities: hotels and guest houses (55–60°C/131–140°F)

Yalova

Sport

Turkey's more esoteric national sports include greased Turkish wrestling,
camel wrestling (see Events) and cirit oyunu, a game with javelins on
horseback. So far as the more conventional sporting activities are concerned many tour operators use hotels which have a wide range of sports
facilities, although the tennis courts, etc. are not always up to European
standards and facilities elsewhere tend to be rather limited outside the
peak holiday season. The tourist offices listed in the Information section
can supply an outdoor pursuits leaflet covering climbing, trekking and river
rafting.

Foreign groups wanting to climb Eastern Anatolia's Mount Ararat (Büyük
Ağrı Dağı, 5165m/16,952ft) and the Cilo-Sat ranges (up to 4135m/13,571ft)
in the Hakkari district require special permission from the authorities concerned. Information can be had from the Turkish Foreign Ministry of Foreign Affairs (Dışişleri Bakanlığı, Ankara; tel. (0–312) 212 51 25).
Before your trip you should also inform the Turkish Mountaineering
Club (Dışışleri Federasyonu, TTGM, Ulus İşhani A-Blok, Ulus, Ankara; tel.
(0–312) 310 15 78) of when and where you intend to climb. They can then
alert the relevant authorities in the region in order for them to be ready to
come to your assistance if necessary.
For your own safety, however, you should never attempt the ascent of any
of Turkey's peaks on your own or without using a local mountain guide.

Mountaineering

Sport fishing without a licence, using a line or net weighing up to 5kg/
11 lb, is allowed in any non-prohibited area. To check on these, and on fish
sizes and maximum catches, contact tourist offices or the Department of
Fisheries of the Turkish Ministry of Agriculture in Ankara (Tarım ve Köyişleri
Bakanlığı, Su Ürünleri Dairesi Başkanlığı). Commercial fishing by foreigners is strictly forbidden.

Fishing

Sport

Aerial sports	Anyone interested in aerial sports such as flying, gliding, hang-gliding, para-sailing, etc. should contact the Turkish Flying Association (THK) in Ankara: Türk Hava Kurumu Genel Başkanlığı, Havacılık Müdürlüğü, Atatürk Bulvarı 33, Opera-Ankara; tel. (0–312) 310 48 40. Courses in these activities can be provided for groups of ten or more people so long as they speak the same language.
Football	Football is one of Turkey's favourite spectator sports, but between June and October Club Palmariva organises a holiday football school near Kemer where soccer enthusiasts can also join in many other sporting activities such as tennis, squash, sailing, water-skiing, etc.
Hunting	Hunting by individuals is banned in Turkey, and foreign visitors can only hunt in parties organised by Turkish travel agencies which have been authorised by the Ministry of Agriculture, Forestry and Rural Affairs. These agencies provide all the information required regarding seasons, authorised zones, permit formalities, etc. A list of such agencies can be obtained from the Union of Turkish Travel Agencies (TÜRSAB, Gazeteciler Sitesi, Haberler Sokak 15, İstanbul-Esentepe; tel. (0–212) 275 13 61, 275 13 97 or 275 11 62, and in Ankara, Atatürk Bulvarı 107/71; tel. (0–312) 418 07 75).
Cruises	Cruises in the Aegean and the eastern Mediterranean usually call in at Turkey's fine harbours such as Kuşadası, Bodrum, Marmaris, Kaş and Alanya. Travel agents specialising in sea cruises will be able to supply you with more detailed information. See also Coastal Shipping.
Sailing	Private yachts require a transit log before entering Turkey's territorial waters where they may remain for up to two years for maintenance or for wintering. Once you have entered Turkish waters you must make your way immediately to an official port of entry to present your transit log and get it endorsed by the proper authorities. These ports of entry are Tekirdağ, İstanbul, Korfez, Bandırma, Çanakkale, Akçay, Ayvalık, Dikili, İzmir, Çeşme, Kuşadası, Güllük, Didim, Bodrum, Datça, Marmaris, Fethiye, Kaş, Finkike, Kemer, Antalya, Alanya, Anamur, Taşucu (Silifke), Mersin, Bodaş (Adana) and İskenderun, and, on the Black Sea, Zonguldak, Sinop, Samsun, Ordu, Giresun, Trabzon, Rize and Hopa.
Rules of navigation	International navigation rules must be scrupulously observed. The Turkish courtesy flag should be flown from 8am to sunset. Avoid zigzagging between Turkish and Greek territorial waters to prevent any misunderstanding, and above all refrain from taking any "archaeological souvenirs" from coastal waters and keeping them on board – the penalty is confiscation of the boat.
Wind and weather conditions	Be sure to check on wind and weather conditions. There is a meteorological bulletin, repeated twice at five minute intervals, on VHF 16 and 67 in English and Turkish for the Mediterranean and Aegean region, broadcast daily at 9am, 12 noon and 3, 6 and 9pm. For further information contact Çevre Bakanlığı Devlet Meteoroloji Genel Müdürlüğü, Kalaba-Ankara; tel. (0–312) 359 75 45 (see also When to Go in this section and Climate under Facts and Figures).
Package sailing holidays and cruises	Sailing holidays cruising around the Turkish coastline and islands of the Aegean and Mediterranean are becoming very popular. Many of the vessels used are new motor yachts built in Turkey on the lines of the traditional wooden "goulets" of Bodrum and Marmaris, with a local crew and able to accommodate up to twelve people.
Blue Voyage (Mavi Yolculuk)	The "Blue Voyage" is a popular week-long sailing cruise along the coast from Çeşme to Antalya operated by various agencies between April and October for groups of 8 to 12 people. A wide spectrum of all kinds of yachts are available at Marmaris – the voyage from here towards Bodrum is particularly enjoyable.

Water sports are clearly the main outdoor pursuit along Turkey's Aegean and Mediterranean coasts, and most of the popular resorts have impressive facilities for windsurfing, water skiing, jetskiing, para-gliding and the like. Snorkelling and scuba diving with amateur equipment is permitted in certain areas for leisure purposes, but since the rules governing diving vary from place to place it is best to find out about them from a national Turkish tourist office (see Information) before leaving home and also to check again with the appropriate authorities, such as the local harbour-master's office, when you get to Turkey.

Water sports and diving

Many parts of Turkey lend themselves to walking and hiking, although there are no marked trails as such. The most attractive regions for this purpose are the alpine meadows and plateaux behind the Black Sea coast, the Uludağ mountains around Bursa (see National Parks) and the countryside around Marmaris. You should take good footwear, a rucksack and waterbottle, warm clothing and protection against the sun and the rain. Enquire about trail maps in bookstores or specialist shops before leaving for Turkey.

Hiking

Turkey's best-known skiing area is in the Uludağ mountains (1900m/6236ft) south-east of Bursa, which has cable-cars, chair-lifts, ski-lifts, ski instructors, ski-hire, etc. Anyone who wants to combine skiing in the morning with a swim in the warm waters of the Mediterranean in the afternoon should opt for Saklıkent (2000–2400m/6564–7877ft; chair-lifts, etc., ski instruction) in March and April since this is within easy distance of the sandy beach at Olympos, west of Antalya. The ski centre on Erciyes Dağı (1800–3000m/5908–9846ft) 25km/15½ miles south of Kayseri has a ski lodge, ski lift, ski instruction, etc. and good snow conditions between November and May. Palandöken (2200–3100m/7220–10,174ft; ski-lift, instruction, etc.) 8km/5 miles south-west of Erzurum makes an ideal location for international skiing events, while another popular ski resort is Köroğlu (1900–2340m/6236–7680ft; ski-lift, ski-hire, instruction) which is some 50km/31 miles south-east of Bolu on the İstanbul to Ankara road.

Winter sports

Taxis

All the larger towns and cities have plenty of taxis. These are yellow and easily identifiable by the "Taksi" sign on the roof. They usually have meters which record the fare according to the distance travelled but it is wise to ask how much this is likely to be before starting the journey.

Turkey's communal taxi, the dolmuş, is an even cheaper alternative to the ordinary taxi cab. Identifiable from their yellow band, these follow set routes with predetermined stops and charge set rates which are fixed by the local authority. A typical route would be from the centre of town to the airport or out to the suburbs and often other places nearby. "Dolmuş" means full and they will carry on picking up passengers until there's no more room. Each passenger pays a set amount according to their destination.

Dolmuş

Minibuses are another cheap way to travel. They stop on request – but only if there's enough room inside – and follow no particular route.

Minibuses

See entry

Tipping

Telephone

Although Turkey's telephone system is still being improved and extended nearly all the main towns already have STD and direct dialling, but since the area codes have recently been reorganised it is adviseable to check locally on the latest situation. Long-distance calls through the operator can be either normal, urgent or lightning.

Public phone booths are yellow and there are plenty of them; there is always one near a post office. To make a call either tokens (jetons) or a phonecard (telefon kartı), both available from post offices, are needed. When dialling direct lift the receiver, wait for the tone, then dial 9 and wait for another tone before dialling the area code followed by the number required.

Long-distance calls via the operator can mean a long wait running into several hours in some cases.
The area code within Turkey for İstanbul is 0–212 or 0–216. For calls to İstanbul from abroad omit the 0, dial the code for international calls, followed by 90 for Turkey then 212 or 216 plus the number required.

International dialling codes from Turkey	Dialling codes for calls from Turkey to:	
	Canada, United States	99 1
	Eire	99 353
	South Africa	99 27
	United Kingdom	99 44

Telegrams | See Postal Services

Time

Turkey observes Eastern European Time which is two hours ahead of Greenwich Mean Time (GMT). From the beginning of April until the end of September the clocks are put forward an hour to Turkish Summer Time which is three hours ahead of GMT.

Tipping

In hotels and at barbers and hairdressers the tip is usually up to 10% of the bill and in restaurants up to 15% if service is not included. Taxi drivers expect a generous rounding up of the fare to the nearest 300 TL.

For hotel porters, etc. the tip is between 500 and 1000 TL but often the amounts for some services (lavatory attendant, etc.) are posted up.

Travel Documents

Passport

Nationals of EC countries, Australia, Canada, the United States and most Western countries normally only require a valid passport to enter Turkey for a stay of up to three months. If travelling overland transit visas are also required for countries such Rumania and Bulgaria. Children under sixteen may be included on their parents' passport but only if they are entering and leaving Turkey at the same time.

Driver and vehicle papers

Drivers must have their driving licence and vehicle registration papers and cars must bear the oval nationality disc. On entering Turkey vehicles of any kind – from caravans and minibuses to motorbikes and mopeds, and including luggage trailers and towed boats – will be entered in the driver's passport. Make sure this is cancelled again when you leave (see also Motoring). If you intend to keep a vehicle in Turkey for longer than three months or to continue on into the Middle East you also require a triptyque or "carnet de passage". These are obtainable in advance from local motoring organisations.

All vehicles must have at least third party insurance. The international green card is compulsory and it must expressly state that it covers the Asian as well as the European part of Turkey. Otherwise you will have to take out a short-term insurance at the frontier.

Vehicle insurance

Because of the poor performance of Turkish insurance it is advisable to try to avoid doing badly out of claims for damage in local accidents by taking out an additional short-term comprehensive and passenger insurance in advance which must be written to cover the whole of Turkey. You should definitely carry written confirmation from your home insurers that the policy cover is valid throughout the country. A police report is necessary for the settlement of any claims.

Turkish Baths

The strict rules of Islam require ritual purification and cleanliness and consequently the "hamam" or public bath-house has been a feature of Turkish life since medieval times. There are usually separate baths for men and women, but if not then there are different times for men and women.

The central hot room, which is surrounded by open cubicles, has a heated slab in the middle – the "göbek taşı" or belly stone – where you sweat wrapped in a "peştamal" (a kind of bath apron) before being rubbed down and massaged by a male or female attendant (tellak or natır) as the case may be. This not only leaves you much cleaner but also gets the circulation going.

There are over a hundred Turkish baths in İstanbul alone, some of them well worth visiting, if only for the architecture (see also Art and Culture, Typical Islamic Buildings).

Turkish Society and the Visitor

The vast majority of Turks are followers of Islam, one of the world's great monotheistic religions (see Facts and Figures, Religion), and their lives as Muslims (believers prefer Muslim or Moslem to the term Mohammedan) are wholly governed by the tenets of their faith. These are based on the rules laid down in the Koran, their holy book, which prescribes absolute obedience to the will of Allah, their one and only God. The precepts of the Koran also embrace the laws derived from the words and deeds of Islam's founder, the Prophet Mohammed (born in Mecca in A.D. 570 and died in Medina in 632).

Islam

Every area of Muslim society is ordered by laws, rules and customs based on the five fundamental duties of the Islamic faith (see also Facts and Figures *Baedeker Special*).

1. Profession of faith (Shahidah): "there is no God but Allah and Mohammed is his prophet".
2. Duty of prayer (Salat): this must be performed five times a day, preceded by ritual cleansing, facing Mecca and using preordained prayers, in Arabic if possible, and in strictly prescribed prayer positions.
3. Almsgiving (Sakat): every Muslim must regularly give alms to the poor and needy (between 2.5 and 10% of their income).
4. Fasting (Saum): Muslims are required to abstain from food and drink and worldly pleasures such as smoking between sunrise and sunset during Ramadan (Ramasan), the ninth month of Islam's lunar calendar.
5. Pilgrimage to Mecca (Hadj): every Muslim who is of age, unless prevented by sickness or poverty, must make the pilgrimage to Mecca once in their lifetime to visit the Kaba, Islam's holiest shrine.

Duties of the faith

| Islamic codes of conduct | Other religious ordinances include bans on drinking alcohol and eating pork, as well as the prohibition of usury and all forms of gambling. Animals must be slaughtered according to fixed rules and no blood or blood products may be consumed. |

Other religious ordinances include bans on drinking alcohol and eating pork, as well as the prohibition of usury and all forms of gambling. Animals must be slaughtered according to fixed rules and no blood or blood products may be consumed.

There are also detailed rules governing bodily purification and the relationships between married people and parents and children.

The husband is the prime member of the family for which he alone is responsible both in fact and in law. The wife remains in the background and her domain is the home and the family. The extended family is the Muslim's accepted territory. Thoughts, feelings and behaviour are geared to the communal unit.

The Islamic world is currently displaying a growing awareness of its own values and potential, and greater emphasis is again being placed on cultural and religious tradition. Yet in the big cities you also encounter modern, more western lifestyles – like any other movement Islam has its progressive forces as well as its conservative fundamentalists.

How to behave as a visitor

If you want to understand the way Muslims behave and to avoid offending them you should bear in mind that they have a different lifestyle and way of thinking from those who are not of their faith. Thus the Turks have different values and customs which, as a visitor to their country, you should respect if you want them to respect you.

Since their religion is so closely bound up with every other aspect of Turkish society, any dismissive remark will readily be regarded as a criticism of the Islamic faith.

Avoid wearing revealing clothing, especially in rural areas, and particularly if you are visiting a mosque. Take off your shoes before entering, do not wear shorts, and cover your head with a scarf if you are a woman. Nonmuslims should also not visit mosques during prayers.

In the more conservative parts of Turkey avoid public displays of affection between the sexes since this will be regarded as promiscuous; eye-contact by foreign women with Turkish men is taboo.

Be extremely cautious about taking photographs of women, children, poor people or beggars. Muslims consider this a slur on a person's dignity and it can lead to very hostile reactions.

Needless to say you will cause offence if you make fun of the sound of the muezzin or Muslim behaviour at prayer, and during Ramadan you should avoid eating and drinking or smoking in public.

The Turks are immensely hospitable and it is considered impolite to refuse an invitation. If you do, be sufficiently apologetic about it. The Islamic code means that friendships are taken very seriously.

If you are invited into a Turkish home you will be treated like a member of the family, and the same generous hospitality will be expected of you if you receive a visit in return.

As a guest do not ask for pork or any alcoholic drinks, but you can eat or drink these if they are put in front of you. An appropriate gift of flowers for the hostess or some other token will be expected when you leave. Never offer money.

When to Go

The spring is the best time to make a tour of Turkey to enjoy the scenery at its freshest and greenest. In summer the heat, dust and drought can make travelling very wearing, and it may often prove difficult to get a room during the peak season. Autumn is also a good time to go if you are prepared not to see the countryside at its best. For swimming seasons see Beaches.

Although prices are lower on both sides of the peak holiday season this also has its disadvantages, such as more building work and routine maintenance and repairs. There are often fewer people about to cater for the visitor which means having to wait longer and many shops, restaurants, etc. are closed.

Before and after the peak season

After the heavy winter rains spring comes to the Mediterranean coast between İzmir and Antakya in early March when the countryside is in bloom with fresh new growth and Turkey's beautiful wild flowers. Spring reaches the coast from İzmir to the Bosporus in mid-March and the Black Sea coast in April. On the other hand the mountain peaks of the Taurus and the Pontus are capped with snow until well into June and this contrast between the white of the mountain tops and the azure blue of the sea makes the Mediterranean coast particularly attractive in April and May. Swimming is possible in the Sea of Marmara from mid-May onwards and in the Black Sea from June.

Spring

The summer drought sets in as early as June and the heat on the coasts is only occasionally tempered by sea breezes. This is the time to opt for the Sea of Marmara or the Black Sea, although it can get oppressively close on the eastern part of the Black Sea coast where the warm wet winds from the sea encounter the mountain barrier of the Pontus. The summer months in Central and Eastern Anatolia are hot and dry, but it can become quite chilly in the evenings on the central plateau.

Summer

Temperatures become tolerable again in the autumn but the heat of summer will have dried up the landscape, leaving it barren and sere.

Autumn

Winter tourism in Turkey is still in its infancy. Although the Turkish Riviera and the Aegean coast often enjoy spring temperatures at this time of year, so far they tend to lack the appropriate facilities. The best months for winter sports (see Sport) are from December to March around Bursa and Ankara and from November to April near Kayseri.

Winter

See Facts and Figures, Climate

Climate

Youth Accommodation

Turkey only has a few youth hostels (talebe yurdu). These are chiefly in Ankara, Bolu, Bursa, Çanakkale, İstanbul, İzmir and Marmaris. Holders of International Student Travel Conference (ISTC) or International Youth Hostel Federation (IYFH) cards enjoy special benefits as well. Young people travelling on a tight budget can also easily find a cheap bed for the night in the more modest guest-houses and hotels (see Hotels).

Youth hostels

Information about holidays for young people, youth camps, staying with host families, etc. can be obtained from tourist information offices (see Information) or from the following organisations:

Information

Gençtur Turizm ve Seyahat Acentesi (tourism and travel agency)
Yerebatan Caddesi 15/3, Sultanahmet-İstanbul;
tel. (0–212) 520 52 74/75 and 526 54 09
(member of the International Youth Hostel Federation)

7 TUR Turizm ve Trade
İnönü Caddesi 31/2, Gümüşsuyu-Taksim-İstanbul;
tel. (0–212) 149 40 90, 149 96 19 and 252 59 21 (4 lines)

Youth Accommodation

Renk Turizm Seyahat Acentesi
Halaskargazı Caddesi 105, Harbiye, İstanbul;
tel. (0–212) 232 23 00 and 224 90 00

Seventur Turizm Seyahat Acentesi
Alemdar Caddesi 2/C, Sultanahmet-İstanbul;
tel. (0–212) 520 95 94 and 512 41 84/85

Information especially about accommodation for young people in Ankara
is obtainable from:

Gençlik ve Spor Genel Müdürlüğü (Gençlik Hizmetleri Daire Başkanlığı)
Rüzgarlı Sokak 10, 2nd floor, Ulus/Ankara;
tel. (0–312) 310 02 19 and 310 22 32/36

Leaflet

The Ministry of Tourism in Turkey also publishes a "Youth Tourism" leaflet
in English containing information about student accommodation (yurtkur),
forest camps, sport camps, special rail fares for young people, etc.: Turizm
Bakanlığı, Turizm Eğitim Genel Müdürlüğü, İnönü Bulvarı 5, Ankara; tel.
(0–312) 212 83 00.

Index

Index

Index

The Principal Places of Tourist Interest at a Glance (continued from p. 6)

*	Page	*	Page
Gölçuk	284	Parhal	200
Gordion	314	Patara	312
Haho	304	Pazar	471
Harput	285	Pessinus	307
Hasankeyf	395	Priene	438
Hierapolis	426	Princes' Islands	342
Hizan	216	Rumkale	215
Hoşap	495	Safranbolu	369
İhlara	139	Sagalassos	244
İmerhevi Valley	199	Samandağ	176
İnebolu	220	Samsun-Dağı National Park	296
İsauria Vetus	209	Sardis	447
İshan	199	Selçuk	293
İzmir	343	Selge	456
Kaçkar Dağlan	200	Sertavul Geçidi	359
Kanlıdivane	459	Side	450
Kapıkaya	133	Sille	388
Karadere	238	Simena	363
Karain Mağarası	181	Sinop	220
Karakuş Tepesi	127	Sivas	460
Karaman	356	Söğüt	211
Kars	359	Soğuksu National Park	172
Kasaba	369	Sultanhanı (Kayseri)	377
Kefkalesi	136	Süphan Dağı	136
Kiz Kalesi	157	Susuz Han	246
Knidos	402	Tarakli	352
Köroğlu Dağlan	238	Tercan	300
Kovada National Park	283	Termessos	180
Kümbet	406	Tigris Tunnel	275
Kuş Cenneti	206	Tilmenhüyük	324
Kuşadası	295	Tırsın Yaylası	320
Labranda	412	Tlos	310
Laodikeia	431	Tokat	466
Mardin	394	Tortum Şelalesi	305
Marmaris	400	Trabazon	472
Midyat	397	Tralles	202
Milas	407	Tunceli	485
Mudurnu	239	Tuz Gölü	388
Muğla	401	Ürgüp	263
Myra	363	Xanthos	311
Namrunkalesi	465	Yağmurdere	318
Narlıkuyu	458	Yalınyazı	472
Nemrut Dağı (Ahlat)	136	Yalova	251
Nysa	421	Yedikilise	497
Obruk	387	Yedisalkım	498
Ören	281	Yılanıkale	123
Öşk	304	Zelve	264
Ortahisar	263	Zigana Geçidi	318

Note: The places listed are merely the most important places of tourist interest in Turkey which are worth a visit. In addition there are very many other significant places and sights to which attention is drawn in the A to Z section of the guide by asterisks.

Notes

Notes

Notes